Chp 12-13 Taos Quiz
              Thur.   20 Question
read chp 14   per chp.

Thur. chp 15-19

                    final 9-19

NET*ability* SERIES

MICROSOFT®
WINDOWS XP PROFESSIONAL

Michael D. Stewart

EMCParadigm

Dedication

This book is dedicated to my family and friends who have asupported me from the start. You all know who you are—thanks for always being there.
—*Michael D. Stewart*

EMCParadigm Publishing Management Team
George Provol, Publisher; Janice Johnson, Director of Product Development; Tony Galvin, Acquisitions Editor; Lori Landwer, Marketing Manager; Shelley Clubb, Electronic Design and Production Manager

Text w/CD ISBN: 0-7638-1954-9

© 2003 by Paradigm Publishing Inc.
Published by **EMC**Paradigm
875 Montreal Way
St. Paul, MN 55102

(800) 535-6865
E-mail: educate@emcp.com
Web site: www.emcp.com

Printed in the United States of America.
10 9 8 7 6 5 4 3 2 1

Table of Contents

Chapter 6
Files and Folders in Windows XP Professional 137

Chapter 7
Printing 171

Chapter 8
Hardware Support 205

Chapter 12
Working Securely 321

Chapter 13
Managing and Maintaining
Windows XP Professional 351

Introduction

Welcome to *NetAbility Series: Microsoft© Windows XP Professional*. The aim of this comprehensive textbook is to teach you how to install, configure, and administer Microsoft Windows XP Professional, to administer a Windows network that includes Windows XP Professional workstations, and to prepare you to take Microsoft's Certification Exam #70-270, titled "Installing, Configuring, and Administering Microsoft Windows XP Professional."

The key to learning Windows XP Professional is to obtain the background knowledge required to understand the operation of the software. Network administration skills are best learned with a combination of hands-on and problem-solving exercises. Hands-on exercises provide you with the opportunity to learn how to perform specific network administrative tasks. Problem-solving exercises provide you with the opportunity to demonstrate critical thinking skills. This text will not only help you with learning the Windows XP Professional operating system, it will also aid you in preparing for the Microsoft certification exam for Windows XP Professional.

EMCParadigm's NetAbility texts help you learn specific subject matter and apply skills as you study to pass vendor-specific certification exams. We have worked from Microsoft's own curriculum objectives to ensure that we clearly explain all key topics. Our aim is to bring together as much information as possible about Windows XP Professional and about Microsoft's certification exams.

Text Features

There are a number of features in *NetAbility Series: Microsoft© Windows XP Professional* to aid you in fully understanding Windows XP Professional concepts:

➤ **Chapter objectives**—Each chapter in this book begins with a detailed list of the topics to be mastered within that chapter. This list provides you with a quick reference to the contents of that chapter, as well as a useful study aid.

➤ **Illustrations and tables**—Numerous illustrations of screenshots and components aid you in the visualization of common setup steps, theories, and concepts. In addition, many tables provide details and comparisons of both practical and theoretical information.

➤ **Step-by-step exercises**—Hands-on exercises that follow the presentation of concepts within the chapters provide immediate reinforcement of the concepts and demonstration and practice of the skills required.

➤ **Notes, tips, and warnings**—Notes present additional helpful material related to the subject being described. Tips from the authors' experience provide extra information about hoe to attack a problem or what to do in certain real-world situations. Warnings are included to help you anticipate potential mistakes or problems so you can prevent them from happening.

➤ **Chapter Summaries**—Each chapter's text is followed by a summary of the concepts it has introduced. These summaries provide a helpful way to recap and revisit the ideas covered in each chapter.

➤ **Review Questions**—End-of-chapter assessment begins with a set of review questions that reinforce the ideas introduced in each chapter. These questions not only ensure that you have mastered the concepts, but are written to help prepare you for the Microsoft certification examination.

➤ **Real-World Projects**—Although it is important to understand the theory behind server and networking technology, nothing can improve upon real-world experience. To this end, along with theoretical explanations, each chapter provides numerous hands-on projects aimed at providing you with real-world implementation experience.

➤ **Glossary**—Definitions of all the terms important to your understanding of Windows XP Professional are in the Glossary at the end of the book.

EMCParadigm Encore! CD Quizzes

NetAbility Series: Microsoft© Windows XP Professional comes with an Encore! Companion CD that provides additional, interactive quizzes and tests with which you can test your knowledge of the concepts in the book. There are two levels of tests: book and chapter, and each level functions in two different modes. In the Practice mode you receive immediate feedback on each test item and a report of your total score. In the reportable Test mode your results are e-mailed both to you and your instructor, highlighting the correct answers.

NetAbility Series Internet Resource Center

You can find additional content and study aids for *NetAbility Series: Microsoft© Windows XP Professional* at the NetAbility Internet Resource Center at www.emcp.com. Students will find course information, tips for taking MCSE exams, additional quizzes, and valuable Web links. Instructors will find Instructor's Guide materials (such as syllabi, teaching hints, model answers for Real World Projects, and additional assessment tools).

CHAPTER ONE

What's New in Windows XP Professional

After completing this chapter, you will be able to:

✓ Explain how Windows XP is easier to use than previous versions of Windows

✓ Explain why Windows XP is a more reliable and dependable operating system than its predecessors and is more resistant to application failure than with previous versions of Windows

✓ Explain how Windows XP is more software- and hardware-compatible than the previous versions of Windows and is a more manageable operating system

✓ Describe some of the new enhanced file and print sharing capabilities of Windows XP

✓ Explain why Windows XP has better Internet integration than previous versions of Windows

✓ Describe the security features available in Windows XP

✓ Describe what remote user support is in Windows XP and how it is used

✓ Describe the updated Help and Support tools that have been implemented in Windows XP

✓ Describe several of the enhanced laptop capabilities introduced in Windows XP

✓ Describe the new and improved networking and communications features of Windows XP

Windows XP Professional is the first operating system release in Microsoft's .NET initiative. Windows XP Professional is based on the fast, stable, secure operating-system core of Windows NT and 2000. It offers compatibility with a broad base of applications and hardware, additional technical-support technology, and a fresh user interface.

Navigating the operating system is also easier thanks to reduced clutter on the desktop and a refined Start menu. Windows XP Professional has excellent system stability. The operating system's application compatibility is far better than that of Windows 2000.

Microsoft has managed to build upon the stability of Windows 2000, while adding a multitude of features that home and business users will embrace with open arms.

Easier to Use

Windows XP is the first step toward Microsoft's new broad set of .NET technologies. Windows XP is built off the code base of Windows 2000. Microsoft has taken steps to ensure that this new operating system is one of the easiest yet for customers to use.

Some of the new features that make it one of the easiest operating systems to use are described in this section.

➤ *Fresh Visual Design*—The first change you will notice when you run Windows XP Professional is the striking difference in the visual design versus the design of Windows 2000 Professional. Although Windows XP Professional is based on the core operating system of Windows 2000, the visual design is a lot cleaner than its predecessor. Many common tasks have been consolidated, which makes for simplified use. New visual styles and themes have been added that use 24-bit color icons and unique colors that can be associated with particular tasks. Visual cues have been added to aid users in navigating this new operating system. Users still have the option to use the classic Windows 2000 Professional interface if they are uncomfortable with the new visual design of XP Professional.

➤ *Redesigned Start Menu*—The Start menu has been redesigned to allow users to place the items that they commonly use on a single window. The menu adapts itself as you work. The five programs that you use most often are displayed first. The files and applications that are used most frequently are grouped together for quicker access. Your default email and Web browser applications are always available through the Start menu, in addition to Help and Support and tools used for configuring your system. As with Windows 2000, the Start menu can be customized by users to meet their specific preferences. Printers, documents, and network connections can be accessed by one click on the new Start menu.

1

➤ *Taskbar Grouping*—Taskbar grouping enables you to maintain a cleaner desktop by grouping open files according to their application type. If you have multiple Excel documents open, they will all appear under one taskbar button and can be tiled, cascaded, or minimized all at the same time.

➤ *Updated Search Companion*—Searching for files and documents has become easier with Windows XP. Search tasks are consolidated, which optimizes the search. Suggestions are even made for refining your search. The Search Companion is optimized to work with the way people use their documents. If a user is looking for a Word document, she does not need to know the file extension or even the complete name of the document. Searching the Internet has also been made easier. Internet searches can be made in plain English.

➤ *Multiple-User Logon Features*—Many organizations may find that it is cost-effective to have multiple individuals using one PC. One of the new improvements added to Windows XP Professional is the ability of multiple users to use the same PC. As each user logs onto the PC, his or her individual and customized settings are saved, including all desktop settings. New users can log onto the PC without having to reboot. The logon screen displays the names of users who are using the PC, and a user can select his logon from the list of names. Any applications the user had open when he logged off will be open still when he logs back on.

➤ *Files and Settings Transfer Wizard*—One of the biggest challenges in migrating from one computer to another is transferring all the files and settings to the new computer. The Files and Settings Transfer Wizard is a new feature that was added to XP Professional to make it easier for users to migrate four types of settings: appearance, action, Internet, and mail.

➤ *Fast Switching*—Fast Switching is a new feature of Windows XP that allows for seamless switching between accounts on a Windows XP Professional computer. It is not necessary to log another user off the computer before you use it. With Fast Switching, users can easily and quickly switch among all open accounts without logging off other users. The new Welcome screen provides information such as how many users are logged on, how many applications are currently running, and if users have new email messages. Fast Switching takes advantage of Terminal Services technology. Each user session is opened as a unique Terminal Services session. Fast Switching is not enabled by default in Windows XP Professional, but it is enabled by default in Windows XP Home. It can be used on an XP Professional computer if the computer is a standalone or workgroup-connected computer. It cannot be used if the computer is a member of a domain.

➤ *Improved Handling of File Associations*—Windows XP aids users in opening files that are not associated with an application. If a user tries to open a file that is not associated with a particular application, Windows XP will send the user to a Web page from which they can download the application that the file is associated with. Many times, files can be associated with more than one application. If a default application has been deleted from the computer, XP will restore the default program and the file association.

➤ *Webview*—Webview, which is similar to the Webview in Windows 2000, provides a way for users to have better access to tasks. It aids in managing the file namespace. When a user selects a file or folder, a list of options is displayed, allowing the user to move, copy, rename, email, or publish the file or folder on the Web.

More Reliable and Dependable

Reliability and dependability are crucial ingredients for the successful operation of any operating system. This section describes some of the reasons why XP is one of the most reliable and dependable operating systems on the market.

Built on New Windows Engine

Windows XP is designed to provide the most reliable computing environment for users. It is built on the 32-bit computing architecture and fully protected memory model of code base of Windows NT and 2000.

Device Driver Rollback

Windows XP will keep a duplicate of certain classes of device drivers when they are installed. If the device driver fails, the system administrator can reinstall or roll back the device driver from the copy. This ensures system stability, much like using the Last Known Good Configuration in Windows 2000 Safe Mode. The copy of the driver is stored in a special subdirectory of the system files.

Enhanced Device Driver Verifier

Drivers used in Windows XP will be the most stable yet available in the Windows environment. The Device Driver Verifier used in Windows XP is based on the verifier found in Windows 2000 and provides for greater stress tests for drivers being installed.

System Restore

This new feature will allow a user to recover a system from a failure or problem. System Restore constantly monitors the system and automatically creates restore

1

points. These restore points are created every day by default in Windows XP Professional and can be used to restore the system to its previous state before the problem occurred. Users can also create and manage their own restore points.

Automatic System Recovery (ASR)

ASR can be used to restore applications. In addition, ASR can be used to back up Plug and Play portions of the Registry and restore this information if needed. ASR is extremely useful in such a situation as when a hard disk fails and you need to restore important configuration parameters.

Reduced Reboots

Due to better stability, users of Windows XP will experience less reboots than with previous versions of Windows. Many applications can be installed without having to reboot the computer.

Improved Code Protection

Windows XP has improved upon code protection in Windows 2000 to ensure that rogue applications don't adversely affect core operating system files. Kernel data structures are read-only, and applications cannot access or corrupt them. Driver code is also read-only and page-protected.

Scalable Memory and Processor Support

Many users will be purchasing XP for use with intensive applications that will require more computing power than is available with previous versions of Windows. Windows XP supports up to 4GB of RAM and two symmetric multiprocessors.

Dynamic Update

During the setup of Windows XP Professional, the operating system will check the Web via the Windows Update Web service for critical system updates that may have been released, and will download them for installation. Stability and reliability are ensured with dynamic updates to applications, device drivers, and fixes for security issues.

AutoUpdate

AutoUpdate can be configured to download updates to the computer system without interruption in a current Web session. If the system is disconnected from the Web, AutoUpdate will resume after it is reconnected.

Windows Update

Windows Update provides a centralized point to find product enhancements, service packs, device drivers, and system security updates. These supplement the extensive library of drivers and files found on the installation CD.

Better Resistance to Application Failure

Protection from application failure is critical in maintaining system stability. Windows XP has several features, described next, that make it resistant to application failure.

Windows File Protection

Protecting system files is critical in any operating system. Windows File Protection prevents core system files from being overwritten. If a system file is overwritten by accident, Windows File Protection will reinstall the file.

Windows Installer Service

To aid in minimizing user system downtime, Windows Installer is an integrated service of Windows XP that can be used to configure, upgrade, and remove programs correctly.

Side-by-Side DLL Support

A new folder in Windows XP, called WinSxS, is used to store versions of Windows XP components that are built to reduce problems with dynamic link libraries, sometimes referred to as DDL hell. Multiple versions of the DDL files are stored in this folder, and Windows XP allows applications to use the exact version of the component that they were tested with. Other applications are not affected.

Most Compatible

One of the main concerns with Windows 2000 when it was first introduced was the numerous application incompatibilities that existed with the new operating system. Windows XP has eliminated many of the software and hardware incompatibilities, as described in this section.

Increased Application Compatibility

One of the major problems with Windows 2000 when it first came out was application compatibility, or lack thereof. Many applications from earlier versions of Windows did not run with Windows 2000. You will not have that problem with Windows XP Professional. Applications that did not run in Windows 2000 will run in XP. New compatibility will be available for third-party applications for home and business users. XP will run most of the top applications that run under Windows 9*x* and almost every application that runs under Windows 2000, with the exception of several backup, anti-virus, and system utilities. An Application Compatibility Toolkit is available for developers to use for applications that were not tested before the release of Windows XP. Application fixes are implemented automatically by the operating system with no user intervention. As newer applications and fixes become available, the application updates can be downloaded from the Windows Update Web site. For earlier versions of applications that do not work for Windows XP, the application can be run in Application Compatibility Mode to emulate the environment of the earlier operating system.

Support for Latest Hardware Standards

Windows XP has been designed to support the latest hardware standards. The following is a partial list of some of the new hardware technology supported by Windows XP Professional:

➤ Universal Disk Format (UDF) 2.01 support for reading DVD disks

➤ Formatting of DVD-RAM drivers on FAT32 file system

➤ IrDA (Infrared Data Association)

➤ USB and PS/2 interface keyboards

➤ IEEE 1394

➤ USB array microphones

➤ Support for high-resolution monitors supporting up to 200 dots per inch (dpi)

➤ Intel Itanium 64-bit processor support

Easier Manageability

XP introduces new ways for managing files, folders, and user desktops. It also introduces new ways to migrate files and settings to computers. This section presents some of the options that are provided in Windows XP for making your network more manageable.

IntelliMirror

When running Windows XP Professional in a network with Active Directory, the IntelliMirror technologies can be used to provide "follow-me" functionality for computer systems. Constant access to all information and software is provided regardless of where a user is connected to the network. Windows XP provides IntelliMirror through user data management, software installation and maintenance, user settings management, and remote installation services.

Group Policy

Group Policy was a key component in Windows 2000 for the administration of users in Windows 2000. This is also true in Windows XP. By utilizing Group Policy, the same settings can be applied consistently to all computers on the network. More than 300 new policies are available in Windows XP Professional in addition to those provided with Windows 2000.

Resultant Set of Policy (RSoP)

RSoP is a tool in Windows XP Professional that provides administrators with the ability to plan, monitor, and troubleshoot Group Policy.

Local Group Policies

Local Group Policy was used in Windows 2000 to let administrators lock down and fine-tune the desktop environment. Windows XP Professional introduces several new Local Group Policies that can be used to customize the user interface, prohibit the use of specific operating systems, and protect against viruses.

User State Migration Tool (USMT)

USMT is a new tool in Windows XP that provides the same functionality as the Files and Settings Transfer Wizard. USMT is designed for administrator use only. Client computers must be connected to a Windows domain controller.

Account Management Enhancements

For computer systems that are not connected to a company network, user account configurations can be changed through the account management feature of the Control Panel. User accounts can be added, deleted, and modified, and passwords can be changed.

Regional Options Enhanced

The regional and language options in the Control Panel have been changed to make adding and changing input languages and keyboard layouts easier for users. Switching between Standards and Formats is made simpler, because the most frequently used options are much easier to find than they were in Windows 2000.

Enhanced File and Printer Sharing

Microsoft has added several new features to enhance file and printer sharing in Windows XP. Some of these options are highlighted next.

1

WebDAV

Publishing data on the Web has been made easier with the introduction of Web Digital Authoring and Versioning (WebDAV) in Windows XP Professional. WebDAV is a technology that is a standard Internet access protocol that travels over existing Internet infrastructures via the Hypertext Transport Protocol (HTTP). Individuals at different locations who want to share and collaborate on files or documents can use WebDAV to accomplish this. Data depositories can be located anywhere on the Internet. Users can access servers on the Web just as they would access any file or server share on a home or corporate network.

Disk Defragmenter Enhancements

The Disk Defragmenter tool has been improved from the original version that was introduced in Windows 2000. Individuals who are members of the Power Users group can schedule disk defragmentation via the Scheduled Tasks feature in the System Tools.

Encrypting of Offline Files Database

One of the big features when Windows 2000 was introduced was Offline Files and Folders. This option gave users the ability to work on company files when not connected to the corporate network. This is a dream for remote users. Windows XP Professional has improved on Offline Files and Folders by allowing the Offline Files database to be encrypted. This database, also known as the Client-Side Cache (CSC), can be encrypted to protect locally cached documents from prying eyes and theft.

Private Access via NetCrawler

Another great tool introduced in Windows XP is NetCrawler. NetCrawler enables users who are unfamiliar with networking to automatically access and configure network devices such as printers. NetCrawler *crawls* or searches, the Entire Network folder and provides links to known devices. NetCrawler is installed by default in the XP Home version and on XP Professional when it is installed in a workgroup mode. NetCrawler does not work when XP Professional is connected to a Windows XP domain.

Fax Sharing

Individuals who need to send and receive faxes can do so easily with the Fax Sharing option in Windows XP Professional. Faxes can be sent using your fax hardware or over a corporate network from Microsoft Outlook or any application that supports printing. Fax Sharing is tightly integrated with the Contact List in Outlook, and individuals can preview faxes before they are sent and receive an email confirmation when the fax is received. XP includes new wizards that make configuring fax software and sending faxes simpler.

Internet Integration

Ease of use and functionality are keywords when describing Internet integration in regard to Windows XP. Even though the changes can't be described as dramatic, there is indeed a new look, and some very nifty features incorporated.

Internet Explorer 6

Internet Explorer 6 (IE6) is included with Windows XP. It incorporates the newer visual look of Windows XP but is not dramatically different under the hood than IE5.5. IE6 does include some advances in media playback and a new Privacy tab that affords the user more control over cookies. A new feature called Auto Image Resize will shrink images that are too large to fit in the browser windows. In addition, Personal Bars have been added to give the user more functionality.

New Explorer Bars

The Explorer Bars, called Personal Bars, are a new feature in IE6. Personal Bars give users quicker access to Web-based functionality without having to open a Web browser. Several Personal Bars are available in IE6, including Search, News, Contacts, Weather, and Media.

Security

Security is always a critical component of any networking environment. This section describes some of the security features inherent in Windows XP.

Single Login with Microsoft Passport

New to Microsoft Windows is the addition of Passport-enabled services. Passport provides a single personalized access point to Web sites with the user's email address.

The Password Wizard in the User Accounts tool in the Control Panel is used to set up a user passport. Once the user information is entered, the user only has to enter his username and password to access all Passport-enabled services. This personal information is protected by encryption technology.

Software Restriction Policies

Administrators can prevent unauthorized applications from running on the network through the use of Software Restriction Policies. A Software Restriction Policy can be configured to allow only trusted applications to be executed on the network.

Increased Virus Protection

For increased protection against virus attacks, Windows XP Professional by default does not allow the execution of email attachments. This is because the majority of viruses that affect computer networks are introduced to the network as attachments via email.

Internet Connection Firewall

A new feature that will benefit small business users of Windows XP Professional is the Internet Connection Firewall. This built-in security feature is basically a dynamic packet filter. Users that are connected directly to the Internet are protected. All unsolicited connections are blocked by the Internet Connection Firewall. It does not provide outbound filtering or application-layer filtering. The logic of Network Address Translator (NAT) is used to validate incoming requests for access to local hosts or the network. The Internet Connection Firewall is available for local area network (LAN), Point-to-Point Over Ethernet (PPPoE), virtual private network (VPN), and dial-up connections.

EFS with Multiuser Support

Encrypted File System (EFS) provides the highest degree of protection against data theft. Data is encrypted with a randomly generated key and is decrypted transparently by the user. Windows XP is the first operating system to allow multiple users to access an encrypted document. EFS services are available via Windows Explorer.

IPSec

IP Security (IPSec) allows for transmission of secure data over the public network. IPSec can be used to ensure that data is safe from the following:

➤ Intrusion during transmission

➤ Interception, viewing, and/or editing

➤ Being captured and replayed to gain sensitive information

IPSec was initially implemented in Windows 2000 as an end-to-end strategy to defend against external and internal network attacks.

Kerberos Support

Kerberos is the core of domain authentication in both Windows 2000 and Windows XP. Kerberos, which is a protocol, uses secret key encryption to protect logon credentials as they traverse a network. Users of Windows XP Professional can be provided single-sign-on to Windows 2000 and XP networks via Kerberos.

Smart Card Support

As with Windows 2000, users of laptop computers can use smart cards to provide a tamper-resistant storage medium for private keys, certificates, and other forms of personal identification. A smart card is an integrated circuit card (ICC) about the size of a credit card. It uses a PIN instead of a password for user identification when logging onto the laptop computer. Smart cards can only be used in a domain environment because Kerberos is used for authentication.

Credential Manager

The Credential Manager feature in Windows XP provides users with a secure store for their user credentials. This can include passwords and X.509 certificates. A single-sign-on is provided for both local and remote users. When a user first attempts to connect, he or she is required to supply credentials to authenticate. Once the credentials are supplied and authenticated, they are saved and can be reused without the user having to reenter them.

Remote User Support

One of the new components of Windows XP is the ability to provide assistance for remote users. This section describes several of the tools that aid in remote administration.

Remote Assistance Tool

Administrators are going to find the Remote Assistance tool to be one of the best features in Windows XP. With Remote Assistance, you can allow another user to control your computer. The other user can view the screen settings and use the mouse and keyboard to access the PC just as if he or she were sitting in front of the PC. This is one of the best troubleshooting tools provided with the new operating system. For extra security, a password can be required before another user can attach to your computer.

Remote Desktop

Suppose that you are traveling and need to access specific files on your home or company network. Remote Desktop, which uses the Microsoft Remote Desktop Protocol (RDP), gives users the capability to access and control their computers over the Internet. Remote Desktop is based on Windows Terminal Services. When applications are run on the remote XP computer, only the keyboard and mouse input and the display output data are transmitted over the network to the remote computer.

The following resources are available within a Remote Desktop connection:

➤ File system redirection

➤ Printer redirection

➤ Port redirection

➤ Audio

➤ Clipboard

Offline Files and Folders

Windows 2000 introduced the world to Offline Files and Folders. A user can specify network-based files that she would like to be able to use even when she is not connected to the network. With the use of Offline Files and Folders, users can work on documents just as if they were still connected to their company network. These files can be synchronized after the user reconnects to the company network.

Virtual Private Networks (VPNs)

Remote users have the capability to transmit secure data to their corporate network through the use of VPNs. A new connection wizard has been provided in Windows XP that simplifies the creating of secure pipelines between a user's laptop computer and a corporate network. VPN in Windows XP supports several ways of creating secure connections, including the Point-to-Point Tunneling Protocol (PPTP), Layer 2 Tunneling Protocol (L2TP), and IPSec.

Enhanced Online Conferencing

Windows XP includes several Telephony Application Programming Interface (TAPI)-based applications, such as NetMeeting, that enable you to create the infrastructure needed to conduct online conferences and provide end-user training. Several of the improvements are listed next.

The following are the improvements in Windows XP for audio conferencing:

➤ Support for new codecs for improved quality and interoperability

➤ Support for DirectSound API

➤ Acoustic echo cancellation

➤ Acoustic gain control

➤ Reduced ambient noise

➤ Improved jitter buffer control

The following are the improvements in Windows XP for video conferencing:

➤ Support for new codecs for improved quality and interoperability

➤ Support for new cameras

➤ Support for DirectDraw API

➤ Support for lip synchronization

➤ Support for larger video sizes

Help and Support

Windows XP makes it easier for users to receive assistance through Help and Support. It has been designed to provide users help through multiple remote and online resources. Users can search across the entire Windows compiled Hypertext Markup Language (HTML) Help file databases.

A number of tools have been integrated into Help and Support, including the System Configuration Utility and Msinfo32.exe, which provides detailed system information about the computer.

Extended Laptop Capabilities

As with its predecessor Windows 2000, Windows XP was designed to optimize laptop computer use. This section describes several enhancements that have been added to expand the capabilities of laptop computing.

Improved Power Management

Individuals who use Windows XP on their laptop computers will notice that they are able to work longer on battery power than they could with previous versions of Windows. Windows XP reduces the amount of power a laptop is using by constantly monitoring the CPU state. More accurate data about the amount of power that is actually left will be provided by the operating system, and this can aid in preventing premature system shutdown. If the battery is nearing its drained state, the laptop can be put into hibernation mode and data on it can be saved.

IrCOMM Modem Driver for IrDA

Users of infrared-enabled cell phones can now use their phones to make modem connections with their laptop computers. Cellular phones that have an IrCOMM virtual serial port can be placed next to the infrared port on the notebook computer and a new network connection can be created. Then, a phone call can be placed, as you would with a modem.

Hibernation

Hibernation was one of the key laptop management features of Windows 2000. Hibernation can provide laptop users with maximum battery life by shutting down the laptop when it is not in use. This can be at a preset time or on demand. Any documents that the user was working on are saved to the hard disk. When the user resumes using the laptop, all applications are opened exactly as they were before the laptop was put into hibernation.

Hot Docking

Hot docking gives the user the ability to dock or undock his laptop without having to change the hardware configuration or reboot. If the docking station configuration has been modified, Windows XP will automatically detect the changes and install the new configuration.

Advanced Configuration and Power Interface (ACPI)

The Advanced Configuration and Power Interface provides the latest in power management for notebook computers. Power management in Windows XP is based on ACPI technology. Windows XP improves on the ACPI foundation of Windows 2000 by providing additional new power management features, which include the following:

➤ Processor power control

➤ CardBus Wake-on-LAN

➤ Wake on Battery

➤ Lid power and display dimming

ClearType

ClearType is a new display technology that is being introduced in Windows XP. ClearType triples the horizontal resolution that is available for rendering text. This produces a much clearer display of text on a liquid crystal display (LCD) screen.

Viewing Web Pages Offline

Laptop and remote users have the capability to take entire Web pages offline for future viewing. When visiting Web sites, a user can simply right-click the Explorer Bar, and a wizard will guide them through setting up Offline Web Page viewing. They can also schedule when Offline Web Pages are updated.

Dual View

Dual View is an extension of the multiple monitor support that was introduced in Windows 98. Many new laptop computers support two interfaces to the same display adapter. With Windows XP, laptop users can enable the two interfaces to display different output at the same time. For example, the laptop computer could be set up to display data on one monitor and run a presentation on the second monitor.

Improved Networking and Communications

Several new components have been integrated in Windows XP to improve both networking and communications capabilities for end users. Several of the key new additions are described in this section.

Integrated WiFi Wireless Network Support

One of the major new enhancements in Windows XP is the improvement in performance in wireless networks. Support for wireless LANs has always been a wish more than a reality in networking environments. This has changed with Windows XP. Several enhancements have been added to Windows XP to aid in deploying wireless networks. Microsoft has adopted and implemented IEEE 802.1X support in Windows XP. IEEE 802.1X is the Enhanced Ethernet and Wireless Security standard for port-based network access control. Wireless Zero Configuration gives users the ability to configure connections to networks without user intervention. Wireless Roaming Support provides the capability to detect the availability of networks.

Network Location Awareness

If a user moves a computer from one location to another, Windows XP provides a way for the operating system to determine the new location of the computer.

Network Bridge

Small business or home users who use dissimilar types of networks can use the Network Bridge to set up and configure their networks. If users want to connect a notebook that is using a wireless infrared network connection to a computer that is using an Ethernet connection, Network Bridge can be used to provide the connection for these two computers.

Network Setup Wizard

Individuals who are new to networking can use the Network Setup Wizard to set up and manage their network. The user will be walked through the key steps necessary for setting up file sharing, printer connections, and Internet connections. Users can automatically set up and configure the network and Internet Connection Sharing (ICS, described next). They do not need to know about network protocols or the physical network requirements.

1

Internet Connection Sharing (ICS)

Small businesses can connect all of their computers to the Internet through a single Internet connection utilizing ICS. This provides an economical way for a business to connect multiple computers to the Internet through only one Internet connection. Users can securely access the Internet through shared DSL, cable modems, or telephone line connections.

UPnP Client Support

A new set of Component Object Model (COM) interfaces have been added to Windows XP to provide support for Universal Plug and Play (UPnP) client support. Windows XP can discover UPnP devices on the network and identify the services the devices provide. Applications only have to be concerned with accessing the available UPnP devices and not the UPnP-specific protocols that are required.

Quality of Service (QoS)

Administrators can control via Quality of Service (QoS) how much network bandwidth is allocated between applications running on the network. Crucial applications can be allocated more bandwidth than less critical applications.

Network Diagnostics Features

Microsoft has added network diagnostic features to Windows XP to aid in diagnosing network problems. The following list identifies some of the features added to enable troubleshooting of small network problems:

➤ The Network Diagnostic Web Page and NetSh helper

➤ Network Connections Support tab

➤ Network Connection Repair link

➤ Task Manager Networking tab

➤ Updated Command Line Network Diagnostics tool

Support for Legacy Protocols

Windows XP has eliminated support for several legacy protocols, including NetBIOS Extended User Interface (NetBEUI) and Data Link Control (DLC). In the 64-bit version of Windows XP, support has been removed for Internet Packet Exchange/Sequenced Packet Exchange (IPX/SPX).

IPv6 Development Stack

Windows XP is the first version of Windows to include a complete version 6 protocol stack. This is in preparation for the future migration to Internet Protocol version 6 (IPv6) networks. IPv6 has the following features:

➤ A new header format

➤ Large address space

➤ Stateless and stateful address configuration

➤ Built-in security

➤ Better support for QoS

Connection Manager

Connection Manager, which is a client dialer and connection management software, is a tool that has been available in previous versions of Windows. Several enhancements have been made to the version that is included in Windows XP:

➤ Connection Manager Administration Kit (CMAK) includes user interface additions that were not in previous versions of Windows

➤ Support for split tunneling

➤ Capability for users to save frequently used settings

➤ Logging capability to aid in troubleshooting

PPPoE Clients

Support for clients to create connections using Point-to-Point over Ethernet (PPPoE) has been added to Windows XP. PTPoE can be used to obtain authenticated access to high-speed data networks.

PVC Encapsulation–RFC 2684

Microsoft has attempted to make DSL simpler to implement in Windows XP with the implementation of PVC Encapsulation–RFC 2684. RFC 2684 implements a common method used by industry carriers to deploy DSL that involves using an NDIS driver that looks like an Ethernet interface but uses DSL/ATM PVC to carry Transfer Control Protocol/Internet Protocol (TCP/IP) frames.

NDIS 5.1 and Remote NDIS

The network interface cards (NICs) and their drivers (NDIS) ensure that the physical network is available to both the operating system and all protocols that are being used in the computer. The NICs have been enhanced in Windows XP to include the following:

➤ Plug and Play and power event notification

➤ Support for send cancellation

➤ Increased statistics capability

➤ Performance enhancement

➤ Wake-on-LAN changes

➤ Support for remote NDIS

Remote NDIS, which is also included as part of Windows XP, enables USB network devices to be attached to a network without the installation of third-party drivers.

Peer-to-Peer Network Support

For organizations that are currently using peer-to-peer networking, Windows XP Professional computers can be easily and seamlessly integrated into their existing network.

Best of Windows XP

Several new technologies have been incorporated into Windows XP, and some of the key ones are described in this section.

Digital Camera Friendly

Several new tools have been added in Windows XP to make it the most digital camera friendly version of Windows yet. These tools include the Scanner and Camera Wizard, Explorer Views, the Photo Printing Wizard, Web Publishing, and Internet Print Ordering.

The Scanner and Camera Wizard eases the task of moving your digital images from your digital camera to your Windows XP computer. This wizard supports removable media connected via USB or those devices that use Windows Image Acquisition (WIA)-compatible drivers.

The new Windows Explorer in XP now understands the Exchangeable Image File format (EXIF) information that is embedded in digital camera JPEG and TIFF images. EXIF is an industry standard that was established in 1995 and is the preferred image format for digital cameras. The majority of digital cameras today use EXIF compressed files. This information can be viewed directly in the file's Property window. Two new views have been added to Explorer: Tile and Filmstrip. Additional buttons have been added for printing, photo finishing, and uploading images to shared photo sites.

The Photo Printing Wizard makes printing your photos a snap. Select the image to print, and click the Print Pictures button. You are then given options regarding the layout for the photo you are printing.

Web Publishing will allow users to *publish* or upload, their images to Web storage sites. Images can be uploaded via MSN, to an XDrive, or to an FTP site of the user's choice.

Internet Print Ordering will allow users to order prints of their images directly from online photo finishers. Currently, only two photo finishers are available for this feature, but this selection is expected to increase with the implementation of Windows XP.

Instant Messenger

Users of Windows XP can communicate instantly online with other Windows XP users through Microsoft Instant Messenger. Instant Messenger allows users to see which users are active on their computers and to send an individual (or a group of individuals) a message or a file. They can even send a message from Instant Messenger to a pager.

Native Support for CD R/W Drivers

Copying compact discs has become as common as copying floppy disks was in previous versions of Windows. Windows XP provides native support for copying CDs. CDs can be copied in CD-R and CD-RW format with the simple drag-and-drop functionality provided to other Windows applications. DVD-RAM drive read and write support is also provided.

Windows Media Player 8

A new version of Windows Media Player debuts with XP. It takes on the new sleek visual style of XP and brings together several digital media technologies, including CD and DVD playback, jukebox management, audio CD creation, and media transfer to portable devices. It includes DVD video playback, CD-to-PC copying of music files, and auto conversion of files to the MP3 format.

Windows Movie Maker

Video lovers will appreciate the basic video editing capabilities included with Windows Movie Maker. Windows Movie Maker 1.1 is an updated version of the digital editing capabilities introduced in Windows Me. Both analog and video data can be captured, edited, and outputted, to a final product in the Windows media format. Users also have the ability to create slideshows from their still images.

New My Music Folder

The My Music folder is the default storage location for music files. When Windows Media Player is used to copy tracks to the computer, an artist folder for the track is automatically created on the computer in the My Music folder.

1

64-Bit Support

For users who have a higher level of demand from the operating system, Microsoft has developed a 64-bit version of Windows XP. The 64-bit Windows XP edition is designed to work with the latest processor family being developed by Intel—the Itanium processor. These chips are being developed to meet the demands for online transaction processing, high-end graphics, and memory-intensive and multimedia applications.

The current 32-bit version of Windows XP supports up to 4GB of system memory. The Windows XP 64-bit edition supports up to 18GB of RAM and 16TB of virtual memory. It supports up to two Itanium processors for maximum performance and scalability.

Improved Backup and Restore Capabilities

Microsoft has made some minor improvements to the Backup and Restore utility that ships with Windows XP. Microsoft has expanded the type of media that users can back up their data to. Users are not limited to floppies or tape media. This is an absolute necessity in the age of CD-RW drives.

Users can run the Backup and Restore tool in Wizard mode, which walks them through the backup process step by step, or in Expect mode, in which they determine manually what to back up and where to back it up.

A new good feature of the Backup and Restore utility is the addition of the Automatic System Recovery Wizard, which gives a user the ability to make a System State backup. The System State contains important Registry information and Windows system files. In the event of a system catastrophe, the system can be restored to its previous state by restoring the System State information.

Windows Product Activation

Licensing of the Windows software has always been a major concern of Microsoft. Individuals would purchase one copy of the Windows operating system and use it on multiple computers. This will no longer be an option with Windows XP. Windows Product Activation is being implemented in Windows XP to ensure that Windows XP products are not being unlawfully copied and installed on more than the number of computers allowed in the product license. It also ensures purchasers that the copy of Windows XP they are buying is a genuine copy.

After the initial installation of XP, an Activation and Registration Wizard is started that prompts the user to enter a product identification code located on the back of the Windows XP CD-ROM jewel case. Once the product identification code is entered, the wizard will attempt to establish an online connection to Microsoft. The computer's configuration is assessed and a unique identification number is assigned to that product identification number. If an online connection can't be made, the user will have to contact a customer service representative at Microsoft to complete the activation. A 30-day grace period exists for activating your new installation of Windows XP. If product activation is not done within that time period, the operating system will stop working.

Chapter Summary

In this chapter, you were introduced to Windows XP Professional. You have learned that it is easier to use than its predecessor, Windows 2000 Professional. It has a new sleek visual design and a redesigned Start menu. The Search Companion has been upgraded to make searching more intuitive. A feature has been added to allow multiple users to log onto the same computer without having to reboot. And a new File and Transfer Wizard has been added to aid in transferring files from one computer to another.

You learned that Windows XP is the most reliable and dependable operating system released to date from Microsoft. It includes the ability to roll back device drivers in the case of system instability. The new System Restore feature will aid in recovering from a system failure. Windows XP has fewer reboots and improved code protection, and has scalable memory and multiprocessor support. Dynamic updates ensure that the latest versions of critical system files are on the computer.

Windows XP Professional is designed to provide better resistance to application failure. Windows File Protection ensures that critical system files are not accidentally overwritten, and the Windows Installer can be used to configure and upgrade key Microsoft programs.

Windows XP is the most hardware- and software-compatible operating system Microsoft has released to date. It includes supports for new hardware technologies, including USB and PS/2 keyboards, IEEE 1394 USB array microphones, and the new Intel Itanium 64-bit processor.

Windows XP provides better ways to manage your network through the use of tools such as IntelliMirror, Group Policy, Resultant Set of Policy, and the User State Migration Tool. The Disk Defragmenter tool has been enhanced, and WebDAV has been added to allow for the sharing and collaboration of files over the Internet. You can now encrypt the Offline Files database for increased security.

Internet Explorer 6 has been included with Windows XP Professional. It includes advances in multimedia playback and a new privacy standard for the use of cookies. Several new Explorer Bars have been added to IE6 to give users quicker access to Web-based functionality without having to open a Web browser.

Windows XP has added several new security features. Individuals can now use the Microsoft Passport to log onto Web sites with their email address and password. An Internet Connection Firewall has been added to the operating system, and EFS now has multiuser support. As with Windows 2000, Windows XP includes IPSec, smart card support, and Kerberos support.

Remote administration tools have been added to Windows XP. The Remote Assistant tool allows the computer to be taken over by a second user (such as an administrator) and worked on just as if the user were physically sitting at the computer console. Another feature, Remote Desktop, gives users access to their home computers remotely over the Internet.

Windows XP has enhanced laptop capabilities with the addition of improved power management, hibernation, hot docking, and ClearType. DualView has been added to enable the laptop computer to display two different outputs at the same time.

Windows XP has improved networking and communications support. Integrated WiFi Network, or IEEE 802 1.X, is supported. With Network Bridge, users can connect dissimilar types of networks. The new Network Setup Wizard makes setting up your home network easy and convenient. You also learned that by using Internet Connection Sharing, multiple computers can share one Internet connection. Network Diagnostic features have been added to aid in troubleshooting network problems, and Windows XP is the first operating system to support the IPv6 Development Stack.

Windows XP is the most digital camera friendly version of Windows to date. Instant Messenger has been added to allow users to communicate online instantly. Native support for CD read/write drives has been added as well as Windows Media Player 8 and Windows Movie Maker 1.1.

Review Questions

1. What new feature in Windows XP Professional uses restore points to recover a system to its previous state after it crashes?

    a. Windows Update

    b. System Restore

    c. Taskbar Grouping

    d. Group Policy

2. Ronald has just installed Windows XP on his new computer. What must he use to register and activate the new operating system?

   a. He must use Windows Product Activation to register the new software with Microsoft.

   b. He must use Windows Update to register the new software with Microsoft.

   c. He can use his Microsoft Passport account to register the software.

   d. He must call Microsoft customer service to register the new operating system.

3. Joann wants to ensure that her recently installed version of Windows XP has the latest service packs installed. What can she use to ensure this?

   a. She can run Windows Product Activation.

   b. She can run System Restore.

   c. She can run Windows Update.

   d. She should copy the latest service pack from the Windows XP Professional CD.

4. What technology introduced in Windows XP allows users to share and collaborate on files on the Internet?

   a. Offline Files and Folders

   b. Fax Sharing

   c. Remote Desktop

   d. WebDAV

5. Jonathan wants to set up his new computer on the network, but he is unsure about what printers exist on the network and how to install the printer drivers for them. What tool can he use to search, locate, and install the print devices?

   a. NetCrawler

   b. Windows Search Companion

   c. The Microsoft Help and Support tool

   d. Credential Manager

6. What new technology by Microsoft gives James the ability to log onto multiple secure Web sites with just his email address and password?

   a. Windows Update

   b. Dynamic Update

   c. Microsoft Passport

   d. WebDAV

1

7. William is traveling and needs to send sensitive company data back to the office. What security feature in Windows XP will allow him to transmit the data over the public Internet without fear of the data being compromised?

   a. IPSec

   b. VPN

   c. IE6

   d. Network Bridge

8. Marshall will be traveling on company business but wants to be able to work on several corporate documents while he is away. Which Windows XP Professional feature will allow Marshall to work on the corporate documents during his travel?

   a. Offline Web page viewing

   b. Offline Files and Folders

   c. ICS

   d. QoS

9. What new laptop feature in Windows XP provides clearer display of text for LCD screens?

   a. Dual View

   b. IrCOMM

   c. Hot docking

   d. ClearType

10. What tool in Windows XP will allow Jeff to back up the System State data on his network?

   a. The Automatic Recovery Wizard

   b. System Restore

   c. The Help and Support tool

   d. Windows Media Player

CHAPTER TWO

Installing Windows XP Professional

After completing this chapter, you will be able to:

✓ Describe the hardware requirements for installing Windows XP Professional

✓ Explain the differences between a clean and an upgrade installation of Windows XP Professional

✓ Explain when to use Winnt.exe versus Winnt32.exe when installing Windows XP Professional

✓ Describe the types of deployment tools available for installing Windows XP Professional

✓ Describe an unattended installation and when to use it

✓ Describe what an answer file is and how it is used in unattended installations of Windows XP Professional

✓ Describe how to use the Windows Setup Manager tool

✓ Explain what a UDF (Uniqueness Database File) is and how it is used in unattended installations of Windows XP Professional

✓ Describe the purpose of the Sysprep tool

✓ Deploy Windows XP Professional using RIS

✓ Deploy Windows XP Professional using SMS

✓ Describe the User State Migration Tool and how it is used during the installation of Windows XP Professional

✓ Uninstall Windows XP Professional

✓ Set up Windows XP Professional in a multiboot configuration

✓ Describe Automatic System Recovery

A s it has done with all versions of Windows, Microsoft has provided multiple ways to install the Windows XP Professional operating system. The installation method you choose will be based on several factors, including whether you are upgrading from an existing operating system or performing a clean installation.

It is expensive and inefficient to manually install an operating system on each computer in your network environment. Administrators can automate an installation of Windows XP Professional by using an answer file, which contains pre-defined settings and answers to the questions that are asked during setup. Optionally, a custom installation can be used to support specific hardware and software configurations.

System Requirements

The first step toward the installation of Windows XP is checking various system requirements to ensure that the hardware you're planning to install the new operating system on is capable of supporting Windows XP.

Hardware Requirements

Microsoft has established specific hardware requirements for the installation of Windows XP. Windows XP will work properly with the minimum requirements, but, for peak operation performance, your computer equipment should meet at least the recommended requirements. Table 2.1 lists the minimum and recommended hardware requirements as specified by Microsoft.

Note: Both single- and dual-processor systems are supported by Windows XP.

Checking the System BIOS

After you have verified that your computer hardware is capable of supporting Windows XP, you need to make sure that the system BIOS is also supported by Windows XP.

Table 2.1   Hardware requirements for installing Windows XP.

Component	Minimum	Recommended
CPU	Intel Pentium 233MHz or higher	Intel Pentium II 300MHz or higher
RAM	64MB	128MB
Hard disk space	2GB with 650MB of free space	2GB of free space
Video	VGA	SVGA
Input	Keyboard and mouse	Keyboard and mouse
For CD-ROM installation	12x or faster CD-ROM or a DVD-ROM	12x or faster CD-ROM or a DVD-ROM
For network installation	Network adapter	Network adapter

The BIOS, or basic input/output system, is responsible for enabling the operating system to communicate with the computer's hardware. The BIOS is used to boot, or start, the computer when you turn it on, and it resides on the motherboard of the computer system. Windows XP, as with Windows 2000, uses Advanced Power Management (APM). To use Windows XP, your computer must contain an Advanced Configuration and Power Interface (ACPI)-compliant BIOS.

If your computer supports ACPI, a BIOS upgrade is not necessary. If it does not support ACPI, you need to check with your computer manufacturer to obtain the proper BIOS upgrade for working with Windows XP.

Warning: Make sure you acquire the correct BIOS for your computer. Installing the incorrect update of the BIOS can cause serious damage to the computer and make it inoperable.

Microsoft provides a tool that can be used to search for computers that are compatible with Windows XP. Check **www.microsoft.com/windows2000/server/howtobuy/upgrading/compat/biosissue.asp** for additional information about BIOS upgrades.

Hardware Compatibility List

The importance of the Hardware Compatibility List (HCL) cannot be stressed enough. The HCL contains a list of the up-to-date supported hardware for Windows XP. Computer devices on the HCL have passed rigorous compatibility tests with the Windows XP operating system. Hardware on the HCL has been designed to work specifically with the new operating system.

The HCL is updated regularly as new systems and peripherals are tested. To obtain the latest version of the HCL, go to **www.microsoft.com/hcl**. Two HCLs exist for Windows XP. One is for the standard Intel Pentium processor, and the second is for the new Intel Itanium processor. Make sure that you are acquiring the correct HCL for the type of processor in your computer.

Check Upgrade Mode

Microsoft provides a tool that enables you to check for potential problems before upgrading to Windows XP. This can be done without actually upgrading your current operating system.

Winnt32.exe in the i386 folder on the Windows XP CD can be run with the **/checkupgradeonly** command-line option to run a test upgrade. This will produce a report called Upgrade.txt that is placed in the system root of the hard drive. This test will flag potential upgrade problems, including hardware compatibility issues and software that might not migrate during the upgrade process.

If incompatibility issues are found, the Upgrade.txt report will identify the problems and display links to Web sites that may provide additional information about the problems. If the incompatibility issues are not resolved, and you try to run the Windows XP setup program, it might not continue until the issue is fixed. If the setup program does continue, software identified as a potential problem might not work after the upgrade.

Backup Files

Use a backup program to save existing user settings and desktop configurations before you upgrade to Windows XP. If you are upgrading from Windows NT or 2000, you can use the Windows Backup and Restore Tool to back up the files to disk, tape, or some other type of backup media.

Scan All Hard Disks for Viruses

You want to scan all hard drives to ensure that they are free from viruses before you start the upgrade. Be sure to disable the virus protection software after you perform the scan and before you start the installation of Windows XP Professional.

Uncompress Drives

If you used third-party utility programs to compress your hard drive, you want to uncompress these drives before you start the installation of Windows XP Professional. You should not upgrade a compressed drive unless it was compressed with the Windows NT NFTS compression feature.

Remove Incompatible Software

If software was identified as incompatible with Windows XP Professional when you ran the checkupgradeonly report, remove that software before you start the installation. The Windows XP Professional setup program might halt if it finds software that it detects will not work properly with the operating system.

Upgrade vs. Clean Install

One of the main questions when preparing to install Windows XP is whether to perform an upgrade of your current operating system or to do a clean install. The type of operating system you are currently using will determine your upgrade options.

Upgrade paths to Windows XP Professional are supported from Windows 2000 Professional, Windows NT 4, Windows Me, and Windows 98. If your operating system is Windows 95, 3.x, or DOS, you will have to do a clean install.

When upgrading to Windows XP, all existing user settings are retained. Applications that were installed before the upgrade will also be retained as long as they are compatible with Windows XP. Performing a clean installation of Windows XP will not retain any user and desktop settings. All applications will have to be reinstalled. You should do a clean install if no other operating system is on the system, the operating system does not support upgrading from Windows XP, or the system needs to support a multiboot configuration.

Hardware Compatibility Issues When Upgrading from Windows Me, 98, 95, and 3.x

If you are upgrading from Windows Me, 98, 95, or 3.x, you might have to download updated drivers before the upgrade will complete. Windows XP does not support the 16-bit virtual device driver mode of these operating systems. Drivers for these operating systems will not migrate, and the setup program will not continue until updated drivers are obtained. Many applications written for these operating systems might not work with Windows XP, including some system tools and network clients.

Upgrading from Windows 2000 and NT 4

The majority of applications for Windows NT 2000 and 4 Service Pack 6 will work with Windows XP. These file systems all share a common operating system kernel, Registry, file system, and security structure. The exception to this is some anti-virus software and some networking software, such as IPX/SPX. The majority of peripherals that worked under these operating systems will also work with Windows XP Professional. If your Windows NT 4 file system is NTFS, it will automatically be converted to the NTFS version used by Windows XP during the upgrade.

File System

If you are upgrading from an earlier version of Windows, such as Windows 95, 98, or 3.x, the file system supported was either FAT16 or FAT32. Windows XP supports both the FAT16 and FAT32 file systems but was designed specifically for the NTFS file system. NTFS has many added benefits over both FAT16 and FAT32, including:

➤ Compression

➤ Disk quotas

➤ File encryption

➤ File and folder permissions

➤ Large disk partitions

If you are planning to install Windows XP in a multiboot configuration with a previous version of Windows, such as Windows 95, you need to use the FAT file system on any partition that Windows 95 needs access to.

Note: If you are trying to upgrade a system that is using Windows 98 compressed drives, the drives will have to be uncompressed before starting the upgrade process.

Installing Windows XP Professional

There are many ways to install Windows XP Professional. The type of installation depends on several factors, including whether you will be performing a clean upgrade versus a new install, the number of workstations that will need to be installed, and the amount of user interaction that you want to take place during the installation.

Winnt vs. Winnt32

To start the Windows XP setup program, you run Winnt.exe or Winnt32.exe depending on the operating system currently on the computer system. If the computer system is running Windows 3.x or MS-DOS, you start the Windows XP setup program by running Winnt.exe from the command line. If the computer system is running Windows 95, 98, Me, NT, or 2000, you run Winnt32.exe from the Run option on the Start menu or from a command line. Both Winnt.exe and Winnt32.exe have several command-line options that can be used to tailor the installation. To see these options, run the executable with the **/?** option at a command line.

If you are familiar with Windows NT or Windows 2000, you will notice that the command-line options available for running Winnt.exe and Winnt32.exe are similar. Microsoft has added three command-line switches to Winnt32.exe with Windows XP Professional:

➤ **/dudisable**—Prevents Dynamic Update from running during the installation of Windows XP

➤ **/duprepare:pathname**—Prepares installation shares so that they can be used with Dynamic Update files downloaded from the Microsoft Update Web site

➤ **/dushare:pathname**—Specifies a share on which the Dynamic Update files were downloaded from the Microsoft Update Web site

Now, look at the steps involved when you install Windows XP Professional from the Windows XP Professional product CD:

1. Start the computer system with the Windows XP Production CD.

2. Select To Setup Windows XP Professional Now.

3. Read and accept the license agreement.

4. Select the partition that you want to install Windows XP Professional on.

5. Select the type of file system for the installation partition.

6. If you want to change the regional settings, click Customize and make the changes.

7. Type your name and organization name.

8. Type the product key.

9. Type the name for the computer and a password for the local Administrator account.

10. Select the date, time, and time zone settings.

11. Choose the type of network settings, and click Next.

12. Enter a workgroup or domain name, and click Next.

13. The computer will restart and the Log On To Windows dialog box will appear.

Selecting the Type of Deployment Tool

Installing Windows XP by running the Windows XP setup program with either the Winnt.exe or Winnt32.exe executable is a viable option when upgrading or doing a clean install on a single computer. Microsoft has provided users with several options for installing the operating system when it involves multiple computers. This section discusses the available installation options.

Bootable CD-ROM

A Windows XP bootable CD-ROM can be used to perform either a clean or an upgrade installation of Windows XP on computers that are not part of a network. When installing from a CD-ROM, the installation process will be quicker, because system files will not have to travel over the network for the installation. The computer must be configured to support booting from CD-ROMs.

Administrators can make image copies of Windows XP on bootable CD-ROMs and use them to provide an automated installation with little or no interaction from users. Scripts can be used to tailor the installation for field offices or remote locations. These scripts can be copied onto a floppy disk and used with the CD-ROMs to provide user-specific settings during the installations.

Network Share

For users who are part of a network or have high-speed connectivity to a network, Windows XP can be installed from a network or distribution share. To install

Windows XP Professional from a network share, the administrator must first set up a distribution share. This distribution share holds the i386 folder from the Windows XP Professional CD. Client computers will connect to the network share to load the operating system. The client computers must have a partition with at least 650MB of free space. Microsoft recommends that you have at least 2GB of free space on the hard drive. The partition should be formatted using FAT32. If the client computer has a network client, connect to the distribution share and run the Windows XP Professional setup program. If the client computer is not configured with a network client, it must be started with a boot disk that will allow it to connect to the network distribution share.

Unattended Installation

If you have a large number of computer systems that need to be upgraded to Windows XP Professional, installing from a bootable CD-ROM might not be the most efficient method for deploying the operating system. An unattended installation is the easiest way to deploy the operating system on multiple systems.

An unattended installation uses scripts to simplify the installation. Microsoft provides a tool called Windows Setup Manager that guides you through the process of creating scripts for unattended installations. Scripts can be configured to run the installation with no user interaction. If some user interaction is required during the installation, the scripts can be configured to prompt for user input when needed.

Unattended installations can be performed with a CD-ROM or from a network share. If you are performing the installation over a network share, you can only perform an upgrade. The computer must already have an operating system installed. You cannot perform a clean installation of Windows XP Professional over a network connection. If you need to perform a clean installation of Windows XP Professional, your computer system must have El-Torito No Emulation CD-ROM boot support, and you need to use the Winnt.sif answer file.

Answer Files

If you have gone through the process of installing any version of Windows, you know that user input is required through a series of graphical user interface (GUI) dialog boxes at specific points during the installation. Answer files provide a way to provide the user input during an unattended installation. The setup program uses the answer file to interact with the distribution folders and provide information that the end user would be prompted for during a typical manual Windows XP Professional installation. The answer file is called Unattend.txt. If you are running a CD-based unattended installation, the answer file is called Winnt.sif.

Note: A sample Unattend.txt answer file is included on the Windows XP CD that can be edited to meet your specific installation requirements with any text editor.

The Windows Setup Manager Wizard will step you through the process of creating an answer file. You should have an understanding of the structure and syntax of the answer file in case you decide to bypass using the wizard and create your answer file with a text editor. The settings in the answer file follow a specific format

```
[section]key=value
```

where **[section]** describes the parameter, **key** defines the name of the parameter, and **value** is the actual configuration settings.

Several sections and items are required in the Unattend.txt file. Table 2.2 lists the required sections and entries, and Listing 2.1 shows a sample answer file.

Listing 2.1   Sample Windows XP Professional Unattend.txt file.

```
[Data]
     AutoPartition=1
     MsDosInitiated="0"
     UnattendedInstall="Yes"

[Unattended]
     UnattendMode=FullUnattended
     OemSkipEula=Yes
     OemPreinstall=No
     TargetPath=\WINDOWS

[GuiUnattended]
     AdminPassword="4FT67"
     EncryptedAdminPassword=NO
     OEMSkipRegional=1
     TimeZone=20
     OemSkipWelcome=1
```

Table 2.2   Required Unattend.txt file sections and entries.

Required Section	Required Entries in Section
[Unattended]	UnattendMode
	Target Path
[GuiUnattended]	AdminPassword
	TimeZone
[Identification]	JoinWorkGroup
[LicenseFilePrintData]	AutoMode
	AutoUsers
[UserData]	ComputerName
	FullName

```
[UserData]
     ProductID=12345-12345-12345-12345-12345
     FullName="Joe Doe"
     OrgName="John's Company"
     ComputerName=JoeD

[Display]
     BitsPerPel=8

[RegionalSettings]
     LanguageGroup=13

[GuiRunOnce]
     Command0="rundll32 printui.dll,PrintUIEntry /in /n
\\Printserver\HPLJIIID"

[Identification]
     JoinDomain=JohnCompany

[Networking]
     InstallDefaultComponents=Yes
```

Windows Setup Manager

Microsoft provides a tool that can be used to edit or create answer files. Windows Setup Manager is located on the Windows XP Professional CD and uses a GUI to walk the user through the process of creating and editing answer files.

Windows Setup Manager can be used to do the following:

➤ Create a new answer file to aid in automating the installation of Windows XP on numerous computers

➤ Extract preconfigured system information to an answer file that can be replicated to other computers

➤ Create a distribution share point

To install Windows Setup Manager, go to the \Support\Tools folder on the Windows XP CD. Locate the Deploy.cab file. Right-click the file, and select Extract. Select the folder to extract the deployment tools to.

Now that you have extracted Windows Setup Manager, take a look at the steps you perform to create an answer file:

1. Go to the folder to which you extracted the Setupmgr.exe file and double-click the file. The Windows Setup Manager Wizard starts. Click Next.

2. You have the option to either create a new answer file or modify an existing one. Select the Create A New Answer File radio button, and click Next.

3. Select the type of product you are creating the answer file for. This can be for a Windows Unattended Installation, a Sysprep Install, or Remote Installation Services. Select Windows Unattended Installation, and click Next.

4. Select the type of platform the answer file is for. You can create answer files for Windows XP Home Edition, Windows XP Professional, Windows 2000 Server, and XP Advanced Server and Data Center Server. Select Windows XP Professional, and click Next.

5. Select the type of user interaction that you want during the Windows installation. Your options are Provide Defaults, Fully Automated, Hide Pages, Read Only, and GUI Attended. Select Provide Defaults, and click Next.

6. You have the option of creating a distribution folder that will hold the Windows XP Professional files or installing from a CD. Select No, This Answer File Will Be Used To Install From A CD, and click Next.

7. Now, you can provide information that would normally be entered by the user through the GUI dialog boxes. Figure 2.1 shows the available options. Select the options you want to add and then click Next.

Note: You must complete the General Settings section at a mimimum when creating the answer file.

8. A dialog box will be displayed prompting you for the location of the answer file—Unattend.txt. Select the location, and click OK.

9. The creation of the answer file is complete, and you can close Windows Setup Manager.

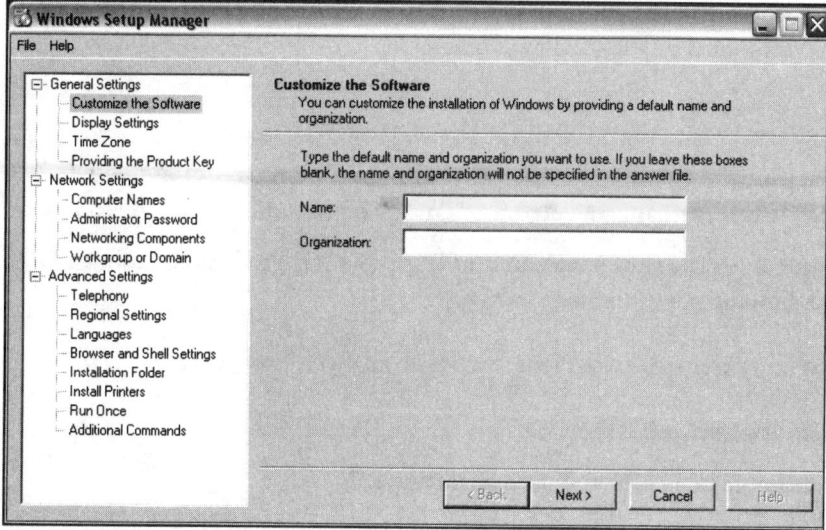

Figure 2.1   Options available through Windows Setup Manager.

Uniqueness Database File (UDF)

The Uniqueness Database File (UDF) is a text file that can be used to supplement an answer file during an unattended installation. You might wonder why you would need to use a UDF file if you already have an answer file. By adding a UDF file to the unattended installation, you can supply specific information during the installation, such as computer names and usernames. The UDF will override the general answers provided by the answer file during the unattended installation.

UDFs can be extremely useful for administrators who have to install a large number of computer systems that have different setup configurations. One point to remember about using a UDF file is that even though you need only one answer file for the unattended installation, you need a separate UDF for each computer or group of computers, because each UDF will contain the unique information for each separate computer or group of computers being installed.

The UDF consists of two sections. The first section is used to specify what sections of data will be either merged or replaced in the answer file. The second section contains the actual data that is being replaced or merged. Strings called *unique IDs* are used to index the UDF, and each computer or group of computers must have a unique ID. The sections that are being replaced are mapped to the unique IDs. The information in the replacement sections is merged or replaced in the answer file during the GUI-mode setup of the unattended installation.

Windows Setup Manager can be used to create UDFs. To create a UDF using Setup Manager, the administrator enters multiple computer names on the Computer Names page. A UDF will be created that contains the unique IDs and the computer names that were entered.

The following command-line switch is used when adding a UDF to your Windows XP Professional unattended installation:

```
/udf:id[,UDF_file]
```

where **/udf:id** specifies the unique ID that will be used during the installation, and **UDF_file** is the name of the of the UDF. This should include the full path.

To start an unattended installation of Windows XP Professional using a UDF, use the following command-line switch:

```
Winnt32 /unattended:unattend.txt /udf:computername,unattend.udf
```

where **unattend.udf** is the UDF.

An example of a UDF is shown in Listing 2.2.

Listing 2.2   Sample UDF file.

```
[UniqueIds]
     JoeD=UserData
     SallyJ=UserData
     BenR=UserData
     Mike1B=UserData
     JoshW=UserData

[JoeD:UserData]
     ComputerName=JoeD

[SallyJ:UserData]
     ComputerName=SallyJ

[BenR:UserData]
     ComputerName=BenR

[Mike1B:UserData]
     ComputerName=Mike1B

[JoshW:UserData]
     ComputerName=JoshW
```

System Preparation Tool

The System Preparation Tool (Sysprep) is designed for administrations who need to deploy a large number of computer systems with the same applications and desktop configurations. With Sysprep, administrators can configure a source computer, take a snapshot of it, and then transfer the image to multiple target computers. This is known as cloning or ghosting.

Sysprep does not actually do the cloning of the system. It prepares the system for cloning. Every computer system in Windows XP must have a unique security ID (SID). If you clone or ghost a target system from a source system without the use of Sysprep, each target system will have the same SID. Sysprep creates a unique SID for each cloned system. You need a third-party utility to do the actual cloning.

Sysprep is found on the Windows XP CD or can be downloaded from **www.microsoft.com/windows2000/downloads/tools/sysprep/default.asp**.

Note: Sysprep cannot be used to upgrade earlier versions of the operating system. Any user-specific settings and data will need to be backed up prior to the installation and then restored following the cloning.

One disadvantage when using third-party cloning tools and Sysprep is that the reference image might be limited by the size of the CD that the image is cloned to.

The following are the steps involved in using Sysprep to clone a Windows XP Professional computer:

1. Log onto the source computer as Administrator.

2. Install Windows XP Professional and any additional applications on the reference or source computer. Verify that the image configuration is correct.

3. Copy the Administrator profile to the Default User profile so that any custom settings will be available to anyone who uses the image. Assign the Everyone permission to the Default User profile.

4. Use Windows Setup Manager to create a Sysprep.inf file. This file is used by setup to automate the Mini-Setup Wizard to complete the installation.

5. Create a folder on the source computer called Sysprep.

6. Copy Sysprep.exe and Setupcl.exe from the Deploy folder on the Windows XP Professional CD to the Sysprep folder.

7. Run the Sysprep utility by selecting Start | Run and, in the Open dialog box, typing "%systemdrive%/sysprep/sysprep.exe".

8. After Sysprep finishes running, the source computer will shut down. It is now ready to be cloned or imaged.

9. Start the source computer and create an image of it using the third-party imaging tool.

10. Store the completed image on a distribution share or on removable media, such as a CD-ROM.

11. Restore the image on the target computer from the distribution share or from the image stored on the CD.

12. Restart the computer, and the Mini-Setup Wizard will run automatically. This will complete the installation of the image.

13. The user will be prompted to input any configuration information that was not included in the answer file.

Sysprep.exe Command-Line Switches

Sysprep.exe can be run with the following command-line switches:

➤ **-quiet**—Runs Sysprep.exe without any on-screen messages

➤ **-reboot**—Forces the computer to restart automatically after the image is installed

➤ **-nosidgen**—Causes Sysprep.exe to run without generating a SID

➤ **-pnp**—Used to install legacy and non–Plug and Play devices

➤ **-forceshutdown**—Forces the computer to shut down after Sysprep is complete

Setupcl.exe

The Setupcl.exe file in the Sysprep folder has two purposes:

➤ It regenerates a new security ID for the computer.

➤ It starts the Mini-Setup Wizard.

Mini-Setup Wizard

The Mini-Setup Wizard starts on the target computer the first time it is booted after the image has been copied to it. The Mini-Setup Wizard prompts for any information that was not provided in the Sysprep.inf file. This could include the following:

➤ Administrator password

➤ Computer name

➤ End-User License Agreement (EULA)

➤ Network settings

➤ Regional options

➤ Time zone selection

➤ Username and company name

Sysprep.inf

Sysprep.inf is used with the Mini-Setup Wizard to provide information needed to complete the installation. Sysprep.inf is an answer file that can be created with any text editor or Windows Setup Manager. Listing 2.3 is an example of a Sysprep.inf file.

Listing 2.3   Sample Sysprep.inf file.

```
[Unattended]
    OemSkipEula=Yes

[GuiUnattended]
    AdminPassword="4Ft6"
    EncryptedAdminPassword=NO
    OEMSkipRegional=1
    TimeZone=35
    OemSkipWelcome=1
```

```
[UserData]
    ProductID=12345-12345-12345-12345-12345
    FullName="John Doe"
    OrgName="Doe Companh"
    ComputerName=JohnD

[Display]
    BitsPerPel=8
    Xresolution=1024
    YResolution=768

[TapiLocation]
    AreaCode=919

[SetupMgr]
    DistFolder=C:\sysprep\i386
    DistShare=whistlerdist

[Identification]
    JoinDomain=DoeCompany

[Networking]
    InstallDefaultComponents=Yes
```

Remote Installation Services (RIS)

Remote Installation Services (RIS) is a feature that was introduced in Windows 2000. RIS enables administrators to simultaneously deploy Windows XP Professional on multiple computer systems from a remote location. A standard Windows XP Professional desktop configuration can be deployed to new desktop computers or to computers that already have an operating system but need to be upgraded to Windows XP Professional.

Three primary components make up the RIS installation process:

➤ Images that can be downloaded and installed on client computers

➤ RIS client computers

➤ RIS servers that run RIS and distribute Windows XP Professional to the client computers

RIS requires the following Windows XP Server services:

➤ *Active Directory*—Locates client computers and RIS servers, and manages the client installations

➤ *Domain Name Service (DNS)*—Required to locate Active Directory

➤ *Dynamic Host Configuration Protocol (DHCP)*—A DHCP server is required to assign IP addresses to client computers

Several services run on the RIS server:

➤ *Boot Information Negotiation Layer (BINL)*—Responds to client requests

➤ *Single Instance Store (SIS)*—Increases free space on the partition that holds the RIS images by replacing duplicate copies of files with links to the original files

➤ *Trivial File Transfer Protocol (TFTP)*—Downloads the Client Installation Wizard to the client computer and starts the installation of the image

Before you can distribute Windows XP Professional using RIS, you need to set up the RIS server, which involves four steps:

1. Install RIS on a Windows XP Server.

2. Configure and start RIS, and create the CD-based images on the RIS server.

3. Authorize the RIS server in Active Directory.

4. Make sure that the users who are performing remote installations have the right to create computer accounts in Active Directory.

RIS Images

Two types of images can be created on a RIS server and used to deploy Windows XP Professional:

➤ *CD-based image*—The default image that is created when the RIS server is configured. It contains only the Windows XP Professional operating system. It is based on the default settings of the operating system. If you need to deploy applications with the CD-based image, you must use Group Policy. This image copies all the files required for the installation on a temporary directory on the target computer before running the setup program.

➤ *RIPrep image*—Based on a preconfigured source computer. It can contain both the Windows XP Professional operating system and additional applications as needed. The image is created using the Remote Installation Preparation Wizard. A RIPrep image deploys faster than a CD-based image because only files necessary for the installation are copied to the client computer.

An answer file can be created using Windows Setup Manager to automate the Client Installation Wizard. These files end in the .sif extension.

Installing a RIS Image on a Client Computer

To install Windows XP Professional using RIS, the client computers must have a network adapter that supports the Pre-Boot execution (PXE) specification. If the adapter doesn't support PXE, you can create a RIS boot disk using the Remote Boot Disk Generator (Rbfg.exe) and boot from it. Users initiate installation by pressing the F12 key after the computer is started. Several events occur when a user presses F12:

1. A DHCP Discover packet requesting an IP address is sent. This packet includes the Globally Unique Identifier (GUID) of the computer.

2. A DHCP server supplies the client computer with an IP address.

3. The RIS server checks Active Directory to make sure that the client computer has been prestaged to receive images from the RIS server.

4. If the client computer has been prestaged, the RIS server will prompt the user to log on using his or her regular account.

5. The user is sent a list of images that can be installed from the RIS server.

Systems Management Server (SMS)

SMS is a set of tools designed for managing networks made up of hundreds to thousands of computers. SMS is a standalone product that must be purchased separately from Microsoft. SMS provides desktop management and software distribution.

If you plan to deploy Windows 2000 XP using SMS, you should already have the SMS infrastructure in place. SMS can only be used to upgrade computers that are currently SMS clients. Distributing Windows XP Professional with SMS can be done automatically on a large scale to several thousand clients. Several tasks are involved in distributing the operating system:

➤ Selecting the computers that are equipped for the upgrade

➤ Distributing the Windows XP Professional source files to all sites

➤ Monitoring the distribution of the operating system to all sites

➤ Providing sufficient rights and permissions to do the upgrade

➤ Automating the initiation of the installation of the software package with the Windows XP Professional operating system

➤ Resolving any problems that occurred during the distribution and installation

SMS can be used to deploy Windows XP Professional on computers that already have an operating system and are part of the SMS environment. It cannot be used to install Windows XP Professional on computers that are not SMS clients or that do not already have an operating system installed.

Software Distribution with SMS

SMS packages are used to distribute software in SMS. A package contains the source files (in this case, the Windows XP operating system installation files) and details regarding how the software distribution process will occur. Each package will contain an SMS program that runs on the target computer and controls the execution of the package. Package source files are copied to Distribution Points, which are shares that are accessed by the client computers. After the package is copied to the Distribution Points, they are advertised to the clients. Advertising tells the client computers that the software is available for the upgrade.

Deploying the Windows XP Professional operating system using SMS provides many benefits that are not available with the other deployment tools, such as RIS and Sysprep. Some of the primary benefits are the following:

➤ Source files use only a fraction of the network bandwidth when they are distributed.

➤ Files can be forwarded at specified hours, such as when most users are not on the network.

➤ Files are checked while they are transferred across the network. Failed packages are retransmitted.

➤ SMS monitors the distribution and sends a status message when each step of the process is completed.

➤ Administrators can select which computers to deploy the upgrade to. Computers that are not ready can be scheduled for deployment at a later time. SMS can also be used to collect inventory information about the computer system as part of the upgrade process.

➤ The installation of the Windows XP Professional operating system can be totally automated, requiring no intervention from users.

➤ SMS has a reporting structure that provides both success and failure statistics about the deployment.

Additional Deployment Tools

All of the tools we just described can be used to deploy Windows XP Professional. Microsoft provides additional tools to aid with the deployment of Windows XP Professional. Some of these tools are meant to be used in a domain environment with Active Directory installed.

User State Migration Tool (USMT)

Windows XP introduces a new tool—USMT—that enables administrators to transfer a user's files and settings to a new computer. USMT provides the same functionality as the Files and Settings Transfer Wizard, but USMT is designed for administrator use only.

The USMT can be used to transfer the user state from computers running Windows 95, 98, Me, NT, and 2000 to a computer running Windows XP Professional. The user state is defined as the user's files, the operating system settings, and any specific settings associated with applications.

The USMT transfers certain settings by default. The following lists the settings that are transferred by default:

➤ Accessibility options

➤ Display properties

➤ Fonts

➤ Network printers and mapped network drivers

➤ Browser and mail settings

➤ Folder and taskbar options

➤ Mouse and keyboard options

➤ Regional settings

➤ Microsoft Office settings

➤ Microsoft Outlook settings

➤ Microsoft Word settings

➤ Microsoft Excel settings

➤ Stored mail and contacts

➤ Microsoft PowerPoint settings

The following folders are transferred by default when using the USMT:

➤ My Documents

➤ My Pictures

➤ Desktop

➤ Favorites

Transferring User Settings Using the USMT Command-Line Tools

Two command-line tools—Scanstate.exe and Loadstate.exe—are used to transfer user state data from one computer to another. Scanstate.exe captures the user settings from the source computer, and Loadstate.exe restores the user settings to the target computer. Administrators can capture settings for a single user or for multiple users by using the command-line tools. To transfer the settings, several resources are required:

➤ A server that both the source and target computers can access, with adequate disk space for the user settings.

➤ A source computer containing the user settings to be transferred.

➤ A target computer running Windows XP Professional. This computer should not have a profile on it for the user who the settings are being transferred for.

➤ Administrative privileges on the target computer.

➤ The account name and password for the user whose settings are being transferred.

Preparing the Server for the Transfer

You must prepare the server for use with the USMT before you can transfer user settings. The source and destination computers must have access to this server. Take a look at the steps required to prepare the server:

1. Create a USMT folder on the server and share it.

2. Give the user whose settings are being migrated Read access to the shared folder.

3. Give the Administrator account on the target computer Read/Write access to the shared folder.

4. Create a folder called MigStore and share it, giving both the migrating user and the administrator on the target computer Read/Write access.

5. Create a folder in the USMT folder and call it Scan.

6. Create a folder in the USMT folder and call it Load.

7. Copy Scanstate.exe and all INF and DLL files from the ValueAdd/USMT folder on the Windows XP Professional CD to the USMT\Scan folder on the server.

8. Copy Loadstate.exe, MigUser.inf, and all DLL files from the ValueAdd/USMT folder to the USMT\Load folder on the server.

After you have prepared the server, you need to scan the user state information on the source computer. Follow these steps to scan the source computer:

1. Log onto the source computer as the migrating user.

2. Map a drive to the USMT folder share on the server.

3. Open a command prompt and go to the USMT folder on the server.

4. Change to the Scan subdirectory.

5. Run Scanstate.exe with the following command-line parameters:

```
Scanstate /i.\migapp.inf /i.\migsys.inf /i.\migfiles.inf /
i.\sysfiles.inf \\<servername>\MigStore
```

6. After the scan is complete, move to the target computer.

Now that you have copied the user settings to the USMT share on the server, you load the settings to the target computer:

1. Log onto the target computer with an account with administrative rights.

2. Confirm that a profile does not already exist on the computer for the migrating user.

3. Map a driver to the USMT share folder on the server.

4. Open a command prompt and go to the USMT folder on the server.

5. Change to the Load subdirectory.

6. Run Loadstate.exe with the following command-line parameters:

```
Loadstate /i.\miguser.inf\\<servername>\MigStore
```

7. When the **Loadstate** process finishes, log off the Administrator account and log on as the migrated user.

8. Verify that the user files and settings have been transferred.

Note: Scripting can be use to incorporate the USMT migration process for large-scale deployments.

Active Directory Migration Tool (ADMT)

The ADMT is a graphical wizard that can be used to migrate users, groups, and computers. Administrators can use it to perform a trial migration to gather information to assess the impact of the migration before it occurs. ADMT can also be used to set file permissions and to migrate Microsoft Exchange Server mailboxes.

The ADMT can be obtained from **www.microsoft.com/windows2000/ downloads/tools/admt/default.asp**.

Active Directory Sizer Tool (ADST)

The Active Directory Sizer Tool (ADST) can be used by administrators and planners to estimate which hardware will be required for deploying Active Directory in your environment. The Active Directory Sizer Tool can aid in estimating the number of domain controllers required, the number of global catalogs per domain required, the amount of memory required, and the amount of network bandwidth utilization.

The Active Directory Sizer Tool can be downloaded from **www.microsoft.com/ windows2000/downloads/tools/sizer/default.asp**.

Active Directory Services Interfaces (ADSI)

ADSI is a single set of directory service interfaces for managing network resources. Administrators can use ADSI to automate tasks such as adding users and groups, and managing printers.

Windows Installer

Windows Installer is a software management tool that manages the installation of software. It also manages the addition and deletion of software and monitors file resiliency. Windows Installer can restore a computer to its original state in the event of an installation failure. It can diagnose and repair corrupted programs and reliably delete unwanted programs. Windows Installer can also be used to support unattended software installations. Windows Installer consists of two components—a client-side installer service (Msiexec.exe) and a Microsoft Software Installation (MSI) package file.

Windows Scripting Host (WSH)

WSH gives administrators the ability to automate deployment tasks through scripts. WSH is a language-independent scripting host that supports Visual Basic, Scripting Edition (VBScript) and Microsoft JScript. Administrators can write scripts to perform repetitive tasks, such as creating new users and backing up the system.

Windows Management Instrumentation (WMI)

WMI can be used by administrators to track, monitor, and control computers and other network devices. WMI is Microsoft's implementation of the Web-based enterprise management architecture for enterprise-level network management. WMI consists of two components—an object repository and the Common Information Mode (CIM) Object Manager. The object repository stores information collected from WMI-manageable hardware and software. The CIM Object Manager collects information from the WMI providers and stores it in the object repository.

Uninstalling Windows XP

After you have upgraded your operating system to Windows XP Professional, if you decide that you do not want to use it, Microsoft provides you with the tools to uninstall Windows XP Professional and return your computer system to its original operating system. To remove Windows XP Professional:

1. Open the Control Panel.

2. Double-click the Add and Remove Programs tool.

3. Click Uninstall Windows XP, and click Continue.

4. Click Yes to confirm to start uninstalling Windows XP Professional.

You cannot uninstall Windows XP Professional if you have made hard disk configuration changes, such as converting the file system from FAT to NTFS. You cannot uninstall Windows XP Professional if you upgraded from Windows NT 4 or Windows 2000 Professional. Any new files that were added after the upgrade will not be deleted when you uninstall Windows XP Professional.

Multibooting Windows XP

Users who have an existing operating system might want to load Windows XP Professional in a multiboot configuration to allow access to the original operating system. Existing applications that are not compatible with Windows XP could still be accessed through the original operating system.

When loading Windows XP in a dual-boot configuration, the active partition must be formatted with the file system that is recognized by both operating systems. If you are setting up a dual-boot configuration with Windows 98 and Windows XP Professional, the active partition must be formatted with the FAT32 file system to allow for access to the Windows 98 operating system.

Table 2.3 shows disk support for multibooting with Windows XP Professional.

Table 2.3   Disk support for multibooting.

Disk Configuration	Requirements for Multibooting
Basic disk	Each operating system must be installed on a separate partition.
Single dynamic disk	Cannot multiboot; only one operating system can be installed.
Multiple dynamic disks	Each dynamic disk can contain Windows XP or 2000; no other operating system can start from a dynamic disk.

Windows Product Activation

Microsoft has implemented Windows Product Activation in Windows XP as an antipiracy measure. Following the installation of Windows XP Professional, the operating system must be activated. The first time a user logs onto the newly installed Windows XP Professional computer, an Activate Windows dialog box appears prompting the user to activate the newly installed copy. A wizard walks the user through the process of activating over the Internet. If the user does not have an Internet connection, he will need to call Microsoft customer service to activate his copy of Windows XP Professional. If the operating system is not activated within a certain time frame, it will stop working.

For large organizations that are automatically deploying large numbers of Windows XP Professional computers, a Volume License Product Key can be used to eliminate the need for individuals to activate each copy of the installation.

Automatic System Recovery

Microsoft implemented ASR in Windows XP Professional to aid in system recovery in the event of hardware failure, such as the loss of a storage device or a system crash. Following the successful implementation of Windows XP Professional, the entire partition should be backed up using the Automated System Recovery Preparation Wizard. The wizard will create an ASR disk that will allow administrators access to the backed up data. The ASR disk contains the ASR state file called Asr.sif and additional files needed to restore the system to its original state. The data must be backed up to media, such as a tape drive or a CD-ROM. The data being back up will be as large as the partition, so you want to ensure that the media you are backing up to has sufficient space for the copy of the image.

Chapter Summary

This chapter introduced you to the various ways to install Windows XP Professional. Microsoft has identified specific hardware requirements for supporting Windows XP Professional. You can run a test upgrade of Windows XP Professional on your computer system to check for potential installation problems.

The type of operating system currently on your computer will determine whether you can upgrade to Windows XP Professional or whether you need to do a clean install. Windows 2000, Windows NT 4, Windows Me, and Windows 98 can all be upgraded to Windows XP Professional.

Windows XP Professional supports the FAT, FAT32, and NTFS file systems. NTFS is the file system of choice because of added security, compression, disk quotas, and file and folder permissions.

Winnt.exe is used to install Windows XP Professional when your computer system is running Windows 3.x or MS-DOS. If your computer is running Windows 95, 98, Me, NT, or 2000 you'll start the installation with winnt32.exe.

There are several ways to perform an unattended installation of Windows XP Professional. The Sysprep tool can be used to deploy a large number of computer systems with the same desktop configuration. A RIS server can be used to simultaneously deploy multiple computer systems from a remote location. AMS can be used to upgrade SMS clients to Windows XP Professional.

The State Migration Tool allows administrators to transfer user files and settings to a computer running Windows XP Professional. Windows XP Professional can be configured to multiboot with other operating systems.

Once Windows XP Professional is installed on a computer, it must be activated. If the operating system is not activated within a specific time frame, it will stop working.

Review Questions

1. Which of the following are minimum hardware requirements for installing Windows XP Professional? [Check all correct answers]

    a. 128MB RAM

    b. CD-ROM drive

    c. VGA monitor

    d. 2GB hard disk space

2. Sally wants to upgrade her computer system from Windows 98 to Windows XP Professional. She is concerned that her system hardware might be a bit outdated and will not support the upgrade. How can she check to see if her computer will support Windows XP Professional?

    a. She can check to see if her hardware is on the Hardware Compatibility List.

    b. She can install Windows XP Professional and hope that it's compatible.

    c. She can't check. She will need to purchase new computer equipment.

    d. She can run Winnt.exe with the **/dudisable** command-line switch to run an upgrade report.

2

3. John wants to upgrade to Windows XP from Windows NT 4. He has several applications that are required for the operation of his business. He wants to ensure that these applications will work after the upgrade. How can John check to make sure that the applications will work after he upgrades his computer system to Windows XP?

p. 29

   a. He can run Windows Product Activation.

   b. He can run Setup.exe with the **/checkupgradeonly** command-line option.

   c. He can run Winnt.exe with the **/checkupgradeonly** command-line option.

   d. He can run Winnt32.exe with the **/checkupgradeonly** command-line option.

4. Which of the following file systems would be the best choice for running on Windows XP?

p. 31

   a. FAT

   b. NTFS

   c. Unix

   d. FAT32

5. Which of the following are benefits of using the NTFS file system over FAT or FAT32 when installing Windows XP Professional? [Check all correct answers]

p. 31

   a. File encryption

   b. Disk quotas

   c. Compression

   d. File permissions

6. Sally wants to upgrade her Windows 95 computer to Windows XP Professional. What executable should she use to perform the upgrade?

p. 30

   a. Winnt32.exe

   b. Setup.exe

   c. Winnt.exe

   d. Setup32.exe

7. Marshall is an administrator for a large travel agency that is planning to upgrade its computer systems to Windows XP Professional. All of the computers are networked, but some do not have CD-ROM drives. How can Marshall upgrade the computer systems without CD-ROM drives to Windows XP Professional?

    a. He can't unless he installs a CD-ROM drive in the computer systems that do not have them.

    b. He can perform the installation over a network share.

    c. He can use the Windows Installer program to push out the operating system.

    d. He can attach a portable tape backup unit to each computer and install the operating system from it.

8. What type of Windows XP Professional installation uses an answer file called Sysprep.inf?

    a. Unattended

    b. RIS

    c. SMS

    d. Sysprep

9. What is the purpose of the Setupcl.exe file? [Check all correct answers]

    a. It starts the Mini-Setup Wizard.

    b. It starts the Windows Product Activation Wizard.

    c. It generates a new security ID for the computer.

    d. It prepares user settings for migration to a new Windows XP Professional computer.

10. What Windows XP Server services are required for installing Windows XP Professional using RIS? [Check all correct answers]

    a. DHCP

    b. WINS

    c. Active Directory

    d. DNS

11. What are the two types of images that can be used to deploy Windows XP Professional using RIS?

    a. CD-based

    b. PXE-based

    c. Floppy-based

    d. RIPrep

12. What does SMS use to distribute software upgrades to SMS client computers?

    a. RPC

    b. Packages

    c. NetBEUI

    d. Distribution Points

13. Sue is the network administrator for a local computer company. She wants to upgrade all of the company computers to Windows XP Professional. The company is purchasing new hardware for the upgrade, because its existing computers do not meet the hardware requirements for Windows XP Professional. Sue wants to be sure that all of the user settings are transferred when the company upgrades to Windows XP Professional. What tool can she use to transfer user settings to the new computers?

    a. RIS

    b. WSH

    c. User State Migration Tool

    d. ADSI

14. What executable is used to scan user state settings on a computer being migrated to Windows XP Professional?

    a. Scanstate.exe   p. 47

    b. Sysprep.exe

    c. Loadstate.exe   p. 47

    d. Mseiexec.exe

15. Billy has upgraded his computer to Windows XP Professional. What is the last step he must perform before using the operating system?

    a. He should reinstall all of his applications.

    b. He should activate the operating system using Windows Product Activation.

    c. He doesn't have to do anything else. Windows XP Professional is ready to use.

    d. He should run Windows Update to check for upgrades to his system files.

Real-World Projects

For the following projects, you need a computer running Windows XP Professional and a computer running a previous version of Windows, such as Windows 98, NT, or 2000. You also need the Windows XP Professional CD.

[handwritten note: Windows button + "E" pulls up windows]

Project 2.1

To use Setup Manager to create a Uniqueness Database File:

1. Double-click Setupmgr.exe.

2. Click Next on the Windows Setup Manager Wizard window.

3. Select the Create A New Answer File radio button, and click Next.

4. Under This Answer File Is For:, select the Windows Unattended Installation radio button, and click Next.

5. Under Select The Platform This Answer File Installs:, select Windows XP Professional, and click Next.

6. Select the user interaction level, and click Next.

7. Select the No, This Answer File Will Be Used To Install From A CD radio button, and click Next.

8. Under Specify The Location Of The Windows Setup File:, select the Copy The Files From CD radio button, and click Next.

9. Select the Create A New Distribution Folder radio button, and click Next.

10. Enter the default name and organization under Customize The Software, and click Next.

[handwritten note: high color 800 x 600 default]

11. Select the display settings, and click Next.

12. Select the time zone, and click Next.

13. Enter the product key for Windows XP Professional, and click Next.

14. Select the Display Settings and click Next.

15. Select the time zone, and click Next.

16. Enter the product key for Windows XP Professional, and click Next.

17. Enter the computer name for the first computer, and click the Add button.

18. Enter each additional computer name, and click the Add button after each entry.

19. When you have finished entering computer names, click the Next button.

20. Enter the administrator password, and click Next.

21. Select the network components, and click Next.

22. Select Domain or Workgroup, and enter the appropriate name. Click Next.

23. Specify any telephony settings, and click Next.

2

24. Select the regional settings, and click Next.

25. Select any languages for the install, and click Next.

26. Select browser and shell settings, and click Next.

27. Select the installation folder, and click Next.

28. If you are installing printers, enter their names, and click Next.

29. Add any command that you want to run once during the installation, and click Next.

30. Enter any additional commands that you want run, and click Finish.

31. Enter a name and location for the file, and click OK.

32. Close Setup Manager.

Project 2.2

To generate a compatibility report:

1. Insert the Windows XP Professional CD into the computer you want to upgrade.

   Installation

2. Go to a command line.

3. Go to the i386 subdirectory on the Windows XP Professional CD.

4. Type "winnt32.exe /checkupgradeonly" and press Enter.

5. In the Microsoft Windows Upgrade Advisor dialog box, select the radio button No, Skip This Step And Continue Installing Windows, and click Next.

6. The system will produce a System Compatibility Report.

7. Click the Finish button after you review the report.

Project 2.3

To use Setup Manager to create a Sysprep.inf file:

1. Double-click Setupmgr.exe.

2. Click Next in the Windows Setup Manager Wizard window.

3. Select the Create A New Answer File radio button, and click Next.

4. Under This Answer File Is For:, select the Sysprep Install radio button, and click Next.

5. Under Select The Platform This Answer File Installs:, select Windows XP Professional, and click Next.

6. In the License Agreement dialog box, select Yes, Fully Automate The Installation, and click Next.

7. Enter the default name and organization under Customize The Software, and click Next.

8. Select the display settings, and click Next.

9. Select the time zone, and click Next.

10. Enter the product key for Windows XP Professional, and click Next.

11. Select the display settings, and click Next.

12. Select the time zone, and click Next.

13. Enter the product key for Windows XP Professional, and click Next.

14. Enter the computer name for the first computer, and click the Add button.

15. Enter each additional computer name, and click the Add button after each entry.

16. When you have finished entering computer names, click the Next button.

17. Enter the administrator password, and click Next.

18. Select the network components, and click Next.

19. Select Domain or Workgroup, and enter the appropriate name. Click Next.

20. Specify any telephony settings, and click Next.

21. Select the regional settings, and click Next.

22. Select any languages for the install, and click Next.

23. Select browser and shell settings, and click Next.

24. Select the installation folder, and click Next.

25. If you are installing printers, enter their names, and click Next.

26. Add any command that you want to run once during the installation, and click Next.

27. Enter any additional commands that you want run, and click Finish.

28. Enter a name and location for the file, and click OK.

29. Close Setup Manager.

CHAPTER THREE

Microsoft Management Console (MMC)

After completing this chapter, you will be able to:

✓ Start the MMC

✓ Add a snap-in to the MMC

✓ Use predefined consoles

✓ Configure a custom console

✓ Distribute a custom console

✓ Create a taskpad and tasks

Managing your computer can sometimes be a tedious and frustrating process. The Microsoft Management Console provides a new way for users to manage their computers and networks.

To manage a computer prior to Windows 2000 and Windows XP, you had to use many tools, and you often had to physically be at the computer you wanted to manage. The MMC provides you with a common interface for all of your management tools. It also allows you to manage your entire network from a single location.

In this chapter, you'll learn how to configure the MMC as well as how to use some of the configuration options available. Creating a custom console by including the utilities you need allows you to complete your work as quickly as possible. You can also create taskpads, which will give you a customized view of a snap-in. In a taskpad, you can create tasks that run common commands or run an external program or script.

The New Administrative Tool

You need a centralized administrative tool to manage your entire network, and now Microsoft has the answer. With the release of Windows 2000, Microsoft took the MMC to the next level. Microsoft first released the MMC with Internet Information Server (IIS) 4. As new BackOffice products have been released, Microsoft has based all of its administrative tools on the MMC (SQL 2000, SMS 2). The current version of the MMC found in Windows XP is 2. Windows 2000 MMC was version 1.2. If you have an MMC on Windows NT, you are probably running version 1. From this point on, all new tools will be based on the MMC. Microsoft has also asked third-party software vendors to integrate their management tools into the MMC.

The MMC brings a completely new world of features and functionality to network administrators. In Windows NT 4, administrators were always opening a new application to perform some task or switching back and forth between windows. For example, if an administrator wanted to create a user account and a share, she would need to open the User Manager application to create the user and open the Server Manager application to create the share.

Some tasks couldn't even be completed unless the administrator was physically at the computer being worked on. With the MMC, all your administrative tasks can be done from a single application, and these tools can be used on your local computer or from a remote computer.

The MMC is really just the framework for other administrative applications. If you run MMC from a command prompt or from the Run dialog box, you will see that the MMC is actually empty (see Figure 3.1).

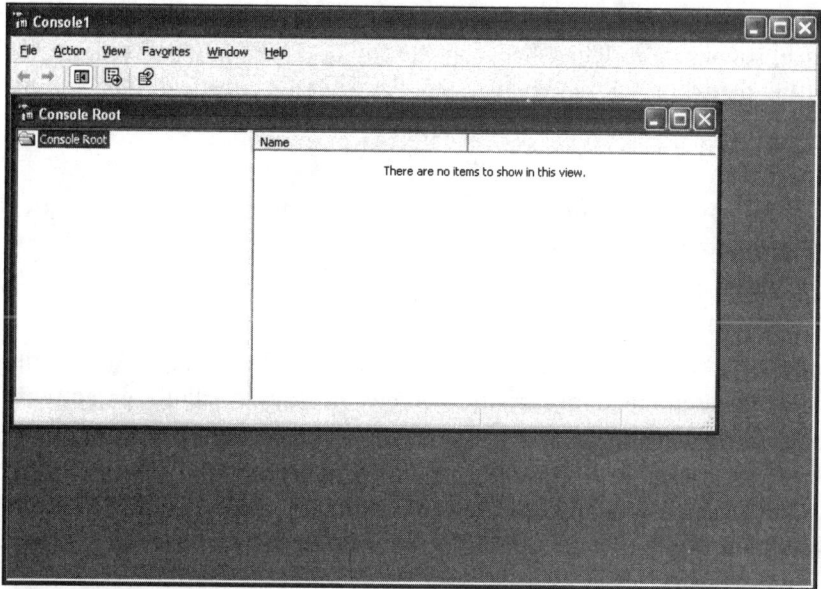

Figure 3.1 The basic MMC window.

To make the MMC useful, you need to add tools to the console. These tools are called *snap-ins*. A snap-in is the core unit of the MMC. As you work with various administrative tools, you will need to add the appropriate snap-in that contains the required functionality to the MMC.

Not only can you add a snap-in to the console, but you can also add folders to organize the snap-ins, and you can add links to Web sites. Besides the advantages that the MMC offers for managing your network, the MMC also provides a consistent look and feel for all of your administrative processes. In the past, every tool had its own program, and many of the programs were very different from each other. The idea behind the MMC is the same as the idea behind other products, such as Microsoft Office. When you switch between Office programs, such as Word, Excel, and PowerPoint, you will notice that the look and feel of these applications are similar, even though these products offer very different features. By making these programs consistent, the user knows how to use all of them simply by learning how to use one of them. The same is true with the MMC. As the MMC gets more popular, its look and feel will remain consistent, so you will always know how to complete an administrative task. You will be able to manage your local system, your network, your database, and your email system from a single standard interface.

Microsoft's goal for all administrative tools as well as the MMC is for them to be entirely based on Internet technologies. However, at this time, Internet technologies are not mature enough to handle some of the more complex tools that you need to manage your network. It is likely that this situation will be resolved soon, with Microsoft and other companies working to develop new standardized Internet tools and applications. The MMC can already display Web pages and can handle anything that your Web browser can handle. Therefore, in the future, you should start to see more snap-ins being ported to the Internet. When this happens, it will allow for many types of network management.

The MMC makes life easier for administrators because they are able to use the MMC from their client workstations. In the past, many administrative tools simply didn't run on some client computers. The MMC now manages all administrative tasks from the client.

The MMC also allows you to create and save your own configuration settings. This is very useful in an organization where you want to allow certain users to manage particular parts of your network. You can now build a custom tool that gives users the specific objects they need to complete the task but does not give them unneeded, extraneous (and, depending on the user's skill-level, potentially dangerous) tools.

Behind the Scenes of the MMC

The MMC is based on the concept of a multiple document interface. Microsoft is pushing third-party software vendors to develop their applications using the MMC as their management tool. A snap-in will have to run in the MMC; it will not run on its own. This concept is similar to Microsoft Word. With Microsoft Word, you can open multiple documents at the same time, but if Microsoft Word is unavailable, you will not be able to use your documents. The documents are dependent on Microsoft Word in the same way snap-ins are dependent on the MMC.

Microsoft has given you a way to create your own snap-ins. The Microsoft Platform Software Developer Kit (MSDK) is available for general use. With this kit, you can design your application with the MMC in mind. For more information on this kit, go to the Microsoft Developer Network Web site at **http://msdn.microsoft. com/library/en-us/mmc/hh/mmc/mmcstart_1dph.asp**.

The MMC is based on Windows Management Services. These services are integrated into the operating system and provide a sophisticated method for developing a management tool. Windows Management Services provides developers with base functionality and access to the operating system to create a new tool.

Windows Management Services consists of three layers. The first, or highest, layer is the presentation layer; this is sometimes referred to as the Presentation services. Developers use this high-level service to tie their application into the operating system. The MMC is part of this layer, along with other automation, scripting, and Extensible Markup Language (XML) services.

The second, or middle, layer is the management logic layer. This layer is divided into two areas. The first area is the value-added management solutions. It consists of task-based solutions provided by Microsoft and third-party software developers. For example, the Group Policy snap-in functions at this level. The second area is the standard management tools area. This area controls the functions of storage management, security management, problem tracking, network quality of service, health monitoring, and change and configuration management.

The last layer of Windows Management Services is the common services layer. This is the lowest layer and provides the base functionality of Windows Management Services. This layer includes services like COM+, Active Directory, Event Notification, Windows Management Instrumentation (WMI), replication, load balancing, and scheduling.

This section provides a fairly brief overview of the architecture of the MMC. The intention is to explain how the MMC works behind the scenes so that you have a better understanding of the MMC concept. Microsoft continues to provide and improve many tools to make the process as easy as possible for developers to create applications for the MMC.

Configuring the MMC

Microsoft has provided some of the most frequently used snap-ins in the pre-configured consoles. To view the pre-configured consoles, click the Administrative Tools icon in the Control Panel. Depending on your needs, these may be sufficient for most of your daily administrative tasks.

Before you can use the MMC, you must add at least one snap-in to it. The MMC offers a great many tools and functions to administrators. After you add a snap-in, you can choose among many options to make the MMC usable to yourself and other administrators. To open the MMC, run the mmc.exe file, which is located in the System32 directory.

Three startup switches are associated with the MMC. The first switch is /a, which opens the MMC in Author Mode and allows you to make changes to previously saved consoles.

The next two switches provide support for later generations of Microsoft operating systems that are 64-bit. First is /64, which opens the 64-bit version of the MMC console. This option is only valid if you are running a 64-bit version of a Microsoft operating system. The other switch is /32, which opens the 32-bit version of the MMC console. This allows a 64-bit Microsoft operating system to run 32-bit snap-ins.

Take a look at the MMC user interface, shown in Figure 3.2, to associate the parts of the MMC with their descriptions in the following list. The MMC is similar in design and function to the Windows Explorer layout.

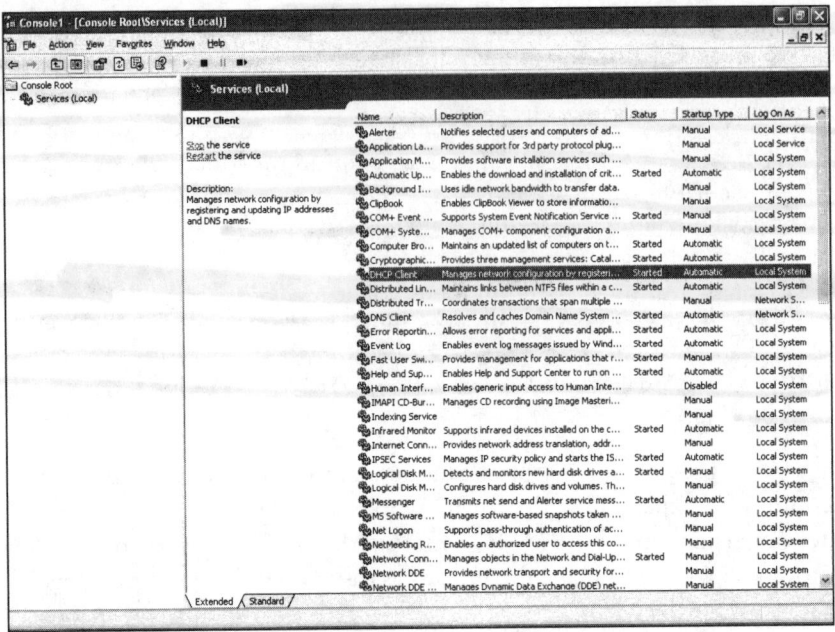

Figure 3.2 An example of the MMC with the Services snap-in loaded.

➤ *Action toolbar*—This menu bar contains the Action, View, and Favorites menus. Below these menus, you will find navigation buttons. Also, notice that as you use different snap-ins, buttons may be added or removed from this toolbar.

➤ *Console tree pane*—This is the left window; it contains the console root, snap-in root nodes, containers, and the Favorites list.

➤ *Details pane*—This window shows the contents of a snap-in, a management utility associated with a snap-in, a Web page, or a taskpad view.

➤ *Main toolbar*—This menu bar contains the Console, Window, and Help menus. This menu is available only in Author Mode or User Mode—Full Access.

Adding and Configuring Snap-Ins

After opening a blank console, add a snap-in. Select File | Add/Remove Snap-In. The Add/Remove Snap-In dialog box is displayed. Click the Add button to get a list of all the loaded snap-ins that are available on the computer. When you add a snap-in, you are usually asked whether you want the snap-in to be directed to the resources of the local computer or want to enter the name of a remote computer you would like to manage. Some of the snap-ins allow you to right-click them to connect the snap-in to a different computer, whereas others might need to connect the snap-in to the other computer at the time you add it. Make sure that when you add the snap-in, you select the checkbox that states the following:

Allow The Selected Computer To Be Changed When Launching From The Command Line. This Only Applies If You Save The Console.

As you add applications to your system, you might notice that new snap-ins are available for you to add to your console. Two tabs are available in the Add/Remove Snap-In dialog box—Standalone and Extensions.

The Standalone tab is the default, which lists the snap-ins that you have already loaded. You can organize your snap-ins by clicking the drop-down button located next to Snap-Ins Added To. From there, you can navigate through the list of snap-ins and folders that you have added to the console. You can load a snap-in inside of another snap-in or add a folder and put specific snap-ins in that folder. Because you can wind up with many snap-ins loaded in a console, folders will enable you to organize them.

No Add Folder button is provided, so you have to add a folder the same way you add a snap-in. In the list of available snap-ins, you will see one called Folder. When you add a folder, it will be called Folder. No way exists to change the name at this point. When you return to the main console window, you can right-click the folder and choose to rename it.

In addition to the available standalone snap-ins are extensions that are associated with them. An extension snap-in is a snap-in that extends the functionality of a standalone snap-in. Some snap-ins can act as standalone snap-ins and extend other snap-ins. By default, when you add a standalone snap-in, all of the extensions to that snap-in are loaded. After you have added the snap-ins, go to the Extensions tab in the Add/Remove Snap-In dialog box and view the extensions that exist or can be loaded. If you want all the extensions loaded, select the Add All Extensions checkbox. You might want to remove some of the extensions that are irrelevant to what you are doing. For example, you might want to remove the Removable Storage Extension setting from Computer Management because you don't have any removable storage to manage (see Figure 3.3). If you later obtain some removable storage, you can then re-enable the extension.

At this point, you should be able to add some snap-ins and organize them into folders efficiently. Many snap-ins are available, and the number grows dramatically as you start adding applications. Therefore, you will want to use folders to plan a useful structure for the snap-ins that you use for a basic console (see Figure 3.4).

You might also want to create some favorite locations in your console. Some of the snap-ins have many layers that you will have to navigate through, and it can be difficult to remember exactly where some options are located. As you find locations that you want to return to, you can create a Favorites list. The Favorites list in the MMC is similar to the concept of Favorites in Internet Explorer. Once you are at a certain location, simply click the Favorites menu and select Add Favorites. The

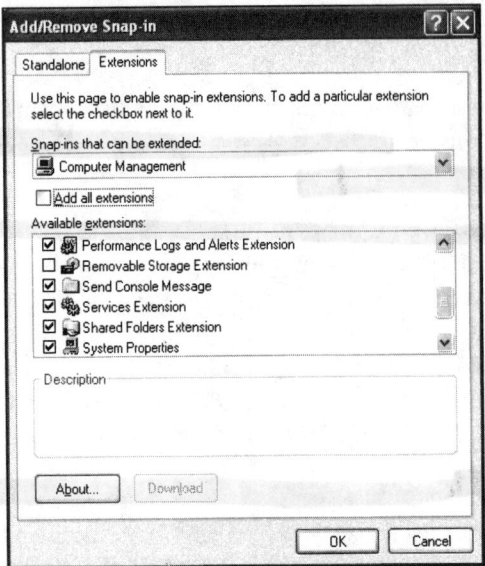

Figure 3.3   The Extensions tab in the Add/Remove Snap-In dialog box.

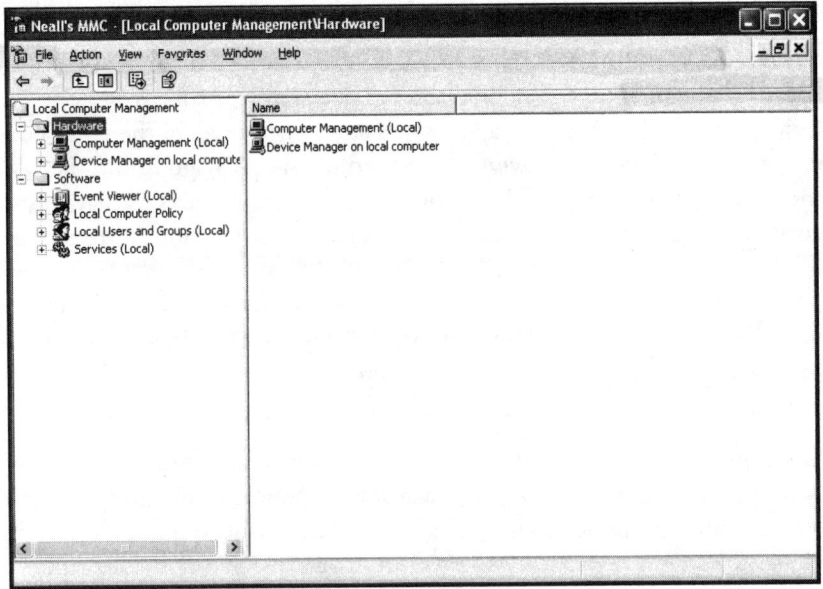

Figure 3.4   A basic console with a few snap-ins loaded and organized into folders.

location will then be displayed in your Favorites list. By clicking a favorite location in the list, you will automatically be taken to that location.

You also might want to open multiple windows to work with your snap-ins. From the Window drop-down menu, you can create multiple windows that allow you to easily switch back and forth between snap-ins that you have loaded. You can also open a new window that uses your current location as the root location for any new windows. Select Action | New Window. This can be useful when you are trying to complete tasks that require you to make changes in multiple snap-ins.

Taskpad View

The taskpad view is another page that you can add to your console. It can contain a snap-in view or tasks. With the taskpad view, you can show the contents of a snap-in in a way that makes it easier for you to view the contents. The tasks allow you to create a shortcut to a task that you created. The task can be a function that you perform often and that requires multiple snap-ins or automates a task for a new user. You might also want to group different tasks into one area. You can create a task that navigates to a particular location in the console, runs a menu command, runs a script, or runs another program. This can be a powerful tool if you use batch files and scripts, which allow you to do just about anything with Windows.

Creating a taskpad view is fairly easy. Navigate to a snap-in and select Action | New Taskpad View. This option starts a wizard that walks you through the process of creating a taskpad view. After you have created the taskpad, you can start the New Task Wizard. See Figure 3.5 for a view of a sample taskpad. The New Task Wizard

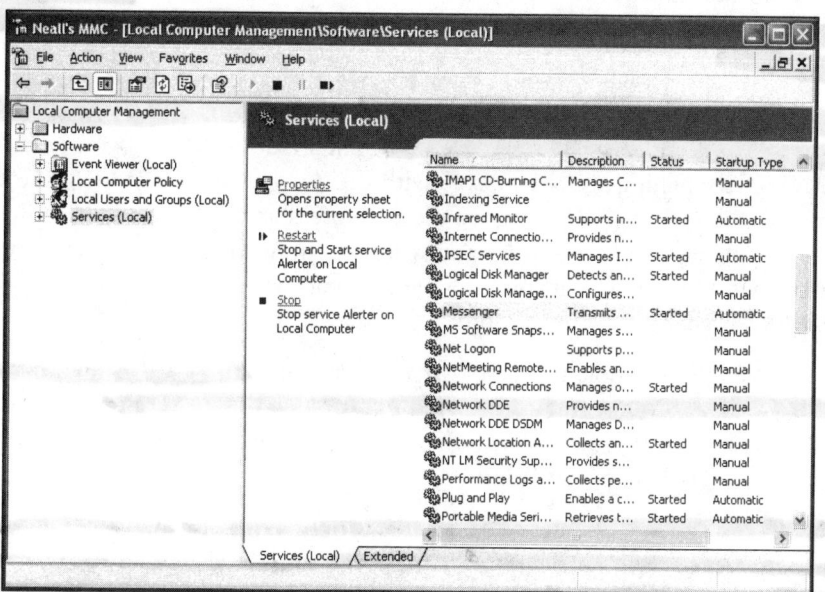

Figure 3.5   A sample taskpad containing a few tasks that can be run.

allows you to create a task in the taskpad view that you just created. You can create three types of tasks:

- ➤ You can navigate throughout the console tree; however, you can only choose a location from the Favorites list.

- ➤ You can create a task that runs one of the commands from the menu.

- ➤ You can create a task that runs a shell command, which is the most powerful task you can create. The shell command option allows you to run a batch file, a script, or a shell command.

Saving a Custom Console

Now that you have spent all this time creating and configuring your console, you will want to reuse your console. You can also distribute your custom console to other users. However, you might not want your console to be modified, so you can provide the use of the same console to multiple people or a specific group.

By default, the console is saved with an .msc extension. This extension is registered with Windows XP, and it automatically opens the file in the MMC. By default, the MMC saves your custom consoles in the following path:

systemdrive\Documents and Settings*user*\Start Menu\Programs\Administrative Tools

After you save the files, they are available to you in the Administrative Tools folder in your Start menu, but they are available only to you. You should consider changing the location if you want other users to access your consoles. If you replace *user* in the previous path with *default user* and save the file, the console will be available to all users.

You can save a console in one of four modes. The first mode is Author Mode. Use this mode when creating a custom console. Enter Author Mode by opening a blank MMC or by opening a saved console with the **/a** option. This mode is the default setting for all new consoles that you create. Note that if you already have the MMC open, any new console that you open will open in Author Mode. When you are in Author Mode and you exit from the console, you will be asked whether you want to save your changes to the console.

You can set your console to one of three other modes. To change the mode for your console, click the File drop-down menu and choose Options. Then, select one of three user modes presented. After you change to any of these user modes, two checkboxes will become available.

The first option allows users to save changes to the console. Users will not be prompted to save their changes; the console will automatically save changes when users close the console. The second option allows users to access the Customize View dialog box.

The three user modes allow users to access a console and use the functionality of the snap-ins that are loaded. However, users will not be able to add any new snap-ins to the console. The following are the three modes:

➤ *User Mode–Full Access*—Users have full functionality of the tools that are available as well as various viewing options. The Save command is not available because only changes that do not affect the snap-ins will be saved.

➤ *User Mode–Limited Access, Multiple Window*—Users are able to access multiple child windows, but they are not able to close them. The same restrictions as Full Access apply. Users are also limited in their access to the console tree.

➤ *User Mode–Limited Access, Single Window*—The same restrictions apply in this mode except that users cannot open any child windows.

Although the MMC is a great tool for administrators, you may not want other users to access it at will. The Group Policy snap-in is the key to restricting this access. Group Policies provide two restrictions to the MMC. The first restricts a user or group of users from opening the MMC in Author Mode. The second restricts access to all or individual snap-ins. To find these options, add the Group Policy snap-in and then navigate down the following path:

User Configuration\Administrative Templates\Windows Components\Microsoft Management Console

The Included Snap-Ins

Now that you understand how to configure and manage the MMC, it is time to actually start using the available tools. Some of the concepts involved in managing the MMC will start making more sense after you start using the console to manage your system. Numerous snap-ins are included with Windows XP Professional. Certainly, these are not all the available snap-ins. You can find many more snap-ins in the .NET Server product as well as in other third-party applications. The following is a list of snap-ins included with Windows XP Professional, accompanied by a short description of each:

➤ *ActiveX Control*—Introduces an ActiveX control at the specified location in the tree.

➤ *Certificates*—Enables you to manage the certificates for a user, service, or computer account.

➤ *Component Services*—Enables you to manage COM and COM+ applications as well as distributed transaction applications.

➤ *Computer Management*—Consists of a collection of the most commonly used snap-ins that you can use for managing your system.

➤ *Device Manager*—Serves as the main tool that you use to manage the hardware on your system. You can use it to scan for new hardware or uninstall hardware. You can also use it to enable or disable hardware.

➤ *Disk Defragmenter*—Enables you to analyze and defragment your hard drive. It is a copy of Diskeeper Lite from Executive Software.

➤ *Disk Management*—Enables you to manage your hard drives. It provides the capability to manage your partitions, drive letters, and dynamic volumes.

➤ *Event Viewer*—Enables you to manage and clear the system, security, and application logs.

➤ *Folder*—Enables you to create folders in the console for organizing your snap-ins.

➤ *Group Policy*—Helps you to manage and create policies that allow you to designate system settings, manage software deployment, and assign scripts.

➤ *Indexing Service*—Enables you to manage the index service and determine which directories you would like to be a part of the index catalog on the local system.

➤ *IP Security Monitor*—Enables you to monitor IP security status.

➤ *IP Security Policy Management*—Enables you to manage Internet Protocol Security (IPSec) policies.

➤ *Link To Web Address*—Enables you to create a Web page link within your console. The Web page will be displayed in the console. This can be useful to link to vendor support pages that have documentation or drivers that you need to configure your system.

➤ *Local Users And Groups*—Enables you to manage and maintain users who are authorized to use the local computer, and manage the local groups and their membership.

➤ *Performance Logs And Alerts*—Enables you to monitor your hardware utilization and configure alerts to notify you when your hardware utilization reaches critical levels.

➤ *Removable Storage Management*—Enables you to set up your removable storage media, such as tape drives and optical disks.

➤ *Resultant Set Of Policy*—Enables you to view the effective results that a particular policy has on a user or computer.

➤ *Security Configuration And Analysis*—Enables you to create a security database. Using a security template, you can compare your system against the template and also have the tool automatically configure the system based on the settings in the template. If you run the analysis, you can view each object and see how it's currently configured, compared to what the template suggests is the best configuration.

➤ *Security Templates*—Contains some pre-configured templates and allows you to create new templates that contain different security options. It doesn't allow you to actually set options, but you can use the templates with the Security Configuration And Analysis tool or set the policies in the Group Policy object.

➤ *Services*—Enables you to manage the services on your system. You can start, stop, and pause the services from here as well as manage when the service starts and, if needed, what user account the service should log onto the system.

➤ *Shared Folders*—Enables you to manage the shares on a computer, the current sessions, and the files a particular user has open. You can disconnect a user from a particular resource and create new shares.

➤ *WMI Control*—Enables you to configure and control the Windows Management Instrumentation (WMI) service.

Throughout the remaining chapters of this book, you will get a better understanding of the full functionality of the snap-ins in the preceding list.

The pre-configured consoles that come with Windows XP Professional are listed next. You will find them in the Control Panel by clicking the Administrative Tools icon in Classic View, or by clicking Performance And Maintenance and then Administrative Tools. You can also choose Performance and Maintenance from Category View in the Control Panel. The preconfigured consoles are:

➤ *Component Services*—Contains the Component Services, Event Viewer, and Services snap-ins. You can use this tool to make sure your services are functioning properly, and, if they are not functioning properly, you can check the Event Viewer for errors.

➤ *Computer Management*—Contains just about every snap-in that you will use to manage your system, including the Computer Management snap-in. It consists of three folders—System Tools, Storage, and Services And Applications (the latter two contain other snap-ins).

➤ *Event Viewer*—Contains the Event Viewer snap-in.

➤ *Local Security Settings*—Contains the Group Policy snap-in.

➤ *Performance*—Contains the System Monitor and the Performance Monitor Logs And Alerts.

➤ *Services*—Contains the Services snap-in.

Note that the Administrative Tools folder has another icon for the Data Sources tool, which you can use to manage connectivity with Open Database Connectivity (ODBC) data sources. This tool does not work with the MMC.

Chapter Summary

Now that you have a better understanding of how the MMC works, you will find that it is a useful and valuable tool. It's a good idea to become familiar with (and, of course, use) the MMC because it's what you will be seeing from Microsoft for the foreseeable future. Obviously, Microsoft will continue to make improvements and changes in the program, but the basic concepts and functionality will probably remain similar to what they are now.

By itself, the MMC really can't do anything; it's there as the interface that the snap-ins use to access the Windows XP operating system. Microsoft has ported virtually every management application into an MMC snap-in. You might still find the occasional application that is not a snap-in, but it seems highly likely that it won't stay that way for long.

The MMC provides a number of configuration options that assist you in making the tool usable for your location. You can restrict user access to the tools with group policies. You can create custom views with the taskpad and launch common routines with tasks in the taskpad. You can use folders to organize your snap-ins, and you can enhance snap-ins by creating links to Web pages that contain useful information. You can also restrict users from modifying your custom console by setting the console to User Mode.

Review Questions

1. Which commands would you use to open the Microsoft Management Console in Author Mode? [Check all correct answers]

   a. **MMC /a**

   b. **MMC**

   c. **MMC /64**

   d. **MMC /author**

2. Which of the following types of tasks can you create within the MMC? [Check all correct answers]

    a. Menu commands

   b. Shell command

   c. Script

   d. Navigate to a favorite

3. You are the lead administrator for a large pharmaceutical company. Due to FDA regulations, you must limit access to Help Desk personnel. You decide to create a custom console for your Help Desk to use. You don't want users to be able to add any new snap-ins to the console. In which mode should you save the console?

p68

   a. User Mode–Full Access

   b. User Mode–Limited Access, Multiple Window

   c. User Mode–Limited Access, Single Window

   d. Author Mode

4. The Help Desk personnel have been complaining that the consoles you created are too limiting. After a meeting with the Help Desk supervisor, you decide to add a little flexibility to the consoles you created. You still don't want users to be able to add any new snap-ins to the console. However, you would like to allow users to open new windows. What mode could you save the console in? [Check all correct answers]

   a. User Mode–Full Access

   b. User Mode–Limited Access, Multiple Window

   c. User Mode–Limited Access, Single Window

   d. Author Mode

5. Still unsatisfied, the members of the Help Desk have threatened to go on strike if you continue to force them to use your restricted consoles. Although you don't like the idea, your boss has now demanded that you give the Help Desk what they want. You decide to give each user an individual copy of the console file. You would also like users to be able to modify the console. In which mode should you save the console?

   a. User Mode–Full Access

   b. User Mode–Limited Access, Multiple Window

   c. User Mode–Limited Access, Single Window

   d. Author Mode

6. Trying to get revenge on the Help Desk personnel, you created another custom console. In this console, you created a number of windows. You don't want Help Desk users to be able to remove any of the windows. In which mode should you save the console?

   a. User Mode–Full Access

   b. User Mode–Limited Access, Multiple Window

   c. User Mode–Limited Access, Single Window

   d. Author Mode

7. You need to manage the hardware on your local system. You need to look at the drivers that the hardware is using and ensure that all the devices are indeed loaded and functioning properly. Which snap-ins can you load to accomplish this? [Check all correct answers]

   a. Component Services

   b. Device Manager

   c. Computer Management

   d. Event Viewer

8. What is the default extension that the MMC uses when saving a custom console?

   P 68

   a. .con

   b. .cus

   c. .msc

   d. .mcs

9. You have created a custom console that some of your users employ. You are receiving complaints that every time your users open the console, it is changed. Your users would like to be able to open new windows within the console as well. Which of the following will you need to do to alleviate your users' concerns?

   a. Select Do Not Save Changes To This Console in the Options dialog box.

   b. Set the mode to User Mode–Full Access.

   c. Set the mode to User Mode–Limited Access, Multiple Window.

   d. Select Allow Users To Customize Views.

10. You are creating a custom console and you realize that you do not want your users to have the full functionality of a particular snap-in. They will need to do certain tasks with the snap-in, but parts of it are not needed. How would you remove some of the functionality?

    *P 70*

    a. Get a modified DLL from the vendor.

    b. Set a Group Policy.

    c. Check the extensions to see if the functionality can be removed.

    d. Get a third-party blocking program.

11. Which of the following external services can you link to with the MMC? [Check all correct answers]

    P 68

    a. SMTP

    b. HTTP

    c. ARP

    d. FTP

12. You would like to set up an easier way to navigate through the snap-in structure to certain areas. Which tool would you use?

    a. Tasks

    b. Links

    c. Views

    d. Favorites

13. You would like to be able to run a script file that you generated from the MMC. Which tool would you use to make this possible?

    a. Tasks

    b. Links

    c. Views

    d. Favorites

14. You are looking at a console, and you realize that the Console drop-down menu isn't available. What do you need to do to make it available?

    a. Restart the MMC.

    b. Reboot the computer.

    c. Open the console in Author Mode.

    d. Open the console file from a fresh MMC instance.

15. You have to physically be at the computer you are managing when using a snap-in in the MMC.

    a. True

    b. False

16. You would like to have access to the system log in the Event Viewer. What snap-ins could you add to a console to accomplish this? [Check all correct answers]

    a. Computer Management

    b. Event Viewer

    c. Services

    d. Disk Management

17. You would like to create a new partition on your hard drive. What snap-ins could you add to a console to accomplish this? [Check all correct answers]

    a. Computer Management

    b. Event Viewer

    c. Services

    d. Disk Management

18. You would like to disable one of your hardware components. What snap-ins could you add to a console to accomplish this? [Check all correct answers]
    a. Computer Management
    b. Device Management
    c. System Information
    d. Disk Management

19. You would like to add a local user to your computer. What snap-ins could you add to a console to accomplish this? [Check all correct answers]
    a. Computer Management
    b. System Information
    c. Local Users And Groups
    d. Services

20. You would like to stop a service on your computer. What snap-ins could you add to a console to accomplish this? [Check all correct answers]
    a. Computer Management
    b. Services
    c. System Information
    d. Component Services

Real-World Project

Steve is working with the rollout team as it puts together a plan to roll out Windows XP Professional. The team is concerned with the level of administrative tools available to the standard user. The team decides that it wants to remove the administrative tools from the users but wants the desktop support staff to be able to access the hardware and system configuration tools for the desktop. The team wants to make sure that the desktop support staff does not have access to other administrative tools and that all staff uses the same tools for ease of training and support later on.

Steve is assigned the task of making sure that all the goals of the team are taken care of when the OS is rolled out. Steve starts by looking at what the desktop support staff is required to do and determining which tools will be needed to accomplish these tasks. After Steve speaks with the staff, he creates a list of snap-ins and a few scripts that the team will run. Steve is now ready to create the console by following the steps in Project 3.1.

Project 3.1

Create a custom console in the MMC:

1. Open the MMC by typing "MMC" in the Run dialog box (accessed by selecting Start | Run).

2. Add two folders to the MMC by clicking the Console menu and selecting Add/Remove Snap-In. Then, click the Add button. Highlight the Folder snap-in and click Add twice. Click the Close button, and then click OK.

3. Rename the root folder *Desktop Support* by right-clicking and then clicking Rename. Rename the two folders you added. Name one *Hardware Support* and the other *Software Support*.

4. From the Snap-Ins Added To drop-down list, select Hardware Support. Add the following snap-ins to the Hardware Support folder:

   ➤ Device Manager

   ➤ Removable Storage

   ➤ Performance Logs And Alerts

   ➤ Disk Management

   Click Close.

5. From the Snap-Ins Added To drop-down list, select Software Support. Add the following snap-ins to the Software Support folder:

   ➤ Event Viewer

   ➤ Component Services

   ➤ Services

   The console should now look like the one shown in Figure 3.6.

6. Set up two Favorites—one to the system error log and the other to the environment variable. Navigate to the Event Viewer and then click the system log. Click the Favorites drop-down list, and click Add To Favorites. Do the same for the environment variables, which are found in System Information—Software Environment.

7. Click the Services icon. Then click the Action drop-down menu and click New Taskpad View.

8. Click Next. Leave the defaults as they are, and click Next again. Again, leave the defaults as they are, and click Next. Change the name to *Service Management*, and click Next. Make sure that the Start New Task Wizard checkbox is selected, and click Next.

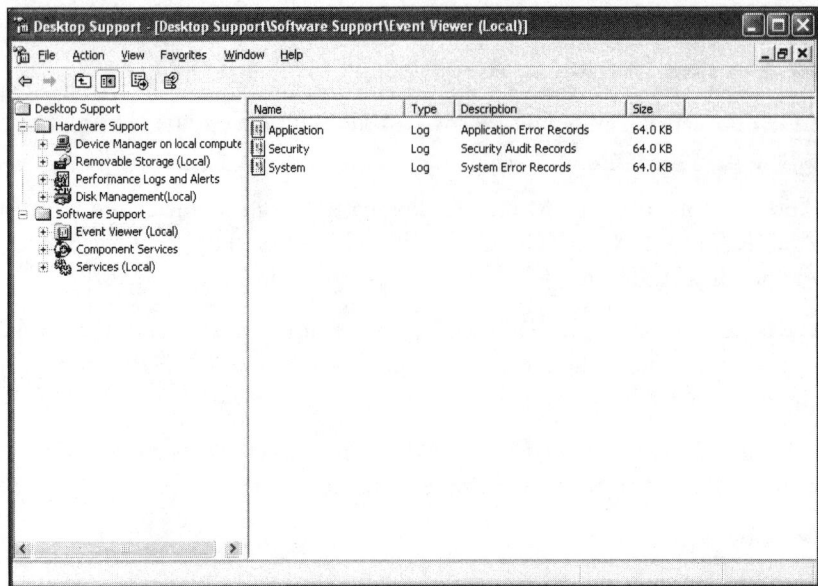

Figure 3.6 Your console should look similar to this after you have completed Step 5.

9. In the New Task Wizard, click Next, click Shell Command, and click Next. Enter the name of the script that was created for your system in the command window, and click Next. Name the task *Script*, and click Next. Then, choose an icon, and click Next. Click Finish.

10. Click the Console drop-down menu, and click Options. Set the console mode to User Mode–Limited Access, Single Window. Also, select the checkbox Do Not Save Changes To This Console. Then, click OK.

11. Click the Console drop-down menu, and click Save. Give the console a name, and click OK.

12. Copy the console file to a secure network location where only your desktop support people will have read access to the file.

Now that Steve has created the custom console, he will need to work with the desktop support team to test it. More modifications might need to be made, but at this point, the team members have a good start and should have the functionality needed to do their job with the new operating system.

CHAPTER FOUR

Managing Disks in Windows XP Professional

After completing this chapter, you will be able to:

✓ Identify the types of disks that are supported in Windows XP Professional

✓ Describe a basic disk and identify when to use it in Windows XP Professional

✓ Describe a dynamic disk and identify when to use it in Windows XP Professional

✓ Describe a master boot record and explain how it relates to disks in Windows XP Professional

✓ Describe a GPT disk and how it is supported in Windows XP Professional

✓ Describe how to manage disks and volumes using the Disk Management snap-in tool

✓ Identify command-line tools that can be used in Windows XP Professional to manage disks

✓ Explain how to use the Disk Defragmenter tool to reduce disk fragmentation

✓ Explain how to defragment a disk from a command line

✓ Explain the various file systems that can be used in Windows XP Professional

Two types of disks are supported in Windows XP Professional—basic disks and dynamic disks. All new disks in Windows XP are initialized as basic disks. Basic disks consist of partitions, and dynamic disks consist of volumes. Disk Management is a GUI-based tool that is used to manage both basic and dynamic disks. Basic disks can be converted to dynamic disks with no loss of data, but all data is lost on a dynamic disk when it's converted to a basic disk. Several tools are provided in Windows XP Professional for managing disks from a command line. These include DiskPart.exe, Fsutil.exe, Convert.exe, and Mountvol.exe. Windows XP Professional supports the FAT, FAT32, and NTFS file systems. NTFS is the file system of choice for XP because of its ability to provide security, disk compression, and disk quotas.

Types of Disks Supported in Windows XP Professional

If you have worked with Windows 2000, you know that it supports two types of disks—basic disks and dynamic disks. This is also the case with Windows XP. Basic disks are similar to the disk structures that were used in Windows NT 4. Dynamic disks are a new type of disk structure introduced in Windows 2000. This section looks at the differences and similarities between basic and dynamic disks in Windows XP Professional.

Basic Disks

When disk drives are initialized in Windows XP, they are done so as basic disks. Basic disks use normal partition tables. They are supported by all versions of Windows, including Windows NT and Windows 2000. A basic disk can hold primary partitions, extended partitions, and logical drives.

Configuration information for basic disks is stored in the master boot record (MBR). This is located on the first sector of the disk. Basic disks can contain volume, mirrored, striped, or RAID 5 sets. Basic disks can be converted to dynamic disks by using Disk Management. If you are planning to run your Windows XP computer in a multiboot configuration with Windows NT, Windows 98, or MS-DOS, you'll want to use basic disks. These operating systems cannot access dynamic disks.

You can create up to four primary partitions or three primary partitions and one extended partition on a basic disk. These can have unlimited logical drives.

Partition Types: Basic Disks

Basic disks can be divided into separate units of storage called *partitions*. Basic disks can have primary partitions, extended partitions, and logical drives.

Primary Partitions

Primary partitions are created from unallocated space on a basic disk. Up to four primary partitions can be created on a basic disk. You cannot subpartition a primary partition. When the computer boots, it searches for the active partition to start the operating system. The computer system can only have one active partition. If you plan to run your computer in a multiboot configuration, having multiple primary partitions allows you to isolate each operating system on a separate partition.

Extended Partitions

An extended partition is a section of a basic disk that can contain logical drives. If you want to have more than four volumes on your basic disk, you would create an extended partition with logical drives. A basic disk can have three primary partitions and one extended partition.

Logical Drives

Logical drives are volumes that are created within extended partitions. You cannot extend logical drives across multiple disks. They can be formatted and assigned drive letters.

Basic disks cannot be used to create multiple volumes or fault-tolerant volumes. You can perform the following tasks only on basic disks:

➤ Create and delete primary partitions

➤ Create extended partitions

➤ Format partitions

➤ Mark a partition as active

➤ Break a mirror from a mirror set

➤ Repair failed legacy fault-tolerant volumes

Dynamic Disks

Dynamic disks were introduced in Windows 2000. Dynamic disks are supported only in Windows 2000 and Windows XP. Unlike basic disks, dynamic disks do not use partitions or logical drives. They use volumes. These volumes are used to subdivide a physical disk into drives identified by letters of the alphabet. Dynamic disks can contain simple volumes, spanned volumes, mirrored volumes, striped volumes, or RAID 5 volumes. Administrators do not have to restart Windows XP when disk and volume management changes are made to dynamic disks.

Dynamic disks do not use the traditional partition scheme that basic disks use. Disk configuration for a dynamic disk is stored in a disk management database. This database occupies the last 1MB of space at the end of the disk. This is totally different from basic disks that store their partition or configuration information in the MBR on the first sector of the hard disk. Dynamic disks cannot be accessed directly by computer systems running MS-DOS, Windows 95, Windows 98, or Windows NT. However, these operating systems can access disk shares on dynamic disks.

The concept of *disk groups* was introduced with dynamic disks. A disk group is a collection of disks that are managed together. Dynamic disks are associated with disk groups. A disk group consists of the computer name plus a suffix of Dg0. Each disk in a disk group stores replicas of the configuration data. Organizing dynamic disks in disk groups helps in the prevention of data loss. A dynamic disk can be moved from one computer to another without the loss of the configuration information.

Tip: If you want to view the name of a disk group, go to the following Registry key: HKEY_LOCAL_MACHINE\ SYSTEM\CurrentControlSet\Services\dmio\Boot_Info\Primary_Disk_Group\Name.

All new disks are initialized as basic disks in Windows XP. You can convert basic disks to dynamic disks using Disk Management. Any disks that are upgraded to dynamic disks will be readable only to the Windows 2000 and Windows XP operating systems. Windows NT and Windows 98 operating systems do not recognize dynamic disks. When you convert basic disks to dynamic disks, the existing partitions are changed, as illustrated in Table 4.1.

The number of volumes you can create on a dynamic disk is only limited to the amount of free space on the disk. The following tasks can only be performed on dynamic disks:

➤ Create and delete simple, spanned, striped, mirror, and RAID 5 volumes

➤ Extend simple or spanned volumes

➤ Remove a mirror from a mirror volume

Table 4.1   Converting basic disks to dynamic disks.

Basic Disk	Dynamic Disk
Primary partition	Volume
System and boot partitions	System and boot volumes
Active partition	Active volume
Extended partition	Volumes and unallocated space
Logical drive	Simple volume
Volume set	Spanned volume
Stripe set	Striped volume
Stripe set with parity	RAID 5 volume
Mirror set	Mirrored volume

➤ Break a mirrored volume into two volumes

➤ Repair mirrored volumes

➤ Repair RAID 5 volumes

➤ Reactivate missing or offline disks

Note: Dynamic disks are not supported on laptop computers, removable media, or disks that use USB or IEEE 1394 interfaces.

Volume Types: Dynamic Disks

Storage on dynamic disks is organized into volumes, unlike basic disks, which are organized into partitions. A volume is a section of a physical disk that operates as a separate disk. Volumes can be created from the free space on one or more disks and can be assigned alphabetic drive letters. Windows XP supports simple, spanned, mirrored, striped, and RAID 5 volumes.

Simple

Simple volumes are created from free space on a single disk. If a simple volume is extended onto additional disks, it becomes a spanned volume.

Spanned

Free or unallocated space from multiple disks can be linked together to create a spanned volume. A spanned volume can use up to a maximum of 32 disks. You must have a minimum of two dynamic disks to create a spanned volume. The unallocated space used to create the spanned volume does not all have to be the same size. Spanned volumes allocate data to one disk until it fills up and then continue to the next disk. They can be extended onto additional disks, but, if you extend a spanned volume, you cannot delete a portion of it without deleting the entire volume. You can only extend spanned volumes if you are using NTFS. The FAT file system does not allow for the extending of spanned volumes.

Mirror

Mirror volumes, or RAID 1, provide fault tolerance. Data is duplicated between two physical disks for redundancy. If one of the disks in a mirror volume fails, the data is still accessible from the other disk. Mirroring only uses 50 percent of the disk space, because data that is written to the primary disk is also written to the secondary disk. You cannot extend mirror volumes.

Note: Mirrored volumes cannot be run on Windows XP Professional. However, an administrator could use a Windows XP Professional computer to create mirrored volumes on Windows XP Server computers and Windows 2000 Server computers.

Striped

A striped volume allocates data evenly across two or more physical disks. If a disk in a striped volume fails, the entire volume is lost. Striped volumes, which are also known as RAID 0, cannot be mirrored or extended.

RAID 5

RAID 5 provides the highest level of fault tolerance. Data in a RAID 5 volume is striped across three or more disks. RAID 5 uses parity to re-create data if one of the disks fails. You cannot extend or mirror RAID 5 volumes. In earlier versions of Windows, RAID 5 was known as *striped set with parity*. The Disk Management tool provided with Windows XP provides limited support for RAID 5 volumes. RAID 5 volumes provide better performance than mirror volumes, but recovery from a failure is slower.

Note: *As with mirrored volumes, RAID 5 volumes cannot be run on Windows XP Professional. However, an administrator could use a Windows XP Professional computer to administer RAID 5 volumes on Windows XP Server computers and Windows 2000 Server computers.*

Some features are common to both dynamic and basic disks. You can perform the following on both:

➤ Check available free space

➤ Check current status

➤ Check disk properties

➤ View volume and partition properties

➤ Establish drive-letter assignments for volumes, partitions, and CD-ROM devices

➤ Establish disk sharing

➤ Assign security to a volume or partition

➤ Upgrade from a basic disk to a dynamic disk or revert from a dynamic disk to a basic disk

You cannot have multiple storage types on one hard disk. A hard disk must be either basic or dynamic. You can have both basic and dynamic disks in the same computer, but they have to be on different hard drives.

Master Boot Record (MBR)

The master boot record is a critical component of the disk structure for basic disks. The MBR is created when a hard disk is partitioned. It contains several important structures, including the master boot code, disk signature, and partition.

The master boot code is responsible for scanning the partition table for the active partition. It locates the starting section of the active partition and loads a copy of the boot sector from the active partition into memory. Finally, it transfers control to the executable code in the boot sector. If the master boot code fails during any of these processes, one of several error messages will be displayed. These could include any of the following:

➤ Invalid partition table

➤ Missing operating system

➤ Error loading operating system

The disk signature is used to identify the disk to the operating system. The operating system also uses the disk signature to retrieve information about the hard disk in the Registry subkey HKEY_LOCAL_MACHINE\SYSTEM\MountedDevices.

The partition table identifies the type and location of partitions on the hard disk. It is a 64-byte structure consisting of four entries, each up to 16 bytes long. Basic disks are the only disk type in Windows XP that uses partition tables.

On disks that support the MBR, you can create up to four primary partitions, or three primary partitions and one extended partition. You can create unlimited logical drives in the extended partition.

GUID Partition Table (GPT)

Starting with the 64-bit version of Windows XP, booting from MBR disks will not be supported. This version requires disks that have GUID partition tables. A GPT disk supports up to 128 partitions, unlike an MBR disk, which only supports up to 4 partitions. GPT is a disk-partitioning scheme that will be used by the Extensible Firmware Interface in Intel's new Itanium-based computers. GPT, in addition to supporting up to 128 partitions on one disk, can support volumes up to 18 exabytes in size.

The 32-bit versions of Windows will not be able to boot, read, or write from a GPT disk.

Managing Disks with Disk Management

Disk Management is an MMC snap-in that is used in Windows XP to manage disks and volumes. Disk Management replaces the Disk Administrator tool that was used in Windows NT 4. If you used Disk Management in Windows 2000, you will be familiar with Disk Management in Windows XP. The snap-in interface is exactly the same, but some functionality has been added to enhance disk management (see Figure 4.1).

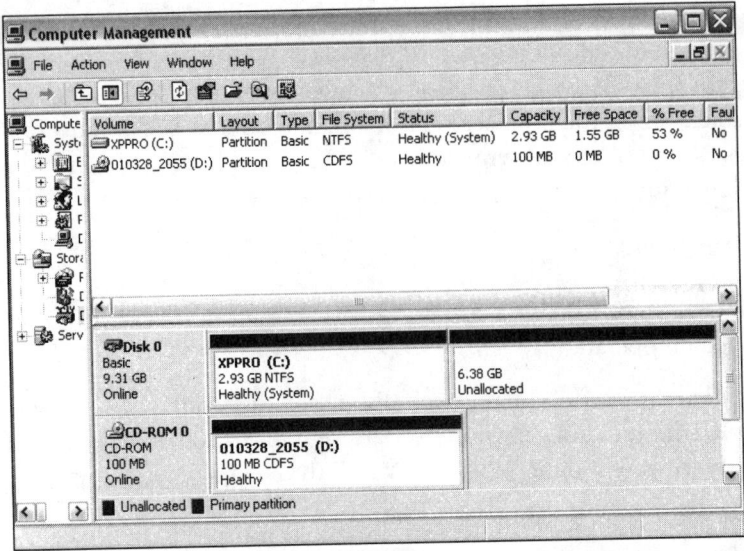

Figure 4.1 Disk Management snap-in tool.

To open Disk Management:

1. Right-click My Computer.

2. Click Manage.

3. Click the plus sign beside the Storage icon to expand it.

4. Click Disk Management.

The Disk Management snap-in consists of three panes that can display disks and volumes in a list or graphical view. Administrators can customize information that is displayed in each pane. They can select colors and patterns to display portions of the disk, such as primary partitions, free space, and extended partitions. You will notice that the first hard disk in your computer is labeled Disk 0. Subsequent disks are Disk 1, Disk 2, and so on. The first compact disc is labeled CD-ROM 0. This number is an object number and cannot be changed in Disk Management.

Disk Management is used to initialize disks. When new disks are introduced into a computer, they are initialized as basic disks. If you want to use dynamic disks, the basic disks must be converted to dynamic disks with Disk Management. You can create volumes with Disk Management that use FAT, FAT32, or NTFS. If you require fault tolerance, Disk Management can be used to create mirror and RAID 5 volumes on Windows 2000 Server, Windows Advance Server, and Windows Data Center computer systems, in addition to Windows XP Server and Windows XP Advance Server.

One of the main advantages of using Disk Management to manage disks is that administrators can perform most disk-related tasks with no interruption to the user. Most configuration changes take effect immediately without the need for a system reboot. Disk Management can be used for both local and remote disk administration.

Disk Management can be used to manage both basic and dynamic disks and volumes. Wizards are provided that step an administrator through the process of creating partitions and volumes and for converting disks from basic to dynamic and from dynamic to basic. Administrators can also use Disk Management to manage disks on remote computers running Windows 2000 or Windows XP. It can be used to mount drives. Local drives can be mounted to an empty drive on a local NTFS volume. Mounted drives afford users more flexibility, because they are not limited to the 26-drive limitation.

Disk Management supports both MBR disks and GPT disks. Disk management can be performed from the command line with the Diskpart.exe tool. This tool is discussed later in this chapter.

Disk Management displays the current status of disks and volumes. This is an extremely important feature when you are trying to troubleshoot disk or volume problems. Table 4.2 lists the status values for disks. Table 4.3 lists the status values for volumes.

Table 4.2   Status values for disks.

Status	Description
Online	The normal status
Foreign	A disk from another computer has been installed in the computer
No Media	No media is in a drive; this only applies to removable media drives
Offline	A disk is not accessible
Online (Errors)	I/O errors have been found on the disk
Unreadable	The disk is not accessible due to hardware failure or I/O errors
Unrecognized	The disk is of an unknown type

Table 4.3   Status values for volumes.

Value	Description
Healthy	The normal status displayed for a volume with no problems
Healthy (Boot)	The normal status for a volume that contains the active primary partition
Healthy (System)	The normal status for a volume that contains the Windows XP installation folder
Failed	The volume can't be automatically restarted
Failed Redundancy	A volume is no longer fault tolerant
Healthy (At Risk)	I/O errors have occurred on the disk that contains this volume
Initializing	The volume is being initialized
Regenerating	Data and parity are being regenerated for a RAID 5 volume
Resynching	Mirrors in a mirrored volume are being resynchronized

Converting from Basic to Dynamic Disk

New disks are initialized in Windows XP Professional as basic disks. You can convert basic disks to dynamic disks at any time by using Disk Management or the DiskPart tool. Converting a disk from basic to dynamic normally will not require a system reboot, with one exception: If the disk you are converting contains the boot or system partition or an active paging file, the computer must be restarted two times before the conversion will take place.

Warning: It is extremely critical to back up all data on a basic disk before you attempt to convert it. This will provide a failsafe in the event that something happens during the conversion process.

When the basic disk is converted, its partitions are changed to simple volumes. The disk will receive a copy of the dynamic disk database. Even though the disk has been converted to a dynamic disk, it will still contain references to partitions in the partition table in the MBR. However, these references will identify these partitions as dynamic volumes, and any new changes to the disk will be written to the Disk Management database at the end of the disk.

Converting from Dynamic to Basic Disk

Converting a dynamic disk to a basic disk is a relatively simple process. But, when you convert a dynamic disk to a basic disk, all data on the disk is lost. It is extremely important that you back up all data on the dynamic disk before you attempt to convert it to a basic disk.

The Disk Management snap-in can be used to convert dynamic disks to basic disks.

Moving Basic Disks

Basic disks can easily be moved from one computer to another. If you need to move a basic disk, you should first physically remove the disk from the computer. Next, install it in the new computer and reboot the computer. The operating system should recognize the new disk after reboot. If it does not recognize the newly installed hard disk after the reboot, select Rescan Disks from the Action menu in the Disk Management snap-in tool.

If you are trying to move a basic disk from a Windows NT 4 computer that is configured as a fault-tolerant set, you must save the configuration data to a floppy before removing the disk. You would then use the Disk Management snap-in to restore the configuration from the floppy to the newly moved disk.

Removing Dynamic Disks

If you decide to remove a dynamic disk from a Windows XP Professional computer, the configuration and volume information is retained by the remaining dynamic disks. The Disk Management snap-in will display the removed disk as Dynamic/Offline, and the disk name will be Missing. To remove this entry, you must remove all volumes on the disk and then use the Remove Disk menu item associated with the disk. Each dynamic disk contains information about the other disks in its disk groups. When the last dynamic disk is physically removed, the missing disk will no longer be displayed in Disk Management.

Moving Dynamic Disks

Moving a disk from one computer from one disk group to another computer with a different disk group results in the disk being identified as Foreign. This disk will stay marked as Foreign until it is manually imported in an existing disk group on the computer. Use the Import Foreign Disks operation to associate the disk with an existing disk group.

Managing Disks from the Command Line

Disk Management is an MMC snap-in that is used to manage both disks and volumes. Included in Windows XP are several command-line tools that can be used to manage disks and volumes from a command prompt. This section looks at some of these tools for managing disks and volumes.

DiskPart

DiskPart (Diskpart.exe) is a powerful command-line disk management tool in Windows XP that administrators can use to manage disks, partitions, and volumes. This can be done from a command line or through scripts. DiskPart is basically a command-line version of Disk Management.

Before DiskPart can be used, an object must be listed and then selected. By selecting an object, it is given focus. DiskPart can operate only on objects that have focus. To specify the disk to work on with DiskPart, you use the disk object number. Object numbering begins with zero, so the first hard disk in the computer is Disk 0.

The **list disk**, **list volume**, and **list partition** commands are used to list the available objects. When the **list** commands are used, the object that has an asterisk next to it is the object that has focus and can be acted on. Table 4.4 lists some of the DiskPart commands and their syntax.

list disk
disk part
list disk

① Start
② run
③ Cmd

Table 4.4   DiskPart commands.

Command	Description
active	Marks the partition as active
add disk=n	Adds a disk
assign [{letter=d|mount=path}]	Changes the drive letter associated with a removable device
break disk=n	Breaks the mirrored volume with focus into two simple volumes; applies only to dynamic disks
clean	Removes all partition or volume information
iconvert basic	Converts an empty dynamic disk to a basic disk
convert dynamic	Converts a basic disk to a dynamic disk
convert gpt	Converts an empty basic disk with the MBR partition style to a basic disk with the GPT partition style; Itanium-based computers only
convert mbr	Converts an empty basic disk with the GPT partition style to a basic disk with the MBR style; Itanium-based computers only
create partition efi [size=n] [offset=n]	Creates an EFI system to a GPT disk; Itanium-based computers only
create partition extended [size=n] [offset=n]	Creates an extended partition on the current drive
create partition logical [size=n] [offset=n]	Creates a logical drive in an extended partition
create partition msr [size=n] [offset=n]	Creates a Microsoft Reserved (MSR) partition on a GPT disk; Itanium-based computers only
create partition primary [size=n] [offset=n]	Creates a primary partition on the current basic disk
create volume raid [size=n] [disk=n]	Creates a RAID 5 volume on the specified dynamic disks
create volume simple [size=n] [disk=n]	Creates a simple volume
create volume stripe [size=n] [disk=n]	Creates a striped volume
delete disk	Deletes a missing dynamic disk from the disk list
delete partition	Deletes the partition with focus on a basic disk
delete volume	Deletes the selected volume
detail disk	Displays the properties of the selected disk
exit	Exits DiskPart
extend [size=n] [disk=n]	Extends the volume with focus
help	Displays a list of available commands
import	Imports a foreign disk group into the local computer's disk group
list disk	Displays a list of disk and information on the disks
list partition	Displays the partition of the current disk
list volume	Lists basic and dynamic volumes on all disks
rem	Identifies comments in a script
remove [{letter=d|mount=*path*[all]}]	Removes a drive letter from the volume with focus
rescan	Locates new disks that have been added to a computer
retain	Prepares an existing dynamic simple volume to be used as a boot or system volume
select disk=[n]	Shifts focus to the specified disk
select partition=[{n/d}]	Shifts focus to the specified partition
select volume=[{n/d}]	Shifts focus to the specified volume

*Note: You cannot format a driver with DiskPart. It does not have a **format** command. You have to exit DiskPart and then run the **format** command from a DOS prompt.*

Fsutil

Fsutil.exe is an extremely powerful tool that should be used only by advanced users, such as administrators. Fsutil can be used to manage reparse points and sparse files, dismount volumes, and extend volumes. Fsutil can be used on both FAT and NTFS. Table 4.5 lists some of the subcommands that can be used on disks and volumes with Fsutil.exe

Convert

Convert.exe is used to convert FAT or FAT32 volumes to NTFS volumes. The command line for converting a FAT volume to an NTFS volume is as follows:

```
convert [drive:] /fs:ntfs [/v]
```

In the preceding line, **drive** specifies the drive to convert to NTFS, and **/fs:ntfs** specifies that the volume be converted to NTFS. Convert.exe can also be run with the **/v** option, which is verbose mode and will display all messages during the conversion process.

Chkdsk

Chkdsk.exe can be used to check disks for errors. If errors are detected, chkdsk will attempt to repair them. Chkdsk can also be used to create and display a status report about the disk.

Table 4.5   Subcommands used with Fsutil.exe.

Command	Description
Behavior	Enables or disables the settings for generating 8.3 character-length file names
Dirty	Queries if a volume's dirty bit is set
File	Finds a file by its SID, sets a file's short name, queries files system statistics
fsinfo	Lists all drives, queries volume information, queries file system statistics
hardlink	Creates a hard link, which is a directory entry for a file
objected	Manages object identifiers
quota	Manages disk quotas on NTFS volumes
reparsepoint	Queries or deletes reparse points
sparse	Manages sparse files
Usn	Manages the update sequence number change journal
volume	Manages a volume, dismounts a volume, queries a volume for available disk space

The command-line options for running Chkdsk are as follows:

```
chkdsk [drive:][[path] filename] [/f] [/v] [/r] [/l[:size]]
```

Chkdsk run by itself produces a status report of the disk. If Chkdsk is run with the **/f** option, it will attempt to fix any errors it finds on the disks. Running Chkdsk with the **/v** option displays all files in every directory as the disk is being checked. If Chkdsk is run with the **/r** option, it will locate bad sectors. On NTFS volumes, you can run Chkdsk with the **/l** option to enable you to change the size of the log file.

Mountvol

Mountvol.exe can be used to create, delete, or list volume mount points. Administrators can use Mountvol to mount local volumes to an existing NTFS folder. No drive letter is associated with the folder. The command line to run Mountvol is as follows:

```
mountvol [drive:]path VolumeName
```

In the preceding command, **path** specifies the existing NTFS directory folder in which the local volume will be mounted, and **VolumeName** is the volume name that is the target of the mount point.

Disk Defragmentation

As with Windows 2000, Windows XP provides a tool that can be used to defragment disks and volumes. Before Windows 2000, users who wanted to defragment their hard disks had to purchase third-party defragmentation utilities. Microsoft introduced Disk Defragmenter in Windows 2000 and enhanced it in Windows XP (see Figure 4.2).

When users create files and folders, the computer tries to save the files in the first contiguous free space that it finds. If not enough free space is available, the computer saves the remaining portion of the file in the next available space. When files are deleted, the empty space that is left is filled in randomly as new files are created. Over time, this causes the disks and volumes to become fragmented. A fragmented drive performs slower, because it has to search out all portions of a file, which might be spread over several areas of a disk or volume.

Disk Defragmenter provided in Windows XP can be used to analyze local disks and volumes. Fragmented files and folders can be consolidated so that they occupy a single contiguous space on the drive or volume. The computer accesses files and folders that are stored in contiguous spaces faster.

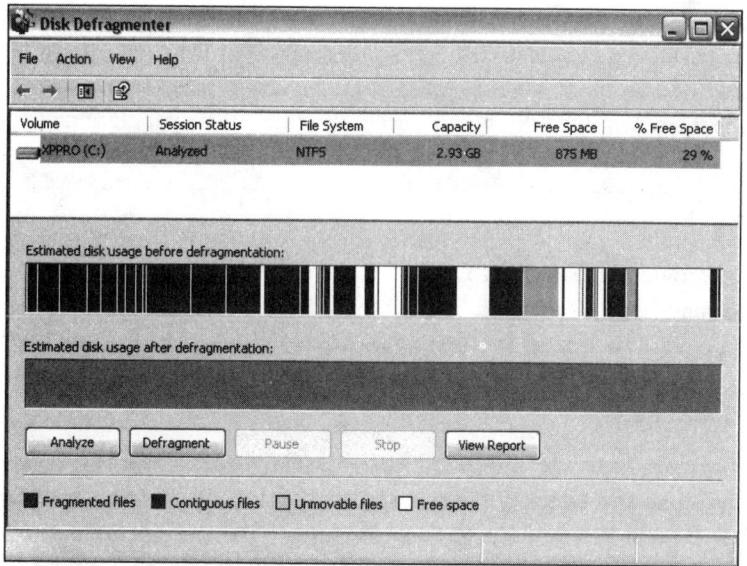

Figure 4.2 Disk Defragmenter utility.

Disk Defragmenter can analyze and defragment volumes formatted with FAT, FAT32, and NTFS.

To determine the amount of fragmentation on computer hard disks, you should first use Disk Defragmenter to analyze the volume. You will be provided with an analysis report that displays detailed information about the volume. The report will provide you with the information of the names of the most fragmented files, the number of fragments for each file, the average number of fragments per file, and the total available free space.

After running the Analysis portion of Disk Defragmenter, you can determine whether it would be beneficial to defragment your volumes. The defragmentation process consolidates free space and makes it more likely that new files will be stored in contiguous space. The length of time the defragmentation process takes depends on several factors, including:

➤ Volume size

➤ Number and size of files on the volume

➤ Amount of fragmentation on the volume

➤ Amount of local system resources available for running Disk Defragmenter

Note: A very large volume could take several hours to defragment.

After a disk or volume has been defragmented, Disk Defragmenter produces a defragmentation report that provides detailed information about the status of the defragmented volume. It can be compared with the analysis report to view improvements that occurred on the volume following the defragmentation.

Defrag Tool

Microsoft has provided administrators with the capability to defragment volumes from the command line. Defrag.exe is a command-line tool that can be used to consolidate files and folders on local volumes. To use Defrag, the volume must have a minimum of 15 percent free space. Otherwise, only a partial defragmentation will be done on the volume.

When Defrag is run from the command line, it displays only a blinking cursor, which indicates that the selected volume is in the process of being analyzed and defragmented. After it has finished, the analysis report and the defragmentation report are displayed. These reports can be saved to a text file by executing Defrag with the following command-line option:

```
Defrag.exe volume /v > filename.txt
```

Defrag can be run with the **/a** option to analyze the volume and display the analysis report. It can also be run with the **/v** option, which displays both the analysis and defragmentation reports. And, it can be run with the **/f** option which forces defragmentation whether the volume needs it or not.

File Systems

Both basic disks and dynamic disks support the FAT16, FAT32, NTFS 4, and NTFS 5 file systems.

FAT

File Allocation Table is a file system that was designed many years ago when hard disks were small in size. It was primarily used on systems running MS-DOS, Windows 3.x, and Windows 95. FAT has several limitations that prohibit it from being a good choice as the primary file system for Windows XP Professional. First, FAT cannot be used on volumes larger than 4GB. This is a major limitation, considering the amount of data that current hard drives can hold. Second, FAT does not support security or file or disk compression. FAT volumes are subject to becoming heavily fragmented when files and folders are created and deleted. FAT can be used, if needed, in Windows XP in a multiboot configuration. FAT supports shared folders. It can be converted to NTFS if more stringent security requirements are needed.

FAT32

FAT32 is supported by Windows 98, Windows 2000, and Windows XP. FAT32 is a more efficient file system than FAT. It supports volumes up to 32GB, though in theory it supports drivers up to 2 terabytes in size. FAT32 uses a smaller disk cluster size than FAT. This makes it a more efficient file system for large volumes. As with FAT, FAT32 does not offer security, other than shared folders. FAT volumes can be accessed only by computers running Windows 95 OSR2, Windows 98, Windows 2000, and Windows XP. It is not the recommended file system for Windows XP Professional, but it could be used in a multiboot configuration if needed.

Note: Microsoft does not recommend running computer systems in multiboot configurations.

NTFS

NTFS is the recommended file system for Windows XP Professional. NTFS supports Encrypting File System (EFS). NTFS is an advanced file system that was specifically designed for Windows NT and Windows 2000. NTFS provides better performance and reliability than FAT and FAT32. It supports compression on both files and folders. It supports the setting of permissions on shares, folders, and files. It manages disk space much more efficiently than either FAT or FAT32. NTFS supports disk quotas that can be used to limit the amount of disk space each user has available to them on the computer. NTFS volumes can't be accessed by MS-DOS, Windows 95, or Windows 98.

Remote Administration

Members of the Administrators group can manage remote computers from their local computers. An administrator can manage disks on Windows XP Professional, Windows XP Server, Windows 2000 Server, and Windows 2000 Advanced Server computers from a Windows XP Professional workstation. The Computer Management tool is used to connect to remote computers to perform disk management.

Disk Cleanup

Disk Cleanup is a utility that was introduced in Windows 98 that allows users to reclaim space on their hard drives. It does this by deleting files that are no longer needed. Disk Cleanup is accessed from the property page of a volume through Disk Management. When you start Disk Cleanup, it calculates the amount of space that it can free up on the volume (see Figure 4.3). The following types of files can be deleted using Disk Cleanup:

➤ Downloaded program files

➤ Temporary Internet files

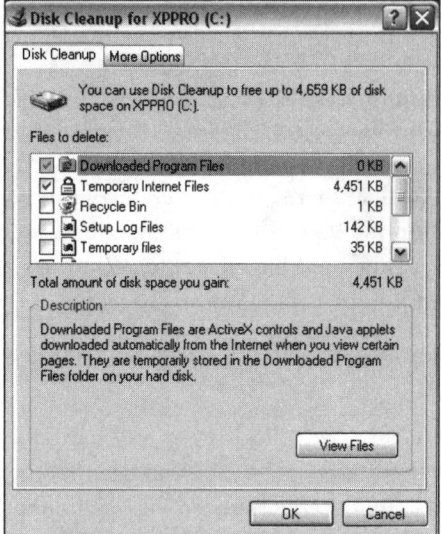

Figure 4.3   Disk Cleanup utility.

➤ Files in the Recycle Bin

➤ Temporary remote desktop files

➤ Temporary files

➤ WebClient/Publisher temporary files

➤ Catalog files for the Content Indexer

➤ Temporary offline files

➤ Offline files

➤ Compressed old files

Disk Cleanup can also be used to free disk space by removing Windows components and installed programs that are not being used. Disk Cleanup can be configured to run automatically when your computer is low on disk space.

Disk Quota

Disk quotas can be used by administrators to track and control user usage on NTFS volumes. This can be done on a per-user basis. When setting disk quotas, two values can be set—a disk quota limit and a disk quota warning level. Disk quotas can be enabled on local and network volumes and removable drives if they are formatted with NTFS (see Figure 4.4).

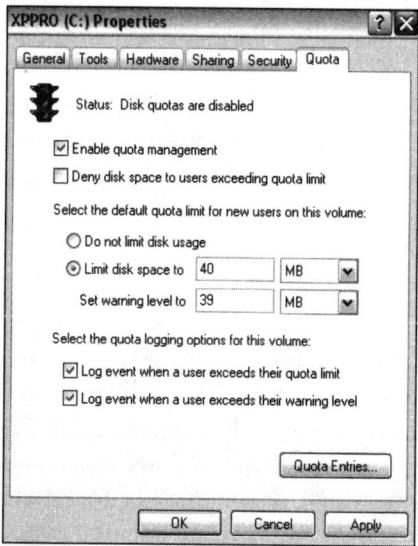

Figure 4.4 Disk Quota utility.

Disk quotas track each user's volume usage individually. Applying limitations to one user will not affect another user. Two events can occur when a user exceeds their disk quota limitations:

➤ An event will be logged to the system log

➤ An event will be logged and disk access will be blocked

If one user has a disk quota limit of 200MB, they will not be able to write additional data to the volume when they reach this limit until they delete or move some existing files.

Administrators can only apply disk quotas to volumes. When applying disk quotas, they are based on file ownership independent of the location of the files and folders on the volume. If a computer has multiple volumes, you can apply disk quotas to each volume. Quotas would be tracked individually for each volume.

To configure disk quotas, administrators can specify two values:

➤ *A quota limit*—The amount of disk space a user is allowed

➤ *A quota threshold*—The condition under which an event will be logged when a user nears the quota limit

Volume usage information for disk quotas is stored by using the security ID (SID). User account names are compared to their SID when quota entries are first made.

You must be a member of the Administrators group to enable disk quotas. When quotas are initially enabled, Windows XP calculates the amount of disk space for users on the volume up to that point. Quota limits and warning levels are applied to current users based on this calculation.

Disk quotas are set using the Disk Management snap-in tool. They can also be managed using the Fsutil command-line utility. Fsutil quotas can be used to create and modify disk quotas, and Fsutil behaviors can be used to change when quota events are logged.

Chapter Summary

Windows XP Professional supports two types of disks—basic disks and dynamic disks. Basic disks are supported in all previous versions of Windows and can hold primary and extended partitions. Basic disks store their configuration information in the MBR. Dynamic disks, which were introduced in Windows 2000, do not store their configuration information in the MBR. It is stored in a Disk Management database at the end of the drive. Dynamic disks contain volumes. These volumes can be simple volumes, spanned volumes, mirrored volumes, striped volumes, and RAID 5 volumes. Basic disks can be converted to dynamic disks, and dynamic disks can be converted to basic disks. When dynamic disks are converted to basic disks, all information on the disks is lost.

The Disk Management snap-in is the main tool available for managing disks. Disk Management can be used to initialize disks, create volumes, display status information of disks and volumes, and troubleshoot disk problems. Administrators can use Disk Management to manage disks on remote computers.

Several command-line tools are provided with Windows XP Professional that administrators can use to perform disk management. DiskPart is a tool that can be used to manage disks, partitions, and volumes from a command line or a script. Fsutil is a tool that is used to manage reparse points and dismount and extend volumes. Convert is used to convert FAT and FAT32 file systems to NTFS. Chkdsk can be used to generate a status report on a disk, check for errors, and repair any errors if they are found. The Mountvol utility enables you to mount local volumes to an empty NTFS folder.

Disks become fragmented over time with the repeated addition and deletion of files and folders. Two tools are provided to defragment hard disks. Disk Defragmenter is a GUI-based tool that can be used to analyze and defragment volumes. A command-line version of the GUI-based Disk Defragmenter tool called Defrag is available for advanced users.

Windows XP Professional supports FAT, FAT32, and NTFS. NTFS is the recommended file system for Windows XP.

Review Questions

1. A basic disk can contain what types of partitions?

    p.80

   a. Simple

   b. Primary

   c. Extended

   d. Striped

2. What type of drive is created on basic disks through an extended partition?

    p.81

   a. CD-ROM drive

   b. Primary partition drive

   c. Logical drive

   d. Dynamic drive

3. Which of the following are not supported in Windows XP Professional?

   p.83

   a. RAID 5 volumes

   b. Simple volumes

   c. Mirrored volumes

   d. Spanned volumes

4. Which of the following is the correct number of partitions supported by basic disks?

   p.80

   a. Five primary partitions

   b. Four primary partitions

   c. Three primary partitions and one extended partition

   d. Two primary partitions and two extended partitions

5. What type of volume can use free space on up to 32 drives?

   p.83

   a. Striped volume

   b. Spanned volume

   c. Striped volume with parity

   d. Simple volume

6. Bob wants to perform disk management but is unable to get the Disk Management snap-in to load. What else can Bob use to perform disk management?

   a. He can use the DiskPart command-line tool.

   b. He can use Device Manager.

   c. He can't. He must get the Disk Management snap-in loaded before he can perform disk management.

   d. He can use the Mountvol.exe tool.

4

7. John is checking the hard disk on several computers in the office, and he notices that one of them is showing a status of Foreign. He is confused as to what this means. What does a status of Foreign tell John about the disk?

     p.87

    a. I/O errors have occurred on the disk.

    b. The disk is of an unknown type.

    c. A disk from another computer has been installed in the computer.

    d. This is the normal disk status.

8. GPT disks are supported by what versions of Windows XP?

     p.86

    a. The 32-bit version of Windows XP Professional.

    b. The 64-bit version of Windows XP Professional.

    c. GPT disks are not supported by Windows XP Professional.

    d. The 32-bit version of Windows XP Server.

9. What is the master boot record?

     p.84

    a. A subpartition on a primary partition on a basic disk.

    b. It contains the master boot code, the disk signature, and the partition.

    c. It is a disk-partitioning scheme that will be used by the Extensible Firmware Interface.

    d. It constantly monitors the disk status of disks in Windows XP Professional.

10. What command-line utility can be used to convert a basic disk to a dynamic disk in Windows XP Professional?

    p.90

    a. Fsutil

    b. DiskPart

    c. Convert

    d. Chkdsk

11. Winston is setting up several new Windows XP Professional computers. They all will contain basic disks, and he knows that they can contain both primary and extended partitions. He's somewhat confused about the number of active partitions that each drive can hold. How many active partitions will Winston be able to set up on the basic disks?

    p.98

    a. Two per disk

    b. One per disk

    c. Three per disk

    d. Zero; basic disks don't have active partitions

12. Sheila wants to defragment her hard drive. She has a very large hard drive, but it is almost full. She wants to use the Defrag.exe command-line utility to perform this operation. What is the minimal amount of free space required for Sheila to run Defrag?

    a. 10 percent

    b. 20 percent

    c. 15 percent

    d. 50 percent

4

13. John wants to determine how much fragmentation has occurred on his hard drive. He doesn't want to defragment it at this time but only wants to get a report about the amount of fragmentation that exists. How can he do this?

    a. He can run Defrag.exe with the **/a** option.

    b. He can run Defrag.exe with the **/v** option.

    c. He can run Defrag.exe by itself.

    d. He can't. He must run the defragmentation utility after he does an analysis of the hard drive.

14. Which of the following file systems do not support file permissions?

    a. NTFS 4

    b. FAT

    c. FAT32

    d. NTFS 5

15. NTFS supports which of the following?

    a. Disk quotas

    b. Compression on files

    c. EFS

    d. Compression on folders

16. What utility will allow administrators to set limits on the amount of disk space users can have on a volume?

    a. Disk Defragmenter

    b. Disk Cleanup

    c. Disk Management

    d. Disk Quotas

17. What types of files can be deleted using the Disk Cleanup utility?

    p 95/
    p 96

    a. Temporary Internet files
    b. System files
    c. Setup log files
    d. Recycle Bin files

18. Administrators can apply disk quotas on which of the following file systems?

    p. 96

    a. FAT
    b. NTFS 4
    c. FAT32
    d. NTFS 5

19. Marie has been given the proper permissions to set disk quotas on several Windows XP Professional computers that are shared by multiple users. Marie has been told that she can do this from a command line. What command-line utility can she use to do this?

    p 98

    a. Convert.exe
    b. Fsutil.exe
    c. Defrag.exe
    d. Chkdsk.exe

20. What is the correct command line to format a FAT32 volume on the D: drive to NTFS?

    p 91

    a. **convert.ext d: /fs**
    b. **convert.exe d: /fs:nt**
    c. **convert.exe c: /fs:ntfs**
    d. **convert.exe d: /fs:ntfs**

Real-World Projects

For all of the following projects, you need a computer running Windows XP Professional. The computer should have at least two hard drives and a CD-ROM drive. At least one of the drives should be formatted with the NTFS file system. These projects are intended to help you better understand some of the disk management tasks that can be performed in Windows XP Professional.

Project 4.1

To convert a basic disk to a dynamic disk using Disk Management:

1. Right-click My Computer.

2. Select Manage.

3. Click the plus sign beside Storage.

4. Select Disk Management.

5. Select the basic disk that you want to convert.

6. Right-click the disk, and select Upgrade To Dynamic Disk.

[handwritten margin note: start admin tools. comp. management. disk management]

[handwritten margin note: don't know run cmd d]

4

Project 4.2

To convert a dynamic disk back to a basic disk:

1. Back up the data on the dynamic disk that will be converted to a basic disk.

2. Go to Disk Management.

3. Right-click the dynamic disks that you want to convert.

4. Select Convert To Basic Disk.

Project 4.3

To use Disk Management to change the CD-ROM drive letter assignment:

1. Open Disk Management.

2. Right-click the CD-ROM drive letter, and select Change Drive Letter And Paths.

3. Click the Edit button.

4. From the Assign Drive Letter drop-down list box, select the new drive letter.

5. Click OK.

Project 4.4

To create a mount point: *[handwritten: accessibility]*

1. Create an empty folder on your NTFS volume. This will become your mount point.

2. Right-click the volume you want to mount, and select Change Drive Letter And Path.

3. Click Add.

4. Click Mount in the following empty NTFS folder.

5. Type in the path to the empty folder you created or click the Browse button to select the folder.

6. Click OK.

Project 4.5

To create a simple volume:

1. Open Computer Management.

2. Click Disk Management.

3. Select unallocated space on the desired disk.

4. Click the Action menu, and select All Tasks.

5. Click Create Volume.

6. When the Create Volume Wizard appears, click Next.

7. Click the Simple Volume radio button on the Select Volume Type window.

8. Click Next.

9. Select the disk on the Select Disks window, and use the Size dialog box to change to the desired volume size.

10. Click Next.

11. Select the drive letter on the Assign Drive Letter Or Path dialog box, and click Next.

12. Select the desired file system from the drop-down menu on the Format Volume window, and click Next.

13. Click Finish on the Completion window.

Project 4.6

To extend a drive:

1. Open Computer Management.

2. Click Disk Management.

3. Click the Action menun and select All Tasks.

4. Click Extend Volume. The Extend Volume Wizard opens.

5. Click Next.

6. Select the drive you want to extend on the Select Disks dialog box.

7. Click Finish to complete the wizard.

CHAPTER FIVE

Customizing Your Desktop Environment in Windows XP Professional

After completing this chapter, you will be able to:

✓ Configure desktop settings in Windows XP Professional

✓ Customize the Start menu

✓ Customize the taskbar

✓ Configure system settings

✓ Use each Control Panel tool

✓ Explain the accessibility options available in Windows XP Professional

✓ Use Remote Assistance to help a user

✓ Explain how Fast Switching is used in Windows XP Professional

Windows XP Professional has a new visual look. When the operating system is initially loaded, the only icon on the desktop is the Recycle Bin. Microsoft eliminated clutter and left it up to users to customize their desktops. The Start menu has been changed to allow users to tailor it to their specific needs. The taskbar has been upgraded with the addition of toolbars that provide users with easy and quick access to the desktop or Web sites. The Control Panel has a new Category View that groups icons together depending on their specific functions. As with all versions of Windows, accessibility options are available to assist users who have special computing needs. Users who need help with the Windows XP Professional operating system can request assistance through the Remote Assistance tool. Designated helpers can open remote sessions to users' computers and perform operations as if they were seated at the computers' consoles.

Configuring Desktop Settings

One aspect that you will notice immediately when you start Windows XP Professional is how different the desktop looks from previous versions of Windows. Microsoft did some market research while developing Windows XP and determined that users were tiring of cluttered desktops. In previous versions of Windows, every application that was loaded added its icon to the desktop by default. When you start Windows XP Professional for the first time, the only icon on the desktop is the Recycle Bin. Microsoft has left the customization of the desktop to users to suit their own needs and wants.

Changing the Display Properties

As with all versions of Windows, users can alter the display properties of their computers to suit their needs. They can change most aspects of the desktop, including the background, dialog boxes, icons, and screen resolution. Windows XP Professional has several themes from which users can choose. These themes consist of predetermined colors, icons, fonts, and desktop backgrounds. Users can modify existing themes or create their own. If a user creates a theme, the theme is saved in the user's My Documents folder. Modified themes are saved in a folder called Current Theme. A modified theme will be lost if a user selects a new theme and does not save the modified theme with a unique name.

A corporation can create themes specific to its company to ensure a unified look on each computer in the corporation. Administrators can prevent employees from changing the themes through the use of mandatory profiles or Group Policy.

Users in Windows XP Professional will find the Windows Classic theme is still available from previous versions of Windows.

Altering the Desktop

The desktop consists of the background and the icons that appear on the desktop. The background was called *wallpaper* in previous versions of Windows. As with the previous versions of Windows, these background images can be stretched across the entire desktop, tiled on the desktop, or centered on the desktop.

When you install Windows XP Professional, the only desktop icon that appears is the Recycle Bin. Users can customize their desktops to include additional icons. These include My Computer, My Network Places, and My Documents. Shortcuts can be added to the desktop with links to frequently used applications and documents. To meet their specific needs, users can change the icons for these shortcuts. Windows XP Professional has included the ability to display Web page content on the desktop. This is especially beneficial for companies that have Web pages. By making the desktop background the company Web page, employees have real-time access to pertinent company information.

5

Screen Savers

Screen savers provide users with additional security. A screen saver can be configured to start after a predetermined period of inactivity. A password could be required before the user can log back onto the computer. This is especially beneficial for users who work on sensitive company data and regularly have to be away from their computers for short periods of time. It can also provide a way for users to protect their personal data from prying eyes.

A new feature has been added to the screen saver options of Windows XP Professional called My Picture Slideshow. Users can integrate personal pictures that they have saved in the My Picture folder into a screen saver slideshow. The slideshow supports transitions and password protection.

Desktop Cleanup

Desktop Cleanup is a new feature in Windows XP Professional that is used to clean all unused icons off the desktop. When you run Desktop Cleanup, it starts a wizard that lists desktop icons that have not been used in the last 60 days. You can use the wizard to remove these icons from your desktop. Desktop Cleanup can be configured to automatically run every 60 days. All icons removed using Desktop Cleanup are stored in a folder called Unused Icons, which is displayed on the desktop.

Individual icons can be removed from the desktop by right-clicking the icon and selecting Delete.

Customizing the Start Menu

The Start menu has been changed in Windows XP Professional to provide users with easier access to their most frequently used programs. Users can tailor the Start menu to their specific needs. If you have used Windows 2000, you will notice that the Start menu looks different in Windows XP (see Figure 5.1).

The Start menu consists of two frames. The left frame contains three sections. The top section contains the default email program and browser and is also used to display pinned programs, which are programs that are manually attached to the Start menu. The second section contains programs that are frequently used. The third section displays the All Programs option that provides access to all programs on the computer.

The right frame contains My Documents, My Recent Documents, My Pictures, My Music, and My Computer. It also contains links to the Control Panel, Printers and Faxes, Help and Support, Search, and Run utilities.

The left side of the Start menu is white and is the user-based portion of the Start menu. The right side is light blue and is the operating system-based section. Users are restricted in how they can modify the light-blue area of the Start menu. The Start menu can be customized for all users on the computer or for individual users. Submenus can be added for easier access to applications that users use more frequently.

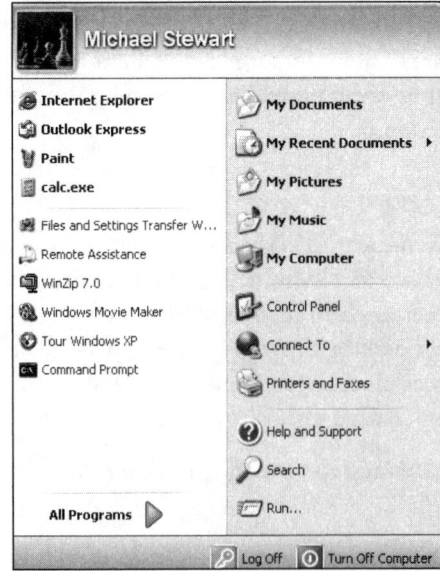

Figure 5.1   The Windows XP Professional Start menu.

Altering the Start Menu Properties

Start menu properties can be changed to suit the needs of users. Users can select whether they want the icons displayed in large or small format. They can select how many programs they want to appear on the Start menu. They can have both their favorite Internet browser and their email program accessible from the Start menu.

The following items can be added to or deleted from the Start Menu to meet the end user's specific wants and needs:

➤ Control Panel

➤ Help and Support

➤ My Computer

➤ My Documents

➤ My Music

➤ My Network Places

➤ My Pictures

➤ Network Connections

➤ Printers and Faxes

➤ Run command

➤ Search

➤ System Administrative Tools

For users who are not comfortable with the new look of the Windows XP Professional Start menu, Microsoft has provided the capability to use the Classic Start menu from Windows 2000. Users can access the taskbar and Start menu properties and can switch from the new Windows XP Start menu to the classic Windows Start menu by clicking the Classic Start menu dialog box button.

Pinning Applications to the Start Menu

Users can "pin" applications to the Start menu. When an application is pinned to the Start menu, the application is always available to the user. Pinning ensures that the application is not hidden when it is not used frequently.

Customizing the Taskbar

The taskbar in Windows XP Professional is very different from the taskbar in Windows 2000 Professional. It consists of three sections, each of which has a specific function (see Figure 5.2).

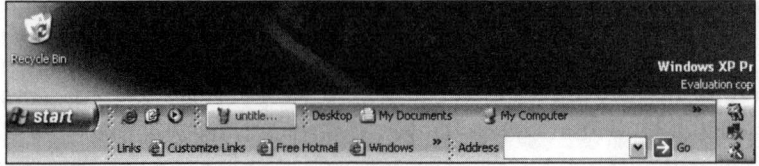

Figure 5.2   The Windows XP Professional taskbar.

The taskbar has a button for each open document. The taskbar could become crowded if each document were displayed individually on it. Microsoft designed the taskbar in Windows XP Professional so documents that run from a single program are grouped together. If the button has a down arrow, this indicates that multiple documents are open for the application. Clicking the arrow displays a list of all the open documents.

The Quick Launch menu allows a user to quickly access her most frequently used programs. This menu can easily be added to any empty space on the taskbar.

The Notification Area is responsible for showing the time and icons that indicate the status of certain events. Microsoft designed this area to hide inactive icons so that the taskbar doesn't become too crowded with notifications, such as new email messages. To view the inactive area on the Notification Area of the taskbar, click the chevron (<). This will display any hidden inactive icons.

The taskbar can be customized to be automatically hidden when it is not in use. Users can also hide inactive icons. The taskbar can be customized further with the addition of toolbars. The following toolbars can be added to the taskbar:

➤ *Address toolbar*—Provides a user with a bar in which he can type the URL for a Web site. Every time a new URL is typed, it is automatically added to the previously created list from which the user can choose.

➤ *Links toolbar*—Provides users with easy access to Web pages.

➤ *Desktop toolbar*—Provides users with instant access to all items on their desktops.

➤ *Language Band toolbar*—Gives users a way to easily switch between languages and keyboard layouts.

➤ *New toolbar*—Enables a user to create links to folders or other resources on the computer.

Customizing the Startup Folder

Users in your organization might use certain programs, such as Microsoft Word, every time they operate their computer. By customizing the Startup folder, you can have such programs start automatically when users log onto their computers. You do this by placing a shortcut to the program in the Startup folder for each user. You can do this for individuals or for all users.

Customizing the My Documents Folder

The My Documents folder is the default location in Windows XP Professional for the storage of user data. The only two accounts that have access to the My Documents folder by default are the user and the administrator.

The My Documents folder is located in Documents and Settings/*username*/My Documents on the local computer. The location of this folder can be changed to an alternative location, such as another hard drive on the computer or a network share on a server.

All folders in Windows XP Professional have attributes that can be changed, including the My Documents folder. Users can customize the following attributes:

➤ Archiving

➤ Compression

➤ Encryption

➤ Indexing

Although it is not recommended, an individual can share his My Documents folder for access by other users on the network. NTFS permissions can be set for user access just like any other shared folder on an NTFS volume. Microsoft recommends that if you want to share files in the My Documents folder, you should create a separate folder, place the files in that folder, and share it.

My Pictures Folder Enhancements

The My Pictures folder was introduced in Windows 2000 and is the default location for storing images. Enhancements have been added to provide users with a better experience when working with scanners, digital cameras, and streaming cameras. Some of the enhancements include the following:

➤ Ability to publish pictures on the Web

➤ Enhanced picture preview capability, including the capability to rotate images

➤ Filmstrip view

➤ Improved thumbnail generation

➤ Links to automatically start wizards when using Windows Image Acquisition (WIA) scanners and cameras

➤ Print Pictures Wizard for printing images to the Web

➤ Slideshow applet

Configuring System Settings

Over time, various factors can cause degradation in system performance for computer systems. Windows XP Professional provides options that can be configured to optimize system performance to keep a computer running at its peak. These operating system settings are applied globally to all users who log on to the computer. You do not have to set individual operating system settings for each user.

Two types of operating system settings can be configured in Windows XP Professional—environment variables, and start and recovery variables.

Configuring Environment Variables

Environment variables provide administrators with the capability to configure a shared computer with variables for each individual user. If a newly installed application requires specific variables for each user, these can be set through the Environment Variables dialog box, shown in Figure 5.3. The two types of environment variables are user variables and system variables. User variables can be used to specify such settings as the location of the current user's temporary files. System variables specify the location for computer files and folders.

User environment variables are stored in the user's profile. Users can modify, add, or remove their own environment variables.

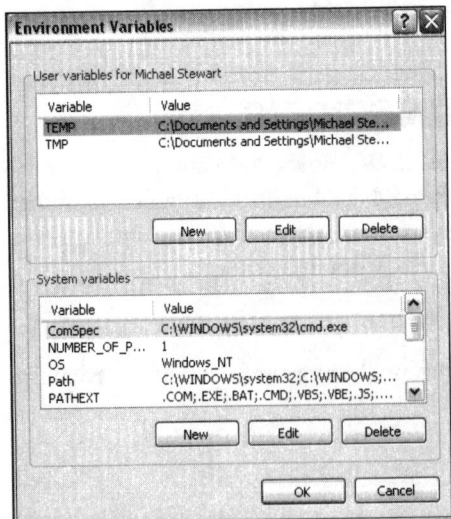

Figure 5.3 Configuring environment variables.

System environment variables are applied system-wide and affect all users on the computer. Administrators are the only ones who can modify, add, or remove system environment variables.

When your Windows XP Professional computer boots, it searches for any environment variables. These variables are set in the following order:

1. Autoexec.bat variables

2. System environment variables

3. User environment variables

If the same environment variables, such as a temp directory location, are set in the Autoexec.bat and in the user environment variable, the user environment variable setting is the setting that will take precedence when the computer boots.

Changing the Startup and Recovery Options

No matter how much preparation and performance tuning you perform on your computer system, it occasionally fails. System failure settings can be configured to determine what action is taken during a system failure or *stop error* (see Figure 5.4). A stop error is a serious error that can cause a system to stop functioning. In Windows XP Professional, the following system failure settings can be configured:

➤ Write an event to the system log to record the source of the stop error

➤ Send an administrative alert via email

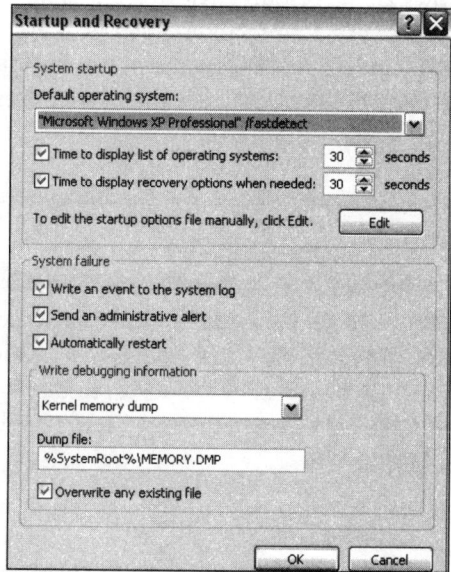

Figure 5.4   System startup and recovery options.

➤ Automatically restart the system

➤ Write debugging information

All versions of Windows provide users with the capability to write debugging information to a file called Memory.dmp. This file can be analyzed or sent to Microsoft technical support to help in determining the problem when a system crashes. Several types of debugging information are available:

➤ *Small memory dump*—Saves the smallest amount of information needed to determine why the system stopped. Requires a paging file of at least 2MB on the boot partition of the computer. Windows XP Professional will create a new dump file every time the system stops. This is different from previous versions of Windows, which require at least two times the size of the paging file to be available on the hard drive for the system to create a memory dump file. For example, if the paging file on a computer is 3MB in size, you need 6MB of disk space to write the memory dump file. Also, you cannot create a new memory file at each system crash for prior versions. The existing file is overwritten.

➤ *Kernel memory dump*—Records only kernel memory. Between 50MB and 800MB of disk space is required to write the kernel memory dump, depending on the amount of RAM in the computer.

➤ *Complete memory dump*—Records the entire contents of system memory. If you decide to record a complete memory dump, you must ensure that the paging file on the boot partition is large enough to hold all the physical RAM plus 1MB.

Two utilities are available in the Windows 2000 Resource Kit to aid in debugging dump files—Dumpchk.exe and Dumpexam.exe. Dumpchk.exe can be used to convert the hexadecimal Memory.dmp file into a text file so that it can be read. Dumpexam.exe is then used to display the contents of the file that was converted using Dumpchk.exe.

Control Panel

The Control Panel contains tools that can be used to change the way Windows XP Professional looks and behaves. The Control Panel has been modified in Windows XP Professional with a new look. A new Category View has been added, which groups similar items together (see Figure 5.5). Users still have access to the classic Control Panel view if they do not want to use the new Category View. The following sections take a look at the Control Panel tools.

Add Hardware

The Add Hardware tool opens to a wizard that allows a user to install hardware and troubleshoot problems she might be having with hardware. When you start the wizard, it searches the computer for any newly installed hardware. If the

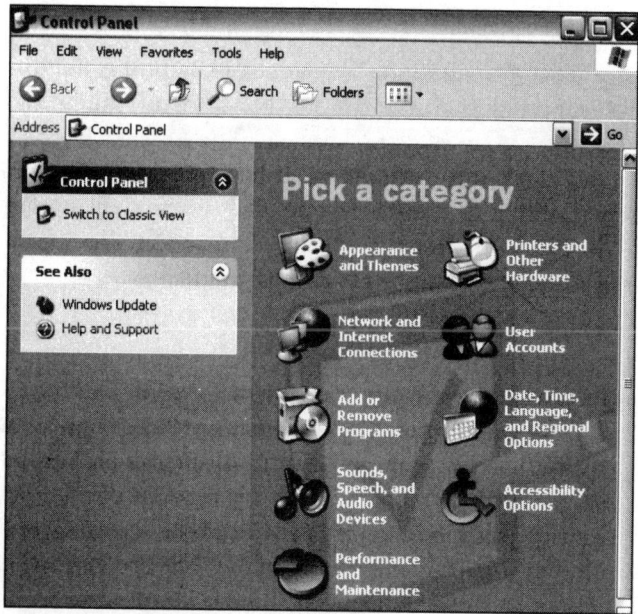

Figure 5.5 The Control Panel Category View.

wizard is not able to identify any newly installed hardware, the user can click Add A New Hardware Device and select the device to install from a list of common hardware types.

Add Or Remove Programs

The Add Or Remove Programs tool is used to change or remove existing programs, add new programs, and add or remove Windows Components.

Administrative Tools

Administrative Tools provides quick access to several tools used to manage a computer. The following tools can be accessed from the Administrative Tools icon in the Control Panel:

➤ Component Services

➤ Computer Management

➤ Data Sources

➤ Event Viewer

➤ Local Security Policy

➤ Performance

➤ Services

Date And Time

Date And Time is used to change a computer's current date and time and to set the time zone the computer is located in. A new feature of Date And Time in Windows XP Professional is the addition of an Internet Time tab. This tab enables you to synchronize your computer clock automatically to an Internet time server. You must be connected to the Internet to use this feature. The system will attempt to synchronize weekly if you have a continuous Internet connection. The Update Now button enables you to synchronize the clock time immediately.

Display

The Display tool is used to configure various components of your Windows XP Professional desktop. You can select from multiple themes or create your own. As with all previous versions of Windows, you can select from various backgrounds for your desktop. You can select a screen saver and specify the amount of time before it is activated. For added security, you can assign a password to the screen saver to protect your computer from prying eyes. New to Windows XP Professional is the ability to use personal pictures to create a picture slideshow screen saver.

Power options for the monitor are configured by clicking the Power button on the Screen Saver tab in the Display Properties dialog box. Users can select from several predefined power schemes or edit an existing power scheme to match their power needs. Both the monitor and hard disks can be configured to be turned off at times specified by the user. You can activate Hibernation mode through the Hibernate tab. When configuring hibernation, you must have a minimal amount of disk space to save the entire contents of the hard drive. The system will specify how much disk space is required for it to go into Hibernation mode.

If you have a UPS attached to your system, you can get status information on it through the UPS tab.

The Appearance tab is used to change the look of your desktop. You can change the color and size of individual desktop items, including the Active Title Bar, Icons, Message Box, Menus, and the Scrollbar.

The Settings tab can be used to change the screen resolution, change the type of display being used by the computer, and troubleshoot any display problems.

Folder Options

The Folder Options tool lets a user tailor how folders are displayed. The General tab lets you specify whether hyperlinks are displayed to common folder tasks or whether the folders are displayed in the Windows Classic view. Folders can be opened in the same or separate windows. Items can be opened with a single click or a double-click.

The View tab lets a user determine which aspects of folders are displayed, such as the full path name or file extensions for known file types. The File Types tab shows registered file types and allows a user to create a new association between file names and extensions.

The Offline Files tab is used to configure the computer so that a user can work with files stored on a company network even when he is not connected to the network.

Fonts

The Fonts tool is used to add and remove fonts. Fonts display text on both the screen and in printing. Windows XP Professional uses three font technologies—outline fonts, vector fonts, and raster fonts.

Game Controllers

The Game Controllers tool is used to configure game controllers that may be installed on the computer. User can also troubleshoot problems with game controllers by clicking the Troubleshoot button in the Game Controllers dialog box.

Internet Options

The Internet Options tool is used to configure Internet properties for Internet Explorer. The General tab can be used to set up a home page when a user starts Internet Explorer. From this tab, users can select where their temporary Internet files are stored and the amount of disk space that is used to store the files. The History folder contains a list of pages that a user has visited. This can be cleared, or the number of days that the pages are recorded in history can be increased or decreased.

The Security tab lets a user customize the security level for various types of Web content zones.

The Privacy tab allows users to determine how Internet Explorer handles cookies when visiting Web sites. Users can configure Internet Explorer to accept, block, or prompt when a Web site requests a cookie.

The Content tab can be used to start or stop Content Advisor, which is used to monitor the type of material being viewed on the Web. The Certificates button is used to display available certificates and to import certificates that might be required when visiting secure Web sites.

AutoComplete stores entries that a user has previously entered and provides a list she can chose from instead of retyping the entry. AutoComplete can be used for Web sites, forms, usernames, and passwords.

The Connections tab is used to set up an Internet connection. This connection can be a dial-up connection, VPN, or LAN connection.

The Programs tab lets a user specify the programs that Windows XP Professional automatically uses for various Internet services. A user can select his preferred HTML editor, email program, newsgroup program, Internet call program, Calendar, Contact list, and Address book.

Keyboard

The Keyboard tool is used to select the character repeat rate and the cursor blink rate. Updated keyboard drivers can be loaded from this tab, and a user can troubleshoot keyboard problems with the Troubleshoot button.

Mouse

The Mouse tool is used to determine how your mouse is configured. For left-handed users, the primary and secondary button can be switched. The double-click speed can be changed to aid users who want to customize the double-clicking response of the mouse. Pointers for the mouse can be selected, and the pointer speed and visibility can be configured to make it easier for users of LCD screens.

Network Connections

Network Connections is used to view the properties of existing network connections and create new connections. Five types of network connections can be created through the Network Connections tool:

➤ Dial-up connections

➤ Direct connections

➤ Incoming connections

➤ Local area connections

➤ VPN connections

For users who want to connect their home or office network to the Internet with only one Internet connection, Network Connections can be used to enable Internet Connection Sharing (ICS). Windows XP Professional includes Internet Connection Firewall (ICF), which can be used in conjunction with ICS to control what information is processed from your network to the Internet. Like ICS, ICF is enabled through Network Connections.

For users who want to set up a home or small business network, the Network Setup Wizard is provided in Windows XP Professional to walk them step by step through the process.

Phone And Modem Options

The Phone And Modem Options tool is used to configure dialing rules and install and troubleshoot modems on the computer.

Power Options

The Power Options tool can be used to configure a power scheme for a computer. Windows XP Professional provides six predefined power schemes that can be used to manage power consumption on your computer. Both the monitor and hard disks can be configured to turn off after a predetermined time to automatically save power. Hibernation can be set on a computer to shut it down after a period of inactivity. When the computer is shut down, everything in memory is stored on the hard drive. When a user returns to the computer, the computer returns to the state it was at when the computer shut down. If your computer has a UPS, it can also be configured through the Power Options tool.

Printers And Faxes

The Printers And Faxes tool is used to set up and remove both printers and fax machines. It also can be used to troubleshoot problems with these devices.

Regional And Language Options

The Regional And Language Options tool is used to set up how programs format numbers, currencies, dates, and time. If a user needs to use multiple languages, they can be added here. Most of the languages that Windows XP Professional supports are added by default when the operating system is installed. If a user needs to use a complex language, such as Chinese or Japanese, he would install it through the Regional And Language Options tool. Text services are also installed through this tool. Text services provide a way for users to add and edit text in documents using keyboards, speech dictation, and digitized handwriting.

Scanners And Cameras

The Scanners And Cameras tool is used to add imaging devices. The Scanner And Camera Installation Wizard will walk a user step by step through the process of adding digital still and video cameras or scanners to her computer. After the imaging device is installed, users can use the Scanners And Cameras tool to download and save pictures to the My Pictures folder. This is the default location for saving images, but users can change this and save to a folder they specify. They can also troubleshoot their image devices through this tool.

Scheduled Tasks

Scheduled Tasks is a program that runs in the background every time Windows XP Professional is started. Users can schedule a script, application, or document to run at a specified time. The Scheduled Tasks tool uses the Scheduled Task Wizard to help a user create a schedule for a task the user wants Windows XP Professional to perform.

A new function that was added with Windows XP Professional is the ability of an administrator to schedule the Disk Defragmenter tool through Scheduled Tasks.

Sounds And Audio Devices

The Sounds And Audio Devices tool is used to configure the audio and voice components of your computer system. Sound schemes can be set up to play specific sounds when a Windows program event occurs. You can also troubleshoot audio devices through the Sounds And Audio Devices Properties dialog box.

Speech

The Speech tool is a new tool added to the Control Panel to control voice properties for text-to-speech translation. You can adjust the speed at which the text-to-speech translation occurs.

System

The Systems tool lets you view and change system properties. The General tab shows the Windows OS version that is being run on the computer. It shows who the software is registered to, the processor type, and amount of RAM in the computer.

The Computer Name tab is used to provide a description for the computer and to add the computer to a workgroup or domain.

The Hardware tab gives you access to the Add Hardware Wizard, the Device Manager, and any hardware profiles that have been configured on the computer.

To use the Advanced tab, you must be logged on as the Administrator or have administrator rights. This tab can be used to configure performance options, such as processor scheduling and memory usage. User profiles for the computer can be edited or deleted. The system startup and recovery options can also be configured on this tab.

The System Restore tab is used to turn on or off System Restore on all drives on a computer. Users can set the amount of disk space that is reserved for System Restore.

The Automatic Updates tab can be used to configure notification when updates are available for the computer.

The Remote Assistance tab is used to allow Remote Assistance invitations to be sent from the computer and to allow other users to remotely connect to the computer.

Taskbar And Start Menu

The Taskbar And Start Menu Properties tool is used to configure how the taskbar is displayed and what appears in the Notification area of the taskbar. Users can use the Start Menu tab to select the classic Windows Start menu or to customize the Windows XP Professional Start menu.

User Accounts

User Accounts is a new Control Panel tool introduced in Windows XP Professional. This tool is used to create user accounts for a computer and to change the properties for these accounts. You can change the way users log on and off. Two options are available for logging on and off—the Welcome screen and Fast User Switching. The Welcome screen allows a user to simply click their account name to log on. With Fast User Switching enabled, computer accounts can be quickly switched from one to another without having to close the program.

Accessibility Options

Windows XP Professional has several accessibility options that are provided to assist individuals with impairments who have special computing needs. These options do not require additional hardware or software. Accessibility options are included to help people with mobility, cognitive, visual, or hearing impairments. Each of these options can be configured individually through the Control Panel (see Figure 5.6). Microsoft has included in Windows XP Professional an Accessibility Wizard that can be used to assist in configuring any of these options. This wizard presents questions to evaluate a user's abilities and then enables the accessibility tools that best fit the needs of the user.

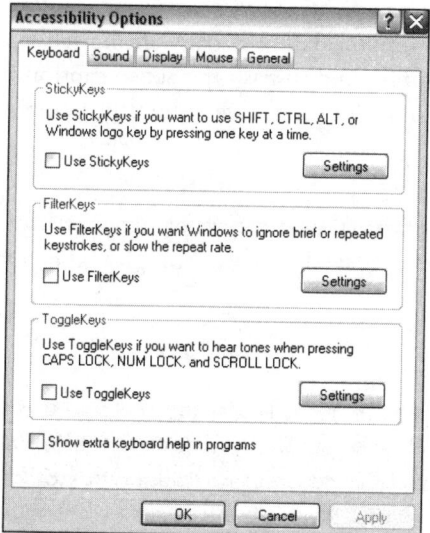

Figure 5.6   Accessibility Options dialog box.

*Note: Additional information about the accessibility options available from Microsoft can be found at **www.microsoft.com/enable**.*

StickyKeys

StickyKeys is useful for individuals who have problems pressing two keys at the same time. After StickyKeys is activated, users can press the Ctrl, Alt, or Shift keys, and those keys will remain active until another key is pressed. StickyKeys can be activated through a shortcut that entails pressing the Shift key fives times. Notifications can be set to show on screen the status that StickyKeys is active, and a sound can be made when the Ctrl, Alt, Shift, or Windows logo key is pressed.

FilterKeys

FilterKeys can be activated to ignore repeated keystrokes. It also can be used to slow the repeat rate when a key is pressed. The shortcut to activate FilterKeys is to hold down the right Shift key for eight seconds. As with the StickyKeys options, notifications can be set to beep when a key is pressed and the status can be shown on the screen when FilterKeys is active.

ToggleKeys

ToggleKeys can be used to emit a sound when the Caps Lock, Num Lock, or Scroll Lock key is pressed. Pressing the Num Lock key for five seconds activates ToggleKeys.

SoundSentry

SoundSentry can be used to have the computer flash a visual warning when a sound is emitted. SoundSentry can be configured to flash the active caption bar, the active window, or the desktop. SoundSentry does not have a shortcut to activate it.

ShowSounds

ShowSounds is used with programs that normally convey information via sound. Using ShowSounds, these sounds can be displayed visually through text captions or informative icons.

Display–High Contrast

High Contrast is used to make it easier for the visually impaired to read the computer screen. Instead of using the normal color schemes, Windows XP Professional can be configured to use fonts and colors that are easier to read. High Contrast has three settings that can be set—white on black, black on white, or a customized color scheme. The keyboard shortcut to activate High Contrast is to press the left Alt, left Shift, and Print Screen keys all at the same time.

Display–Cursor Options

The cursor blink rate and the cursor width can be changed through the Cursor Options on the Display tab in the Accessibility Options dialog box.

MouseKeys

When MouseKeys is activated, users can use the numeric keyboard to move the mouse across the screen. The point speed and acceleration rate can also be changed through MouseKeys. Press the left Alt, left Shift, and Num Lock keys at the same time to activate MouseKeys.

SerialKeys Devices

For users who are unable to use standard devices, such as the keyboard and mouse, SerialKeys can be used to support alternative input devices on the computer's serial port. Serial devices can be configured on any available serial ports on the computer.

Magnifier

The Magnifier accessibility tool is provided to give visually impaired users a way to make the screen more readable. The Magnifier can be used to change the magnification level of the screen, and to change the size, position, and color scheme of the magnification window. Tracking options are available to let the magnifier follow the mouse pointer as it moves across the screen or follow text as it is being edited.

On-Screen Keyboard

The On-Screen Keyboard provides a virtual keyboard that the mobility impaired can use to input data with a pointing device or joystick. The On-Screen Keyboard has three typing modes:

➤ *Clicking mode*—The user clicks the on-screen keys to type text.

➤ *Hovering mode*—The user can type a key by using a mouse or joystick to point to the key.

➤ *Scanning mode*—The On-Screen Keyboard scans the keyboard and highlights areas when the user types keyboard characters by pressing a hot key.

Narrator

Narrator is designed for visually impaired computer users. It is a text-to-speech utility that reads the contents of active windows. Narrator was designed to work specifically with WordPad, Notepad, all Control Panel programs, and Internet Explorer. Narrator can be customized to have new windows and menus read when they are displayed. Characters can be read aloud as they are typed. The mouse pointer can be configured to follow active items on the screen. The user can also adjust the volume, pitch, and speed of the text-to-speech translation.

Utility Manager

The Utility Manager can be used to stop or start accessibility programs. The Narrator, Magnifier, and On-Screen Keyboard are all available from the Utility Manager. By using the Utility Manager, users can configure these tools to start automatically when they log onto their computer.

User Profiles

When a user first logs onto a Windows XP Professional computer, a profile is created for the user. This profile contains all of the user's settings for the computer, including his desktop configuration, regional settings, network and printer connections, and Start menu settings. Each user that logs onto the computer is given her own profile. This profile is stored in the Documents and Settings*username* folder.

Windows XP Professional utilizes several types of profiles:

➤ *Default user profile*—Used by all users on the computer. This is the default profile that is used to make a user's profile when they log onto the computer the first time.

➤ *Local user profile*—Created from a copy of the default user profile and is stored on the local computer. Any changes a user makes to the desktop environment are saved to this profile.

➤ *Roaming user profile*—Created by an administrator. This profile is stored on a server and is available to the user from whatever computer he logs onto. Roaming profiles allow users to maintain their personalized user settings. A user can log onto multiple computers and still have his same desktop settings. Any changes made to the user's roaming profile will be saved when the user logs off.

➤ *Mandatory user profile*—Can be used by an administrator to ensure that users always have the same desktop settings no matter what computer they log on from. Users can make changes to the desktop settings, but they are not saved when the user logs off. Mandatory user profiles are created by changing the user profile name from Ntuser.dat to Ntuser.man.

Group Policy

If your Windows XP Professional computer is part of a domain, Group Policy can be used to define the desktop environment. Group Policy requires Active Directory for implementation. Group Policy can be used to configure user desktop settings, environment variables, and system settings. It also can be used to restrict user access to files and folders. When Group Policy settings are applied with local user profile settings, the Group Policy setting will override the local user profile settings.

Remote Assistance

5

Remote Assistance is a new tool introduced in Windows XP Professional that can be used to remotely provide help to users who need assistance with their Windows XP Professional computer.

With Remote Assistance, a support person can chat with a user who needs help, look at the user's desktop, take control of the desktop, and send and receive files from the user.

In previous versions of Windows, SMS (System Management Server) was used to provide administrators with the ability to connect to and take control of a user's workstation. SMS is an extra package purchased separately from the Windows operating system. It also required an SMS infrastructure before it could be used.

Remote Assistance provides a way for users who are having problems working with Windows XP Professional to get the help they need from more experienced users or IT professionals. To use Remote Assistance, the user who needs help must initiate a remote access session. A session is initiated in three stages:

1. The user who needs help sends an invitation.

2. An individual who has been designated as a helper responds to the request.

3. The user who needs help responds by accepting the helper's assistance.

Users can request help through instant messaging, email, or an invitation saved in a shared folder.

When a remote session is established, each individual sees the Remote Assistance console (see Figure 5.7). The console has two panes. The smaller of the two panes contains the helper's chat area. This is where messages are sent and received between the user and the helper. The second pane contains the user's screen area. This pane is used by the helper to view the user's screen.

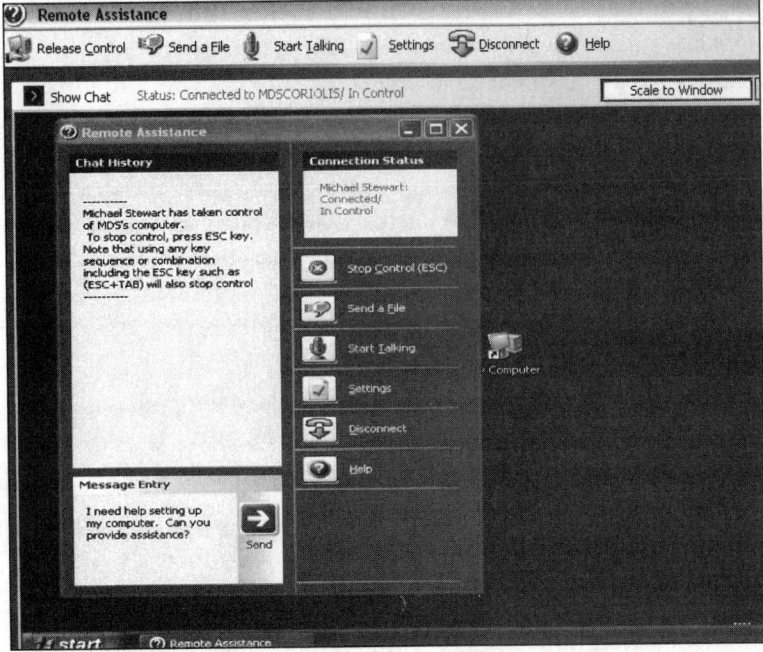

Figure 5.7 Remote Assistance console.

The Remote Assistance console contains several controls:

➤ *Disconnect*—Disconnects the session

➤ *Send A File*—Sends a file from the user's computer to the helper's computer

➤ *Settings*—Enables the user and helper to adjust the sound quality and resize the console

➤ *Start Talking*—Provides voice communications (if the computers support voice capabilities)

➤ *Take Control/Release Control*—Sends a request from the helper to the user to share control of their computer or to release control of the user's computer

When a helper is connected to a user's computer, the helper and user are sharing control of the mouse and keyboard. Only one person should try to control the computer at a time. Some users might be concerned about relinquishing control of their computer to someone else. A user who has requested help can terminate the Remote Assistance session at any time by pressing the Esc key or clicking the Disconnect control. Helpers are not allowed to copy files to a user's hard drive. The user requesting help can only send files to the helper; he cannot receive files. The helper does not have the ability to take sole control of the user's computer. Control during the Remote Assistance session is always shared between the user and the helper.

For additional security, a user who is sending an invitation to request help can require that a password be provided before the helper can connect to the session.

Fast Switching for Multiple Users

Fast Switching is a new feature in Windows XP Professional that allows for the sharing of one computer by multiple users. With Fast Switching, a new user can log onto a computer that is currently being used by another user and not affect the applications the current user is running. The current user does not have to log off and can leave open whatever applications or documents they were working on (see Figure 5.8).

Fast Switching utilizes Windows Terminal Services to provide each user with their own session. Each session is run as a separate unique Terminal Services session. Each session requires a minimum of 2MB of RAM. This does not take into account any programs that are running during a session.

Note: Fast Switching does not work in a domain environment.

Chapter Summary

This chapter looks at how a user can customize her desktop in Windows XP Professional. When Windows XP is initially installed, the only icon that is loaded on the desktop is the Recycle Bin. Microsoft eliminated icon clutter on the desktop in response to customer requests for a cleaner desktop work environment. Microsoft has left the customization up to the user.

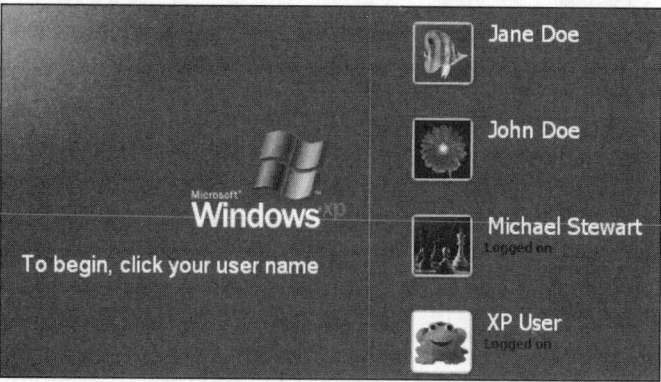

Figure 5.8   Using Fast Switching to log onto a Windows XP Professional computer.

As with all versions of Windows, users can modify the display properties, including the background, all dialog boxes, and icons. They can select from new themes that have been included in Windows XP Professional. The Start menu has a new look. It now consists of two panes. The white pane is the user-based side of the Start menu, and the light-blue side is the OS-based section. Users can customize the white pane by adding items, such as the Control Panel, My Documents, My Computer, and Network Connections. The OS-based side can be modified only slightly.

The taskbar has been enhanced to allow for more functionality than in previous versions of Windows. It has a Quick Launch menu that provides quicker access to frequently used applications. Toolbars can be added to give users instant access to their desktop or Web sites.

As computer systems run over time, they can suffer from degradation in performance. OS variables can be set to ensure that a computer is always running at its peak performance. Environment variables can be set to allow specific variables to be configured on a per-user basis.

Variables can be set through the Startup And Recovery options to determine how a system reacts if it encounters an unexpected shutdown. An event can be written to the system log for further analysis, an administrative alert can be sent via email, or the system can reboot itself automatically. The system can also be configured to write debugging information to three types of dump files for later analysis and problem solving.

The Control Panel has been enhanced with a new look for Windows XP Professional. Users can now use the new Category View that groups similar items together. Most of the tools have the same functionality as they did in Windows 2000. A new tool—User Accounts—has been added to allow for the creation of user accounts. It also is used to control how users log onto the computer—through the Welcome screen or through Fast Switching.

As with all versions of Windows, Windows XP includes accessibility options to assist computer users who have special computing needs. Tools are provided for users with cognitive, mobility, visual, and hearing impairments.

Any time a new user logs onto a Windows XP Professional computer, a user profile is created for the user. The profile contains settings for the user, such as their desktop environment, network connections, and printer connections. Four types of profiles are available—default user profile, local user profile, roaming user profile, and mandatory user profile.

Users who need help for their computer can get it remotely in Windows XP Professional through Remote Assistance. A user can send an invitation to an individual who has been designated as a helper and request help. The helper will establish a remote session to the user's computer. After the remote session is established, the helper can use the user's computer just as if he were setting at the console.

Review Questions

1. John is the system administrator for his company, which has upgraded all of its Windows 2000 Professional computers to Windows XP Professional. When it rolled out the upgrade, it configured the computers so that all users will have the same desktop configuration. What user profile should John use to ensure that users are not able to change the desktop environment?

   a. Roaming

   b. Local user

   c. Mandatory

   d. Default user profile

2. Julie wants to be able to quickly access Web sites she uses every day. How can Julie set up her Windows XP Professional computer so that the Web sites she uses frequently are easily accessible?

   a. She can add a Web site shortcut to her desktop for the sites she frequently visits.

   b. She can add a Program shortcut to her desktop to load Internet Explorer, and then she can search for the Web sites.

   c. She can't. She will have to open Internet Explorer or another browser and manually search for the Web sites.

   d. She can change her display so that it always shows the Web sites she wants to visit.

3. Mary is the system administrator for several companies. She supports a senior citizens recreation center that has just installed Windows XP Professional on its computers. Several of the users are complaining that they are having problems with the keyboards, which don't seem to be entering input when they type. What accessibility option can Mary implement on the computers to help the senior citizens with their typing problem?

   a. SoundSentry

   b. ToggleKeys

   c. MouseKeys

   d. FilterKeys

4. The Utility Manager can be used to provide access to which accessibility options? [check all correct answers]

   a. SerialKeys

   b. Magnifier

   c. On-Screen Keyboard

   d. StickyKeys

5. William has several programs that he uses all the time and wants them to appear on his Start menu when he logs onto his Windows XP Professional workstation. How can William set up his computer to ensure that the programs he uses frequently are always available on the Start menu?

a. He can add the programs as a shortcut to the desktop.

b. He can pin the programs to the Start menu.

c. He can add a submenu to the Start menu and place the programs in the submenu.

d. He doesn't have to do anything. When he uses the programs, they will automatically appear on the Start menu.

6. Samantha needs quick access to several company Web sites periodically during the day. Sherman, the system administrator for the company, has informed Samantha that she can configure the taskbar on her Windows XP Professional computer for quick access to the Web sites. What toolbar would Samantha add to the taskbar to give her access to the company Web sites?

a. Address

b. Links

c. Desktop

d. Language Band

7. Ronce is installing a new application on all the Windows XP Professional computers in the office. The application was custom-designed for each individual who uses it. Ronce is going to set some variables for each computer that are specific to each user. Where can Ronce set the user-specific variables for use with the new application?

a. In the Environment Variables dialog box in the System tool in the Control Panel.

b. In the Autoexec.bat file for each user.

c. In the Systems Variables dialog box in the System tool in the Control Panel.

d. He can alter each individual's user profile.

8. Billy's company recently upgraded several of its computers from Windows 98 to Windows XP Professional. Periodically, a few of the computers have been crashing. Billy wants to be able to monitor each box when this happens. What system failure settings can Billy implement on the boxes that are crashing to aid in troubleshooting the problem? [check all correct answers]

   a. He can have the system write an event or system stop error to the system log.

   b. He can configure the system to send him an administrative alert when it stops.

   c. He can configure the system to automatically reboot after the crash.

   d. He can configure the system to write debugging information to a memory dump file.

9. Bonnie was inputting some data into a spreadsheet on her computer when it crashed. After she rebooted it, she checked the system log and noticed that the system wrote a memory dump file after the crash. What tools can Bonnie use to analyze the information in this file and try to understand why her system crashed? [check all correct answers]

   a. DiskPart.exe

   b. Dumpchk.exe

   c. Dumpexam.exe

   d. Chkdsk.exe

10. Alicia is the system administrator for her company, and the company has just upgraded all of its Windows 98 and Windows 2000 Professional workstations to Windows XP Professional. Alicia has several users who are always requesting help using their computers. What tool introduced in Windows XP Professional will enable Alicia to remotely help users who are having problems with their computers?

   a. Remote Desktop

   b. Remote Assistance

   c. Group Policy

   d. SMS

11. Sally has used an existing theme on her Windows XP Professional computer to create a new one. The next day when Sally uses her computer, she notices that the theme she created is not there. What happened to the theme Sally created?

    a. Sally did not give the theme a unique name when she created it, and it was not saved.

    b. Sally is not able to modify any of the existing themes in Windows XP Professional.

    c. Sally did not save the new theme in the Document and Settings folder on her computer.

    d. Group Policy is implemented on the network, preventing her from creating themes.

12. Rhonda is part of a small office that recently upgraded its workstations to Windows XP Professional. All of the computer users need access to the Internet, but only one computer currently has Internet access. How can Rhonda and the other computer users gain access to the Internet?

    a. They can implement Internet Connection Sharing on the network.

    b. They can implement Internet Connection Firewall on the network.

    c. They can connect modems to the computers that need Internet access.

    d. The only individual who will have access to the Internet is the one using the computer that is currently connected to the Internet.

13. Winston is sharing a computer with three other users. What new feature in Windows XP Professional will allow multiple users to share the same computer?

    a. Remote Assistance

    b. Fast Switching.

    c. Remote Desktop

    d. Terminal Services

Real-World Projects

For all of the following projects, you need a computer running Windows XP Professional. For the Remote Assistance project, it would be beneficial to have access to a second Windows XP Professional computer on a home or small business network. These projects are designed to help you become proficient in configuring the desktop environment in Windows XP Professional.

Project 5.1

To select a theme for your desktop environment:

1. Right-click an empty area on the desktop.

2. Select Properties.

3. Click the Themes tab of the Display Properties.

4. Click the down arrow under Themes.

5. Select the theme you want for the desktop.

6. Click OK.

Project 5.2

To add a Web site as a shortcut on your desktop:

1. Open Internet Explorer.

2. Go to the Web site that you want to add to the desktop as a shortcut.

3. Right-click anywhere on the Web site page.

4. Select Create Shortcut.

5. Click OK.

Project 5.3

To add a new keyboard layout:

1. Click Start | Control Panel.

2. Double-click Regional And Language Options.

3. Select the Languages tab.

4. Click the Details button.

5. In the Text Services And Input Languages dialog box, select the language for the keyboard layout under Settings.

6. Click the Add button.

7. In the Add Input Language dialog box, click the down arrow under Keyboard Layout/IME.

8. Select the keyboard layout from the drop-down list.

9. Click OK.

10. Click OK to close the Text Services And Input Languages dialog box.

11. Click OK to close the Regional Language Options dialog box.

Project 5.4

To change from the Windows XP Professional Start menu to the Windows classic Start menu:

1. Right-click the Start button, and select the Start Menu tab.

2. Click the Classic Start Menu button.

3. Click OK.

Project 5.5

To pin the calculator to the Start menu:

1. Select Start | Search.

2. Under What Do You Want To Search For?, click All Files And Folders.

3. Under All Or Part Of The File Name, enter "calc" and click Search.

4. On the right Search pane under Name, right-click Calc.exe.

5. Select Pin To Start Menu.

6. Close the Search Results dialog box.

Project 5.6

To add toolbars to the taskbar:

1. Right-click an empty area on the taskbar.

2. Place your mouse over Toolbars.

3. Select the toolbars to add to the taskbar.

Project 5.7

To change the location of the My Documents folder:

1. Click the Start menu.

2. Right-click My Documents.

3. Select Properties.

4. Under Target Folder Location on the Target tab of the My Documents Properties dialog box, click the Move button.

5. Select the new location for the My Documents folder.

6. Click OK.

7. Click OK to close the My Documents Properties dialog box.

Project 5.8

To configure your computer to write debugging information to a kernel memory dump file:

1. Click the Start menu.

2. Select Control Panel.

3. Double-click the System icon.

4. Select the Advanced tab.

5. Under Startup And Recovery, click the Settings button.

6. Click the down arrow under Write Debugging Information.

7. Select Kernel Memory Dump.

8. Click OK.

9. Click OK to close the System Properties dialog box.

5

CHAPTER SIX

Files and Folders in Windows XP Professional

After completing this chapter, you will be able to:

✓ Explain the purpose of the My Documents, My Pictures, and My Music folders

✓ Customize folder views

✓ Apply NTFS file and folder permissions to files and folders

✓ Describe shared folders

✓ Share a folder

✓ Use Offline Files and Folders

✓ Explain the purpose of the Offline Files Database

✓ Explain what compression is and how it is used in Windows XP Professional

Windows XP Professional makes managing your files and folders easier with enhancements that build on the support that was introduced in Windows 2000. New ways are provided for viewing, arranging, and managing files and folders. They can be shared on local computers, on networks, and on the Web, and their access can be controlled through user and group permissions. In this chapter, we look at some of the features that are implemented in Windows XP Professional for file management.

Files and Folders Overview

The majority of tasks in Windows XP Professional require working with files and folders. Folders are used as storage devices for files. Windows XP Professional provides users with several predefined folders that have specific functions, such as the My Documents folder and the My Pictures folder. Users can create, manage, and delete their own files and folders.

My Computer

My Computer provides access to a computer's hard drives, any removable storage devices, and mapped network drives (see Figure 6.1). From the System Tasks pane, users can access the Systems Properties dialog box and view system information. They can click Add Or Remove Programs to add and remove programs and Windows components. They can also access the Control Panel by clicking Change A Setting.

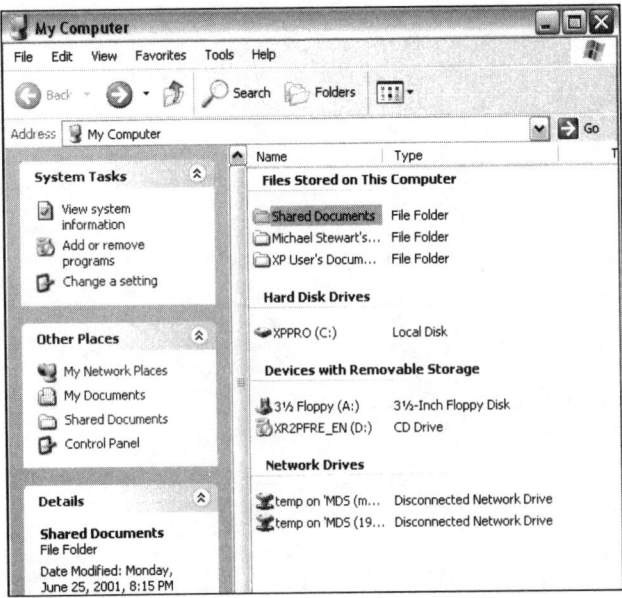

Figure 6.1 My Computer.

The Address bar allows users to quickly access desktop shortcuts, such as My Documents, the Shared Documents folder, the Control Panel, and My Network Places.

The Explorer Bar can be used to open a pane on the left side that allows users to view their folders in a hierarchical manner. It can be used to open the Search Companion to search for files, folders, pictures, music, videos, computers, and people. The History pane can be used to show files and folders that have been used for any period from the current day up to three weeks ago. The Explorer Bar is accessed from the View menu.

My Documents Folder

The My Documents folder is the default storage location for users' files. The content of the My Documents folder is stored on a per-user basis. If multiple individuals share a computer, they each will have their own My Documents folder. The My Documents folder is a system folder. It can't be deleted, but it can be renamed or redirected. The My Documents folder has two subfolders—the My Pictures folder and the My Music folder.

The My Documents folder is accessed from the Start menu. You will notice that it looks different from the My Documents folder in previous versions of Windows (see Figure 6.2).

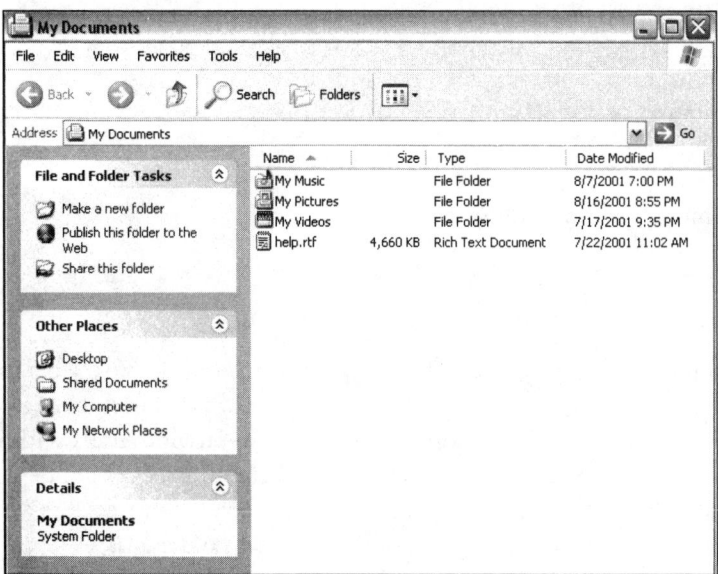

Figure 6.2   The My Documents folder.

The first aspect you will notice about the My Documents folder is that it consists of two panes. The right pane contains the actual content of the folder and the My Pictures and My Music folders.

The left pane consists of three sections. The first section is called File and Folder Tasks. In this section, you can rename, move, copy, and delete folders. You can publish a folder to the Web or share the folder for others to use. You can also email the folder's content to another user. The second section—called Other Places—provides quick access to the desktop, the Shared Documents folder, My Computer, and My Network Places. The last section—Details—provides information about the file or folder that is highlighted in the right pane.

The My Documents, My Pictures, and My Music folders are all personal folders. These folders can be shared so that anyone can access them. They can also be made private so that only the user of the folder has access to it.

My Pictures Folder

The My Pictures folder is a subfolder of the My Documents folder. The My Pictures folder was introduced in Windows 2000 and is the default storage area for graphics and digital images. When you save images from your digital camera or scanner, they are automatically stored in the My Pictures folder. With the My Pictures folder, users can do the following:

➤ Share pictures with other users

➤ Send photos via email

➤ Publish pictures on the Web

➤ Print pictures

➤ Order prints of pictures online

➤ View pictures in a slideshow

➤ Use a picture as the desktop background

The My Pictures folder, like the My Documents folder, consists of two panes (see Figure 6.3). The right pane contains the actual content of the folder. The left pane contains four sections. The first section—Picture Tasks—provides users with instant access to tasks related to their images. They can view their images as a slideshow, order prints of their images online, print their images, or save an image as a desktop background. The second section consists of the File and Folder Tasks, where users can rename, move, copy, and delete image files. They can also publish their images on the Web. The third section—Other Places—provides instant access to the My Documents folder, the Shared Pictures folder, My Computer, and My Network Places. The fourth section—Details—provides detailed information about the image file that is highlighted.

Figure 6.3   The My Pictures folder.

My Music Folder

New to Windows XP Professional is the My Music folder, which is the primary storage location for a user's music files, such as downloaded MP3 files. The My Music folder works in conjunction with Windows Media Player, which is used to play video, audio, and mixed-media files. It can be used to copy files from a CD or download music from the Internet. These files are stored by default in the My Music folder.

The My Music folder consists of two panes (see Figure 6.4). The right pane contains the actual music files. The left pane consists of four sections. The first section is called Music Tasks, and users can use it to play their audio files or shop online for music. The other three sections are the same as in the My Documents and My Pictures folders—File and Folder Tasks, Other Places, and Details.

For every CD track you copy to your computer, Windows XP Professional automatically creates a folder in the My Music folder for the artist. A subfolder is created for each artist that is downloaded or copied to the computer.

As with the My Pictures folder, users can share their files from the My Music folder.

Figure 6.4 The My Music folder.

Shared Documents Folder

Windows XP Professional automatically creates a Shared Documents folder, which is used to share files with other users. The Shared Documents folder contains a Shared My Pictures folder and a Shared My Music folder.

My Network Places

My Network Places provides a user with access to resources on the network and other networks that the computer is connected to. It also provides a list of all shared computers, files, and printers.

The History Folder

The History folder tracks the history of documents that the user has opened and Web sites that the user has recently visited. The History folder can be accessed by selecting it from the toolbars in Windows Explorer. The History folder can be viewed by Date, Site, Most Visited, or Order Visited Today.

Windows Explorer

Windows Explorer is the primary tool for managing files and folders. By default, when you open Windows Explorer, it opens to your Start menu. Windows Explorer can be used to customize folders and to set folder options. Windows

Explorer is accessed by selecting Start|All Programs|Accessories|Windows Explorer. As an alternative, users can right-click the Start menu and select Explore.

Note: Files with the system and hidden attributes do not appear by default in Windows Explorer. These files are not accessible so users do not inadvertently erase or modify them.

Files and Folder Views

Windows XP Professional provides users with several ways to view and arrange their files and folders. Users can change the way files are viewed by selecting the View menu option. The following views are available:

➤ *Thumbnails*—Displays the images the files or folders contain so that the contents of the file or folder can be easily identified. The name of the file or folder is displayed under the thumbnail.

➤ *Tiles*—Displays files and folders as icons that are larger than those normally displayed in Icons view. For folders, the name of each folder is displayed to the right of its icon. For files, the sort information that the user selected is displayed under the file or folder name.

➤ *Filmstrip*—Available only in folders that have pictures or images. All images appear as a single row of thumbnail images. Left and right arrow buttons are available that enable a user to scroll through the images one at a time. Double-clicking an image opens it in the Windows Picture and Fax Viewer (see Figure 6.5). By using the Windows Picture and Fax Viewer, a user can zoom an image in and out, rotate the image, and delete, print, or copy the image.

Figure 6.5 Windows Picture and Fax Viewer.

➤ *Icons*—Displays both files and folders as icons. No other information about the file or folder is displayed.

➤ *List*—Displays all files and folders as a list of small icons. This view is good to use if you have many files and folders and you want to scan them for specific file or folder names. Files and folders in List view cannot be displayed in groups.

➤ *Details*—Provides detailed information about files and folders. Users can determine the type and amount of information that is displayed in Details view by selecting View|Choose Details, which opens the Choose Details dialog box, from which users can select from various display options (see Figure 6.6).

➤ *Show In Groups*—Displays files and folders in groups. Windows XP Professional will group the files and folders according to the selected sort option. If a user has sorted the icons by name and selects Show In Groups, the files and folders will be displayed in alphabetical groups, as shown in Figure 6.7.

Customizing Folders

All folders in Windows XP Professional can be customized for a user's particular needs. Folders are customized through Tools|Folder Options or through Customize This Folder.

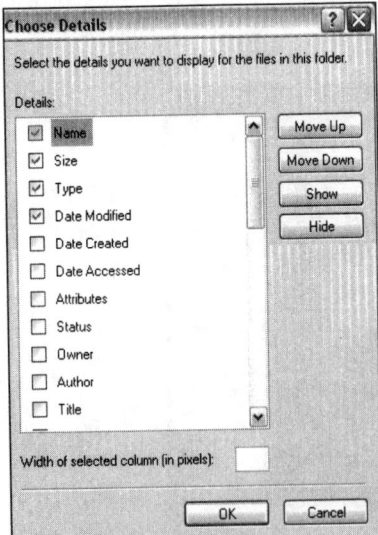

Figure 6.6 The Choose Details dialog box for Details view.

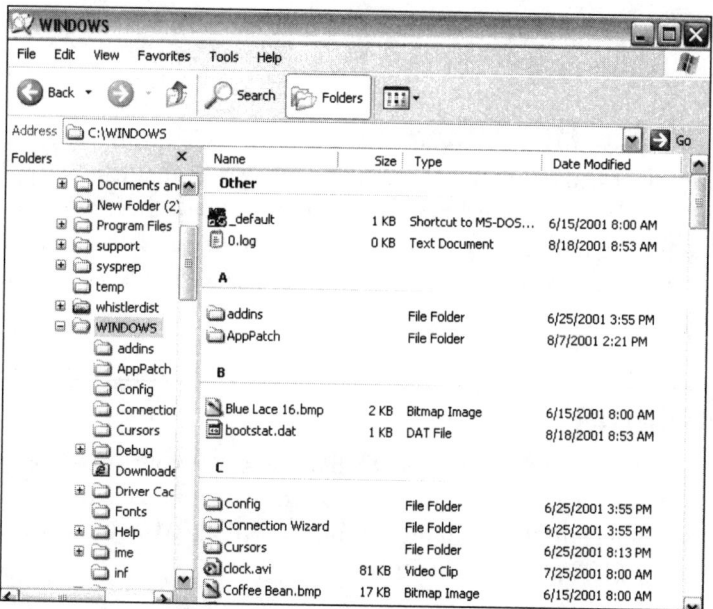

Figure 6.7   Files shown in groups and sorted by name.

Configuring Folder Options

Folder views and preferences are configured by selecting Tools|Folder Options. This selection has four tabs—General, View, File Types, and Offline Files.

The General tab has three sections. The first section—Tasks—is used to configure hyperlinks to common folder tasks or to select to display the folders in the Windows classic view. In the Windows classic view, the folders do not look or work like Web pages. They appear as classic Windows folders. The second section—Browse Folders—allows a user to open each folder in the same window or in separate folders. Click Items As Follows is the last section under the General tab. Using this option, users can configure items to be opened with a single click or a double-click.

The View tab has two sections. The first section—Folder Views—is used to apply the current folder view to all folders on the computer. The Advance Settings section has numerous options that can be set to determine how folders are displayed.

The File Types tab lists the registered file types for Windows XP Professional. This includes the file name extension and the association between the file name extension and the file type. New file types can be registered by clicking the New button and entering the file extension. Newly entered file extensions can be associated with specific file types by selecting the file type in the Associated File Type drop-down box.

The Offline Files tab is used to configure computers so that users can continue to work on their network files even when they are not connected to the network.

Offline Files is not available if Fast Switching is being used on the computer. The Offline Files and Folders feature is discussed later in this chapter.

Using Customize This Folder

Customize This Folder can be used to select folder templates that can be applied to folders. Windows XP Professional has seven templates that can be applied to a folder and any subfolders in it. Under Folder Pictures, users can select a picture to identify a folder when it is being displayed in Thumbnails view. Users can also change the default "folder" icon through this wizard.

NTFS Permissions

One of the major benefits of using the NTFS file system on your Windows XP Professional computer is having the ability to control which users and groups have access to files and folders on the computer. Windows XP, like Windows NT and Windows 2000, uses file and folder permissions.

File Permissions

File permissions are used to control access to files on a computer system. By setting up file permissions, an administrator can control the level of access that users and groups have to files on the computer. Auditing can be set up to detect and record user and group access. The five types of NTFS file permissions are Full Control, Modify, Read and Execute, Read, and Write. Table 6.1 lists the NTFS file permissions and the access that is allowed with each.

Folder Permissions

Folder permissions are used to control access to folders on a computer system and the files and subfolders contained within the folders. The six types of NTFS folder permissions are Full Control, Modify, Read and Execute, List Folder Contents, Read, and Write. Files and subfolders by default inherit the permissions of their parent folder. Table 6.2 lists the NTFS folder permissions.

Table 6.1   NTFS file permissions.

NTFS File Permission	Type of Access Given to User or Group
Full Control	Change permissions, take ownership, and perform all actions permitted by the other NTFS file permissions
Modify	Modify and delete files; all actions permitted by the Write and the Read and Execute permissions
Read	Read a file and view file attributes
Read and Execute	Run applications; perform all actions permitted by the Read permission
Write	Overwrite a file, change the file attributes, and view file ownership

Table 6.2   NTFS folder permissions.

NFTS Folder Permissions	Type of Access Given to User or Group
Full Control	Change permissions, take ownership, delete subfolders and files, and perform all actions allowed by the other NTFS folder permissions
List Folder Contents	View the names of files and subfolders
Modify	Delete the folder and perform all actions allowed by the Write and the Read and Execute permissions
Read	See files and subfolders, and view folder ownership, permissions, and attributes
Read and Execute	Move folders and perform all actions allowed by the Read and the List Folder Contents permissions
Write	Create new file and subfolders, change folder attributes, and view folder ownership and permissions

Special File and Folder Permissions

Special file and folder permissions can be used in Windows XP Professional when administrators find that the regular file and folder permissions do not provide the access control they want for their users or groups. Special permissions for files and folders are set in the Permission Entry For dialog box for the file or folder. This dialog box is accessed by clicking the Advanced button on the file or folder's Properties dialog box and then clicking the View/Edit button. Table 6.3 lists the special permissions that can be associated with NTFS file and folder permissions.

Table 6.4 lists each standard file and folder permission and its associated special permission.

Table 6.3   Special NTFS file and folder permissions.

Special Permission	Purpose
Change Permissions	Allows or denies permission to change files and folders
Create Files/Write Data	Create Files allows or denies permission to create files within folders (applies to folders only); Write Data allows or denies permission to make changes to files and overwrite existing content (applies to files only)
Create Folders/Append Data	Create Folders allows or denies permission to create folders within folders (applies to folders only); Append Data allows or denies permission to make changes to the end of files (applies to files only)
Delete	Allows or denies permission to delete files or folders
Delete Subfolders and Files	Allows or denies permission to delete subfolders or files
List Folder/Read Data	List Folder allows or denies permission to view file names and subfolder names; Read Data allows or denies permission to view data in files (applies to files only)
Read Attributes	Allows or denies permission to view the attributes of files or folders
Read Extended Attributes	Allows or denies permission to view extended attributes of files or folders
Read Permissions	Allows or denies permission to read files or folders
Take Ownership	Allows or denies permission to take ownership of files or folders
Traverse Folder/Execute File	Allows or denies permission to move through folders; takes effect only when the user or group is not granted the Bypass Traverse Checking right
Write Attributes	Allows or denies permission to change attributes of files and folders
Write Extended Attributes	Allows or denies permission to change the extended attributes of files or folders

6

Table 6.4   Special permissions associated with file and folder permissions.

Special Permission	Full Control	Modify	Read and Execute	List Folder Contents	Read	Write
Change Permissions	X					
Create Files/Write Data	X	X				X
Create Folders/Append Data	X	X				X
Delete	X	X				
Delete Subfolders and Files	X					
List Folder/Read Data	X	X	X	X	X	
Traverse Folder/Execute File		X	X	X	X	
Read Attributes	X	X	X	X	X	
Read Extended Attributes	X	X	X	X	X	
Read Permissions	X	X	X	X	X	X
Take Ownership	X					
Write Attributes	X	X				X
Write Extended Attributes	X	X				X

Inherited Permissions

Window XP includes two types of permissions—explicit and inherited. Explicit permissions are set when an object, such as a file or folder, is created. Inherited permissions are propagated to an object from a parent object, such as a subfolder receiving permissions from its parent folder. Files and subfolders by default inherit permissions from their parent folders.

If you do not want files or subfolders to inherit the permissions of a parent folder, select the Security tab in the Property dialog box for the file and folder and uncheck the Allow Inheritable Permissions From Parent To Propagate To This Object checkbox.

The following are some key pointers to consider when setting up NTFS permissions for users and groups on a network:

➤ Give users only the access they need. If users need the Read and Execute permission, it would be overkill to give them Full Control.

➤ Create a group and give the group permission to the resource. Add those users who need access to the resource to the group. Give individuals permissions to resources only when absolutely necessary.

➤ When assigning permissions to data or application folders, assign the Read and Execute permission to the Users groups. This will prevent data and applications from being deleted.

➤ Deny permissions to a specific user or group only when absolutely necessary. The Deny permission overrides all other permissions.

➤ Educate users on how to assign permissions to the file and folders they create.

Access Control Lists

An access control list (ACL) is a list of access control entries that define what actions are allowed, denied, or audited for users or groups. Two ACLs are contained in an object's security descriptor—a discretionary ACL (DACL) and a system ACL (SACL).

Every file and folder on an NTFS volume has an ACL that lists every user and group that has been granted access to the file or folder. The ACL also contains the type of access these users or groups have been granted. When users or groups attempt to access a file or folder, the ACL for the file or folder must have an access control entry (ACE) for the user account. If no ACE exists in an ACL, the user account will not have access to the resource.

Access Control Entries

Access control entries are entries in the ACL that contain the SID for a user or group. They also contain an access mask that is used to determine which actions are allowed, denied, or audited for the user or group.

Security Identifiers

Security identifiers (SIDs) are created when an account or group is created on a computer. The SID for a local account is created by the Local Security Authority (LSA) and stored in the Registry. Every SID is unique for the account or group it was created for. No two accounts or groups can share the same SID. SIDs for domain accounts are generated by the Domain Security Authority and stored in Active Directory.

SIDs are used with the following access control components: access tokens, security descriptors, and ACEs. Table 6.5 lists some of the well-known SIDs.

Table 6.5   Well-know SIDs.

SID	Description
Anonymous Logon (S-1-5-7)	Any user who has connected to the computer without supplying a username or password
Authenticated Users (S-1-5-11)	Users who have been authenticated
Creator Owner (S-1-3-1)	The generic user Creator Owner
Everyone (S-1-1-0)	The generic group Everyone
Interactive (S-1-5-4)	Anyone who logs on locally or through a Remote Desktop connection
Network (S-1-5-2)	Users who log on through a network connection
Terminal Users (S-1-5-13)	Users who log onto a Terminal Services server

Access Tokens

Access tokens contain information about the identity and access privileges associated with an account. An access token contains the SID for the user account, SIDs for the security groups that include the user, a list of privileges held on the local computer by the user, and the user's primary security group.

Security Descriptors

Security descriptors contain information about an object's access control. When a user attempts to open a file, the computer system will check the security descriptor of the file to see whether the user is allowed to open it. Usually, security descriptors contain information regarding the object owner, which users and groups have Allow and Deny access to the object, which users and groups should have their access audited, and inheritance information about the object. The security descriptor consists of the owner of the object, the owner's primary group, the DACL, and the SACL.

Discretionary Access Control List

The DACL is the part of the security descriptor that contains ACEs that grant or deny user or group access to an object. The owner of an object is the only one who can change the granted or denied permissions in a DACL. Owners can share control of objects to other users by granting Change Permissions to objects.

System Access Control List

The SACL is the part of the security descriptor that determines what events are audited for users or groups. Like the DACL, the SACL contains ACEs. It is different from the DACL in that, instead of controlling access to an object, it is used to audit objects. The ACEs in the SACL are used to determine whether an event is written to the system log on the success or failure of an event.

How Access Control Works

When a user initially logs onto a computer, the user's SID is encapsulated into an access token. When the user attempts to open a file or folder, her access token is presented and an access check is done between the access token and the object's security descriptor. The access token contains the user's SID that identifies the groups the user is a member of. The security descriptor contains a DACL with the ACE that specifies the access rights that are allowed or denied to users or groups.

The security subsystem checks the object DACL looking for an ACE that applies to the user trying to access the file. If it finds an Allow entry for the user, the user is allowed access to the file. If a Deny entry is found for the user, the user is not allowed access to the file. If no entry is found in the ACE for the user, she is denied access to the file.

File Ownership

Whenever an object, such as a file or folder, is created, the person who created it is automatically the owner of the object. The owner of the object determines how permissions are applied to it and who has access to the object.

Ownership of objects can be transferred in two ways. First, the creator of an object can grant the Take Ownership permission to another user who he wants to have ownership of the file or folder. Second, an administrator can take ownership of an object. Although an administrator can take ownership of an object, he cannot transfer the ownership to another user. Only the creator of an object can grant Take Ownership permission for the object to another user.

To determine the owner of a file, follow these steps:

1. Right-click the file.

2. Select Properties.

3. Select the Security tab.

4. Click the Advanced button.

5. Select the Owner tab. The owner of the file is listed under Current Owner Of This Item.

Auditing

Auditing provides a way for administrators to confirm the identity of users and groups who are attempting to access computer resources. To set up auditing, an administrator must first determine what objects she wants to audit. Next, she must decide what users and groups to audit, and the types of actions to audit. Once auditing is configured, administrators can track the activity through the Security Log in the Event Viewer.

Before file or folder access can be audited, Audit Object Access must be enabled in Group Policy or the Local Security Policy. Once this is enabled, an administrator can select the file or folder they want audited and the users or groups whose actions they want to audit. Both failed and successful attempts can be audited.

Shared Folders

Shared folders are used to provide users with access to files and folders over the network. Shared folders can contain applications or programs, data, or a user's personal data. Before users can gain access to shared folders, they must have the appropriate permissions to access the folders.

Shared Folder Permissions

Shared folder permissions are applied to folders only. They cannot be applied to individual files. If you want to restrict access to individual files, you should consider placing the folder on an NTFS partition and using NTFS file permissions to restrict access to the individual files.

If a user has access to the computer console, shared folder permissions do not apply. Shared folder permissions only work when folders are accessed over a network.

If your computer only has a FAT partition, using shared folders is the only way to secure the folders. NTFS permissions cannot be used on FAT partitions.

By default, when a folder is shared, the Everyone group has Full Control permission to the folder. This means that everyone on the network has immediate access to the shared folder. You should always assign permissions to the group or individuals that you want to have access to the folders and remove the Everyone group from the shared folder.

Note: When a folder is shared, the folder's icon appears in Windows Explorer with a hand holding the folder.

Three permissions can be applied to shared folders—Read, Change, and Full Control. Table 6.6 lists the shared folder permissions and the level of access that each allows.

Shared folder permissions can be allowed or denied (see Figure 6.8). You normally would only deny permissions to an individual or group when it is necessary to override a permission they have as part of a group that has been given the Allow permission to the shared folder.

Table 6.6   Shared folder permissions.

Shared Folder Permission	Action Allowed by User or Group
Change	Create folders, add files to folders, change data in files, change file attributes, delete files and folders, and perform all actions permitted by the Read permission
Full Control	Change file permissions, take ownership of files, and perform all tasks permitted by the Change permission
Read	Display folder's name, file names, file data, and attributes; run program files; and change folders within the shared folder

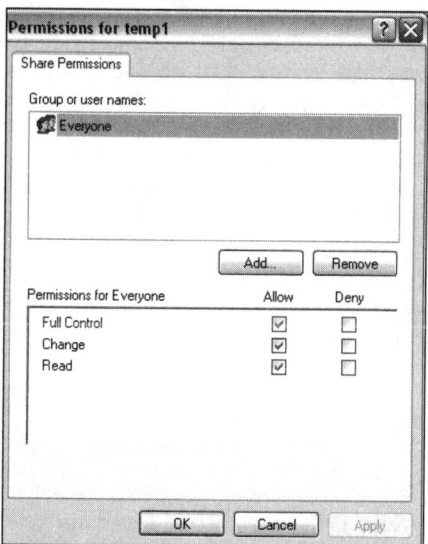

Figure 6.8   Assigning share permissions for a shared folder.

Special Shares

Windows XP Professional, like previous versions of Windows, automatically shares certain folders for administrative purposes. These shares are hidden from anyone who might be browsing the network. The share name is appended with a dollar sign ($) that hides the share. The following administrative folders are shared by default in Windows XP Professional:

➤ *C$, D$, and so forth*—The root of each volume on the hard disk that automatically shared. The share name is the drive letter with the appended dollar sign. Administrators who connect to this share have full access to the entire volume. These shares are used to allow administrators to connect to remote computers and perform administrative tasks

➤ *ADMIN$*—The system root folder that is normally C:\winnt by default. Only members of the Administrators group have Full Control permission to this share

➤ *IPC$*—Used by named pipes and is essential for communication between applications on the computer. Also used during remote administration of computers and for viewing shared resources

➤ *PRINT$*—Used during the remote administration of printers

Creating a Shared Folder

To share a folder, you must have the appropriate permissions on the computer where the folder exists. To share a folder, follow these steps:

1. Open Windows Explorer or My Documents.

2. Right-click the folder that you want to share.

3. Click Properties.

4. Click the Sharing tab (see Figure 6.9).

5. Click Share This Folder.

6. Enter a name for the shared folder in the Share Name text box.

7. Enter any additional comments or descriptions in the Comment text box.

8. Select the number of users that you want to have access to the shared folder in the User Limit box.

9. Click the OK button.

Assigning Permissions to Shared Folders

After you have configured your shared folder, you need to specify which users or groups on the network will have access to the shared folder. Assigning shared folder permissions to the shared folder does this. The Permissions button on the Sharing tab of the shared folder's Properties dialog box is used to set permissions on how

Figure 6.9 The Sharing tab in a folder's Properties dialog box.

users can access the shared folder over the network. The Permissions button opens the Share Permissions dialog box, which allows you to determine which users or groups will have access to the shared folder, and the level of permissions that will be assigned to them (see Figure 6.8 shown earlier in this chapter).

Remember to remove the Everyone group from the Share Permissions. If you don't, anyone with the capability to log onto the network will have access to the shared folder.

Combining Shared Folder Permissions and NTFS Permissions

Because shared folders provide only limited access control, administrators can secure resources further by also using NTFS permissions. Shared folder access is applicable only if a folder is accessed via a network. NTFS permissions are applicable regardless of whether the folder is accessed via a network or locally.

Administrators can use NTFS permissions on files and subfolders within shared folders. A different NTFS permission can be applied to each individual file or folder, depending on the level of access needed. When shared folder permissions are combined with NTFS permissions, the most restrictive permission is the overriding permission.

Managing Shared Folders

The Shared Folders tool is used by administrators to administer and monitor local and remote shared folders. Shared Folders is located under System Tools in Computer Management. By utilizing Shared Folders, administrators can create, view, and set permissions for shared folders; view a list of all users who are connected to a computer over the network; and view a list of files opened by remote users.

Shared Folders consists of three sections (see Figure 6.10):

➤ *Shares*—Shows the name of the shared folder, the actual path to the folder, the type of network connection, the number of user connections to the share and any comments that describe the share.

➤ *Sessions*—Lists the name of any user who is connected to the shared folder, the name of the computer that the user is connecting from, and the type of network connection being used to connect to the share. It also shows how long in hours and minutes the user has been connected to the share, how much idle time has elapsed since the user last initiated an action, and whether the user is connected as a guest.

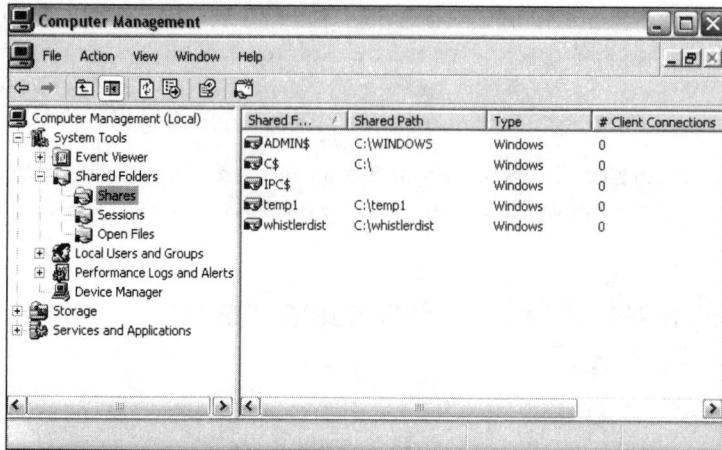

Figure 6.10 Shared Folders, which is used to create, view, and set permissions for shared folders.

➤ *Open Files*—Lists the name of any open files in the shared folder, the name of the user who is accessing the file, the type of network connection being used to access the file, the number of locks on the resource, and the permissions that were granted to the user when the resource was opened.

Managing Shared Folders from a Command Line

For advanced users such as administrators, shared folders can be created, deleted, and managed from a command line in addition to through Windows Explorer and the Shared Folders tool. The following command-line options are available for managing shared folders on a Windows XP Professional computer:

➤ **Net share**—Displays shared resources

➤ **Net share** *sharename*—Displays the network share, the path to the network share, the number of users connected to the share, and the maximum number of connections allowed to connect to the share

➤ **Net share** *sharename* **/USERS:numbers**—Specifies the number of users who can access the shared resource at the same time

➤ **Net share** *sharename* **/UNLIMITED**—Specifies that an unlimited number of users can access the share

➤ **Net share** *sharename* **/REMARKS**—Adds a descriptive comment about the shared resource

➤ **Net share** *sharename* **/DELETE**—Stops the sharing of the shared resource

➤ **Net share** *sharename* **/CACHE:Manual**—Enables manual offline caching

➤ **Net share** *sharename* **/CACHE:Automatic**—Enables automatic offline caching

➤ **Net use** *servername**sharename*—Connects to a shared resource

Offline Files and Folders

The Offline Files and Folders feature was introduced in Windows 2000 to provide users with the ability to work on network files when they are not connected to the network. This feature is extremely useful for both users of portable computers and users who have unstable network connections. Users work with the network files using Offline Files and Folders the same way they would if they were connected to the network. When the users reconnect to the network, the files they have been working on are synchronized or updated to reflect any changes.

Files and folders on any computer on a Microsoft network that supports server message block (SMB) File and Print Sharing can be made available for offline use. This includes files on Windows 95, 98, NT 4, and 2000 computers. You cannot use Offline Files and Folders on Novell networks or any Windows 2000 computers running Terminal Services.

Before you can use Offline Files and Folders, your computer must be configured for its use. To configure a computer to use Offline Files and Folders, follow these steps:

1. Open My Computer or Windows Explorer.

2. Select Tools|Folder Options.

3. Select the Offline Files tab (see Figure 6.11).

4. Check the Enable Offline Files checkbox.

Note: *Offline Files and Folders is not available if Fast Switching is being used on the Windows XP Professional computer.*

The following several options are available for configuring the computer for Offline Files and Folders:

➤ *Synchronize all offline files when logging on*—When a user logs on, the locally cached copy of files are synchronized with the network version of the files.

➤ *Synchronize all offline files before logging off*—When a user disconnects from the network, the locally cached files are synchronized with the network version of the files.

➤ *Display a reminder every* xx *minutes*—Displays a reminder to a user that he is working on an offline file for *xx* minutes.

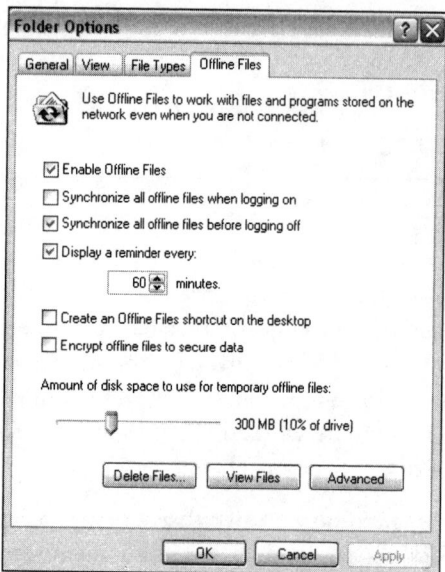

Figure 6.11 Offline Files tab in a folder's Properties dialog box.

➤ *Create an Offline Files shortcut on the desktop*—Allows a user to create a shortcut to the offline file on the desktop

➤ *Encrypt offline files to secure data*—A new feature in Windows XP that prevents intrusion to a user's files by encrypting them

➤ *Amount of disk space to use for temporary offline files*—Enables users to control how much disk space is used by the locally cached files

Files that are marked for offline use are cached (or stored) in a database on the local hard drive. Any changes made to a file when the computer is offline are saved to the local database and synchronized when the computer is reconnected to the network. Three types of caching are available:

➤ *Automatic caching of documents*—All files are made available when working offline. Older versions of files are automatically deleted to make room for the newer versions. The network version of a file is always available.

➤ *Automatic caching of programs and documents*—Recommended for read-only documents or for when users need to continue to run an application off the network even after they have disconnected from the network. As with automatic caching of documents, older versions of files are automatically deleted to make room for newer versions.

➤ *Manual caching of documents*—A user must specify the files that she wants cached for offline use. The network version of a file always is available.

By default, manual caching of documents is enabled when a folder is shared in Windows XP Professional. To select the type of caching for a folder, follow these steps:

1. Right-click the shared folder, and click Properties.

2. Select the Sharing tab.

3. Click the Caching button.

4. Select the type of caching under the Setting drop-down menu.

5. Click OK to close the Cache Settings dialog box, and click OK to close the folder's Properties dialog box.

Certain types of files cannot be cached. These include the following file types:

➤ DB

➤ LDB

➤ MDB

➤ MDE

➤ MDW

➤ PST

➤ SLM

The Offline Files Database

Offline files are stored in a hidden database on the local drive in a directory on the %systemroot% called CSC, which stands for *client-side caching*. This directory contains all the offline files requested by users on the computer. To access this folder in Windows Explorer, you have to go to Folder Options and uncheck the Hide Protected Operating System Files (Recommended) checkbox. You must be an administrator to access the CSC directory.

The amount of disk space reserved for offline files is 10 percent of the hard disk space. This can be changed through the Offline Files tab under Folder Options in Windows Explorer or My Computer.

In Windows 2000, you could not encrypt the Offline Files Database. Any user with Administrator rights could view documents in the CSC directory. This has been changed in Windows XP Professional. The Offline Files Database can now be encrypted to protect user's offline files and folders. The CSC directory must be on an NTFS volume for encryption to be used. You cannot encrypt files or folders on FAT or FAT32 volumes.

Microsoft provides a tool for moving the cache directory. The Offline Files Cache Mover is available from the Windows 2000 Resource Kit. The file name for the tool is Cachemov.exe. The cache directory can only be moved to another fixed disk.

Offline Web Pages

Files and folders are not the only items that can be made available for users offline. Web pages can also be configured for access when users are not connected to their networks. Users of Microsoft Internet Explorer can make entire Web pages available for offline viewing. A wizard walks a user through the steps for making the Web content available when the user is working offline.

Synchronization Manager

Synchronization Manager is a tool provided to help users control when their offline files are synchronized with their network counterparts (see Figure 6.12). Synchronization Manager can be configured to synchronize files in the following instances:

➤ When a user logs on or off her computer, or both

➤ When the computer is idle

➤ At predefined scheduled times

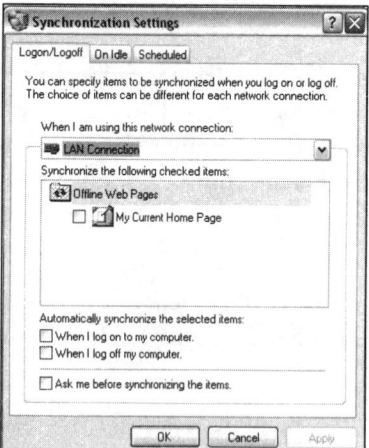

Figure 6.12 The Synchronization Settings dialog box.

NTFS File and Folder Compression

Compressing files and folders reduces the amount of disk space required for storage. Windows XP Professional supports two types of compression—NTFS compression and Compressed (Zipped) Folders.

Your hard drive must be formatted with NTFS to support compression. FAT and FAT32 drives do not support compression. Files, folders, and entire NTFS volumes can be compressed in Windows XP Professional.

Users can access and use compressed files without having to decompress them. When a user opens a compressed Word document, the document is automatically uncompressed and recompressed when it is saved and closed. The entire process is transparent to a user. He never realizes that he is working on a compressed file.

Windows XP Professional allocates disk space for compressed files by their uncompressed file size. If a user attempts to copy or move a compressed file to an NTFS volume that does not have enough space to accommodate it in its uncompressed state, it will not be copied or moved. The volume must have enough space to accommodate the file in its uncompressed state.

Files and folders are compressed through Windows Explorer. For easier identification, they can be displayed in an alternate color.

Files and folders can also be compressed using the Compact.exe command-line utility. The following options are available for compressing files using this utility:

```
compact [/c|/u] [/s[:dir]] [/a] [/q] [/i] [/f] [filename[...]]
```

The parameters are described in the following list:

➤ *None*—Used without parameters, **compact** displays the compression state of the current directory

➤ **/c**—Compresses the specified directory or file

➤ **/u**—Uncompresses the specified directory or file

➤ **/s:*dir***—Specifies that the requested action (compress or uncompress) be applied to all subdirectories of the specified directory or of the current directory if none is specified

➤ **/a**—Displays hidden or system files

➤ **/q**—Reports only the most essential information

➤ **/I**—Ignores errors

➤ **/f**—Forces compression or uncompression of the specified directory or file
This is used in the case of a file that was partly compressed when the operation
was interrupted by a system crash. To force the file to be compressed in its
entirety, use the **/c** and **/f** parameters, and specify the partially compressed file

➤ *Filename*—Specifies the file or directory. You can use multiple file names and
wildcard characters (* and ?)

Copying and Moving Compressed Files and Folder

The following are a few key points to know when copying or moving compressed
files or folders:

➤ A file that is copied from one location on an NTFS volume to another location on the same volume inherits the compression of the target folder

➤ A file that is copied from one NTFS volume to another NTFS volume inherits
the compression of the target folder

➤ A file that is moved from one location on an NTFS volume to another location on the same volume retains its compression state

➤ A file that is moved from one NTFS volume to another NTFS volume inherits
the compression state of the target folder

➤ Any compressed file or folder that is copied or moved from an NTFS volume
to a FAT or FAT32 volume loses its compressed state. Neither FAT nor FAT32
supports compression

Compressed (Zipped) Folders

Compressed (Zipped) Folders is a new feature introduced in Windows XP Professional that allows users to compress folders and the files they contain. Compression
reduces the amount of disk drive space required to save the files and folders. The
Compressed (Zipped) Folder is identified by a folder with a zipper icon (see
Figure 6.13).

Files in compressed folders can be opened or run directly from the compressed
folder without decompressing them. Files and folders created with Compressed
(Zipped) Folders are compatible with other third-party Zip utilities. To compress
individual files, create a compressed folder, and move the files you want compressed
to that folder.

For added security, users can protect compressed folders with passwords.

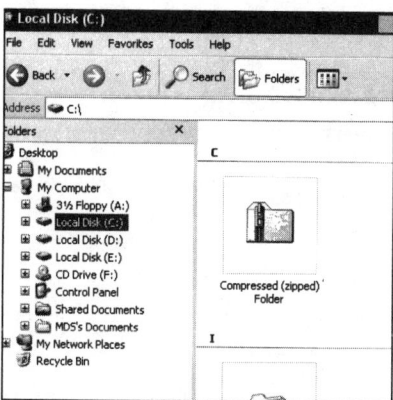

Figure 6.13   A Compressed (Zipped) Folder.

6

Searching for Files and Folders

Windows XP Professional makes it easier for users to search for files and folders locally on their computers and over networks. The Search Companion (see Figure 6.14) can be accessed through My Computer, My Network Places, My Documents, the Start menu, and Windows Explorer.

Indexing Service

The Indexing Service provides a way to quickly access information through the Search Companion. The Indexing Service extracts information from documents and organizes the information in a way that makes searching easier through the

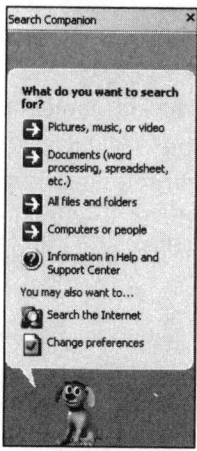

Figure 6.14   The Search Companion.

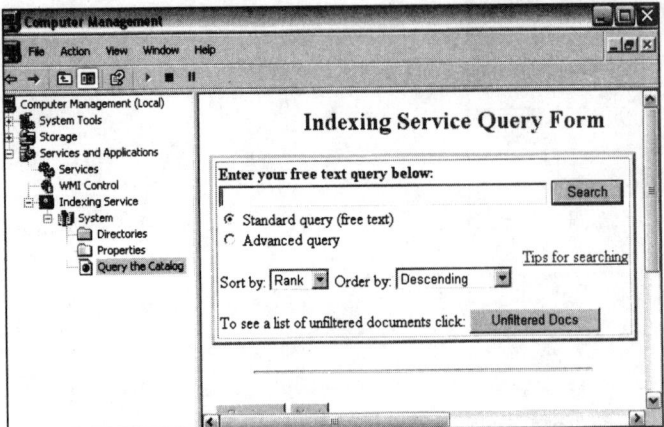

Figure 6.15 The Indexing Service.

Search Companion, the Indexing Service Query Form (see Figure 6.15), or a Web browser, such as Internet Explorer.

The Indexing Service can index HTML, text, and Microsoft Office 95, 98, 2000, and XP documents. It can also index Internet mail and news.

The Indexing Service is designed to run continuously in Windows XP Professional with little maintenance from users.

When the Indexing Service is installed, it creates a default catalog called System. Users can add or delete catalogs, and modify any existing catalogs. By default, the System catalog contains all directories on the local hard disk.

Chapter Summary

This chapter looked at the various ways to work with files and folders in Windows XP Professional. The My Documents folder is the default storage location for users' documents. Each user who logs onto the computer will have their own My Documents folder. The My Pictures folder is used to store images saved from scanners and digital cameras. The My Music folder is new to Windows and is the primary storage location for downloaded music files or files copied from audio CDs.

Windows XP Professional provides several ways for users to view their files and folders. They can view them in Thumbnails, Tiles, Filmstrip, Icons, List, or Details view. Users can customize how folders are displayed. Folders can be viewed as Web pages or in the classic Windows format.

NTFS permissions provide additional security on a computer. Windows XP Professional supports file and folder permissions. The five file permissions are Full Control, Modify, Read and Execute, Read, and Write. The six folder permissions are Full Control, Modify, Read and Execute, List Folder Content, Read, and Write. Special permissions are available when administrators want to provide more security than is provided with the standard file and folder permissions.

Shared folders are used to provide users with access to files and folders over a network. Before users can access a shared folder, they must have the appropriate permissions. Shared folder permissions only apply to folders. If users want to assign permissions to the files within the folders, they have to use NTFS permissions on the files. The Shared Folders tool is used by administrators to manage shared folders on a network.

Offline Files and Folders provides users with the ability to work on network-based files when they are not connected to the network. When users reconnect to the network, their files and folder are synchronized with their network counterparts. Synchronization Manager can be used to control when file synchronization occurs.

Files, folders, and NTFS volumes can be compressed to conserve disk space. Compression can only be used on NTFS volumes. FAT and FAT32 do not support file and folder compression.

Review Questions

1. Donavan has recently used Windows Media Player to download music files from the Internet to his computer. He can't seem to find the files. Where should he look for the music files?

   a. My Documents folder

   b. My Pictures folder

   c. My Music folder

   d. Windows Temp folder

2. What option in Windows Explorer will let users track the documents they have opened and Web pages they have visited?

   a. Toolbars

   b. Address Bar

   c. History folder

   d. Favorites

3. What folder view will allow Jenny to display the contents of each file in the folder as an image?

   a. List

   b. Tile

   c. Thumbnail .

   d. Icons

4. Which of the following file permissions is the most restrictive?

   a. Read

   b. Write

   c. Full Control

   d. Read and Execute

5. Which of the following permissions are special file and folder permissions that can be used when standard file and folder permissions do not provide sufficient access control? [Check all correct answers]

   a. Read Attributes

   b. Modify

   c. Write Attributes

   d. Read and Execute

6. What are access control entries?

   a. They are created when accounts are created, and they are unique for each account.

   b. They are a list of ACEs that define which actions are allowed or denied for users or groups.

   c. They are entries in the ACL that determine which actions are allowed or denied by users or groups.

   d. They contain information about a user's access control.

7. What is used to audit object access?

   a. DACL

   b. SACL

   c. SID

   d. Security Descriptor

8. What object in Group Policy or Local Security Policy must be enabled before auditing of files and folders can occur?

   a. Audit Policy Change

   b. Audit Account Management

   c. Audit Policy Change

   d. Audit Object Access

9. Which of the following are valid shared folder permissions? [Check all correct answers]

   a. Read Attributes

   b. Full Control

   c. Read

   d. Change

10. When Windows XP Professional is installed, certain shares are created for administrative purposes. Which of the following shares provides the Administrators group full access to the system root folder?

   a. IPC$

   b. NETLOGON$

   c. ADMIN$

   d. C$

11. What section of Shared Folders will allow administrators to see which users are connected to folders that are shared on the network?

   a. Shares

   b. Sessions

   c. Files

   d. Open Files

12. Which command line would allow an administrator to delete a share named OLDSHARE on the network?

   a. **net share oldshare /delete**

   b. **net share oldshare**

   c. **net share /connect**

   d. **net share oldshare /remarks**

6

Real-World Projects

Joan's company has just implemented a new network with both Windows 2000 and Windows XP computers. Many of the users are working from remote locations and use laptop computers when they are not in the office. The main files that everyone needs to work with on a daily basis are located on the company network. Joan has volunteered to help those users who will be traveling to configure their new workstations. She wants to set things up so that they are able to work on company files even when they are not connected to the company network. She also wants to ensure that user data is protected on laptop computers since many users sometimes work from locations that have little or no security.

Project 6.1

To share a folder and configure it for Offline Files and Folders use:

1. Open Windows Explorer.

2. Create a new folder called My Offline Folder.

3. Right-click My Offline Folder, and select Sharing.

4. Select the Share This Folder radio button.

5. Click the Caching button.

6. Ensure that the Allow Caching Of Files In This Shared Folder checkbox is checked.

7. Click OK to close the Caching Settings dialog box.

8. Click OK to close the My Offline Folder Properties dialog box.

Project 6.2

To make a Web page available for offline viewing and to create a schedule for updating the page:

1. Open Internet Explorer.

2. Go to the Web page that you want to have available when you are offline.

3. Click Add To Favorites on the Favorites menu.

4. Check the Make Available Offline checkbox.

5. Click the Customize button.

6. Select whether the page contains links to other pages, and click Next.

7. Select I Would Like To Create A New Schedule, and click Next.

8. Enter the number of days and the time that you want the page updated, and click Next.

9. If the site requires a password, enter it and the username, and click Finish.

Project 6.3

To prepare the My Offline Folder you created in Project 6.1 for auditing to monitor user access:

1. Open the Control Panel.

2. Double-click Administrative Tools.

3. Double-click Local Security Policy.

4. Click the plus sign (+) by Local Policies.

5. Click Audit Policy.

6. Double-click Audit Object Access in the right pane.

7. Under Audit These Attempts, select both the Success and Failure checkboxes, and click OK.

8. Close the Local Security Settings dialog box.

9. Close Administrative Tools.

10. Open Windows Explorer.

11. Right-click the My Offline Folder folder, and select Properties.

12. Select the Security tab.

13. Click the Advanced button.

14. Click the Audit tab.

15. Click the Add button.

16. Enter the name of the users or groups that you want to audit access for on this folder.

17. Select the type of access to monitor, and click OK.

18. Click OK to close the Advance Security Settings Properties dialog box.

19. Click OK to close the My Offline Folder Properties dialog box.

records of logins

Project 6.4

To encrypt the Offline Files Database:

1. Open My Computer or Windows Explorer.

2. Select Tools|Folder Options.

3. Select the Offline Files tab.

4. Check the Encrypt Offline Files To Secure Data checkbox.

5. Click OK.

6. Close My Computer.

others that would log in

CHAPTER SEVEN

Printing

After completing this chapter, you will be able to:

✓ Understand the Windows XP printing process

✓ Install and configure Windows XP printers

✓ Monitor and manage print jobs

✓ Enforce printer access through permissions

✓ Understand and install advanced printing configurations

✓ Troubleshoot common printing issues

P rinting, in addition to file sharing, is the most commonly used network application. For years, people have been exhorting the coming of the paperless office;
however, many of us realize that it is merely a myth. Thanks to low-cost laser
printers, printing and overall paper use is higher than ever. Windows XP supplies an
easily implemented printing solution that supports a variety of clients, including
Windows XP, Windows NT 4/3.51, Windows 95/98, Windows For Workgroups,
MS-DOS, Macintosh, Unix, and Novell NetWare.

Printing Overview

Windows XP is an excellent printing platform, both locally and across a network.
By combining a variety of software and hardware components, Windows XP
provides a robust and versatile printing environment. It also provides support for
almost all printers on the market. Although it might appear to be overly complex,
in reality, printing in Windows XP is extremely easy to install and configure.

First, review the following terms, which you will see mentioned throughout this
chapter:

➤ *Local printer*—A printer that is attached to a local computer.

➤ *Network printer*—A printer that is directly attached to a network.

➤ *Print device*—The physical hardware device used for printing.

➤ *Print driver*—A software component that enables applications to communicate
properly with the associated print device.

➤ *Print jobs*—A file that is created by an application to be sent to a print device.
A print job contains the information (printer commands and data) for the print
device to create a finished printed sheet.

➤ *Print queue*—A list of print jobs waiting to be sent to a print device. As print
jobs are sent to a print device, the print server queues the jobs. After a job is
completed, the next job in the queue is sent to the print device.

➤ *Print server*—A computer that hosts one or more print devices. A print server
holds the spool files for the printer and manages the print queue.

➤ *Print spooler*—A software component that receives, stores, and distributes print
jobs. A print spooler places print jobs in the print queue. When the print
device is available, the print spooler sends the next print job to the print
device. The Windows XP printing process actually has two spoolers—the
client-side spooler and the server-side spooler. These two components interact
to make network printing possible.

➤ *Printer*—The most commonly mistaken term in the Windows XP printing
process. A printer represents the software interface between the print device
and the clients, not the actual physical printer (the print device).

The Windows XP Printing Process

To the unfamiliar eye, the printing process might seem like magic. The Windows XP printing process, however, is a powerful and flexible operation (see Figure 7.1). This section reviews the general architecture of the process and defines the various components involved. Although a user does not need to know this much detail

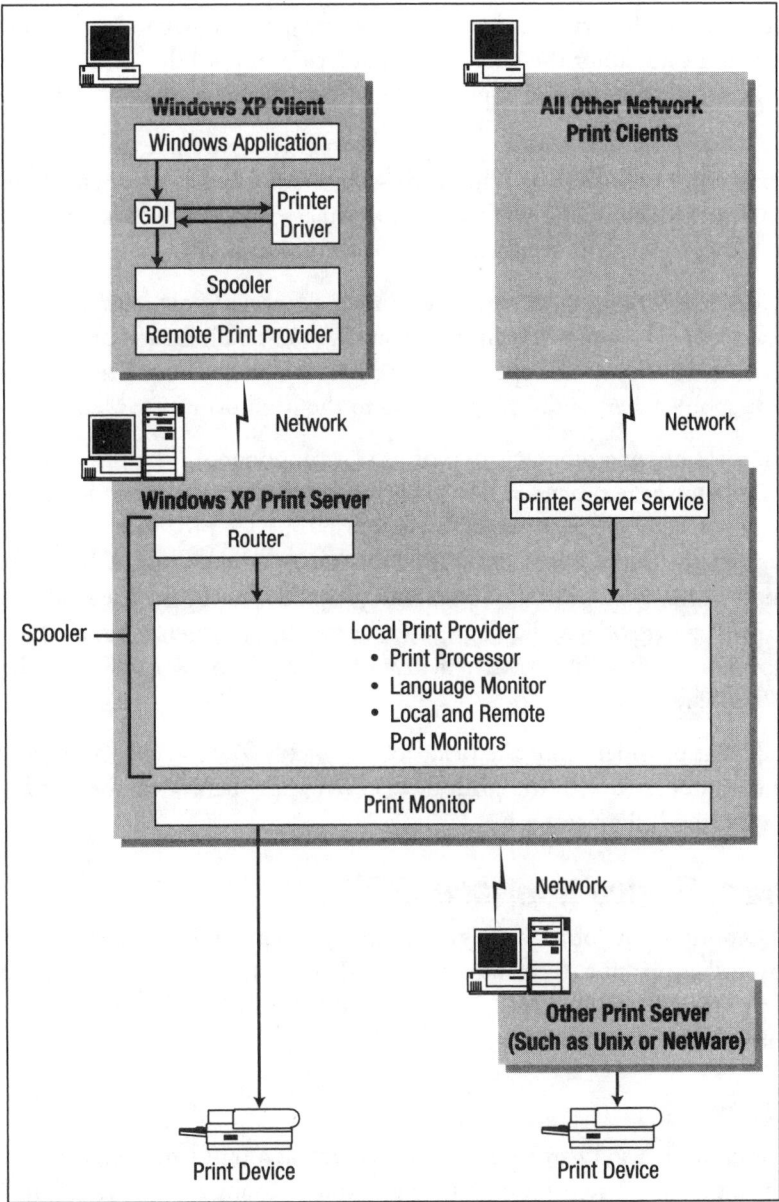

Figure 7.1   The Windows XP printing process.

about the process, an administrator familiar with it will be better prepared to troubleshoot printing issues.

The printing process begins when a user chooses to print a document at a client workstation. The application on the client calls the graphical device interface (GDI), which in turn calls the print driver for the selected print device. After obtaining device-dependent information from the print driver, the GDI renders the print job using the print device's supported printer language. Once complete, the application calls either the client-side spooler (Winspool.drv) if the printer is local or the server-side spooler (Spoolsv.exe) if the printer is a network printer.

For local printers, the client-side spooler contacts the server-side spooler via remote procedure calls (RPCs). The server-side spooler makes an application programming interface (API) call to the *print router* (Spoolss.dll). The print router then sends the print job to the *local print provider* (Localspl.dll).

For network printers, the print router examines the *remote print providers* to see if they are available. The remote print provider (Win32spl.dll) creates an RPC connection to the server-side spooler located on the print server. The print server's server-side spooler then sends the print job to the local print provider.

The local print provider contacts two of its subcomponents—the print processor and the separator page processor. The print processor alters the print job according to the document's data type. If needed, the separator page processor adds separator pages. A separator page is more commonly known as a *banner page*, which includes information about who printed the job and when. Separator pages can also be used to have the print provider switch languages between jobs (such as from PCL to PostScript). The local print provider then writes the job to a spool file and keeps track of the job.

The local print provider sends the print job to the *port monitor*. The port monitor's job is to communicate with the print device. When the print device is available, the port monitor sends the print job.

Graphical Device Interface (GDI)

The GDI controls how objects are graphically represented. This includes the video display as well as printing. In printing, the GDI contacts the print driver of the selected printer to determine the fully qualified pathname of the printer and the appropriate printer language to use.

Print Drivers

The print driver is a software component that acts as a translator between the GDI and the print device. The print driver understands the language of the print device, allowing computer commands to be translated into printer-specific commands.

Because it is a translator, multiple drivers need to be installed if multiple print devices or operating systems are used. Windows XP ships with three generic drivers that provide basic functionality for most print devices:

➤ *HPGL/2 Plotter Driver*—This print driver is used for plotters that support the HPGL/2 plotter language.

➤ *PostScript Printer Driver*—This print driver supports Adobe v4.3 PostScript printer description (PPD) files.

➤ *Universal Printer Driver (Unidriver)*—This print driver supports most printers.

Print Spooler

The print spooler is actually a group of components that work together to provide spooling services. There is a client-side spooler (Winspool.drv) if the printer is local, or a server-side spooler (Spoolsv.exe) if the printer is a network printer.

Print Router

The print router takes the print job from the GDI and locates an available print provider that can handle the print job. Once the print provider is located, the print router sends the job to the local print provider (for local printing) or to a remote print provider (for network printing).

Remote Print Providers

A remote print provider is located on the client-side spooler. Its function is to relay a print job to the local print provider on a remote print server.

Local Print Providers

The local print provider does most of the work in the spooler. It receives the print job, writes it to a spool file, and keeps track of the file. The local print provider also contains two subcomponents—the print processor and the separator page processor.

Port Monitors

Windows XP includes a number of port monitors to enable printing in various network environments:

➤ *AppleTalk Port Monitor*—This port monitor allows you to view and manage queues on AppleTalk (Macintosh) networks.

➤ *Local Port Monitor*—This is the preferred local port monitor in Windows XP. This port monitor is used when a print device is attached to the LPT or COM port.

- ➤ *NetWare Port Monitor*—This port monitor enables you to view and manage NetWare queues.

- ➤ *Standard TCP/IP Port Monitor (SPM)*—This is the preferred network port monitor in Windows XP. It uses the Simple Network Management Protocol (SNMP) to configure and monitor printer ports.

Print Job Formats

Print jobs can be created in a variety of formats, depending on the environment being used:

- ➤ *Enhanced Metafile (EMF)*—The default print job format in Windows XP and Windows 2000. This print job format is generated by the GDI. Once the print job is sent to the spooler, control of the application is returned to the user.

- ➤ *PSCRIPT1*—The print job format used by Macintosh printers using Level 1 monochrome PostScript printing. The print job is translated into a bitmap by the spooler, allowing the print job to be printed on non-PostScript print devices.

- ➤ *RAW*—For non-Windows XP clients, such as Windows NT 4 and Windows 95, RAW is the default print job format. The RAW format is created by the print driver.

- ➤ *RAW (FF Appended)*—The same format as RAW, with the exception that a form feed (FF) has been appended to the job. This might be necessary with a print device that doesn't print the last page of the print job.

- ➤ *RAW (FF Auto)*—The same format as RAW, but the spooler checks the print job for a form feed. If no form feed is present, the spooler automatically adds it.

- ➤ *Text*—This print job only contains ASCII text. The print job is printed using the print device's default font.

The Printers and Faxes Folder

The Printers and Faxes folder is where all activities relating to printing in Windows XP can be found. In this folder, a user can add a printer via the Add Printer Wizard or modify the properties of printers already installed. To call the Printers and Faxes folder a *folder* is really a misnomer. Actually, it should be called the Printers and Faxes Control Panel. Besides adding and modifying printers, the Printers and Faxes folder also controls the print server properties for the computer.

As with almost anything else in Windows XP or Windows 2000, you can open the Printers and Faxes folder in a variety of ways. To find the Printers and Faxes folder, select Start|Printers And Faxes, or follow these steps:

1. Select My Computer on the Start menu.

2. Click Control Panel.

3. In the Control Panel, find the Printers And Other Hardware applet, and click it.

4. Click View Installed Printers Or Fax Printers.

After the initial install of Windows XP Professional, the Printers and Faxes folder is empty (see Figure 7.2). To install a printer, click Add A Printer under the Printer Tasks box on the left. This starts the Add Printer Wizard, which is used to install local printers or attach to existing network printers. The printer can then be managed or shared at that point.

Installing Printers

Several ways exist to install printers in Windows XP Professional. Depending on the situation, one of the following methods might be used.

Plug and Play

One of the easiest and most convenient methods of installing a printer in Windows XP is by using Plug and Play. The Plug and Play specification allows a computer to automatically detect and configure components that have been added. This specification also includes printers, where Plug and Play automatically adds the printer

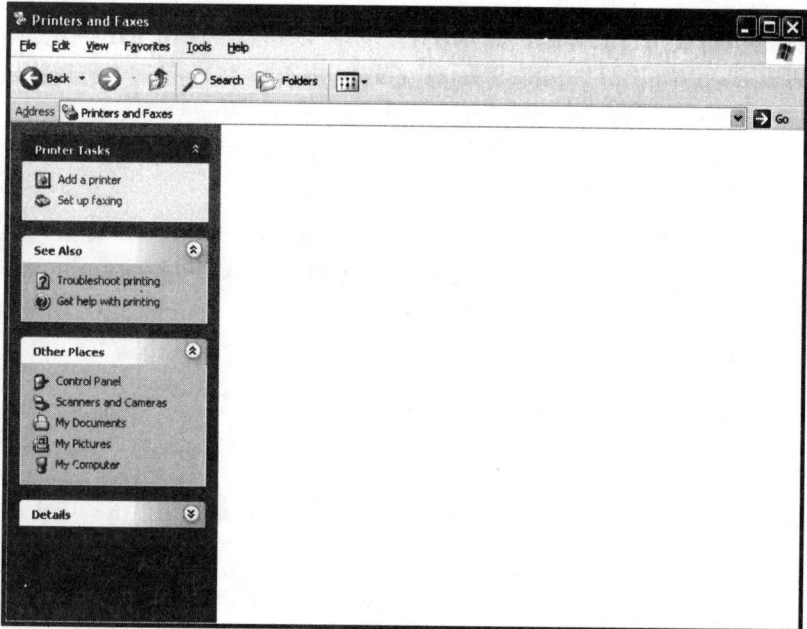

Figure 7.2 The Printers and Faxes folder.

and installs the appropriate printer drivers. It's important to remember that Plug and Play works only for printers directly attached to the computer (a local printer). It will not work for network printers.

Plug and Play is extremely easy to use. Simply plug the printer into the computer. Plug and Play begins to initialize the printer and to install the printer drivers. It also allocates any needed resources. Amazingly, no reboot is necessary. All Plug and Play-compatible printers use Institute of Electrical and Electronics Engineers (IEEE) 1394 cables, universal serial bus (USB) cables, or Infrared Data Association (IrDA).

Although Plug and Play works 99 percent of the time, in a few situations, it will not work. Usually, this occurs because the printer itself is older and doesn't support the Plug and Play specification.

If the printer isn't automatically installed after being connected, Plug and Play can be started manually by forcing Windows XP to look for new hardware using the Add Hardware Wizard or by restarting Windows XP (the operating system looks for new hardware at bootup). Another possibility is to use the Add Printer Wizard. If any of these methods detects the printer, Plug and Play finishes the installation.

Another possible installation problem might be the lack of a printer driver. Although Windows XP ships with drivers for many popular printers, the print driver for a printer being installed might not be included. In that case, the user needs to supply the print driver when prompted.

Using the Add Printer Wizard

In all situations, the Add Printer Wizard can be employed to install local printers, even after Plug and Play has failed to install the printer. When a local printer is installed via the Add Printer Wizard, a logical printer is created that connects to the physical print device.

To start the Add Printer Wizard, simply click Add A Printer under Printer Tasks in the Printers and Faxes folder. You are then prompted for configuration information relating to the printer, such as the following:

➤ Select the port that the printer is attached to.

➤ Select the printer's manufacturer and model.

➤ Enter a name for the printer.

➤ Specify whether the printer should be the default printer for the workstation.

➤ Specify whether the printer should be shared.

➤ Supply the share name.

➤ Optionally, supply location and description information for the printer (which can help users identify the printer).

➤ Print a test page to verify proper installation of the printer.

Once complete, the new logical printer will have an icon in the Printers and Faxes folder (see Figure 7.3). Applications will now be able to utilize the printer, unless, of course, the application itself has special needs.

Using Windows Update

Windows XP comes with a dandy new feature that takes a lot of the headache out of searching for new drivers. First included in Windows 2000, this feature is called Windows Update. Windows Update is an online extension of Windows XP (see Figure 7.4). Windows Update contains a list of fixes, enhancements, and updates to the Windows XP operating system. If you need a printer driver that wasn't shipped with Windows XP, you can try Windows Update to see if the driver has been added.

Because Windows Update is an online extension, Internet connectivity via analog modem, cable modem, or digital subscriber line (DSL) is required. Additionally, as always, you must be either an administrator or a user with administrative permissions to update system files and drivers. Windows Update can be started by selecting Start|All Programs|Windows Update. When connected, the Windows Update

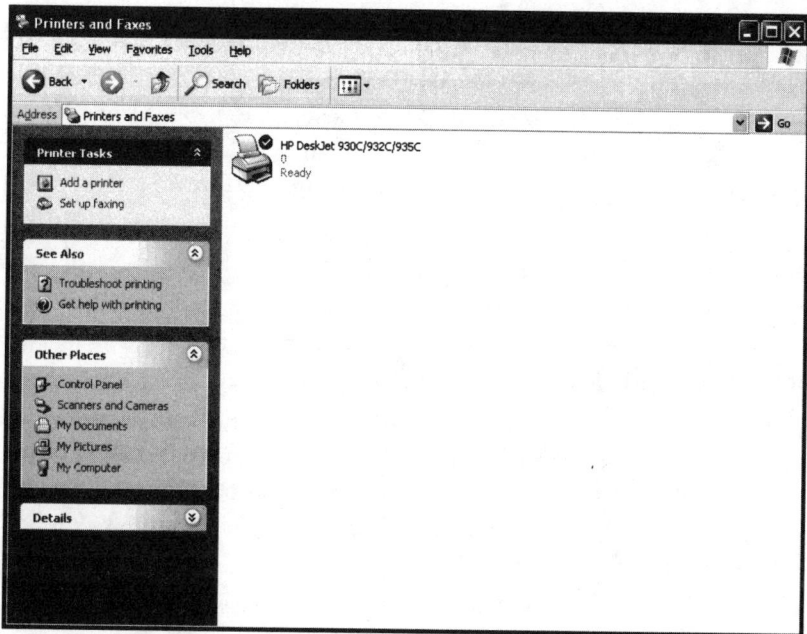

Figure 7.3   A new printer in the Printers and Faxes folder.

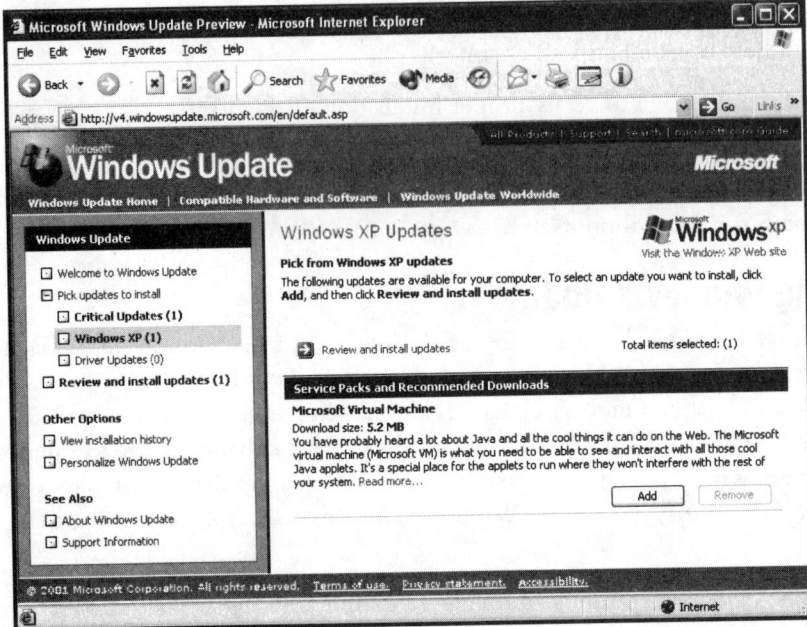

Figure 7.4 Windows Update.

Web site will be displayed. Select Scan For Updates, and Windows Update scans your computer to determine which components have been installed and presents a list of components that were updated or can be added. Windows Update has various categories of components—Critical Updates, Windows XP, and Driver Updates. In the case of printers, view the Drivers Updates category and see whether your printer has been added. If listed, select the printer driver. You can then decide on which other components to install. Windows Update then downloads the selected components and automatically installs them.

Note: *Windows Update does not send any scanned information to Microsoft. It is only used to determine what is necessary to keep your computer up-to-date.*

Installing Network Printers

The real power in networking is the capability to share network resources with other users. A printer is one such commonly shared resource. Installing network printers in Windows XP can be accomplished in a number of ways. Some of these are familiar and are the same as those in Windows NT and Windows 95/98. Some features are new to Windows XP.

Using the Add Printer Wizard

You can use the Add Printer Wizard to add a network printer in the same way as you add a local printer. The only difference is that when you are asked whether you want to install a local printer or a network printer, you specify network printer. Depending on your computer's domain/workgroup configuration, you will then be given three choices to locate a network printer:

➤ Find a printer using Active Directory.

➤ Enter the printer's Universal Naming Convention (UNC) name, or click Next to browse.

➤ Enter the printer's Uniform Resource Locator (URL) to connect to a printer via the Internet or an intranet.

Using Point and Print

Point and Print is a great feature that can be used on network printers. It significantly simplifies the network printer installation for users, much as Plug and Play does for local printers. This in turn reduces the administrative overhead required in configuring and maintaining printers.

Point and Print allows users to install a printer from across a network. Users simply "point" to a print server and select the printer they would like to install. The print server sends important configuration information to the workstation, including the following:

➤ Print drivers

➤ Location of the print drivers (the server where they are stored)

➤ Printer model

To install a printer using Point and Print, follow these steps:

1. Find the print server where the printer is located by using Find|My Network Places or entering its UNC in the Run dialog box or the Add Printer Wizard.

2. Double-click the server, and then double-click the server's Printers and Faxes folder.

3. Right-click the desired printer, and click Connect.

Internet Printers

Another exciting feature found in Windows XP is the ability to print to a URL over an intranet or the Internet. This is possible via the use of the Internet Printing Protocol (IPP), which is defined in a set of RFCs (2565, 2566, 2567, 2568, and 2569).

IPP might someday replace the fax machine and email when its ease of use is considered. Rather than sending a fax via long distance or sending an email with an attachment, a user can simply use a Web browser to view the print server to which the recipient's printer is attached. From the list of printers displayed, the user can select the appropriate printer and print the document. The user doesn't need to worry about long-distance costs or whether the recipient received and opened the email.

On the print server, IPP requires Internet Information Services (IIS) for either Windows XP Professional or Windows .NET Server to be installed. Jobs are submitted using IPP 1 as the protocol, which controls job configuration information (job name, paper tray, duplexing, notification, and so on). The Hypertext Transport Protocol (HTTP) transmits the print job from the client to the print server.

With IPP, the user's Web browser provides the necessary interface (via Active Server Pages) to view the printer status, perform installation and configuration, print the job status, and print the job submission (see Figure 7.5).

Installing an Internet printer is much like installing a local printer, except that the port that the printer is attached to is an IP address or URL. To applications, the Internet printer appears the same as a local printer (see Figure 7.6).

To install an Internet printer, follow these steps:

1. Open Internet Explorer.

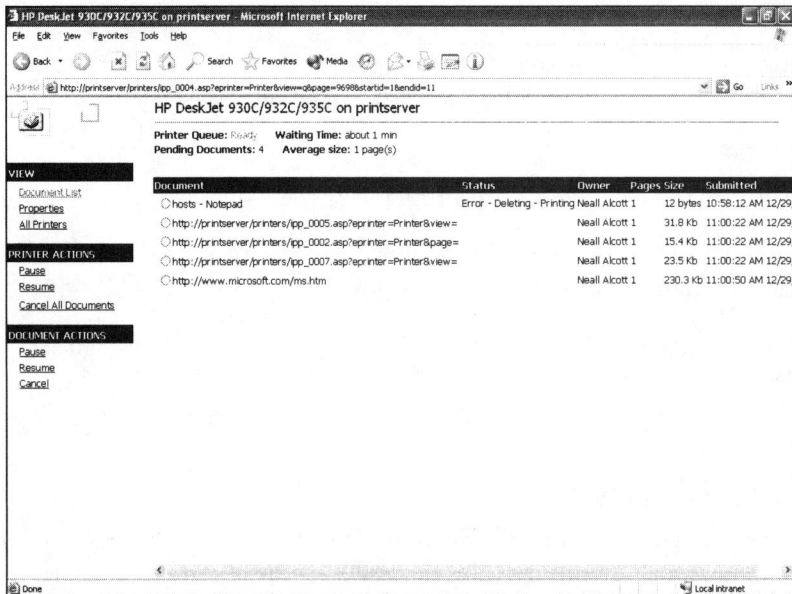

Figure 7.5 The status screen of an Internet printer.

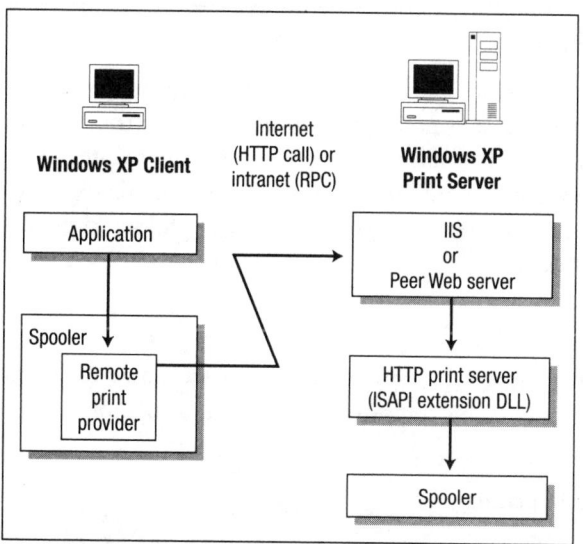

Figure 7.6   Internet printing process.

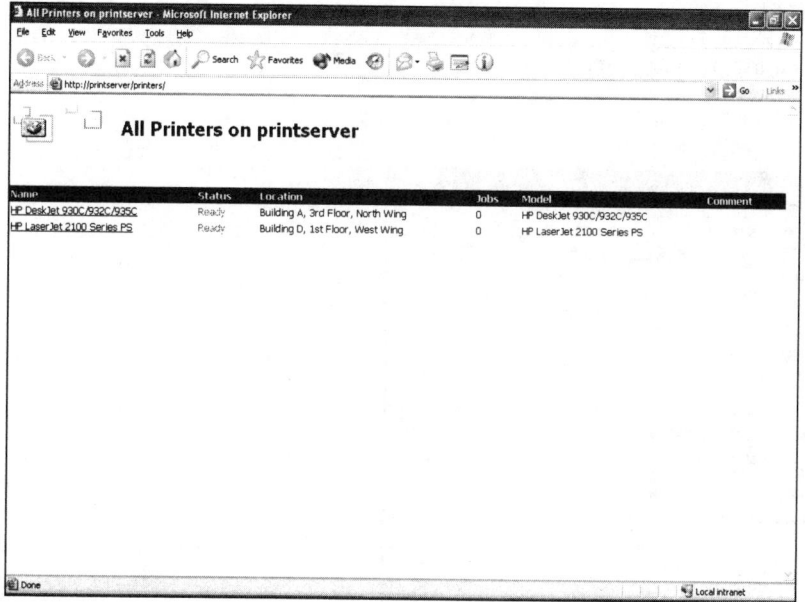

Figure 7.7   Connecting to an Internet printer.

2. In the Address box, type the print server's URL or IP address followed by "/printers", and press Enter. For example, enter "http://*printserver*/printers".

3. Select the printer you want to print to, and click Connect (see Figure 7.7).

After the Internet printer is installed, it will appear in the Printers and Faxes folder like any other installed printer.

Configuring Printers

After a printer has been installed, an icon representing the logical printer appears in the Printers and Faxes folder. Further configuration of printer settings (port settings, device settings, and so on) can be accomplished via the printer's Properties dialog box. Several methods are available to access the Properties dialog box, but the most common method is to open the Printers and Faxes folder, right-click the printer, and select Properties.

The General Tab

The General tab, shown in Figure 7.8, displays basic information about the installed printer, such as the printer model and supported features. It also allows you to do the following:

➤ Specify the name of the printer.

➤ Specify the location of the printer (for example, *1ˢᵗ Floor, Bldg. 110*).

➤ Add any additional comments (for example, *Call Neall Alcott @ x5555 for assistance*).

➤ Set any printing preferences.

➤ Print a test page.

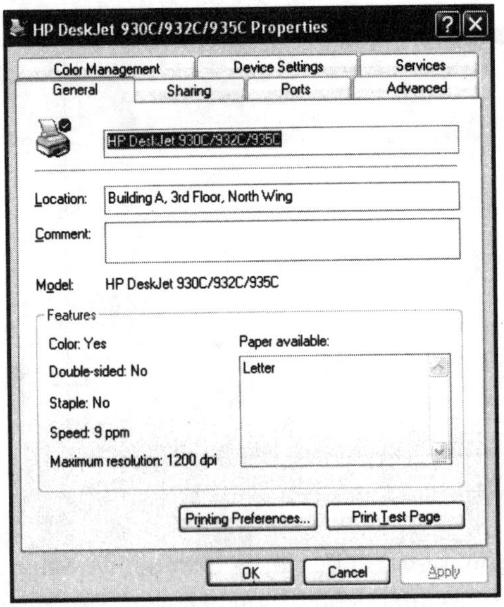

Figure 7.8 The General tab.

Printing Preferences

The Printing Preferences dialog box enables a user to specify print settings that will be maintained across multiple documents. This dialog box determines the default print job settings, although they can be overridden by using the Print dialog box.

The Printing Preferences dialog box is activated by clicking the Printing Preferences button on the General tab or by right-clicking a printer in the Printers and Faxes folder and selecting Printing Preferences. This dialog box consists of two tabs—Layout and Paper/Quality. An Advanced button might also be available, if the printer supports advanced features, as described here:

➤ The Layout page allows you to specify the orientation (Portrait or Landscape) of the page as well as the ordering of pages when printed (front to back/back to front).

➤ Pages Per Sheet allows you to print multiple pages of a document to a single piece of paper.

➤ The Paper/Quality page can be used to specify information such as the default paper tray, print quality (Draft/Normal/Best), and color or black and white settings.

The Sharing Tab

The Sharing tab is used to designate whether a printer will be shared with other users on the network (see Figure 7.9).

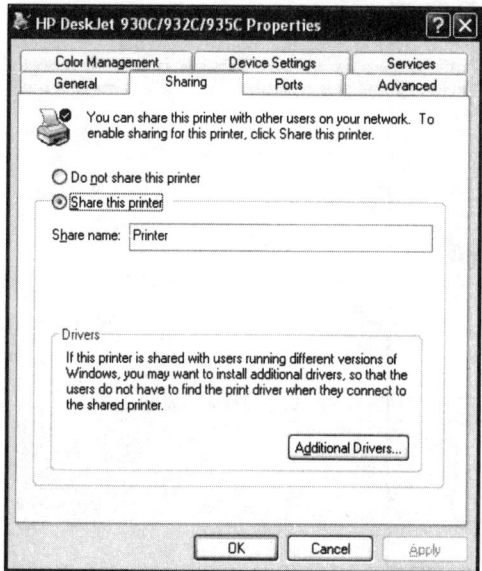

Figure 7.9   The Sharing tab.

By default, a printer is not shared. To share a printer, select the Share This Printer radio button, and enter the printer's share name. The share name is limited to 80 characters, so a very descriptive name can be entered. In practice, however, the name should be kept to a smaller standard, especially if older clients, such as Windows 3.*x* and MS-DOS, are in the environment. These clients cannot see names longer than eight characters with a three-character extension (for example, Printer.pcl); you'll need to make sure that the old MS-DOS 8.3 naming convention is used.

Additional print drivers can be added for other operating systems, such as Windows NT 3.51/4 and Windows 95/98.

The Ports Tab

The Ports tab, shown in Figure 7.10, is used to configure printer ports on the local machine. On this tab, you can do the following:

➤ Select the port or ports a printer will print to

➤ Add, delete, and configure local ports

➤ Enable bidirectional support

➤ Enable printer pooling

Printer pooling is an advanced concept and will be discussed in the "Printer Pooling" section later in this chapter.

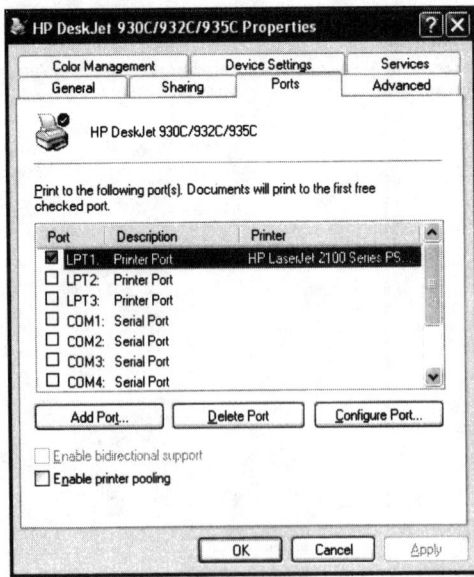

Figure 7.10 The Ports tab.

The Advanced Tab

On the Advanced tab (see Figure 7.11), features such as scheduling, priorities, and spooler settings can be found.

Scheduling

Scheduling allows an administrator to specify when a printer is available for use. This feature can be useful if an organization wants to limit printer use to standard business hours or if the printer is maintained during certain hours. If any print jobs are sent to the printer when the printer is unavailable, the jobs will sit in the spooler until the printer becomes available again.

This feature is also beneficial when used to manage large print jobs. In this case, an administrator can create two logical printers both pointing to the same print device. The first logical printer is used for regular print jobs and is always available. The second logical printer is used for large print jobs and is available only after business hours. Users are instructed to send all large print jobs to the second logical printer. This way, large print jobs won't overburden the print device during normal work hours when other users are printing regular print jobs.

An administrator can specify whether a printer is always available or whether a printer is only available within a specified time frame.

7

Figure 7.11   The Advanced tab.

Priorities

Priorities can be defined per logical printer. If multiple logical printers point to the same physical print device, priorities can determine which logical printer will print first. Priorities can range in descending order from 99 through 1, with 99 having the highest priority.

As an example, a printer might be used by two groups of employees—supervisors and workers. The supervisors may want their print jobs to print sooner, so they have the administrator set the priority for their logical printers to 99. Because the default priority is 1, the workers' logical printers don't need to be modified. When one of the supervisors prints, her print job will be processed first because supervisors have a higher print priority. The workers' print jobs remain in the spooler until the print device is finished printing the supervisor's job.

Spooler Settings

Spooler settings determine if and how the spooler should be employed. Using the spooler allows a document to be printed in the background. This is accomplished by first storing the print job on the hard drive, after which it is sent to the print device.

Select Spool Print Documents So Program Finishes Printing Faster on the Advanced tab to enable spooling. When this option is selected, you can have the spooler wait until after the last page is spooled before printing or have printing begin immediately.

Select Print Directly To The Printer to disable spooling and have the print job sent immediately to the print device.

When spooling is enabled, a number of additional options are available, such as these:

➤ If a user sends a print job that needs a different type of paper than the one loaded into the print device, the print device stops printing all jobs until the requested paper is installed. To make printing more efficient, the print processor can check the print job's destination print device to see if its settings match the settings needed by the print job. If a mismatch exists, the spooler holds mismatched documents until all other documents have been printed.

➤ By selecting Print Spooled Documents First, the spooler prints jobs that have completed spooling. Incomplete jobs, even those with a higher priority, will be printed after the complete jobs.

➤ The user can specify that the spooler not delete print jobs from the queue after they are printed. This allows the job to be printed again via the queue and not from the application.

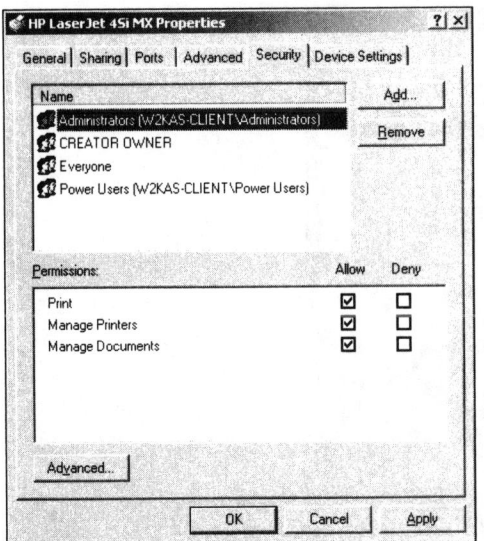

Figure 7.12   The Security tab.

The Security Tab

The Security tab controls the access control list (ACL) for the printer (see Figure 7.12). This tab provides access to the list of users or groups permitted to use the printer as well as the type of access they have been granted.

Three rights can be granted to a user:

➤ *Manage Documents*—The user can change the properties of a job, manipulate jobs in the queue, and change printing defaults.

➤ *Manage Printers*—The user can administer the printer, including printing defaults, creating a printer share, modifying printer properties, and deleting a printer.

➤ *Print*—The user can submit print jobs to the printer and view the list of print jobs in the queue.

Advanced Security

By clicking the Advanced button, more security options can be viewed or modified, such as special permissions, auditing, and ownership.

The Permissions tab gives a more granular view of the ACL, displaying the type of access granted, the user to whom it is granted, the right granted, and where the permissions are applied (see Figure 7.13). To view which permissions are granted for the Print, Manage Printers, and Manage Documents rights, select a user with that right, and click View | Edit (see Figure 7.14). You can also add or remove users from the ACL from this dialog box.

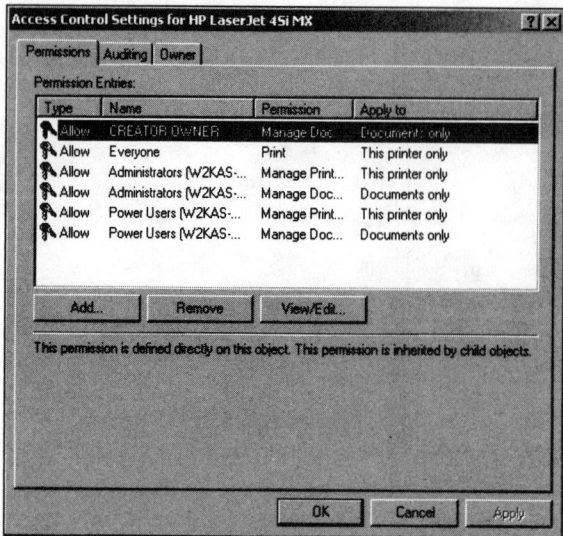

Figure 7.13 The Permissions tab.

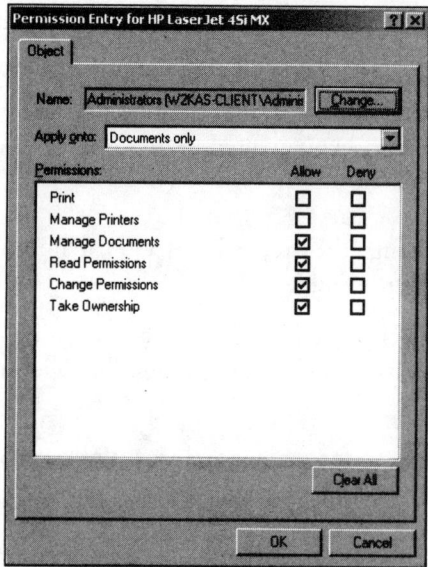

Figure 7.14 Viewing a user's permissions entry.

The Auditing tab controls which events are audited for a specific printer object. Auditing is useful for tracking a printer's usage. This dialog box allows you to specify which types of access should be audited for which groups (see Figure 7.15). Auditing can be set to take place if the object is successfully or unsuccessfully accessed. Events that have been audited can be viewed with the Event Viewer.

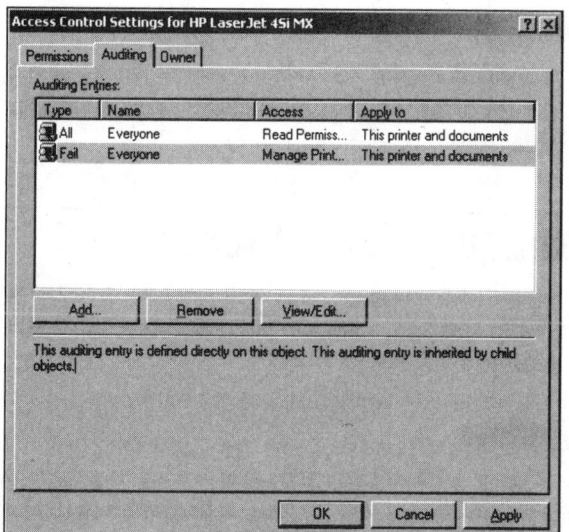

Figure 7.15 The Auditing tab.

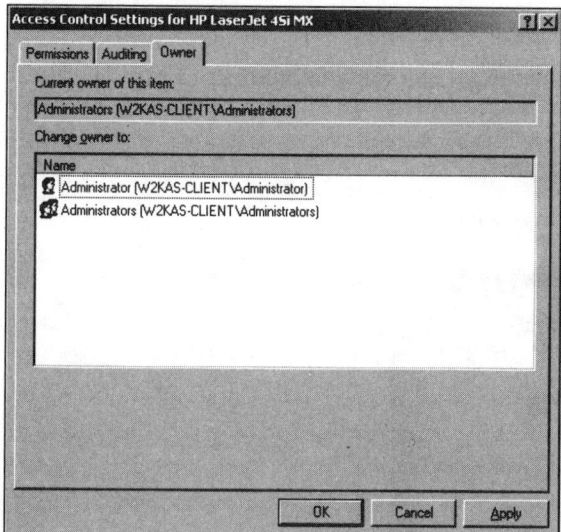

Figure 7.16 Viewing and modifying ownership.

The Owner tab displays which user is the current owner of the printer object (see Figure 7.16). If you have Take Ownership permission, you can take ownership of the object by selecting your user or group account and clicking Apply or OK. A common situation in which ownership needs to be taken occurs when the previous owner's account has been deleted and the current administrator does not have the proper rights to an object. Because an administrator has the Take Ownership right, the administrator can take ownership of the object and grant himself access.

The Device Settings Tab

The Device Settings tab, displayed in Figure 7.17, allows you to specify and configure device-specific settings for the print device. This includes items such as paper tray selection, printer resolution, font cartridges, and so on.

Monitoring and Managing Print Jobs

After a printer has been installed and configured, you will need to monitor and manage print jobs that have been sent to the queue. The following sections explain the features that help you to do so.

The Print Queue Window

The Print Queue window displays a list of print jobs that are waiting to be printed (see Figure 7.18). Each print job in the list will include information such as the following:

➤ *Document Name*—Name of the document

➤ *Owner*—User who sent the document to the printer

➤ *Pages*—Number of printed pages and the total number of pages in the document

➤ *Port*—Printer port being used

➤ *Size*—Document size in kilobytes

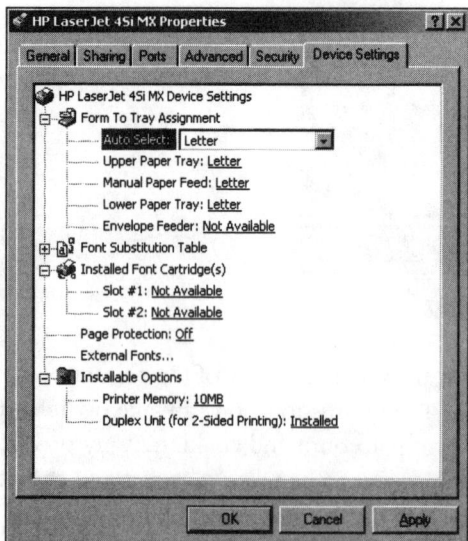

Figure 7.17   The Device Settings tab.

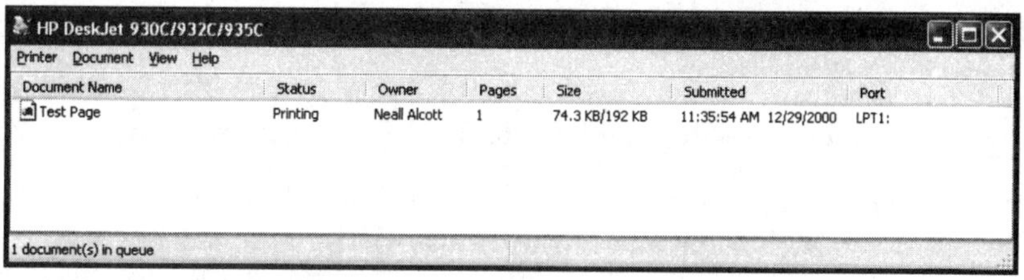

Figure 7.18 The Print Queue window.

➤ *Status*—Current status (Spooling, Paused, or Printing) of the document

➤ *Submitted*—Time and date that the document was sent to the printer

Besides simply providing a list of print jobs, the Print Queue window allows a user or administrator to manage the print jobs in the queue. A regular user, by default, is given only the Print right. This allows a user to submit his or her print jobs and modify the printing preferences for those jobs only. Administrators, on the other hand, are granted the Manage Printer and Manage Documents rights. These rights give administrators full control of the print queue. They can submit, modify, and delete any print job in the queue. They can also modify or delete the printer itself. Table 7.1 lists the printer permissions and their capabilities.

Managing print jobs can be accomplished by selecting the desired print job and selecting one of the following commands on the Document drop-down menu:

➤ *Cancel*—Stops the printing of a print job and deletes it from the queue.

➤ *Pause*—Suspends the printing of an already printing print job or pauses a print job in the queue.

➤ *Restart*—Starts a print job from the beginning, allowing the entire print job to be reprinted in the event of a print device error.

➤ *Resume*—Allows a paused print job to be released.

Table 7.1 Printer permissions.

Capabilities	Print	Manage Documents	Manage Printers
Print documents	X	X	X
Pause, resume, restart, and cancel the user's own print jobs	X	X	X
Connect to a printer	X	X	X
Control print job settings for all jobs		X	X
Pause, restart, and delete all print jobs		X	X
Share a printer			X
Modify printer properties			X
Delete printers			X
Modify printer permissions			X

Managing the entire print queue is attained by using the following commands on the Printer drop-down menu:

➤ *Cancel All Documents*—Stops and deletes all print jobs from the queue.

➤ *Pause Printing*—Suspends the printing of all print jobs in the queue. Any print jobs submitted after the queue is paused will still be accepted, but not printed. To release the pause, simply reselect Pause Printing on the Printer drop-down menu.

➤ *Set As Default Printer*—Designates a printer as the default printer for a workstation. All print jobs sent without specifying a print device are sent to the default printer. After setting a printer as the default printer, a checkmark will be displayed next to the command on the Printer drop-down menu. To change the default printer, select another printer as the default.

Note: Pausing or canceling print jobs will not instantly stop all printing at the print device. If the print device has a significant amount of RAM, printing might continue until all print jobs are removed from its memory. Simply turning off the print device and clearing any paper jams will remove any jobs from memory.

Managing the Print Server

In addition to managing print jobs and printers, you can manage the overall operation of the print server. All changes made to the print server affect all attached logical printers. Management of the print server is provided via the Printers and Faxes folder's File drop-down menu. From this menu, select Server Properties.

The Forms Tab

When the Print Server Properties dialog box is displayed, the first tab shown is the Forms tab (see Figure 7.19). This is where forms for the print server are defined. A form defines the dimensions of the paper (letter, legal, A4, and so on) and the margins for the right, left, top, and bottom of the paper. From the Forms tab, you can do the following:

➤ Define a new form by specifying the form name, paper size, and margins.

➤ Delete forms from the print server.

The Ports Tab

The Ports tab is used to configure printer ports on the local machine. On this tab, you can perform these tasks:

➤ Select the port or ports the printer will print to.

➤ Add, delete, and configure local ports.

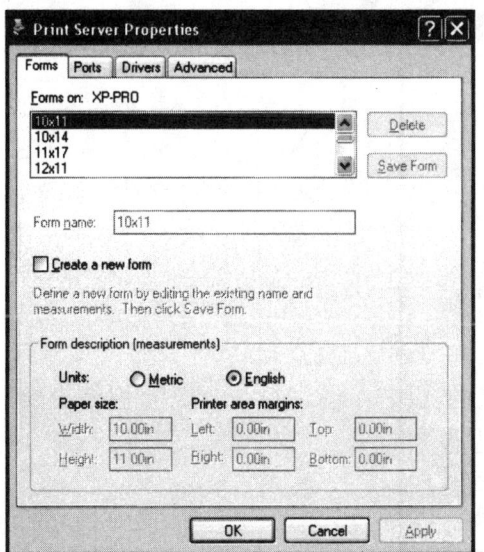

Figure 7.19 The Forms tab in the Print Server Properties dialog box.

The following ports can be added to a Windows XP Professional workstation:

➤ *Local Port*—This gives you the ability to connect to a network printer via its UNC name (such as *servername**sharename*).

➤ *Standard TCP/IP Port*—Sometimes referred to as a Line Printer Remote (LPR) port, the standard TCP/IP port gives you the ability to print directly to TCP/IP-enabled devices. To configure this port, you must specify the IP address or hostname of the printer, along with an optional device name.

The Drivers Tab

The Drivers tab, shown in Figure 7.20, provides a centralized area where you can view, add, remove, and update any print drivers installed. It lists the printer model and the operating system that the installed print driver supports.

The Advanced Tab

The Advanced tab, shown in Figure 7.21, is used to manage advanced properties of the print server. On the Advanced tab, you can perform these tasks:

➤ Specify the spool folder location where print jobs are kept before being sent to the print device. The default location is %systemroot%\System32\spool\PRINTERS.

➤ Enable logging of spooler events (Errors, Warnings, Informational) in the event log.

Figure 7.20 The Drivers tab in the Print Server Properties dialog box.

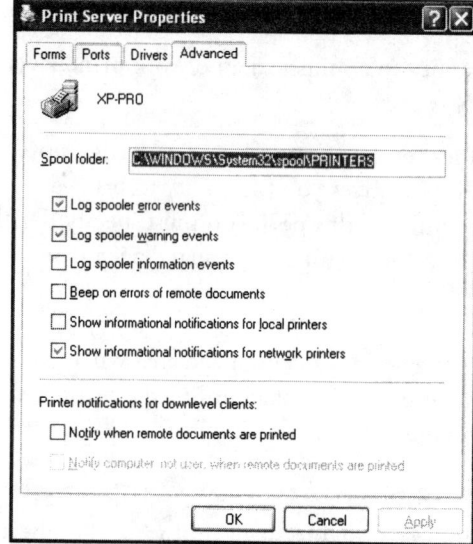

Figure 7.21 The Advanced tab in the Print Server Properties dialog box.

➤ Enable the computer to beep when it encounters an error with a remote document.

➤ Send a notification to a user when a remote document is printed.

➤ Send a notification to the computer when a remote document is printed.

Printer Pooling

Printer pooling is an advanced printing technique that allows two or more identical print devices to be associated with a single logical printer (see Figure 7.22). This technique helps alleviate printing bottlenecks in situations where many print jobs are being sent to one printer. By attaching multiple identical print devices, the logical printer can send one print job to one print device and send the next print job to another available print device.

The print devices need to be identical because the print jobs are formatted for a particular device's features. If different print devices are in the same printer pool, print output might not be the same.

To create a printer pool:

1. Add a printer using the Add Printer Wizard.

2. After the printer is created, right-click the printer, and select Properties.

3. Select the Ports tab, and select the Enable Printer Pooling checkbox.

4. Select the ports that the print devices are attached to.

5. Click OK.

7

Troubleshooting

Troubleshooting printers can really be an art, considering the many components—both software and hardware—that come together to produce a final product. As such, the key to troubleshooting printer problems is to be patient and methodical. Test a component and observe how it behaves. The following list contains some common questions to address when troubleshooting:

➤ *Is one user having the problem, or is the same problem affecting all jobs going to the printer?* This is *the* first question to ask. Observe the environment. If a single user is complaining that the printer is down but other users are sending and printing their jobs, the problem is with the user. It could be an issue with the user's configuration, a permissions issue, or a training issue.

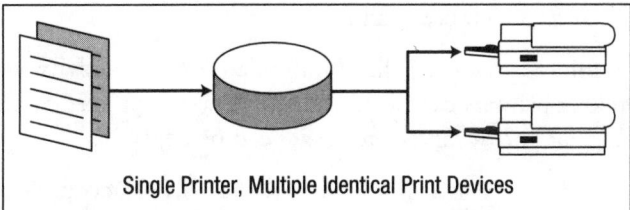

Single Printer, Multiple Identical Print Devices

Figure 7.22   Printer pooling.

➤ *Is the printer plugged in, both power and communications cables?* Always start with the simple solutions first, no matter how simple they seem. It's obvious if the printer has lost power, but a loose cable (network or printer) can cause the printer to stop communicating. By verifying and reseating the cables, you can eliminate bad connections from the equation.

➤ *Is a printer jam or other physical problem causing the printer to not print?* This is another simple problem, but one that can cause users to complain that the printer is down. Verify that the printer has no physical problems.

➤ *Does the printer have network connectivity?* With network printers, it's important to verify that they have network connectivity. Try pinging the printer's IP address. If you get no response, verify that the printer's network configuration is correct.

➤ *Are print jobs getting to the queue?* Using the printer's Print Queue window, verify that print jobs are actually reaching the queue. You can also see whether the print queue is paused or jobs are just sitting there waiting to be serviced.

➤ *Are the print jobs stalled in the queue?* If the print jobs are stalled in the queue, try restarting the Print Spooler service on the print server.

➤ *Does enough free disk space exist on the print server or workstation to spool the print jobs?* Verify that plenty of disk space is available for printing operations. If not enough disk space is available, move the spool folder location, which is found on the Server Properties Advanced tab.

Chapter Summary

Printing is one of the most important components in a networking environment. Everyone, from the people in the mail room to the president of the company, uses this service. Windows XP provides a robust printing architecture that supports multiple operating systems, such as Windows 2000, Windows NT 4/3.51, Windows 95/98, Windows For Workgroups, MS-DOS, Macintosh, Unix, and Novell NetWare.

The Windows XP printing process is comprised of many parts, mostly software (with the exception of the print device). The combination of these components creates a logical printer, from which users print.

The Printers and Faxes folder is the centralized hub of all printing activity in Windows XP. In this folder, printers can be added and removed, printer configurations can be modified, and print server properties can be adjusted.

Installing a printer in Windows XP is a simple process that can be accomplished in several ways. Using the Add Printer Wizard, a user is walked through the steps required to install the printer. Using Point and Print, a user simply browses to the printer via My Network Places and connects to the printer. Windows XP automatically installs the print driver. Finally, Plug and Play can install local printers upon detection.

Through the Print Queue window, print jobs can be paused, canceled, and resumed. The queue itself can also be paused or resumed, affecting all print jobs in the queue.

Printer pooling is an advanced printing feature that helps alleviate printing bottlenecks in networking environments.

Review Questions

1. Which print process component provides device-specific information to the GDI?

   a. Local print provider (Localspl.dll)

   b. Client-side spooler (Winspool.drv)

   c. Port monitor

   d. Print driver

2. For printer pooling, what do the print devices need to be or have?

   a. Identical

   b. Parallel cables

   c. HP printers

   d. PostScript

3. Where can additional print drivers be installed for other operating systems? [check all correct answers]

   a. Sharing tab in the printer's Properties dialog box

   b. Advanced Properties tab

   c. Control Panel

   d. Drivers tab in the Print Server Properties dialog box

4. Which of the following statements is correct?

   a. Internet Printing can be used with the IPX protocol.

   b. Internet Printing is not standardized.

   c. Internet Printing requires IIS on the print server.

   d. Internet Printing requires SQL Server.

5. Where is the default spooler located?

   a. %systemroot%\spooler\FILES

   b. %systemroot%\System32\spool\PRINTERS

   c. %systemroot%\System\spool\PRINTERS

   d. %systemroot%\System32\spool\JOBS

6. Windows XP does not support which of the following print job formats?

   a. PSCRIPT1

   b. RAW (AF)

   c. EMF

   d. RAW

7. If print jobs are stalled in the print queue, what can be done to get them printed?

   a. Restart the print spooler service.

   b. Redirect the print jobs to another print device.

   c. Delete the printer and re-create it.

   d. Use another print driver.

8. Which port monitor is the preferred port monitor for network printing in Windows XP?

   a. NLSP

   b. SPM

   c. SNMP

   d. TCP/IP

9. Which statement best describes the difference between a logical printer and a physical printer?

   a. A logical printer represents all software components belonging to the Windows XP printing process. The physical printer, known as a print device, is the actual hardware.

   b. A physical printer represents all software components belonging to the Windows XP printing process. The logical printer, known as a print device, is the actual hardware.

   c. Both printer types are exactly the same.

   d. A logical printer represents the components on the client side of the printing process. The physical printer represents the components on the server side of the printing process.

10. When using Windows 3.*x* or DOS clients, how many characters should the print share name use?

  a. 255

  b. 31

  c. 11

  d. 5

p.186

11. A print jam occurs in the middle of a very long document. After fixing the print jam, what command do you use to continue printing the document?

  a. Restart on the Document menu

  b. Restart on the Printer menu

  c. Resume on the Printer menu

  d. Resume on the Document menu

12. To print to an Internet printer, TCP/IP must be installed. True or False?

  a. True

  b. False

7

13. What can you do if the print server has run out of disk space?

  a. Move the spool folder to another drive with free space.

  b. Pause some print jobs to allow others to print.

  c. Restrict the number of users using the printer.

  d. Send the print jobs to another printer port.

 p.198

14. The Pause Printing command:

  a. Stops the print device from printing immediately.

  b. Stops the print queue from sending data to the print device.

  c. Stops new jobs from entering the print queue.

  d. Allows jobs in the queue to print, but pauses any new jobs.

p.194

15. You have a network with 100 Windows NT 3.51 clients. You install three Windows XP computers to the network to be used as print servers. What must you do to enable the clients to print to these servers?

  a. Install the Windows NT 3.51 print drivers on each of the print servers.

  b. Map a network drive from each client computer to the new printer servers.

  c. On each client computer, create a share name for each of the printers.

  d. On each print server, create a client account for each client with the appropriate printer permissions.

16. Your supervisor demands that his print jobs be printed before anyone else's. What must you do?

    a. On his computer, configure his logical printer's priority to 1.

    b. On all computers except his, configure the logical printers' priority to 99.

    c. On his computer, configure his logical printer's priority to 99.

    d. On all computers except his, configure the logical printers' priority to 1.

17. Where can forms be added to a print server?

    a. Advanced Properties tab in the Printer Properties.

    b. Forms cannot be added.

    c. Forms tab in the Print Server Properties dialog box.

    d. Device Settings tab in the Printer Properties.

18. To manage their own print documents, what right do users need?

    a. Manage Documents

    b. Print

    c. Manage Printers

    d. Full Control

19. All Windows XP printing requires the TCP/IP protocol. True or False?

    a. True

    b. False

20. Which tab controls auditing?

    a. Security

    b. General

    c. Advanced Properties

    d. Ports

21. If a print job is paused, what happens to other print jobs in the queue?

    a. They continue to print.

    b. They wait for the paused print job to be resumed.

    c. They are hidden in the queue.

    d. Their priority is raised.

22. The print spooler service can be stopped and started using which utility?

    a. Printers and Faxes folder

    b. Services applet

    c. Add/Remove Hardware applet

    d. Windows NT Explorer

23. What happens if the printer's port is set to FILE?

    a. The print job is sent to the spooler as a file.

    b. The print job is saved to the %systemroot% directory.

    c. The user is prompted for a file name.

    d. The user must cut and paste the file into the spooler.

24. Which components are part of the local print provider?

    a. Print router

    b. Print processor

    c. Separator page processor

    d. GDI

Real-World Projects

7

Your boss has just notified you that you will be receiving the company's first Windows XP Professional workstation. He wants you to test the printing capabilities of the new operating system.

After receiving the workstation, you attach an HP LaserJet 5000 laser printer to the computer and begin the installation process. The workstation's computer name is W2K.

Project 7.1

To install a locally attached printer:

1. Open the Printers and Faxes folder by clicking Start|Printers And Faxes.

2. In the Printers and Faxes folder, click Add Printer under Printer Tasks to start the Add Printer Wizard.

3. The Welcome screen is displayed. Click Next.

4. The Local or Network Printer screen asks if the printer to be installed is a local or network printer. Select Local Printer, and clear the Automatically Detect And Install My Plug And Play Printer checkbox. Click Next.

5. Select LPT1 as your printer port, and click Next.

6. Select the correct print driver for the print device. Select HP as the manufacturer and HP LaserJet 5000 Series PS as the model. Click Next.

7. Name the printer, and click Yes to make the printer the default printer for the workstation.

8. On the Sharing screen, select Do Not Share This Printer. Click Next.

9. Click Yes to send a test page to the print device. Click Next.

10. Click Finish to complete the installation.

After installing the printer, you need to share the printer so that other employees in the department can access it. The environment is a mix of Intel-based Windows 98 and Windows NT 4 workstations. Presently, your department uses a workgroup security structure.

Project 7.2

To share a local printer:

1. Open the Printers and Faxes folder by selecting Start|Printers And Faxes.

2. Right-click the icon for the printer, and click Sharing. The Sharing tab is displayed.

3. Select the Shared As radio button, and enter "LJ5000" as the share name.

4. Click Additional Drivers. The Additional Drivers dialog box is displayed.

5. Select both the Intel Windows 95 or 98 and the Intel Windows NT 4 drivers, and click OK. If prompted, insert the Windows XP CD-ROM.

6. Click OK to complete the operation.

You must now connect the department's workstations to the printer share you just created.

Project 7.3

To connect to a printer share:

1. Open the Printers and Faxes folder by selecting Start|Printers And Faxes.

2. In the Printers and Faxes folder, double-click the Add Printer icon to start the Add Printer Wizard.

3. The Welcome screen is displayed. Click Next.

4. This screen asks if the printer to be installed is a local or network printer. Select Network Printer. Click Next.

5. Locate a network printer. Select Type The Printer Name, or click Next to browse for a printer. Enter "\\W2K\LJ5000" and click Next.

6. Select the correct print driver for the print device. Select HP as the manufacturer and HP LaserJet 5000 Series PS as the model. Click Next.

7. Click Yes to make the printer the default printer for the workstation. Click Next.

8. Click Finish to complete the installation.

Users in your department can now start sending print jobs to the printer.

CHAPTER EIGHT

Hardware Support

After completing this chapter, you will be able to:

✓ Describe the new hardware support provided in Windows XP Professional

✓ Describe the digital media support provided in Windows XP Professional

✓ Describe the power management features of Windows XP Professional

✓ Describe the enhanced monitor support of Windows XP Professional

✓ Explain how to install and troubleshoot hardware devices in Windows XP Professional

✓ Describe driver rollback and how it is used in Windows XP Professional

✓ Describe the purpose of driver signing in Windows XP Professional

✓ Explain how to install a local printer

New Hardware Support

Windows XP Professional improves upon the hardware support that was introduced in Windows 2000. In this chapter, we look at some of the new hardware
devices that can be used with the Windows XP Professional operating system.

USB

USB support was implemented in the Windows family starting with Windows 98.
USB is an external bus that eliminates the need for installing internal cards to
attach peripheral devices. USB is totally Plug and Play compliant and devices can
be configured immediately after they are connected to the computer. No reboot of
the computer is required to use the device.

USB is supported in Windows XP Professional through the Windows Driver
Model (WDM). This model allows developers to write a single device driver that
can be used by multiple operating systems, including Windows 98, Windows 2000,
and Windows XP. USB has several advantages over standard internal adapter cards:

➤ All USB devices use the same standard type of I/O connection.

➤ Multiple USB devices can be plugged into a single USB port. USB uses a
   tiered topology, which allows for the connection of a maximum 127 devices to
   one USB bus.

➤ USB devices are hot-pluggable.

USB supports two data transfer rates. Devices that do not require a large amount of
bandwidth can run at 1.5MBps. Devices that require a higher bandwidth can
operate at speeds up to 12MBps.

Many types of USB devices are available that you can purchase and add to your
existing system. These include keyboards, mice, disk drives, CD-ROM drives, DVD
players, modems, monitors, printers, scanners, and digital cameras. Interfaces are also
available for connection to Digital Subscriber Line (DSL), Integrated Services
Digital Network (ISDN), and digital Private Branch Exchanges (PBXs). For
additional information about USB, visit **www.usb.org**.

IEEE 1394

IEEE 1394 provides a convenient and cost-effective method for connecting high-
speed consumer devices, such as scanners, VCRs, digital cameras, and DVD players.
IEEE 1394 is a serial bus that provides high-speed Plug and Play capability for
high-bandwidth devices. Both Windows ME and Windows 2000 include support
for IEEE 1394, and many PC vendors have already adopted it as a standard and are
shipping Windows-based PCs with IEEE 1394 buses.

IEEE 1394 is a peer-to-peer bus that runs independently of the system processor. USB devices cause additional demand on the system processor as each new device is added to the USB bus. This is not a problem with IEEE 1394 devices, because they don't require system processor support to run.

IEEE 1394 supports connecting up to 63 devices to one IEEE 1394 bus. Up to 1,023 buses can be interconnected to provide connectivity for over 64,000 devices. IEEE 1394a supports three bus transfers rates—100Mbps, 200Mbps, and 400Mbps. IEEE 1394b will support bus transfer rates of 800Mbps through 3,200Mbps. As with USB, IEEE 1394 supports both isochronous and asynchronous data transfer protocols and the devices are hot-pluggable.

IEEE 1394 will eventually become the industry standard for interconnecting digital devices. Manufacturers are already delivering IEEE 1394-enabled devices to consumers. Some of these devices are listed in Table 8.1.

TCP/IP networking is easier in Windows XP with IEEE 1394. Users can connect their computers to a TCP/IP network via the IEEE 1394 bus with no additional hardware or device driver requirements. Internet Connection Sharing (ICS) is also supported on these connections.

In addition to TCP/IP networking capability, additional capabilities over those available in Windows ME and 2000 have been implemented in Windows XP with IEEE 1394. These include:

> Support for high-end audio and video devices

> Support for MPEG-2 streams for digital video systems and satellite transmission

> Driver support for legacy devices not IEEE 1394-compliant

> Resource management of digital video applications to ensure guaranteed bandwidth

> Connection management

Table 8.1   IEEE 1394-enabled devices.

End User Electronics	Computers and Peripherals
Audio equipment	Telephony adapters
Digital cameras, TVs, and VCRs	Cable modems
Digital satellite receivers	CD-ROM drives, DVD-ROM drives
DVD players	Network interface adapters
Speakers	Personal computers
TV tuners	Printers
Video cameras	Scanners

➤ Support for the creation of virtual devices

➤ The ability to bridge TCP/IP to a wireless IEEE 802.11b network or a standard Ethernet network

HID Support

As with Windows 98 and Windows 2000, Windows XP Professional provides support for Human Interface Devices (HIDs). The HID specification is a standard for a variety of input devices, including keyboards, mice, pointing devices, joysticks, and game pads. These devices can be plugged into the computer system via USB ports, and used immediately.

Currently HID controls have been defined for the following devices:

➤ Simulation devices

➤ Virtual reality devices

➤ Sport-equipment devices

➤ Consumer appliance devices

➤ Advanced game controllers

HID devices can also be connected to the computer via ports other than USB ports such as the IEEE 1394 bus.

UPnP

When Plug and Play (PnP) was introduced in Windows, it made setting up and configuring computer devices easier for end users. A user could attach a PnP-compatible device, such as a printer, and the computer system would automatically detect the device and install the appropriate device drivers for it. Windows XP improves on PnP with the introduction of Universal Plug and Play (UPnP). UPnP detects not only local peripheral devices, but also network-wide attached devices.

UPnP is designed for zero configuration. Devices that are attached to the network can dynamically join the network, automatically obtain an IP address, identify their capabilities to the network, and detect other devices on the network.

UPnP is an open network architecture that provides vendors the capability to create APIs to suite their particular needs. UPnP uses the standard TCP/IP and Internet protocols. Devices can be attached to the network with just about any type of communications media, including wireless, phone lines, IrDA, Ethernet, and IEEE 1394. UPnP provides true peer-to-peer networking connectivity.

The following lists some of the protocols that are used to implement UPnP:

➤ *TCP/IP*—The TCP/IP protocol stack is the basis on which the other UPnP protocols are built. Several protocols in this stack can be used by UPnP devices, including TCP, UDP, ICMP, ARP, and IP.

➤ *HTTP, HTTPU, and HTTPMU*—HTTP is a core component of UPnP for Internet access. HTTPU and HTTPMU are variations of HTTP that are used by SSDP.

➤ *Simple Service Discovery Protocol (SSDP)*—Built on HTTPU and HTTPMU and defines how network services are discovered on the network.

➤ *Generic Event Notification Architecture (GENA)*—Used to provide the ability to send and receive UPnP event notifications.

➤ *Simple Object Access Protocol (SOAP)*—Is becoming the standard for communicating over the Internet and defines the use of XML and HTTP for executing remote procedure calls.

➤ *Extensible Markup Language (XML)*—Is replacing HTTP as the universal format for data on the Web.

Certain steps are involved when a new UPnP device is added to the network:

1. Addressing. The device must be assigned an IP address before it can be recognized on the network. This can be obtained from a DHCP server. If no DHCP server is available, the device uses Auto IP to obtain an IP address.

2. Discovery. After the device obtains an IP address, it advertises its services to a control point on the network. This step is handled by SSDP.

3. Description. The control point retrieves the device's description from the URL provided by the device.

4. Control. After the control point has the device's description, which includes a list of commands for the device, the control point attempts to take control of the device by sending an action request in XML format to the device's service.

5. Eventing. The description of the device contains a list of actions that the service will respond to. The service updates this list by sending event messages.

6. Presentation. The control point loads the URL for the device into a browser, and the user can control and view status information on the device.

For additional information on UPnP, check the Universal Plug and Play Forum at **www.upnp.org**.

8

IrDA

IrDA is a protocol that supports data transmission over point-to-point infrared devices at speeds of between 9.6Kbps and 4Mbps. This data transmission occurs over the infrared port, which is the small semitransparent red window that is located on a notebook computer. Windows CE was the first Windows operating system to provide built-in IrDA support. Subsequently, this capability was included with Windows 98, Windows ME, Windows 2000, and Windows XP.

IrDA consists of a set of mandatory protocols and a few optional protocols. The mandatory protocols are Physical IrDA Data Signaling, IrDA Link Access Protocol (IrLAP), and IrDA Link Management Protocol (IrLMP). The optional protocols include Tiny TP, IrCOMM, IrNET, and IrTran-P.

In Windows XP, the IrDA protocol has been enhanced to provide infrared-enabled devices with the capability to connect to the Internet or a network through a dial-up network profile or a LAN access networking profile.

In normal dial-up networking, the computer uses a modem to connect to the network. With dial-up networking over IrDA, the computer uses a cellular phone as the modem. The user places the infrared-enabled cellular phone next to the infrared port on the computer and creates the connection via the built-in modem. IrCOMM is the protocol used to provide this capability.

LAN access networking is provided over IrDA through the IrNET protocol and PPP. This connectivity can be between two computers (peer-to-peer) or between one computer and a network access point. An IrNET connection can only be made between Windows XP and Windows 2000 computers. Windows 98 and Windows ME do not support the IrNET protocol.

IrCOMM

IrCOMM is a family of protocols that run over IrDA. IrCOMM emulates RS-232 serial ports. The IrCOMM driver works on top of your existing Windows XP driver and adds a new virtual COM port to access your infrared adapter.

IrCOMM provides four service types or classes—3-Wire raw, 3-Wire, 9-Wire, and Centronics. The Windows XP implementation of IrCOMM supports the IrDA 9-Wire specification, allowing control-line information to be sent over the infrared link. IrCOMM is intended for legacy applications—applications that know about serial or parallel ports but know nothing about IrDA protocols.

Captured Still Images Support—Windows Image Acquisition (WIA)

Windows Image Acquisition (WIA) provides support for devices that capture still images, such as scanners and digital cameras. WIA is based on the Microsoft Still

Image Architecture that was introduced in Windows 98. Programs such as Microsoft Picture It use WIA to communicate with these devices.

Microsoft has attempted to make it easier for users in Windows XP by adding extensions to the Windows Explorer interface for interacting with WIA devices. When a user installs a device such as a digital camera, an icon is automatically added to My Computer. Users can interact with the camera or pictures on the camera from this icon (see Figure 8.1).

The Scanners and Cameras folder in the Control Panel is used to install and configure WIA devices, such as flatbed scanners, handheld scanners, and digital cameras. The Scanner and Camera Wizard is used to retrieve and manipulate images from supported devices. The wizard presents the user with specific options depending on the type of device being accessed. If the user is accessing a scanner, he can scan, zoom, adjust settings such as Brightness and Contrast, and select the image type (see Figure 8.2). If the user is accessing a still digital camera, she can select pictures, rotate them, and view specific information on each picture. From the wizard, users can name and save the images to the My Pictures folder or another folder of their choice.

WIA supports Plug and Play for USB, SCSI, and IEEE 1394 buses.

Microsoft has added several features to enhance end user usage of WIA devices. The My Pictures folder, which was initially introduced in Windows 2000, is linked to automatically launch the Scanner and Camera Wizard if a WIA device is installed

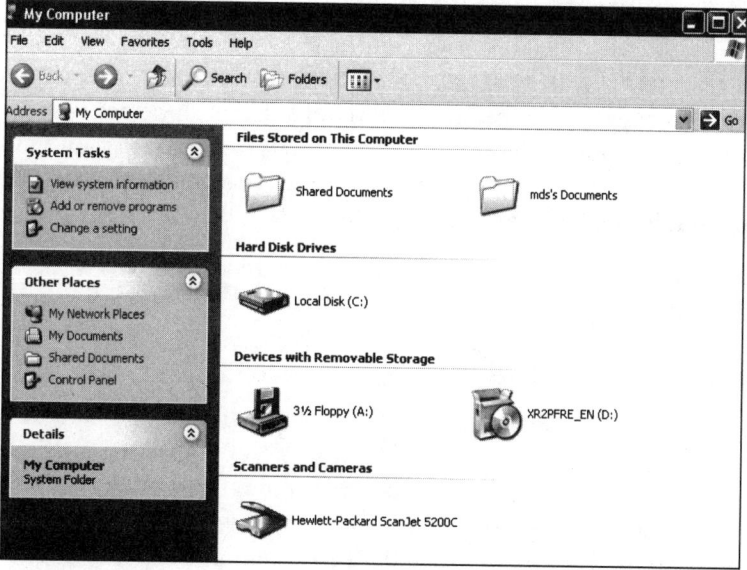

Figure 8.1 Scanner listed in My Computer.

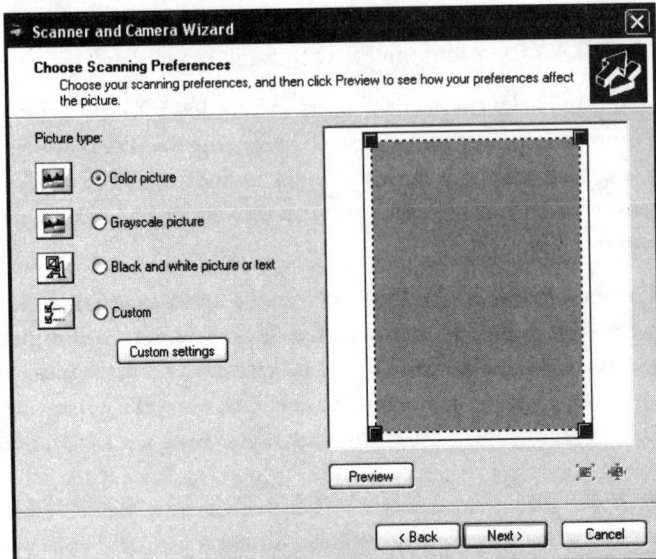

Figure 8.2   The Scanner and Camera Wizard.

on a computer. A slideshow applet has been added so that users can create slideshows from their pictures. The preview window allows pictures to be rotated and more file types have been included for viewing. Users can actually print their pictures from the preview window.

Users can enjoy their pictures via their desktop by saving them as a screensaver. The My Picture Screensaver enables users to create their own screensaver with transitions and password protection.

Microsoft Paint has been enhanced to support WIA. If a WIA device is enabled on the computer, a menu item—From Scanner Or Camera—is enabled on the Microsoft Paint File menu. Users can easily retrieve pictures directly from the device through this menu option (see Figure 8.3).

For additional information about Windows Image Acquisition, visit **www.microsoft. com/hwdev/wia**.

Windows XP 64-bit Edition

Windows XP is the first operating system from Microsoft that will support the new Intel Itanium processor family. This new 64-bit version of Windows is designed to provide support for users who have more demanding computing needs. Windows XP 64-bit Edition is for users who have exceeded the capabilities of the 32-bit version and need advanced scalability, large memory support, and the increased floating-point performance that can be provided by the Itanium family of processors.

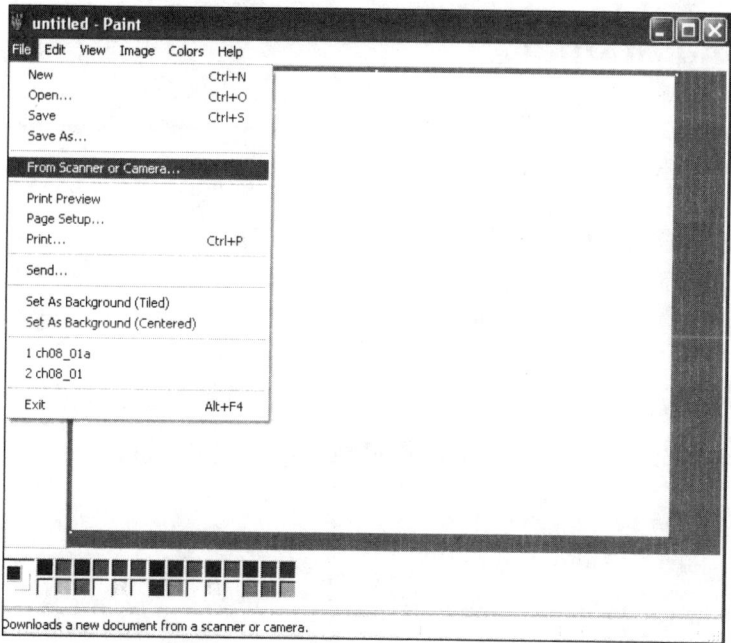

Figure 8.3   The From Scanner Or Camera menu option in Microsoft Paint.

The current 32-bit version of Windows XP supports up to 4GB of memory. Windows XP 64-bit Edition will support up to 16GB of memory. In theory, it is capable of supporting up to 16TB of RAM. It also is capable of supporting up to two symmetric Intel Itanium processors for maximum scalability and performance.

The 64-bit edition of Windows XP requires a 64-bit motherboard and chipset from Intel or one of the original equipment manufacturers (OEMs) that will be supporting it. Table 8.2 lists the requirements for using Windows XP 64-bit Edition.

The same features that are supported in the 32-bit version of Windows XP will be supported by the 64-bit version, including security, multimedia, directory service, and Plug and Play. Although the 64-bit hardware will work with 32-bit applications, users will find that their 32-bit applications will perform better on 32-bit hardware. Unless they have a need for memory support over 2GB, users might find it more beneficial to stay in the Windows XP 32-bit environment.

Table 8.2   System requirements for Windows XP 64-bit Edition.

Device	Mimimum	Recommended
Memory	1GB RAM	1GB RAM
Processor	733MHz Intel Itanium	800MHz Intel Itanium
Video	VGA	3-D graphics

Digital Media Support

Windows XP Professional improves on the previous versions of Windows with additional support for digital audio and video devices. As with Windows 2000, the Windows Driver Model (WDM) is the basis for this support.

Windows Media Player 8

Windows XP Professional includes Windows Media Player 8 (see Figure 8.4). WMP 8 provides many multimedia functions in one tool. With WMP 8, users can do the following:

➤ Play and copy CDs

➤ View information about CDs from the Internet

➤ Play DVDs

➤ Listen to Internet radio stations

➤ Copy audio and video files to portable devices

➤ Search for media files on the Internet

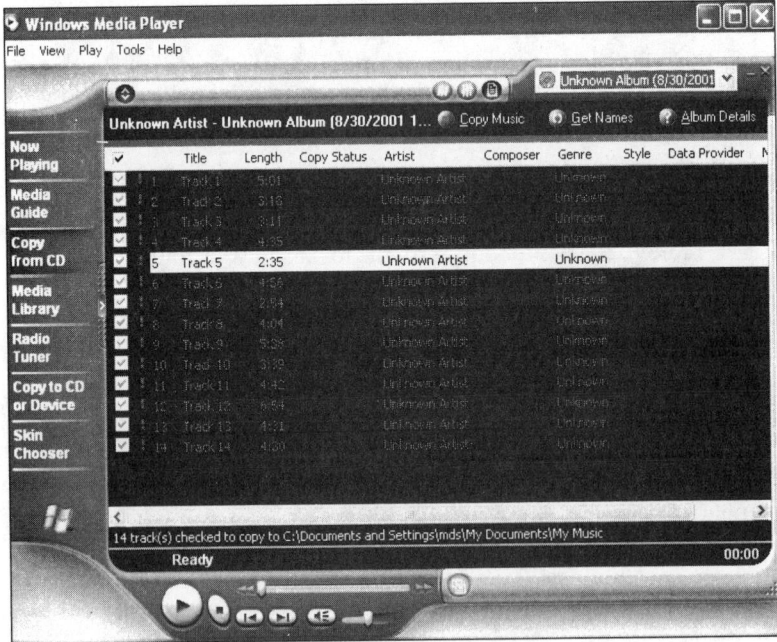

Figure 8.4 Windows Media Player 8.

Windows Movie Maker

Windows Movie Maker provides video capture and file creation and simple editing of audio and video files. Movie Maker can import all file formats and compression types that are supported by DirectShow, but it can only produce output in the Windows Media format.

Digital Photo Support

Digital photography is easier with Windows XP Professional. Users can shoot pictures with their digital cameras and immediately use the photos. Windows XP is compatible with a large number of the latest digital cameras currently on the market. If the camera has a USB connection, a user can plug it into the computer, and a wizard will walk him through the steps for obtaining the pictures from the camera.

Photos are saved by default in the My Pictures folder. When photos are transferred from the digital camera, Windows XP creates a new subfolder within the My Pictures folder in which to store them. If you have a network or Internet connection, the photos can be saved to the network or published directly on the Web.

Photos can be sent via email, printed to a local printer, or stored on a CD. You can even send photos via email to a Web-based photo-processing service, which can print the photos on paper and mail them back to you or a party of your choice.

Digital Rights Management

Support is provided to allow artists and record companies to protect their music or data through Digital Rights Management. Digital Rights Management enables creators and distributors of music or other digital content to encrypt their property and assign rules regarding how it can be used. These rules can be used to determine such things as how the content can be played, the types of devices it can be played on, and the number of times that it can be played. Windows XP can be used to ensure that users don't circumvent the rules that were assigned by the creator of the content.

CD Burning

Windows XP Professional enables users to master or burn CDs in the CD-R and CD-RW formats. Users can create CDs by using the drag and drop functionality of Windows or the CD Writing Wizard (see Figure 8.5). When creating CDs, Windows XP first premasters the CD image to the local hard drive. It then streams the data to the CD burner for recording. Users can create a complete copy of a CD or use the conventional copy-and-paste or drag-and-drop methods to copy individual sound files from the music library to the CD.

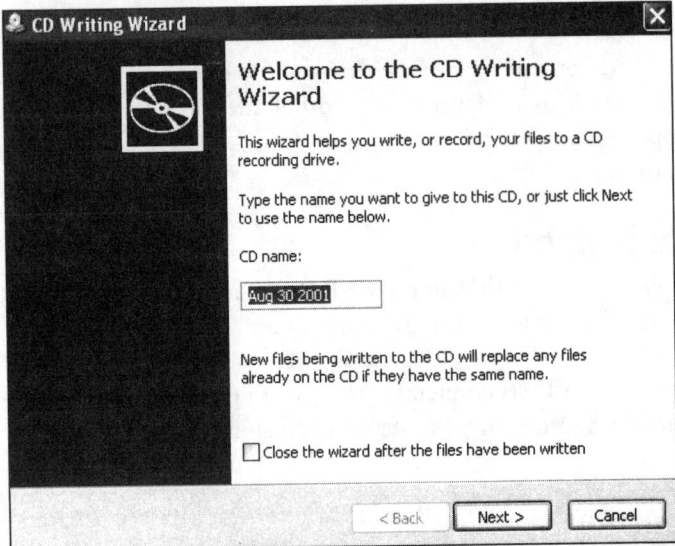

Figure 8.5 The CD Writing Wizard.

Windows XP Professional supports the Redbook audio, and data disk format uses the Juliet and IOS 9660 file system. All Microsoft operating systems and portable MP3 players can read CDs created using these formats.

Windows Media Player 8 can also be used to copy audio files. When recording CDs, Windows XP uses the *track-at-once* method. With track-at-once, when files are copied to the CD, they cannot be deleted or modified. This is true even if they are recorded on CD-RW discs. However, if you want to reuse the discs, they can be completely erased and reused. Windows Media Player copies CDs using the Redbook format, which can be read by any standard CD player.

DVD

Windows 2000 introduced support for digital video discs (DVDs). DVD technology is currently supported for movie playback and storage as well as writeable devices. The DVD file system is based on the Universal Disk Format (UDF), which is the successor to the CD-ROM File System (CDFS). Windows XP Professional supports DVD in the following formats:

➤ *DVD-RAM*—A DVD disc that supports multiple recording capabilities, such as those with magneto-optical (MO) discs. DVD-RAM also requires third-party software to operate with Windows XP Professional.

➤ *DVD-ROM*—A DVD disc that contains data that can be read by a DVD-ROM drive. A DVD-ROM can have up to 17GB of data storage space.

➤ *DVD-Video*—A DVD disc that contains full-length motion pictures. The pictures can be played on a computer's DVD-ROM drive or on a home DVD-video player.

➤ *DVD-WO*—A DVD disc that is similar to CD-recordable discs insofar as it supports one-time recording of data to the disc. A DVD-WO requires third-party software to operate with Windows XP Professional.

A DVD drive and decoder are needed on your computer to use DVD-video. The decoder can be a hardware decoder card, a software decoder card, or a combination of both. Windows Media Player 8 can be used to view DVDs in Windows XP Professional.

Windows XP improves on the DVD that was introduced in Windows 2000 by including native read and write support for DVD-RAM drives. Windows XP Professional has support for FAT32 on DVD-RAM. If your computer is running the FAT32 file system, you can mount and format FAT32 on the DVD-RAM disk in a super-floppy format. This DVD can be used in any common media drive.

DirectX

8

Windows XP Professional has support for DirectX 8. DirectX is an interface between programs and the computer's sound and video adapters that enhances the multimedia capabilities of the computer. Applications that are written for DirectX don't have to be concerned with what sound or graphics adapter is in the computer. DirectX takes care of determining the hardware capabilities of the computer and sets the parameters of the program to match them.

DirectX is involved in many aspects of providing multimedia capabilities for the computer, including 3-D rendering, video playback, audio effects, still and motion capture, and networking for multiplayer games. DirectX 8 is comprised of the following components:

➤ *Direct3D*—Provides access to the 3-D rendering functions built into the video adapter.

➤ *DirectDraw*—Provides fast access to the video adapter. It provides a way for programs to gain access to the advanced features of the video device without the need for additional information from the user on the device's capability.

➤ *DirectInput*—Provides input for programs that use joysticks, keyboards, and force-feedback game controllers.

➤ *DirectMusic*—Works with digital audio and supports input in the Musical Instrument Digital Interface (MIDI) format in both compressed and uncompressed audio formats.

➤ *DirectPlay*—Supports game connectivity over the Internet, a LAN, or a modem.

➤ *DirectShow*—Provides high-quality capture and playback of multimedia files. It supports the following formats: Advanced Streaming Format (ASF), Audio-Video Interleaved (AVI), Digital Video (DV), Motion Picture Experts Group (MPEG), MPEG Audio Layer 3 (MP3), and WAV files.

➤ *DirectSound*—Provides access to the audio adapter's sound mixing, playback, and capture capabilities.

DirectX 8 can be downloaded from **www.microsoft.com/directx**.

Note: DirectX 8 will overwrite any earlier version of DirectX that is on the computer system. Also, DirectX 8 cannot be uninstalled. It is a system component, and if you want to remove it from your computer system, you have to do a complete reinstall of the Windows XP Professional operating system.

The DirectX Diagnostic Tool (Dxdiag.exe) is installed directly from DirectX and can be used to diagnose problems and test the functionality of DirectX.

Power Management

As with Windows 2000, Windows XP provides power management for both desktop and mobile computers. Windows XP power management is based on the ACPI specification. Computer systems that are designed using this specification allow the operating system to manage and coordinate power needs for the system.

The Application Configuration and Power Interface (ACPI) specification is based on the OnNow initiative. This is a design initiative that specifies that the computer is available immediately from a low-power state, much like the instant-on capabilities that exist now with TVs and VCRs. To use power management in Windows XP, the computer BIOS must support ACPI.

ACPI-compliant computers coordinate the power requirements for the system. Power is directed to those peripherals as they need it. Devices such as hard drives can be put in a low-power state when they are not being accessed. Windows XP has several power management features, including:

➤ Improved startup and shutdown performance

➤ Improved power efficiency

➤ Wake-on support

➤ Processor power control

➤ Power management for individual devices

➤ Power management for applications

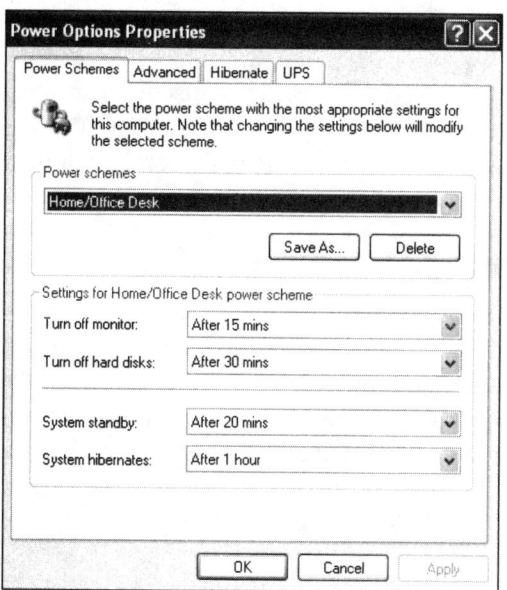

Figure 8.6 The Power Options Properties tool in the Control Panel.

8

Windows XP provides users the ability to manage power consumption by the computer through the Power Options Properties tool in the Control Panel (see Figure 8.6). There are several predefined power schemes that a user can choose from. If none of the power schemes provided in Windows XP Professional meet their specific needs, users can create their own schemes through the Power Options Properties tool.

Enhanced Monitor Support

Multiple-monitor support has been available since Windows 98. Windows 2000 Professional provided support for the connection of up to 10 monitors. Users could create a desktop that displayed a single large document or spreadsheet across multiple monitors. When the computer is configured in a multiple-monitor configuration, one monitor always acts as the primary display and holds the Windows Logon dialog box. Windows XP Professional has improved on multiple-monitor support with the addition of Dualview.

Dualview is like the multiple-monitor support that was provided in Windows 2000 Professional with one exception—the video adapter can be configured to display different outputs at the same time. Many high-end video adapters support the connection of two or more monitors to the same interface. With Dualview, users can display one document on the first video output port and a different document on each subsequent video output port.

The Display tool in Control Panel is used to configure the computer for multiple-monitor support. To use multiple monitors, the computer must have a Peripheral Component Interconnect (PCI) or Accelerated Graphics Port (AGP) adapter. The monitor must have the capability to run in GUI mode and must have the appropriate Windows XP Professional drivers that will enable it as a secondary display.

Installing Hardware Devices

Windows XP Professional supports many types of hardware devices. A hardware device is any physical device that is attached to the computer. This can be a device that was installed when the computer was originally manufactured or peripherals that were added by the user after purchase. When working with any computer system, it is important to know how to install and troubleshoot internal and external hardware components.

Plug and Play Devices

Plug and Play devices are the easiest to install in Windows XP Professional. Plug and Play was introduced in Windows 98 and has been improved on with each subsequent release of Windows. When a Plug and Play device is connected to the computer, Windows XP will automatically detect the device. It will install the necessary drivers for the device and update the system with this new configuration.

If Windows XP does not automatically detect a Plug and Play device, the user will have to use the Add Hardware Wizard to manually install and configure it (see Figure 8.7). Normally, Windows XP will detect Plug and Play devices that are

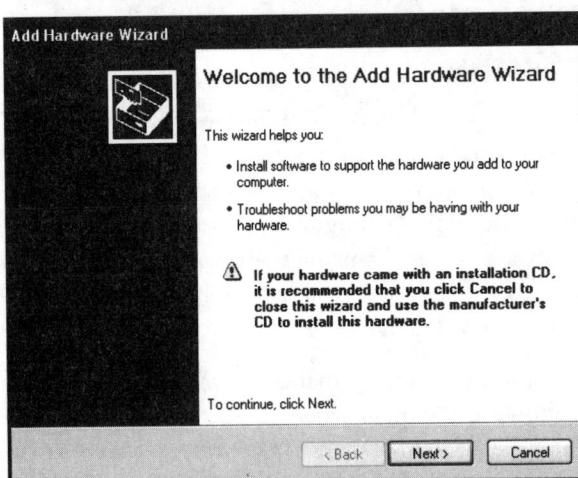

Figure 8.7　The Add Hardware Wizard.

connected to a system via USB, IEEE 1394, and SCSI buses. For PCI and ISA Plug and Play devices, the user will have to shut down the computer, install the adapter, and restart the computer. The operating system should detect the device and start the installation procedure.

When Plug and Play devices are installed, the operating system assigns the appropriate system resource for the specific channels and addresses needed for the device to operate. Users must be members of the Administrators group to install Plug and Play devices.

Non-Plug and Play Devices

Non-Plug and Play devices are not automatically detected by the operating system. They must be manually configured before Windows XP can use them. To install a non-Plug and Play device, you first must be a member of the Administrators group. After you have the device connected to the computer, use the Add Hardware Wizard to identify the type of hardware you are installing (see Figure 8.8). Install the Windows XP Professional CD or the CD or disk provided by the hardware manufacturer to load the appropriate device drivers. Following the installation of the device drivers, Windows XP should configure the devices for use with the system.

When installing a non-Plug and Play device, the setup program provided with the device might try to use specific resources that the device needs to communicate with Windows XP Professional. If these resources are already being used by another device in the computer, you might have to manually configure resources for the device by using Device Manager.

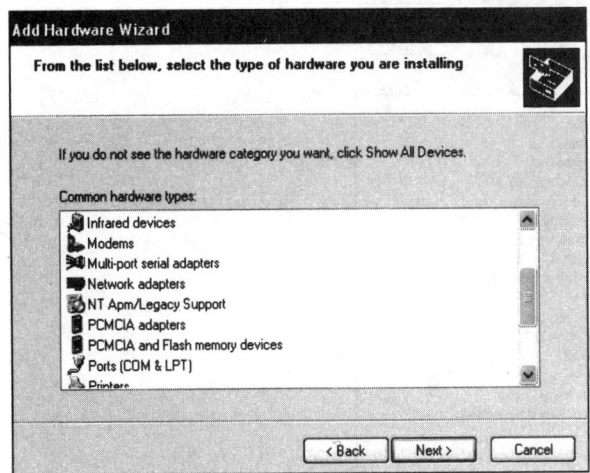

Figure 8.8 Hardware types in the Device Manager.

Device Manager

Device Manager is the tool used to manage devices in Windows XP Professional. Device Manager can be used to view properties of devices, enable and disable devices, see a list of devices that are installed on the computer, troubleshoot devices, and update device drivers (see Figure 8.9). To access Device Manager:

1. Right-click My Computer.

2. Click Manage.

3. Click Device Manager under System Tools.

Device Manager shows a list of the active devices that are installed on the computer. This list is called the *device tree*. The device tree is created in RAM every time the computer is started or when a dynamic change is made to the system. This information is based on configuration information stored in the Registry.

Each branch in the tree is called a *device node*. If you double-click the device node, you will be presented with a list of devices installed under that node. Bus devices are also listed in Device Manager.

Before the advent of Plug and Play, system resources had to be manually configured on the computer for each device so that they didn't conflict with other devices. System resources include the input/output (I/O) port addresses, the interrupt request lines (IRQs), direct memory access (DMA), and reserved memory. With Plug and Plug devices, system resources are automatically determined and configured by the operating system. If you are installing non-Plug and Play devices, you

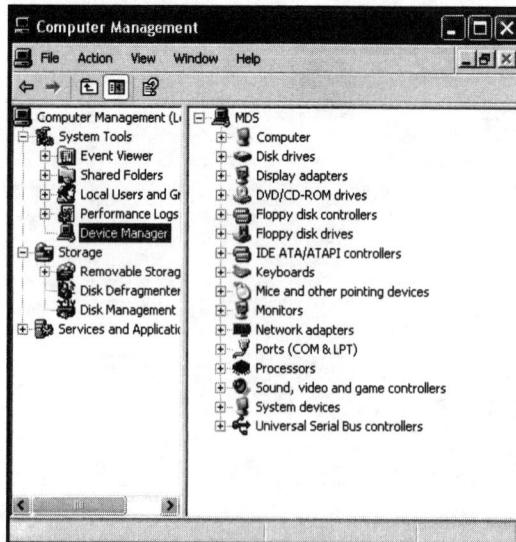

Figure 8.9 Device Manager.

might have to configure the system resources for the device in Device Manager. You can view the system resources for your computer by selecting View | Resources By Type.

Device Manager can be used to print system reports. Select Action | Print to print a system summary, an output of selected devices, or a complete report of all devices and the system summary. This report can also be printed to a file for later viewing if a printer is unavailable.

Hidden Devices

By default, some devices are not shown in Device Manager. Devices that have been removed from the computer are hidden in Device Manager. Even though these devices are no longer attached to the computer, the device drivers for the devices might still be on the computer. Also, non-Plug and Play devices are hidden from user view. These devices are known as nonpresent devices. Users can configure Device Manager so that they can view these nonpresent devices by selecting View | Show Hidden Devices.

8

Updating Device Drivers

Devices drivers are required by all hardware devices attached to a computer. A device driver tells the operating system how to communicate with the device. Device drivers are supplied by the manufacturer of the hardware device. Normally, these drivers are installed with little or no intervention from the user.

Periodically, manufacturers update device drivers to correct problems or bugs that have been discovered with the device or to enhance the functionality of the device. Device drivers can be updated in Windows XP Professional from the Microsoft Windows Update Web site. When a user accesses the Update Web site, drivers on the user's computer are compared with drivers on the Update site. If newer drivers are found on the site, they are downloaded to the user's computer and installed automatically. The Update Driver button on the Driver tab of the Properties dialog box of the device is used to connect to the Windows Update Web site (see Figure 8.10).

Device drivers that are provided from the Windows Update Web site are assigned a unique, four-part identification number. This number is called the hardware ID and ensures that the drivers are of the highest quality and reliability. When a user connects to the Web site to update her device drivers, the hardware ID of both device drivers is compared. All Windows XP Professional device drivers are stored in a single file called Driver.cab. If a newer version exists on the Web site, the CAB file is downloaded and installed.

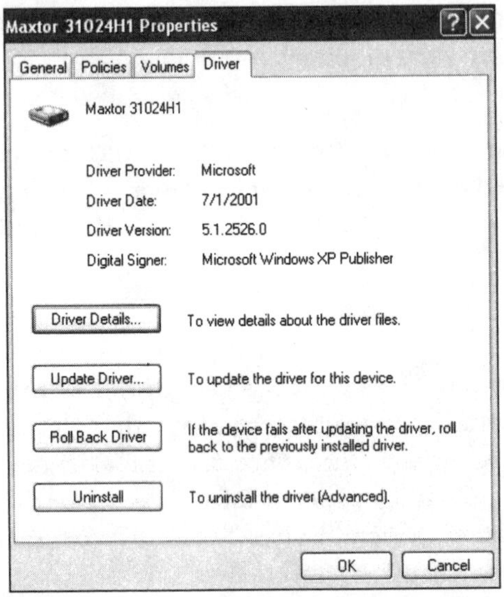

Figure 8.10 Properties dialog box for a hardware device.

Driver Rollback

What happens if you install a new device driver and the device stops responding or locks the computer? In previous versions of Windows, you would have to try to uninstall the current device driver and reinstall the previous device driver, if you had it. Windows XP Professional introduces a new system recovery tool call Driver Rollback that will allow users to reinstall the last-known functioning device driver for a device.

You could roll back to the previous version of the device driver by clicking Roll Back Driver on the Driver tab in the device's Properties dialog box (refer to Figure 8.10). By default, Windows XP Professional backs up all original driver files on the computer the first time a user updates an existing driver. The following are the original driver files:

➤ *.sys*—The system configuration file

➤ *.inf*—The information file for the device

These files are stored in the %systemroot%\system32\reinstallbackups subdirectory on the local hard drive. If no backup driver exists for a device driver that you are trying to roll back, Windows XP Professional will state that rollback is not available for that device driver.

Note: Printer drivers cannot be rolled back. They are configured through Printers and Faxes, and only device drivers that are configured through Device Manager can be rolled back with Driver Rollback.

Changing Resource Settings

If you use Plug and Play devices in your computer system, you should never have to manually configure system resource settings. Plug and Play devices do not have default resource settings assigned to them. Windows XP Professional identifies the devices that are currently installed in a system and allocates system resources to newly installed Plug and Play devices as needed. Non-Plug and Play or legacy devices might be configured to use a specific system resource, such as an IRQ that might conflict with one that has been assigned by the operating system to another device. You might have to manually configure the device so that it works properly with your computer system.

Administrators can manually change system resource settings using Device Manager or Registry Editor. Device Manager is the tool of choice for configuring resource settings. Before you make any type of device configuration change, make sure that you back up the System State Data on your computer so that you can restore it to the original settings if needed. You should change resource settings only if absolutely necessary. Changing the wrong settings can cause the system to function improperly or not at all. If you must make changes to system resource settings, follow these steps:

1. Open My Computer.

2. Select Manage.

3. Select Device Manager.

4. Right-click the device that you want to change the resource setting for, and click Properties.

5. Select the Resource tab.

6. Uncheck Use Automatic Settings.

7. Click the Change Settings button.

8. Change the conflicting resource, and click OK.

9. Restart Windows XP Professional.

Driver Signing

Starting with Windows 2000, Microsoft started digitally signing system files and device drivers. Drivers that have been digitally signed have been tested and verified for running on the Windows XP Professional operating systems. Drivers that have been signed have passed compatibility tests administered by the Windows Hardware Quality Lab.

All drivers on the Windows XP Professional CD and from the Windows Update Web site are digitally signed. This is a requirement from Microsoft. When a device driver is digitally signed, cryptographic information is stored in a catalog, or CAT, file. A CAT file is created for every driver that has a digital signature from Microsoft. The information in a CAT file identifies that the driver has been tested and verified by the Windows Hardware Quality Lab. No change is actually made to the binary device driver file. The CAT file is referenced in the driver's INF file.

As with Windows 2000, Windows XP can be configured to notify a user if a program attempts to install an unsigned driver. Several options are available that can be configured if an application or user attempts to install unsigned drivers. The operating system can be configured to install all device drivers regardless of whether they have been digitally signed. It can be configured to display a warning message indicating that the driver is not digitally signed. It can also be configured to block all drivers from being installed that have not been digitally signed. Figure 8.11 shows the Driver Signing Options dialog box used to select the type of file signature verification.

Note: The default setting for file signature verification is Warn.

Windows XP Professional includes a tool that can be used to verify the digital signatures of files. The File Signature Verification tool is a command-line tool that scans a computer system and identifies signed and unsigned files. The tool is started by typing "sigverif" from a command line or from the Run command on the Start menu (see Figure 8.12). A log file named Sigverif.txt records information about files that were scanned. It is located in the %systemroot% folder and contains the filename, the modification date, the version number of the file, the signed status, and the file location.

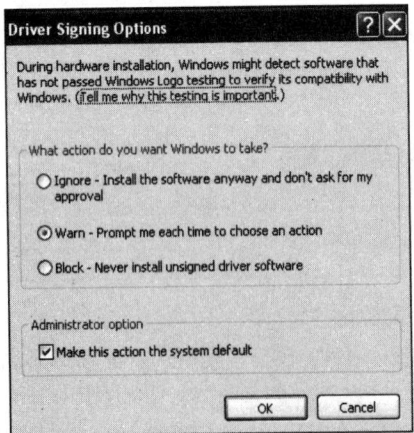

Figure 8.11 Driver Signing Options dialog box.

Figure 8.12   The File Signature Verification tool.

Surprise Removal of Devices

A surprise removal occurs when a device is removed from a computer before it is stopped. This is called surprise removal because it is an unexpected event to the operating system. Windows XP is better able to handle surprise removal of devices than previous versions of Windows. Surprise removal of a device in Windows 95 and Windows 98 could cause damage to both the operating system and the computer hardware. Manufacturers took steps when developing hardware for Windows XP to reduce damage to devices and the computer when surprise removal of devices occurrs.

The surprise removal of a device from a computer can cause the system to become unstable. The system might stop responding to the device or it might even lock up and have to be rebooted. Plug and Play devices are detected and configured automatically by Windows XP Professional. These devices have been designed for surprise removal from the system without system interruption. The types of Plug and Play devices that support surprise removal include all USB devices, IEEE 1394 devices, PC cards, and CardBus devices.

In previous versions of Windows, a surprise removal of a device resulted in a Surprise Removal pop-up message, reminding users that they should stop the device before removing it (see Figure 8.13). This pop-up message has been removed in Windows XP. Even though certain devices are designed for surprise removal with no effect on the operations of the computer, you should notify the operating system before you remove or unplug a device. In the notification area of the Taskbar is an icon called Safe Removal. This icon can be used to safely remove a Plug and Play device. When you want to remove a Plug and Play device, right-click the Safe Removal icon, and select the device you want to remove.

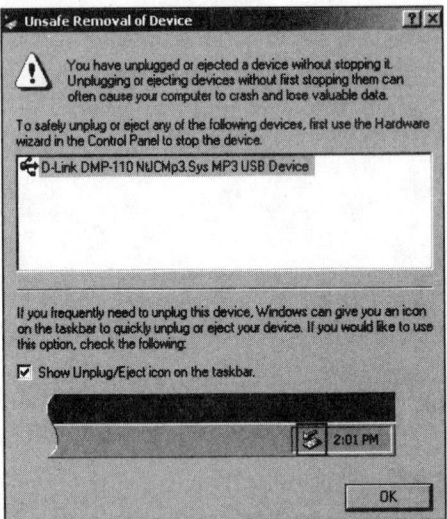

Figure 8.13 Surprise removal warning message.

Installing a Local Printer

Installing a local printer is a relatively simple procedure. If the printer is Plug and Play compliant, plug your printer into the computer and the installation process will start automatically. Windows XP Professional will install the appropriate print drivers. A reboot of the computer is not required when installing a Plug and Play printer.

If the printer is not Plug and Play compliant, or for some reason the installation of a Plug and Play printer fails, you will have to use the Add Printer Wizard to install the printer. To access the Add Printer Wizard, select Start|Printers And Faxes and double-click Add A Printer (see Figure 8.14). You can also access the Add Printer Wizard through the Control Panel. Only local printers can be installed using Plug and Play. If you have a network printer that you want installed, you must use the Add Printer Wizard. Network printers cannot be installed using Plug and Play.

Windows XP Professional automatically detects printers that connect to the computer via USB ports. Printers that are connected via a serial or parallel port require installation using the Add Printer Wizard. If you need to install updated print drivers on your computer, you must be logged on as an administrator or be a member of the Administrators group. Print drivers are installed from the Properties dialog box of the printer. This is accessed through Printers and Faxes. If you have problems when you try to install a new or updated print driver, you cannot use Driver Rollback to return to the previous print driver. Driver Rollback can only be performed on devices that are installed through the Device Manager. All printers are installed through Printers and Faxes.

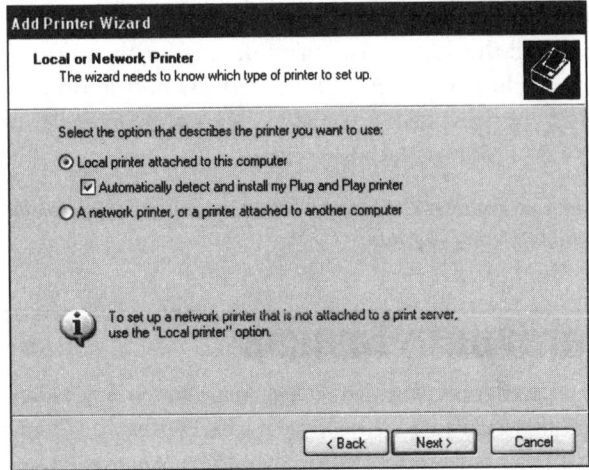

Figure 8.14   The Add Printer Wizard.

A local printer on your computer can be shared so that others on the network can access it (see Figure 8.15). To share a local printer, follow these steps:

1. Open Printers and Faxes.

2. Right-click the printer you want to share.

3. Select the Sharing tab.

4. Click Share This Printer, and enter a name for the shared printer.

5. Click OK.

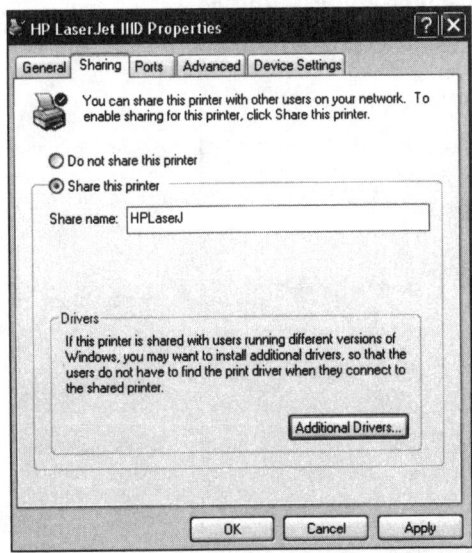

Figure 8.15   The Sharing tab in a printer's Properties dialog box.

If your shared printer is going to be accessed by operating systems other than Windows XP, you need to install the appropriate print drivers for the other operating systems. You can do this by clicking the Additional Drivers button on the Sharing tab in the printer's Properties dialog box. You can install printer drivers for the Windows 95/98/ME/NT 4/2000 operating sytems.

Note: Keep in mind that when users are accessing your printer, you will notice a degradation in your system performance while they are printing.

Troubleshooting Hardware Devices

The most common cause of problems found with using hardware devices in Windows XP results from using hardware that is not on the Hardware Compatibility List (HCL). The first step that you should take to avoid hardware problems is to only use devices that are on the latest HCL.

Device Manager can be used to view information about devices and as an aid in troubleshooting device problems. Users can access the Properties dialog box for devices from Device Manager. From this dialog box, users can view the status of each inidividual device and see whether any conflicts exists between the device in question and other devices in the computer. They can update device drivers or roll back drivers if updating device drivers was unsuccessful. As with Windows 2000, a troubleshooter is provided to help resolve device problems (see Figure 8.16).

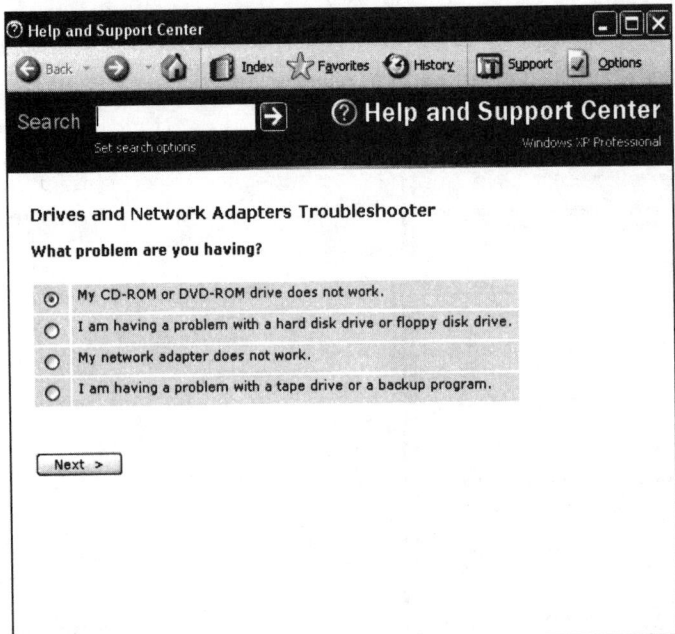

Figure 8.16   Help and Support Center troubleshooter.

Diagnostic Boot Options

If Windows XP Professional does not boot properly, users have several boot options to aid them in troubleshooting:

➤ *Debugging Mode*—Starts Windows XP Professional and sends debugging information through a serial port to another computer.

➤ *Enable Boot Logging*—Windows XP professional is started normally, but all drivers and services are logged in systemroot\ntbtlog.txt.

➤ *Enable VGA Mode*—Windows XP Professional is started with the basic VGA driver.

➤ *Last Known Good Configuration*—Starts Windows XP Professional with the last-known good configuration, which the operating system saved before its most recent shutdown. Registry settings are restored to the state the operating system was in before its last shutdown.

➤ *Safe Mode*—Windows XP Professional is started with the minimum number of files and drivers.

➤ *Safe Mode with Command Prompt*—Starts Windows XP Professional with the minimal files and drivers, and it boots to a command prompt.

➤ *Safe Mode with Networking*—The same as Safe Mode, but includes networking support.

➤ *Start Windows Normally*—Starts Windows XP Professional in normal operating mode.

➤ *Reboot*—Reboots the computer.

➤ *Recovery Console*—Only available if it has been installed on the computer; allows administrators to enable and disable services, format drives, and read and write data to the local drive.

To start Windows XP Professional in Safe Mode, press F8 when prompted for the operating system.

Chapter Summary

In this chapter, we looked at the various types of hardware support provided in Windows XP Professional. USB device support was introduced in Windows 98. Windows XP Professional supports USB devices through the Windows Driver Model (WDM). Many types of USB devices are available that can be plugged directly into your computer and used immediately. These include keyboards, CD-ROM and DVD drives, printers, scanners, and cameras.

IEEE 1394 is the new standard for interconnecting digital devices. IEEE 1394 is a peer-to-peer bus that runs independently of the system processor. This means that these devices do not cause a performance hit on the system when they are running. Up to 63 devices can be connected to one IEEE 1394 bus, and up to 1,023 buses can be interconnected for support of over 64,000 devices.

As with Windows 2000, Human Interface Devices are supported in Windows XP. These devices include simulation, virtual reality, sport-equipment, and consumer appliance devices. HIDs are connected to the computer via USB or IEEE 1394 ports.

Universal Plug and Play (UPnP) is introduced in Windows XP. With UPnP, a user can attach a PnP-compatible device anywhere on the network and it will be detected and automatically installed just as a local PnP printer would be on a local computer. TCP/IP is the foundation protocol on which UPnP operates, but it also uses HTTP, HTTPU, SSDP, GENA, SOAP, and XML.

Support for infrared devices is provided by the IrDA protocol. Devices with infrared ports can transmit data between them at speeds up to 4Mbps. IrDA consists of several protocols, including IrCOMM, which is used by legacy applications and uses virtual RS-232 ports to access the infrared adapter on a computer.

Still images are supported in Windows XP Professional through Windows Image Acquisition. The Scanner and Cameras folder in the the Control Panel is used to install and configure WIA devices. The My Pictures folder is the default storage location for images.

Windows XP is the first operating system from Microsoft that will support the new Intel Itanium processor. This 64-bit version of Windows will provide support for up to 16GB of RAM to meet the demands of users who require more processing power than is currently available with the 32-bit version of Windows XP.

Digital media support has been enhanced with the inclusion of Windows Media Player 8, Windows Movie Maker, and digital photography support. Windows XP Professional makes it easier for users to work with both audio and digital media. Users can play and record CDs with their writable CD-ROM driver or with Windows Media Player 8. Media Player can also be used to view DVDs.

Power management in Windows XP Professional is based on the ACPI specification, just as it was in Windows 2000. With ACPI, the operating system manages the power consumption of various system components. Devices that are not being used can be put into a low-power state until they are needed.

Device Manager is used to manage devices in Windows XP Professional. Users can view the status of individual devices, enable or disable devices, and troubleshoot devices through Device Manager. Users can connect to the Windows Update Web site through Device Manager to update device drivers for their hardware devices.

Review Questions

1. What is the maximum number of USB devices that can be interconnected via one USB port in Windows XP Professional?

    p 204

    a. 10

    b. 125

    c. 127

    d. 55

2. What specification allows developers to create device drivers that are usable across multiple operating system platforms?

    p 206

    a. WDM

    b. WAI

    c. WIA

    d. IEEE 802.11a

3. Both USB and IEEE 1394 support which types of data transfer modes? [Check all correct answers]

    a. Isochronous

    b. Synchronous

    c. Asynchronous

    d. Interactive

4. Which bus transfer speeds does IEEE 1394a support? [Check all correct answers]

    p 207

    a. 12Mbps

    b. 100Mbps

    c. 400Mbps

    d. 1.5Mbps

5. Which of the following is becoming the universal format for data on the Web?

    209

    a. XML

    b. HTTP

    c. HTTPS

    d. HTTPU

6. What new technology provides automatic detection and configuration of hardware devices on a network?

    208

    a. Print Crawler

    b. UPnP

    c. USMT

    d. Remote Assistance

7. Ronald has an IEEE 1394 bus in his computer and wants to connect several devices to it. What is the maximum number of devices that Ronald can connect to one IEEE 1394 bus in Windows XP Professional?

   a. 152

   b. 10

   c. 62

   (d.) 63

8. What protocol is the foundation for Universal Plug and Play in Windows XP Professional?

   a. IPX/SPX

   (b.) TCP/IP

   c. NetBEUI

   d. HTTPS

9. Which of the following hardware devices causes the least amount of performance degradation to the computer's central processing unit?

   a. USB devices

   b. IEEE 1394 devices

   (c.) HIDs

   d. IrDA devices

10. What is the first step that occurs when an UPnP device is connected to the network for the first time?

    a. Eventing

    (b.) Addressing

    c. Discovery

    d. Control

11. What does the acronym SSDP stand for?

    a. Standard Service Discovery Protocol

    (b.) Simple Service Discovery Protocol

    c. Shared Service Distant Protocol

    d. Session Service Discovery Process

12. Julie wants to transfer some files to several of her coworkers who are using notebook computers. All of the computers have infrared ports, and Julie figures it will be easier and faster to transfer the data via these ports. Julie is running Windows XP Professional on her notebook. Her coworkers are running a mix of operating systems. Which of the following operating systems can make an IrDA connection to Julie's computer? [Check all correct answers]

   a. Windows 98
   b. Windows ME
   c. Windows XP Professional
   d. Windows 2000 Professional

13. IrCOMM provides four types of service classes that can be used when emulating RS-232 ports on a computer. Which of the following classes is supported by Windows XP Professional?

   a. Centronics
   b. 9-Wire
   c. 3-Wire raw
   d. 3-Wire

14. Rashed has just installed a new USB scanner on his Windows XP Professional computer. What Control Panel applet can he use to control the parameters for the newly installed scanner?

   a. Scanners and Printers
   b. Power Options
   c. Scanners and Cameras
   d. Sounds and Multimedia

15. Becky wants to purchase a new computer to use for some Web development she has been assigned to do at work. She believes that she is going to need more memory than is currently available with the 32-bit version of Windows XP. She will be working with data sets over 5GB in size. What is the maximum amount of RAM that is available on a computer that is running the 64-bit version of Windows XP?

   a. 4GB
   b. 12GB
   c. 16GB
   d. 32GB

8

16. Winston has just purchased a new computer that came pre-installed with Windows XP Professional. Winston wants to be able to view on his new computer some DVDs he just purchased. What digital media provided in Windows XP Professioal can be used by Winston to view his DVDs?

    a. Scanner and Camera Wizard

    b. Windows Media Player 8

    c. Windows Movie Maker

    d. CD-writeable drive

17. What file system is Digital Video Disc based on?

    a. CDFS

    b. NTFS

    c. UDF

    d. FAT32

18. Power management in Windows XP Professional is based on what specification?

    a. APM

    b. WIA

    c. ACPI

    d. WDM

19. What tool is provided to assist in troubleshooting and testing the functionality of DirectX?

    a. Dxdiag.exe

    b. DiskProbe.exe

    c. Chkdsk.exe

    d. Diskpart.exe

20. Jim is the systems administrator for his company and has just upgraded all computers to Windows XP Professional. He wants to be sure that users are not able to download and install system files or device drivers that have not been tested and approved to work in the Windows XP environment. What can Jim enable on each computer to ensure that only digitally signed files are loaded on the computers?

    a. He can configure driver signing on each computer.

    b. He can use Group Policy to ensure that only digitally signed files are loaded on the computers.

    c. He can use driver rollback to ensure that only digitally signed files are installed on the computers.

    d. He can't do anything. Once he upgrades the computers to Windows XP Professional, he is at the mercy of his users.

Real-World Projects

Renee is the systems administrator for his company, which is in the process of upgrading all of its Windows 98, Windows NT, and Windows 2000 workstations to Windows XP Professional. Renee has decided to roll out the installation to a pilot group before he attempts to upgrade the entire company. Renee wants all of the computers standardized to make troubleshooting easier for the help desk who will be supporting them. For part of this setup, he wants to be sure that the help desk is able to determine what types of hardware devices have been installed on each computer. He wants only digitally signed system files and device drivers to be on each computer. Several of the users in the office will need to use mulitple monitors on their computers when they travel to give company presentations.

Project 8.1

To configure Device Manager to always display nonpresent or "hidden" devices:

1. Right-click My Computer.

2. Click Properties.

3. Click the Advanced tab.

4. Click the Environment Variables button.

5. Under User Variables For *User_name,* click New.

6. In the New User Variable dialog box, under Variable Name, type "DEVMGR_SHOW_NONPRESENT_DEVICES".

7. In Variable Value, enter 1.

8. Click OK to close the New User Variable dialog box.

9. Click OK to close the Environment Variables dialog box.

10. Click OK to exit the Systems Properties dialog box.

Project 8.2

To configure Windows XP Professional to block the installation of all files and device drivers that have not been digitally signed by Microsoft:

1. Open My Computer.

2. Select Properties.

3. Select the Hardware tab.

4. Click Driver Signing.

5. Select Block—Never Install Unsigned Driver Software.

8

6. Click OK to close the Driver Signing Options dialog box.

7. Click OK to close the Systems Properties dialog box.

For the following projects, you first are going to install a second video adapter into your computer and configure it for use with multiple monitors. The video adapter should be a PCE or AGP adapter. You also need a secondary monitor for connecting to the second video adapter that you are going to install. After you complete Project 8.3, you will change the primary display for your computer in Project 8.4. You will make the secondary monitor that you installed in Project 8.3 the primary monitor.

Project 8.3

To install a second video adapter into your computer and configure it for use with multiple monitors:

1. Turn off the computer.

2. Install the PCI or AGP video adapter.

3. Connect the second monitor to the newly installed video adapter.

4. Turn on your computer. Windows XP Professional should recognize the newly installed monitor and will install the appropriate drivers.

5. Open Control Panel.

6. Double-click Display.

7. Click the Settings tab.

8. Click the monitor icon for the second monitor.

9. Select the Extend My Windows Desktop Onto This Monitor checkbox, and click Apply.

10. Select the resolution and color depth for the second monitor.

11. Click OK to close the Display Properties dialog box.

Project 8.4

To change the primary display for your computer and make the secondary monitor installed in Project 8.3 the primary monitor:

1. Open Control Panel.

2. Double-click Display.

3. Click the Settings tab.

4. Click the monitor icon for the secondary monitor that you installed in Project 8.3.

5. Select the Use This Device As The Primary Monitor checkbox, and click OK.

CHAPTER NINE

Networking

After completing this chapter, you will be able to:

✓ Define the basic components of a network

✓ Configure local area connections

✓ Configure remote connections

✓ Configure virtual private network connections

✓ Configure Internet Connection Sharing

✓ Configure Internet Connection Firewall

S ince the beginning of time, the human race has been driven to communicate. Cavemen drew on the walls of caves in prehistoric times. Around 5000 B.C., the Egyptians developed hieroglyphics. The first books started to appear around A.D. 70. In 1452, Johann Gutenberg conceived of movable type and a mass-production papermaking technique, setting the stage for the printing press. The first computer, basically a mechanical machine, was invented in the mid-1800s. A little more than a century later, the Internet was born.

Networking Overview

Today, networking is so pervasive that it's hard to believe that just 10 years ago, many people didn't even know what the Internet was, let alone have access to it. Today, the Internet is used for nearly everything—communication, research, commerce, weather, and so on. All this is possible through the advent of computer networking.

With the release of the .NET Framework, Microsoft is planning to build a new Internet-based platform. This platform will create an integrated, service-oriented Web platform where users can access standard applications over the Web.

Networking Defined

A *network* is a group of computers connected via an electronic medium and associated hardware devices. The computers might share a common operating system, such as Windows XP, but, more importantly, they must be running a common network protocol.

Network protocols process requests from computers and handle the delivery of data from one computer to another. Network protocols have many functions. Some connection-oriented network protocols—such as TCP and SPX—will retransmit any data that is corrupted or lost. Other network protocols are known as unreliable or non-connection-oriented. These protocols—such as IP and IPX—are only concerned with the transmission of data, not whether data gets to its destination. The network protocol can also send notification messages when a data connection fails or a computer cannot be found.

Networking Hardware

Various types of hardware make networking possible. Working together, these hardware components create a synergistic entity that brings a network to life. Although they might not all be required in some network designs, they all play an important role in a network.

Network Media

The *network media* provides the physical path on which communication occurs. Two classes of network media exist—bound and unbound.

Bound network media essentially consists of wired-based media. This includes the following:

➤ *Unshielded twisted-pair (UTP) cabling*—By far the most common network medium. Originally used for telephone wiring, it has long held its place in the world of networking. UTP cabling consists of two or more insulated copper wires that are twisted together and wrapped in insulation. It is not shielded against interference, such as electromagnetic interference (EMI) or radio frequency interference (RFI). By twisting the wires together, susceptibility to EMI is reduced. UTP is classified using a five-level categorization. The categories designate the number of twists per foot and the grade of insulation. Cat 1 is the lowest grade of UTP cabling. It works well for voice use only. Cat 3 is voice grade but can be used for data. Cat 5 is recommended for data use. Cat 5 provides data capacity to 100Mbps. UTP is extremely cost-effective in LAN environments.

➤ *Shielded twisted-pair (STP) cabling*—Provides better protection for data lines than UTP because it is shielded. The shielding is added under the outer jacket of the cabling with a drain wire that connects the shielding to an electrical ground. The shielding traps any EMI or RFI, which is then dissipated into the ground. STP typically forms the foundation of Token Ring networks. STP provides data capacity to 155Mbps. Because of the additional shielding, STP is a more expensive alternative than UTP.

➤ *Coaxial cabling*—Provides higher bandwidth than UTP or STP, although it is not as flexible when designing the physical layout of a network. Coaxial cabling consists of two conductors. The first conductor is typically a solid copper wire that runs in the center of the cable. This conductor is surrounded by insulation. The outer conductor, which is a wire mesh, surrounds the insulation. Coaxial resists EMI and RFI better than UTP or STP. Although coaxial is typically used for television and cable transmissions, in LAN environments, it is used in a bus configuration.

➤ *Fiber-optic cabling*—Doesn't experience any of the problems faced by the other bound media. Fiber optics uses light pulses instead of electrons to transmit data. It is not affected by EMI or RFI, it has much higher bandwidth, and it can be used in distances measured in kilometers, not meters. The downside of fiber optics is its high cost. It is typically used as a high-speed network backbone.

9

Unbound network media consists of wireless media. This area of technology is constantly expanding, but it includes radio, microwave, and infrared. Unbound network media allows a network to span larger geographic distances.

➤ When used as a networking media, radio tends to be used in the unregulated radio bands—902 through 928MHz, 2.4GHz, and 5.72 through 5.85GHz. These bands are used because they have few restrictions and no licensing fees placed on them. Systems based on radio can operate at 1Mbps through 10Mbps. These speeds are increasing with the latest advancements in technology.

➤ Microwave operates at frequencies that are higher than those used in radio. The frequency ranges are from 6GHz through 11GHz and from 21GHz through 23GHz for ground-based microwave, and from 11GHz through 14GHz for satellite microwave.

➤ Infrared communication is essentially unbound fiber-optic technology. Similar to fiber optics, infrared relies on light to send data back and forth. Infrared cannot pass through walls or solid objects; it is usually used in line-of-sight applications. The following are the two types of infrared communications:

  ➤ *Point-to-point infrared*—The most typical infrared application. It can be used between two systems, such as a laptop and a laser printer. By lining up the infrared ports between the two systems, the laptop can create a connection with the printer and send print jobs to it.

  ➤ *Broadcast infrared*—Used when an access point is installed in a room, typically on the ceiling, and communicates with multiple infrared receiving devices. Because the light is highly diluted throughout the room, bandwidth is very low.

Hubs

A *hub* is a network device that provides a central point of connectivity to a physical network. Each individual computer connects to the hub with its own network cable. Network traffic that enters the hub is replicated and sent to every port in the hub.

Bridges

A *bridge* is a network device that connects two or more physical networks. The bridge maintains a table consisting of hardware addresses. When the bridge receives a *frame* from one physical segment, it checks the destination hardware address for the frame against the table. A frame is a segment of data that includes source and destination hardware addresses. Picture a frame as though it's a postal envelope, in which you place your letter (the data). You then address the envelope (the frame) with the recipient's mailing address (the destination hardware address) and your return address (the source hardware address). If the hardware address is located on the other side of the bridge, it allows the frame to cross. If it isn't, the frame is not permitted to cross.

Switches

A *switch* is a network device that combines the features of bridges and hubs. Like a hub, a switch contains ports that interconnect multiple computers or physical networks. Like a bridge, a switch analyzes the destination hardware address in a frame and sends the frame out the appropriate port. Because the frame is not replicated on all ports (like a hub), using a switch results in greater bandwidth for individual workstations.

Routers

A *router* is a network device that connects two or more logical networks. A router maintains a routing table that tells the router which logical networks it knows the routes to. When the router receives a packet, it analyzes the packet's logical destination address to determine where it should route the packet. If the router is aware of a route to the destination, it forwards the packet to the next hop according to the routing table. If the router is not aware of a suitable route, the router discards the packet and sends a notification to the sender that the destination was not reachable.

Types of Networks

Networks are organized according to their desired function. Consider, for example, the administrative model and geographic locations.

Workgroup Networks

A *workgroup*, also known as a *peer-to-peer network*, is the simplest type of network. Workgroup networks are ideal for file and print sharing among a small number of users and computers. Typically, workgroup networks are used in homes and small offices, where a centralized administrative model is not required. A workgroup is a group of computers associated by name only. All computers in a workgroup maintain their own security database. As a result, user administration is more complex because a user needs to have valid user accounts on each computer. Most peer-to-peer networks are based on Windows 98 or Me as well as Windows 2000 or Windows XP Professional.

Domain-Based Networks

Domain-based networks are common in larger businesses. Domain-based networks are used for many network applications, such as file and print sharing, and also messaging, database, and intranet applications. Domain-based networks benefit from a centralized administration, which results in a stronger security model and efficient user administration. A user requires a single user account to access network resources. Domain-based networks are usually built using NetWare, Unix, Windows NT, and Windows 2000, or a combination of these operating systems. With the release of Windows 2000, Microsoft introduced a new version of a domain-based network—Active Directory. Microsoft will be releasing the next version of its domain-based operating system—.NET Server—in 2002.

Windows XP Component Architecture

Windows XP supports a modular component architecture to support networking. These components are all software-based. Figure 9.1 shows the components from bottom to top.

Network Driver Interface Specification (NDIS) Layer

The NDIS layer provides a way for a network transport protocol (TCP/IP, NWLink, or NetBEUI) to communicate with a network adapter. This layer contains the drivers that communicate directly with the network adapters.

Network Protocol Layer

The Network Protocol layer provides services that allow data to be sent across the network. These protocols include IP, NWLink, NetBEUI, AppleTalk, Infrared Link Access Protocol (IrLAP), Asynchronous Transfer Mode (ATM), and Data Link Control (DLC).

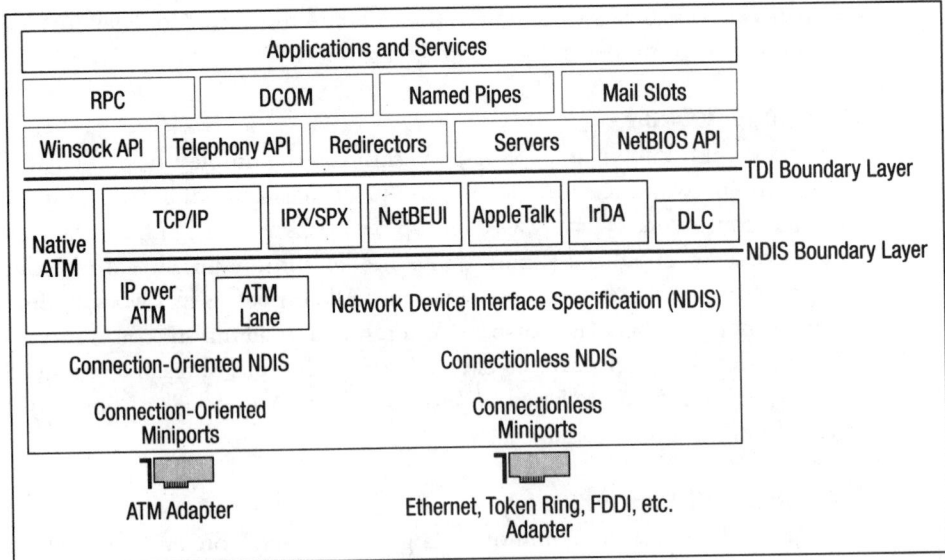

Figure 9.1   Windows XP component architecture.

Transport Driver Interface Layer

The Transport Driver Interface (TDI) layer provides an interface between the Network Protocol layer and the Network Application Programming Interface layer. This allows an application programming interface (API) to operate independently of any particular network protocol.

Network Application Programming Interface Layer

The Network Application Programming Interface layer is a set of APIs that applications can use to access network services. These APIs provide a set of standard routines that the applications can use to perform low-level network activities. By employing APIs, the application doesn't need to contain its own code to perform network functions. APIs include Winsock, NetBIOS, Telephony, Messaging, and WNet.

Interprocess Communications Layer

The Interprocess Communications (IPC) layer supports applications that rely on communications for client/server and distributed processing technology. Some of these services include remote procedure calls (RPC), Named Pipes, Mailslots, the Distributed Component Object Model (DCOM), and the Common Internet File System (CIFS).

Basic Network Services Layer

Basic Network Services support user applications by providing networking services. These services include simple I/O requests, such as reading and writing to a file across the network. Services at this layer include the Server service, Workstation service, and Network Resource Access.

Creating and Managing Connections

In today's networking environments, a workstation might be required to connect to a number of different types of networks. Windows XP allows a number of connections to be created. These include local area connections or LAN-based connections, remote connections, VPN connections, and direct connections. All connections are created in the Network Connections folder (see Figure 9.2).

Local Area Connections

Local area connections are LAN-based connections and are the fastest connection type. These connections use one of the following communication methods: Ethernet, Token Ring, cable modem, Digital Subscriber Line (DSL), Fiber Distributed Data Interface (FDDI), IP over ATM, wireless, IrDA, T1, and frame relay.

Figure 9.2 The Network Connections folder.

A local area connection is created by default for each network adapter installed in the system. For example, if a Windows XP-based computer contains two network adapters, two local area connection icons will be displayed in the folder. To modify an existing local area connection, you need to right-click the connection and select Properties. The Local Area Connection Properties dialog box is displayed (see Figure 9.3).

The Local Area Connection Properties dialog box shows which network adapter is being used by the connection. It also displays the components that are in use with this connection. The components are divided into three categories—Clients, Services, and Protocols.

Clients

A client is a software component that provides access to computers and files on a LAN. The following clients are shipped with Windows XP:

➤ *Client for Microsoft Networks*—Provides access to all Microsoft-based file and print services, such as Windows 95/98 or Windows NT. The client sends requests to the servers using the Server Message Block (SMB) protocol.

➤ *Client Services for NetWare*—Provides access to all NetWare file and print servers. This client sends requests to the servers using the NetWare Core Protocol (NCP).

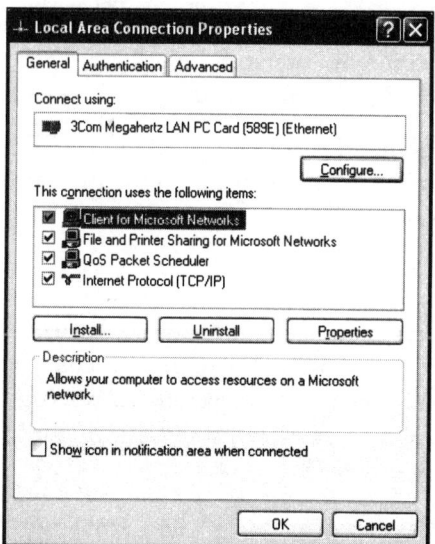

Figure 9.3 The Local Area Connection Properties dialog box.

Services

A service is a software component that provides additional features to the operating system, such as file and print sharing. The following services are shipped with Windows XP:

➤ *File and Printer Sharing for Microsoft Networks*—Essentially, this server service allows a Windows XP–based system to share its files and printers across a network.

➤ *QoS Packet Scheduler*—Quality of Service (QoS) allows an administrator to control bandwidth on a network. For example, if a user needs to use a network-intensive application, such as Voice over IP (VoIP), QoS can be implemented to prioritize VoIP traffic over regular network traffic.

➤ *Service Advertising Protocol*—This service collects and distributes SAP information and responds to client SAP requests. Used on a NetWare IPX-based network, SAP creates a list of services available on the network and their corresponding IPX internetwork addresses.

Protocols

A protocol is a software component that allows a computer to communicate with other computers on a network. A protocol is a common language that computers use for communication. The following protocols are shipped with Windows XP:

➤ *NWLink (IPX/SPX)*—NWLink, more commonly known as IPX/SPX, allows a Windows XP-based computer to communicate with Novell NetWare networks. A routable protocol can be used in small, medium, or large networks.

➤ *TCP/IP*—By far the most commonly used protocol in the world, TCP/IP allows a Windows XP-based computer to communicate via the Internet or across a LAN. It is a routable protocol.

Remote Connections

Remote connections provide a network connection for mobile users who need to dial in to their corporate LAN. Most corporations have a dial-in infrastructure that supports remote access with modems and integrated services digital network (ISDN) lines. Remote connections can also be employed to establish a connection to the Internet via an Internet service provider (ISP).

When creating a remote connection with Windows XP, you have two choices: connect to a private network or connect to the Internet. In most operating systems, there is no difference between the two. In Windows XP, however, File and Print Sharing for Microsoft Networks is automatically disabled if a connection to the Internet is created. This protects your computer from unauthorized access via the Internet.

To create a remote connection to a private network, follow these steps:

1. Open the Network Connections folder by selecting Start|Control Panel|Network And Internet Connections.

2. From the Pick A Task list, select Create A Connection To The Network At Your Workplace. The New Connection Wizard starts.

3. On the Network Connection Type screen, select Dial-up Connection, and click Next.

4. If you have more than one modem or interface, the Select A Device screen will appear. On the Select A Device screen, the devices currently installed in the computer and that are capable of establishing remote connections are displayed (see Figure 9.4). Select the device you want to use, and click Next.

5. On the Connection Name screen, you must name the remote connection. When you open the Network Connections folder, you will see a connection icon with its name. Type "Dial-up to Corporate Network" and click Next.

6. You must now enter the phone number of the dial-up connection to the private network. Specify the phone number and, if required, its area code in the appropriate box. Also, make sure you include any extra numbers or codes, such as "1" or a code to disable call waiting. Click Next.

7. Finally, the wizard will end. Click Finish to complete the wizard and to create the new dial-up connection.

Virtual Private Network Connections

A VPN is a private network that uses a public network infrastructure, such as the Internet (see Figure 9.5). Because using a public network infrastructure creates a security risk, a VPN relies on a tunneling protocol to maintain privacy and security. With a VPN, a user can connect to the corporate LAN and access resources and data as though they were directly connected. The connection is secure because the tunneling protocol encrypts and encapsulates the data at one end of the connection and decrypts the data on the other end of the connection.

Windows XP supports two tunneling protocols to create a VPN environment—Point-to-Point Tunneling Protocol (PPTP) and Layer 2 Tunneling Protocol (L2TP).

PPTP

PPTP is a simple, yet secure, way of creating a VPN for clients. PPTP is a TCP/IP protocol that can encapsulate TCP/IP, IPX/SPX, and NetBEUI protocols. Using the authentication, encryption, and compression capabilities of the Point-to-Point Protocol (PPP), Windows XP clients with a PPP connection to an ISP can take advantage of the security found in PPTP to connect to their corporate LANs.

L2TP

L2TP, which combines the features of PPTP and Layer 2 Forwarding, developed by Cisco Systems, is another tunneling protocol. L2TP is similar to PPTP, but uses the

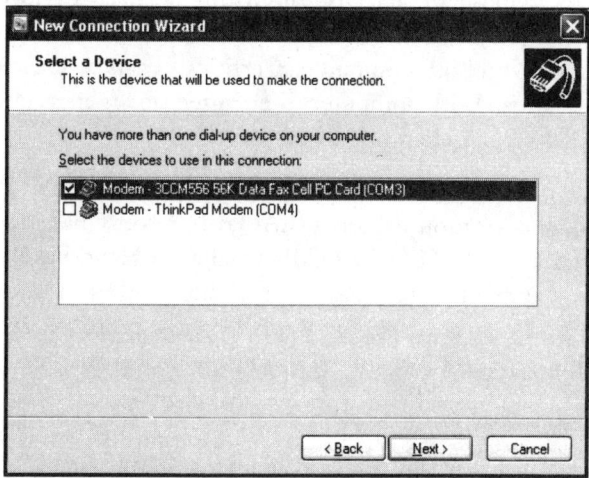

Figure 9.4   Selecting a remote connection device.

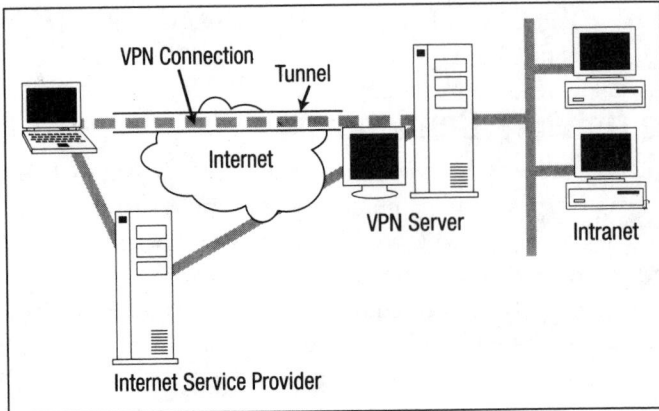

Figure 9.5 A virtual private network.

User Datagram Protocol (UDP), which is a connectionless transport protocol. Although L2TP was designed to run over a number of different networks—such as frame relay, ATM, and X.25—in Windows XP, L2TP supports only IP networks.

Because L2TP itself doesn't provide data encryption, L2TP relies on Internet Protocol Security (IPSec). IPSec is a group of open standards that define methods of using public key cryptography for secure IP connections. IPSec is discussed in the "Data Encryption" section later in this chapter.

When a connection is created between two computers using L2TP and IPSec, it goes through two stages:

1. Both computers—the VPN client and the VPN host—are authenticated. This is known as *mutual authentication*. At this stage, the two computers exchange computer certificates to establish an IPSec Encapsulating Security Payload (ESP) security association (SA). In order for the exchange to occur, a computer certificate must be installed on both computers. Certificates can be created by using the Certificates snap-in. Both computers then agree on an encryption algorithm, a hash algorithm, and encryption keys.

2. The user is authenticated via the user authentication protocols found in PPP, including Extensible Authentication Protocol (EAP), Microsoft Challenge Handshake Authentication Protocol (MSCHAP), Challenge Handshake Authentication Protocol (CHAP), Shiva Password Authentication Protocol (SPAP), and Password Authentication Protocol (PAP). These protocols are discussed in the "Authentication Protocols" section later in this chapter.

To create a VPN connection, follow these steps:

1. Open the Network and Dial-up Connection folder by selecting Start|Control Panel|Network And Internet Connections.

2. From the Pick A Task list, select Create A Connection To The Network At Your Workplace. The New Connection Wizard starts.

3. On the Network Connection screen, select Virtual Private Network Connection, and click Next.

4. On the Connection Name screen, you must name the VPN connection. When you open Network And Internet Connections, you will see a connection icon with its name. Enter "VPN to Corporate Network" and click Next.

5. On the Public Network screen, you must specify whether Windows XP Professional will initiate a dial-up connection to the Internet. If your computer has an "always-on" Internet connection—such as a cable modem or DSL connection—select Do Not Dial The Initial Connection. If you use a modem to connect to the Internet, select the appropriate dial-up connection. To create a dial-up connection, refer to the "Remote Connections" section earlier in this chapter.

6. On the VPN Server Selection screen, enter the name or IP address of the computer that will be hosting the VPN connection. Click Next.

7. Finally, the wizard will end. Click Finish to complete the wizard and to create the new VPN connection.

By default, the VPN connection is set to Automatic, in which L2TP is attempted first and then PPTP. If you are sure of the type of VPN connection to use, configure the setting to L2TP or PPTP by following these steps:

1. Open the Network and Dial-up Connection folder by selecting Start|Control Panel|Network And Internet Connections.

2. From the Or Pick A Control Panel Icon list, select Network Connections.

3. Right-click the desired VPN connection and select Properties.

4. The Virtual Private Connection Properties dialog box is displayed. Select the Networking tab (see Figure 9.6).

5. On the Type Of VPN drop-down list, select PPTP or L2TP.

6. Click OK to save your selections.

Direct Connections

Another type of remote connection supported by Windows XP is a direct connection. Direct connections are typically used to synchronize information between a personal digital assistant (PDA)—such as a Palm Pilot or Windows CE device—and a desktop computer. Windows XP supports three direct connection types—serial, infrared, and parallel.

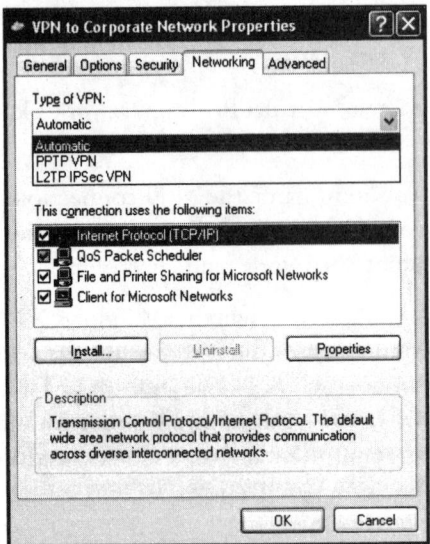

Figure 9.6   Setting the tunneling protocol.

Security for Remote Connections

Now that you have reviewed several methods of creating a remote connection using Windows XP, you need to consider an issue that is becoming more and more important in today's networking environments—security. Because the very nature of remote connections means that users from outside the corporate LAN can establish a connection and access the network's resources, it is important that measures are in place to verify that the user is permitted access. It is also important to ensure the integrity of the data being transmitted.

Authentication

Authentication is the process in which a system validates a user's logon credentials. In other words, a user's username and password are compared to an authoritative database, such as Windows 2000's Active Directory or the Security Accounts Manager (SAM) found in Windows NT 4. If the credentials match those in the database, access is granted. If they do not match, access is denied.

Interactive Authentication

Interactive authentication occurs when a user logs in at the keyboard of a Windows XP computer. The WinLogon process passes the user's credentials to the Local Security Authority (LSA), which then attempts to verify them. If the credentials match, WinLogon creates an interactive session on the computer and provides access. If they do not match, access is denied.

If the account is issued on the local computer where the logon is occurring, the LSA verifies the credentials. If the account is issued from another security entity—such as a domain—the LSA contacts the issuing authority for verification.

Network Authentication

Network authentication occurs when a user attempts to access any network resource or service. This type of authentication can be provided by Kerberos, Secure Sockets Layer/Transport Layer Security (SSL/TLS), and Windows NT LAN Manager (NTLM), which is used by Windows NT 4. Windows 2000 and Windows XP use Kerberos by default.

If users access a local account (one that was issued by the LSA) when logging on, they will be prompted for a username and password whenever they attempt to access network resources. Users who log in with a domain account do not receive such challenges if the resource being accessed trusts the domain.

Authentication Protocols

Authentication protocols are responsible for the transmission and reception of usernames and passwords.

PAP

PAP is the least sophisticated authentication protocol. It transmits passwords in plaintext (unencrypted). PAP tends to be the least common denominator in authentication protocols, and it is used when two computers cannot negotiate a more secure means of authentication.

SPAP

SPAP is a proprietary authentication protocol used to connect Windows XP dial-in clients to a Shiva dial-in server.

CHAP

Designed to address some of the concerns associated with transmitting passwords via plaintext, CHAP uses an encrypted authentication based on a hashing method known as Message Digest 5 (MD5). CHAP operates by having the server send a challenge to a client computer. The client computer, using MD5, hashes both the challenge and the password and sends the hashed result to the server. The server, knowing the challenge and the user's password from its security database, creates its own hash. The server then compares the two hashes. If the hashes match, the requested access is permitted. Because CHAP operates in this way, the password itself is never actually transmitted across the network.

9

MSCHAP

MSCHAP uses the same challenge-response type of authentication found in CHAP. Instead of MD5, MSCHAP uses MD4 for its hashing method.

MSCHAPv2

MSCHAPv2 provides more advanced features than CHAP or MSCHAP. These features include mutual authentication, stronger initial data encryption keys, and different encryption keys for sending and receiving data.

The MSCHAPv2 authentication process operates as follows:

1. The server sends a challenge to the client that includes a unique session identifier and an arbitrary challenge string.

2. The client sends a response with a username, an arbitrary peer challenge string, a hashed copy of the challenge string, the peer challenge string, and the user's password.

3. The server receives and checks the response from the client. It then sends a response to the client containing an indication of whether the authentication was successful.

4. The client verifies the authentication response from the server. If authentication is successful, the client begins to use the connection. If authentication fails, the client terminates the connection.

MSCHAPv2 also allows users to change their passwords when the passwords expire.

EAP

EAP is an extension to PPP that works with dial-in, PPTP, and L2TP clients. EAP allows additional authentication methods with PPP. These methods include smart cards, such as Secure ID, public key authentication, and certificates. EAP is generally used in VPN networks that require stronger authentication methods.

To configure the authentication protocol used by a remote connection, follow these steps:

1. Open the Network and Dial-up Connection folder by selecting Start|Control Panel|Network And Internet Connections.

2. From the Or Pick A Control Panel Icon list, select Network Connections.

3. Right-click the desired VPN connection, and select Properties.

4. The VPN Properties dialog box is displayed. Select the Security tab.

5. Select Advanced, and then click the Settings button. The Advanced Security Settings dialog box is displayed (see Figure 9.7).

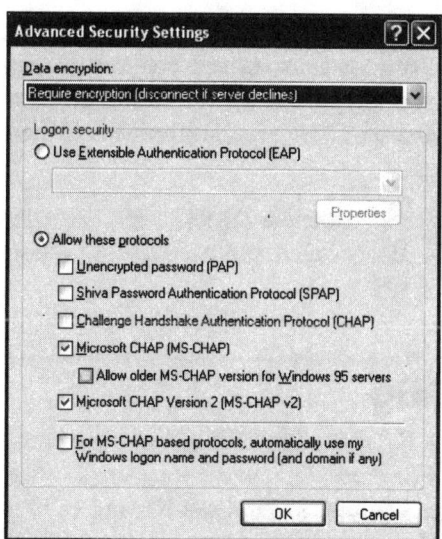

Figure 9.7   The Advanced Security Settings dialog box.

6. Select EAP or one of the other authentication methods.

7. Click OK to save your selections.

Data Encryption

Data encryption is a way to secure the actual transmission of the data across a network. Data is encrypted using a key algorithm, which can only be decrypted by a computer with the appropriate key. Windows XP supports two types of data encryption—Microsoft Point-to-Point Encryption (MPPE) and IPSec.

MPPE

MPPE uses Rivest-Shamir-Adlemen (RSA) RC4 encryption. MPPE can be used only if EAP-TLS, MSCHAP, or MSCHAP v2 is used for authentication.

MPPE can use 40-bit, 56-bit, or 128-bit encryption keys. The client and the server negotiate the encryption key, and the highest key supported by both is used. If the server requires a key higher than the client can support, the connection is terminated. Windows XP supports all three MPPE encryption keys.

IPSec

IPSec is a group of services and protocols that use cryptography to protect data. Typically used for L2TP-based VPNs, IPSec provides machine-level authentication and data encryption.

Because IPSec is implemented at the Internet layer of the OSI model, IPSec encapsulates data provided from upper-layer applications and becomes transparent to the user. In this way, IPSec packets are encrypted at the transmitting end of a connection and decrypted at the receiving end. The encapsulated data is then presented to the upper-layer applications.

IPSec uses Data Encryption Standard (DES) and triple DES (3DES) encryption. DES uses a 56-bit encryption key, while 3DES uses a 168-bit encryption key. Windows XP supports both DES and 3DES.

Internet Connection Sharing

ICS is a new feature found in Windows XP that allows a single computer to host an Internet connection for a network. For example, if you have a small office with 10 computers, only one of the computers (running Windows XP and ICS) would require a physical dial-up connection. The other nine computers would be ICS clients and would access the Internet via the ICS computer.

ICS provides IP address allocation, network address translation (NAT), and name resolution services for all ICS clients. Clients can use Internet applications (such as Internet Explorer and Outlook) as though the computers themselves were connected to the Internet. If the ICS connection to the Internet isn't active when one of the clients attempts access, ICS automatically dials the ISP and creates the connection. The client is then able to access the requested Internet resource.

Note: ICS is not available on Windows XP Professional 64-bit.

Configuring ICS

A computer running ICS needs two connections—one for the internal network (the connection for computers in the office) and one for the connection to the Internet.

To enable ICS, follow these steps:

1. Create a remote connection to the Internet as described earlier in this chapter.

2. Open the Network Connections folder by selecting Start|Connect To|Show all Connections.

3. On the File drop-down menu, select Network Setup Wizard. The Network Setup Wizard will start. Click Next.

Note: This feature is not available if your computer is part of a domain.

4. A reminder screen will be displayed telling you to review the network creation checklist. Click Next.

5. The Select A Connection Method dialog box will be displayed. Select the first option, This Computer Connects Directly To The Internet. The Other Computers On My Network Connect To The Internet Through This Computer (see Figure 9.8). Click Next.

6. Select which network connection (your Internet connection) will be used for ICS (see Figure 9.9).

7. Complete the Network Setup Wizard.

By enabling ICS, the computer automatically becomes a Dynamic Host Configuration Protocol (DHCP) server for the office network. DHCP automatically assigns

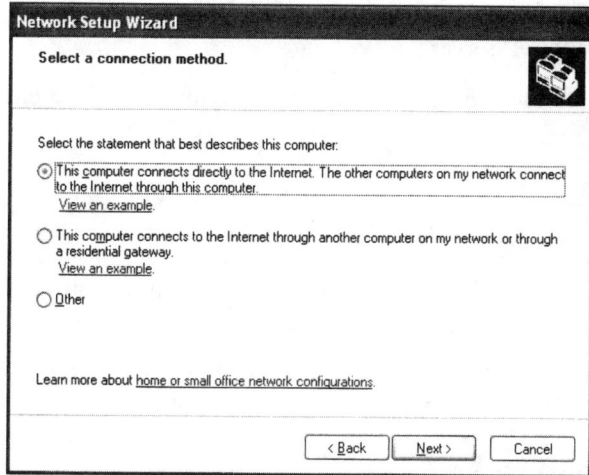

Figure 9.8   Enabling ICS.

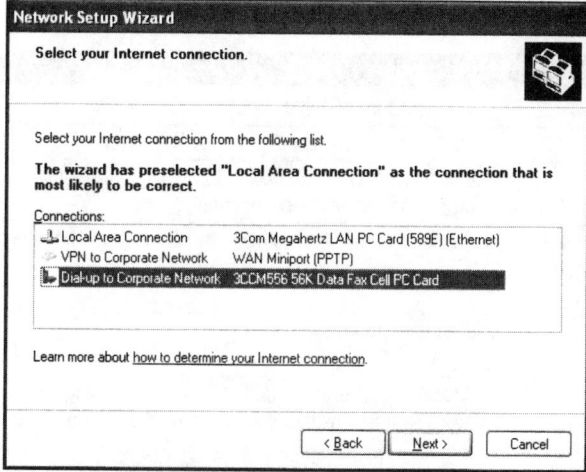

Figure 9.9   Selecting a network connection for ICS.

IP addresses to the hosts on the office network along with TCP/IP configuration information, such as DNS servers. Table 9.1 displays the settings that are configured when ICS is enabled. Note that the default settings cannot be modified, nor can any particular service, such as DHCP or DNS Proxy, be disabled.

Configuring ICS Clients

Configuring ICS clients is simple. Verify that the ICS client is configured as follows:

➤ The local area connection is using Client for Microsoft Networks, Internet Protocol (TCP/IP), and File and Printer Sharing.

➤ TCP/IP is configured to obtain an IP address and DNS server addresses automatically from a DHCP server.

After verifying that the previous settings are correct, configure the ICS client as follows:

1. Start Internet Explorer.

2. On the Tools drop-down menu, select Internet Options.

3. In the Dial-up Settings dialog box, select Never Dial A Connection. Click LAN Settings.

4. In the Automatic Configuration dialog box, select Automatically Detect Settings. Clear the Use Automatic Configuration Script checkbox.

5. In the Proxy Server, clear the Use A Proxy Server checkbox. Click OK to close the LAN Settings dialog box. Click OK to close the Internet Options dialog box.

[handwritten annotation: "Private network '192'"]

Table 9.1   ICS settings.

Item	Configuration	Description
IP address	192.168.0.1	IP address for the office network adapter
Subnet mask	255.255.255.0	Subnet mask for the office network adapter
Autodial	Enabled	If an Internet connection is not present, ICS autodials the modem to create the connection
Static default route	Created when the dial-up connection is established	Provides a default route from the office network to the Internet
Internet Connection Sharing Service		Starts automatically
DHCP Allocator	Enabled	Allocates IP addresses from 192.168.0.2 through 192.168.0.254, with a subnet mask of 255.255.255.0
DNS Proxy	Enabled	ICS receives DNS queries from clients and forwards them to a DNS server

At this point, the ICS client can access and browse the Internet using the ICS host. Note that the previous steps configure only Internet Explorer. If other applications, such as Outlook, need to be configured, refer to the instructions for the application.

Internet Connection Firewall

The Internet Connection Firewall (ICF) is a new feature found in Windows XP. With the expansion of the Internet and broadband Internet access (always-on access), many home computer users started to seek out ways to protect their home computers from hackers and malicious access via the Internet.

For many years, many organizations and corporations have been using *firewalls* to protect their networks. A firewall is a security system that acts as a boundary between a corporate network and the public network (the Internet). The firewall contains a set of rules, also called access lists, that determine who can access the network as well as what types of access are permitted. For example, the firewall might let Web traffic (which communicates on TCP/IP port 80) through so users outside the firewall can access certain Web sites. The firewall can also limit access to specific IP addresses.

Several third-party software vendors released a number of *personal firewalls* designed to provide limited firewall security to home computers. As this demand became more and more evident, Microsoft implemented its own personal firewall into the Windows XP Professional operating system.

Note: ICF is not available on Windows XP Professional 64-bit.

Configuring ICF

ICF can be used with ICS to provide security for the ICS server hosting the Internet connection. It can also be used separately from ICS to protect an individual computer if desired.

1. Open the Network Connections folder by selecting Start|Connect To|Show All Connections.

2. Right-click your Internet connection, and select Properties.

3. Select the Advanced tab. Check the Internet Connection Firewall box to enable ICF (see Figure 9.10).

4. Click Settings to configure ICF.

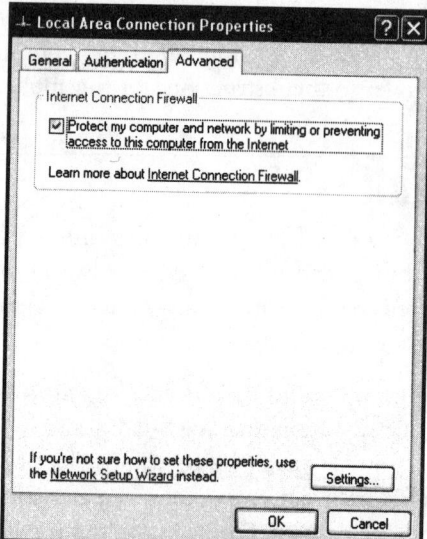

Figure 9.10   Enabling ICF.

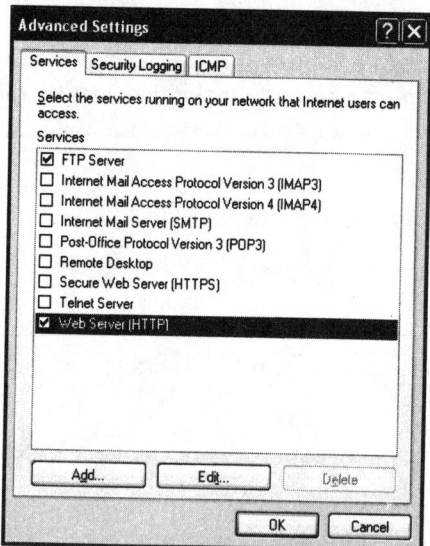

Figure 9.11   Configuring ICF settings.

5. The Advanced Settings dialog box will be displayed. From the Services tab, you can select which network services/protocols will be granted access through the firewall (see Figure 9.11). For example, if you want to allow FTP and Web traffic through your firewall, check both FTP Server and Web Server (HTTP).

6. When you select a service, a new dialog box called Service Settings will be displayed (see Figure 9.12). This allows you to determine where the traffic should be directed. For example, if you had a Web server called **webserver. helpandlearn.com**, you would enter the name of the Web server. All Web traffic through the firewall would be directed to this Web server. Click OK to close the Service Settings dialog box.

7. Select the Security Logging tab (see Figure 9.13). This tab allows you to configure what events and types of information ICF should write to a log file. You should periodically review these logs to determine if your firewall has been compromised or attacked.

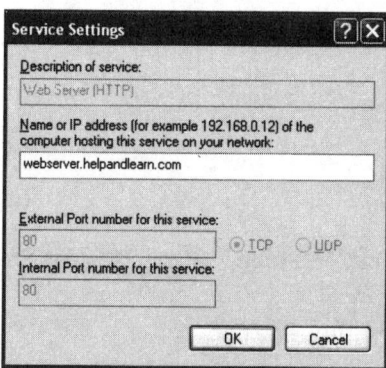

Figure 9.12 Configuring individual ICF service settings.

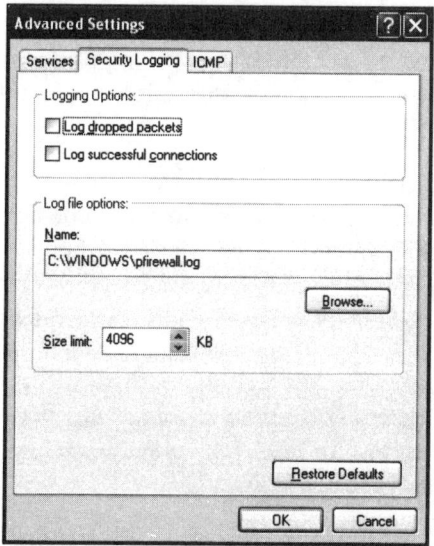

Figure 9.13 Configuring ICF security logging options.

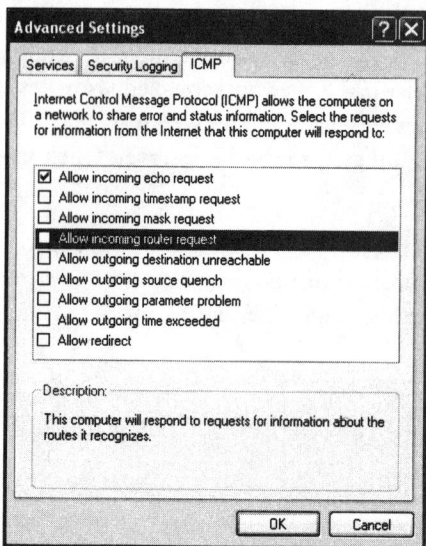

Figure 9.14 Configuring ICF ICMP settings.

8. Select the ICMP tab (see Figure 9.14). The Internet Control Message Protocol (ICMP) is used by TCP/IP-based computers to disclose error and status information. You can fine-tune the types of ICMP messages you want your computer to respond to.

Chapter Summary

In this chapter, you learned that Windows XP is a robust networking platform. Microsoft provides the means to connect a Windows XP Professional computer to practically every networking environment.

A number of devices are combined to form a functional network. The network media facilitates the network communication. The network media can be bound or cabling, or it can be unbound, such as radio, microwave, or infrared. A hub is a network device that provides a central point of connectivity for several workstations. A bridge connects two or more physical network segments and divides traffic according to the physical addresses of the hosts on each segment. A switch operates much like a hub except that it also operates like a bridge, where it divides traffic according to the destination's physical address. This results in greater bandwidth for individual workstations. A router connects two or more logical networks and divides the traffic according to the logical network address.

Two network administration models are supported by Windows XP. The first is the workgroup, which is a collection of network computers by name only.

A workgroup has a noncentralized administration, in which each computer maintains its own database of user accounts. The second is a domain-based network, which is a group of network computers that share a common database of user accounts. This results in a centralized administrative model.

Windows XP is based on a software component architecture to provide network connectivity. This architecture has several levels, starting with the NDIS layer. This layer consists of the network adapter drivers. The next layer is the Network Protocol layer, which provides services for network communication. Windows XP supports TCP/IP, NWLink, NetBEUI, AppleTalk, IrDA, ATM, and DLC. The TDI layer provides an interface between the Network Protocol layer and the Network Application Interface layer. TDI allows upper-layer applications to operate independently of any particular protocol. The Network Application Programming Interface layer is a set of APIs that contain common routines, which applications can employ to use the network. The IPC layer supports applications that rely on bidirectional communication, typically client/server-based applications. The Basic Network Services layer supports applications by providing basic networking services, such as drive mapping and file I/O requests across the networks.

Windows XP supports a number of network connections, both local and remote. This gives Windows XP the capability to connect to a number of varied networking environments. Windows XP supports local area connections over Ethernet, Token Ring, FDDI, ATM, IrDA, T1, and frame relay.

Remote connections can be dial-up or VPN connections. For dial-up connections, Windows XP provides the capability to connect either to private networks or to the Internet via an ISP. If the connection is to the Internet, Windows XP automatically disables File and Printer Sharing to protect the workstation from unauthorized access. Windows XP is capable of creating VPN connections via the use of tunneling protocols, such as PPTP and L2TP. A VPN provides a secure, private network connection via a public infrastructure, such as the Internet.

To provide security for remote connections, Windows XP supports a number of authentication protocols—PAP, SPAP, CHAP, MSCHAP, MSCHAPv2, and EAP. Data encryption is supplied by using either MPPE or IPSec.

Windows XP provides a feature that allows a single computer to host an Internet connection that other computers on the network can share and utilize. When this service—called ICS—is enabled, the ICS host becomes a DHCP server that provides IP addresses to the internal network. It also provides a DNS proxy that accepts name resolution requests from the network and directs them to a DNS server.

Windows XP provides a new service known as Internet Connection Firewall (ICF), which provides a security system to protect the computer from malicious Internet access.

Review Questions

1. Which authentication protocol provides unencrypted transmission of passwords?

    a. L2TP

    b. ISDN

    c. PAP

    d. CHAP

2. Which network device provides a central point of network connectivity and replicates any signals received to all ports?

    a. Switch

    b. Hub

    c. Router

    d. Gateway

3. Which network model is based on separate account databases being maintained by each computer?

    a. Domain

    b. Client/server

    c. Distributed

    d. Workgroup

4. Which network service allows an administrator to control the bandwidth usage on a network?

    a. SAP Agent

    b. Throttle Service

    c. File and Printer Sharing for Microsoft Networks

    d. QoS Packet Scheduler

5. Which network clients are included with Windows XP?

    a. Client for Linux Networks

    b. Client Services for NetWare

    c. Client for Microsoft Networks

    d. AppleTalk Client Services

6. Which tunneling protocol relies on IPSec to provide data encryption?

    a. L2TP

    b. IPSec

    c. PPTP

    d. PPP

7. With CHAP, when is a password transmitted across the network?

    a. During the challenge

    b. During the response

    c. Never

8. What is the function of the NDIS layer of the Windows XP Component Architecture?

    a. Provides a design structure for network adapters

    b. Provides a connectivity between network protocols and APIs

    c. Provides services between network adapters and network protocols

    d. Provides communications from APIs to network adapters

9. Which authentication protocol is used with smart cards?

    a. PPTP

    b. EAP

    c. VPN

    d. MSCHAPv2

10. Which network device connects two or more physical networks?

    a. Bridge

    b. Hub

    c. Gateway

    d. Router

11. A Windows XP computer hosting ICS can be configured with a DHCP address. True or False?

    a. True

    b. False

12. You have some clients that need to connect to your corporate network using third-party communication software. The server they are dialing into supports MSCHAPv2. What other authentication protocol should you configure the server to use?

    a. MSCHAPv2 only

    b. CHAP

    c. MSCHAP

    d. PAP

9

13. Which network protocols provide connectivity between Windows XP Professional and Novell NetWare 5?

   a. NWLink

   b. TCP/IP

   c. NetBEUI

   d. DLC

14. The Windows XP Component Architecture is comprised of what type of components?

   a. Software

   b. Hardware

   c. Network

   d. Both software and hardware

15. Which network device connects two or more logical networks?

   a. Bridge

   b. Hub

   c. Gateway

   d. Router

16. Windows XP supports only local area and remote connections. True or False?

   a. True

   b. False

17. Which connection media cannot be used for a local area connection?

   a. ATM

   b. Ethernet

   c. X.25

   d. Token Ring

18. Which network device provides a centralized point of network connectivity and routes signals received to the proper destination port only?

   a. Router

   b. Gateway

   c. Switch

   d. Bridge

19. Which network protocol provides connectivity between Windows XP Professional and Novell NetWare 3.12?

    a. NWLink
    b. TCP/IP
    c. NetBEUI
    d. DLC

20. Which protocol is not shipped with Windows XP?

    a. AppleTalk
    b. NetBEUI
    c. LocalTalk
    d. TCP/IP

21. Which network model is based on a centralized account database being shared by all member computers?

    a. Domain
    b. Client/server
    c. Centralized
    d. Workgroup

22. What is the function of the Network Protocol layer of the Windows XP Component Architecture?

    a. Provides services that facilitate the transmission of data across a network
    b. Provides services between transport protocols and network adapters
    c. Provides communication paths between APIs and network adapters
    d. Provides services that facilitate the communication of data via network adapters

Real-World Projects

You have just been assigned to a team to redesign your corporation's remote access capabilities. You have been assigned the task of determining and configuring the dial-in clients.

Project 9.1

To create a remote dial-up connection:

1. Open the Network Connections folder by selecting Start|Connect To|Show All Connections.

2. Select Create A New Connection from the left-hand menu. The Network Connection Wizard starts. Click Next.

3. On the Network Connection Type screen, select Connect To The Network At My Workplace, and click Next.

4. On the Network Connection screen, select Dial-up Connection. Click Next.

5. On the Select A Device screen, the devices currently installed in the computer that are capable of establishing remote connections are displayed (refer to Figure 9.4). Select the device you want to use, and click Next.

6. The next screen to be displayed is the Connection Name screen. Enter "Remote Access to Corporate Network" and click Next.

7. This screen is for entering the phone number of the dial-up connection to the private network. Specify the phone number and area code in the appropriate box. Click Next.

8. Click Finish to complete the wizard.

After consulting with the security engineer on the team, you decide that you want to use VPN connections for the remote clients. The security engineer configures the dial-in architecture to use L2TP for the tunneling protocol. The IP address for the server hosting the VPN connection is 10.123.1.1.

Project 9.2

To create a remote VPN connection:

1. Open the Network and Dial-up Connection folder by selecting Start|Control Panel|Network And Internet Connections.

2. From the Pick A Task list, select Create A Connection To The Network At Your Workplace. The New Connection Wizard starts.

3. On the Connection Name screen, type "VPN to Corporate Network" and click Next.

4. On the Network Connection screen, select Virtual Private Network Connection, and click Next.

5. On the Public Network screen, select the appropriate dial-up connection. Click Next.

6. On the VPN Server Selection screen, type "10.123.1.1". Click Next.

7. Finally, the wizard will end. Click Finish to complete the wizard and to create the new VPN connection.

Next, you need to configure the VPN connection to use L2TP as the tunneling protocol.

Project 9.3

To select L2TP for the remote VPN connection:

1. Right-click the VPN connection, and select Properties.

2. The Virtual Private Connection Properties dialog box is displayed. Select the Networking tab.

3. From the Type Of VPN drop-down list, select L2TP.

4. Click OK to save your selections.

After the project is complete, you are assigned a small project. This project consists of establishing Internet connectivity for a small office. Because the clients' computers use Windows XP Professional workstations, you decide to use Internet Connection Sharing. You order a DSL line from a local provider.

Project 9.4

To install ICS:

1. Open the Network Connections folder by selecting Start|Connect To|Show All Connections.

2. Rename the local area connection on the Windows XP Professional machine to "Office Network". Power down the computer.

3. The DSL line requires the use of a second network adapter. Install the second network adapter. Power up the computer, and install the network adapter's device driver if Plug and Play does not detect it.

4. On the File drop-down menu, select Network Setup Wizard. The Network Setup Wizard will start. Click Next.

5. A reminder screen will be displayed telling you to review the network creation checklist. Click Next.

6. The Select A Connection Method dialog box will be displayed. Select the first option, This Computer Connects Directly To The Internet. The Other Computers On My Network Connect To The Internet Through This Computer. Click Next.

7. Select which network connection (your Internet connection) will be used for ICS.

8. Complete the Network Setup Wizard.

Next, you need to configure the clients on the office network.

9

Project 9.5

To configure ICS clients:

1. Open the Network Connections folder by selecting Start|Connect To|Show All Connections.

2. Right-click the client's network connection, and select Properties.

3. Select Internet Protocol, and click the Properties button.

4. Verify that the system is set to obtain an IP address automatically from a DHCP server. Also, verify that it will obtain DNS server addresses automatically.

5. Start Internet Explorer.

6. On the Tools drop-down menu, select Internet Options.

7. In the Dial-up Settings dialog box, select Never Dial A Connection. Next, click LAN Settings.

8. In the Automatic Configuration dialog box, select Automatically Detect Settings. Clear the Use Automatic Configuration Script checkbox.

9. In the Proxy Server dialog box, clear the Use A Proxy Server checkbox. Click OK to close the LAN Settings dialog box. Click OK to close the Internet Options dialog box.

CHAPTER TEN

A TCP/IP Primer

After completing this chapter, you will be able to:

✓ Define an IP address

✓ Determine a basic subnet mask

✓ Identify the network ID and broadcast ID

✓ Identify the class of an IP address

B eginning with Windows 2000, Microsoft based all of its operating systems' networking capabilities on Transmission Control Protocol/Internet Protocol (TCP/IP). Previously, its operating systems used NetBIOS and other protocols, such as NetBEUI and IPX/SPX. With the explosion of the Internet, Microsoft realized that customers required a native TCP/IP implementation.

Although this is not a book about TCP/IP, understanding it is essential to knowing Windows XP Professional. TCP/IP is considered an *open protocol*. In other words, it is a vendor-neutral, nonproprietary protocol. It was developed and has since been improved upon by many people and organizations. Hence, it is an open protocol; anyone can suggest a change or an improvement.

TCP/IP is made up of Request for Comments (RFC) documents, each of which provides the details of different portions of the protocol. Most of these documents are very clear as to what they are trying to accomplish and how TCP/IP works. These source documents will become useful to you as you continue to work with TCP/IP. You can find the RFCs in many locations on the Internet by searching for "RFC" on any of the major search engines. A good search engine for looking up RFC documents is **http://sunsite.cnlab-switch.ch/cgi-bin/search/ standard/nph-findstd?show_about=yes**. You might also want to check **www. rfc-editor.org**, which has the RFCs and information about how to publish an RFC. You'll also find some of the more interesting and important RFCs on this book's companion CD-ROM.

As you look through the RFCs, you will see many different names and compa-nies—names such as Microsoft, Cisco, Novell, Sun Microsystems, and others—that have created the TCP/IP protocol. The advantages to this are that no one vendor can control what happens with the protocol, and all can take advantage of the protocol's strengths and weaknesses.

This chapter provides a basic overview of some of the protocol's major aspects. If you are familiar with TCP/IP, this chapter might not offer you much new informa-tion. If, however, you are new to TCP/IP, it should give you a strong beginning. A great deal of information is available on TCP/IP; this chapter is by no means meant to be a complete reference on the subject. We recommend that you study this topic in more depth; many TCP/IP-specific books are currently available.

IP Addresses

The IP address is the basis for how the TCP/IP protocol functions on your net-work. Every computer and peripheral device that wants to communicate on the network must contain a unique IP address. An IP address is a *logical* address, meaning that it is not fixed with a piece of hardware. Each IP address must be unique to the network. For example, one system can be using an address; if that system removes itself from the network, another system could start using that address and the device communicates without any problems. If two systems attempt to use the same IP address, an IP address conflict will occur. One or both will not be able to communicate with other systems on the network.

An IP address is a 32-bit binary number. Always remember this. That is how computers, routers, and software view IP addresses. For humans, however, IP addresses are represented in dotted-decimal format. In dotted-decimal format, an IP address is made up of four octets (8 bits for each octet times 4 octets equals 32 bits). Each octet contains a number from 0 through 255. The range of possible addresses is therefore 0.0.0.0 through 255.255.255.255. No number in an octet can be larger than 255 because the IP address is actually a binary number. Remember that the dotted-decimal format of the IP address is just a representation of the binary IP address to make our life easier, but the computer always looks at the address in the binary representation. To fully understand IP addressing, you must figure out how to convert an address from decimal to binary and back.

In a binary number, each number can be either a 0 or a 1 only. For example, if the number, or bit, is 0, the bit is considered "off." If the bit is 1, it is considered "on." If you start at the right of the binary number, the first bit has a value of 1, the second has a value of 2, then 4, then 8, then 16, and so on. Each bit to the left is double the amount of the bit before it. An octet has only 8 bits total. If the value is a 1 in the binary address, you add the number to the total. If the value is 0, you do not. So, if all eight places have a value of 1, the total is 255: 128+64+32+16+8+4+2+1=255.

10

The easy way to convert a number to its binary format is to use the Windows Calculator. After starting Calculator, go to the View menu and click Scientific. Type a number and then click the Bin radio button. This shows the representation of the number you typed, in binary. You also can type a binary value into Calculator and then click the Dec radio button to get the decimal value of the number.

Note: If you are using Calculator to convert decimal numbers to binary, be aware that it shows only the numbers that are relevant. Therefore, when you work with the binary values, you must place the leading zero in there so that you have eight places in every IP address. For example, if you use Calculator to convert the number 61 to binary, the result is 111101. This result has only six places. To make this a valid IP octet, you need to add the two leading zeros to make an eight-place total, with a result of 00111101.

Therefore, if you see an IP address of 210.164.87.218, you can convert it into the binary address of 11010010.10100100.01010111.11011010. Although the average user never needs to know how to do this, it becomes important later, when you start calculating routes for packets and troubleshooting TCP/IP-related issues.

Subnet Masks

The *subnet mask* is used to allow different groups of IP addresses to be divided into networks. After you have divided IP address ranges into networks, you can route among them. All IP addresses require a subnet mask.

Every IP address has two parts to it—the network portion and the host portion. The subnet mask defines which part of the IP address is network and which is host. The subnet mask is defined by starting at the far left of the four octets and placing a value of 1 in each binary placeholder (a series of contiguous 1s). As an example, if the subnet mask is 255.255.0.0, the binary equivalent of the number is 11111111.11111111.00000000.00000000. If the subnet mask is 255.255.240.0, the binary equivalent is 11111111.11111111.11110000.00000000.

The subnet mask should match the IP address, and wherever there is a bit with the value of 1 in the subnet mask (i.e., contiguous 1s), it means that the value in the IP address is part of the network ID. Where there is a bit with the value of 0 in the subnet mask (i.e., contiguous 0s), that portion of the IP address is part of the host portion. So, if a subnet mask is 255.0.0.0, then any time the IP address has the same number in the first octet, all of those addresses are considered to be on the same network. Then, for example, the network consists of the IP address range w.0.0.0 through w.255.255.255. If a subnet mask is 255.255.0.0, then when the first two octets contain the same number, the IP addresses are on the same network. Then, the network consists of the IP address range w.x.0.0 through w.x.255.255.

Note: Throughout this chapter, when w.x.y.z is used in an IP address, it is used as a generic placeholder and will represent any valid IP number.

When you start getting into partial octet subnetting, or values in the subnet mask other than 255, things can get a little more complicated. This topic is a little too advanced for the space available here, so look at RFCs 950, 1878, and 1219 for more information about this topic.

Network IDs and Broadcast IDs

After you calculate the range of values for your network, there are two addresses that you cannot use. The first and last addresses in every network range are reserved. The first address in every network is the *network ID*. This number is used to refer to a whole range of addresses. You often see this in routers and other similar devices. If your subnet mask is 255.255.255.0, the network ID is w.x.y.0.

The last address in every network is the *broadcast ID* for the network. If a packet needs to reach all computers on a network, then the destination address for the packet is the last address in the network. If your subnet mask is 255.255.255.0, the broadcast ID of the network is w.x.y.255.

Classes of Addresses

If you are going to use your IP address on the Internet, you need to have a unique IP address. If your company is going to go on the Internet, you might need multiple IP addresses, and this is where the classes of addresses come in. Three classes of addresses are available for use on the Internet and within your private company. The classes are simply there as a way of distributing multiple IP addresses to a particular company or organization. Table 10.1 lists the network IDs that are available, the number of networks available for each class of address, and the number of hosts available in each network. The Class A network 127.0.0.0 is reserved for local loopback and interprocess communications on a local computer.

Address Resolution Protocol

The IP address is a logical address, which means that it can be used on any system. It is not tied to a particular piece of hardware. The problem with this is that at some point when you send a packet from one system to another, the packet needs to know what piece of hardware to send the packet to. The Address Resolution Protocol (ARP) maps an IP address to a media access control (MAC) address. A MAC address is hard-coded into a network card. Every network card has a unique MAC address when it comes from the manufacturer. The local computer sends out an ARP request broadcast packet. The packet basically asks who is using the destination IP address. When the device using the IP address receives the packet, it returns a packet with its MAC address, at which point the two systems can begin to communicate. For more information about ARP, refer to RFC 826.

10

Dynamic Host Configuration Protocol

After you have determined what IP addresses you are going to use on your network, you must decide how you are going to assign the addresses to your clients. You might have only a few devices that you need to assign addresses, or you might have hundreds of devices to assign. You can manually assign the IP addresses to your clients. If you decide to take this course, you must keep track of the IP addresses that you assign. If you don't keep track of where you are assigning your addresses, it can be difficult to track down duplicate addresses. It can also be difficult if you ever change your addressing scheme, because you must visit every device on the

Table 10.1   Classes of addresses.

Class	IP Network ID Range	Subnet Mask	Networks Available	Hosts Available
A	1.0.0.0 through 126.0.0.0	255.0.0.0	126	16,777,214
B	128.0.0.0 through 191.255.0.0	255.255.0.0	16,382	65,534
C	192.0.0.0 through 223.255.255.0	255.255.255.0	2,097,052	254

network. As networks continued to grow, many administrators and engineers realized that a better solution was required. In steps DHCP.

The Dynamic Host Configuration Protocol (DHCP) enables you to automatically distribute IP addresses to your clients. On a DHCP server, you must define a *scope* of addresses. The scope contains a range of IP addresses available to be distributed along with the subnet mask. Each scope also has a *lease time*, which is the time that a client can use a distributed address; after that time, the client must get a new address. You can also define other scope options to be distributed with the address. You can distribute things like a default gateway, a Windows Internet Name Server (WINS) server address, and a domain name system (DNS) server address.

After a client computer receives an address from a DHCP server, it keeps this address for the time of the lease. When half the time of the lease has expired, the client attempts to renew the lease on the address it has been given. As long as everything is the same, the address should be renewed. If the address cannot be renewed for whatever reason, the client waits until seven-eighths of the time has expired and then tries to renew the address again. If this is still unsuccessful, then when the time has expired, the client releases its address and requests a new one from a DHCP server. The client will also try to renew its address whenever the system is booted.

If you want to check to see that you did get an address and what options were set, you can run **ipconfig** from the command prompt. Doing so gives you your current IP address, subnet mask, and default gateway. To get a more complete picture of your TCP/IP settings, run **ipconfig /all**. Entering this lists all the relevant IP settings that have been made on your system. You should note that if you have two or more network cards or a network card and a modem, each of these can have different settings and each is listed under the devices title. This can also present a decent amount of data, and it might scroll off the screen. You should make sure you can scroll in your command prompt.

You can get rid of an IP address and request a new one manually if you would like to. This is a useful troubleshooting tool because sometimes an address is not distributed properly, and requesting a new one fixes the problem many times. To get rid of your IP address, run the **ipconfig /release** command. If you run **ipconfig** at this point, you will see that your current address is 0.0.0.0, which means you won't be able to connect to anything on the network until you get a new address. If you run **ipconfig /renew**, your system requests a new IP address from the DHCP server. For more information about DHCP, refer to RFC 2132.

Routing

Routing is another one of those topics that can become very large and very complex. This section deals with how clients interact with routers. The basic idea behind a routed network is that you want to reduce the amount of broadcast traffic. A router does not forward broadcast packets, so those packets are confined to the subnet where they started. The problem with this is that the client still needs to be able to find and communicate with devices that are on different subnets.

Based on the IP address of a destination device, a local computer can determine whether a destination is on the local subnet or a remote subnet. The local computer uses a process called *Anding*. To And IP addresses, you need to first convert both the local and destination addresses as well as the subnet mask to binary. In the first step, the computer lines up the local address with the subnet mask. Any time both bits have a 1 value, a 1 value is put in the result; if there is any other combination, a 0 is placed in the result. The first part of the process is to And the local IP address against the subnet mask, as follows:

```
11000000.10101000.11010100.10000011   Local IP Address
11111111.11111111.00000000.00000000   Subnet Mask
11000000.10101000.00000000.00000000   Result
```

Now the system needs to get a result set with the destination address and the local subnet, as shown here:

```
11000000.10101001.11010100.10000011   Destination IP Address
11111111.11111111.00000000.00000000   Subnet Mask
11000000.10101001.00000000.00000000   Result
```

Now that the system has the two result sets, it compares them. If they are the same, the system knows that the destination address is on the local subnet. If the result sets are different, the system knows that the destination address is on a remote subnet.

If the local system determines that a destination address is on a remote subnet, it forwards the packet to the default gateway. The default gateway, which is a router, then transfers the packet to the network where it belongs. The local computer's only responsibilities here are to determine whether the destination is local or remote and, if the destination is remote, to let the default gateway find out how to get the packet to its destination. After the router receives the packet, it might have to do a great deal to get the packet to its destination. The routers on your network might communicate with one another to determine the best way for the packet to get to its destination.

Routing is a huge topic, and dozens of RFCs define various aspects of routing. Take a look at RFCs 1518 and 1519.

10

Name Resolution

TCP/IP addresses are not very friendly to most users. Certainly, the Internet probably wouldn't have taken off as it has if everyone had to remember an IP address. Imagine the commercial for some company saying "Just go to 10.187.42.16" instead of "Just go to company.com."

Being able to use a name instead of an IP address makes it dramatically easier for a user to be able to use the network. Microsoft currently uses two types of name resolution. Windows XP supports NetBIOS name resolution and hostname resolution. Both of these simply resolve a name to an IP address for a system, so it is redundant to have both. Microsoft has decided to phase out NetBIOS name resolution and to use hostname resolution instead. NetBIOS name resolution is still in Windows XP; although you cannot use this form of name resolution, it's included for backward compatibility.

NetBIOS Name Resolution

A number of possible steps are involved when you are resolving a NetBIOS name to an IP address. Each Windows computer uses the computer name as its NetBIOS name. To resolve a name, the system goes through the following steps by default:

1. Checks the NetBIOS name cache.

2. Queries the WINS server.

3. Sends a local broadcast.

4. Checks the LMHOSTS file (described in the "LMHOSTS File" section later in this chapter).

5. Checks the HOSTS file (described in the "HOSTS File" section later in this chapter).

6. Queries DNS.

You can change the order of the preceding steps, although they seem to work best for most systems in this order.

Name Cache

The NetBIOS name cache on a local system stores the names you have recently resolved. The idea here is that after you resolve a name, you are likely to use that name again in the near future. The NetBIOS name cache stores the names you have resolved for 10 minutes by default.

The NBTSTAT.exe utility allows you to work with the name cache. Table 10.2 lists the options of this utility.

Table 10.2   The switches for the NBTSTAT utility.

Parameter	Definition
-a *remotename*	Lists the remote computer's name table given its name
-A *IP Address*	Lists the remote computer's name table given its IP address
-c	Lists the current contents of the name cache, giving the IP address and name for each system you have resolved
-n	Lists local NetBIOS names
-R	Purges the local cache and then reloads the LMHOSTS file
-r	Lists names resolved by broadcast and via WINS
-S	Lists client and server sessions, displaying remote computers by IP address
-s	Lists client and server sessions, displaying remote computers by name if it can resolve them
-RR	Sends Name Release packets to WINS and then starts Refresh

Note: The switches shown in Table 10.2 are case-sensitive and can give very different results if the case is not followed. Replace the placeholder information (which is in italics) with the actual remote name and IP address.

WINS

WINS is a NetBIOS name server that stores NetBIOS names and their IP addresses. If a client is configured with a WINS server address, the client registers its name and IP address with the server when the system boots. When the system shuts down, it tells the WINS server that it is doing so, and the server removes the name from its list.

After a client registers itself with the WINS server, it can then resolve names from the server. Although the WINS server readily resolves a name to an IP address, it can also handle requests for services. When a client comes online, it tells the WINS server about all the services it can handle. This way, when a client needs to find a domain controller to authenticate it to the network, it can simply ask the WINS server for a domain controller in the network to which it would like to authenticate. If you look at the WINS database of information, you might notice that a particular computer name is listed multiple times. The difference between ComputerName[20h] and ComputerName[1Bh] is the sixteenth character of the name, which has a value of 00-FF in hexadecimal form (this always indicates a resource type). Table 10.3 defines the sixteenth characters that are available and when they are used. These services are registered only if the particular service is active on your network.

The advantage of working with a WINS server is that it dynamically builds its table of names and addresses. The client also needs to be configured with the address of the WINS server so that clients on multiple networks can use the same WINS server. The clients can also resolve the names of computers on remote networks:

10

Table 10.3   The types of services that can be registered in a WINS server.

Format	Description
Computer_name[00h]	This is the name registered by the workstation service and is usually referred to as the NetBIOS name.
Computer_name[03h]	This name is registered by the messenger service.
Computer_name[06h]	This name is registered by the Routing and Remote Access Service.
Domain_name[1Bh]	This is registered by a Windows NT 4 domain controller.
Computer_name[1Fh]	This is registered by the Network Dynamic Data Exchange (NetDDE) Service.
Computer_name[20h]	This is registered by the Server service.
Computer_name[21h]	This is registered by Remote Access Service (RAS) clients.
Computer_name[BEh]	This is registered by the Network Monitoring Agent Service.
Computer_name[BFh]	This is registered by the Network Monitoring utility.
Username[03h]	This is the username of the currently logged-on user.
Domain_name[00h]	This is registered by the workstation service to receive browser broadcasts.
Domain_name[1Ch]	This is registered for use by the domain controllers.
Domain_name[1Dh]	This is registered for use by the Master Browser.
Group_name[1Eh]	This is a normal group.
Group_name[20h]	This is an Internet group used for administrative purposes.
MSBROWSE[01h]	This is registered by the Master Browser for each subnet.

Local Broadcasts

A local broadcast is made to find a computer that responds to the NetBIOS name request. The issuing computer sends a message to every computer. The receiving computers check whether they have the matching name in the request, and, if they do, they send back a response with the IP address.

The problem with a local broadcast is that your routers are probably not configured to forward these broadcast packets, so, if the computer you are looking for is on the other side of a router, you receive no response. This is why you should implement a WINS server on a routed network.

LMHOSTS File

The LMHOSTS file is a static file that is located on the local system. A sample named Lmhosts.sam is located in the c:\windows\system32\drivers\etc directory. This is also where you must place an LMHOSTS file if you are going to use one. For an LMHOSTS file to work, it must be named *LMHOSTS* with no extension.

The LMHOSTS file is a text file that has some NetBIOS names and their IP addresses. For the most part, you simply enter an IP address followed by a NetBIOS name. You can include a number of options with the LMHOSTS file. If you follow a NetBIOS name with **#PRE**, that particular entry is preloaded into the NetBIOS name cache when the system boots. You might want to add this kind of entry for computers you will be accessing regularly. You can also follow a NetBIOS name with **#DOM:<*domain*>**, replacing ***domain*** with the domain name for a domain controller. You may want to do this in a situation in which you would like a domain controller to be the preferred option for login authentication.

If you have multiple entries for a particular system, only the first entry is used. When a computer goes through the LMHOSTS file, it starts at the top and then stops as soon as it finds the entry that it's looking for.

The problem with using LMHOSTS is that it is a static file. Therefore, you shouldn't place any entries in this file for systems that are getting their addresses from a DHCP server, because their IP addresses will change over time. The other issue is that each computer on your network has its own LMHOSTS file, so, if you want to make a change, you must either change every computer or direct your LMHOSTS file to include information from a network LMHOSTS file.

Hostname Resolution

Hostname resolution is a huge topic in and of itself. You can find books dedicated just to this topic. This section focuses on the client's perspective in name resolution. The advantage of using hostname resolution is that just about all systems that support TCP/IP use hostname resolution. The Internet uses hostname resolution and the idea of domains and subdomains. A *domain name* is a construct such as **company.com**, and the hostname is whatever comes before the domain. So, if you see an address like **www.company.com**, then the domain name is company.com and the hostname is **www**.

To resolve a hostname, the system goes through the following steps by default:

1. Checks the HOSTS file.

2. Queries DNS.

3. Checks the NetBIOS name cache.

4. Queries the WINS server.

5. Sends a local broadcast.

6. Checks the LMHOSTS file.

These settings can be changed, but they seem to work best for most environments.

HOSTS File

The HOSTS file is very similar to the LMHOSTS file. As with the LMHOSTS file, the entries in the HOSTS file consist of an IP address followed by a hostname. That's it for the HOSTS file. As with the LMHOSTS file, only the first entry for a hostname is used if you have multiple entries for a host.

For a system to use the HOSTS file, the file must be named *Hosts*, with no extension, and placed in the c:\windows\system32\drivers\etc folder. The file is a simple text file that you can open and edit with Notepad or any other available plain text editor.

DNS

Working with and managing a DNS server can be a very complicated task. This section covers using DNS from the client perspective and assumes that the DNS servers have been configured appropriately. Generally, as long as the client computer has been configured with the appropriate IP address of the DNS server, the client's system can resolve a hostname to an IP address. The client needs only to be configured with the address of one DNS server; if the DNS server does not have the address for which the client is looking, the DNS server checks with other DNS servers to resolve the name.

If the DNS server that you are using supports dynamic registration, Windows XP can register its hostname when the client boots up. If for some reason you want to change your hostname when it has been registered dynamically, run the **ipconfig /registerdns** command.

For more information about DNS, see RFCs 1034, 1035, and 2181. You can also reference the documentation for the DNS server that you are using.

Chapter Summary

TCP/IP is a large topic. Most people don't think it's as complex as it is because, after all, it is just a protocol. Well, it is more than that. Although TCP/IP allows you to have two or more devices connect and transfer data, it also routes your information around a large network and transfers data in different ways.

This chapter does not go into a great amount of detail about some of the topics; it is meant as an overview. After reading this, hopefully you will be motivated to study TCP/IP more. Microsoft has determined that TCP/IP is going to be the basis of all Windows-based operating systems beginning with Windows 2000. In fact, you cannot have an Active Directory network without TCP/IP. TCP/IP is certainly the most-used protocol in the world at the current time, so you must understand it well. You might want to start with RFC 1180, which is a tutorial on TCP/IP.

Review Questions

128 64 32 16 8 4 2 1 (handwritten)

1. Convert the following IP address to binary: 37.162.47.96.
   a. 00100101.10100010.00101111.01100001
   (b) 00100101.10100010.00101111.01100000
   c. 00100101.10101010.00101111.01100001
   d. 00100101.10100010.00101111.01100011

2. Convert the following IP address to binary: 218.47.236.118.
   a. 11011011.00101111.11101100.01110110
   b. 11011010.00101111.11101101.01110110
   c. 11011010.00101111.11101100.01110111
   (d) 11011010.00101111.11101100.01110110

3. Convert the following IP address to binary: 18.247.136.128.
   a. 00010011.11110111.10001001.10000000
   b. 00010010.11110111.10001000.10000001
   (c) 00010010.11110111.10001000.10000000
   d. 00010010.11110111.10001010.10000001

4. Convert the following binary address to decimal:
   11011001.11111101.00100110.11101110.
   (a) 217.253.38.238
   b. 216.253.68.236
   c. 217.253.36.64
   d. 216.253.64.230

5. Convert the following binary address to decimal:
   10011001.11111100.00100111.01101110.
   a. 151.234.92.111
   b. 212.92.66.84
   c. 118.215.183.99
   (d) 153.252.39.110

6. Convert the following binary address to decimal:
   10011101.11001100.00111111.11011110.
   (a) 157.204.63.222
   b. 137.202.73.222
   c. 157.204.63.232
   d. 117.202.73.222

10

7. Your address is 192.168.2.37, and your subnet mask is 255.255.255.0. The destination address is 192.168.1.64. Is this address local or remote?

   a. Local

   b. Remote

8. Your address is 192.168.2.37, and your subnet mask is 255.255.0.0. The destination address is 192.168.1.64. Is this address local or remote?

   a. Local

   b. Remote

9. Your address is 11000000.10101000.00000010.00100101, and your subnet mask is 11111111.11111111.11111111.00000000. The destination address is 11000000.10101000.00000001.01000000. Is this address local or remote?

   a. Local

   b. Remote

10. Your address is 11000000.10101000.00000010.00100101, and your subnet mask is 11111111.11111111.00000000.00000000. The destination address is 11000000.10101000.00000001.01000000. Is this address local or remote?

    a. Local

    b. Remote

11. You are trying to resolve a NetBIOS name. The computer you are trying to reach has entries in both the WINS server and the LMHOSTS file, but the entries are different. Which entry is used?

    a. WINS.

    b. LMHOSTS.

    c. Neither is used.

    d. Both are used.

12. You are trying to resolve a host's name. The computer you are trying to reach has entries in both the DNS server and the HOSTS file, but the entries are different. Which entry is used?

    a. DNS.

    b. HOSTS.

    c. Neither is used.

    d. Both are used.

13. You are having trouble communicating, and you realize that you do not have an IP address. You are on a network that is using DHCP. What command requests a new IP address?

    a. **ipconfig /registerdns**

    b. **ipconfig /release**

    c. **ipconfig /renew**

    d. **ipconfig /flushdns**

14. You have changed the hostname of your local computer, and you would like to add this new hostname to a DNS server that supports dynamic updates. What command should you use to update this entry without rebooting the system?

    a. **ipconfig /registerdns**

    b. **ipconfig /release**

    c. **ipconfig /renew**

    d. **ipconfig /flushdns**

15. You want to check which DNS and WINS server has been distributed to the local computer via DHCP. What command allows you to see this information?

    a. **ipconfig /registerdns**

    b. **ipconfig /displaydns**

    c. **ipconfig /showclassid**

    d. **ipconfig /all**

16. You have received an IP address from a DHCP server. When does the local system try to renew this address? [Check all correct answers.]

    a. When half the lease time has expired.

    b. When seven-eighths of the lease time has expired.

    c. When the lease time expires.

    d. You must renew the address manually.

    e. When the system reboots.

17. You have recently accessed a system using a NetBIOS name, and then you changed the IP address of the remote system. Now, you cannot access the system, and you notice that the wrong name is being resolved. What can you do from the local computer to resolve the name properly?

    a. Run the command **NBTSTAT –r**.

    b. Run the command **NBTSTAT –R**.

    c. Add an entry to the LMHOSTS file.

    d. Add an entry to the HOSTS file.

10

18. You are trying to resolve a hostname, and you have multiple entries for the hostname. Which of the following provides the name resolution for the local system if all options have entries for the host?

    a. DNS

    b. WINS

    c. Local broadcast

    d. HOSTS file

19. IP addresses are logical addresses that need to be mapped to a physical piece of hardware. Which of the following allows that to happen?

    a. DHCP

    b. DNS

    c. WINS

    d. ARP

20. Where should your HOSTS file and LMHOSTS file be placed for the system to use them?

    a. c:\windows\system32\drivers

    b. c:\windows\system32

    c. c:\windows\system32\drivers\etc

    d. c:\windows\system32\wins

Real-World Projects

Nora's company has decided to implement TCP/IP as its protocol. Nora has been assigned the responsibility of making sure that the workstations on the network can communicate. Other people are responsible for making sure the routers communicate and for setting up the server components. Nora will decide how to distribute the IP addresses to the clients and what settings should be in place.

Nora decides that the company will be better served by using DHCP instead of manually assigning the addresses. A few of the workstations will require a static IP address, so those will be configured separately. To handle the name resolution, Nora must make a few decisions. First, Nora decides to look at NetBIOS name resolution. The network is divided into three subnets, so relying on broadcast traffic will not work. She realizes that if she decides to implement LMHOSTS for the network, problems might occur because she has decided to use DHCP to distribute the addresses, and LMHOSTS is a static file. Nora checks with the server group and finds that it can install a WINS server, so she gets the IP address of the server and uses that for NetBIOS name resolution.

As far as hostname resolution is concerned, Nora realizes that implementing the HOSTS file will cause the same problems as implementing LMHOSTS. Therefore, the only alternative is to implement DNS. She checks with the server group again and finds out the current domain name it is using and the address of the DNS server. She also finds out that the DNS server being used supports dynamic updates, and thus she convinces the server group to enable this feature.

Nora then consults with the router group and gets the IP addresses for the routers and the ranges of addresses that she is allowed to use for the clients.

Now that Nora has the addresses and the name resolution addresses, she puts these together to determine the scope for DHCP. Nora lists the options that are needed for each scope and has the server team enter them into the DHCP servers. Nora decides to have a short lease time on the DHCP servers so that if changes need to be made, they can go into effect quickly.

After the servers have been configured, she starts setting up the client workstations to obtain their IP addresses automatically through DHCP.

Project 10.1

To configure Windows XP Professional to obtain a DHCP address:

1. Select Start|Control Panel.

2. Double-click Network And Internet Connections.

3. Right-click Local Area Connection and choose Properties.

4. Highlight Internet Protocol (TCP/IP), and click Properties.

5. Select Obtain An IP Address Automatically.

6. Select Obtain DNS Server Address Automatically.

7. Click OK twice.

A few clients are running a special piece of software that requires that they have a static IP address. Nora configures these systems by following the steps in Project 10.2.

Project 10.2

To configure Windows XP Professional with a static IP address:

1. Select Start|Control Panel.

2. Double-click Network And Internet Connections.

3. Right-click Local Area Connection, and choose Properties.

4. Highlight Internet Protocol (TCP/IP), and click Properties.

10

5. Select Use The Following IP Address.

6. Enter the workstation's IP address, subnet mask, and default gateway.

7. Select Use The Following DNS Server Address.

8. Enter the IP address of the DNS server.

9. Click OK two times.

Now that Nora has the systems up and running, she is finding that some of the computers have authentication to the wrong domain controller. She decides to implement an LMHOSTS file on these computers to point them to the proper domain controller.

Project 10.3

To create an LMHOSTS file that specifies a domain controller and preloads the entry:

1. Open Notepad.

2. Type the following line into Notepad:

```
IP Address      domain controller        #PRE #DOM:domainname
```

Replace *IP Address* with the IP address of the domain controller, *domain controller* with the name of the domain controller, and *domainname* with the name of the domain.

3. Save the file as *lmhosts*.

4. Copy the file to c:\winnt\system32\drivers\etc.

CHAPTER ELEVEN

Mobile Users

After completing this chapter, you will be able to:

✓ Describe the power management options available for mobile computing

✓ Explain how to configure a power scheme

✓ Describe how to use Offline Files and Folders

✓ Describe how to configure remote connections

✓ Describe how to make a direct connection to another computer

✓ Explain the purpose of Remote Desktop

✓ Explain the purpose of Fast Startup

✓ Explain the purpose of Stored User Names and Passwords

Due to technological advances and decreases in pricing, laptop computers are becoming more common in the workplace and at home. Many companies understand the benefits of having the portability that laptop computers provide, and they are issuing them, instead of desktop computers, to employees. Windows XP Professional has improved the features that made Windows 2000 such a good operating system for mobile computing. In this chapter, we look at the enhancements that have been included in Windows XP Professional for using laptop computers.

Configuring Hardware for Mobile Computing Use

Windows XP Professional uses Plug and Play to automatically detect devices that are connected to and running on a notebook computer. In most cases, if a notebook computer is used in different work environments, Windows XP will load the appropriate device drivers for the environment the notebook computer is being used in. If Windows XP is unable to automatically detect the hardware settings, the user might have to set up hardware profiles for each work environment.

Hardware Profiles

Notebook computers are used at work, at home, and on the road. Users might find that they have different hardware configuration needs depending on where they are using their notebook computers. Hardware profiles provide users with the capability to have different setup configurations for each work environment.

Users might have to log onto a network when they are in the office to access resources. When they are working from home and are not connecting to the company network, they do not need the network logon screen. Therefore, they could create different hardware profiles for work and home. A hardware profile determines which device drivers to load when a computer starts. If a user creates a profile for home with no network connectivity, the device drivers for the network card are not loaded.

When you initially install Windows XP Professional, a default hardware profile is created. If you are using a desktop computer, the default profile is called Profile 1. On notebook computers, the default profiles are Docked Profile and Undocked Profile. If multiple profiles are on your computer, you can designate which profile will be used every time the computer starts. You can also have Windows XP Professional query you as to which profile you want to use at system startup.

Docking Stations

Many notebook computers on the market today can be used with *docking stations*. A docking station is an accessory that a notebook computer fits into to give the notebook computer the same functionality as a desktop computer. With the addition of a docking station, notebook computer users can use standard-size keyboards, mice, and monitors. Some manufacturers also include *port replicators* with their docking stations. Port replicators provide additional functionality and can include input/output devices, such as PC slots, Ethernet ports, and external parallel and serial ports.

Users have three ways that they can dock or undock a notebook computer from a docking station:

➤ *Cold dock*—Occurs when a notebook is shut down before it is inserted or removed from the docking station.

➤ *Warm dock*—Occurs when a notebook computer has been put into Standby mode first before it is inserted or removed from the docking station.

➤ *Hot dock*—Occurs when a computer is running and is removed from or inserted into the docking station.

How a user undocks a notebook computer is dependent on the type of docking station being used. Windows XP Professional has built-in support for most docking stations, and users can eject or undock their computers by using the Undock PC command on the Start menu. When this option is used, a message appears on the screen indicating that it is safe to undock the notebook computer from the docking station. Some manufacturers have included eject buttons on docking stations that can be used to undock a notebook computer from a docking station. Users should check the owner's manual for the docking station for the appropriate docking and undocking procedures.

Windows XP Professional was designed to automatically detect most docking stations. If for some reason it does not, the user might have to configure a hardware profile for the docking station.

11

Warning: If your computer has been put into Hibernation mode, do not undock it from the docking station. When the computer is put into Hibernation mode, the system state, which includes the hardware configuration, is saved to a file. When the computer resumes operation from Hibernation mode, if the hardware configuration has changed, the system could become erratic.

Users cannot put their portable computers in Standby or Hibernate mode and then undock them. Windows XP Professional will not be able to unload the device drivers for the docking station if the computer is running in either of these modes. This could affect the system and cause it to act erratically when the computer is undocked.

Power Management for Mobile Computing

Users of portable computes have different power needs than desktop computer users. Power management is important for portable computers, especially when they are runnning on battery power. Portable computer users don't want resources that are not required at a specific time to be taxing the limited available power resources.

When purchasing a notebook computer for use with Windows XP Professional, consumers should look for one that supports the Advanced Configuration and Power Interface (ACPI) specification. Although Windows XP Professional supports Advance Power Management (APM), only computers that are ACPI-compliant can benenfit from all the power management options that are available for both notebook and desktop computers.

To determine whether your computer is ACPI-compliant, take these steps:

1. Open Device Manager.

2. Select Devices By Connection on the View menu. If the computer is ACPI-compliant, you should see in the right pane Advanced Configuration and Power Interface (ACPI) PC.

Power Schemes

Power schemes are provided as part of power management in Windows XP Professional. Portable computer users can utilize power schemes to determine what devices a computer turns off when it enters Standby or Hibernation mode. Six predefined power schemes are provided in Windows XP Professional. If one of the provided power schemes does not meet the specific needs of a portable computer user, the user can create his or her own using one of the predefined schemes as a template. Table 11.1 lists the six predefined power schemes that are available in Windows XP Professional.

Table 11.1   Power schemes.

Power Scheme	Description
Home/Office Desk	Maintains constant power to the system and the hard disk when the computer is on AC power. This is the default scheme.
Portable/Laptop	Turns the computer off after from 5 to 30 minutes of inactivity.
Presentation	Keeps the computer from going into Standby mode. This is appropriate for presentations when you do not want the computer display to cut off.
Always On	Provides constant power to the system, whether it is running on AC or battery power. The Standby time is disabled, and the hard disk timer is increates.
Minimal Power Management	Maintains constant power to the hard disk and the system when the computer is running on AC power. Timed hibernation is disabled.
Max Battery	Puts the computer into Power Saving mode after a short period of inactivity.

Note: By default, all computers are enabled with the Home/Office Desk power scheme. This should be changed by portable computer users, because this power scheme is not designed to optimize battery power.

The Presentation power scheme is a good scheme to use if you do not want a portable computer to go into Standby or Hibernation mode. The Presentation scheme provides constant power to the computer and prevents it from going into either Standby or Hibernation mode.

After you have selected a power scheme, you can control how long before the monitor and hard disks are turned off. These settings can be individually configured, and different settings can be made for when the computer is running on AC power versus batteries.

Remember that the power options available on your notebook computer depend on the specific hardware configuration that it supports. Windows XP Professional detects what is available on your computer and displays only those options that are supported.

Power Saving Options

Windows XP Professional has two power saving options that can be enabled to conserve battery power when you are not using your notebook computer. These two options are Standby and Hibernation.

Standby

When a notebook computer is configured for Standby mode, the entire operating system can be put into a low power state. This means that devices that are not being used are not draining power from the batteries. When the computer is put into Standby mode, all systems, including the monitor and hard disks, are put into a low power state. When the user logs back onto the computer, the desktop is returned to the state it was in before the computer was put in Standby mode.

Note: If you lose power to a computer while it is in Standy mode, all unsaved data will be lost.

Standby mode is enabled by default on APCI- and APM-compliant notebook computers. The computer can be enabled to require that users enter a valid username and password when returning from Standby mode.

Hibernation

If you are concerned about losing data when your computer goes into a low power state, you should configure it to use Hibernation mode instead of Standby mode. When a notebook computer goes into Hibernation mode, the entire desktop is saved to the hard disk, including anything the user was working on at the time.

11

When the user logs back onto the computer, the desktop is restored to the exact state it was in before the computer was put in Hibernation mode.

Before Hibernation mode can be used on a notebook computer, the user must ensure that sufficient disk space exists on the hard disk. The computer must have an amount of free space on the hard disk equal to the total amount of RAM in the system. This is needed because when the system is put into Hibernation mode, everything in RAM is saved to the hard disk for later retrieval when the user logs back on. Users can view on the Hibernation tab in the Power Options dialog box how much disk space is currently available on the hard drive and how much disk space is required to use Hibernation mode.

Hibernation mode is not enabled by default in Windows XP Professional. It must be enabled through Power Options in the Control Panel. When a user logs back onto a computer from Hibernation mode, the user is required to enter a valid username and password. This is enabled by default and cannot be changed in Hibernation mode.

Both Standby and Hibernation modes can be configured to start from one minute to six hours of inactivity on a portable computer.

Battery Monitoring

Notebook computers that are ACPI-compliant include the capability for users to monitor the battery status of their computers. This is extremely helpful insofar as a user does not have to guess how much time he or she has left to use the computer before it must be connected to an AC source for battery recharging.

A battery icon is displayed on the taskbar that gives users a direct indication of the current battery level. This icon must be enabled before it will appear on the taskbar.

Power Button

If your notebook computer is ACPI-compliant, Windows XP Professional enables you to specify what action is taken when the power button is pressed. The power button can be configured to put the computer in Standby mode, to put it in Hibernate mode, or to shut it down completely. If the computer is shut down by pressing the power button, the user is not prompted to save any data that he or she is working on. The computer is immediately powered down. The power button can also be configured to ask the user which available option to take when the button is pressed.

New Power Features Added with Windows XP

Several new power management features have been added to support the features that were introduced in Windows 2000. These features are described next.

Processor Power Control

With procesor power control, the CPU speed can be reduced when the notebook computer is running on battery power. Normally, the CPU runs at full speed when the notebook computer is running on AC power. By running the CPU at a slower speed when the computer is on battery power, the user extends the amount of time available for the battery use.

Wake-on-LAN

With Wake-on-LAN technology, administrators can better manage notebook computers that are connected to their networks. If a computer is running in Standby mode, the administrator can "wake up" the computer and perform administration functions, such as software installation. After the software is installed, the computer can be returned to its Standby state.

Wake on Battery

Wake on Battery can be used to conserve battery resources by putting the system into Hibernation mode when the system detects that the battery is hitting a critical low in its power state while the system is running in Standby mode.

Lid Power/Display Dimming

The display can be powered off when the lid of a notebook computer is closed. The LCD can also be dimmed when the computer is running on battery mode. When the computer is connected to an AC source, the LCD will return to its original brightness.

Suspend USB Ports

For computers with multiple USB ports, the operating system can turn off individual ports to conserve power.

Offline Files and Folders

Offline Files and Folders is discussed in Chapter 6. It provides users with the ability to work with their company network files and folders when they are disconnected from the network. This is an especially important tool for mobile computer users who work away from the office for periods of time. This enables mobile users to work on networked versions of their files when they are not connected to the network.

When a networked version of a file is made available offline, a copy of the file is cached to the user's local hard drive. The user works on the file just as if he or she were connected to the network. When the user is reconnected to the network, the locally cached copy of the file is synchronized with the network version. If both

11

the network version and the locally cached version of the file have been worked on, Windows XP will ask the user to choose which file should be kept. A user can also keep both versions by renaming one of the files.

After files are made available on a shared network folder for offline use, the client computer must be configured to use them. Users must set up their notebook computers for offline file use before they will be able to cache the files to their local hard disk (see Figure 11.1). To configure a notebook computer for offline file use, follow these steps:

1. Click Start.

2. Double-click My Computer.

3. Select Tools.

4. Select Folder Options.

5. Select the Offline Files tab.

6. Make sure that the Enable Offline Files checkbox is checked.

7. Click OK to close the Folder Options dialog box.

8. Close My Computer.

If a user is working with a networked file and she gets disconnected from the network for one reason or another, how will she know if she is working on the

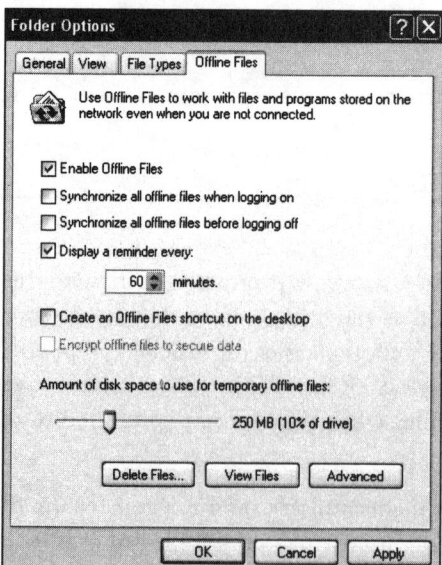

Figure 11.1 Offline Files tab in the Folder Options dialog box.

networked version of the file or the locally cached version? Windows XP Professional can be configured to provide a warning message if a notebook computer is disconnected from the network. Windows XP Professional provides two options for how your computer will behave when the network connection to offline files is lost. The first option will notifiy you by stating that the network connection has been lost and you can continue working on the locally cached copy of the files. The second warning option will make offline files unavailable if the network connection is lost.

Synchronizing Offline Files and Folders

The key to using Offline Files and Folders is to keep the network and cached copies synchronized so that the user always has access to the most current copy. When a user initially configures his notebook computer for offline file use, he is given two options as to when his files can be synchronized. The options are located on the Offline Files tab of the Folder Options dialog box in My Computers. Users can choose to have their files synchronized when they log onto the network or when they log off (refer to Figure 11.1).

The Synchronization Manager tool on the Accessories menu can be used to specify additional options for synchronizing files and folders (see Figure 11.2). This tool scans the computer system for changes. If any changes are detected, the resources are automatically updated. An option is available to prompt users before the Synchronization Manager synchronizes the items.

11

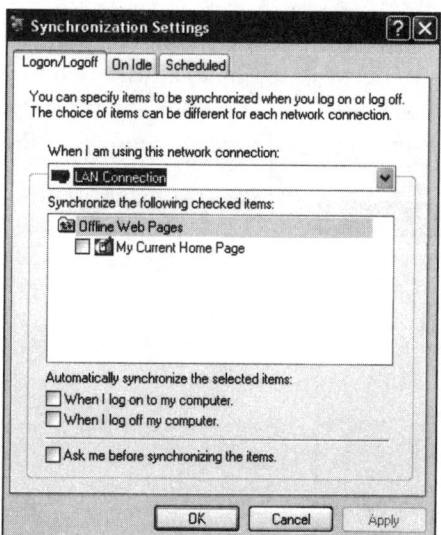

Figure 11.2   Synchronization Settings in the Synchronization Manager tool.

Users can schedule when items are synchronized. The Scheduled Synchronization Wizard can be used to configure the times when items are synchronized (see Figure 11.3). You might not want to synchronize offline files during heavy network traffic periods. You could schedule the synchronization to take place during off-peak hours, such as late at night or when there is less activity on the network. You can also specify to synchronize during periods of system inactivity.

Notebook computer users sometimes don't have the best network connections. Many times, while traveling, they may have to connect to the office network through a slow dial-up connection. With the Synchronization Manager, notebook computer users can synchronize their files dependent on the type of network connection they are currently using. They can specify that large files only be synchronized when the notebook computer is connected to the network with a high-speed connection.

Security is always an important issue, especially when using portable computers. You do not want unauthorized users to gain access to sensitive company or personal data. In Windows 2000, you had no way to ensure that your locally cached offline files were secure from prying eyes. Windows XP Professional has tightened security, by adding the capability to encrypt offline files. EFS can be used to encrypt the Offline Files database (refer to Figure 11.1). Remember, though, that EFS works only on the NTFS file system. If your notebook computer is formatted with FAT or FAT32, you will not be able to encrypt your offline files.

Remote Access Connections

Many notebook computer users work from home, remote client locations, or both. These users often need the same access to network resources as users who work in the office and are directly connected to the office network. Windows XP Professional provides notebook computer users with several ways to connect to their

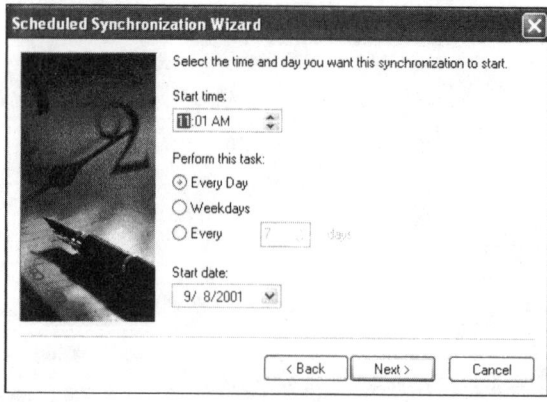

Figure 11.3 The Scheduled Synchronization Wizard.

company network. For a user to connect to a company network, he must first configure an outbound connecton on his notebook computer. This outbound connnection is used to connect to a remote access server for the company network. Windows XP Professional provides support for three types of outbound connections—Internet connections, connections to private networks, and advanced connections. These connections are configured using the New Connection Wizard (see Figure 11.4).

Internet Connections

The Internet connections option is used to create dial-up connections and broadband connections. A dial-up connection is used to connect users to their company network through the public switched telephone network (PSTN) via an Internet service provider (ISP). The most common type of dial-up connection is made with a modem and a standard analog telephone line.

A broadband connection is used to connect a computer to a company network or remote access server by use of a cable or DSL modem. This type of connection provides faster access than a dial-up connnection. The only problem with using a broadband connection such as a cable or DSL modem is that these types of connections might not always be available. Many hotels are now including high-speed data access capabilities in their rooms for business travelers who have the need for faster Internet connections than can be provided though an analog telephone line.

Connections to Private Networks

Making a connection to a private network provides access to a private network via a dial-up connection or a VPN. The dial-up connecton can be made using a

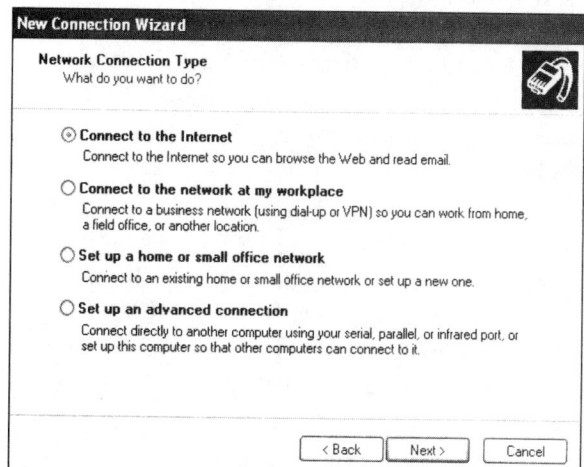

Figure 11.4 The New Connection Wizard.

modem and analog telephone line or an ISDN phone line. A VPN connecton can be initiated through a local ISP to the private network via the Internet. By using a local ISP, users will not have to incur costly long-distance charges.

Advanced Connections

An advanced connection is used to configure a computer to accept incoming connections through a telephone line or over the Internet. Using this option, users can also configure a direct connection to another computer through a parallel, serial, or infrared port.

Remote Access Protocols

After you determine the type of connection that a notebook computer will make to the company network, you must establish the connection. Remote access protocols are used to establish a connection between the remote access server on the company network and a notebook or client computer. Windows XP Professional supports the following remote access protocols for dial-up connections.

Point-to-Point Protocol

PPP enables remote clients from various vendors to communicate and operate together in a network. PPP replaces SLIP and is the basis for both PPTP and L2TP. PPP supports several authentication schemes, including PAP and CHAP. PPP is the most commonly used protocol today for dial-up connections.

Serial Line Internet Protocol

SLIP is an older protocol that was originally developed for use in the Unix environment. SLIP only supports the TCP/IP protocol and has been replaced with PPP. Windows XP Professional can act as a SLIP client but not a SLIP server. SLIP is mainly used with Telnet.

Remote Access Service

RAS is an older protocol that was primarily used in earlier versions of Windows to provide access for remote clients. RAS allowed remote clients to connect to remote servers over standard telephone lines, ISDN lines, and X.25 switching networks. RAS was replaced by Routing and Remote Access Service (RRAS) starting with Windows 2000. Windows XP Professional supports RAS for connecting to remote access servers running older versions of Windows, such as NT 3.51, Windows for Workgroups, and LAN Manager.

VPN

A virtual private network (VPN) is a way for remote clients to securely connect to a private network over the shared public network. If a company has a large number of remote clients that need to connect to the company network, a VPN is a cost-effective alternative to using a dial-up remote access network. A VPN creates a tunnel, which is a secure communication route on an existing network. Data is encapsulated into PPP data packets and transmitted across this tunnel.

VPN connections can be made by dialing a local ISP or through an Internet connection. If a remote client is creating a VPN connecton through its ISP, it first makes the connection to the ISP and then makes another call to the remote access server using either the PPTP or L2TP protocol. Both of these protocols are installed by default in Windows XP Professional.

VPN Protocol

Both PPTP and L2TP can be used in Windows XP Professional to create a secure VPN tunnel to transmit data over an unsecure network.

Point-to-Point Tunneling Protocol

PPTP is an extension of PPP and encapsulates IP data packets into PPP frames to create a tunnel for secure communication. PPTP provides authentication through the same authentication methods as PPP, including PAP, CHAP, and MS-CHAP. PPTP requires an IP-based network and does not support header compression. It does not support IPSec, and encryption is provided via standard PPP methods.

Layer 2 Tunneling Protocol

L2TP is the second protocol that can be used to create VPNs over public networks. As with PPTP, L2TP supports the same authention methods as PPP. L2TP can be tunneled over a wide range of connection media, unlike PPTP, which can only be tunneled over IP. L2TP supports header compression and supports tunnel authentication using IPSec.

Authentication Protocols

When a remote user is trying to connect to a remote server, the user must be authenticated just as if she were connected to the office LAN. After the user is authenticated, she can access resources on the network that she has the appropriate permissions for.

Standard Authentication Protocols

As in Windows 2000, Windows XP Professional has several standard authentication protocols that can be used to perform remote client user authentication. A description of these protocols follows.

Password Authentication Protocol

PAP uses unencrypted, clear-text passwords to authenticate users. PAP is the least secure authentication method available in Windows XP Professional. It is normally only used if the remote access client and server cannot negotiate a higher form of authentication.

Shiva Authentication Protocol

SPAP is used by Shiva clients to dial in to a remote access server. SPAP is more secure than PAP because it encrypts a user's password.

Challenge Handshake Authentication Protocol

CHAP is more secure than PAP and uses the industry-standard Message Digest 5 (MD5) encryption scheme to negotiate a secure form of authentication. MD5 is a hashing scheme that transforms a password into a unique form that cannot be changed back to its original form. A CHAP authentication session consists of the following steps:

1. The remote client connects to the remote server.

2. The remote server challenges the remote client by sending a session ID and an arbitrary string of characters called a challenge string.

3. The remote client uses MD5 and sends to the remote server the username, an encrypted form of the remote server's challenge, the session ID, and the password.

4. The remote server checks the response from the remote client; if it is valid, the connection is allowed.

CHAP is normally used by clients that are not running a Microsoft operating system. It is supported by both RAS and RRAS.

Microsoft Challenge Handshake Authentication Protocol

MS-CHAP was created as an extension of CHAP to allow for the authentication of remote Windows workstations. MS-CHAP is basically Microsoft's version of CHAP. It uses a challenge response packet that is specifically designed for Microsoft operating sytems. An MS-CHAP authentication session consists of the following steps:

1. The remote client connects to the remote server.

2. The remote client requests authentication from the remote server.

3. The remote server sends the remote client a challenge consisting of a session identifier and an arbitrary string of characters called a challenge string.

4. The remote client returns to the remote server a response consisting of the username plus a one-way encryption of the password, the session ID, and the challenge string.

5. The remote server checks the response from the remote client; if it is valid, the connection is allowed and the remote client is authenticated.

MS-CHAPv2

MS-CHAPv2 is the latest version of MS-CHAP. MS-CHAPv2 supports two-way (or mutual) authentication and is more secure than MS-CHAP. MS-CHAPv2 uses separate cryptographic keys for transmitting and receiving user data. It is the most secure form of authentication available in Windows XP Professional.

Extensible Authentication Protocol

EAP was designed in response to user demand for remote access authentication using third-party security devices, such as smart cards. EAP is an extension of PPP and enables a remote server and client to negotiate the type of authentication method that will be used for the session. Windows XP Professional supports EAP using the following methods.

Message Digest 5 Challenge Handshake

MD5-CHAP uses the MDR hash algorithm to encrypt usernames and passwords. MD5 takes the user data (username and password) and produces a128-bit nonreversible message digest. This message digest is unique, and it is computationally infeasible to determine what the data is, based on the message digest. Another user would not be able to decipher the username and password based on the message digest.

Transport Layer Security

TLS provides connection security in a way that prevents eavesdropping or message forgery. TLS is composed of two layers—the TLS Record Protocol and the TLS Handshake Protocol. The TLS Record Protocol provides connection security and ensures that the connection is private and that it is reliable. It uses symmetric cyptography for data encryption. TLS is used for security devices, such as smart cards.

Third-party Authentication Methods

Manaufacturers can use EAP to provide their own authentication methods.

11

Smart Cards

A smart card is a small device about the size of a credit card that contains an embedded integrated circuit. Smart card use was first introduced in Windows 2000 Professional as an important part of the public key infrastructure that was integrated in Windows 2000. This support is also provided in Windows XP.

A smart card stores private and public key information, passwords, and other personal user information. Smart cards provide a tamper-resistant storage method for protecting user data, such as passwords. It provides a way for remote users to take their logon information with them to use on their computers, whether they are at home, at work, or on the road.

To use a smart card, you must install a smart card reader on your notebook computer. Windows XP Professional automatically detects Plug and Play smart card readers. Windows XP Professional can use smart cards to authenticate users in two ways—interactive logon and remote access. An interactive logon occurs when a user inserts a smart card into the smart card reader and the operating system prompts the user for the PIN. With remote access authentication, two steps are involved. In the first step, authentication is performed on the remote server, and remote access policies are applied to the remote client. The second step occurs on the network, and the EAP_TLS protocol is used for authentication.

Data Encryption

Data encryption is used to encrypt data sent between a remote client and a remote server. This remote data encryption only occurs on the communications link between the server and the client. If end-to-end encryption is required, users should considering using IPSec.

Data encryption over dial-up remote connections is made possible via PPP and the MS-CHAP authentication protocols. If the remote server requires data encryption, and the client cannot perform the required encryption, the connection will be terminated.

Network connections in Windows XP Professional supports two types of data encryption between remote access servers and clients—MPPE and IPSec.

Microsoft Point-to-Point Encryption

MPPE is based on the Rivest-Shamir-Adleman (RSA) RCA stream cipher and uses either 40-, 56-, or 128-bit secret keys. MPPE secret keys are generated when using the EAP-TLS, MS-CHAP, or MS-CHAP v2 authentication method. Using MPPE with the 128-bit secret key provides the strongest level of encryption for moving data across a PPTP connection on a VPN. You must use the same level of encryption on the two computers or they will not be able to communicate.

Internet Protocol Security

IPSec is used to negotiate a secure connection between a remote server and a remote client. IPSec secures data at the IP level and uses the DES or Triple DES encryption algorithm. DES uses 56-bit encryption, and Triple DES uses 168-bit encryption. IPSec is used with L2TP to provide a tunnel to securely transmit data packets over an IP network.

The type of encryption method used by a VPN is determined by the type of server that it is being connected to. If a remote client computer is trying to connect to a PPTP server, then MPPE encrytion is used. If the remote client is tying to connect to an L2TP server, then IPSec encryption is used. If the VPN is configured for automatic detection, L2TP with IPSec is attempted first. If this is unsuccessful, then PPTP is used.

Callback

The Callback feature in Windows XP Professional is a useful feature that can be used to reduce company telephone charges when remote users are on company travel. With the Callback feature, a remote client calls a remote server. The remote server disconnects the call and re-calls the remote client at a predetermined number. This provides added security in that only users from specific numbers will be able to access the remote server.

Callback privileges are determined by the remote access server administrator (see Figure 11.5). The administrator can deny a user the ability to use Callback, allow

11

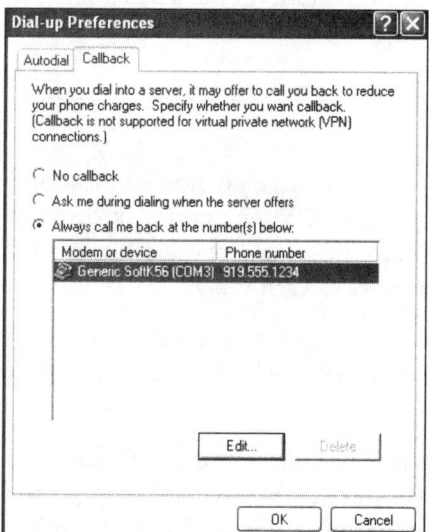

Figure 11.5   Callback options in the Dial-Up Preferences dialog box.

the remote user to set his Callback options, or require that the Callback feature always be used with a particular telephone number.

Multilink Connections

Network connections can be used to dynamically control the use of multilink, which enables users to combine multiple physical links into one logical link. By combining two or more communications ports into a single port, the amount of bandwidth available to a computer is increased. Multilink can combine multiple modem, ISDN, or X.25 lines for increased throughput. Windows XP Professional uses PPP Multilink and Bandwidth Allocation Protocol to provide multilinking.

Point-to-Point Protocol Multilink

PPP Multilink is used to combine multiple modem and IDSN lines into a single virtual data connection. PPP Multilink is an extension of PPP and basically is inverse multiplexing of PPP communication links. Multiple physical links are inversely multiplexed together to form a single logical high-bandwith connection. To use PPP Multilink, it must be enabled on both the remote client and remote server computers.

Bandwidth Allocation Protocol

BAP provides additional functionality to PPP Multilink by eliminating wasted bandwidth. With BAP, administrators can configure the PPP Multilink server to dynamically add or drop links on demand. BAP is especially useful to consumers who are being charged by the amount of bandwidth they are using. Links that are not being utilized can be dynamically dropped.

Direct Cable Connections

The New Connections Wizard can be used to make a physical connection to another computer. This can be another notebook computer, a desktop computer, or another device, such as a palm computer. To make a direct cable connection, the two computers must be in physical proximity to each other.

A direct connection can be made using a serial cable, DirectParallel cables, an IDSN device, or an RS-232 null mode. DirectParellel cables use standard ECP parallel ports.

When you create a direct connection, one computer acts as the host and the other acts as the guest (see Figure 11.6). To configure a computer as a direct connection host, you must have administrator rights on the computer. You do not need administrator rights if you are configuring the computer as a direct connection guest. You can also specify which users can connect to the computer through this connecton.

When a computer is configured as a direct connection host, the connection for it appears as an incoming connection in the Network Connections window (see Figure 11.7).

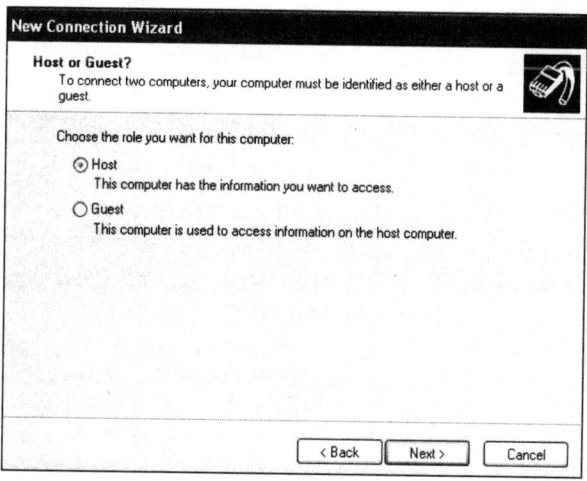

Figure 11.6 The New Connection Wizard for direct cable connections.

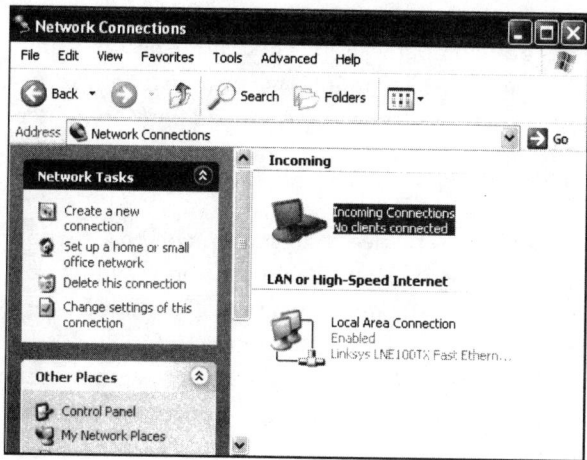

Figure 11.7 Network Connections with an incoming connection.

Remote Desktop

Remote Desktop is a new feature introduced in Windows XP Professional that will allow users to connect to their desktop computers from remote locations. Users can access their files and folders just as if they were working from the desktop console. Remote Desktop is a great tool for remote users who travels and needs access to files on their home computer.

A Windows XP Professional computer that is running Remote Desktop can be accessed from the Internet using any Windows-based client. Remote Desktop can be used even when the remote client only has access via a low-bandwidth connection, because only the keyboard, mouse, and display information are transmitted over the connection.

The Remote Desktop Protocol (RDP) enables Windows-based clients to communicate with the Windows XP Professional computer that is running Remote Desktop. RDP can be used across any TCP/IP connection, including dial-up, LAN, WAN, ISDN, VPN, and DSL.

Fast Startup

Microsoft found that one of the major complaints users had about its computer systems was the amount of time it took for the OSs to start. This could be from a cold boot or from Standby or Hibernation mode. The Windows XP development team took steps to make fast startup for computers a reality. Startup times are especially important for notebook computer users. These users do not want to have to wait long periods of time to use their computers when returning from Standby or Hibernation mode. Windows XP Professional, when used with computers that are ACPI-compliant, wakes from Standby mode in only a few seconds. Waking from Hibernation mode takes less than 30 seconds.

Windows XP Professional includes several design improvements that support fast startup. Windows XP supports the Simple Boot Flag specification, which reduces the amount of time the BIOS spends peforming a self test. The boot loader, or NTLDR, optimizes disk reads by caching files and the directory metadata, which reduces time spent for disk seeks. Load time for the operating system is optimized by delaying the loading of processes and services that are not required at boot time.

New Usability Features

New features have been added to Windows XP Professional to make using portable computers easier for remote users.

ClearType

ClearType provides mobile computer users with better resolution for their LCD screens. This new technology triples the horizontal resolution that is used on notebook computers. Text that is displayed on an LCD screen with ClearType is much clearer.

Automatic Connection for Networks

Users of notebook computers can use them as standalone machines at home or connected via a docking station to their company network while at work. Windows XP Professional simplifies configuring your mobile computer with automatic configuration. When a notebook computer is attached to a company network, Windows XP Professional will try to automatically configure it with the appropriate settings for working on the network. If a DHCP server is unavailable to provide an IP address, the computer will be automatically assigned a private IP.

Dualview

Dualview enables a mobile computer user to utilize two monitors on his notebook computer at the same time. One document can be displayed on the LCD screen of the notebook computer while another document is displayed on a monitor attached to the external monitor port.

Stored User Names and Passwords

When a user logs onto her computer, she supplies a username and password. This information is authenticated using the local SAM on a standalone computer and using Active Directory in a domain environment. Remote users might need to log onto different resources that require a separate set of usernames and passwords. Windows XP Professional includes a feature that enables users to store multiple credentials that can be unique for each resource they are trying to connect to. Stored User Names and Passwords stores usernames and passwords for multiple servers. Users can store a different set of logon credentials for each server they need to connect to (see Figure 11.8).

When a user attempts to connect to a network, Windows XP Professional will supply the current username and password for authentication. If this password and username do not have sufficient rights for logon, Stored User Names and Passwords will attemp to provide a username and password that have sufficient logon rights. The information in Stored User Names and Passwords can be saved as part of a user's profile and used from any computer that is used to log onto the network.

By using Stored User Names and Passwords, mobile computer users do not have to log off their computer when they need to supply a different set of logon credentials to a remote server. Any number of usernames and passwords can be stored and used as needed.

11

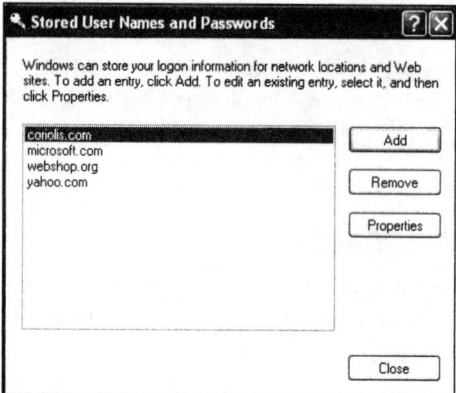

Figure 11.8 Stored User Names and Passwords.

Chapter Summary

This chapter examines how Windows XP Professional can enhance the mobile computing experience for remote users. Hardware profiles can be used to provide remote users with the option to set up different configurations for each of their work environments. Users can have one hardware configuration for work if they are using a notebook computer with a docking station and have a second hardware configuration for when they are using the notebook remotely.

Power management in Windows XP Professional is supported through the ACPI specification. Several predefined power schemes have been included that a user can select to aid in power management on a notebook computer. Two power saving options—Standby mode and Hibernation mode—can be configured to conserve battery power by putting devices that are not being used into a low-power state. Several new power management features have been added with Windows XP, including processor power control, Wake-on-LAN, Wake on Battery, and display dimming.

Offline Files and Folders is used to provide remote users with the capability to work on their networked files and folders when they are not connected to the network. The files are cached to their local hard disk and synchronized with their networked counterparts when the user reconnects to the network.

Network connections provides several ways for remote users to connect to company networks and the Internet. Dial-up connections can be made with standard analog telephone lines through an ISP. A broadband connection can be made to a network through devices, such as cable or DSL modems. A VPN can be created if a user needs a secure connection to a network.

Windows XP Professioal supports PPP, SLIP, and RAS for dial-up connections. PPTP and L2TP are the protocols that are used to create secure VPN tunnels over an unsecured public network. Several authentication protocols are used to perform remote client user authentication. They include PAP, SPAP, CHAP, and MS-CHAP. MPPE and IPSec are used to provide data encryption between remote clients and servers.

Remote Desktop can be used remotely to allow remote users to access their desktop computers from the Internet using any Windows-based client computer. Remote Desktop is based on the Windows Terminal Services technology and uses RDP for connectivity.

Review Questions

1. What feature in Windows XP Professional will allow a notebook computer user to set up different configurations for work and home?

   a. Network Connections

   b. Hardware profiles

   c. Device Manager

   d. Add Hardware Wizard

2. Jeannie has a notebook computer that she uses both at home and work. Jeannie is frustrated with the small keyboard and monitor on her notebook and is considering purchasing a desktop computer. What can Jeannie purchase to use with her notebook computer that will provide her with the same functionality that she would have if she were to purchase a regular desktop computer?

   a. Nothing she can purchase will give her the same functionality as a desktop computer.

   b. A new desktop computer.

   c. A palm-type computer.

   d. A docking station.

3. What statement describes the process that occurs when William plugs his portable computer into its docking station while it is not turned on?

   a. Warm dock

   b. Hot dock

   c. Cold dock

   d. System lock

4. Which of the following protocols allows for the dynamic adding or dropping of links on a modem pool that is configured for multilink?

   a. PPP

   b. RAS

   c. BAP

   d. MPPE

5. Ron is on company travel and needs to connect to the company intranet to transfer some client files that will be needed for a meeting tomorrow morning. The hotel he is staying in has told him that he will be assessed a per-minute fee for each call he makes from his room. Ron does not have access to his local ISP from this hotel. How can Ron get the files transferred without incurring extensive long-distance charges?

   a. He can use the Callback feature for dial-up connections in Windows XP Professional.

   b. He can trying emailing the files back to the office.

   c. There is nothing he can do that won't cost him additional charges.

   d. He can select the option in the New Connection Wizard to select an ISP.

6. Which of the following data encryption methods can be used on a VPN tunnel that is utilizing the IPSec protocol? [Check all correct answers]

   a. DES

   b. Triple DES

   c. MD5-CHAP

   d. TLS

7. Regina supports a large number of remote users. She periodically has to log onto 15 remote access servers to ensure that they are servicing the remote users. Regina has different logon accounts on 12 of the 15 servers. What feature in Windows XP Professional will allow Regina to have multiple server logon accounts, each with a unique password?

   a. Users and Password

   b. User Accounts

   c. Stored User Names and Passwords

   d. Remote Assistance

8. Julie has just purchased a new notebook computer that came preinstalled with Windows XP Professional. She is planning to give her old notebook computer to her little sister who is going away to college in the fall. Julie has several very large databases that she needs to transfer to her new computer before she gives her old computer to her sister. The new computer does not have a writeable CD-ROM drive, and the majority of the files she needs to transfer are over 5MB. What options are available to allow Julie to transfer her files to the new notebook computer?

   a. Julie can use Direct Connections under Network Connections to connect the two computers and transfer the files.

   b. Julie can try to email the file to the new computer over the Internet.

   c. Julie can install a tape backup unit on the first computer, save the files to a tape, and then connect the tape backup unit to the second computer and restore the files to it.

   d. She can purchase a new CD-ROM drive for the computer that has write capability.

9. Betsy is the system administrator for a large insurance company. The company has just implemented a large number of Windows XP Professional computers that are used by the agents when they are in the field. When the agents are in the office, they usually have their notebook computers attached to the network. Many of the users have configured their computers to go into Standby mode after five minutes of inactivity. Betsy needs to push out via the network a new software application that the agents will be required to use. What Windows XP Professional technology will ensure that Betsy will be able to push out the software to both the desktop computers and the agents' notebook computers?

   a. Wake on Battery

   b. Remote Desktop

   c. SMS

   d. Wake-on-LAN

11

10. Wills is using several files that have been cached from the network to the local hard drive on his portable computer. He needs to synchronize them with their network counterparts but doesn't want his computer slowed down while it is trying to synchronize the files. How can Wills continue to use his computer with minimal interference and still get his files synchronized with the ones on the network?

    a. He can use the Synchronization Manager and schedule the files to be synchronized when he logs onto the computer.

    b. He can use the Synchronization Manager and schedule the files to be synchronized during periods of inactivity.

    c. He can use the Synchronization Manager and schedule the files to be synchronized when he logs off the computer.

    d. He can't. He will have to take the performance hit on his computer when the files are synchronized with their network counterparts.

11. Jill needs to transfer some important company files to her manager before tomorrow night. She has remote access to the company network but wants to make sure that the files are securely transmitted over the Internet. What kind of connection should Jill set up to securely transfer the files to the company network?

    a. Dial-up connection via an analog telephone line

    b. Dial-up connection using a VPN

    c. Direct connection to another computer

    d. Dial-up connection to a local ISP

12. Which of the following authentication protocols supports mutual authentication?

    a. PAP

    b. SPAP

    c. MS-CHAPv2

    d. EAP

13. Which of the following remote access protocols is used primarily with the Telnet application?

    a. PPP

    b. RAS

    c. SLIP

    d. PPTP

14. Jonathan has just installed Windows XP Professional on his portable computer. He is an accountant and uses his computer to work on and store client data. Jonathan works away from the office a lot and usually runs his computer on batteries when he is not in the office. He wants to make sure that he doesn't lose any important client data if the battery power becomes low on the computer. What can he do to ensure this?

   a. He can configure the portable computer to operate in Standby mode.

   b. He can configure the portable computer to operate in Hibernation mode.

   c. He can periodically back up the client data while he is working on it.

   d. He can create a power scheme to automatically save the client data.

15. PPTP can be used on which types of networks?

   a. AppleTalk

   b. IPX/SPX

   c. IP-based

   d. Unix

16. Morris has been given permission to work from home for a couple of weeks to help his wife who just had a baby. He needs to periodically access the computer in his office during the day to connect to the company mainframe. What Windows XP Professional tool will allow Morris to connect to the mainframe application on his desktop computer in the office?

   a. Desktop Assistant

   b. Synchronization Manager

   c. Telnet

   d. Remote Desktop

11

17. Susan has to give a presentation to a group of lawyers on some research she just completed for them. The presentation is on her notebook computer and was created in a PowerPoint presentation that runs automatically. She needs to continue working on some other projects during the time the presentation is running. How can she accomplish this?

   a. She can use Dualview and run the presentation on an external monitor attached to her notebook computer while she works on her other projects using the notebook's LCD display.

   b. She can use a second computer—one for the presentation and one to continue working on.

   c. There is no way that she can continue working on her projects while she is giving the presentation to the lawyers.

   d. Susan can reschedule the presentation to another time when she is not working on her computer.

18. What feature in Windows XP Professional can be used to protect users' locally cached offline files and folders?

  (a.) EFS

  b. NTFS

  c. Shared Folders

  d. Disk Compression

19. Ronald is giving a speech to prospective clients in an attempt to acquire more business for his company. The majority of his presentation is on his portable computer, and he will be using it for at least four hours to demonstrate some of the new features of the software his company is developing. Ronald wants to make sure that the portable computer does not go into Standby mode during the time he is demonstrating the software to the prospective clients. What power scheme should he set on the computer before he gives the presentation?

  a. Home/Office Desk

  b. Portable/Laptop

  c. Max Battery

  (d.) Presentation

20. What protocol is used to provide the Terminal Services services in Remote Desktop?

  a. TCP/IP

  b. RPC

  (c.) RDP

  d. MPPE

Real-World Projects

Ronald is the systems administrator for a major insurance company in the southwest portion of the country. The company has just purchased a large number of Windows XP Professional computers to be used by its agents when they go into the field to help with claims. Some of the users have specific requests regarding how they want their notebook computers configured before they receive them.

Project 11.1

To create a hardware profile for a notebook computer:

1. Click Start.

2. Click Control Panel.

3. Double-click System.

4. Click the Hardware tab.

5. Click Hardware Profiles.

6. Click Docked (Current) under Available Hardware Profiles.

7. Click Copy.

8. Type the name of the new hardware profile, and click OK.

9. Under When Windows Starts, select a startup option.

10. Reboot the computer.

11. Select the new profile you just created when the computer starts up.

12. Click Start.

13. Click Control Panel.

14. Double-click System.

15. Select the Hardware tab.

16. Click Device Manager.

17. Select a device(s) in Device Manager to enable or disable with this profile.

18. Select one of the following options under Device Usage:
    - ➤ Use this device (enabled)
    - ➤ Do not use this device in the current hardware profile (disabled)
    - ➤ Do not use this device in any hardware profile (disabled)

19. Click OK.

20. Close the Device Manager.

21. Close Systems Properties.

Project 11.2

To create a power scheme for your portable computer:

1. Click Start.

2. Click Control Panel.

3. Double-click Power Options.

4. Select the power scheme that you want to use as your template from Power Schemes.

11

5. Select After 20 Mins under Turn Off Monitor.

6. Select After 30 Mins under Turn Off Hard Disks.

7. Click the Save As button.

8. Enter a name for the new power scheme in Save This Power Scheme As, and click OK.

9. Select After 30 Mins under Turn Off Hard Disks.

10. Your new power scheme is listed under Power Schemes. Click OK to close the Power Options dialog box.

Project 11.3

For this project, you will configure two computers to use a direct cable connection for the transfer of data files. The first computer is the host or source computer, and the second computer is the guest or destination computer.

To configure the host computer:

1. Log onto the source computer as Adminstrator or as an account with administrative privileges.

2. Select Start|Control Panel.

3. Double-click Network Connections.

4. Select Create A New Connection under Network Tasks.

5. The New Connection Wizard is started. Click Next on the Welcome page.

6. Select Set Up An Advanced Connection, and click Next.

7. Select Connect Directly To Another Computer, and click Next.

8. Select Host, and click Next.

9. Select the connection device to be used under Device For This Connection, and click Next.

10. Select the users that will be able to connect to this computer, and click Next.

11. Click Finish.

To configure the second computer as a guest for a direct cable connection:

1. Log onto the destination computer. You do not have to be logged on as Adminstrator to set up a guest direct cable connection.

2. Select Start|Control Panel.

3. Double-click Network Connections.

4. Select Create A New Connection under Network Tasks.

5. The New Connection Wizard is started. Click Next on the Welcome page.

6. Select Set Up An Advanced Connection, and click Next.

7. Select Connect Directly To Another Computer, and click Next.

8. Select Guest, and click Next.

9. Enter the name of the computer you are connect to under Computer Name, and click Next.

10. Select the connection device that will be used under Select A Device, and click Next.

11. Click Finish.

11

CHAPTER TWELVE

Working Securely

After completing this chapter, you will be able to:

✓ Describe the security groups that are included in Windows XP Professional

✓ Describe the security policies that are available in Windows XP Professional

✓ Describe the security features that are available in Windows XP Professional

✓ Explain how to use the Security Configuration and Analysis snap-in tool

✓ Describe Public Key Infrastructure and how it is implemented in Windows XP Professional

U sers should take the necessary precautions to protect their computers from data loss and intrusion by unauthorized sources. Windows XP Professional provides several methods that can be used to ensure that your data is not compromised when working locally, on a network, or over the Internet. In this chapter, we examine some of the security features included in Windows XP Professional.

Security Groups

Windows XP Professional has several built-in security groups that are automatically created when you install the operating system. These security groups can be used to give users the permissions to access resources locally and on the network. Each built-in group has rights to perform specific tasks. These groups are described next.

Administrators

The Administrators group is the most powerful group and has full access to all resources on a computer. Members of the Administrators group can perform the following functions:

➤ Install the operating system and various components, including device drivers

➤ Install Service Packs

➤ Upgrade and repair the operating system

➤ Configure operating system parameters, such as policies and access control

➤ Take ownership of files

➤ Manage security and auditing logs

➤ Perform system backups and restores

Users

Members of the Users group have full control over their data files but cannot remove applications that have been installed by members of the Administrators group or other users. By default, members of the Users group have read-only permissions for most of the OS. They cannot modify any system-wide settings, OS files, or application files that they did not install. They have permission to shut down workstations but not servers. Users group members can create local groups, but can only manage the local groups that they create.

Guests

The Guests group is for users who need one-time access to a workstation. This group has the least amount of permissions but its members can shut down the system on a workstation. The Guest account is disabled by default.

Backup Operators

The Backup Operators group has the permission to back up and restore all files and folders on a computer, regardless of the permissions protecting the files. Its members can shut down the computer but cannot change any security settings. Read and Write permissions are required to back up and restore files. Users who are made members of the Backup Operators group are able to read individual user's files. Thus, special consideration should be given when deciding which users are given membership to this group.

Power Users

Power Users have more permissions than members of the Users group but fewer permissions than members of the Administrators group. They can perform most tasks except for those specifically reserved for the Administrators group. Members of the Power Users group can perform the following functions:

➤ Run applications

➤ Install programs and applications that do not modify system files

➤ Customize printers, power options, date, time, and other Control Panel resources

➤ Create and manage local user accounts and groups

➤ Stop and start system services not configured to start by default

➤ Remove users from the Power Users, Users, and Guests groups

Power Users group members cannot add themselves to the Administrators group and cannot access user data on NTFS volumes.

Replicator

The Replicator group does not contain any actual user accounts. It is used by a domain user account that logs onto the Replicator services of a domain controller to support directory replication functions.

Special Groups

Several other groups are created by default when Windows XP Professional is installed, in addition to the security groups previously described.

Interactive

The Interactive group includes any users who are currently logged onto the computer. If the computer was upgraded from a previous version of Windows to Windows XP, members of the Interactive group will be added to the Power Users group.

12

Network

Any uses who are accessing a computer over a network are members of the Network group.

Terminal Server User

Any users who are currently logged on a computer that is running Terminal Services in application serving mode are members of the Terminal Server User group. If Terminal Services is running in remote administration mode, users who are logged onto the computer will not be members of the Terminal Server User group.

Group Policy

Group Policies give administrators the capability to manage and define different components of a user's desktop environment. Administrators can use Group Policies to apply security policies to both domain-based and local workstations.

Group Polices are created using the Group Policy snap-in, which can be used to create policy settings for the computer configuration or the user configuration (see Figure 12.1). Computer-configured Group Policies take effect when a computer is started. User-configured Group Policies take effect when a user logs onto the computer.

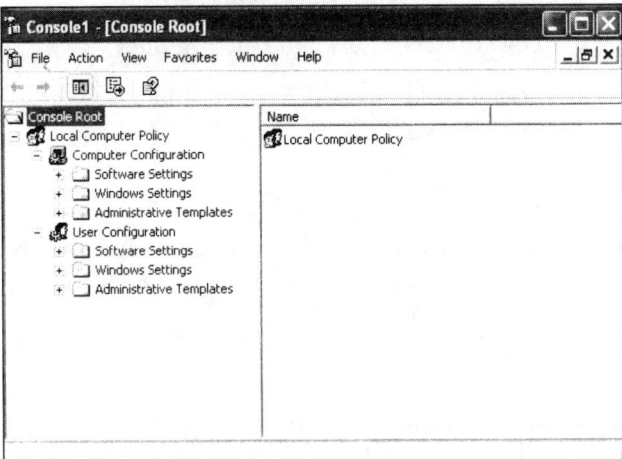

Figure 12.1   Group Policy snap-in tool.

Security Policies

Security Policies are a subset of Group Policies and are configured on individual computers using the Local Security Policy, which is accessed through Administrative Tools in the Control Panel (see Figure 12.2). Security settings that are configured through the Local Security Policy take effect immediately on the computer.

Account Policies

Account Policies are used to configure password and account lockout policies. The following Account Policies can be configured.

Password Policy

➤ Enforce password history

➤ Maximum password age

➤ Minimum password age

➤ Minimum password length

➤ Password must meet complexity requirements

➤ Store password using reversible encryption

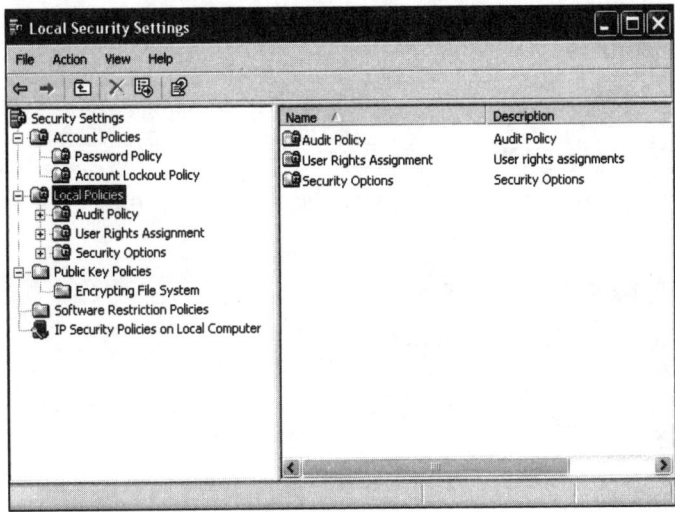

Figure 12.2   Local Security Settings for Local Security Policy.

Account Lockout Policy

➤ Account lockout duration

➤ Account lockout threshold

➤ Reset account lockout counter after

Local Policies

Local Policies are used to configure auditing, user rights, and additional security options. The following Local Policies can be configured.

Audit Policy

➤ Audit account logon events

➤ Audit account management

➤ Audit directory service access

➤ Audit logon events

➤ Audit object access

➤ Audit policy change

➤ Audit privilege use

➤ Audit process tracking

➤ Audit system events

User Rights Assignment

Thirty-seven user rights assignment policies can be configured. Some of these are the following:

➤ Access this computer from the network

➤ Allow logon through Terminal Services

➤ Back up files and directories

➤ Create a pagefile

➤ Deny logon locally

➤ Restore files and directories

Security Options

Sixty-two security options can be configured for local and domain-based workstations (see Figure 12.3). The following are some of the optional settings that can be configured to enhance security on local workstations:

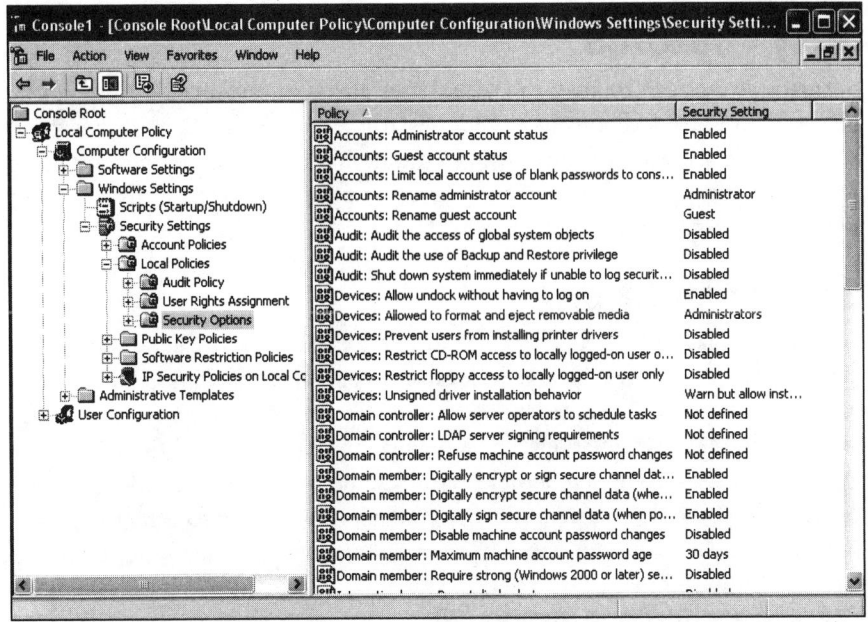

Figure 12.3 Security Options under Local Computer Policy.

➤ *Ctrl+Alt+Delete*—If this policy is enabled, users are required to use the Ctrl+Alt+Delete key combination to log onto the workstation. By using this option, you are ensured that users are being authenticated by either a local SAM for a standalone workstation or Active Directory in a domain environment. This option can also be used to lock a workstation when the user has to leave the work environment for any period of time.

➤ *Clear virtual memory pagefile*—When Windows XP Professional is shut down, it does not clear the virtual memory pagefile. This file could be accessible to users who are not authorized to view it and could therefore pose a security risk.

➤ *Message text for users attempting to log on*—Companies can post a message to users logging onto their computers to remind them that they are to be used only for business purposes.

➤ *Limit local account use of blank passwords to console logon only*—If this option is enabled, remote users who are trying to log onto the computer via Telnet or Terminal Services must have a nonblank password. Blank passwords would only be allowed if entered directly from the computer console.

➤ *Do not display last username*—The name of the last user who logged onto a Windows XP Professional computer is displayed by default in the Log On To Windows dialog box. For security reasons, administrators might want to disable this so that unauthorized users do not see valid user accounts displayed on the screen.

12

Security Features

Security groups can be used to control user access to resources. Group Policies can be used to define and control a user's desktop environment. Windows XP includes several other security features to aid in protecting resources on your network. Administrators can use security templates to apply predefined security configurations to workstations and servers.

Security Templates

Security templates are included in Windows XP Professional to allow administrators to create and apply Security Policies to local and domain-based workstations. The predefined templates included can be customized by the system administrator and applied to one or multiple workstations. These templates can be imported to the Local Security Policy of the local computer. Templates can also be used as a baseline for creating an analysis of a computer's current security configuration. All the security templates discussed next are located in the *%systemroot%*\security\templates subdirectory.

Default Security (Setup security.inf)

Setup security.inf is the default security template that is applied when Windows XP Professional is installed. This template could be used as part of a disaster recovery operation if you needed to return a system to the state it was in when the operating system was initially installed.

Compatible (Compatws.inf)

The Compatws.inf security template applies strict security settings to members of the Users group and gives the Power Users group security settings that are compatible with the Users group in Windows NT 4. It is assumed that if an administrator is applying the compatible security template, she does not want users to be members of Power Users. For this reason, all members of the Power Users group are removed.

Secure (Secure*.inf)

Secure.inf provides stronger password, account lockout, and audit settings than the default and compatible security templates. It limits the use of LAN Manager and NTLM authentication protocols. It provides stronger restrictions on anonymous users, such as users accessing from untrusted domains.

Highly Secure (Hisec*.inf)

The Hisec.inf security template requires strong encryption and signing on all network communications. Computers configured with the highly secure template will only be able to communicate with other computers with the same template.

They also will not be able to communicate with computers running Windows 95, 98, or NT. All members of the Power Users group are removed when this template is applied.

System Root Security (Rootsec.inf)

The system root security template, new to Windows XP (all the other security templates were introduced in Windows 2000), specifies root permissions for the system drive. It can be used to reapply these permissions if, for some reason, they have been changed or inadvertently modified.

Security Configuration and Analysis

The Security Configuration and Analysis snap-in can be used to both analyze a computer's current security settings and apply any of the predefined security templates or custom templates created by an administrator (see Figure 12.4). The Security Configuration and Analysis tool can be used to import and export security templates to a local workstation, and to analyze the current security configuration of the computer. This analysis is provided with recommendations on how to bring the system up to a proposed level of security. It also is a troubleshooting tool that can be used to resolve any security discrepancies revealed during the analysis.

Secedit.exe

Secedit.exe is a command-line tool that can be used to automate the task of analyzing system security. It is extremely useful for administrators who have a large number of computers that they want to analyze but only want them analyzed during off-peak hours. Secedit.exe can be called from a script or batch file or run

12

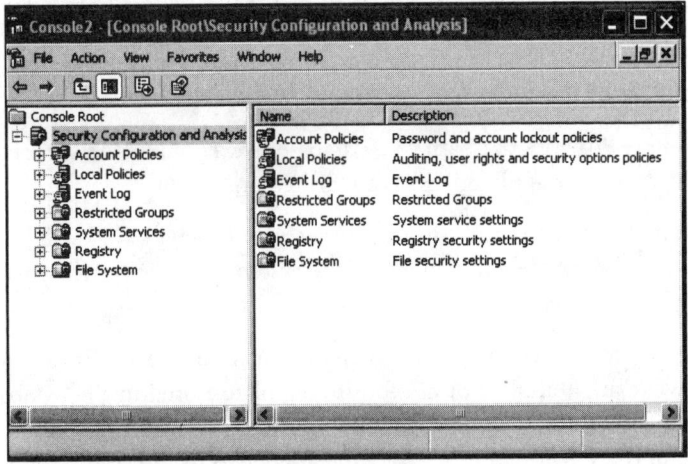

Figure 12.4   Security Configuration and Analysis snap-in.

dynamically from a command line to compare the computer system's current security configuration against at least one of the security templates.

The following are the command-line options for configuring Secedit.exe to analyze security on a computer system:

```
secedit /analyze [/DB file name ] [/CFG file name ] [/log log path]
[/verbose] [/quiet]
```

The following is a list of the individual command-line parameters:

➤ **/DB** *file name*—Provides the path to a database that contains the stored configuration against which the analysis will be performed. This is a required argument.

➤ **/CFG** *file name*—Provides the path to the security template that will be imported into the database for analysis. Only valid when used with the **/DB** parameter.

➤ **/log** *log path*—Provides the path to the log file for the process. If this is not provided, the default file is used.

➤ **/verbose**—Requests more detailed progress information during the analysis.

➤ **/quiet**—Suppresses screen and log output. You will still be able to view analysis results using Security Configuration and Analysis.

The following are the command-line options for configuring Secedit.exe to configure security on the computer system:

```
secedit /configure [/DB file name ] [/CFG file name ] [/overwrite][/areas
area1 area2...] [/log log path] [/verbose] [/quiet]
```

The following is a list of the individual command-line parameters:

➤ **/DB** *file name*—Provides the path to a database that contains the security template that should be applied. This is a required argument.

➤ **/CFG** *file name*—Provides the path to the security template that will be imported into the database and applied to the system. Valid only when used with the **/DB** parameter.

➤ **/overwrite**—Specifies whether the security template in the **/CFG** argument should overwrite any template or composite template stored in the database instead of appending the results to the stored template. If this is not specified, the template in the **/CFG** argument will be appended to the stored template. Valid only when the **/CFG** argument is also used.

➤ **/areas** *area1 area2...*—Specifies the security areas to be applied to the system. The default is "all areas." Each area should be separated by a space.

Access Control

Access Control in Windows XP is based on authentication and authorization. Authentication confirms the identity of users who are trying to access a computer. Authorization verifies that the user who has been authenticated has the correct permissions to access a resource. Two types of authentication are provided in Windows XP Professional—interactive logon and network authentication.

Interactive Logon

Interactive logon authentication confirms a user's identification to either the local computer or a domain account. In a domain environment, the user logs onto the network using Single Sign-On (SSO) credentials stored in Active Directory. As with Windows 2000, Kerberos v5 is used for authentication in Windows XP.

On a local computer, a user's identification is confirmed based on credentials stored in the Security Accounts Manager (SAM). The SAM is the local security account database.

Network Authentication

Windows XP uses network authentication to confirm a user's identification to any network resources he is trying to access. The user must supply a username and password before he is granted access to the resources. Users in domain-based environments do not see the network authorization when they are logging onto the network. Windows XP can provide network authentication through several methods, including Kerberos, NTLM, and smart cards.

Auditing Security Events

Auditing is a critical security component in the Windows XP environment. By enabling auditing, administrators can monitor the resources that are being accessed on the computer and the users who are accessing them. Auditing enables you to track user and group access to files, folders, and other objects.

All audited events are written to the security log. An audit entry that is written to the security log contains the action that was performed, the name of the user who performed the action, and whether the event was a success or failure when it occurred.

Before you can audit objects, you must specify in an audit policy the type of auditing you want to implement. The types of events that can be audited are listed next. For each item, you can audit the success and/or failure of the audit event:

➤ *Account logon events*—Audit each instance of a user logging onto or logging off of a computer.

12

➤ *Account management*—Audit account management events, such as an account being created, changed, or deleted; an account being renamed, disabled, or enabled; or a password being changed.

➤ *Directory service access*—Audit the event of a user accessing an object in Active Directory.

➤ *Logon events*—Audit the instance of a user logging onto or logging off of a computer.

➤ *Object access*—Audit the event of a user accessing an object, such as a printer or a file or folder.

➤ *Policy change*—Audit the incidence of changes to user rights assignment policies, audit policies, or trust policies.

➤ *Privilege use*—Audit every instance of a user exercising a user right.

➤ *Process tracking*—Audit event tracking information, such as program activation.

➤ *System events*—Audit events such as a user restarting or shutting down a computer or any event that affects the system security log.

User Rights

User rights define the actions users or groups can perform. These are defined by the system administrator who applies them to the user accounts. User rights are different from permissions. Permissions are applied to objects. Even though user rights can be applied to individual users, best practice is to apply the rights to a group and then add users to the group. If a user is the member of multiple groups, her rights are cumulative from all of her group memberships.

As with Windows 2000 Professional, Windows XP Professional supports two types of rights—privilege rights and logon rights. A *privilege right* allows a user to perform specific tasks on the network or local computer. A *logon right* specifies how a user can log onto a system.

Permissions

Permissions define which objects users or groups can access. Permissions can only be applied on NTFS volumes. Permissions can be applied to files and folders for local computer and network resources. File permissions include Full Control, Modify, Read & Execute, Read, and Write. Folder permissions include Full Control, Modify, Read & Execute, List Folder Contents, Read, and Write. Permissions that are set on parent folders are inherited by files and subfolders created under the parent folders. For more information about file and folder permissions, refer to Chapter 6.

Public Key Infrastructure

Public Key Infrastructure (PKI) is the core of Windows XP security. PKI generally is used to describe policies and standards that regulate certificates and public and private keys. By implementing a PKI on their Windows XP networks, administrators can provide users with smart card logon capabilities, secure email, digital signatures, and client authentication through Secure Sockets Layer and Transport Layer Security.

For a better understanding of security in Windows XP, you need to understand public key security. Two types of encryption are used in public key security—private key encryption, also known as symmetric encryption, and public key encryption, also known as asymmetric encryption. With private key encryption, one secret key is used to encrypt and decrypt data; the same private key used to encrypt data is used to decrypt it. Public key encryption uses two keys, one public and one private. The two keys are mathematically related to each other. One key encrypts the data, whereas the other decrypts it. This public key technology is used by the following services in Windows XP:

➤ Network logon authentication

➤ Routing and Remote Access Service (RRAS)

➤ User authentication based on EAP and TLS

➤ Communication over PPTP and L2TP

➤ Microsoft Internet Information Server (IIS)

➤ Encryption File System (EFS)

➤ IPSec

Certificates

Certificate services can be implemented by a system administrator to deploy a PKI on a network. Public keys are published using certificates. A certificate is a digitally signed entity statement that binds a public key to the entity that holds the identity of the individual who has the corresponding private key. Certificates can be used for a variety of purposes, including authenticating a Web server, signing, sending secure email, and implementing IPSec and Transport Layer Security. Certificates used in Windows XP Professional are based on the X.509 v3 certificate standard.

Certificates can be used for identification and trust establishment for the secure exchange of information between users, computers, and services such as IPSec. Some applications use certificates to verify that they are accessing information on the computer from a trusted source. Certificates are also used by email programs, such as Outlook 2000 or Outlook Express, when users send encrypted or signed messages.

Certificates are stored in plaintext and normally contain the following items (see Figure 12.5):

➤ Public key value

➤ Identification information, such as the subject's name and email address

➤ Validation period

➤ Issuer's identification information

➤ Digital signature of the issuer

Certificates are valid only for a specified time period. If the certificate expires, it cannot be reissued. A new certification request must be submitted by the subject.

A certificate store is used in Windows XP Professional to house certificates locally on a computer. Certificates are stored in the Documents and Settings\ *username*\ApplicationData\Microsoft\SystemCertificates\My\Certificates for each user profile. It is possible to have certificates in the certificate store that have been issued from various certificate authorities (CAs). Certificates housed in the certificate store can come from one of four places:

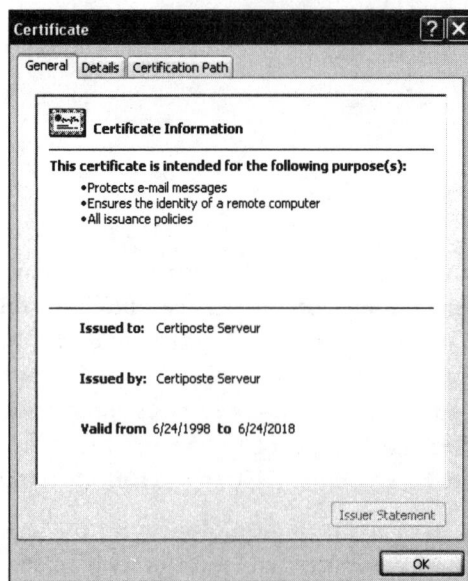

Figure 12.5 Certificate contents.

➤ The certificates were included on the Windows XP Professional CD and were installed when the operating system was installed.

➤ The user connected to a Web application that required an SSL session, and a certificate was stored on the computer.

➤ The user accepted a certificate during the installation of software or received an encrypted email.

➤ The user requested a certificate from a CA.

Certificates are displayed in the certificate store by logical store or purpose. Table 12.1 outlines how certificates are displayed in the certificate store.

The Certificates snap-in tool can be used to view, import, and export certificates that are in a user's certificate store (see Figure 12.6). It also can be used to request new certificates from CAs.

Table 12.1   Description of certificates in the certificate store.

Displayed By	Folder Name	Description
Logical store	Personal	Lists certificates with private keys that the user has access to
Logical store	Trusted Root Certification Authorities	Lists certificates from trusted CAs
Logical store	Enterprise Trust	Is a container for certificate trust lists
Logical store	Intermediate Certification Authorities	Lists certificates issued to subordinate CAs
Logical store	Trusted People	Lists certificates from explicitly trusted people
Logical store	Other People	Lists certificates from implicitly trusted people
Logical store	Trusted Publishers	Lists certificates from CAs that have been trusted by Software Restriction policies
Logical store	Disallowed Certificates	Lists certificates that are not to be trusted
Logical store	Third-Party Root Certification Authorities	Lists trusted root certificates from CAs other than Microsoft
Logical store	Certificate Enrollment Requests	Lists pending or rejected certificate requests
Logical store	Active Directory User Object	Lists certificates published in Active Directory
Purpose	Server Authentication	Lists certificates server programs use to authenticate themselves to clients
Purpose	Client Authentication	Lists certificates client programs use to authenticate themselves to servers
Purpose	Code Signing	Lists certificates associated with key pairs used to sign active content
Purpose	Secure Email	Lists certificates associated with key pairs used to sign email messages
Purpose	Encrypting File System	Lists certificates associated with key pairs used to encrypt/decrypt data by EFS
Purpose	File Recovery	Lists certificates associated with key pairs used to recover encrypted data by EFS

12

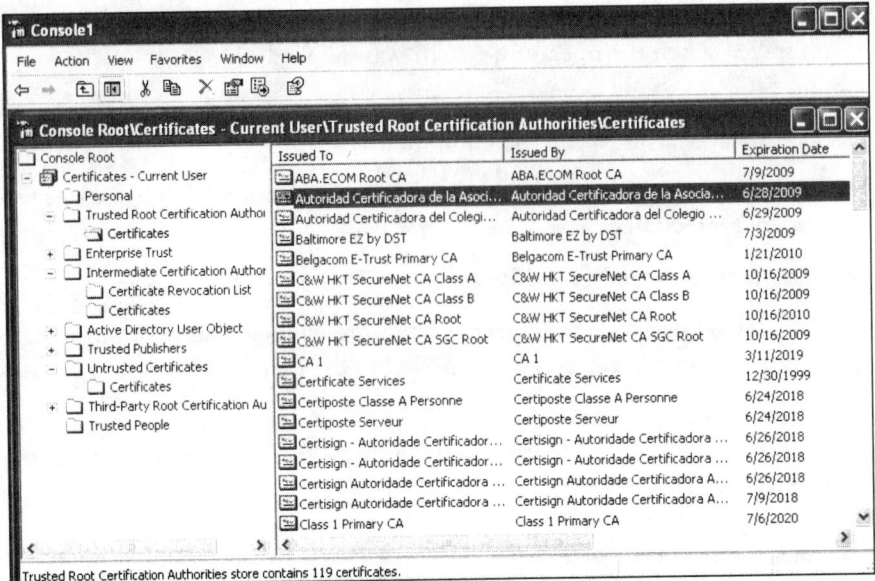

Figure 12.6 Certificates snap-in tool.

Windows XP Professional supports user certificate Auto-Enrollment, which was introduced in Windows 2000. Auto-Enrollment requires Active Directory and Group Policy. Certificates can automatically be renewed for a user if the appropriate certificate template has been specified in Active Directory. This is especially useful for remote users trying to facilitate VPN connections using RRAS.

EFS

Encryption File System was introduced in Windows 2000 to provide users with the capability to encrypt their files on NTFS volumes. EFS is transparent to an end user. The user who encrypts the file can work with it just as they would with any other file or folder. They can open and close it as they normally would. If an individual who did not encrypt a file tries to open it, he will receive a message indicating that access to the file is denied.

Files and folders can only be encrypted on NTFS volumes. You cannot encrypt files on FAT or FAT32 volumes. If an encrypted file is moved to a FAT or FAT32 volume, it will become decrypted.

If a user wants to move an encrypted file to another folder, she must use the Edit, Copy, and Paste commands. If she tries to move encrypted files using drag-and-drop, the file might not stay encrypted when it is moved to the new folder.

System files and compressed files cannot be encrypted.

Files can be encrypted in two ways in Windows XP Professional. They can be encrypted via a file's Properties page or by using the Cipher.exe command-line tool. To encrypt a file via the file's Properties page, follow these steps:

1. Open Windows Explorer.

2. Select the file you want to encrypt.

3. Right-click the file, and select Properties.

4. Click the Advanced button.

5. Select the Encrypt Contents To Secure Data checkbox, and click OK.

6. Click OK to close the file's Properties dialog box.

Table 12.2 lists the command-line options for encrypting a file or folder using Cipher.exe.

If a folder is encrypted, all files and subfolders in the folder are encrypted. Any files added to the folder after it is encrypted will also be encrypted.

The following process occurs when a file is encrypted using EFS:

1. The data in the file is copied to the system's temporary directory in plaintext form as a temporary file.

2. An encryption key is randomly generated to encrypt the data.

3. A Data Decryption Field (DDF) is created. This contains both the file encryption key and the recovery agent's public key.

4. The encrypted data is written back to the file with the DDF.

5. The temporary file is deleted.

Table 12.2   Command-line options for Cipher.exe.

Option	Description
pathname	Specifies a file or folder
/a	Specifies the operation for files as well as for folders
/e	Encrypts the specified folders
/d	Decrypts the specified folders
/f	Forces encryption of all specified directories even if they have already been encrypted
/h	Displays files with hidden or system attributes
/i	Continues encrypting even if Cipher.exe finds errors
/q	Causes Cipher.exe to report only essential information
/s:folder	Performs the specified operation on folders in the specified folder and all subfolders
/?	Displays user help

12

Public key cryptography is used to encrypt files with EFS. It uses keys that are obtained from a certificate from a user or CA. To use EFS, all users must have EFS certificates. If a user does not have access to a CA, the operating system will automatically assign self-signed certificates. For security reasons, the certificate and private key should be exported to a floppy disk or some other type of removable media and stored in a secure location.

Note: EFS only encrypts data that is stored on the hard disk. If you need to transport encrypted data over a TCP/IP network, you need to use another method, such as IPSec, PPTP, or WebDAV (Web-based Distributed Authoring and Versioning).

If the user who creates an encrypted file leaves or loses his private key, the data can still be recovered from the encrypted file. EFS includes built-in data recovery. A recovery policy is used to designate a user as a recovery agent. This agent is authorized to decrypt the data that was encrypted by another user. The recovery policy is configured locally for standalone computers and through Group Policy on a domain. Before a recovery agent can decrypt encrypted data, she must be issued a recovery certificate. Recovery certificates are issued by a CA and managed by the Certificates snap-in tool.

Several new features of EFS have been implemented in Windows XP Professional that were not available with the Windows 2000 version, including:

➤ Encrypted files can be displayed in an alternate color in Windows Explorer.

➤ Individuals can encrypt files that they do not own as long as they have the Write Attributes, Create Files/Write Data, and List Folder/Read Data permissions to the files.

➤ Additional users can be authorized to have access to an encrypted file. Before they can be added, they must have a valid EFS certificate in Active Directory.

➤ Offline Files and Folders can be encrypted using EFS.

➤ EFS over WebDAV is available.

IPSec

Internet Protocol Security is a suite of services and security protocols that provide user-level authentication and data encryption. IPSec is used with VPN connections that use the L2TP protocol. IPSec uses the standard authentication protocols, including EAP, MS-CHAP, and PAP. An IPSec Security Association (SA) determines the type of encryption that is used for IPSec. This SA consists of a destination address, a security protocol, and a Security Parameters Index (SPI), which is a unique identification value. The encryption can be DES, which uses a 56-bit key, or Triple DES (3DES), which uses two 56-bit keys.

IPSec is configured using IPSec policies, which can be stored in Active Directory or locally in the Registry for a computer that is not part of a domain. The IPSec Policy Management snap-in is used to create and manage both domain-based and local IPSec policies. The type of IPSec policy that is implemented determines the level of security that is used for the communications sessions. This can be either low or high.

Several components are installed in Windows XP when IPSec is implemented:

➤ *IPSec Policy Agent service*—Retrieves policy information and passes it on to the various IPSec components that require it to perform their services. This service appears as IPSEC Services in the list of system services.

➤ *Internet Key Exchange (IKE)*—Before information can be exchanged between two computers, an SA must agree on how the information will be exchanged and protected. The IKE provides this function.

➤ *Key Protection*—Several features enhance the strength of keys being used, including key lifetimes, session key refresh limits, the use of Diffie-Hellman groups, and perfect forward secrecy.

➤ *IPSec driver*—Compares inbound and outbound packets against a filter list and performs filter management.

Smart Cards

Support for smart cards is a key feature that has been integrated into the Windows XP PKI. A smart card is a credit card-sized device that can store public and private keys, passwords, and additional personal user information. Smart cards can be used in Windows XP for certificate-based authentication and SSO to an Active Directory domain.

Smart cards use personal identification numbers (PINs) instead of passwords. If the correct PIN is not entered in a predetermined number of tries, the smart card is locked. To use a smart card on your computer, you must have a smart card reader. Normally, a user would use the Ctrl+Alt+Delete key combination to log onto the computer. To initiate the logon process with a smart card, the user inserts the smart card into the smart card reader. She is prompted to enter the PIN. If the PIN entered is valid, the user is logged on.

Microsoft suggests that you only use smart card readers that are Plug and Play–compliant and have been tested by the Hardware Quality Lab. Windows XP Professional supports standard Personal Computer/Smart Card (PC/SC)-complaint Plug and Play smart cards and smart card readers. These devices conform to the IOS 7816-2 and 7816-3 standards. Smart card readers are controlled through Windows device drivers and attach to computers through standard ports, such as RS-232, PCMCIA, PS/2, and USB.

12

Smart cards use certificates and the EAP protocol for authentication when used in a domain environment. The certificate can be stored in the certificate store on the local computer or on the smart card itself. The Certificate Services Web page and the Smart Card Enrollment Station can be used to issue smart card certificates to users.

The New Connection Wizard is used to enable smart card support. If you have a smart card reader attached to a computer and you create a new connection using the wizard, Windows XP will detect the reader and prompt you for the authentication method that it should use for the connection. To enable smart cards on a network connection, follow these steps:

1. Select Start|Settings|Control Panel.

2. Double-click Network Connections.

3. Select the network connection on which you want to enable smart card support.

4. Select Change Settings Of This Connection under Network Tasks.

5. Click the Security tab.

6. Under Validate My Identity As Follows, select Use Smart Card.

7. Click OK.

Kerberos

Kerberos 5 is the default protocol used when a Windows XP computer is trying to authenticate to a Windows 2000 domain. Kerberos is known as a "shared-secret" or mutual-authentication protocol. It verifies both the identity of the user and the network services that he has access to.

Three elements are essential to Kerberos authentication—the client, the server, and the Key Distribution Center (KDC). The KDC acts as a trusted intermediary and is actually a service that runs on a domain controller. It issues a ticket-granting ticket (TGT) that contains encrypted data about the user. The TGT gets a service ticket (ST) that provides access to the network services.

The Kerberos authentication process is as follows:

1. A client requests authentication from an authentication server.

2. The server creates two session keys. These keys are sent to the client in an encrypted message that contains the client's private key and the server's encrypted private key.

3. Copies of the session key are sent to the server from the client. The server uses its private key to open the encrypted key.

4. The client is verified and can now communicate with the server and access the appropriate resources.

Windows XP has a Kerberos policy that is defined at the domain level. This policy is implemented by the domain's KDC and is stored in Active Directory. The following Kerberos policies are available:

➤ *Enforce User Logon Restrictions*—By default, this is enabled, and it verifies that the user who is trying to access the computer has either the Log On Locally or Access This Computer From The Network rights.

➤ *Maximum Lifetime For Service Ticket*—Defines the maximum lifetime for the service or session ticket. The default is 10 hours.

➤ *Maximum Lifetime For User Ticket*—Defines the maximum lifetime for the user ticket or TGT. The default is 10 hours.

➤ *Maximum Lifetime For User Ticket Renewal*—The default setting for user ticket renewal is seven days.

➤ *Maximum Tolerance For Computer Clock Synchronization*—The default setting for computer clock synchronization is five minutes.

Chapter Summary

This chapter looked at some of the security features of Windows XP Professional. Several built-in security groups are automatically installed when the operating system is installed. Security groups are used to control access to resources. The Administrators group is the most powerful of the groups and has full access to all resources. The Users group has full control over its data and has read-only permissions to the rest of the OS. Individuals can be included in the Guests group for one-time access to a computer. The Backup Operators group has the necessary Read and Write permissions to back up and restore all files on a computer. Members of the Power Users group have more access than most of the other groups except for the Administrators group.

Group Policies can be used to control user access to resources on local computers and networked computers. Security policies are a subset of Group Policies. Security Policies can be configured on both local and domain-based workstations. Windows XP Professional includes security policies to control account access, auditing, and user rights to resources.

Several predefined security templates are included in Windows XP to allow administrators to apply security policies to users' workstations. Setup security.inf is the

12

default security template that is applied to computers when Windows XP Professional is initially installed. The Security Configuration and Analysis snap-in tool is used to both analyze security on computers and apply predefined or customized security templates. Secedit.exe is a command-line tool that can provide the same functionality.

Access control is provided through authentication and authorization. Authentication is the process of confirming the identity of individuals who are trying to access a computer. Authorization verifies that individuals who have been authenticated are given access to the resources that they have the appropriate permissions for.

Administrators can use auditing to monitor user access to objects on a network. All auditing events are written to the security log. Administrators can audit the success and/or failure of events.

PKI is a core component of security in Windows XP. Windows XP uses public key technology to provide security services for users. These services include certificates, EFS, IPSec, and smart cards.

Review Questions

1. Jerrold wants to increase the security on his Windows XP Professional workstation and has decided to use the highly secure template on his system. What operating systems will he not be able to communicate with if he installs this template? [Check all correct answers]

   a. Windows 2000

   b. Windows 95

   c. Windows XP

   d. Windows NT

2. William is visiting the corporate office for a day and needs to access some public files on the corporate network. William does not have an account on the corporate network because he normally works from a remote location in another city. How can William be given access to the public files on the corporate network?

   a. William can be made a member of the Administrators group.

   b. William can be made a member of the Guests group.

   c. William can be made a member of the Power Users group.

   d. William can't be given access to the public files on the corporate network.

3. What tool is used to perform a security analysis on a Windows XP Professional computer?

    a. Computer Management snap-in tool

    b. Group Policy snap-in tool

    c. Security Configuration and Analysis snap-in tool

    d. Security Templates

4. Which of the following are authentication methods that are provided with Windows XP? [Check all correct answers]

    a. Interactive Logon

    b. Network Authentication

    c. MS-CHAP

    d. Remote Authentication

5. Joan has been given the assignment of ensuring that all data on the network has been backed up to removable media and stored offsite for safekeeping. What group should she be made a member of to complete this task?

    a. Users

    b. Administrators

    c. Backup Operators

    d. Network

6. What protocol is used to authenticate Windows XP Professional users in a Windows 2000 domain environment?

    a. EAP

    b. PPTP

    c. Kerberos

    d. NTLM

12

7. Rena is a member of the Users group. She has created several local groups on the network that are no longer needed. Jill also has several local groups that she wants deleted from the network. Because Rena will be accessing the network to delete her local groups, Jill has asked her to do the same for her. Rena will be able to delete the local groups she created and the local groups that Jill created. True or False?

    a. True

    b. False

8. Ron is the system administrator for his company. He is going to a class for two days but needs to add several new users to the network. Ron has decided to let Mary add the users because he will not have time before he leaves for his class. What group should Ron make Mary a member of so that she can add the users to the network?

   a. Interactive

   b. Users

   c. Administrators

   d. Power Users

9. John wants to determine who is accessing certain files on the network. What type of events should he audit?

   a. System events

   b. Logon events

   c. Object access

   d. Account logon events

10. Marcy is accessing the corporate LAN from her notebook computer. What group is she a member of?

   a. Network

   b. Interactive

   c. Users

   d. Replicator

11. What service issues ticket-granting tickets?

   a. KDC

   b. Certificate Authority

   c. Certificate Store

   d. ADSI

12. Smart cards use which protocol to authenticate users?

   a. PPTP

   b. CHAP

   c. BAP

   d. EAP

13. What IPSec component performs packet-filter management?

    a. IPSec driver
    b. Key Protection
    c. IPSec Policy Agent service
    d. Internet Key Exchange

14. Both encrypted and compressed files can be shown in color in Windows Explorer. True or False?

    a. True
    b. False

15. Joan is running out of disk space on her local hard drive. She has a folder that contains a large number of encrypted files. Joan can save some disk space by compressing the folder containing the encrypted files. True or False?

    a. True
    b. False

16. What is the purpose of the certificate store in Windows XP Professional?

    a. It is the storage location for certificates.
    b. It is used to manage certificates.
    c. It is where a user can acquire a certificate for use on a network.
    d. It is used to encrypt data before it is transmitted over the Internet.

17. What determines the type of encryption that is used by IPSec on a VPN connection?

    a. IPSec policies
    b. IPSec driver
    c. Security Association
    d. Public Key Cryptography

18. Andrew wants to use the extra security features that are provided with EFS. His computer is running Windows XP Professional but is using a FAT32 partition. Andrew can use EFS to encrypt his files on his system with its current configuration. True or False?

    a. True
    b. False

12

19. Certificates that are used in Windows XP are based on which industry standard?

   a. IEEE 1394

   b. X.500

   c. X.25

   d. X.509 v3

20. What are two types of encryption used in public key security? [Check all correct answers]

   a. Public key

   b. MPPE

   c. EAP

   d. Private key

Real-World Projects

John is the system administrator for his company, which has had a recent problem with hacking from internal and external sources on the network. John has been told by his bosses to look at the security on all the company computers and to make any necessary changes to ensure that all computer systems comply with new security initiatives that will be implemented by the company.

Project 12.1

To configure Windows XP Professional to show encrypted files and folders in color:

1. Click Windows Explorer.

2. Select Folder Options.

3. Click the View tab.

4. Select Show Encrypted Or Compressed NTFS Files In Color under Advanced Settings.

5. Click OK.

6. Exit Windows Explorer.

Project 12.2

To create a test document, encrypt it, and then examine it using Windows Explorer to ensure it is being displayed in an alternate color:

1. Open Windows Explorer.

2. Create a temp folder, if you do not already have one.

3. Create a text file in the temp folder, and name it "Efs.txt".

4. Right-click the new file, and select Properties.

5. Click the Advanced button.

6. Under Compress Or Encrypt Attributes, select Encrypt Contents To Secure Data, and then click OK.

7. Click OK. You will receive a warning message stating that you have chosen to encrypt a file that is not in an encrypted folder. Select Encrypt The File Only, and click OK.

8. Open Windows Explorer and go to the temp folder. The Efs.txt file that you just encrypted should be shown in color in Windows Explorer.

Project 12.3

To give additional users access to the encrypted file you created in Project 12.2:

1. Open Windows Explorer.

2. Right-click the encrypted file.

3. Select Properties.

4. Click the Advanced button.

5. Click the Details button.

6. Click the Add button.

7. Select the user's certificate that you want to use to share access to the file, and then click OK.

8. Click OK to close the Advanced Attributes property dialog box.

9. Click OK to close the file's property dialog box.

Note: Remember that the user to whom you are giving access to the encrypted file must have a certificate to access the file.

Project 12.4

To enable auditing of the file you encrypted in Project 12.2:

1. Click Start|Settings|Control Panel.

2. Double-click Administrative Tools.

3. Double-click Local Security Policy.

12

4. Click the + by Local Policies.

5. Select Audit Policy.

6. Double-click Audit Object Access.

7. Select Success And Failure under Audit Object Access, and click OK.

8. Close the Local Security Settings dialog box.

9. Open Windows Explorer.

10. Select Tools And Folder Options.

11. Select the View tab.

12. Make sure that Use Simple File Sharing (Recommended) is unchecked under Advanced Settings.

13. Click OK.

14. Right-click the encrypted file.

15. Select the Security tab.

16. Click the Add button to add the users or groups that you want to audit for file access.

17. Click OK to close the file's Property dialog box.

Project 12.5

To use the Security Configuration and Analysis snap-in to perform a security analysis on your workstation:

1. Click Start|Run.

2. Enter "mmc" and click OK.

3. Select File And Add/Remove Snap-in.

4. Click the Add button.

5. Under Available Standalone Snap-in, select Security Configuration And Analysis, and then click Add.

6. Click Close.

7. Click OK.

8. Click Security Configuration And Analysis in the MMC.

9. Select Action.

10. Select Open Database.

11. Enter the name "Analysis" in File name, and click Open.

12. Select the Compatws template, and click Open.

13. Select Action And Analyze Computer Now.

14. Enter a path to the error log file, and click OK.

Windows XP performs a security analysis on the workstation. The settings can be reviewed using the Security Configuration and Analysis snap-in tool.

12

CHAPTER THIRTEEN

Managing and Maintaining Windows XP Professional

After completing this chapter, you will be able to:

✓ Use Scheduled Tasks to schedule a program to run at a predetermined time

✓ Describe the System Information tool and how it is used in Windows XP Professional

✓ Explain how to use Task Manager to monitor system performance

✓ Explain how System Monitor is used to monitor system performance

✓ Explain how Performance Logs and Alerts is used to monitor system performance

✓ Describe the types of event logs in Windows XP Professional

✓ Explain how to use Event Viewer to view and manage event logs

✓ Describe the performance options that are included to improve system performance

Monitoring system performance is a crucial component of preventive system maintenance. You should take proactive actions to diagnose and troubleshoot system problems before they occur. Windows XP Professional includes many tools that you can use to manage and maintain your system. This chapter looks at some of these tools.

Scheduled Tasks

Scheduled Tasks enables you to schedule programs or tasks to run at a predetermined time. It runs as a service in Windows XP Professional and is started automatically at boot. With Scheduled Tasks, a user or administrator can schedule a task to run once, daily, weekly, monthly, or at certain times, such as system startup. Tasks can be changed, stopped, or customized to run at a scheduled time.

The Schedule Tasks Wizard is a GUI-based tool that walks you through the process of creating a schedule. The wizard first asks for the program that you want the Scheduled Task to run. You then enter a name for the task and the timeframe for when the task will be performed. The following options are available:

➤ Daily

➤ Weekly

➤ Monthly

➤ One time only

➤ When my computer starts

➤ When I log on

You select a start time and start date, and then enter the username and password for the user who will be running the tasks. The wizard displays the task that has been created with the scheduled time for it to run.

Several advanced options are available for further configuring Scheduled Tasks (see Figure 13.1). If the task was scheduled to run only once, users can select the Delete The Task If It Is Not Scheduled To Run Again checkbox to delete the task file from the computer's hard disk after it has run. Users can specify that a task be stopped after it has been running for a period of time. They can also schedule tasks to run only if the computer is idle. The amount of idle time that must pass before the tasks begin can be specified, and the tasks can be stopped if the user starts using the computer while the tasks are being run. Laptop users can configure a Scheduled Task to not run if the computer is running on batteries. The tasks can also be stopped if the laptop goes from AC to battery power. If the computer is in Standby mode, its mode can be changed to allow the tasks to be run.

In previous versions of Windows, the **AT** command was used to schedule tasks. This tool is still available in Windows XP and works with the Scheduled Tasks GUI-based tool. Any schedules that are created with the **AT** command show up in the Scheduled Tasks with a name that starts with *At* (see Figure 13.2). The task can

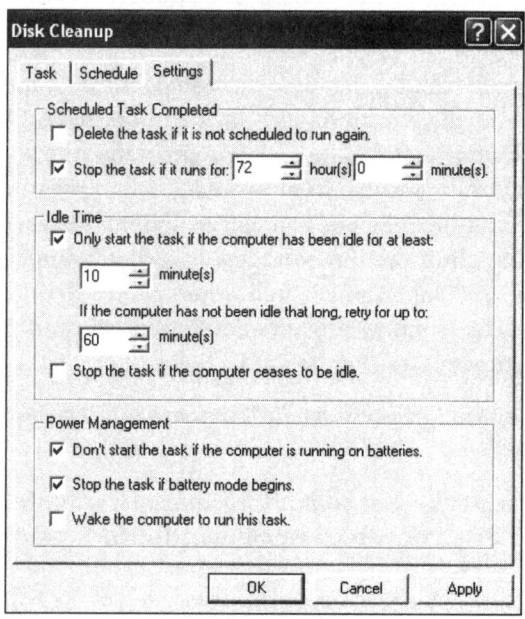

Figure 13.1 The advanced settings that can be configured for a Scheduled Task.

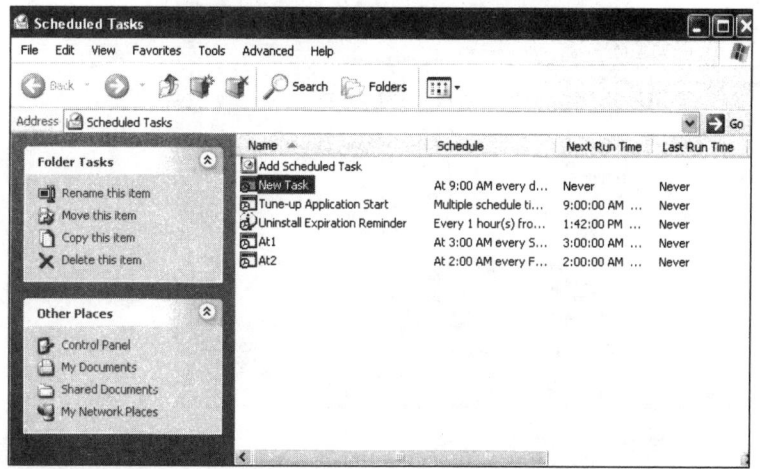

Figure 13.2 AT tasks in the Scheduled Tasks.

be viewed in Scheduled Tasks, but if it is modified, it will be upgraded to a normal task and will no longer be visible from a command line with the **AT** command.

A command-line tool Schtasks.exe can also be used to schedule tasks.

System Information

System Information provides a user with detailed information about his computer's configuration. System Information collects and displays information that can be used as an aid when diagnosing and troubleshooting system problems. It is a Windows-based tool that displays the information in two panes. The first pane, on the left side of the window, contains the following categories: System Summary, Hardware Resources, Components, Software Environment, Internet Settings, and Applications (if Microsoft Office 2000 and similar applications are installed). The second pane, on the right side of the window, provides detailed information about the item that is selected in the left pane (see Figure 13.3).

To access the System Information tool, select Start|All Programs|Accessories| System Tools|System Information.

The System Information tool can also be started from a command line or the Run dialog box by typing "msinfo32". The following sections describe the System Information components.

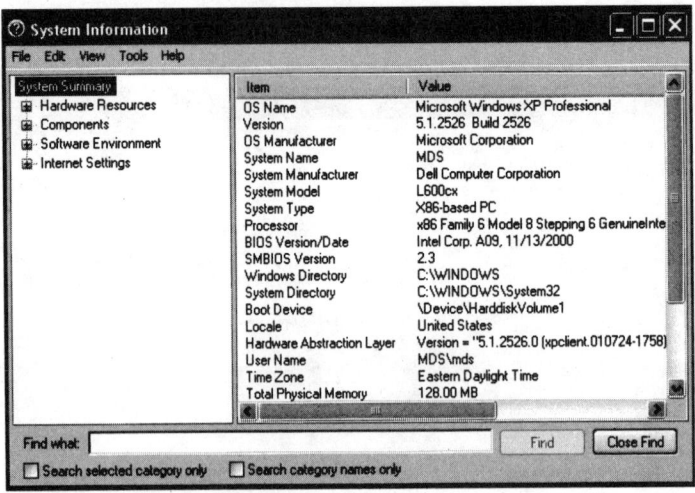

Figure 13.3   The System Information tool.

System Summary

System Summary provides a user with general information regarding the computer and the operating system. The following is the information provided by System Summary:

➤ OS name, version, and manufacturer

➤ Computer system name, manufacturer, model, and type

➤ Processor type

➤ BIOS version

➤ Operating system directory location

➤ Locale and time zone

➤ Hardware Abstraction Layer

➤ Username

➤ Total amount of physical memory and available amount

➤ Total amount of virtual memory and available amount

➤ Page file size and location

Hardware Resources

Hardware Resources is used to view hardware-specific settings on a computer. The following categories are included:

➤ *Conflicts/Sharing*—Identifies any hardware conflicts that exist between devices. This section should be checked if a user is having problems with a device to make sure that no sharing conflict exists with another device in the system, such as two devices trying to use the same IRQ.

➤ *DMA*—Direct Memory Access channels are used by devices to transfer data to and from memory. This information is processed without passing through the CPU. This means that devices can communicate without any additional burden being put on the CPU. Table 13.1 lists the eight DMA channels and their typical uses.

➤ *Forced Hardware*—Refers to devices that have to be configured manually. These devices are usually legacy devices that are not Plug and Play compatible.

➤ *I/O*—Input/output is the communication channel that is used by hardware devices. I/O channels represent locations in memory that are designated for use by each device to communicate with other devices in the computer.

13

➤ *IRQs*—Interrupt requests are channels used by devices to signal the CPU to get its attention. Standard computer architecture has 16 IRQs, and the lower the interrupt number, the higher the priority. Table 13.2 lists the standard IRQs and their typical uses.

➤ *Memory*—A memory address is a portion of memory that is allocated for a device. Each device has its own range of memory that it uses to communicate with other devices and the operating system.

Table 13.1   DMA channels and their typical use.

DMA Channel	Typical Use
0	Memory refresh
1	Sound card, SCSI host adapter, network card
2	Floppy disk controller
3	None
4	None; cascade for DMAs 0–3
5	Sound card
6	None
7	None

Table 13.2   IRQs and their use.

IRQ	Priority	Typical Default Use
0	1	System timer
1	2	Keyboard controller
2	N/A	Cascade for IRQs 8–15
3	11	COM2
4	12	COM1
5	13	Sound card, network card
6	14	Floppy disk controller
7	15	LPT1
8	3	Realtime clock
9	4	Open
10	5	Open
11	6	Open
12	7	PS/2 mouse
13	8	FPU/NPU math coprocessor
14	9	Primary IDE channel
15	10	Secondary IDE channel

Components

The Components section provides information about the following components that may be installed on a system:

➤ *Display*—Lists the video card type and current video configuration

➤ *Infrared*—Lists infrared device information

➤ *Input*—Lists keyboard and pointing device information

➤ *Modem*—Lists modem specifications

➤ *Multimedia*—Lists sound card information, including audio and video codecs and the CD-ROM drive letter and model

➤ *Network*—Lists network adapter, protocol, and WinSock information

➤ *Ports*—Lists serial and parallel port information

➤ *Printing*—Lists installed printers and print drivers

➤ *Problem Devices*—Lists any devices that have been flagged in Device Manager for problems

➤ *Storage*—Lists information on hard and floppy drives and removable media

➤ *USB*—Lists USB controllers and drivers

Software Environment

The Software Environment section provides information about the software that is running on a computer. Users can use this section to see what modules and services are running. Information regarding the following devices can be viewed:

➤ *Certified Drivers*—Lists information about signed drivers

➤ *Environment Variables*—Lists all system environment variables and their values

➤ *Loaded Modules*—Lists loaded DLLs and programs with version number, size, file data, and path

➤ *Network Connections*—Lists all mapped network connections

➤ *OLE Registration*—Lists OLE associations

➤ *Print Jobs*—Lists open print jobs

➤ *Program Groups*—Lists all known existing program groups for all users

➤ *Running Tasks*—Lists all processes currently running on the system

13

➤ *Services*—Lists all available system services and their current run status

➤ *Startup Programs*—Lists programs that start automatically when the system boots

➤ *System Drivers*—Lists the system drivers that are currently running

➤ *Windows Error Reporting*—Contains information about faults that are reported in the event log

Internet Settings

The Internet Settings section contains information about the Web browsers that are installed on a computer. Included is summary information about the version and build, the file version of files that are associated with the browser, and additional configuration information.

Applications

An Applications section is added to the System Information tool if any version of Office 2000 is installed on the computer. The Office suite applications are listed with summary information about each one.

A full system report can be saved to a text file and stored for later reference. It also can be printed, but this document could be extremely large, depending on the type and amount of hardware and software installed on the system.

Several troubleshooting tools are accessible from the System Information tool via the Tools menu. These include the following:

➤ Network Diagnostics

➤ System Restore

➤ File Signature Verification Utility

➤ DirectX Diagnostic Tool

➤ Dr. Watson

Task Manager

Task Manager provides dynamic information about processes and applications that are running on a computer system. It can be used to provide an overall view of a system's performance. It can also be used to terminate applications and processes that have stopped responding to a system or to start new programs. If the computer is connected to a network, Task Manager can be used to view the network status.

Task Manager can be started by using any of the following methods:

➤ Press Ctrl+Shift+Esc.

➤ Right-click the taskbar, and select Task Manager.

➤ Press Ctrl+Alt+Delete, and select Task Manager.

➤ Enter "taskmgr" at a command prompt or in the Run dialog box.

Task Manager consists of five tabs—Applications, Processes, Performance, Networking, and Users (see Figure 13.4), each of which is described next.

Applications Tab

The Applications tab is used to monitor applications that are currently running. It can be used to start or stop programs and to switch among applications that are running. The Applications tab should be the first place to look for help in troubleshooting nonresponsive applications or programs. The status of all currently running applications are listed as either Running or Not Responding. Applications whose status is Not Responding can be terminated by clicking the End Task button. You can also identify the processes that are associated with the application. Right-click the application, and select Go To Process. Task Manager will switch to the Processes tab, and the associated processes will be highlighted.

Processes Tab

The Processes tab shows all *processes* that are running on a system. A process is basically a program that performs a task. Processes can run in the foreground or the

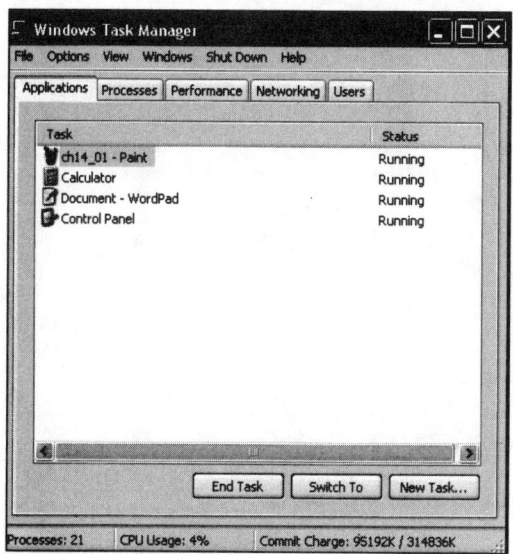

Figure 13.4 Task Manager.

background. Every application has at least one process associated with it. Many times, multiple processes are associated with a single application that is running. Processes run in their own *address space,* which is memory that is dedicated to the process. The Processes tab is useful for determining whether a process is using an excessive amount of CPU time. Measures are displayed on the Processes tab and contain information about the processes that are running. Task Manager can be configured to display up to 25 different measures for each process (see Figure 13.5). To select the measures that are viewed on the Processes tab:

1. Select View | Select Columns.

2. Put a check by the measure items that you want to view on the Processes tab, and click OK.

Several measures are displayed by default on the Processes tab of Task Manager:

➤ *CPU*—The amount of CPU time that the process is currently using.

➤ *CPU Time*—The total amount of CPU time that has been used by the process since it was started.

➤ *Mem Usage*—The amount of main memory that is in use by the process, displayed in kilobytes.

➤ *PID*—The Process Identifier is a unique identifier of each process that is running.

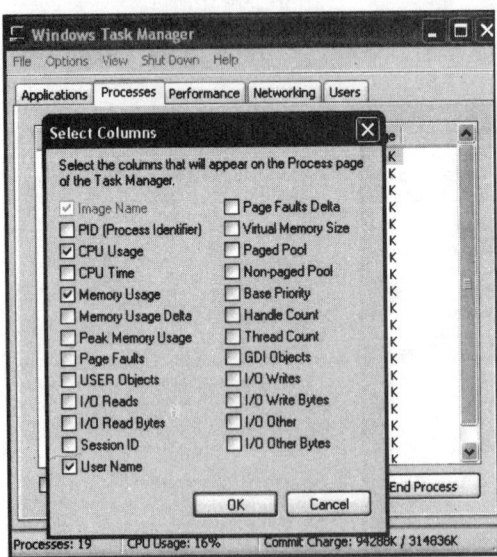

Figure 13.5   Measures that can be displayed on the Processes tab.

When a process is started, it is assigned a base priority by the operating system. This priority can be changed to make the process run faster or slower. However, keep in mind that changing the priority of a process might affect other processes that are running on the system. To change the priority of a process:

1. Right-click the process, and select Set Priority.

2. Select the priority from the drop-down list.

The rate at which Task Manager updates a selected counter or measures can be controlled with the Update Speed option in the View menu. The following update speeds can be selected:

➤ *High*—Updates the counters every half-second

➤ *Normal*—Updates counters once per second

➤ *Low*—Updates counters every four seconds

➤ *Paused*—Does not update counters automatically; F5 must be pressed to update counters

Performance Tab

The Performance tab is used to monitor the current performance of a computer. CPU Usage displays the current processor usage. CPU Usage History is a graphical snapshot of the processor history usage. MEM Usage displays the current memory usage. MEM Usage History provides a graphical representation of the memory usage. Several measures can be viewed via this tab:

➤ *Commit Change*—Displays three areas related to virtual memory. The first area in Commit Change shows the total amount of virtual memory available on the system. The second area, Limit, shows the amount of virtual memory that can be committed to all processes running on the system without having to enlarge the paging file. The third area, Peak, shows the maximum amount of virtual memory that has been used during the current session.

➤ *Kernel Memory*—Displays three areas relevant to paged memory. Total displays the sum of all paged and nonpaged memory. Paged displays the size of the paged memory pool. Nonpaged displays the size of the nonpaged memory pool.

➤ *Physical Memory*—Displays three areas of physical memory. The first area displays the total amount of physical RAM installed in the computer. The second area displays the total amount of RAM that is available for processes. The third area displays the amount of RAM that is released to file cache on demand. All of these are displayed in kilobytes.

➤ *Totals*—Displays the number of handles, threads, and processes currently running.

13

Networking Tab

The Networking tab is a new tab added to Task Manager in Windows XP. This tab enables a computer user to monitor statistics about any network connections that are currently in use. If you have multiple network connections, each will be displayed with its own graphical representation. This tab is only available if the system has a network adapter installed. Twenty-six column headings can be displayed below the graph (see Figure 13.6). Table 13.3 lists and describes the default measures that are enabled for a LAN connection.

The Networking tab is configured to collect data only when Task Manager is open. This helps to conserve memory resources on the system. This can be changed by selecting the Tab Always Active option on the Options menu.

Users Tab

If Fast Switching is enabled on a computer, an additional tab is included in Task Manager. This is the Users tab (see Figure 13.7), which displays the name of the

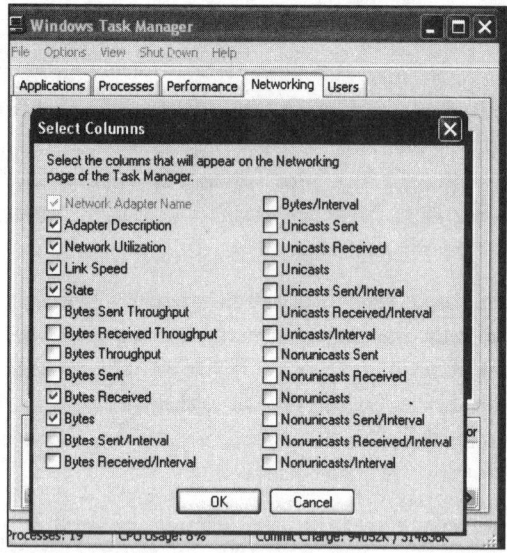

Figure 13.6 Measures that can be added to the Networking tab.

Table 13.3   Default measures that are displayed on the Networking tab.

Colume Name	Description
Bytes/Interval	The total number of bytes received and sent on the connection in the polling time interval
Link Speed	Connection speed of the interface taken from the initial connection speed
Network Adapter	Name of the network adapter in the Network Connections folder
Network Utilization	Network utilization percentage based on the initial connection speed for the interface

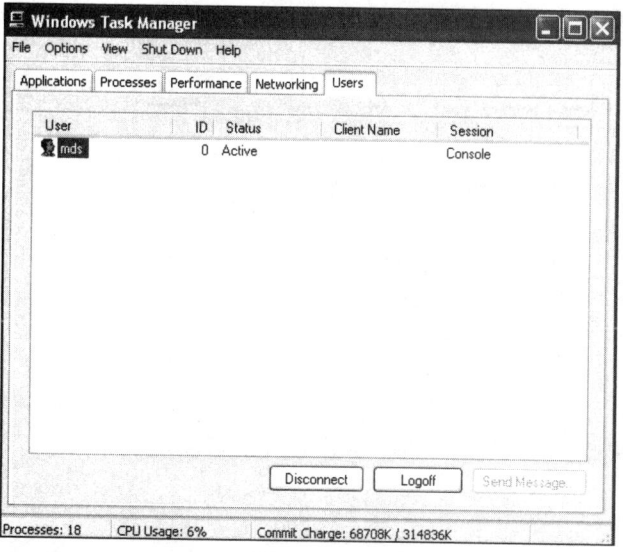

Figure 13.7   The Users tab in Task Manager.

user or users who are accessing the computer. It can be used to send a message to these users and disconnect or log them off of the computer. Remember that Fast Switching works only on computers that are members of a workgroup or on standalone computers. Fast Switching is not available on computers that are connected to a domain.

Performance and Maintenance Tools

In addition to Task Manager, two other tools are provided in Windows XP Professional to provide administrators and users with the ability to monitor resources on their computers. These are System Monitor and Performance Logs and Alerts. Both of these tools are accessed from the Performance tool that is included with Administrative Tools in the Control Panel. They can also be accessed by typing "perfmon.msc" in the Run dialog box.

System Monitor

System Monitor is used to collect and display data about the hardware resources on local or remote computers. A user can define the type of data that is displayed in the System Monitor graph (see Figure 13.8). System Monitor is used to do the following:

➤ Collect and display realtime performance data

➤ Display data from a current or previous counter log

➤ Present the collected data in a printable graph, histogram, or report view

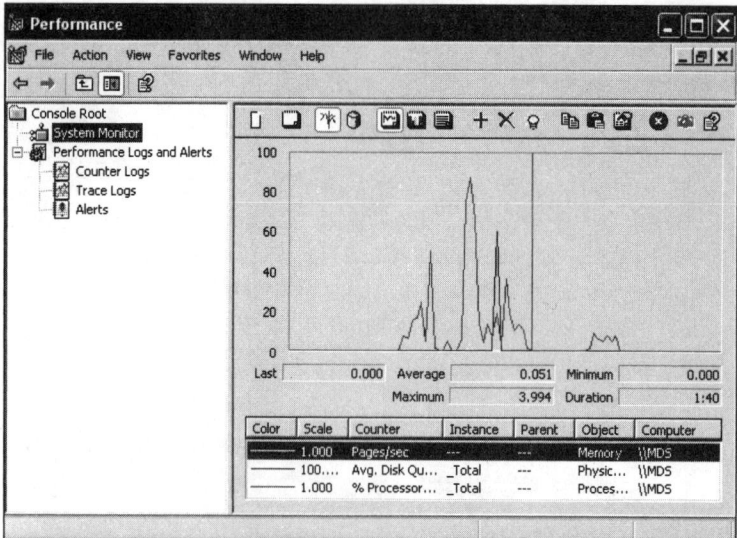

Figure 13.8 System Monitor graph.

➤ Create HTML pages from performance views

➤ Create monitoring configurations that are reusable with the Microsoft Management Console

System Monitor opens to a blank graph. To aid in monitoring data using System Monitor, some predefined settings are provided under Counter Logs. These counters are Memory\Pages/sec, PhysicalDisk(Total)\Avg. Disk Queue Length, and Processor(Total)\%Processor Time.

The functionality of System Monitor can be accessed from the toolbar. Table 13.4 lists the buttons on the System Monitor toolbar and the functions they perform.

Table 13.4 System Monitor toolbar icons and their functions.

Icon	Function
New Counter Set	Clears the current counters from the display and starts over from scratch.
Clear Display	Clears the display of the activity, but does not remove any of the counters.
View Current Activity	Enables you to add counters and view the results in realtime. All the activity displayed is current and no log of the information is kept.
View Log File Data	Enables you to display data from a log file that you have created. When you click this button, you are asked to select a log file that you would like to use.
View Chart	Displays the result of the counters in a line chart.
View Histogram	Displays the result of the counters in a column chart.
View Report	Displays the result of the counters in report format.

(continued)

Table 13.4   System Monitor toolbar icons and their functions *(continued)*.

Icon	Function
Add	Enables you to add counters to your display. The counters that you add can be for your computer or another computer.
Delete	Deletes the selected counter from the display.
Highlight	Highlights the selected counter in the display.
Copy Properties	Copies the properties to the clipboard.
Paste Counter List	Pastes the information from the clipboard into the counter list.
Properties	Enables you to change the appearance of System Monitor. You can change the font or the colors, change the scale of information, and give titles to the axes of the chart.
Freeze Display	Enables you to stop System Monitor from collecting data and leave the current results on the screen.
Update Data	Works in conjunction with Freeze Display. After you have frozen the display, you can click this to manually update the data displayed on the screen.
Help	Displays Help for System Monitor.

Windows XP Professional collects performance data from various components of the system. Performance objects are built into the system that corresponds to various hardware components and resources, such as the processor, hard drives, and memory. Performance counters are data objects that are associated with each performance object. The type of performance counter that is selected is dependent on the type of problem that the administrator or user is trying to resolve. Table 13.5 lists counters that would prove beneficial in troubleshooting system problems.

Table 13.5   Performance counters to use for investigating performance problems.

Type of Problem	Counter
Memory bottlenecks	Memory\Available Bytes Memory\Pages/sec
Disk bottlenecks	PhysicalDisk\ % Disk Time and % Idle Time PhysicalDisk\ Disk Reads/sec and Disk Writes/sec PhysicalDisk\ Avg. Disk Queue Length LogicalDisk\ % Free Space
Processor bottlenecks	Processor\ Interrupts/sec Processor\ % Processor Time Process(*process*)\ % Processor Time System\ Processor Queue Length
Network bottlenecks	Network Interface\ Bytes Total/sec, Bytes Sent/sec, and Bytes Received/sec *Protocol_layer_object*\ Segments Received/sec, Segments Sent/sec, Frames Sent/sec, and Frames Received/sec
Printer bottlenecks	Print Queue\ Bytes Printed/sec Print Queue\ Job Errors

13

Performance Logs and Alerts

Performance Logs and Alerts is similar to System Monitor in that it is used to collect and display data about system resources. It includes some other capabilities in addition to those provided with System Monitor:

➤ Data can be collected in SQL database format.

➤ Counter data that is collected can be viewed in realtime and after it has been collected.

➤ Data is collected whether or not a user is logged on the computer that is being monitored, because logging runs as a service.

➤ Start and stop times for logging can be defined as well as file names and sizes for automatic log generation.

➤ Multiple logging sessions can be managed from a single console window.

➤ Alerts can be set on counters that specify actions to be performed when a selected counter's value exceeds or falls below a predefined setting.

Two types of logs are provided in Windows XP Professional—counter logs and trace logs. Counter logs sample data based on the performance counters and objects that have been selected. This data is collected at predefined update intervals. Trace logs don't sample the data. They track the data from start to finish. Alerts can be configured when certain counter values are met. The triggered alert can be configured to send an email message to an administrator or user, run a specific program, or start a log.

Event Logs

Event logs are used to monitor events that occur on a system, such as system startup and shutdown, user activity, and the accessing of resources. Event log activity is recorded in three logs in Windows XP:

➤ *Application log*—Logs events that are generated by applications on the system. This could be a SQL database logging its activities as it processes data during a session. The types of events that are written to the application log are determined by the application developers of the software. Dr. Watson errors are also written to the Application log. Dr. Watson is a program error debugger that can be used by technical support groups to diagnose a program error for a computer.

➤ *Security log*—Records security events on a system. This includes logging users logging on and off of the system and any activities related to resources, such as file creation and deletion. The Security log is the only log that is accessible by system administrators exclusively. Users who do not have administrative rights are not able to view the Security log.

➤ *System log*—Records events that are generated by the operating system. The success or failure of device drivers loading is one example of the type of event that is recorded in this log. Items that are logged in the system log are predetermined by Windows XP Professional.

When developers are writing for Windows XP, they determine what system and application events are written to the log files. Each log file contains specific information about the event that it has recorded. Three types of events can be written to the System and Application log files:

➤ *Error events*—This is the most serious type of event. This event indicates that a significant problem has occurred on the system that requires immediate attention.

➤ *Information events*—Monitor the successful operation of a device driver, application, or other service. When a computer system starts, an information event is written to the System log to indicate that the Event Log service has started successfully.

➤ *Warning events*—Indicate potential problems and should be looked at to help defer future problems.

If security logging is enabled through local or Group Policy, two additional types of events are written to the event logs—Success Audit and Failure Audit. Success Audit logs successful access attempts. Failure Audit logs access attempts that failed.

The Event Log service is a system function that starts automatically at system startup and logs event activity to the event log. Event Viewer is used to view the event logs (see Figure 13.9). To open Event Viewer:

1. Select Start|Control Panel.

2. Double-click Administrative Tools.

3. Double-click Event Viewer.

13

To open Event Viewer from a command prompt or the Run dialog box, type "eventvwr".

Event Viewer does not restrict users to viewing just log files on their local computer. Users who have access to remote computers can use Event Viewer to view the event logs on those computers also. To view the event logs on a remote computer:

1. Open Event Viewer.

2. Right-click Event Viewer (Local), and select Connect To Another Computer.

3. Enter the name of the remote computer in the Another Computer text box, and click OK.

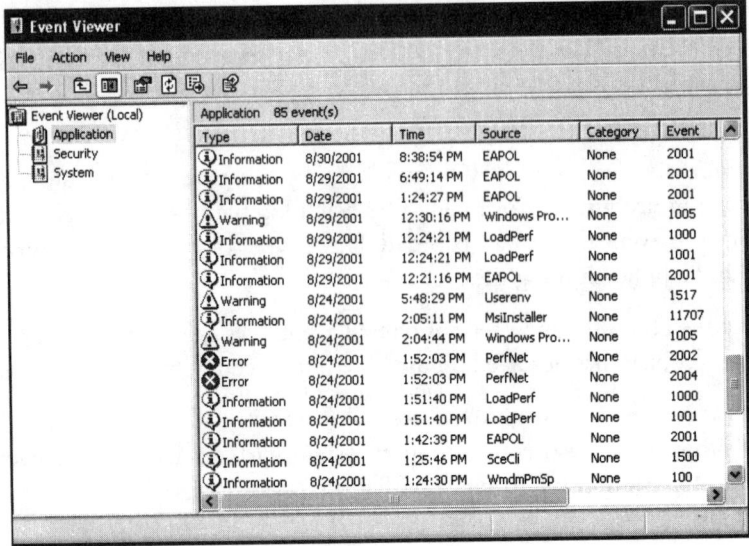

Figure 13.9   Event Viewer.

The event logs can be searched for specific events by using the Find command on the View menu. Event logs can be searched by event types and source, categories, event ID, username, and computer name. You can even search for specific text in the event log by entering that text in the Description text box (see Figure 13.10).

During the course of a computer session, the event logs can contain an extremely large amount of event data. To aid in the analysis of this data, specific events can be filtered in Event Viewer. By default, all data in Event Viewer is shown. Users can

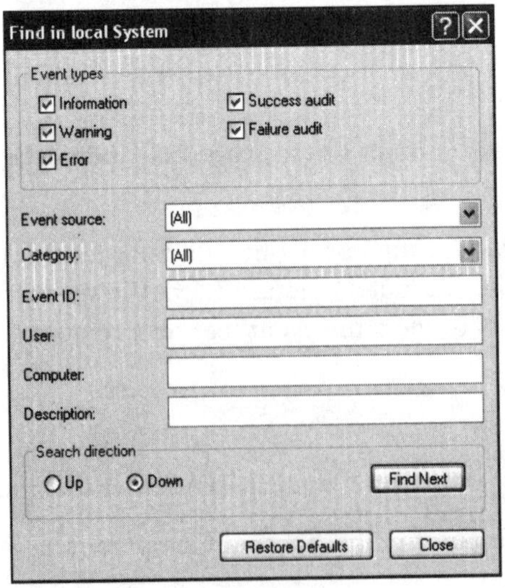

Figure 13.10   Description Box.

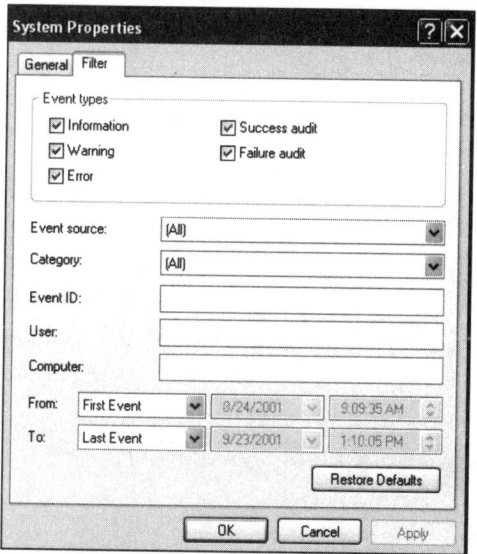

Figure 13.11   Filter options for Event Viewer.

select View|Filter to filter the types of events that are displayed in Event Viewer. Figure 13.11 shows the options that are available for filtering event log data in Event Viewer.

Over time, the size of event logs can become extremely large, depending on the amount of activity that is being monitored on the computer. The size of event logs can be limited if hard disk space on the computer is an issue. The default size of all event logs is 512KB. This size should prove sufficient if the computer is not monitoring a lot of event activity. If the computer is monitoring an excessive amount of event log data, you might want to increase the size of the event logs. Each log can be configured to be from 64KB to 4GB in size. Users can also select the action that is taken in Windows XP when the event logs become full:

➤ *Do Not Overwrite Events (Clear Log Manually)*—If this option is selected, the data in the log files is never overwritten, and the log files have to be manually cleared.

➤ *Overwrite Events As Needed*—This option will overwrite data in the log file as soon as the log file reaches its maximum log size.

➤ *Overwrite Events Older Than x Days*—This option will overwrite the data in the log file after a predefined number of days.

Many companies find it beneficial to archive the event logs so that they have an audit trail for later analysis. Each event log can be saved in one of three file formats:

➤ *Comma-delimited text-file format*—Can be imported into a spreadsheet or database program. The names of these files end with the .csv extension.

➤ *Log-file format*—Can be viewed in Event Viewer. The names of these files end with an .evt extension.

➤ *Text-file format*—Can be read in any text editor, such as Microsoft Word. The names of these files end with a .txt extension.

Users can determine the items that are displayed in Event Viewer by selecting View|Add/Remove Columns. By default, all columns are displayed, but users might want to remove some columns that contain information that they don't need or use. All columns can also be sorted by clicking the title bar of the column heading. This action changes the sort order of the columns from descending to ascending and vice versa.

Using Performance Options to Improve Performance

Administrators can configure additional options to improve system performance in Windows XP Professional. Processor scheduling, memory usage, and virtual memory can be configured on the Performance Options property sheet (see Figure 13.12). To access this sheet:

1. Right-click My Computer.

2. Select Manage.

3. Right-click Computer Management (Local), and select Properties.

4. Select the Advanced tab.

5. Click Settings under Performance.

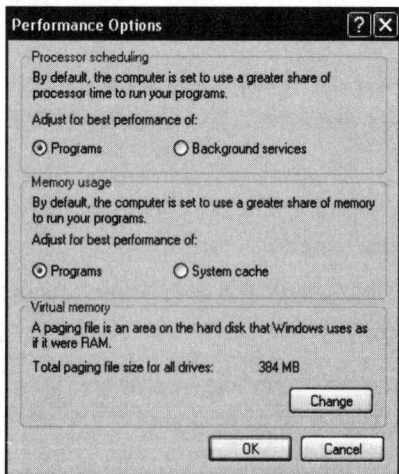

Figure 13.12   Performance Options property sheet.

Use the following:

➤ *Memory Usage*—Memory usage can be optimized for either applications or system cache. If the option is selected to optimize for applications, the application that is running in the foreground will receive priority use of the system's RAM. If this option is selected, the application will run faster. If the option is selected to optimize for system caching, more RAM is allocated for swapping page files. This enables data to be moved from the hard disk to RAM and is beneficial when multiple applications are running.

➤ *Process Scheduling*—Process scheduling can be optimized for either applications or background services. If the option is selected to optimize for applications, any program running in the foreground will be allocated more processor resources. If the option is selected for background services, all programs that are running on the system receive the same amount of processor resources.

➤ *Virtual Memory*—Virtual memory is the temporary storage area on the hard disk or disks that is used to run programs that need more memory than the computer physically has. Virtual memory basically is the size of the page file. The recommended size for the page file is 1.5 times the amount of physical RAM in the computer. A small page file can limit the amount of data that is stored and can cause degradation in system response time. If the system has multiple hard disks, performance can be improved by having a page file on each hard disk. Several options are available for configuring the page file size. If Custom Size is selected, the user can specify the size of the paging file. If System Managed Size is selected, Windows XP Professional manages the page file size. If No Paging File is selected, then no page file is configured on the hard disk.

Where the page file is placed can also have an effect on system performance. For the best performance, Microsoft suggests that you do not place a paging file on the hard disk that contains the operating system in a multiple-disk system. If the computer system consists of a single hard disk, the paging file should be on the same partition as the operating system for peak performance.

13

Chapter Summary

This chapter looks at some of the ways to manage and maintain Windows XP Professional. Scheduled Tasks can be used to schedule programs—such as a backup program—to run at predefined times determined by a user or system administrator. Programs can be scheduled to run once, daily, weekly, monthly, or at other predetermined times.

Users can review detailed information about their computer systems by using the System Information tool. This tool is divided into categories that provide specific information about various system components. The categories include System Summary, Hardware Resources, Components, Software Environment, and Internet Settings.

Users can acquire dynamic information about the processes and applications that are running on their system by using Task Manager. Task Manager consists of several tabs, each with its own functions. The Application tab is used to monitor applications that are currently running. The Processor tab shows individual processes that are running on the system. The Performance tab displays the current system performance. The Network tab displays network connection statistics.

System Monitor is a performance tool that, along with Performance Logs and Alerts, can be used by administrators to monitor computer resources. Windows XP Professional collects performance data from system components, and these can be monitored using either of these tools.

The event logs are used to monitor events that occur on the system. Three event logs are included in Windows XP Professional. The System log records system events that are generated by the operating system. The Application log records events that are generated by applications on the system. The Security log records security events on the system. The Security log can only be viewed by users with administrative privileges.

Review Questions

1. What Windows XP Professional tool can be used to run programs automatically at a predefined time?

   a. Task Manager

   b. Performance Logs and Alerts

   c. Scheduled Tasks

   d. Task Scheduler

2. What tool can Bill use if he wants to monitor the network connections on his computer?

   a. Shared Folders

   b. Network tab on Task Manager

   c. Applications tab on Task Manager

   d. Event Viewer

3. What types of devices are displayed in the Forced Hardware section of the System Information tool?

  a. Plug and Play—compliant devices

  (b.) Any hardware devices that had to be manually configured

  c. Newly installed hardware devices

  d. Devices that have been disabled on the system

4. Tom feels he might be having a problem with the RAM in his computer. What performance counters can he check to see if he has a potential memory problem on his computer? [Check all correct answers]

  (a.) Processor\% Processor Time

  b. Memory\Available Bytes

  c. System\Processor Queue Length

  (d.) Memory\Pages/sec

5. What tool can Jill use to see who has been logging onto the network server?

  (a.) Security log

  b. Application log

  c. System log

  d. Replication log

6. Which of the following events in Event Viewer would warrant immediate attention from a user or administrator?

  a. Warning

  (b.) Error

  c. Information

  d. Success Audit

7. Data in the event logs can be archived for later analysis. True or False?

  (a.) True

  b. False

8. William has scheduled backups to run on his system using the **AT** command. He wants to start using Scheduled Tasks, included in Windows XP Professional, because of its nice GUI-based interface. William will not be able to use Scheduled Tasks to run programs that were configured using the **AT** command. True or False?

  a. True

  (b.) False

13

9. What components in System Information will provide a user with information about the hard disks on her computer?

   a. Components

   b. Software Environment

   c. Internet Settings

   d. Applications

10. Applications can be scheduled to run using Scheduled Tasks at which of the following times? [Check all correct answers]

    a. Monthly

    b. Hourly

    c. Weekly

    d. At system shutdown

11. Greg wants to save the event log data from his computer. What format can he save this data in? [Check all correct answers]

    a. .evt

    b. .txt

    c. .dat

    d. .exe

12. What is typed at a command line to start Task Manager?

    a. task.exe

    b. taskmgr.exe

    c. eventvwr.exe

    d taskman.exe

13. Ronda is using the System Information tool and notices that she does not have an Application section, whereas her coworker John does on his computer. Why does Ronda not have this section in her System Information tool?

    a. She does not have any applications installed on her computer.

    b. She does not have any version of Microsoft Office installed on her system.

    c. She must go to the Options menu of System Information to enable this section.

    d. John's computer is configured differently than Ronda's; she will have to reconfigure her computer to see this section.

14. All applications that are running on the computer system show one of two
    states in Task Manager—either Running or Not Responding. True or False?

    a. True

    b. False

15. What tab in Task Manager is displayed only if Fast Switching is enabled on the
    computer?

    a. Applications

    b. Users

    c. Networking

    d. Processes

16. What can be configured to provide more memory than is physically available
    on a computer system?

    a. EMS memory

    b. Virtual memory

    c. XMS memory

    d. Disk quotas

17. What can be set to ensure that a database program that is running will not be
    interrupted by other applications competing for processor time?

    a. Set memory usage to optimized for applications.

    b. Set memory usage to optimized for system cache.

    c. Configure the page file size to be 2.5 times the amount of RAM in the
       computer.

    d. Set process scheduling to be optimized for applications.

18. What tool is used to view event logs on a computer?

    a. Event Viewer

    b. Scheduled Tasks

    c. MMC

    d. Computer Management

13

19. What counter would Stan look at to determine the amount of memory that is
    being used by individual processes?

    a. CPU time under the Processor tab of Task Manager

    b. Mem Usage under the Processor tab of Task Manager

    c. I/O Reads under the Processor tab of Task Manager

    d. Thread Count under the Processor tab of Task Manager

20. The Event Log is a service that must be started manually before data is written to event logs. True or False?

    a. True

    b. False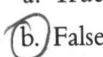

Real-World Projects

Jim has been given the responsibility of managing the Windows XP Professional workstations in his company. He doesn't know what type of shape the computers are in, because many of the users have had little training since the machines were upgraded from Windows 98 and Windows 2000. Jim would like to run the Disk Cleanup utility on all the workstations to eliminate any unnecessary temp and log files. He wants to schedule this to occur during off hours so that it doesn't affect user work production.

Jim also wants to check the event log files on all the computers to make sure that users are not receiving errors that they are not telling him about. He knows that when Windows XP Professional was installed, it was configured with the default installation options. He will need to increase the size of the event log files, because the default log size is not sufficient to hold the amount of event log data that he expects each computer to produce.

Project 13.1

To schedule Disk Cleanup to run once monthly on your computer:

1. Select Start|All Programs|Accessories|System Tools|Scheduled Tasks.

2. Double-click Add Scheduled Tasks.

3. Click Next on the Scheduled Task Wizard.

4. Select Disk Cleanup under Application, and click Next.

5. Leave the default name, and select Monthly.

6. Click Next.

7. Select 9:00 pm under Start Time.

8. Select the date to start the Disk Cleanup. For this project, select the second Monday of the month.

9. Make sure that checkmarks appear by each month.

10. Click Next.

11. Enter the username and password for the scheduled task, and click Next.

12. Click Finish.

Project 13.2

To search the event log for specific event types that occurred during a specified time period:

1. Select Start|Run.

2. Type "eventvwr" and click OK.

3. Select the System Log.

4. Select View|Filter.

5. Uncheck all the items under Event Types except for Warning and Error.

6. In From, select Events On, and enter a date and time.

7. In To, select Events On, and enter a date and time.

8. Click OK.

Only the items that match those listed in the filter are now displayed in Event Viewer.

Project 13.3

To change the size of the event logs:

1. Select Start|Run.

2. Type "eventvwr" and click OK.

3. Right-click the System log, and select Properties.

4. Change the maximum log size to 1,000KB under Log Size.

5. Right-click the Application log, and select Properties.

6. Change the maximum log size to 500KB under Log Size.

7. Select Overwrite Events Older, and enter 14 days.

8. Click OK.

9. Right-click the Security log and select Properties.

10. Change the maximum log size to 2,000KB under Log Size.

11. Select Do Not Overwrite Events (Clear Log Manually).

12. Click OK.

13

Project 13.4

To create a counter log:

1. Select Start | Control Panel.

2. Double-click Administrative Tools.

3. Double-click Performance.

4. Double-click Performance Logs And Alerts.

5. Click Counter Logs to highlight it.

6. Right-click and select New Log Settings.

7. Enter a name for the new settings in the Name text box, and click OK.

8. Click Add Objects on the General tab.

9. Select the performance objects you want to add and click the Add button after selecting each item.

10. Click Close when you have finished adding performance objects.

Project 13.5

To add a counter to the log that you created in Project 13.4:

1. Select Start | Control Panel.

2. Double-click Administrative Tools.

3. Double-click Performance.

4. Double-click Performance Logs And Alerts.

5. Double-click Count Logs.

6. Double-click the log file that you created in Project 13.4.

7. Click Add Counters on the General tab.

8. Click Select Counters From Computer.

9. Select the performance objects to monitor under Performance Object.

10. Select the counters you want to monitor from Select Counters From List and click Add after selecting each item.

11. Click Close.

12. Click OK.

CHAPTER FOURTEEN

System Recovery

After completing this chapter, you will be able to:

✓ Prevent and troubleshoot system problems

✓ Plan backup strategies

✓ Perform backups using Windows XP Professional Backup

✓ Perform restores using Windows XP Professional Backup

✓ Use Safe Mode options to boot a troublesome system

✓ Access and use the Recovery Console

✓ Use the ERD and the emergency repair process

Usually, a Windows XP Professional-based system runs pretty much flawlessly; however, there are times when a system doesn't work, and you, as an administrator, need to take certain actions to restore services. You might be aware of what caused the problem, such as faulty hardware or a misbehaving application, or you might not. If you are not aware of the cause, you'll need to troubleshoot the situation to determine what is at fault.

Prevention of System Problems

Basically, you need to be aware of three types of system problems:

➤ Device driver problems

➤ System file problems

➤ Hardware-related problems

Device Driver Problems

By far, the most common system problems are device driver problems, which can result when a new device and its associated device driver are installed in a Windows XP Professional machine. A device driver is a small application that allows Windows XP Professional to communicate with a hardware device. The device driver might be incompatible with Windows XP. It maight also conflict with other device drivers by overwriting their memory address spaces.

To prevent problems with device drivers, an administrator should do the following:

➤ *Read the documentation for configuration and compatibility information that shipped with the device.* Also, always read any addenda or readme files for changes and notifications that have occurred since the shipped documents were published.

➤ *Check the Hardware Compatibility List (HCL) to verify that Microsoft has certified the device.* The HCL can be obtained from the Windows XP Professional CD-ROM or from Microsoft's Web site (**www.microsoft.com/hcl**).

➤ *Obtain the latest device driver from the manufacturer.* Check the manufacturer's Web site for the latest device driver as well as any notices or alerts about potential problems with the device driver.

To correct problems with device drivers, an administrator should do the following:

➤ *Check the Event Viewer if the system boots.* By checking the Event Viewer, an administrator might be able to determine what is causing a device driver to fail; for example, it could be an interrupt conflict or a missing system file. Once the cause is determined, the administrator can take steps to resolve the situation.

➤ *Restart the computer using the Last Known Good Configuration.* This restores Registry settings that Windows XP Professional saved during the last successful boot. If the administrator recently changed the configuration, this setting should restore the old configuration, allowing the computer to boot.

➤ *Restart the computer in Safe Mode.* In Safe Mode, Windows XP Professional will load using basic system files and device drivers only. Drivers and system files for base video, mouse, keyboard, and storage media will be loaded. No system files or drivers will be loaded for networking services. Booting in Safe Mode allows an administrator to double-check configuration settings and reinstall the device driver if necessary.

➤ *Obtain the latest device driver from the manufacturer.* The administrator can check the manufacturer's Web site for the latest device driver and install the new device driver.

System File Problems

If device driver problems are the most common problems, then system file problems are by far the most annoying and difficult to troubleshoot. If system files become corrupt or damaged, a computer might not run properly. It is also possible for system files to become mismatched—that is, a version of a system file might conflict with other system files. System files include the following:

➤ The Registry

➤ DLL files

➤ Operating system files

➤ Device drivers

➤ Boot files

To prevent problems with system files, an administrator should do the following:

➤ *Perform regular backups that include the System State information.* The System State information includes the boot files, the Registry, performance counter configuration information, and the Component Services Class registration database.

➤ *Use an uninterruptible power supply (UPS) to protect computers from power surges and outages.* System files can be corrupted if power failures occur during file write operations.

To correct problems with system files, an administrator should do the following:

➤ Check the Event Viewer.

➤ Restart the computer using the Last Known Good Configuration.

14

➤ Restart the computer in Safe Mode.

➤ Restore the System State from a recent backup.

Hardware-Related Problems

Hardware-related problems can occur with a hard drive, a network card, memory, a CPU, or other hardware devices.

To prevent hardware-related problems, an administrator should do the following:

➤ *Check the Event Viewer.* By checking the Event Viewer, an administrator will be able to observe problems as they develop.

➤ *Perform regular backups that include the System State information.* The System State information includes the boot files, the Registry, performance counter configuration information, and the Component Services Class registration database.

➤ *Use a UPS to protect computers from power surges and outages.* System files can be corrupted if power failures occur during file-write operations.

➤ *Implement fault tolerance.* An administrator can implement fault tolerance on some hardware devices, such as hard disks.

Backup Strategies

One of the most important aspects to recovering a Windows XP Professional configuration is to perform regular backups. A regular backup helps prevent data loss caused by faulty hardware, user error, power outages, virus infections, and so on. These days, computer data is an integral part of a business, and, as such, a company's backup strategy needs to be carefully planned and executed.

Windows XP Professional supports the following backup types:

➤ *Copy*—Backs up all selected files and does not mark the files as backed up.

➤ *Daily*—Only backs up files that have changed that day and does not mark the files as backed up.

➤ *Differential*—Only backs up files that have changed since the last normal backup and does not mark the files as backed up.

➤ *Incremental*—Only backs up files that changed since the last normal or incremental backup, and marks the files as backed up by setting the files' archive bits.

➤ *Normal*—Backs up all selected files and marks each file as backed up by setting the file's archive bit.

One of the first details to consider is what needs to be backed up and how important the data is. Any data that changes frequently and is critical to the business should be backed up on a daily schedule using the Normal backup type. This data would include network file servers, information stores, databases, and so on. Any data that is lost or corrupted can be restored to the state of previous backups. One problem with performing Normal backups with a large amount of data everyday is the amount of time and backup capacity needed. In spite of this, most organizations opt for the daily backup schedule if their equipment and backup capacity allows for it.

Any data that is static or changes infrequently does not need to be backed up as vigorously. An example of this would be a user's workstation. If the user stores data files on a network share, that data is backed up daily from the file server. Because data is not stored on the workstation, a Normal backup can be performed once a month with Incremental backups performed nightly. This gives the user or administrator the ability to restore the system and most files.

Using Windows XP Professional Backup

Windows XP Professional ships with Microsoft Windows Backup 5 (see Figure 14.1). This full-featured graphical utility allows an administrator to perform backup and restore operations to a variety of backup media. Backup also includes the Windows XP Professional Job Scheduler for automating the execution of backup jobs.

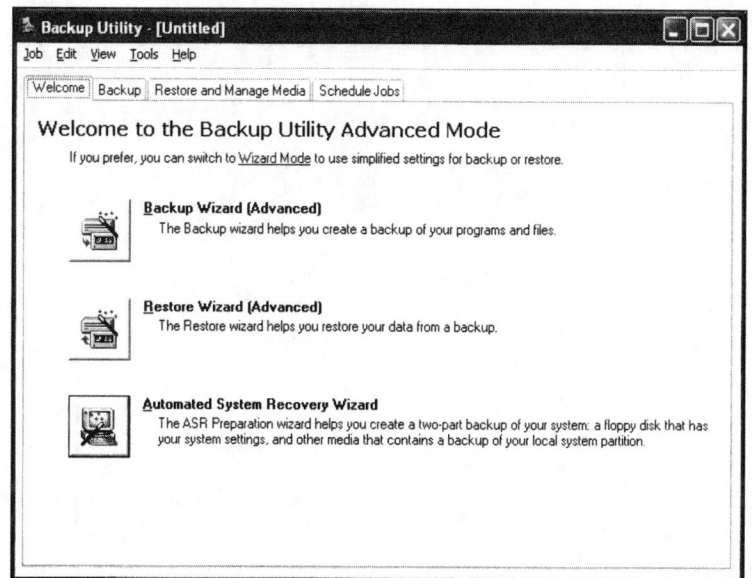

Figure 14.1 Microsoft Windows Backup Utility.

All file systems that are supported by Windows XP Professional are also supported by Backup. When Backup backs up data, all attributes and security permissions are also preserved.

Removable Storage

The management of backup tapes and disks is performed using the Removable Storage Console (see Figure 14.2). Backup media is allocated according to media pools. When a user configures Backup for a backup job, the user must specify which media pool Backup should allocate media to. This is a significant change from previous versions of Backup found in Windows NT.

For example, in earlier versions of Backup, a user would specify any available tape cartridge when configuring backup jobs. If the user wanted to perform backups every night, the user would create a single job.

In the new Backup, tapes are managed by Removable Storage. A user must select a media pool to back up the data to. After the media pool is selected, Removable Storage determines which tape is available to be written to.

Backup

Creating a backup job is fairly simple. A user has two choices—use the Backup Wizard found on the Welcome page or choose to back up manually from the Backup tab. From the Backup tab (see Figure 14.3), take these steps:

1. Select the drivers, directories, files, and/or System State to be backed up.

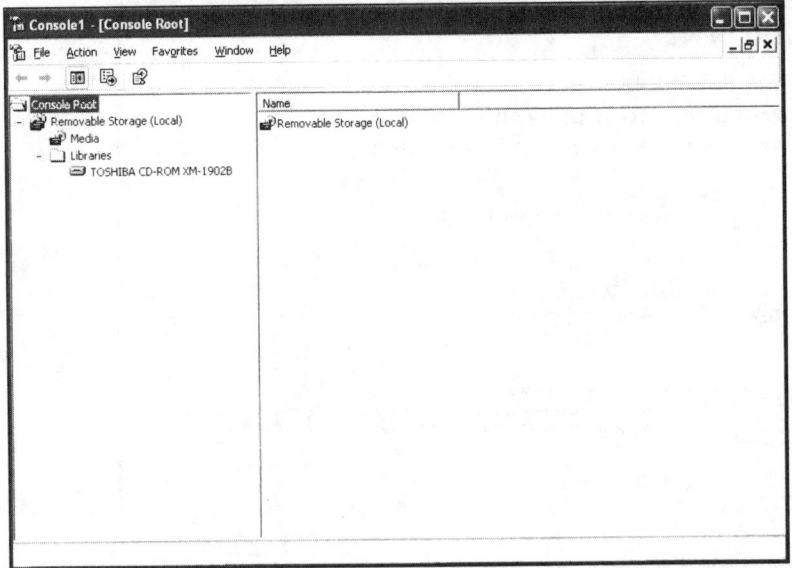

Figure 14.2 The Removable Storage Console.

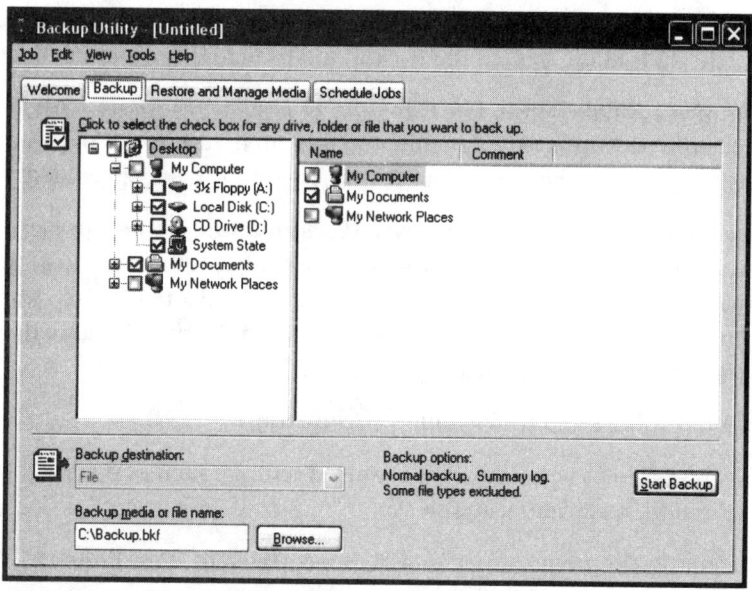

Figure 14.3 Manually configuring a backup job.

2. Select the backup destination in the Backup Destination drop-down list box. This designates which media pool will be used. Remember that the media pools are managed by Removable Storage Service. If the media pool selected is File, the user can enter the file name and destination.

3. Click the Start Backup button. The Backup Job Information dialog box is displayed (see Figure 14.4). The following information can be supplied:

   ➤ *Backup Description*—Allows you to enter a useful description for the backup job; for example, Full Backup/March 13, 2001.

   ➤ *Append This Backup To The Media*—Allows the backup job to be appended or added to an existing backup media.

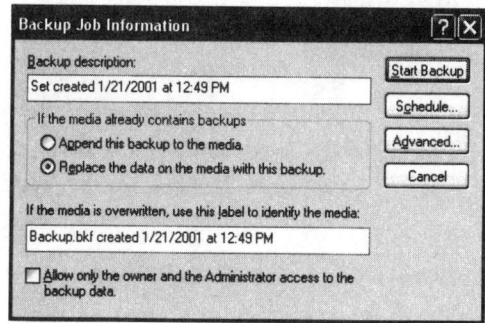

Figure 14.4 The Backup Job Information dialog box.

➤ *Replace The Data On The Media With This Backup*—Causes Backup to erase any existing backup data on the backup media before writing the new data.

➤ *If The Media Is Overwritten, Use This Label To Identify The Media*—Allows you to label the backup media. Labeling the backup media causes the tape to be erased, so it cannot be used when the backup job is being appended.

➤ *Allow Only The Owner And The Administrator Access To The Backup Data*— Allows the tape to be secured. Only members of the Administrators group or the Creator/Owner of the tape will be able to restore the data. If the backup job is being appended, this option cannot be used because the security for the tape has already been created.

➤ *Schedule*—Allows you to schedule a backup job.

➤ *Advanced*—Allows you to specify advanced settings, such as the backup type, compression, verification, and so on.

To set the default Backup type, select Tools|Options|Backup Type. From the Backup Type page, you can select the desired Backup Type.

To back up data, a user must be a member of the Administrators or Backup Operators group.

Backing Up and Restoring System State Information

In previous versions of Windows NT, Backup could back up and restore the Registry and system files. Starting with Windows 2000, Backup backs up these items in what is known as the System State. The System State includes the following items:

➤ Boot files

➤ System files

➤ Windows File Protection (WFP) protected files

➤ Performance counter configuration information

➤ Component Services Class registration database

➤ The Registry

When System State is selected for backup, all of the preceeding items are backed up. Backup will not allow individual items to be selected. To back up the System State, follow these steps:

1. Click Start|Programs|Accessories|System Tools, and select Backup.

2. Go to the Backup tab. Select the System State checkbox.

When the System State checkbox is selected, the System State is backed up along with any other files selected in the backup job.

If a user wants to restore the System State, the user must be a member of the Administrators group. During a restore, the Registry and system files can be restored to an alternate location. The Component Services Class registration database can only be restored to its original location.

Restore

Restoring data is as simple as backing it up. Again, as with a backup, a user has two choices—use the Restore Wizard found on the Welcome page or restore manually from the Restore tab.

From the Restore and Manage Media tab, a list of media pools is displayed (see Figure 14.5). To restore data, the user selects the media pool that contains the appropriate backup set. After the media pool is displayed, the user can select the backup set and the desired files. To restore data, the user must be a member of the Administrators or Backup Operators group.

Warning: When backing up encrypted files (EFS), user keys and certificates should also be backed up. When encrypted files are restored, they remain encrypted; only the user with the correct key can decrypt the file. The Certificate Console furnishes ways to export keys to removable media, such as floppy disks.

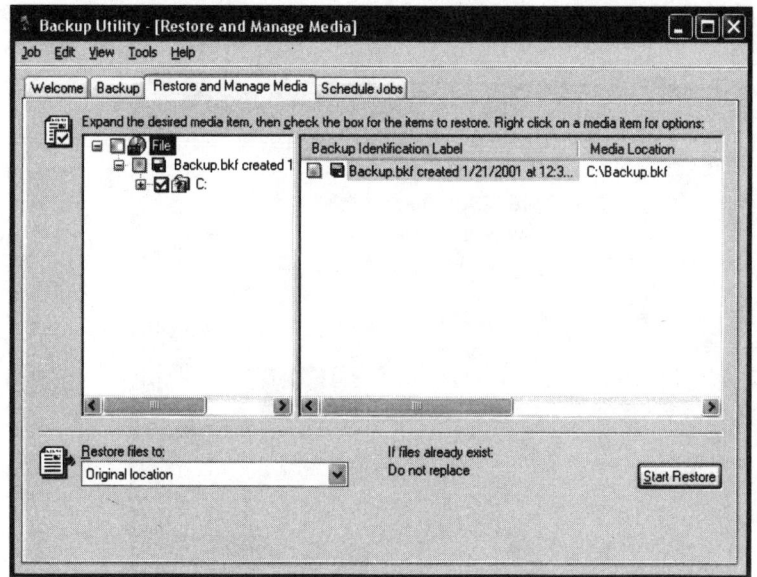

Figure 14.5   Manually configuring a restore job.

Schedule Jobs

To schedule backup jobs, users have a variety of options to customize job schedules to suit their needs. The Schedule Jobs tab displays a monthly calendar (see Figure 14.6).

To schedule a backup job, take these steps:

1. From Backup, select the Schedule Jobs tab.

2. Select the day that the backup job should start running. Click Add Job.

3. The Backup Wizard will start. Click Next.

4. Specify what should be backed up:

   ➤ Back up everything on my computer

   ➤ Back up selected files, drives, or network data

   ➤ Only back up the System State data

5. Click Next.

6. Select the backup media type and the backup media.

7. Select the type of backup to be performed (Normal, Copy, Incremental, Differential, or Daily) from the drop-down list.

8. Click Next.

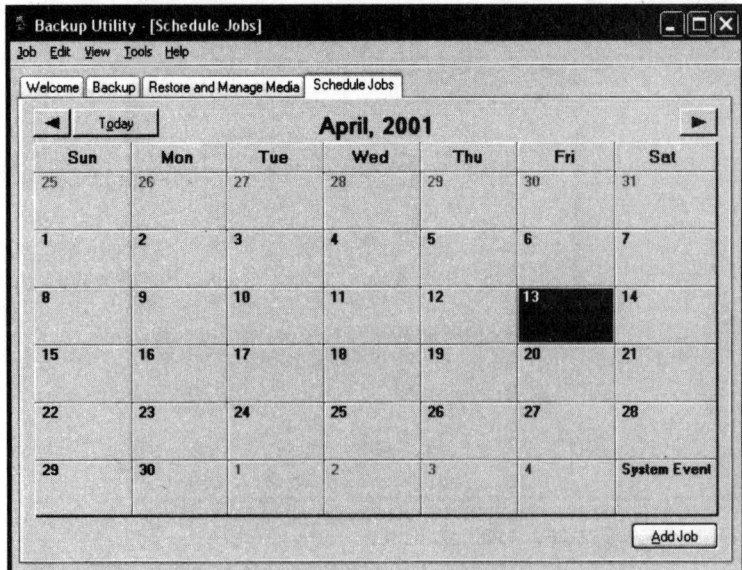

Figure 14.6   The Schedule Jobs tab.

9. Specify verification and compression options. Click Next.

10. Select whether the backup job should be appended to or overwrite the media. Click Next.

11. Enter backup and media labels if desired. Click Next.

12. Select Later to specify a time for the backup job to start. Click Set Schedule.

13. From the Schedule Job dialog box, select the Schedule Task from the drop-down list:

   ➤ Daily

   ➤ Weekly

   ➤ Monthly

   ➤ Once

   ➤ At System Startup

   ➤ At Logon

   ➤ When Idle

14. Click OK. Click Next.

15. A summary of the scheduled backup job will be displayed. Click Finish to schedule the job.

Using Safe Mode Options

Safe Mode is a tool that allows a user to control how Windows XP Professional starts. Although this tool was first introduced in Windows 95, it was never added to Windows NT 4. With Windows NT, a user had a limited number of options available for diagnosing and troubleshooting system problems that were possibly related to device drivers and system files. Problems with these types of files can prevent a computer from booting properly, so Safe Mode allows a user to boot a computer with the minimum required drivers and system files.

To access the Safe Mode boot menu, press F8 when the message *For troubleshooting and advanced startup options for Windows, press F8* is displayed. You can then select the Safe Mode option you would like to use or press ESC to return to the boot menu. After pressing F8, the following will be displayed:

```
Windows Advanced Options Menu
Please select an option:

    Safe Mode
```

14

```
Safe Mode With Networking
Safe Mode With Command Prompt

Enable Boot Logging
Enable VGA Mode
Last Known Good Configuration (your most recent settings that worked)
Directory Services Restore Mode (Windows domain controllers only)
Debugging Mode

Start Windows Normally
Reboot
Return to OS Choices Menu
```

```
Use the up and down arrow keys to move the highlight to your choice.
```

To enter an option, use the arrow keys to highlight the option, and press Enter. You then can select from the following modes:

➤ *Safe Mode*—Loads Windows XP Professional with a minimum number of basic device drivers and system services to load the operating system. No other services or applications are started.

➤ *Safe Mode With Networking*—Loads the same devices and services as Safe Mode, but also loads drivers and services associated with networking. This option allows an administrator to access resources on the network. No other services or applications are started.

➤ *Safe Mode With Command Prompt*—Loads the same devices and services as Safe Mode, but loads Cmd.exe instead of Explorer.exe as the user shell.

➤ *Enable Boot Logging*—Boots the system under normal conditions (all device drivers and services designated to start automatically will be loaded). It creates a log file called Ntbtlog.txt that logs the name and status of device drivers in memory. The log file is stored in the %systemroot% folder.

➤ *Enable VGA Mode*—Starts the system using the basic VGA mode. This option is useful when you are experiencing video driver problems.

➤ *Last Known Good Configuration*—Starts the system using the last successfully started system configuration.

➤ *Directory Services Restore Mode (Windows Domain Controllers Only)*—As indicated in the option name, this mode is used only on Windows 2000 or .NET domain controllers. It doesn't apply to Windows XP Professional.

➤ *Debugging Mode*—Starts Windows XP Professional in kernel debug mode. This mode is useful in troubleshooting, where another system (the debugger) can break into the Windows XP Professional kernel for precise analysis.

The Recovery Console

Another exciting feature in Windows XP Professional is the Recovery Console, a command-line interface that an administrator can use to access the hard disk of a Windows XP Professional system. Windows XP Professional does not need to be operating when using the Recovery Console, so it is very useful in troubleshooting and recovery situations.

The Recovery Console provides access to the file systems on a hard disk, whether it is FAT, FAT32, or NTFS. With this level of access, an administrator can access files and directories. More importantly, the administrator has the capability to start and stop services and therefore repair the system.

Starting the Recovery Console

The Recovery Console can be accessed from the Windows XP Professional installation CD-ROM or from the Windows XP Professional Setup floppy disks. It can also be installed to the local hard disk by typing the following command at a command prompt:

```
D:\I386\WINNT32.EXE /cmdcons
```

In this prompt, *D:* represents the CD-ROM drive where the Windows XP Professional installation CD-ROM is located.

Note: *The Recovery Console cannot be installed on a mirrored disk. To install the Recovery Console on the system, break the mirror, install the Recovery Console, and re-create the mirror.*

To start the Recovery Console using the installation media, take these steps:

1. Boot the computer from the Windows XP Professional installation CD-ROM or from the Windows XP Professional Setup floppy disks. At the Setup Notification screen, press Enter.

2. On the Welcome To Setup screen, press R to repair a Windows installation.

3. Select the Windows XP Professional installation you want to repair, and press Enter.

4. Enter the password for the local administrator account.

To start the Recovery Console that was installed to the local hard disk, take these steps:

1. Boot the computer. At the Operating System selection screen, select Microsoft Windows Recovery Console.

14

2. Select the Windows XP Professional installation you want to repair, and press Enter.

3. Enter the password for the local administrator account.

Using the Recovery Console

The Recovery Console is a command-line interface. Most of the commands are derived from MS-DOS commands, so, if you are familiar with MS-DOS, you can figure out what a command does. If you are not sure what a command does, help can be obtained by typing the command followed by /?. Table 14.1 lists the commands supported by the Recovery Console.

Table 14.1 Recovery Console commands.

Command	Description
Attrib	Changes attributes on one file or directory
Batch	Executes commands specified in a text file
Bootcfg	Boots configuration and recovery
Cd/chdir	Displays the name of the current directory or switches to a new directory
Chkdsk	Checks a disk and displays a status report
Cls	Clears the screen
Copy	Copies a single file to another location
Del/delete	Deletes one file
Dir	Displays a list of files and subdirectories in a directory
Disable	Disables a Windows system service or driver
Diskpart	Manages the partitions on your hard disk volumes
Enable	Enables a Windows system service or driver
Exit	Exits the Recovery Console and restarts the computer
Expand	Expands a compressed file
Fixboot	Writes a new boot sector onto the system partition
Fixmbr	Repairs the master boot code of the boot partition
Format	Formats a disk for use with Windows
Help	Displays information about commands supported by the Recovery Console
Listsvc	Lists all available services and drivers on the computer
Logon	Lists the detected installations of Windows and requests the local administrator password for those installations
Map	Lists the drive letter to physical device mappings that are currently active
Md/mkdir	Creates a directory
More/type	Displays a text file to the screen
Net Use	Maps a network share to a drive letter
Rd/rmdir	Removes (deletes) a directory
Ren/rename	Renames a single file
Set	Displays and sets Recovery Console environment variables
Systemroot	Sets the current directory to %systemroot%

By default, the Recovery Console only permits access to the following directories:

➤ %systemroot%

➤ Root directory of local disks

➤ \cmdcons and any subdirectories

➤ Directories on floppy disks and CD-ROMs

Access can be gained to other directories by changing the local Group Policy settings as described in the following steps:

1. Select Start|Run, and enter "MMC".

2. Click the Console drop-down menu, and select Add/Remove Snap-In.

3. Click Add.

4. From the list of snap-ins, select Group Policy, and click Add.

5. The Select Group Policy Object dialog box will be displayed. Verify that Local Computer is listed, and click Finish.

6. Click Close on the Add Stand-Alone Snap-In dialog box.

7. Click OK to close the Add/Remove Snap-In dialog box.

8. Double-click Local Computer Policy.

9. Double-click Computer Configuration.

10. Double-click Windows Settings.

11. Double-click Security Settings.

12. Double-click Local Policies.

13. Select Security Options.

14. Double-click Recovery Console: Allow floppy copy and access to all drives and all folders.

15. The Local Security Policy Setting dialog box will be displayed. Select Enabled, and click OK.

The **set** command is disabled by default. Once this access has been granted via Group Policy, the **set** command is enabled. The following **set** command can provide several functions:

```
Set [variable = value]
```

14

In the preceding command line, *variable* can be the following:

➤ **AllowWildCards**—Enables wild-card support for some commands, such as **copy**.

➤ **AllowAllPaths**—Provides access to all files and folders on the system.

➤ **AllRemovableMedia**—Allows files to be copied to removable media, such as floppies.

➤ **NoCopyPrompt**—Causes the confirmation prompt during overwrites to be disabled.

Recovering the Boot Configuration by Using the Recovery Console

Problems with the boot configuration found in the Boot.ini file can be remedied by using the Recovery Console. The boot configuration can be recovered by using the **BOOTCFG** command, which contains several parameters to assist you in recovering from a boot configuration failure. Table 14.2 lists and describes the **BOOTCFG** parameters.

Warning: When using **BOOTCFG /rebuild**, always make a backup copy of your Boot.ini file. You can accomplish this from the Recovery Console by using the **copy** command.

Replacing the Registry by Using the Recovery Console

Problems with the Registry can be remedied by using the Recovery Console. Registry files can be replaced by using the **copy** command. Backup copies of the Registry files are kept in either the %systemroot%\repair folder or the %systemroot%\repair\regback folder.

To replace the Registry using the Recovery Console, follow these steps:

1. Start the Recovery Console, and enter the local administrator password.

Table 14.2   BOOTCFG parameters.

Command	Description
Bootcfg /add	Adds a Windows OS to the boot list
Bootcfg /default	Sets the default boot entry
Bootcfg /disableredirect	Disables redirection of the boot loader
Bootcfg /list	Lists all current entries for the boot list
Bootcfg /rebuild	Searches through all Windows installations and prompts for which to add
Bootcfg /redirect [PortBaudRate] [useBiosSettings]	Enables the redirection of the boot loader to the specified location
Bootcfg /scan	Scans all disks for all Windows installations and displays the results

2. You will start in the %systemroot% directory (for example, C:\WINDOWS). Enter the following commands:

```
cd repair\regback
copy filename C:\WINDOWS\SYSTEM32\CONFIG
```

Here, *filename* is the name of the Registry file to be copied. You should rename the current Registry files before replacing them. In case a problem occurs, this gives you the opportunity to return to the system's original condition.

Warning: Files located in %systemroot%\repair\regback represent the Registry state the last time that the System State was backed up. Any changes made to the Registry files since then will be lost.

Disabling a Device Driver or Service by Using the Recovery Console

Problems with device drivers and services can be remedied by using the Recovery Console as well. By using the **enable** and **disable** commands, troublesome device drivers and services can be disabled. To disable a device driver using the Recovery Console, take the following steps:

1. Start the Recovery Console, and enter the local administrator password.

2. You will start in the %systemroot% directory (for example, C:\WINDOWS). Type "listsvc" to obtain a list of currently installed device drivers and services. Locate the name of the troublesome device driver.

3. Enter the following command:

```
disable servicename
```

Here, *servicename* is the name of the device driver and service. For example, if you needed to disable the device driver for a 3Com Network Adapter, you would enter:

```
disable EL90BC
```

The following output will be displayed:

```
The registry entry for the EL90BC service was found.
The service currently has a start_type SERVICE_DEMAND_START.
Please record this value.

The new start_type for the service has been set to SERVICE_DISABLED.
The computer must now be restarted for the changes to take effect.
Type EXIT if you want to restart the computer now.
```

14

4. The **disable** command will display the current start type. Write this down so that you know what it should be set back to when it is enabled.

5. Type "exit" to restart the computer.

To enable a device driver using the Recovery Console, follow these steps:

1. Start the Recovery Console, and enter the local administrator password.

2. You will start in the %systemroot% directory (for example, C:\WINDOWS). Enter the following command:

```
enable EL90BC SERVICE_DEMAND_START
```

The following output will be displayed:

```
The registry entry for the EL90BC service was found.
The service currently has a start_type SERVICE_DISABLED.
Please record this value.

The new start_type for the service has been set to
SERVICE_DEMAND_START.
The computer must now be restarted for the changes to take effect.
Type EXIT if you want to restart the computer now.
```

3. Type "exit" to restart the computer.

Using System Restore

A new tool found in Windows XP Professional is System Restore. System Restore allows you to restore the operating system to a previous point without jeopardizing or losing a user's personal data, such as email, Internet Favorites, and documents.

The previous point is known as the Restore Point. Windows XP Professional uses System Restore to automatically create Restore Points both daily and whenever a significant event occurs, such as the installation of a new application or device driver.

You can also manually create a Restore Point to protect your system. For example, if you are about to upgrade an application, you could create a Restore Point to guarantee that you will be able to restore the system in the event that the upgrade fails. It is therefore good practice to create a Restore Point before making any significant configuration change to a system.

To create a Restore Point, follow these steps:

1. Select Start|All Programs|Accessories|System Tools|System Restore.

2. Select Create A Restore Point, and click Next.

3. Enter a description for the Restore Point. For example, enter "Before new NIC driver installation".

4. Click Create.

5. Click Close.

If you find you need to revert to a particular Restore Point, follow these steps:

1. Select Start|All Programs|Accessories|System Tools|System Restore.

2. Select Restore My Computer To An Earlier Time, and click Next.

3. From the calendar, select the date that contains the desired Restore Point (see Figure 14.7). Click Next.

4. Click Next.

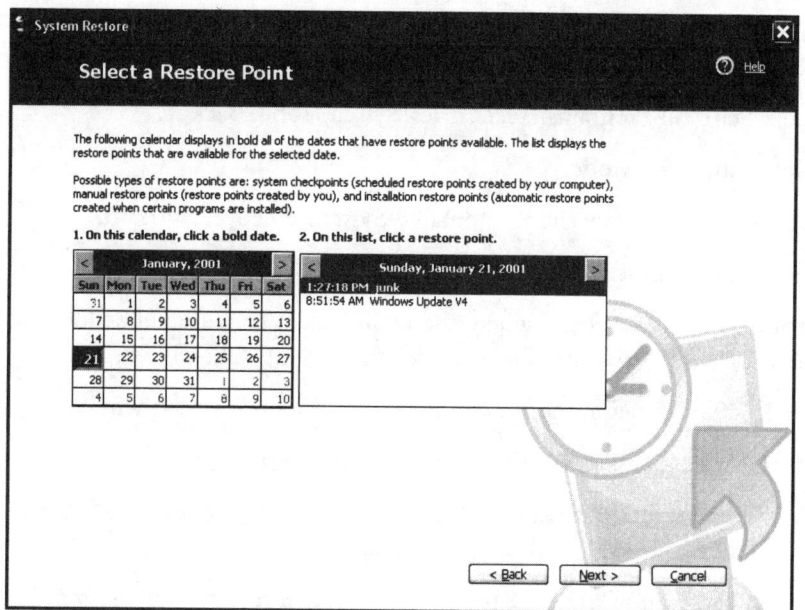

Figure 14.7   Using System Restore to revert to a Restore Point.

Using Automated System Recovery

The Automated System Recovery (ASR) process allows you to restore a Windows XP Professional system to the condition the system was in when the ASR disks were created. The ASR disks contain files and information needed to restore a damaged or seriously malfunctioning system. Before initiating the ASR process, verify that your system is functioning properly and fully.

The first portion of the ASR process is the creation of the backup. This backup includes two sets of backup media. First is a system backup placed on high-density media, such as CDR, tape, or hard disk. The second component is the ASR disk.

Because the high-density media will contain the partition that Windows XP Professional was installed in, you need to verify that your media will be able to hold this data. In other words, if the partition you are backing up contains 11GB of data, your media will need to be at least 11GB.

The ASR floppy disk is created at the end of the ASR process. It contains the ASR state file called Asr.sif as well as several other files. These files are used to restore the system to its original system state.

To run the ASR process, you need to start the Automated System Recovery Wizard as described here:

1. Click Start|All Programs|Accessories|System Tools|Backup.

2. Click Advanced Mode.

3. On the Welcome tab, click Automated System Recovery Wizard.

4. The wizard will start. Click Next.

5. First, you need to specify where the main system backup will be located. Select the destination drive and file name for the backup. Click Next.

6. Click Finish to begin the backup. A Backup Progress screen will be displayed.

7. Insert a high-density 3.5-inch floppy disk when prompted.

8. The wizard will now create the ASR disk. Label the floppy *ASR Disk* along with the current date, and store it in a safe, secure place.

The second portion of the ASR process is the actual recovery of a system. To recover a system, perform the following steps:

1. Boot from the Windows XP Professional Installation CD-ROM.

2. When prompted, press F2 to begin the ASR process.

3. When prompted, insert the ASR floppy disk to begin the restore.

Note: The ASR process has replaced the emergency repair disk (ERD) process found in Windows 2000 and earlier versions of the Windows NT operating system. The ERD process only backed up certain files to restore System State, while ASR performs a complete system backup.

Chapter Summary

Recovering a Windows XP Professional installation can be a real lifesaver. Luckily, Windows XP Professional comes with a number of utilities to help an administrator diagnose, troubleshoot, restore, and recover a Windows XP Professional system.

Before attempting to recover a system, the administrator needs to diagnose the problem. The types of problems encountered in Windows XP Professional generally fall into three categories—device driver problems, system file problems, or hardware problems. Each category has its own methods for diagnosing and remedying problems.

Windows XP Professional includes a full-featured backup utility, simply called Backup. The Backup Utility allows data to be backed up to any removable media. Once the data is backed up, individual files or even the full system can be restored. This can include the System State, which includes the Registry, boot files, system files, Windows File Protection (WFP) protected files, performance counter configuration, and the Component Services Class registration database.

Windows XP Professional now includes Safe Mode options upon boot. These options allow an administrator to start a Windows XP Professional system with the minimum required device drivers and services. These options are useful when diagnosing and repairing a troublesome workstation.

Another new feature in Windows XP Professional is the Recovery Console, a command-line interface that provides an administrator with access to the file system, whether the file system is FAT, FAT32, or NTFS. An administrator can also start and stop device drivers and services with the Recovery Console. It is a powerful tool that might be able to repair a system that previously would have required a full restore.

Finally, this chapter covered the Automated System Recovery (ASR) process, which enables an administrator to completely repair a damaged Windows XP Professional system.

14

Review Questions

1. The ASR disk is a bootable floppy disk. True or False?

   a. True

   b. False

2. What is the easiest way to recover boot files that are missing or corrupt?

   a. Reinstall the operating system.

   b. Copy the files from a Windows NT workstation.

   c. Use the ASR process.

   d. Run the **SYS** command in the Recovery Console.

3. How can you back up the Windows XP Professional Registry?

   a. Use the ERD.

   b. Boot using Safe Mode With Registry Backup.

   c. Export the Registry to tab-delimited text files.

   d. Perform a backup using the Backup Utility, and select the System State.

4. Which service or device driver is not loaded when booting in Safe Mode?

   a. Mouse device driver

   b. Logical Disk Manager services

   c. Network Adapter device driver

   d. Basic VGA device driver

5. What is one method of starting the Recovery Console?

   a. Boot the system with the ERD.

   b. Boot the system with the Windows XP Professional installation CD.

   c. Press F8 when starting.

   d. Boot with an MS-DOS disk.

6. Which Windows XP Professional repair option allows an administrator to disable a device driver?

   a. Safe Mode

   b. Emergency repair disk process

   c. Recovery Console

   d. Safe Mode With Command Prompt

7. Backup found in Windows XP Professional does not support which of the following media?

   a. QIC tape

   b. DLT tape

   c. Floppy

   d. CD-ROM

8. Using Recovery Console, which directories can be accessed? [Check all correct answers]

   a. %systemroot%

   b. Directories on floppy disks and CD-ROMs

   c. The root directory of local disks

   d. \cmdcons and any subdirectories

9. If the Safe Mode startup option Enable Boot Logging is selected, where is the log file stored?

   a. %systemroot%

   b. C:\ntbtlog.txt

   c. %systemroot%\repair

   d. The Event Viewer

10. You are having difficulties with an application in Windows 2000. It has corrupted some application-specific device drivers that are causing the system to crash. You need to install a service pack for the application that will fix the problem, but it only resides on a network share. How can you utilize the system to get to and install the service pack?

    a. Boot with Safe Mode.

    b. Boot with Safe Mode With Command Prompt.

    c. Use the Recovery Console.

    d. Boot with Safe Mode With Networking.

14

11. The ERD contains a compressed copy of the Windows XP Professional Registry. True or False?

    a. True

    b. False

12. How do you access Safe Mode options in Windows 2000?

    a. Press F8 on the OS selection menu.

    b. Boot with the ERD.

    c. Select the Restart In Safe Mode option upon shutdown.

    d. Press Ctrl+Alt+Esc.

13. When restoring the Registry using the emergency repair disk process, from where is the Registry restored?

    a. ERD

    b. Backup tape

    c. %systemroot%\repair\regback

    d. %systemroot%\repair

14. When restoring the System State to a Windows XP Professional system, individual Registry files can be selected. True or False?

    a. True

    b. False

15. Which Recovery Console command can be used to set the start_type of a service or device driver?

    a. **Enable**

    b. **Set start_type**

    c. **Start_type**

    d. **Re-enable**

16. Which Safe Mode startup option provides you with a list of loaded device drivers and services?

    a. Safe Mode

    b. Enable Boot Logging

    c. Safe Mode With Networking

    d. Debugging Mode

17. Which Recovery Console command creates a new boot sector on the system partition?

    a. **Fixmbr**

    b. **Fixboot**

    c. **Fixbootsector**

    d. **Fixsys**

18. You need to restore the Registry on your Windows XP Professional system. You boot the system using the Windows XP Professional installation CD and access the Recovery Console. You change to the %systemroot%\repair directory and notice that there is no regback subdirectory. Why is this so?

    a. The Recovery Console does not provide access to the regback directory.

    b. An ERD has not been created.

    c. The System State has never been backed up.

    d. The **Set** command must be run first.

19. The Recovery Console does not allow full access to which file system?

    a. FAT

    b. FAT32

    c. NTFS

    d. CDFS

20. How do you install the Recovery Console as a startup option?

    a. From a command prompt, type "D:\I386\WINNT32 /cmdcons".

    b. In the Control Panel, select Recovery Console from Windows Setup.

    c. It cannot be installed as a startup option.

    d. Reinstall Windows XP Professional, and select Recovery Console from Advanced Options.

Real-World Projects

You have just been given a new Windows XP Professional-based workstation. Although your workstation is connected to the network, you prefer to save your data to the local hard disk. The workstation includes an internal DLT tape drive.

You want to create a backup schedule where a Normal backup occurs every Friday night with Differential backups taking place Monday through Thursday. No backups will be performed on the weekend. You want to back up everything on your workstation, including the System State.

Project 14.1

To create a scheduled Normal backup:

1. Select Start|All Programs|Accessories|System Tools|Backup to open the Backup utility.

2. On the Welcome screen, click the Backup tab.

3. On the left pane, select the local disk to be backed up (C:). Also, select the System State to back up the Registry and related system files.

4. Select DLT from the Backup destination drop-down list.

5. Click Start Backup.

6. The Backup Job Information dialog box will be displayed. Enter "Full Normal Friday Backup" in the Backup description box.

7. Select Replace The Data On The Media With This Backup. This will overwrite any data on the DLT tape.

14

8. Click Schedule. A warning will be displayed to notify you that you must save the backup selection before proceeding. Click Yes to save the selection. The Save Selections dialog box will be displayed. Enter "Friday-Normal" as the file name. Click OK.

9. The Set Account Information dialog box will be displayed. Enter the user account that the backup job will use as a security context when run. Remember that the user account must be in the Administrators group because the System State is also being backed up. By default, the local Administrator account is selected. Enter the administrator password and verify the password. Click OK.

10. The Schedule Job Options dialog box will be displayed. Enter "Friday-Normal Backup" in the Job name box. Click Properties to schedule the job.

11. The Schedule Job dialog box will be displayed. From the Schedule Task drop-down list, select Weekly. Clear the default selection Monday checkbox, and select the Friday checkbox. In the Start Time box, enter "10:00 P.M.". Click OK to save the scheduled job. Click OK to close the Schedule Job Options dialog box.

Next, you need to create the Daily Differential backup job.

Project 14.2

To create a scheduled Differential backup:

1. Select Start|All Programs|Accessories|System Tools|Backup to open the Backup utility.

2. On the Welcome screen, click the Backup tab.

3. In the Job drop-down menu, select Load Selections. Select FridayNormal.bks because it contains the desired job selection set (Local C: and the System State).

4. Select DLT in the Backup Destination drop-down list.

5. In the Tools drop-down menu, select Options. In the Default Backup Type drop-down list, select Differential. Click OK to close the Options dialog box.

6. Click Start Backup.

7. The Backup Job Information dialog box will be displayed. Enter "Daily Differential Backup" in the Backup description box.

8. Select Append This Backup To The Media. This will append the backup job to any data on the DLT tape.

9. Click Schedule.

10. The Schedule Job Options dialog box will be displayed. Enter "Daily Differential Backup" in the Job name box. Click Properties to schedule the job.

11. The Schedule Job dialog box will be displayed. In the Schedule Task dropdown list, select Weekly. Keep the default selection of Monday and also select the Tuesday, Wednesday, and Thursday checkboxes. In the Start Time text box, enter "10:00 P.M.". Click OK to save the scheduled job. Click OK to close the Schedule Job Options dialog box.

You have a Windows XP Professional workstation that will be used for testing new applications and hardware. You want to use the Recovery Console to help troubleshoot any problems resulting from the testing.

Project 14.3
To install the Recovery Console:

1. Open a command prompt by selecting Start | Run. Type "cmd" in the Run dialog box. Click OK.

2. Insert the Windows XP Professional Installation CD in the CD-ROM drive. At the command prompt, type "*D:*\I386\WINNT32.EXE /cmdcons" (where *D:* is the letter of the CD-ROM drive), and press Enter.

3. A dialog box will be displayed, asking if you want to install the Recovery Console on the hard disk. Click Yes.

4. The Windows XP Professional Setup Wizard will start to install the necessary files. Click OK when the wizard is finished.

After installing a new Adaptec SCSI adapter in your system along with its associated device drivers, strange application faults start occurring. After rebooting your system, Windows XP Professional will not boot normally. Because the SCSI adapter's device driver was the last change made to the workstation, you decide that you want to disable it using the Recovery Console.

Project 14.4
To disable a device driver using the Recovery Console:

1. Boot the computer. At the Operating System selection screen, select Windows XP Professional Recovery Console.

2. Type the number for the Windows XP Professional installation, and press Enter.

3. Type the password for the local administrator account installation, and press Enter.

14

4. At the Recovery Console command prompt, type "listsvc" to display a list of all device drivers and services installed. From the list, identify the troublesome device driver, aic78xx.

5. At the command prompt, type the command "disable aic78xx". The following text is displayed:

```
The registry entry for the aic78xx service was found.
The service currently has a start_type SERVICE_DEMAND_START.
Please record this value.

The new start_type for the service has been set to SERVICE_DISABLED.
The computer must now be restarted for the changes to take effect.
Type EXIT if you want to restart the computer now.
```

6. Type "exit" at the command prompt to restart the workstation.

After restarting, the workstation boots normally. You check the Adaptec Web site and find a technical article describing the problem with the device driver. You download the updated device driver and install it on the workstation. You will not see the previously encountered problems resurface.

CHAPTER FIFTEEN

The Windows Network Environment

After completing this chapter, you will be able to:

✓ Identify the types of networks found in Windows XP Professional

✓ Identify and access network resources

✓ Join a workgroup or domain

✓ Implement Group Policies on a local computer

✓ Configure network protocols in a Windows network

Many organizations and individuals find that networks are beneficial, because they use resources, such as disk space and printers, in a cost-effective manner. A company with 20 computers in a nonnetworked environment would need to use more costly measures to access resources. For example, it would need to purchase 20 individual printers for the computers or resort to printer sharing using an unreliable patchwork of switchboxes and cables. To share files, it would have to resort to "sneakernet," in which individual users copy files to floppy disks and walk them to other computers. Using sneakernet is very inefficient because the computers end up with multiple copies of the same files. Another problem with sneakernet is that file size is limited to whatever can fit on a floppy. Other more advanced features found in networks, such as email and databases, are not even possible in nonnetworked environments.

This chapter will introduce you to the Windows XP Professional network environment.

Networking and Communications

Most Microsoft operating systems include built-in networking support. Windows 95/98, Windows NT 3.51/4, Windows 2000, and Windows XP provide networking capabilities that many organizations use for network services. Because Microsoft operating systems are widely used, chances are that the network you will be attaching Windows XP Professional to will be a Microsoft Windows network.

Although Windows XP Professional is a great standalone platform, its power is truly found when it is attached to a network. In a network environment, it can take advantage of myriad network resources, including file and print servers, databases, messaging, application servers, intranets, and, perhaps most important, the Internet. Windows XP Professional provides file and print sharing, peer Web services, and many other network features.

Accessing Network Resources

Windows XP Professional can access many network resources straight out of the box. Microsoft wisely included support for the most popular network protocols, such as TCP/IP, NWLink (IPX/SPX), and NetBEUI. By supporting these protocols, Windows XP Professional can speak the same language as the servers supplying network resources, such as databases and messaging. For example, a client/server-based database might use TCP/IP via a particular port to facilitate communication between the client and the server. Messaging applications typically use Simple Mail Transport Protocol (SMTP), a member of the TCP/IP protocol suite, to send email across the network.

Although a network protocol allows Windows XP to speak the same language as other network resources, a network client provides the functionality and access to these network resources. Microsoft includes network clients that allow Windows XP Professional to access file and printing resources on Novell NetWare networks, Unix networks, and, of course, Microsoft networks. A client/server database would include its own client software. Messaging resources can be accessed from a number of clients that support SMTP, such as Netscape Communicator and Microsoft Outlook. Table 15.1 lists the network clients supported by Windows XP.

This chapter focuses on the default client found in Windows XP—Client for Microsoft Networks. Chapter 16 focuses on Client Services for NetWare, and Chapter 17 covers Microsoft Windows Services for Unix 2.

Microsoft Networks

More often than not, Windows XP Professional computers will be connected to a Microsoft network. The network might be built around any of the Microsoft operating systems—Microsoft LAN Manager, Windows 3.*x*, Windows for Workgroups, Windows 95, Windows 98, Windows NT 4, or Windows 2000.

Microsoft networks use the Common Internet File System (CIFS) protocol. CIFS is a file and printer sharing protocol that allows a computer to access files and folders on remote computers. Computers using CIFS communicate using four basic command types—session control, file, printer, and message. CIFS is identical to the Server Message Block (SMB) protocol found in Windows NT.

Networks are organized according to their desired function. Details to consider when organizing a network are the administrative model and geographic locations involved.

Types of Network Environments

Two types of network environments are found in Microsoft networks—workgroup-based networks and domain-based networks. These environment types are based on the security structure of the network.

Table 15.1   Windows XP-supported network clients.

Client	Network Protocols	Description	Other Information
Client for Microsoft Networks	TCP/IP, NWLink, NetBEUI	Used for accessing file and print services for Microsoft Networks	Included with Windows XP (installed by default)
Client Services for NetWare	NWLink	Used for accessing file and print services on Novell NetWare services	Included with Windows XP
Microsoft Windows Services for Unix 2	TCP/IP	Used to provide functionality between Unix hosts and Windows 2000 computers	Included as an add-on pack
Windows 2000 Services for Macintosh	TCP/IP, AppleTalk	Allows Windows 2000 clients and Macintosh clients to share files over TCP/IP or AppleTalk	Found in Windows 2000 Server and Windows 2000 Advanced Server

15

Workgroup-Based Networks

A workgroup-based network is a single subnet, peer-to-peer network. A workgroup is simply a logical grouping of computers that allows a small number of users to share network resources, such as disk space and printers. Security is decentralized, and each computer in the network maintains its own security database. In order to access resources on a computer, a user needs a valid user account and password on that computer.

Workgroup-based networks are ideal for a small office or home, where users want to share resources and security is not the greatest concern. Workgroups typically consist of no more than 10 computers.

Joining a Workgroup

By default, a Windows XP Professional computer becomes a member of the workgroup named WORKGROUP. Only a user account that is a member of the Administrators group can change workgroup membership. A Windows XP Professional computer can change workgroup membership via two methods—by using the Network Identification Wizard or by manually joining a workgroup.

The Network Identification Wizard, shown in Figure 15.1, provides a simple interface that allows a Windows XP Professional computer to join a workgroup. To start the Network Identification Wizard, follow these steps:

1. Click Start. Right-click My Computer, and select Properties.

2. Select the Computer Name tab.

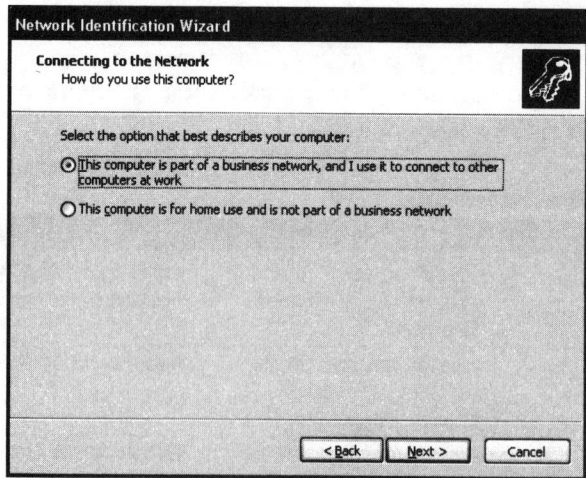

Figure 15.1   The Network Identification Wizard.

3. Click Network ID, and then click Next.

4. Select This Computer Is Part Of A Business Network, And I Use It To Connect To Other Computers At Work. Click Next.

5. To join a workgroup, select My Company Uses A Network Without A Domain. Click Next.

6. Enter the name of the workgroup. Click Next.

7. Click Finish, and restart the computer.

To manually join a workgroup, follow these steps.

1. Click Start. Right-click My Computer, and select Properties.

2. Select the Computer Name tab. Select Change.

3. The Computer Name Changes dialog box is displayed. In the Member Of section, select Workgroup.

4. Enter the name of the workgroup. Click OK.

5. Click OK to close the Computer Name Changes dialog box.

6. Click OK to close the System Properties dialog box.

7. Click Yes to restart the computer.

Domain-Based Networks

A domain-based network is also a logical grouping of computers, with the notable exception that they all share a common security database. This allows a user to have a single user account that, when granted the proper access, can utilize any resources in the domain.

The security database for the domain is housed on domain controllers. These are servers that manage all interactions, such as authentication, account creation and deletion, auditing, and the granting or revoking of rights.

If a domain contains more than one domain controller, the security database is replicated between them. This provides fault tolerance and scalability. If a domain controller fails, the other domain controllers can continue to authenticate users. It provides scalability by distributing the authentication load across multiple domain controllers.

15

Two models of domain-based networks exist. The older model, found in Windows NT 4, is known as a Windows NT 4 Domain, or simply a Domain. The new model is found in Windows 2000 and is called Active Directory.

Windows NT 4 Domains

Windows NT 4 Domains are created with the installation of a Windows NT 4 Server designated as a primary domain controller (PDC). On the PDC resides a read/write copy of the Security Accounts Manager (SAM). The SAM is the security database for the domain. When a user account is created or modified, the result is saved to the SAM located on the PDC.

To create fault tolerance and scalability in a Windows NT 4 Domain, another type of domain controller can be added. This domain controller is known as a backup domain controller (BDC). A BDC houses a read-only copy of the SAM. If the PDC goes down, the BDCs will continue to authenticate users, although changes or additions cannot occur. A BDC can also be promoted to function as the PDC.

Active Directory

Active Directory is the domain-based security model found in Windows 2000. Active Directory is known as a directory service. A directory service provides a place to store information about a network, such as user accounts, computer accounts, files, printers, and applications.

Unlike a Windows NT 4 Domain, which contains a single read/write copy of the SAM, Active Directory is known as a *multiple master database*. The domain controllers in Active Directory all have read/write access to the directory service.

Active Directory is also more organized than a Windows NT 4 Domain. Active Directory can contain separate trees, domains, and organizational units (OUs) that can mimic the organizational or geographical structure of a company.

Joining a Domain

Whether joining a Windows NT 4 Domain or Active Directory, the method is the same. Only a user account that is a member of the Administrators group can add or remove a computer from a domain. As with workgroup-based networks, a Windows XP Professional computer can be added or removed from a domain via two methods—by using the Network Identification Wizard or by manually joining a domain.

The Network Identification Wizard provides a simple interface that allows a Windows XP Professional computer to join a domain. To start the Network Identification Wizard, follow these steps:

1. Click Start. Right-click My Computer, and select Properties.

2. Click the Computer Name tab.

3. Click Network ID, and then click Next.

4. Select This Computer Is Part Of A Business Network, And I Use It To Connect To Other Computers At Work. Click Next.

5. Click Next.

6. To join a domain, select My Company Uses A Network With A Domain. Click Next.

7. Enter the name of the domain and a valid user account and password. Click Next.

8. Click Finish, and restart the computer.

To manually join a domain, follow these steps:

1. Click Start. Right-click My Computer, and select Properties.

2. Click the Computer Name tab. Select Change.

3. The Computer Name Changes dialog box is displayed. In the Member Of section, select Domain.

4. Enter the name of the domain and a valid user account and password. Click OK.

5. Click OK to close the Computer Name Changes dialog box.

6. Click OK to close the System Properties dialog box.

7. Click Yes to restart the computer.

Account Authentication

Whether joining a workgroup or domain, a computer needs to be protected from unauthorized access. Microsoft networks use account authentication to secure a computer and the resources it contains. Account authentication is the process of verifying a user's identification supplied by the user against the information found in the security database. Once verified, the user is allowed to access resources according to the permissions granted. If authentication fails, the user is denied access.

Authentication in workgroup-based networks occurs at the local account database on each computer. Authentication in domain-based networks occurs at the domain controllers.

Beginning with Windows 2000, Kerberos v5 authentication protocol is the default authentication method. Kerberos is a standard security protocol supported by many vendors and operating systems.

Windows XP Professional also supports Windows NT LAN Manager (NTLM) security for authentication to Windows NT 4 Domains. When logging into a Windows NT domain, Windows XP Professional will first attempt to use Kerberos. If it fails to find the Kerberos Key Distribution Center on the domain controller, it will attempt to use NTLM and the SAM.

15

Logon Names

Windows XP and Windows 2000 require every user who attempts to access resources to have a valid and unique logon name. A logon name identifies the user to the operating system. In Windows XP and Windows 2000, a user can have two types of logons—a SAM Account Name and a User Principal Name (UPN).

Recall from the first part of this chapter that user accounts in Windows NT are stored in the SAM. The SAM is a security accounts database containing user accounts, group accounts, passwords, and so on. A SAM Account Name is used to provide compatibility with older Windows NT 4 domains and workgroups. In Windows NT 4, each logon name in the SAM must be unique. In other words, if there are two users, one named Mike Witherspoon and another named Mike Walters, only one of them can have the logon name MIKEW. The other user would need to have a logon name that incorporates a middle initial or some other variation to make it unique.

The UPN is a feature found in Windows 2000 and Active Directory. It is used in addition to the SAM Account Name. The UPN looks exactly like an Internet email account. The UPN consists of the username followed by the @ sign followed by the UPN suffix. The suffix is typically the Active Directory domain in which the logon name is found. For example, if Mike Witherspoon had a logon name in the Active Directory domain helpandlearn.com, his UPN would be mikew@helpandlearn.com.

The UPN is a shortened version of the Distinguished Name and the Relative Distinguished Name. The Distinguished Name uniquely identifies an object in Active Directory by including the full path to its location. The Distinguished Name includes the common name of the object as well as the names of all organizational and domain units that contain the object. For example, the Distinguished Name of Mike Witherspoon, a member of the Engineering department at helpandlearn.com, is cn=Mike Witherspoon, ou=engineering, dc=helpandlearn, dc=com (cn designates the common name, ou designates the organizational unit, and dc designates the domain component).

The Relative Distinguished Name is an attribute of the object that the object itself is naming. For example, given the Distinguished Name of cn=Mike Witherspoon, ou=engineering, dc=helpandlearn, dc=com, the Relative Distinguished Name is Mike Witherspoon. The maximum length of the Relative Distinguished Name is 255 characters.

As you can see, the Distinguished Name must be unique in Active Directory because it points to a single object. The Relative Distinguished Name need only be unique at its current organizational level. In other words, only one Mike Witherspoon object can be in the engineering ou, but another Mike Witherspoon object can be in other ous, such as marketing.helpandlearn.com.

Group and System Policies

Starting with Windows NT 4, Microsoft introduced the System Policy Editor. The System Policy Editor allowed an administrator to specify user and computer configuration settings in the Registry. Administrators could then enforce and control the user's work environment. This in turn helped reduce the administrative costs caused by a user changing or misconfiguring (breaking is more like it!) the system.

Windows XP and Windows 2000 include a new utility called the Group Policy snap-in. It provides the same basic functionality as the System Policy Editor but is expanded to include a broad range of user environment options. To access the Group Policy snap-in, follow these steps:

1. Select Start|Run. In the Run dialog box, type "MMC" and click OK.

2. On the File pull-down menu, select Add/Remove Snap-In.

3. In the Add/Remove Snap-In dialog box, click Add.

4. In the Add Standalone Snap-In dialog box, select Group Policy from the list of snap-ins. Click Add.

5. When prompted to store the Group Policy in Active Directory or on the local computer, select Local Computer. Click Finish.

6. Click Close to close the Add Standalone Snap-In dialog box.

7. Click OK to close the Add/Remove Snap-In dialog box.

Remember to save the MMC you've just created. When finished, the Group Policy MMC should look like Figure 15.2.

A Group Policy is an object that gets associated with a particular domain or OU in Active Directory or in a local computer. In Windows XP Professional, this discussion focuses on the Local Computer Policy.

The Local Group Policy allows an administrator to make the following changes to a local computer:

➤ Define security settings

➤ Modify more than 450 operating system components

➤ Specify scripts for computer startup and shutdown and user logon and logoff

Windows XP Professional stores Group Policy objects in the %systemroot%\System32\GroupPolicy directory.

The following discussion walks through some Group Policy examples.

15

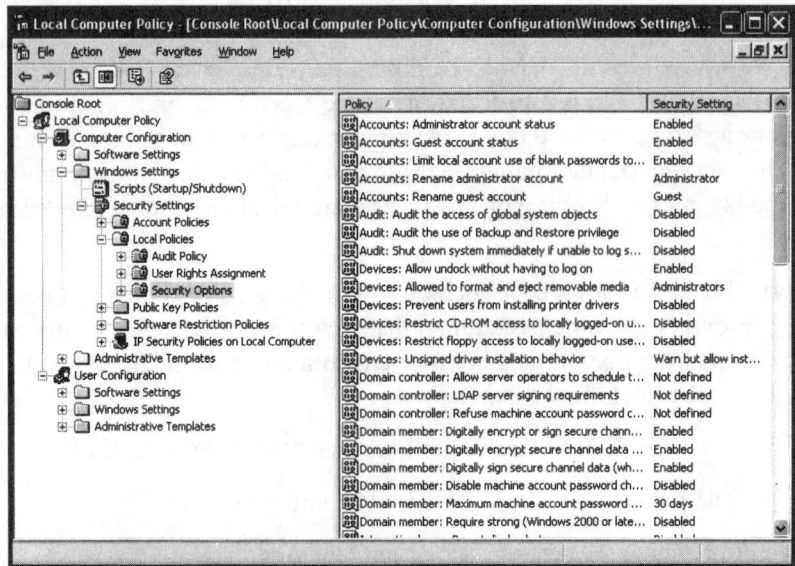

Figure 15.2 The Group Policy snap-in dialog box.

Pretend you are the administrator for a corporate LAN. The CFO of the company is concerned about the loss of production output for a particular department. The CFO discovers that a number of employees in the department have been changing the configurations on the workstations. These changes are breaking some of the applications, which in turn results in downtime. The CFO wants you to take measures that will limit the number of changes that can be made.

You decide that you will implement a Group Policy that will eliminate access to the Control Panel, the Run dialog box, My Network Places, Registry tools, and the command prompt. To accomplish this, follow these steps:

1. Start the Group Policy MMC you created earlier in the chapter.

2. In the left pane, select User Configuration. Expand Administrative Templates, and select Desktop.

3. In the right pane, double-click the Hide My Network Places icon on the desktop. Select Enable. This hides the My Network Places icon, which prevents users from browsing the network. Click OK.

4. In the left pane, select Start Menu and Taskbar. Select Remove Run menu from Start menu. Select Enable. This removes the Run menu from the Start menu and the New Task (Run) option from Task Manager. Click OK.

5. In the left pane, select Control Panel. Double-click Disable Control Panel. Select Enable. This hides the Control Panel from users. If you want to limit access to only a few applets on the Control Panel, you could choose Hide Specified Control Panel Applets instead. Click OK.

6. In the left pane, select System. Double-click Disable Registry Editing Tools. Select Enable. This disables access to Regedit.exe and Regedt32.exe. Click OK.

7. Again under System, double-click Disable The Command Prompt. Click Enable. This eliminates access to the command prompt, where a user could enter other commands, such as **Net**, in an attempt to circumvent your Group Policy. Click OK.

Test the Group Policy by logging on as a regular user. Notice that the Control Panel, the Run dialog box, and My Network Places are all hidden. Next, try opening the command prompt. You should get a message stating that it has been disabled by the administrator. Finally, try running Regedit.exe. It too displays a message stating that it has been disabled by the administrator.

Group Policy is a powerful tool for locking down Windows XP Professional configurations. Although it is more commonly used in domain-based networks, it can also be used in workgroup or standalone environments. Group Policy can save an administrator a lot of time when trying to troubleshoot items broken by a renegade user. It also allows users to do what they are paid to do—work.

Logon Scripts

Logon scripts are typically batch files or scripts (Windows Scripting Host, VBScript, or JavaScript) that are used to configure a user's work environment. Items, such as mapped network drives and printers, are set up automatically. This saves users valuable time and also standardizes their configurations.

Typically, logon scripts are used in domain environments, where the logon script resides on a domain controller. As a user logs on, the logon script executes and configures the user's environment. Logon scripts are executed after the Group Policy has been applied.

15

Getting Connected

If you want to start using network resources, you need to connect to the network. A number of ways are available to accomplish this, depending on your situation.

Local Area Connection

If you need to connect to a LAN, you need to create a Local Area Connection. A Local Area Connection is created automatically when a network adapter is installed in the Windows XP Professional-based computer. For example, if you have one network adapter installed, there is one Local Area Connection found in the Network Connections folder. If two network adapters are installed, there are two Local Area Connections.

To open the Network Connections folder, select Start | Connect To | Show All Connections. By default, Windows XP configures the Local Area Connection with the following items:

➤ Client for Microsoft Networks

➤ File and Printer Sharing for Microsoft Networks

➤ QoS Packet Scheduler

➤ TCP/IP

Depending on your situation, this may be all the network components you need. However, your situation might require the use of another network protocol, network client, or service. So, the next section explores the Local Area Connection interface and defines some of the items found there. Figure 15.3 displays the Local Area Connection Properties dialog box.

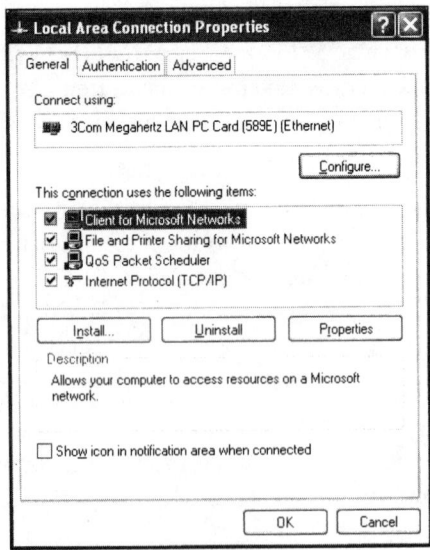

Figure 15.3 Local Area Connection Properties dialog box.

Configuring Network Protocols

A network protocol facilitates communication between computers on a network. Before you can start accessing network resources, you need to configure your network protocol. Windows XP includes support for a number of network protocols. The three covered here—TCP/IP, NWLink (IPX/SPX), and NetBEUI—are the most common network protocols found in LAN environments.

TCP/IP

Transport Control Protocol/Internet Protocol is a protocol suite that forms the foundation of many of today's corporate internetworks and, most importantly, the Internet. Refer to Chapter 10 for a thorough and detailed explanation of the TCP/IP protocol suite.

To install TCP/IP in Windows XP, follow these steps:

1. Open the Network Connections folder by selecting Start|Connect To|Show All Connections.

2. Right-click the desired Local Area Connection, and select Properties.

3. Click Install in the Local Area Connection Properties dialog box.

4. Select Protocol from the Select Network Component dialog box. Click Add.

5. In the Select Network Protocol dialog box, select Internet Protocol (TCP/IP). Click OK.

6. Reboot.

The Dynamic Host Configuration Protocol (DHCP) is a protocol that was designed to make the configuration of TCP/IP hosts much simpler. DHCP is a client/server protocol, where the DHCP client (a TCP/IP host) requests TCP/IP configuration information from a DHCP server. The DHCP server is configured by an administrator with scopes (which are ranges of available IP addresses) along with other TCP/IP configuration items.

A number of items can be configured via DHCP:

➤ Default gateway

➤ DNS server IP addresses

➤ IP address

➤ Subnet mask

➤ WINS server IP addresses

15

If a DHCP server is available on your network, you probably will use it to configure TCP/IP. Windows XP Professional defaults to obtaining an IP address automatically via DHCP (see Figure 15.4).

If you want to use a static IP address configuration, you must specify the configuration information manually. From the Internet Protocols (TCP/IP) Properties dialog box, select Use The Following IP Address and specify a valid IP address, subnet mask, and, if in a routed environment, the default gateway IP address.

By clicking the Advanced button on the Internet Protocols (TCP/IP) Properties dialog box, you can configure more advanced TCP/IP settings. Figure 15.5 displays the first tab displayed in the Advanced TCP/IP Settings dialog box. The IP Settings tab is used to configure IP addresses, subnet masks, and default gateways.

To add an IP address and subnet mask for this network connection, click the Add button, and enter the IP address and the appropriate subnet mask. You can add more than one IP address in Windows XP. A typical application for this would be a Web server using virtual Web sites. Each Web site would be bound to a separate IP address.

Finally, enter the default gateway address. Windows XP also allows you to specify a Metric for this interface. A Metric, sometimes referred to as a *hop*, indicates the cost of using the routes associated with this interface. The Metric is placed in the Windows XP routing table. If there are multiple routes to a destination, the interface with the lowest Metric is chosen for the route. The default value for the Metric is 1.

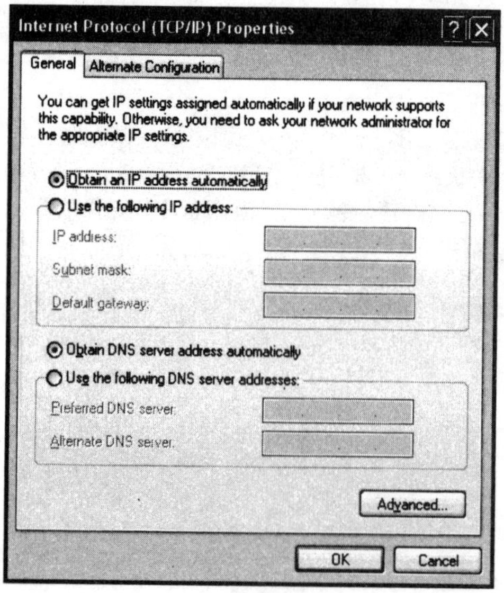

Figure 15.4   Internet Protocol (TCP/IP) Properties dialog box.

The next tab that is displayed is the DNS tab (see Figure 15.6), which is used to configure hostname resolution. The upper portion of the page is used to specify the IP addresses for DNS servers. These DNS servers resolve hostnames to IP addresses.

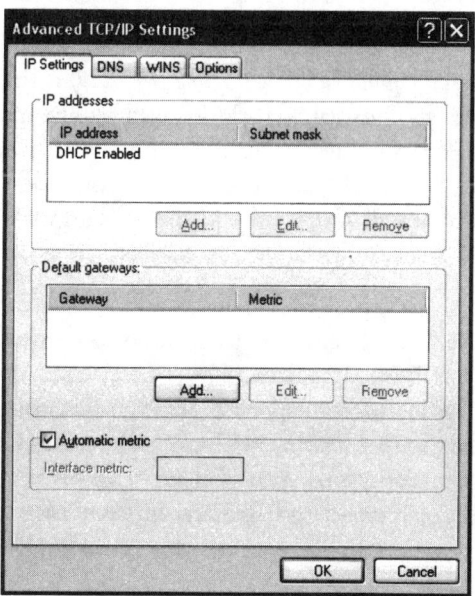

Figure 15.5   The IP Settings tab in the Advanced TCP/IP Settings dialog box.

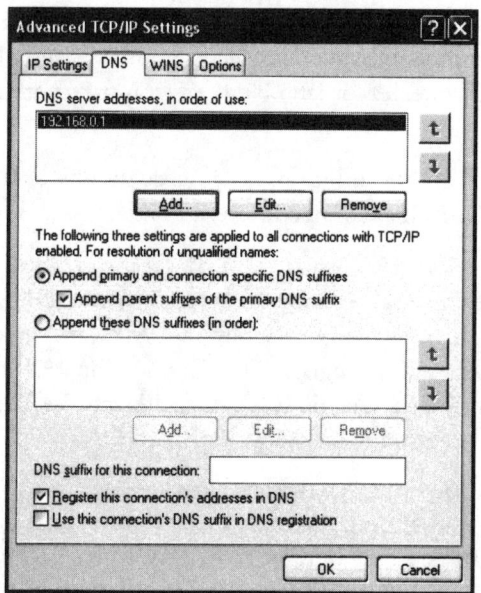

Figure 15.6   The DNS tab in the Advanced TCP/IP Settings dialog box.

15

For example, when you enter **www.microsoft.com** into your Web browser, your system queries a DNS server to resolve this address into an IP address. The DNS server might know the address, or, if it doesn't, it can query another DNS server to resolve the name. When the DNS server receives the response, it forwards the resolution to your system.

Two types of DNS names exist. The *fully qualified domain name (FQDN)* is the unique name of the host. It starts with the hostname, includes all the domains, and finally ends at the root domain. For example, if your computer's hostname is lab1 and it is located in the mycompany.com domain, the FQDN would be lab1.mycompany.com. The *unqualified name* is simply the hostname without the domain names. So, in the previous FQDN example, the unqualified name is simply lab1.

The other settings on the DNS tab tell the system how to respond to unqualified name resolution requests and Dynamic DNS. The first setting—Append Primary And Connection Specific DNS Suffixes—specifies that resolution of unqualified domain names be limited to the domain suffixes of the primary and connection-specific suffixes. For example, suppose your system's FQDN is lab1.mycompany.com. If you attempt to connect to lab5.mycomputer.com, you can simply specify lab5. Your system automatically appends your primary DNS suffix, mycomputer.com, to the request.

The next setting—Append These DNS Suffixes (In Order)—specifies that resolution of unqualified domain names be limited to the specific DNS suffixes listed. The primary and connection-specific suffixes are ignored. For example, if you add bldg1.mycompany.com and bldg2.mycompany.com to the list and type "ping lab3" at a command prompt, Windows XP queries for lab3.bldg1.mycompany.com and lab3.bldg2.mycompany.com.

You can specify a connection-specific DNS suffix on this page as well by entering the DNS suffix in the DNS Suffix For This Connection text box.

The final two settings on this page refer to Dynamic DNS. Dynamic DNS allows a system to register its own hostname in the DNS tables. Before Dynamic DNS, the hostnames had to be entered manually into the DNS tables by LAN administrators. To enable Dynamic DNS registration, select Register This Connection's Addresses In DNS. If you also specified a connection-specific DNS suffix, select Use This Connection's DNS Suffix In DNS Registration to register that suffix as well.

The next tab is the WINS tab (see Figure 15.7), which is used to configure NetBIOS name resolution. The first portion of the WINS tab is for specifying the IP addresses for WINS servers. A WINS server resolves NetBIOS names to IP addresses. For example, when you map a drive to a network share on another

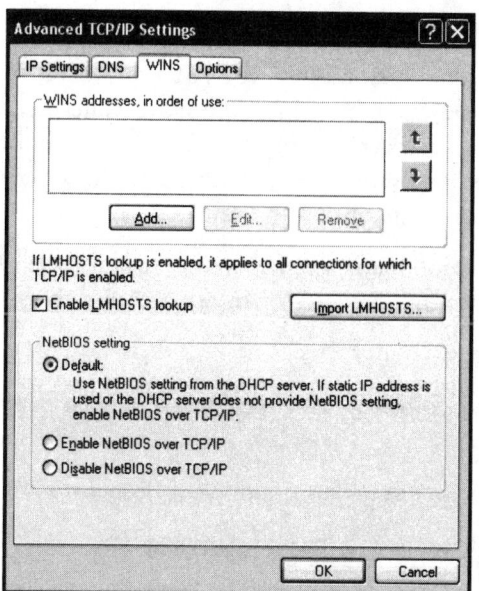

Figure 15.7 The WINS tab in the Advanced TCP/IP Settings dialog box.

Windows XP machine, Windows XP queries the WINS server to resolve this address into an IP address.

If you are using an LMHOSTS file for NetBIOS resolution as well, enable LMHOSTS lookup.

The final option specifies whether NetBIOS resolution over TCP/IP will be used on this computer. This option is included because Windows XP relies on DNS for name resolution, not NetBIOS. If you are operating in a pure Windows XP environment, you can disable NetBIOS resolution. However, it is important to realize that you might have applications that rely on NetBIOS. If you disable it, these applications will be broken. Refer to the applications' documentation to determine if NetBIOS is required.

The final tab in the Advanced TCP/IP Settings dialog box is for configuring optional components, such as IPSec and TCP/IP Filtering. IP Security (IPSec) is a group of services and protocols that use cryptography to protect data. Typically used for L2TP-based VPNs, IPSec provides machine-level authentication and data encryption. TCP/IP Filtering allows you to enable or disable specific TCP and UDP ports. This setting is used to secure TCP/IP traffic entering the computer by allowing or disallowing the processing of traffic on those ports.

15

NWLink (IPX/SPX)

NWLink is Microsoft's fully compatible version of the IPX/SPX protocol. IPX/SPX is a proprietary protocol designed for use in Novell NetWare-based networks. NetWare 4.x and earlier networks relied on IPX/SPX for communications. The latest version of NetWare, NetWare 5, is the first version that operates using TCP/IP as its primary network protocol.

NWLink is a routable network protocol that is suitable for any size network. The only caveat with NWLink is that it cannot be used for Internet connectivity.

To install NWLink, follow these steps:

1. Open the Network Connections folder by selecting Start|Connect To|Show All Connections.

2. Right-click the desired Local Area Connection, and select Properties.

3. Click Install in the Local Area Connection Properties dialog box.

4. Select Protocol from the Select Network Component dialog box. Click Add.

5. In the Select Network Protocol dialog box, select NWLink IPX/SPX/ NetBIOS Compatible Transport Protocol. Click OK.

6. Reboot.

Compared to TCP/IP, NWLink is a snap to implement and configure. NWLink has only three configurable components—internal network number, frametype, and external network number. NWLink uses these components to communicate with computers on the same logical network.

The internal network number is used for internal routing purposes—that is, among the network-related processes within the computer. It is only used if you are running an application, such as File and Print Services for NetWare. By default, Windows XP sets the internal network number to 00000000.

A frame is a logical contiguous group of bits. Frames form the data that is being transmitted on a network. The frametype specifies the structure of the frames. There are different frametypes depending on the networking media being used. Windows XP supports the following frametypes: Ethernet II, Ethernet 802.3, Ethernet 802.2, Ethernet 802.2 SNAP, 802.5, and 802.5 SNAP. Table 15.2 lists the network topologies and their supported frametypes.

Table 15.2 Supported network topologies and frametypes.

Network Topology	Supported Frametypes
Ethernet	Ethernet II, Ethernet 802.3, Ethernet 802.2, Ethernet 802.2 SNAP
FDDI	Ethernet 802.3, Ethernet 802.2, Ethernet 802.2 SNAP
Token Ring	802.5 and 802.5 SNAP

In Windows XP, the default setting for frametype is AutoDetect. When Windows XP is set to autodetect the frametype, it selects the first one detected and sets it to that frametype. Usually, this is sufficient for most networking implementations. However, some environments might have legacy equipment that requires specific frametypes to be implemented. In this case, you must specify each frametype to be used. For example, if you are installing a Windows XP Professional workstation in an environment that uses both Ethernet 802.3 and Ethernet 802.2, you would need to specify both frametypes.

The external network number is used for addressing and routing purposes. The external network number is associated with physical network adapters and networks. All computers on the same network that use a given frametype must have the same external network number to communicate with each other. The external network number must be unique to the IPX internetwork.

NetBEUI

NetBIOS Extended User Interface is one of the earliest network protocols available. NetBEUI is a simple protocol meant to be used in small networks with less than 200 computers, although, in all actuality, it is usually used in small workgroup environments with less than 10 computers. Because NetBEUI does not have any layer 3 components, it is nonroutable. It is included with Windows XP for compatibility with legacy systems, such as LAN Manager and Windows for Workgroups. NetBEUI is also supported by the Windows 9x and Windows NT families of operating systems.

To install NetBEUI, follow these steps:

1. Open the Network Connections folder by selecting Start|Connect To|Show All Connections.

2. Right-click the desired Local Area Connection and select Properties.

3. Click Install in the Local Area Connection Properties dialog box.

4. Select Protocol in the Select Network Component dialog box. Click Add.

5. In the Select Network Protocol dialog box, click Have Disk.

6. Insert the Windows XP Professional installation CD-ROM. Browse to D:\VALUEADD\MSFT\NET\NETBEUI, and click Open.

7. Click OK.

8. Select NetBEUI Protocol. Click OK.

9. Reboot.

You don't need to configure anything with NetBEUI. It doesn't get any simpler than that!

Chapter Summary

This chapter covers many of the aspects of working with Windows XP Professional in a Windows network environment. The chapter begins with a discussion of the methods used to access network resources with Windows XP Professional. Windows XP can access and exploit many types of network resources, including file and print servers, databases, messaging, application servers, intranets, and the Internet.

Windows XP includes many of the components that make network connectivity possible. These components include various networking protocols, such as TCP/IP, NWLink (IPX/SPX), DLC, AppleTalk, and NetBEUI. Networking protocols allow computers to communicate in exactly the same way as people use language to communicate. If two people speak English, they can communicate. If two computers speak TCP/IP, they can communicate.

Another essential networking component is the network client. A network client allows a computer to access network resources, such as file and print services. Windows XP ships with support for a number of networks, including Client for Microsoft Networks and Client Services for NetWare Networks. Windows XP also supports, through add-on packages, Unix (via Microsoft Windows Services for Unix 2) and Macintosh (via Windows 2000 Services for Macintosh).

A Microsoft network uses the CIFS protocol to provide network access to file and printer shares. This protocol allows a client computer to open, read, write, and close a file on a file server.

Microsoft networks support two types of network environments—workgroups and domains. Workgroups are peer-to-peer networks grouped logically, without a centralized security database. To access resources on the computers in a workgroup, you need a valid logon with each computer. A domain is a logical grouping of computers with a centralized security database. Windows XP Professional can be a member of a workgroup or a domain.

The process in which a user, using a logon name and password, is validated by a security database is known as authentication. Windows XP supports two methods of authentication—NTLM for older Windows NT 4 domains and Kerberos for Windows XP. Windows XP includes support for System Policies and Group Policies. System and Group Policies allow an administrator to specify user and computer configuration settings in the Registry. These settings help an administrator enforce and control a user's work environment. System Policies were first introduced in Windows NT 4. Beginning with Windows 2000, Group Policies have been expanded and have replaced the functionality of System Policies.

The chapter concludes with an overview of the three most popular network protocols used in Windows XP—TCP/IP, NWLink, and NetBEUI.

Review Questions

1. Which of the following TCP/IP components cannot be configured via DHCP?

   a. IP address

   b. Subnet mask

   c. Default gateway

   d. MAC address

2. David Murphy has a user account in the domain mycompany.com. His username is dmurphy. What is his UPN?

   a. dmurphy@mycompany.com

   b. .dmurphy.mycompany.com

   c. cn=dmurphy, dc=mycompany, dc=com

   d. dmurphy/mycompany.com

3. What is the default authentication method for Windows XP?

   a. NTLM

   b. Kerberos v5

   c. Kerberos v4

   d. NTLM2000

4. In a domain-based network, a user needs only a single logon to access domain resources. True or False?

   a. True

   b. False

5. You are connecting a Windows XP Professional workstation to a Token Ring network that uses NWLink. What frametype should be specified?

   a. 802.5

   b. Ethernet 802.2

   c. Ethernet 802.5

   d. Ethernet 802.3

6. A WINS server is used for what type of name resolution?

   a. IP address to NetBIOS name

   b. Hostname to IP address

   c. IP address to hostname

   d. NetBIOS name to IP address

15

7. When configuring TCP/IP on a Windows XP Professional in a nonrouted environment, what items need to be specified? [Check all correct answers]

   a. IP address

   b. Subnet mask

   c. Default gateway

   d. DNS server address

8. To access resources on a NetWare network, what components need to be installed? [Check all correct answers]

   a. NWLink

   b. Client Services for NetWare

   c. NetWare for Windows Networks

   d. TCP/IP

9. Which object uniquely identifies a user object in Active Directory?

   a. Relative Distinguished Name

   b. UPN

   c. Distinguished Name

   d. SAM Account Name

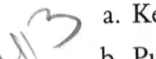

10. To receive an IP address via DHCP, you select which of the following?

    a. Use DHCP For IP Addresses in the Control Panel

    b. Obtain An IP Address Automatically in the Internet Protocol (TCP/IP) Properties dialog box

    c. **IPCONFIG /RELEASE** from a command prompt

    d. Obtain An IP Address Automatically in the Network Control Panel

11. If a Windows XP Professional workstation is attempting to authenticate with a Windows NT 4 domain, what authentication method will it use?

    a. Kerberos

    b. Public key cryptology

    c. NTLM

    d. Domain

12. A DNS server is used for what type of name resolution?

    a. IP address to NetBIOS name

    b. NetBIOS name to IP address

    c. Hostname to IP address

    d. Computer name to IP address

13. Windows XP uses what protocol to open and close files on a Microsoft network?

    a. TCP/IP

    b. NetBEUI

    c. NWLink

    d. CIFS

14. Windows XP Professional stores Group Policy objects in which location?

    a. Active Directory

    b. C:\WINNT

    c. %systemroot%\GroupPolicy

    d. % systemroot%\System32\GroupPolicy

15. Which groups can add a Windows XP Professional computer to a domain?

    a. Administrators

    b. Users

    c. Power Users

    d. Server Operators

16. Which network client is not supported by Windows XP?

    a. Client for Microsoft Networks

    b. Client Services for NetWare

    c. Microsoft Windows Services for Unix 2

    d. Client Services for AS400

17. You are attempting to connect a Windows XP Professional computer to a network that uses NWLink as its networking protocol. Because of legacy applications, the network uses two frametypes, Ethernet 802.2 and Ethernet 802.3. Which frametypes need to be specified on the workstation?

    a. Ethernet 802.2

    b. AutoDetect

    c. Ethernet 802.3

    d. Ethernet 802.2 and Ethernet 802.3

18. A workgroup is a logical grouping of computers sharing a centralized security database. True or False?

    a. True

    b. False

15

19. What types of logons are found in Windows XP? [Check all correct answers]

    a. SAM Account Name

    b. Relative Distinguished Name

    c. Distinguished Name

    d. UPN

20. Given the Distinguished Name of cn=MichaelGrift, ou=Lab5, ou=Research, dc=NewYork, dc=Pharmaco, dc=com, what is the Relative Distinguished Name?

    a. MichaelGrift@Pharmaco.com

    b. MichaelGrift

    c. Lab5

    d. MichaelGrift.Lab5.Research.NewYork@Pharmaco.Com

Real-World Projects

You have just received your first Windows XP Professional computer. After unpacking the computer, you need to attach and configure it to your company's Windows network.

The corporate network uses TCP/IP. After talking with the network administrator, you find out that, at this time, the corporation has not implemented DHCP. The network administrator gives you the following information:

```
IP address              10.0.26.5
Subnet Mask             255.0.0.0
Default Gateway         10.0.0.1
Preferred DNS Server    10.0.0.10
Alternate DNS Server    10.0.0.11
Primary WINS Server     10.0.0.20
Secondary WINS Server   10.0.0.21
```

Project 15.1
To configure TCP/IP in Windows XP Professional:

1. Click Start|Connect To|Show All Connections.

2. Right-click Local Area Connection, and select Properties.

3. Select Internet Protocol (TCP/IP), and then select Properties. The Internet Protocol (TCP/IP) Properties dialog box is displayed.

4. Select Use The Following IP Address. For the IP address, enter "10.0.26.5" Enter "255.0.0.0" as the subnet mask and "10.0.0.1" as the default gateway.

5. Select Use The Following DNS Server Addresses. For the Preferred DNS Server, enter "10.0.0.10", and for the Alternate DNS Server, enter "10.0.0.11".

6. Click the Advanced button to open the Advanced TCP/IP Properties dialog box.

7. Select the WINS tab to display the WINS properties page.

8. Click Add to enter a WINS server IP address. Enter "10.0.0.20", and click Add. Click Add again to enter the other WINS server IP address. Enter "10.0.0.21", and click Add.

9. On the same tab, select Enable NetBIOS Over TCP/IP.

10. Click OK to close the Advanced TCP/IP Properties dialog box.

11. Click OK to close the Internet Protocol (TCP/IP) Properties dialog box.

12. Click OK to close the Local Area Connection Properties dialog box.

After you configure TCP/IP, it's time to have your computer join the corporation's domain. To join a domain, the account you are using must be a member of the Domain Admins group or have been granted the Add A Machine To The Domain user right.

You call the network administrator to let him know that you need to add the computer to the domain. He tells you that the domain name is CorpDomain. There is a special user account called AddMachine with the password AddMore. The account has the Add A Machine To The Domain user right.

Project 15.2

To join a domain with Windows XP Professional:

1. Click Start. Right-click My Computer, and select Properties.

2. Click the Computer Name tab. Select Change.

3. The Computer Name Changes dialog box is displayed. In the Member Of section, select Domain.

4. Enter "CorpDomain" as the name of the domain.

5. When prompted, enter "AddMachine" as the user account and "AddMore" as the password. Click OK.

6. You should get a message welcoming you to the domain. Click OK.

7. Click OK to close the Identification Changes dialog box.

15

8. Click OK to close the System Properties dialog box.

9. Click Yes to restart the computer.

After you have joined CorpDomain, you want to map some network drives to shares on servers named CorpServer1 and CorpServer2. The following list contains the shares and their corresponding drive mappings:

```
H:      \\CorpServer1\Data
K:      \\CorpServer1\Finance
Y:      \\CorpServer2\Marketing
```

Project 15.3

To map network drives with Windows XP Professional:

1. Click Start. Right-click My Network Places, and select Map Network Drives.

2. Select H: from the Drive Letter drop-down list. Type "\\CorpServer1\Data" in the folder. If needed, you can also browse the network.

3. Click Finish.

4. Repeat the process for the remaining network drives.

CHAPTER SIXTEEN

The Novell NetWare Environment

After completing this chapter, you will be able to:

✓ Identify the members of the NetWare family

✓ Configure IPX

✓ Configure the client for NetWare networks

✓ Access NetWare resources

✓ Troubleshoot NetWare connectivity problems

Novell NetWare, once a powerhouse in the world of local area networks (LANs), is a family of robust network operating systems. Novell was one of the first companies to realize that organizations could benefit greatly by pooling their resources. Connecting a group of PCs together on a LAN, users were able to share data and printers quickly and easily.

An Overview of Novell NetWare

NetWare has always been based on a dedicated PC-based server. The first version of NetWare, released in 1984, ran on an IBM PC XT using the Intel 8086 processor. It was a multitasking operating system, so it was perfect for LANs, on which it could handle multiple connections and requests simultaneously. NetWare, a centralized server-based network operating system (NOS), cannot be used as a workstation operating system.

By creating a NOS that provided file and print services in a secure fashion, Novell quickly cornered the networking market. Throughout the years, Novell continued to enhance NetWare, further pushing the envelope. Many of the newer NOSs, including Windows NT and Windows 2000, owe their very existence to the path forged by Novell NetWare.

Novell NetWare 3.12

In 1993, Novell introduced NetWare 3.12, which was a powerful, standalone server NOS that provided file, print, and application services. NetWare 3.12 used a concept known as the *Bindery*. This contained all of the user and group accounts as well as users' passwords and trustee assignments. *Trustee assignments* are comparable to access control lists (ACLs) in Windows 2000. They provide the access list to server objects, such as files, directories, print queues, and so on. Internet Protocol Exchange/Sequenced Packet Exchange (IPX/SPX) was the default network protocol for NetWare 3.12. IPX/SPX is a proprietary network protocol, designed by Novell.

All NetWare 3.12 servers, because they were standalone, contained their own Bindery. In other words, if a user wanted to access files on two separate NetWare 3.12 servers, he or she would need a user account on each server. This is analogous to the *Workgroup* network type in Windows 2000, wherein each computer manages its own local security database. As networks grew, the Bindery approach to network security became increasingly unwieldy. Thus, Novell went back to the drawing board.

Novell NetWare 4.*x*

With NetWare 4.*x*, Novell unveiled a new concept in networking—the directory service. NetWare Directory Services (NDS) created a global directory of network objects. These network objects included users, groups, servers, volumes, organizational units (OUs), and so on. NDS allowed a user to have a single user account, through which he or she could access any network resources.

NDS organizes these objects using a tree-style architecture. An NDS tree is divided into two object types—containers and leaf objects. *Container objects* are used to organize resources. An NDS tree is usually divided into OUs (container objects that can hold other OUs or leaf objects) that represent a group of resources or geographic locations. For example, an NDS tree might have OUs that represent major cities, such as New York, Chicago, Philadelphia, and Los Angeles. Any resources— such as servers, volumes, and printers—located in those cities would be placed in the OU. These resources are known as *leaf objects.* Items such as user accounts, servers, volumes, printers, and so on are considered leaf objects.

In NDS, a user logs in to the NDS tree, not into an individual server. When logging in, the user needs to specify a *default context,* which points to the location in the NDS tree (the container object) of the user's user object. For example, if a user account called Joe is located in an OU called Users, and Users is located in the Philadelphia OU, Joe's default context is USERS.PHILADELPHIA.

All the NDS objects are stored in a database, which is then replicated to all servers within the tree. By replicating the database, NDS increases both the performance of user login authentication and fault tolerance. The database is replicated to all servers, so if any server goes down, users can still log into the tree. Therefore, the tree won't go down.

Although NDS greatly improved the NetWare operating system, NetWare still suffered from a major drawback—it was dependent on IPX/SPX. With the growing popularity of the Internet and open standards such as Transmission Control Protocol/Internet Protocol (TCP/IP), NetWare's dependence on a proprietary protocol such as IPX/SPX quickly became a liability. Microsoft, realizing the importance of the Internet, steered its NOSs, such as Windows 95 and Windows NT, toward adopting TCP/IP. This gave Microsoft a toehold against the supremacy of NetWare in the NOS market.

So again, Novell went back to the drawing board.

Novell NetWare 5.*x*

In 1999, Novell introduced the latest addition to the NetWare family, NetWare 5.*x*. NetWare 5.*x* continues the formidable advancement that Novell has achieved with NDS. In NetWare 5.*x*, NDS is improved, with the capability to hold over a billion objects! For an organization with a large, enterprise network, this new version of NDS provides plenty of capacity for growth and change.

16

More important, NetWare 5.*x* was completely redesigned to use TCP/IP as its core network protocol. This allows NetWare 5.*x* servers to be used as Web and FTP servers on the Internet. It also allows many corporate networks to run more efficiently with only one network protocol—TCP/IP.

Although NetWare lost its market dominance to Windows NT, it is still widely used in many businesses and organizations. The jury is still out on NetWare 5.*x*. It is being deployed, although not at a blistering pace. NetWare 4.*x* is the most popular version of NetWare, and, even though NetWare 3.12 is older, many organizations still use it. This is why we cover Windows XP Professional in a NetWare environment. Odds are, you will need to connect a Windows XP Professional computer to a NetWare network at some point in your career.

The IPX/SPX Protocol Suite

Before delving into the client components, let's spend some time detailing the protocol suite that NetWare depends upon for communication. The IPX/SPX protocol suite is a descendant of another protocol—Xerox Network Systems (XNS). This protocol was developed by the Xerox Corporation as a client/server protocol. IPX/SPX supports a number of different network media, such as Ethernet/Institute of Electrical and Electronics Engineers (IEEE) 802.3, Token Ring/IEEE 802.5, and Fiber Distributed Data Interface (FDDI).

The protocol suite itself is composed of a number of protocols that together form the functionality required by the NetWare OS. When you install NWLink (described later in this chapter) on Windows XP Professional, only some of these protocols (IPX and SPX) are implemented. The others are needed only for server and routing functions.

IPX

IPX is a network protocol that operates on Layer 3 of the Open System Interconnection (OSI) model. This protocol makes it possible for packets to be routed across an internetwork. It is a connectionless protocol, meaning that it does not require the use of a virtual circuit for connectivity. It does not provide any error correction or flow control. IPX is analogous to the IP protocol found in the TCP/IP protocol suite.

Network addressing with IPX is represented in a hexadecimal format and, like IP, consists of two parts—the IPX network number and the node number. The IPX *network number* is 32 bits long and is assigned by the network administrator. The *node number* is 48 bits long and is derived from the network adapter's media access control (MAC) address. As a result of using the MAC address for the node number, IPX does not need to use any type of address translation. IP, on the other hand, requires the use of another protocol—Address Resolution Protocol (ARP).

SPX

SPX is a connection-oriented protocol located on Layer 4 of the OSI model. SPX is considered a reliable protocol because it requests that missing datagrams be retransmitted. SPX is typically used for applications that require a continuous connection between the client and server.

SAP

Service Advertising Protocol (SAP) is used by network devices to advertise the services they provide. Devices such as file servers and print services use this protocol. These devices send out SAP advertisements every 60 seconds. The services being advertised are represented by a SAP identifier, a hexadecimal number. For example, a file server has a SAP identifier of 4, while a print server has a SAP identifier of 7.

RIP

Routing Information Protocol (RIP) is used for route and router discovery with IPX. RIP is used in internetworks. Without RIP, an administrator would need to configure static routes for each logical network. With RIP, a router will send its routing table to its neighbors every 30 seconds. This allows a router or server to build a routing table to determine where to forward IPX packets.

Operating Windows XP and NetWare Together

When using Windows XP Professional on a NetWare network, you have two choices for connectivity. First, you can use Client Services for NetWare (CSNW), a network component that is installed on each workstation. Once it is installed, the Windows XP Professional computer can access NetWare resources on the network. This option gives you the best performance and speed when accessing NetWare resources.

Another alternative is to install Gateway (and Client) Services for NetWare (GSNW). This network component is installed on either Windows 2000 Server or Windows .NET Server. It's a gateway to NetWare servers through which Windows clients can access NetWare resources. This can be a useful alternative. If you don't want to install CSNW on every Windows machine, you need only install GSNW on one Windows 2000 server. The downside of this approach is that performance takes a hit. It creates a funnel effect because the Windows 2000 server running the gateway must host all connections to NetWare resources.

NWLink (IPX/SPX)

Regardless of which client you decide to use, you need to use NWLink as the network protocol. Although Microsoft did its best to confuse everyone by referring

16

to IPX/SPX as NWLink, make no mistake: the protocols are the same. NWLink is simply Microsoft's implementation of IPX/SPX. Let's spend a few moments discussing the different parameters in NWLink that you need to configure.

Internal Network Numbers

The *internal network number* is used for internal routing purposes (among the network-related processes within the computer). This is used only if you are running an application such as File and Print Services for NetWare. By default, Windows XP sets the internal network number to 00000000. Normally, the internal network number does not need to be changed.

Frametypes

A *frame* is a logical contiguous group of bits. Frames form the data that is being transmitted on the network. The *frametype* specifies the structure of the frames. Different frametypes exist, depending on the networking medium being used. Windows 2000 supports the following frametypes: Ethernet II, Ethernet 802.3, Ethernet 802.2, Ethernet 802.2 SNAP, 802.5, and 802.5 SNAP. Table 16.1 lists the network topologies and their supported frametypes.

On Ethernet, NetWare uses a few different frametypes, depending on the version of NetWare. NetWare 3.11 and earlier (that's not a typo; Novell changed the default frametype at NetWare 3.12!) use Ethernet 802.3. In NetWare 3.12 and later, Novell decided to use Ethernet 802.2. Also, remember—of course—that NetWare 5.*x* uses TCP/IP as the default network protocol, so this discussion does not apply unless it is running IPX/SPX.

In Windows XP, the default setting for Frametype is Autodetect. When Windows XP is set to autodetect the frametype, it selects the first one detected and sets it to that frametype. Usually, this is sufficient for most networking implementations. However, some environments might have legacy equipment that requires specific frametypes to be implemented. In this case, you must specify each frametype to be used. For example, if you are installing a Windows XP Professional workstation in an environment that uses both Ethernet 802.3 and Ethernet 802.2, you must specify both frametypes.

External Network Numbers

The *external network number* is used for addressing and routing purposes. It is associated with physical network adapters and networks. All computers on the same

Table 16.1   Supported network topologies and frametypes.

Network Topology	Supported Frametypes
Ethernet	Ethernet II, Ethernet 802.3, Ethernet 802.2, and Ethernet 802.2 SNAP
FDDI	Ethernet 802.3, Ethernet 802.2, and Ethernet 802.2 SNAP
Token Ring	802.5 and 802.5 SNAP

network that use a given frametype must have the same external network number to communicate with each other. The external network number must be unique to the IPX internetwork. This is analogous to the network portion of an IP address.

Client Services for NetWare

CSNW is the client component installed on a Windows XP Professional computer that allows it to access NetWare resources. CSNW accomplishes this by allowing the Windows XP Professional computer to communicate directly with the NetWare server using the NetWare Core Protocol (NCP). NCP facilitates the opening, closing, writing, and so on of files between the client and server, as shown in Figure 16.1.

When you are installing CSNW, you must configure a number of items, discussed in the next few sections.

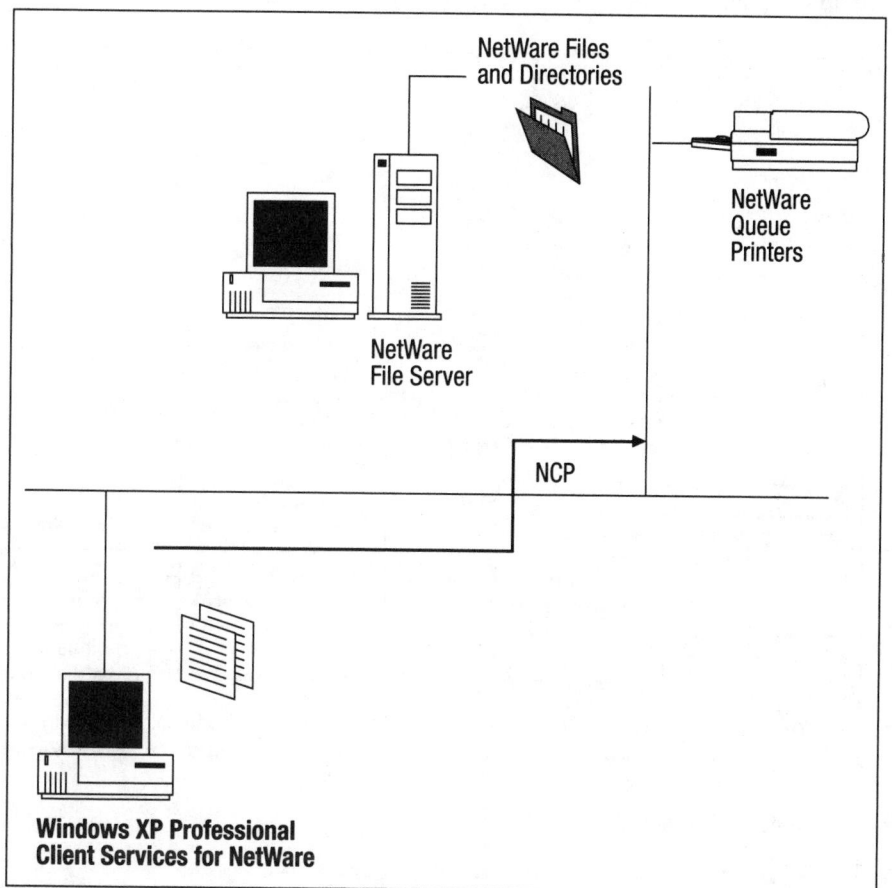

Figure 16.1   Using CSNW to access NetWare resources.

Preferred Server or Default Tree and Context

To access NetWare resources, a user needs to be authenticated. The first component—Preferred Server or Default Tree and Context—is used for authentication to the NetWare server (in Bindery mode) or the NDS tree.

Preferred Server is used when you are authenticating to a NetWare server running in Bindery mode. NetWare 3.12 and earlier rely on the Bindery for user authentication. Later versions of NetWare, including NetWare 5.x, can also run in Bindery mode. Regardless of the version of NetWare, if it's running in Bindery mode, you need to specify a Preferred Server.

Default Tree and Context is used when you are authenticating to an NDS tree. NetWare 4.x and later support NDS for user authentication. The Default Tree is simply the name of the NDS tree to which you want to be authenticated. The context is the location in the NDS tree where your user account is located. Figure 16.2 illustrates the concept of the Default Tree and context.

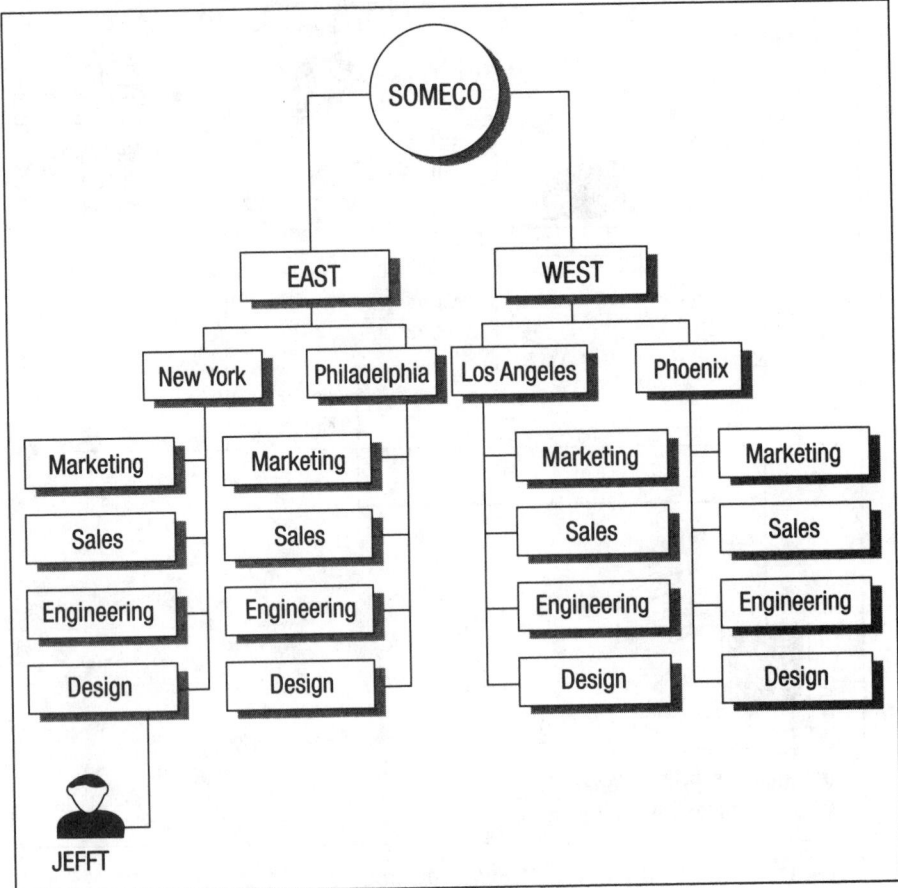

Figure 16.2 The NDS tree structure.

NDS is always described as an upside-down tree. At the top is the root object of the tree. This is the NDS tree's name. In Figure 16.2, the tree's name is SOMECO. This would be entered as the Default Tree. Spreading out below the root object are various OUs. We need to determine the context for the user account JEFFT. In Figure 16.2, JEFFT is located in ou=design.ou=newyork.ou=east.o=someco. Specifying the context like this is known as specifying the *typefull name format*. The o= type in the typefull name signifies the NDS tree name. A much simpler form is the *typeless name format*, which would be .design.newyork.east.someco.

Run Login Script

A NetWare login script, much like a Windows logon script, is a series of commands that are used to configure a user's environment. The login script is executed each time the user logs in. A login script is used to set up network and search-drive mappings, printers, and environment variables. It can also be used to distribute software updates, such as the latest virus definitions for antivirus software.

If you want the NetWare login script to execute on a Windows XP Professional computer with CSNW installed, simply select the radio button for Run Login Script.

Installing CSNW

To install CSNW, follow these steps:

1. Open the Network Connections folder (choose Start|Connect To|Show All Connections).

2. Right-click Local Area Connection, and select Properties.

3. Click Install.

4. The Select Network Component Type dialog box is displayed. Select Client, and click Add.

5. The Select Network Client dialog box is displayed. Select Client Services For NetWare. Click OK.

6. Windows XP Professional now installs CSNW. NWLink is also installed (if it wasn't previously).

7. If prompted, restart the computer.

8. The Select NetWare Logon dialog box is displayed.

   If you are connecting to a NetWare server that is running in Bindery mode, select Preferred Server. From the drop-down list, select the NetWare server on which your user account is located. Windows XP Professional generates this list by compiling what is known as a SAP list. NetWare servers use SAP broadcasts via IPX to advertise their file and print services.

16

If you are connecting to a NetWare server that is running NDS, select Default Tree And Context. Enter the name of the tree and the context where your user account is located.

Finally, if you want to execute the NetWare login script, select Run Login Script.

9. Click OK to save your settings.

Figure 16.3 shows that the following components were added after these nine steps were completed:

➤ Client Services for NetWare

➤ NWLink NetBIOS

➤ NWLink IPX/SPX/NetBIOS Compatible Transport Protocol

Gateway (and Client) Services for NetWare

GSNW allows a Windows 2000 server or Windows .NET server to act as a gateway to NetWare resources on a network. This allows Windows XP Professional computers to access NetWare resources without having CSNW installed. Figure 16.4 illustrates how GSNW operates on a network.

The gateway translates Common Internet File System (CIFS) requests sent by Windows computers into NCP requests that the NetWare servers understand. The NetWare servers then respond with NCP requests to the Windows server that hosts

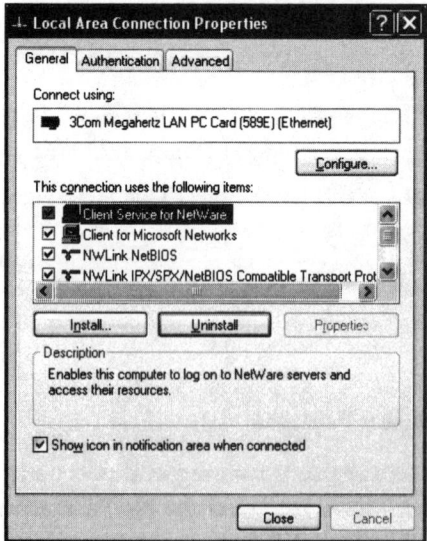

Figure 16.3 Client Services for NetWare.

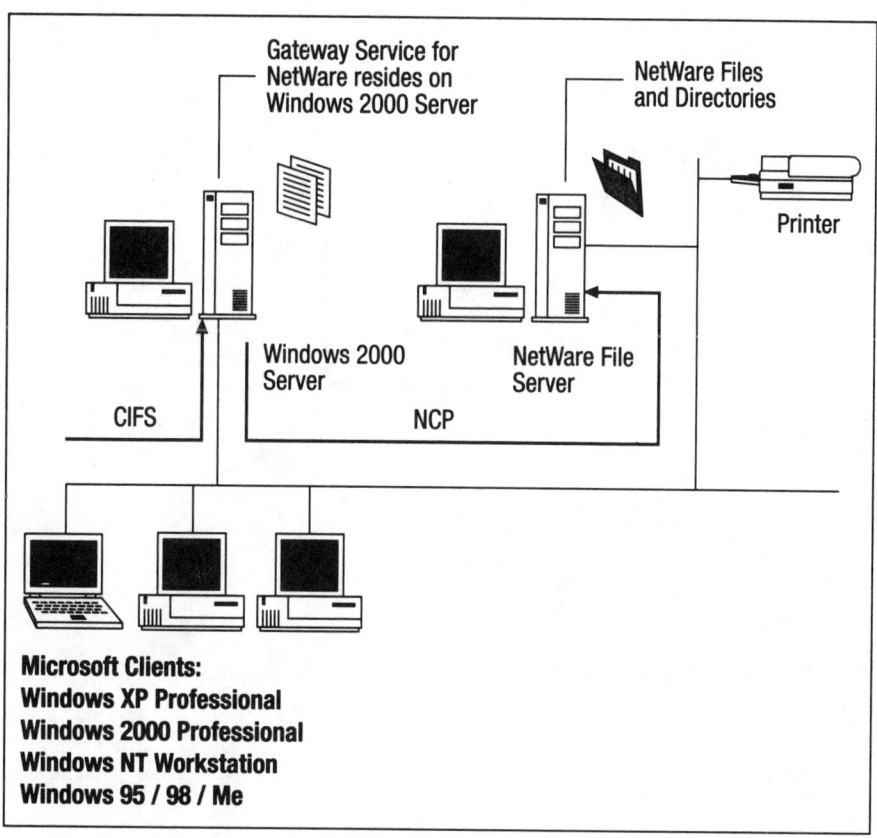

Figure 16.4   Using GSNW to access NetWare resources.

the gateway. The gateway translates the NCP requests back into CIFS requests and sends them to the Windows XP Professional computers, as shown in Figure 16.5.

Using the gateway alleviates many of the concerns about supporting multiple clients on workstations. The technical staff needs to be trained to support Client for Microsoft Networks as well as CSNW. With the gateway, most of the staff needs to support only Client for Microsoft Networks. Another more critical concern is supporting multiple network protocols on the network infrastructure. Windows XP Professional computers that are running both clients need TCP/IP to connect to Microsoft Network resources and need NWLink to connect to NetWare resources. Using both of these might cause the network to take a performance hit if the network infrastructure has limited bandwidth.

Installing GSNW

To install GSNW on a Windows 2000 server, follow these steps:

1. Open the Network And Dial-Up Connections folder (select Start|Control Panel|Network And Internet Connections).

16

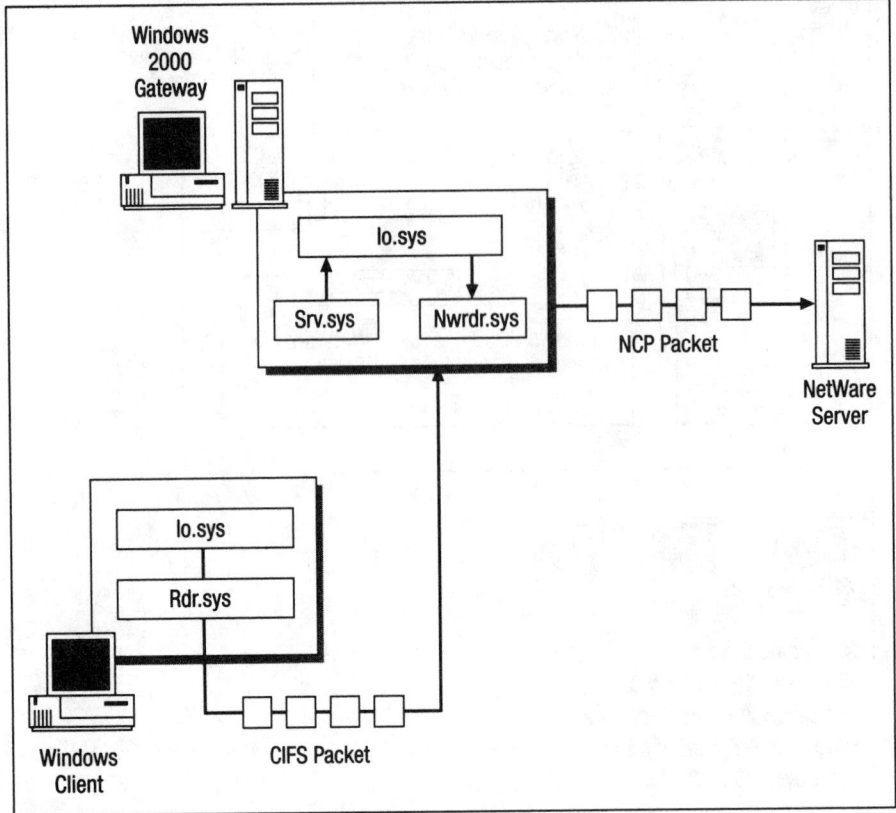

Figure 16.5 Converting CIFS requests to NCP requests.

2. Right-click Local Area Connection, and select Properties.

3. Click Install.

4. The Select Network Component Type dialog box is displayed. Select Client, and click Add.

5. The Select Network Client dialog box is displayed. Select Gateway (And Client) Services For NetWare. Click OK.

6. The Windows 2000 server now installs GSNW. NWLink is also installed (if it wasn't previously installed).

7. The Select NetWare Logon dialog box is displayed.

   If you are connecting to a NetWare server that is running in Bindery mode, select Preferred Server. From the drop-down list, select the NetWare server on which your user account is located. Windows XP Professional generates this list by compiling what is known as a SAP list. NetWare servers use SAP broadcasts via IPX to advertise their file and print services.

If you are connecting to a NetWare server that is running NDS, select Default Tree And Context. Enter the name of the tree and the context where your user account is located.

Finally, if you want to execute the NetWare login script, select Run Login Script.

8. Click OK to save your settings.

9. Reboot your computer if prompted.

10. Open the Control Panel (select Start|Settings|Control Panel).

11. Double-click the GSNW applet.

12. Click Gateway to configure GSNW.

13. Click Enable Gateway to start GSNW.

14. In Gateway Account, enter the NetWare user account you created. Also, enter and confirm the password for the user account.

15. Click Add to begin mapping network drives to NetWare volumes.

16. The New Share dialog box is displayed. Enter the share name. This is the name that Windows XP Professional computers see when browsing the Windows 2000 server that hosts the gateway.

17. Enter the network path to the NetWare resource. The path needs to be entered in Uniform Naming Convention (UNC) format. For example, if you want to access the volume DATA on a NetWare 3.12 server named NW312, the UNC path is \\NW312\DATA.

18. On the drop-down list, select the local drive letter that you want to map the drive to. Click OK to save the settings.

19. Click OK to close the Configure Gateway dialog box.

20. Click OK to close the Gateway Services For NetWare dialog box.

Configuring GSNW

Before actually configuring GSNW on the Windows 2000 server, you need to prepare the NetWare server or NDS tree. First, create a unique NetWare user account using either NetWare Administrator (NetWare 4.*x* or later) or SYSCON (NetWare 3.12 or earlier). The gateway uses this account to authenticate to the NetWare network. The password for this account must match the password used to configure the gateway. Next, create a unique NetWare group called NTGATEWAY. Assign the appropriate trustee assignments for the NTGATEWAY

16

group to any NetWare resources to which the gateway will provide access. Make the NetWare user account a member of the NTGATEWAY group.

The initial configuration of GSNW is exactly like that of CSNW (you need to configure the client with Preferred Server or Default Tree and Context). Using this and the NetWare user account authenticates the gateway with NetWare resources.

After the gateway is authenticated, you can configure the gateway to host connections to NetWare resources. Configuring the gateway is relatively simple. The Windows 2000 Server that is running the gateway maps one of its drives to a NetWare volume. The mapped drive is then shared on the Microsoft Network. Windows XP Professional computers see the share as a resource on the Windows 2000 server, although it is actually a volume located on a NetWare server.

Accessing NetWare Resources

After you have installed CSNW, accessing NetWare resources is a lot like accessing resources on Microsoft networks. Many of the NetWare utilities have functional equivalents in Windows 2000 or Windows XP. Table 16.2 lists some of the NetWare utilities and their Windows 2000/XP counterparts.

As you can see, most of the functionality for NetWare networks can be accomplished by using the **net** command in Windows. You can also use My Network Places or the Add Printer Wizard to browse and connect to NetWare file and print servers.

Accessing NetWare Resources

To access NetWare files, folders, printers, and volumes, simply map a network drive to the resource. You can accomplish this either via My Network Places or by using the **net use** command at a command prompt.

To connect to a volume via My Network Places, follow these steps:

1. Double-click My Network Places.

Table 16.2   NetWare utilities and their Windows 2000/XP counterparts.

Task	NetWare Utility	Windows 2000/XP Counterpart
View NetWare resources on the network	SLIST	**net view /network:nw**
Log in and log off the NetWare network	ATTACH, LOGIN, or LOGOUT	**net use**
Map network drives to NetWare volumes	MAP	**net use**
Map a local printer port to a NetWare printer	CAPTURE	**net use**
View current logon and configuration	WHOAMI	**net config workstation** or **net config server**

2. Double-click Entire Network, and then double-click NetWare or Compatible Network.

3. Browse through the NetWare network to locate the volume to which you want to map a drive. When you have located it, right-click the volume, and select Map Network Drive. Select an available drive letter from the drop-down list, and click OK.

To connect to a volume via the **net use** command, follow these steps:

1. Open a command prompt (select Start|Run, type "cmd", and then press Enter).

2. Type "net use [*drive_letter*]: *Servername**Resourcename*".

Here is a description of the preceding syntax:

➤ *[drive_letter]*—The letter of the local drive to be mapped to the volume

➤ *Servername*—The name of the NetWare server that contains the volume

➤ *Resourcename*—The name of the volume or print queue

For example, if you want to map drive Z: to the volume MYDATA on the NetWare server PRODUCT, you can enter "net use Z: \\PRODUCT\ MYDATA".

Accessing NetWare Print Queues

To access NetWare printers, you can use the Add Printer Wizard or the **net use** command.

Using the Add Printer Wizard, take these steps:

1. Open the Printer folder (select Start|Settings|Printers).

2. Double-click Add Printer to start the Add Printer Wizard. Click Next.

3. Click Network Printer. Click Next.

4. Type the UNC path to the network printer, or click Next to browse the network.

5. Click Next to finish the Add Printer Wizard.

Using the **net use** command, follow these steps:

1. Open a command prompt (select Start|Run, type "cmd", and then press Enter).

2. Type "net use [*lpt_port*]: *Servername**Printer*".

16

Here is a description of the preceding syntax:

➤ *[lpt_port]*—The LPT port (for example, LPT1, LPT2) to be mapped to the printer

➤ *Servername*—The name of the NetWare print server

➤ *Printer*—The name of the printer

Troubleshooting NetWare Problems

Connecting Windows XP Professional computers to Novell NetWare servers is a relatively simple task. However, something inevitably goes wrong, and, as an administrator, you must diagnose and fix whatever problems pop up. This section reviews some of the areas where connectivity problems tend to arise.

Are Client Services for NetWare and NWLink Installed?

Always remember to start with the simplest solution when troubleshooting. If a user cannot access NetWare resources, verify that CSNW and NWLink are installed. To do so, first, open the Local Area Connection Properties dialog box and visually inspect that these two components are installed. If they are not installed, go through the installation procedure described in the previous section, "Installing Client Services for NetWare."

Next, check that the CSNW service is started, by following these steps:

1. Open the Services applet (select Start|Programs|Administrative Tools| Services).

2. Find Client Services For NetWare and verify that it states *Started* in the Status column.

3. If it isn't started, right-click the service, and select Start.

Is NWLink Configured Correctly?

Remember that in order for two computers to communicate via NWLink, they must both be using the same frametype and external network number. Novell NetWare 3.11 and earlier use Ethernet 802.3 as their default frametype. NetWare 3.12 and later use Ethernet 802.2. If you are connecting to either of these versions of NetWare, you can leave the Frame Type field set to Autodetect. However, if you need to connect to servers that are using both frametypes, you must manually add both Ethernet 802.2 and Ethernet 802.3. You must also verify that the external network number matches the external network number configured on the NetWare servers.

Is the Preferred Server or Default Tree and Context Correct?

To authenticate to the NetWare network, you must configure CSNW for the Preferred Server or Default Tree and Context. If you are connecting to a NetWare server that supports Bindery mode, select the Preferred Server whose Bindery contains your NetWare user account.

If you are connecting to a NetWare 4.*x* or later server running NDS, enter the name of the Default Tree and specify the context where your NetWare user account is located.

Chapter Summary

This chapter covered many aspects of working with Windows XP Professional in a Novell NetWare environment. Novell NetWare, once the undisputed market leader in LAN technology, is a powerful and versatile NOS. NetWare comes in three flavors that all operate in a centralized server architecture.

NetWare 3.12 is deployed as a standalone server NOS that provides fast and efficient file, print, and application services. This version of NetWare uses what is known as the Bindery, which contains all user and group accounts as well as passwords and trustee assignments.

With NetWare 4.x, Novell introduced a new concept in local area networking—the directory service. NDS creates a global directory of network objects, which is then replicated and distributed among all NetWare 4.*x* servers. This type of architecture improved authentication speed and fault tolerance.

The architecture of NDS is known as a *tree*. Objects in an NDS tree can be one of two types—container or leaf. There are two container-type objects—an organization (O) object that represents the top level of the NDS tree and an OU. Container objects can contain other OUs or leaf objects. Leaf objects represent actual resources—such as users, groups, servers, or printers—on a network.

NetWare 5.*x* is the first version of NetWare to not rely on IPX/SPX as its network protocol. It relies on the network protocol that built the Internet—TCP/IP. NetWare 5.*x* also introduced an improved version of NDS that could support a billion objects in the tree.

16

IPX/SPX was the default network protocol for NetWare 3.12 and NetWare 4.*x*. It is a proprietary network protocol whose predecessor, XNS, was developed by Xerox. IPX/SPX is a routable network protocol, meaning that you can develop and deploy large internetworks. NWLink is Microsoft's implementation of IPX/SPX.

When needing to interconnect NetWare networks with Windows 2000, a network designer has two choices—use CSNW or use GSNW.

CSNW is installed on a Windows XP Professional computer. The client, along with NWLink, gives the workstation access to NetWare resources on the network. This configuration gives the workstation its best network performance.

GSNW takes a different approach, installing the gateway on a Windows 2000 or Windows .NET server. Windows clients can then access NetWare resources. The gateway accomplishes this by converting CIFS requests sent by Windows clients into NCP requests that the NetWare servers understand. The NetWare servers respond by using NCP, which the gateway converts back into CIFS. The gateway then sends the requested data to the Windows clients. This solution eliminates the need to install two clients and two network protocols on the Windows workstations. The downside of this solution is that it does not perform as well as CSNW, because all workstations are sharing a single gateway connection.

Review Questions

1. When you are configuring Gateway (and Client) Services for NetWare, what item is required?

   a. A valid NetWare user account that is a member of the NTGATEWAY group on NetWare.

   b. A valid NetWare user account that is a member of the NTGATEWAY group on Windows 2000.

   c. A valid Windows 2000 user account that is a member of the NTGATEWAY group on Windows 2000.

   d. A valid Windows 2000 user account that is a member of the NTGATEWAY group on NetWare.

2. NetWare 3.12 is fault tolerant because the Bindery is replicated and distributed to all NetWare 3.12 servers on the network. True or False?

   a. True

   b. False

3. What represents the location of a user account in NDS?

   a. Login

   b. Common Context

   c. Default Tree

   d. Context

4. When you are connecting to a NetWare 3.12 server, what two network components need to be installed on a Windows XP Professional workstation? [Check all correct answers]

   a. Client Services for NetWare

   b. Client for Microsoft Networks

   c. TCP/IP

   d. NWLink

5. You need to connect to the NetWare 5.*x* server DATASRV. This server is using a Bindery context for user authentication. How does Client Services for NetWare need to be configured?

   a. Preferred Server

   b. Default Tree

   c. Context

   d. NetWare 5 Context

6. You are installing Gateway (and Client) Services for NetWare. The gateway needs to be configured to access resources on NetWare 3.11, NetWare 3.12, and NetWare 4.*x* servers. How does the frametype for NWLink need to be configured? [Check all correct answers]

   a. Autodetect

   b. Ethernet 802.2

   c. Ethernet 802.3

   d. Autoswitch

7. What is the name of the NetWare group that Gateway (and Client) Services for NetWare uses?

   a. NTGATEWAY

   b. NWGATEWAY

   c. NSGATEWAY

   d. NMGATEWAY

8. You use a DOS application that prints to the LPT1 printer port. Unfortunately, you cannot upgrade this application because the company that produced it went out of business. You need print jobs from this application to go to a NetWare printer named PRT1 on NetWare server PRINTSRV. What command do you use?

   a. **capture LPT1: \\PRINTSRV\PRT1**

   b. **map LPT1: \\PRINTSRV\PRT1**

   c. **net use LPT1: \\PRINTSRV\PRT1**

   d. **LPT1:=\\PRINTSRV\PRT1**

16

9. When you are installing Gateway (and Client) Services for NetWare, all Windows XP Professional workstations need to install NWLink as well. True or False?

   a. True

   b. False

10. The internal network number normally does not need to be changed. True or False?

    a. True

    b. False

11. In Windows 2000, what command allows you to map the network drive Y: to the volume DATASTORE on NetWare 3.12 server NW312?

    a. **net use \\nw312\datastore Y:**

    b. **net use Y: nw312\\datastore**

    c. **net use Y: \\nw312\datastore**

    d. **map root Y: nw312:datastore**

12. You need to install a Windows XP Professional workstation on IPX subnet B4, which contains no NetWare servers. The NetWare servers are located on IPX subnet B1. What do you need to set the external network number to for NWLink?

    a. B4

    b. B1

    c. B★

    d. Autodetect

13. When you are connecting to a NetWare 3.12 server, what needs to be configured on Client Services for NetWare?

    a. Default Tree and Context

    b. Default Context

    c. Preferred Server

    d. Default Tree

14. What did Novell first introduce with the NetWare 4.x operating system?

    a. TCP/IP

    b. NDS

    c. Bindery

    d. NetBIOS support

15. What is the name of the object that stores all user and group accounts, passwords, and trustee assignments in Novell NetWare 3.12?

    a. XNS

    b. NDS

    c. Bindery

    d. Ethernet 802.2

16. Your user account is DAVIDS. Your account is located in an OU named ENGINEERING, which itself is located in another OU named PARIS. The NDS tree is named SOMECO. What is your typefull context?

    a. ou=ENGINEERING.ou=PARIS.o=SOMECO

    b. cn=DAVIDS.ou=ENGINEERING.ou=PARIS.o=SOMECO

    c. .ENGINEERING.PARIS.SOMECO

    d. DAVIDS.ENGINEERING.PARIS.SOMECO

17. You are the network administrator for a large corporation. Your company has recently acquired a smaller company whose network uses NetWare 4.*x* servers. The management of your company wants employees to access the data on the NetWare servers; however, it does not want another network client deployed. What should you do?

    a. Install only Client Services for NetWare on workstations that require access.

    b. Install a Windows XP Professional computer with Gateway (and Client) Services for NetWare.

    c. Install a Windows 2000 server with Gateway (and Client) Services for NetWare.

    d. Migrate all NetWare data to Windows 2000 servers.

18. How does Gateway (and Client) Services for NetWare operate?

    a. It translates SMB to NCP.

    b. It translates CIFS to NCP.

    c. It translates TCP to NCP.

    d. It translates SPX to NCP.

19. When you are configuring Gateway (and Client) Services for NetWare, how do Windows 2000 clients locate NetWare resources?

    a. By connecting to shares on the Windows 2000 server

    b. By connecting to volumes on the NetWare server

    c. By mapping a network drive to the NetWare volume

    d. By mapping a network drive to the NetWare server

16

20. What command can be used to view NetWare resources on a network via a command prompt?

    a. **net use /network:nw**

    b. **net /network:nw**

    c. **net view /network:nw**

    d. **net view /network:netware**

21. You are installing Client Services for NetWare on your Windows XP Professional workstation. You need to access NetWare 3.11 servers. Which frametype do you use?

    a. Ethernet 802.2

    b. Ethernet 802.5

    c. Ethernet 802.3

    d. Ethernet 802.4

22. When you are connecting to a NetWare 5.x server, what needs to be configured on Client Services for NetWare? [Check all correct answers]

    a. Default Tree

    b. Preferred Server

    c. Common Name

    d. Context

23. Which version of NetWare was the first NetWare operating system with the capability to be used as a Web server on the Internet?

    a. NetWare 2.2

    b. NetWare 3.12

    c. NetWare 4.x

    d. NetWare 5.x

24. Objects in an NDS tree can be of which two types?

    a. Container

    b. User

    c. Leaf

    d. Common

25. Which version of the Novell NetWare operating system relies on the Bindery for storing user and group account information?

    a. NetWare 5.x

    b. NetWare 4.1

    c. NetWare 4.11

    d. NetWare 3.12

Real-World Projects

You work for a large corporation whose network includes Windows XP, Windows 2000, and Novell NetWare 4.*x* servers. The NDS tree is called SOMECO. Your NetWare user account is located in the .SALES.MIAMI container. You have been given a Windows XP Professional workstation to use to access the corporate network. It has already been configured to access the corporate Windows domain. You need to install and configure Client Services for NetWare.

Project 16.1

To install and configure Client Services for NetWare:

1. Open the Network And Dial-Up Connections folder (choose Start|Control Panel|Network And Internet Connections).

2. Right-click Local Area Connection, and select Properties.

3. Click Install.

4. The Select Network Component Type dialog box is displayed. Select Client, and click Add.

5. The Select Network Client dialog box is displayed. Select Client Services For NetWare. Click OK.

6. Windows XP Professional now installs CSNW. NWLink is also installed (if it wasn't previously).

7. The Select NetWare Logon dialog box is displayed.

   The corporate network is using NetWare 4.*x*, so you need to specify Default Tree and Context.

   Enter the name of the tree: SOMECO.

   Enter the context: .SALES.MIAMI.

   You are concerned about conflicts, so you do not want to execute the NetWare login script. Verify that Run Login Script is not selected.

8. Click OK to save your settings.

9. Reboot if prompted.

Next, you want to map to some volumes on the NetWare network. The volumes are listed below:

Y: \\MIAMISRV\DATA

K: \\NYSRV\DATA

Q: \\LASRV\DATA

16

Project 16.2

To map drives to NetWare resources:

1. Open a command prompt (select Start|Run, type "cmd", and then press Enter).

2. Type "net use Y: \\MIAMISRV\DATA".

3. Type "net use K: \\NYSRV\DATA".

4. Type "net use Q: \\LASRV\DATA".

One of the applications you use is a DOS application. This DOS application is set up to print to LPT2 only. You want to send some print jobs from this application to a printer located in Philadelphia. The printer's name is LASER1, and it is located on the PHILLYSRV print server.

Project 16.3

To map printer ports to NetWare printers:

1. Open a command prompt (select Start|Run, type "cmd", and then press Enter).

2. Type "net use LPT2: \\PHILLYSRV\LASER1".

CHAPTER SEVENTEEN

The Unix Networking Environment

After completing this chapter, you will be able to:

✓ Identify the origins of the Unix operating system

✓ Identify the Unix variants

✓ Install and configure Services for Unix

✓ Access files and directories on Network File System (NFS) servers

✓ Host files and directories on an NFS network

The Unix operating system is a powerful and versatile operating system that can handle many of the roles needed in today's enterprise network environment. Unix achieves this power from its utilities and scripting tools as well as from its support for powerful hardware systems. It also supports a large number of programming languages, which allows programmers and administrators to customize and automate many tasks.

Most important, Unix is arguably the operating system of the Internet. Most large commercial Web sites use Unix because of its powerful features and scalability. Consequently, it is imperative that Microsoft provide a means to integrate Windows 2000 and Windows XP into an existing Unix network infrastructure.

History of Unix

The history of Unix begins in the early 1960s as a project headed by AT&T. The goal of this project was to develop an operating system that could be deployed throughout the United States. In other words, AT&T wanted to accomplish with computer services what it had achieved with its national telecommunications network. During this early development, Unix was unwieldy and difficult to use and maintain.

In the early 1970s, the C programming language was introduced. With the power of C, the architects of Unix rebuilt the entire operating system. By using C, Unix became much more flexible and easily modifiable. This allowed administrators and programmers to develop solutions to many of the problems encountered in a networking environment.

Because licenses for Unix were either very inexpensive or free, many universities adopted the operating system. As more and more students who were exposed to it started moving into the business industry, Unix began infiltrating corporate networks.

Unix Variants

Unix combines open standards, such as C and TCP/IP, along with a common command set. Because Unix was developed using open standards, eventually many different flavors of Unix were available on the market. These Unix variants have all been developed for a special need in the Unix market. Because of the expense in upgrading and implementing new hardware, the different flavors of Unix allow different hardware platforms to be used.

Linux

Linux is by far the most widely used Unix variant for Intel-based hardware platforms and is a freely distributed Unix operating system. Linux is also available on other platforms, such as the Motorola Power PC, Digital Alpha, Sun Sparc, and

MIPS. Because it is free and runs on the Intel platform, many people simply download Linux from the Internet and install it on their home PC.

Solaris

Solaris is a version of Unix developed by Sun Microsystems. It is primarily run on Sun workstations and hardware; however, it has also been ported to the Intel platform.

HP-UX

HP-UX is another version of Unix, which was developed by Hewlett-Packard (HP) for its workstations and servers.

Introducing Services for Unix 2

As Windows NT and Windows 2000 were adopted and implemented into more and more networking environments, Microsoft introduced Services for Unix 2 as a way for these operating systems to connect with Unix servers and workstations. Services for Unix 2 is a robust add-on package that provides many components that allow Windows NT/2000/XP computers to be integrated into a Unix-based networking environment.

Table 17.1 lists the components found in Services for Unix 2 as well as with which operating systems the component is compatible. The following components are included with Services for Unix 2 and provide connectivity services:

Table 17.1   Windows operating systems compatibility chart in relation to Services for Unix 2.

Component	NT 4 Workstation	NT 4 Server	XP Professional	2000 Server
Client for NFS	X	X	X	X
Server for NFS	X	X	X	X
Gateway for NFS		X		X
Telnet Client	X	X	X	X
Telnet Server	X	X	X	X
Server for NIS				X
Server for PCNFS	X	X	X	X
User Name Mapping	X	X	X	X
Password Synchronization		X		X
Server for NFS Authentication		X		X
Remote Shell Service	X	X	X	X
CRON Service	X	X	X	X
ActiveState ActivePerl 5.6	X	X	X	X
Unix Shell and Utilities	X	X	X	X

17

➤ *Client for NFS*—Allows Windows-based computers to access Unix or Windows NFS servers.

➤ *Server for NFS*—Enables a Windows NT server or a Windows 2000 server to act as an NFS server, exporting Windows directories as NFS file systems.

➤ *Gateway for NFS*—Acts as a bridge between Unix-based NFS servers and Windows clients. The Gateway for NFS server presents NFS file systems as shared directories. Windows clients can then access NFS data without requiring Client for NFS to be installed.

➤ *Telnet Client*—Enables a Windows NT/2000/XP computer to make a Telnet connection to a remote computer.

➤ *Telnet Server*—Provides a Windows NT/2000/XP computer with the capability to host a Telnet session from a Telnet client.

The remaining components included with Services for Unix 2 provide administrative functions:

➤ *Server for PCNFS*—Supports an authentication method originally found in Services for Unix 1. Services for Unix 2 provides another authentication method—User Name Mapping.

➤ *Server for NIS*—Enables a Windows NT server or a Windows 2000 server to act as an NIS server. This allows a domain controller to act as a master NIS server, thus integrating Active Directory domains and NIS domains.

➤ *Password Synchronization*—Enables users to maintain a single password for both Windows domains and Unix systems.

➤ *User Name Mapping*—Creates a map that associates Windows and Unix user accounts, which allows users to log onto Unix resources without needing a separate Unix user account.

➤ *Remote Shell Service*—Enables a user to execute commands on a remote computer.

➤ *CRON Service*—Serves as a scheduling utility that allows commands to be executed at specified times and dates.

➤ *ActiveState ActivePerl 5.6*—Enables Perl scripts to be executed on a server.

➤ *Unix Shell and Utilities*—Provides the Korn shell that allows Unix scripting and Perl scripting.

System Requirements

To install Services for Unix 2, your computer requires the following:

➤ Windows NT/2000/XP operating system

➤ 60MB free disk space

➤ 16MB RAM (in addition to the operating system's minimum recommendations)

➤ CD-ROM drive

➤ Network adapter

Installing Services for Unix 2

Services for Unix 2 is available as an add-on pack for Windows NT 4/2000/XP. It does not support the clustering feature found in Windows NT 4 Enterprise or Windows 2000 Advanced Server. Also, it does not run on Windows 95 or Windows 98. To install Services for Unix 2, take these steps:

1. Start the Services for Unix 2 installation routine. The Services for Unix Setup Wizard starts. Click Next.

2. On the Customer Information screen, enter your username and company name. You also need to enter the 25-character product key. You can find this key on the back of the Services for Unix 2 CD case. Click Next.

3. The License and Support screen appears. This screen displays the End User License Agreement (EULA). If you enjoy this type of reading material, take the time to read the entire EULA. Click I Accept The Agreement, and then click Next. (Of course, if you don't agree with the EULA, click I Don't Accept The Agreement. If you select this option, the wizard exits the installation without installing the software.)

4. The Installation Options screen is then displayed. You can select either a standard installation or a customized installation. The Standard Installation option installs certain components depending on the operating system the computer is running. If your computer is running Windows NT Workstation 4 or Windows 2000 Professional, the following components are installed during a standard installation:

   ➤ Telnet Client

   ➤ Telnet Server

   ➤ Unix Shell and Utilities

   ➤ Client for NFS

17

If your computer is running Windows NT Server 4 or Windows 2000 Server, the following components are installed during a standard installation:

➤ Telnet Client

➤ Telnet Server

➤ Unix Shell and Utilities

➤ Server for NFS

If your computer is also a domain controller, Server for NFS Authentication is also installed. A customized installation allows you to specify which components you want to install.

Select Standard Installation, and click Next.

5. The User Name Mapping screen appears. This screen is used to specify the name of a User Name Mapping server. If you know the name of the server, enter it. If you are not sure of the server's name, leave it blank. You can configure this item later. Click Next.

At this point, the wizard begins installing the components selected.

You can administer the components in Services for Unix 2 from the Services for Unix Administration console, an MMC-based utility that provides an interface to manage the components found in Services for Unix 2. To start the console, select Start|Programs|Services For Unix|Services For Unix Administration. See Figure 17.1 for a display of the Services for Unix Administration console.

Accessing Files Using NFS

NFS is a standard client/server protocol used to access files across a Unix-based network. NFS is defined in Request for Comments (RFCs) 1094 and 1813.

NFS is analogous to the native network file sharing protocol found in Windows 2000—Common Internet File System (CIFS), formerly known as Server Message Block (SMB). It provides a common language that allows both Unix and Windows computers to open, close, read, and write files across the network.

Client for NFS

Client for NFS allows a Windows NT4/2000/XP computer to access files on an NFS server (see Figure 17.2). Much like accessing files on a Microsoft-based network, Client for NFS allows a user to connect to and disconnect from NFS

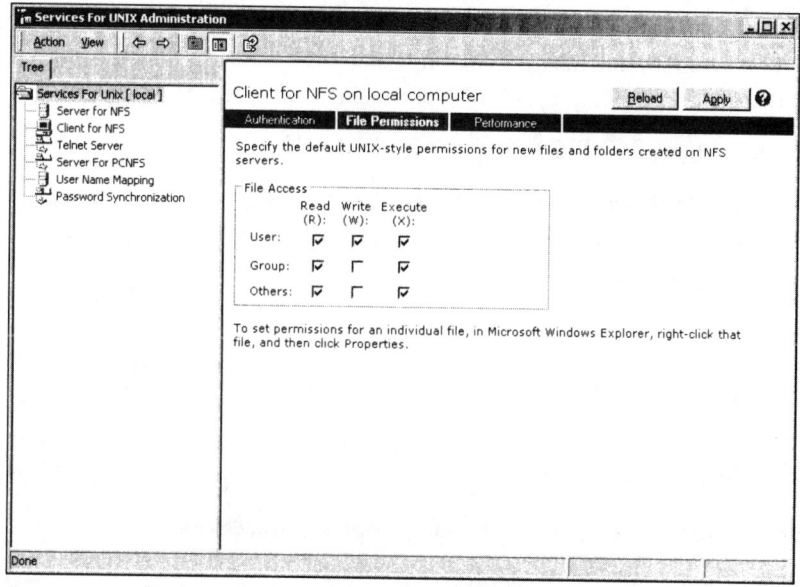

Figure 17.1   The Services for Unix Administration console.

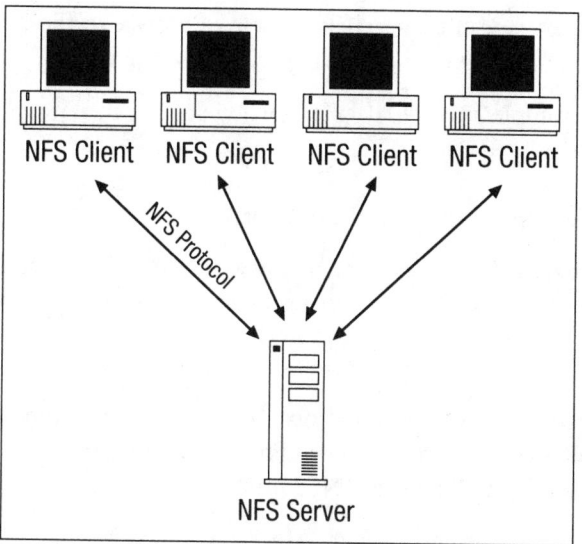

Figure 17.2   Accessing NFS files using Client for NFS.

17

shares. These connections can be created either by using the command prompt (that is, **\\servername\share**) or by browsing My Network Places. Client for NFS provides a new selection in My Network Places called NFS Network.

To configure Client for NFS, follow these steps:

1. Open the Windows Services for Unix Administration console (click Start|Programs|Services For Unix).

2. Click Client For NFS.

3. Click the Authentication tab.

4. Type the name of the mapping server you want to use for authentication, and then click Apply.

To map a network drive to an NFS share, follow these steps:

1. Open Windows Explorer (click Start|Programs|Accessories).

2. On the Tools menu, click Map Network Drive.

3. In the Drive list, click the drive letter to use.

4. To locate the NFS share, you can either click Browse to browse to the NFS share, or, in Folder, type the path to the share. Specify the path as

   serverName:/path (for example: nfsserv:/data/export)

   or as

   \\serverName\path (for example: \\nfsserv\data\export)

5. To connect using a different NFS username or password, click Connect Using A Different Username, and type the NFS username and password. Click OK.

Server for NFS

Server for NFS allows NFS clients to access files on a Windows 2000 computer (see Figure 17.3). These NFS clients can be either Unix-based workstations or Windows 2000 computers running Client for NFS.

To configure Server for NFS, follow these steps:

1. Open the Windows Services for Unix Administration console (click Start|Programs|Services For Unix).

2. Click Server For NFS.

3. Click the Authentication tab.

4. Type the name of the mapping server you want to use for authentication, and then click Apply.

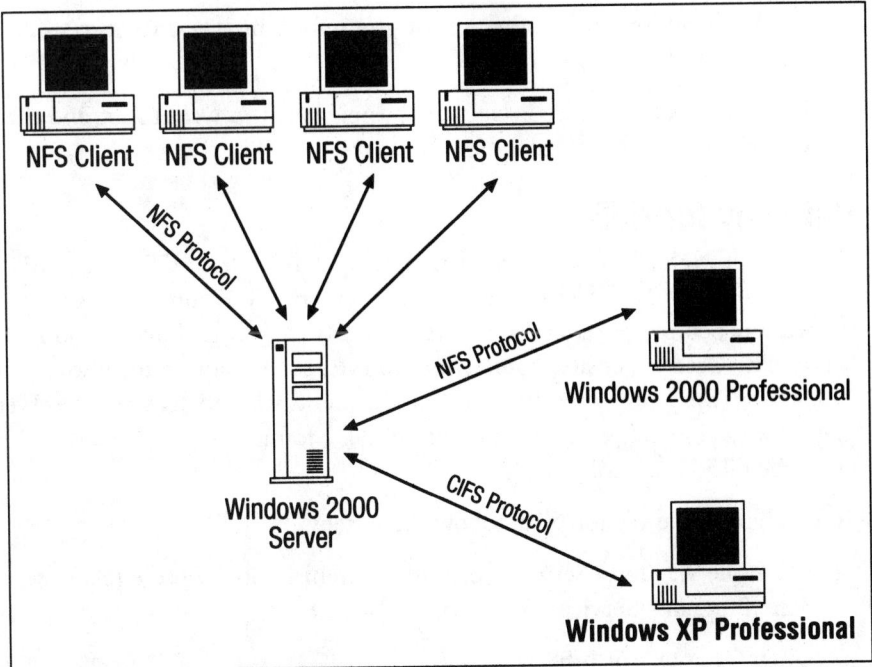

Figure 17.3 Hosting NFS files using Server for NFS.

To create an NFS share, take the following steps:

1. Start Windows Explorer.

2. Locate the directory you want to share. In the details pane, right-click the directory.

3. Click Sharing.

4. Click NFS Sharing.

5. Click Share This Folder, and, in the Share Name text box, type a share name.

To set up NFS permissions on an NFS share, follow these steps:

1. Start Windows Explorer.

2. Locate the directory you want to share. Right-click the directory for which you want to set permissions.

3. Click Sharing.

4. Click NFS Sharing. If the folder is not already being shared, click Share This Folder.

17

5. Click Permissions. Select the user or group for which you want to set permissions.

6. In the Type Of Access list, select the permissions you want to set, and then click OK twice to exit the dialog box.

Gateway for NFS

Gateway for NFS allows Windows-based computers without Client for NFS installed to access NFS files located on NFS servers (see Figure 17.4). Comparable to Gateway Services for NetWare, Gateway for NFS is loaded on a Windows 2000 Server. The Gateway creates connections to NFS servers and in turn hosts these connections as shares. When Windows-based clients want to access NFS servers, they make a connection to the appropriate share found on the Gateway server using the CIFS protocol.

To configure Gateway for NFS, follow these steps:

1. Open the Windows Services for Unix Administration console (click Start|Programs|Services For Unix).

2. Click Gateway For NFS.

3. Click the Authentication tab.

4. Type the name of the mapping server you want to use for authentication, and then click Apply.

To set up an NFS share on the Windows network, follow these steps:

1. Start Gateway for NFS Configuration.

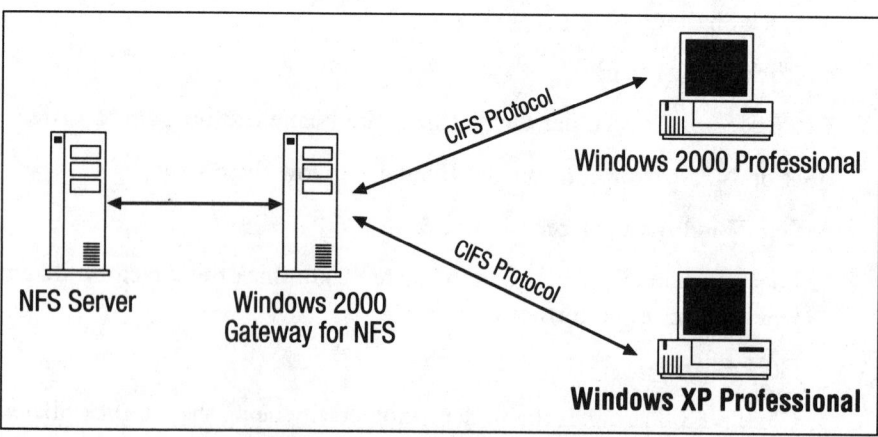

Figure 17.4   Using Gateway for NFS to access NFS files.

2. To connect to an NFS share, you can do one of the following:

➤ Double-click Default LAN in the Network Resources list. Next, double-click the server that contains the directory, and then click the desired directory name.

➤ Enter the name of the NFS server and the exported directory into the Network Resource text box.

3. In the Share Name text box, enter the name of the drive you are going to share. Note that this is the share name by which the Windows clients will gain access to the resource.

4. In the Drive list, click the drive letter you want to assign to the NFS share.

5. Use the Comment text box to enter a brief description about the network share.

6. If you want to limit the number of users that can connect to the share, click Allow, and in the Users text box, type the number of users to allow. If it doesn't matter, click Maximum Allowed.

7. Click Permissions.

8. In Gateway For NFS Share Permissions, select the user or group that you want to set permissions for.

9. In the Type Of Access list, select the permissions you want to assign.

Authentication Using Services for Unix 2

User authentication can quickly become a problem in a network where multiple security authorities are present. For example, if a user needs to access data on both Unix and Windows 2000 servers, the user would need user accounts in both Active Directory and Network Information Service (NIS). NIS is a security database used in Unix environments.

Resembling Active Directory, NIS is structured in an NIS domain, where NIS clients perform lookup services on NIS servers. The NIS servers hold the NIS lookup database. The database itself is replicated among the NIS servers.

Server for NIS

Server for NIS is another component found in Services for Unix 2. It integrates Active Directory and NIS by allowing an Active Directory domain controller to act as a master NIS server. This permits an Active Directory administrator to create, modify, and delete user accounts in both security domains.

17

Server for PCNFS

Server for PCNFS allows a user to supply his or her Unix username and password to be authenticated. Once verified, the Windows 2000 server running Server for PCNFS returns the user identifier (UID) and group identifier (GID). The user's computer then connects to the Unix server.

Server for PCNFS was first included in Services for Unix 1. It relied on Unix servers to run the PCNFS daemon. It is included in Services for Unix 2 to provide support for earlier Services for Unix clients.

Password Synchronization

Another task that users in a multiple network infrastructure find difficult is maintaining multiple passwords. If users change their Unix password, they need to either change their Windows password to match or remember both passwords.

One way to simplify this task is through password synchronization, which provides a means of keeping these passwords the same. When a user changes his or her password in Active Directory, the Unix password is also changed automatically. Password synchronization can also be configured to work in the opposite direction: When a user changes his or her Unix password, the Windows password is updated as well.

User Name Mapping Server

User Name Mapping provides a way to create maps between Windows and Unix user and group accounts. For example, a Windows user account is mapped to a Unix account. When a user (running either Client for NFS, Server for NFS, or Gateway for NFS) attempts to access data on a Unix server, the client contacts a User Name Mapping server, which in turn matches the Windows account to the appropriate Unix account.

Remote Administration Using Services for Unix 2

One of the great features found in many of the Unix variants, but unfortunately not found in many of the Windows operating systems, is the ability to remotely administer and run applications. Unix includes a utility called Telnet that allows a user or administrator to run applications on a remote computer. Telnet is a command-line-based interface. Services for Unix 2 includes an improved Telnet Client and adds a Telnet Server to the Windows NT and Windows 2000 operating system.

Telnet Client

The Telnet Client allows a user to connect via the Telnet protocol (port 23) to a remote computer over a TCP/IP-based network. The remote computer needs to be running a Telnet Server that hosts the Telnet connection. The Telnet Client can also be used to access other server-based applications, such as SMTP and POP3. To do this, simply specify the IP address for the server and the port address for the application. For example, SMTP uses port 25, and POP3 uses port 110.

The Telnet Client operates in two modes when connecting to a remote computer—command mode and session mode. Command mode allows a user to open or close a connection, set Telnet options, or change the display properties. In session mode, the Telnet Client opens a connection to the remote computer, allowing the user to execute any character-based applications on the remote computer. The following list describes the Telnet commands:

➤ **Close**—Closes or ends an existing Telnet connection.

➤ **Ctrl+]**—Goes to the Telnet command prompt from a connected session.

➤ **Display**—Used to view the current operating parameters for a Telnet Client. The following operating parameters are available: WILL AUTH (NTLM Authentication), WONT AUTH, WILL TERM TYPE, WONT TERM TYPE, LOCALECHO off, and LOCALECHO on.

➤ **Enter**—Used from the command prompt to go to the connected session.

➤ **ESCAPE Character**—Sets the key sequence to use for switching from session to command mode. For example, type "set escape", press Ctrl+X, and then press Enter. This will set Ctrl+X as your escape character.

➤ **LOGFILE FileName**—Sets the file to be used for logging Telnet activity. The log file is a text file that is saved to your local computer. Logging automatically begins when this option is set.

➤ **LOGGING**—Turns on logging.

➤ **Open**—Used to establish a Telnet connection to a host. Syntax: **Open** *hostname*, where *hostname* is the name of the Telnet Server.

➤ **Quit**—Exits Telnet.

➤ **Set**—Used to set the terminal type for the connection, set authentication to NTLM, set the escape character, turn on local echo, and set up logging.

➤ **SET LOCALECHO**—Turns on local echoing.

➤ **SET NTLM**—Turns on NTLM. While you are using NTLM Authentication, your username and password are automatically verified. Therefore, you are not prompted for a logon name and password.

➤ **SET TERM {*ANSI* | *VT100* | *VT52* | *VTNT*}**—Sets the terminal type to the appropriate terminal type.

17

➤ **Status**—Determines whether the Telnet Client is currently connected.

➤ **Unset**—Turns off local echo or sets authentication to logon/password prompt.

➤ **UNSET LOCALECHO**—Turns off local echoing.

➤ **UNSET NTLM**—Turns off NTLM.

➤ **?/help**—Prints Help information.

Telnet Server

The Telnet Server hosts connections from remote Telnet Clients. The Telnet Clients can run applications on the Telnet Server. Please note that applications that interact with the desktop cannot be executed via Telnet.

Some licensing issues must be considered when using the Telnet Server in Services for Unix 2. With each Windows 2000 installation, there is one license for Telnet Server. However, this means that several Telnet Clients can be connected to the Telnet Server. Table 17.2 lists the maximum number of Telnet Client connections available for each Telnet Server.

Chapter Summary

In this chapter, the history and origins of the Unix operating system (as it was developed in the early 1960s at AT&T) were discussed. Also discussed were some of the Unix variants from the different Unix vendors, such as HP and Sun.

Next, Services for Unix 2 was introduced as Microsoft's solution to facilitate the integration of Windows NT and Windows 2000 into an existing Unix environment. This was followed by a brief description of the components found in Services for Unix 2.

The subsequent section described the various methods of accessing and hosting NFS data on a network. Client for NFS allows a Windows NT or Windows 2000 computer to access NFS data on the network. Server for NFS allows a Windows NT or Windows 2000 computer to host NFS data on the network, just like a

Table 17.2 Maximum number of Telnet Client connections.

Operating System	Maximum Number of Connections
Windows 2000 Server	Number of client access licenses installed
Windows 2000/XP Professional	10
Windows NT Server 4	Number of client access licenses installed
Windows NT Workstation 4	10

Unix-based NFS server. And, the Gateway for NFS component allows a Windows NT or Windows 2000 server to act as a gateway for other Windows clients to connect to NFS data.

The methods of integrating authentication services between Active Directory and Unix were described. Server for NIS allows a Windows 2000 domain controller to participate in an NIS domain, thereby synchronizing Active Directory and NIS user accounts automatically. User Name Mapping server creates a user map between Windows and Unix accounts.

The Telnet Client and Telnet Server were discussed. These components allow a user or administrator to execute applications on a remote computer.

Review Questions

1. Which Intel-based Unix variant is distributed freely via the Internet?

   a. Linux

   b. HP-UX

   c. AIX

   d. SunOS

2. Which component allows Windows NT/2000/XP computers to directly access files on an NFS network?

   a. Server for NFS

   b. Client for NFS

   c. Gateway for NFS

   d. NFS Direct for Windows

3. Services for Unix is included with Windows 2000. True or False?

   a. True

   b. False

4. How much free disk space is required to install Services for Unix 2?

   a. 100MB

   b. 40MB

   c. 80MB

   d. 60MB

17

5. What is the standard file sharing protocol found on Unix-based networks?

   a. SMB

   b. NCP

   c. CIFS

   d. NFS

6. Which Services for Unix component integrates Active Directory domains and NIS domains?

   a. Server for PCNFS

   b. Server for NIS

   c. Password Synchronization

   d. User Name Mapping server

7. Which component creates user maps between Windows user accounts and Unix user accounts?

   a. User Name Mapping server

   b. Server for NFS

   c. Server for PCNFS

   d. Server for NIS

8. What is the maximum number of connections the Telnet Server can host on a Windows 2000 Professional workstation?

   a. The total number of client access licenses installed

   b. 1

   c. 10

   d. None; it cannot be installed on Windows 2000 Professional

9. If you are installing Services for Unix 2 on a Windows 2000 Professional workstation and select Standard Installation, which component is not installed?

   a. Client for NFS

   b. Telnet Client

   c. Telnet Server

   d. Server for NFS

10. Which utility allows a user to connect and execute applications on a remote computer?

   a. Server for NIS

   b. Remote Server

   c. Telnet Server

   d. Telnet Client

11. Which Services for Unix component allows a Windows NT or Windows 2000 server to export Windows directories as NFS file systems?

    a. Server for NFS

    b. Client for NFS

    c. Gateway for NFS

    d. Windows for NFS

12. Which company spearheaded development of the Unix operating system in the early 1960s?

    a. Microsoft

    b. Sun

    c. AT&T

    d. HP

13. Which Telnet Client command creates a connection between the client and the Telnet Server?

    a. **Connect computername**

    b. **Open hostname**

    c. **Open connection**

    d. **Connect hostname**

14. Which utility provides a command-line interface that allows a user to execute character-based applications on a remote computer?

    a. Telnet Server

    b. Telnet Client

    c. Shell

    d. Explorer

15. Which component is included with Services for Unix 2 to provide support for earlier Services for Unix 1 clients?

    a. Server for PCNFS

    b. Server for NIS

    c. Password Synchronization

    d. User Name Mapping server

16. Windows users attempting to access files on NFS shares do not need another user account. True or False?

    a. True

    b. False

17

17. If you are performing a standard install of Services for Unix on a Windows 2000 domain controller, which component is also installed?

 a. Telnet Server

 b. Server for NFS Authentication

 c. Server for NFS

 d. Unix Shell and Utilities

18. Gateway for NFS can be installed on a Windows 2000 Professional computer. True or False?

 a. True

 b. False

19. What programming language is closely related to the Unix operating system?

 a. Java

 b. Visual Basic

 c. C

 d. Cobol

20. Which Services for Unix component allows Windows computers to access NFS using the CIFS protocol?

 a. Client for NFS

 b. Server for NFS

 c. Gateway for NFS

 d. Telnet Server

Real-World Projects

You work for a large corporation whose network includes Windows 2000/XP, Windows NT 4, and Unix-based servers. You are given a Windows XP Professional workstation to use to access the corporate network. It has been configured to access the corporate Windows domain. Your boss notifies you that you will also need to access data on the Unix servers. Consequently, you need to install and configure Services for Unix 2.

Project 17.1

To install and configure Services for Unix 2:

1. Start the Services for Unix 2 installation routine. The Services for Unix Setup Wizard starts. Click Next.

2. On the Customer Information screen, enter your username and company name. You also need to enter the 25-character product key. You can find this key on the back of the Services for Unix 2 CD case. Click Next.

3. The License and Support screen appears. This screen displays the End User License Agreement (EULA). If you enjoy this type of reading material, take the time to read the entire EULA. Click I Accept The Agreement, and then click Next. (Of course, if you don't agree with the EULA, click I Don't Accept The Agreement. If you select this option, the wizard exits the installation without installing the software.)

4. The Installation Options screen appears. You can select either a standard installation or a customized installation. Selecting Standard Installation installs the following components:

   ➤ Telnet Client

   ➤ Telnet Server

   ➤ Unix Shell and Utilities

   ➤ Client for NFS

5. The User Name Mapping screen appears. This screen is used to specify the name of a User Name Mapping server. If you know the name of the server, enter it. If you are not sure of the server's name, leave it blank. You can configure this item later. Click Next.

After Services for Unix is installed, you need to configure Client for NFS so you can access the data stored on NFS shares. You first need to configure where your user account should be authenticated. After discussing this with the LAN administrator, you learn that there is a User Name Mapping server called usermap.ourco.com.

Project 17.2

To configure authentication in Client for NFS:

1. Open the Windows Services for Unix Administration console (select Start|Programs|Services For Unix).

2. Click Client For NFS.

3. Click the Authentication tab.

4. Type the name of the mapping server you want to use for authentication, "usermap.ourco.com". Click Apply.

17

After your authentication settings have been configured, you need to map a network drive to the NFS data. Your boss tells you that the data is located on the server corpdata.ourco.com in export data/export. You want to map this export to the drive letter F.

Project 17.3

To map a network drive using Client for NFS:

1. Open Windows Explorer (select Start|Programs|Accessories).

2. On the Tools menu, click Map Network Drive.

3. In the Drive list, select drive F.

4. To locate the NFS share, you can either click Browse to browse to the NFS share, or, in Folder, type the path to the share. Specify the path as "corpdata.ourco.com/data/export".

5. Click OK.

CHAPTER EIGHTEEN

Configuring Internet Explorer 6

After completing this chapter, you will be able to:

✓ Use Internet Explorer

✓ Configure Internet Explorer 6

✓ Customize security settings in Internet Explorer 6

Internet Explorer 6 Overview

Internet Explorer 6 is the latest version of Microsoft's Internet browser. It is built into Windows XP Home Edition and Windows XP Professional. It can also be used on Windows 98, 2000, NT, and Me. Internet Explorer 6 includes many new features that continue to push the envelope when it comes to browsing technologies.

The first aspect you will notice about Internet Explorer 6 is the new interface design, shown in Figure 18.1. This interface mirrors the look and feel of the Windows XP interface. The buttons on the browser toolbar are more stylized, and all components of the browser—such as dialog boxes, toolbars, list boxes, scroll bars, and menus—have been updated.

Internet Explorer 6 includes new privacy features. These tools enable you to protect your privacy by controlling the personal information that Web sites attempt to collect about you. The World Wide Web Consortium (W3C) is currently developing technologies relating to Internet privacy. Internet Explorer 6 supports these technologies, called Platform Privacy Preferences (P3P).

Internet Explorer 6 also includes an Image toolbar, shown in Figure 18.2, which is displayed whenever you place your mouse over an image on a Web site. It enables you to save, email, or print the image. It also enables you to view all the images in your My Pictures folder.

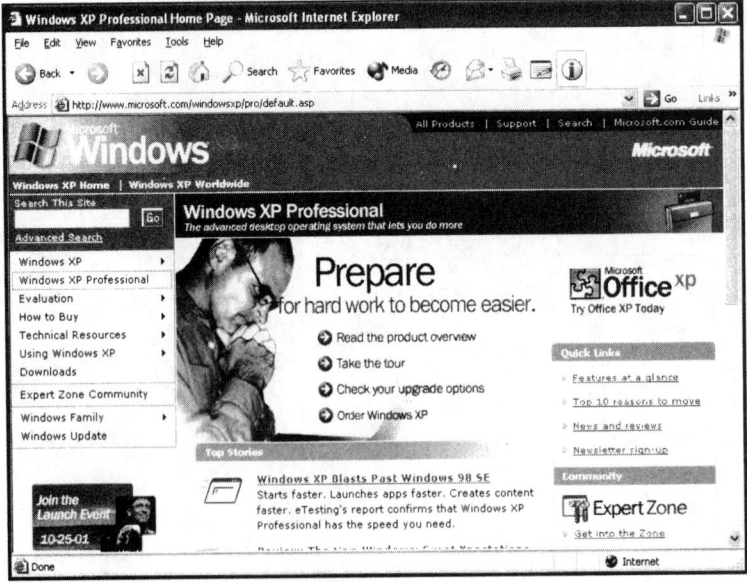

Figure 18.1   The new Internet Explorer 6 interface.

Figure 18.2   Web image with the Image toolbar displayed.

Internet Explorer 6 will also automatically resize Web images that are too large to display in your browser window. This helps eliminate the need to use the scrollbars to view portions of a very large image.

The recommended system configuration for Internet Explorer 6 is Windows XP or Windows 2000 with 128MB of RAM. The basic system requirements for these operating systems will be fine for Internet Explorer 6. For the other operating systems, the memory requirements differ. For Windows 98 and Windows 98 SE, a minimum of 16MB of RAM is required. For Windows NT and Windows Me, a minimum of 32MB of RAM is required. Windows NT also requires Service Pack 6a to be installed.

Configuring Internet Explorer 6

Straight out of the box, Internet Explorer 6 is configured to accomplish most tasks for novice and serious Web surfers. But, you might encounter situations in which you need to customize the Internet Explorer 6 configuration. The following sections walk you through the various configuration tabs and provide a description of their functions.

To access these configuration tabs, open Internet Explorer. On the Tools menu, select Internet Options. You can also access these tabs via the Control Panel, by selecting Network And Internet Connections|Internet Options.

General Tab

The General tab is used to modify the basic configuration of Internet Explorer 6 (see Figure 18.3). Here, you can specify the Home Page, which is the default Web site that Internet Explorer loads when first started. If you click the Use Current button, the current Web page that is displayed in Internet Explorer is made the Home Page. If you select Use Default, the **www.msn.com** Web site is made the Home Page. Finally, you can also choose that no Home Page be displayed, by clicking the Use Blank button.

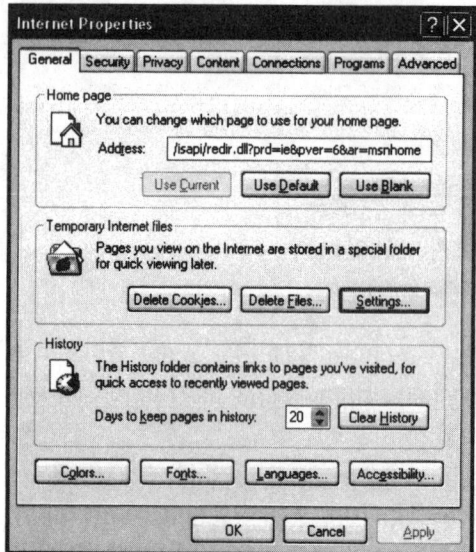

Figure 18.3 The General tab.

You can also manage your temporary Internet files on the General tab. Internet Explorer automatically caches to your hard drive the Web pages that you visit. These cached files end up as temporary Internet files. On the General tab, you can delete the files to free up disk space on your computer. You can also delete any cookies that have been written to your computer. Cookies are used by Web sites to track your usage and visits, as well as to store other information about you. You can also configure how and when temporary Internet files are created and the amount of disk space they can use (see Figure 18.4).

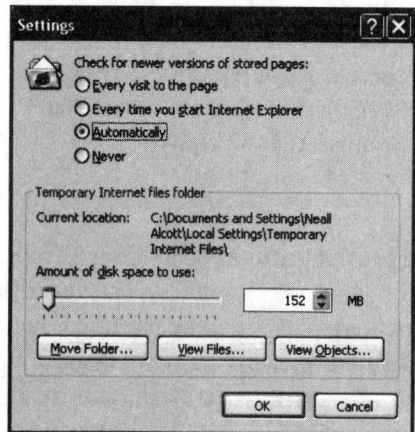

Figure 18.4 Configuring temporary Internet file usage.

The General tab provides you with a means to configure your History folder. The History folder contains links to Web pages that you've visited. You can specify the amount of time that items in the History folder should be retained. By default, items are kept for 20 days.

Finally, the General tab is used to configure the overall appearance of Internet Explorer, such as its colors, fonts, languages, and accessibility options.

Security Tab

The Security tab is used to specify security settings for Internet Explorer (see Figure 18.5).

Content Zones

Internet Explorer uses a concept known as *Web content zones* to specify security settings for various Web sites. The following are the four Web content zones:

➤ *Internet*—Includes all Web sites that haven't been placed within the other Web content zones. The security settings for this content zone prompt the user before downloading signed ActiveX controls. They also enable file downloads and disable the downloading of unsigned ActiveX controls.

➤ *Local Intranet*—Intended for Web sites that are internal to your organization. Click the Sites button to define which Web sites will be included in this zone (see Figure 18.6). The security settings for this content zone prompt the user before downloading signed ActiveX controls. They also enable file downloads and disable the downloading of unsigned ActiveX controls.

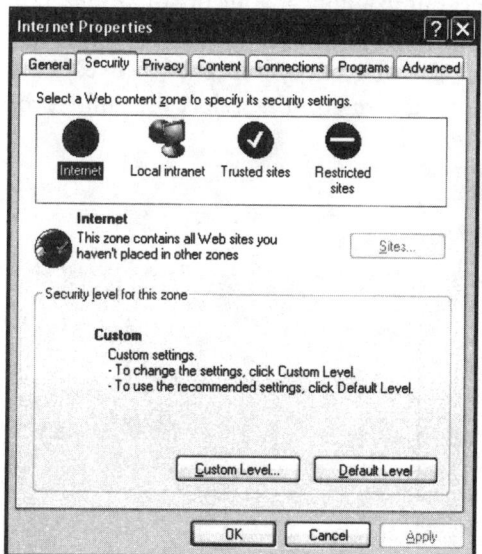

Figure 18.5   The Security tab.

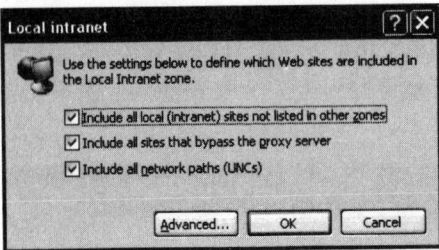

Figure 18.6 Defining the Local Intranet content zone.

➤ *Trusted Sites*—Should contain Internet Web sites that you trust. For example, you can place in this content zone Web sites that you trust will not damage your computer. Click the Sites button to define which Web sites will be included in this zone (see Figure 18.7). Web sites in this content zone must use HTTPS by default. The security settings for this content zone enable you to download and run signed ActiveX controls as well as download files. If the Web site you are accessing attempts to download an unsigned ActiveX control, you will be prompted.

➤ *Restricted Sites*—Should contain sites that you do not trust and that could potentially damage your computer. Click the Sites button to define which Web sites will be included in this zone. The security settings for this content zone disable all ActiveX controls, disable file downloads, and disable Java support.

Customizing Security Settings

You might encounter situations in which you need to customize the security settings for a particular content zone. For example, if your organization's Internet Web site is using an unsigned ActiveX control on a Web page, you might need to loosen security settings to enable the downloading of unsigned ActiveX controls for the Local Intranet content zone. To accomplish this, select the desired content

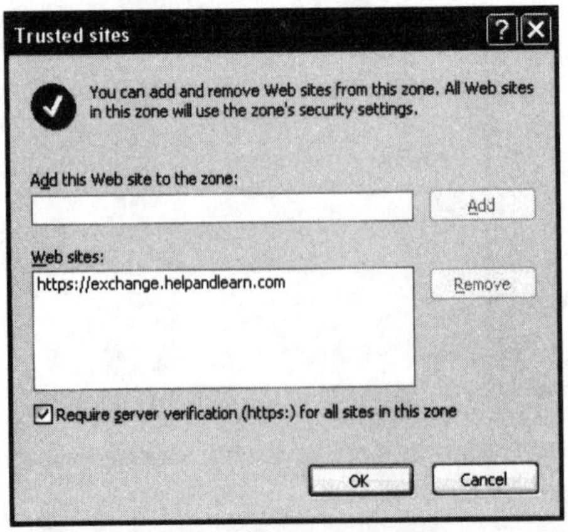

Figure 18.7 Defining the Trusted Sites content zone.

zone. Next, click the Custom Level button to access the Security Settings dialog box (see Figure 18.8). In this dialog box, you can specify how different aspects of Internet Explorer will handle security. If you want to restore the default security settings for a content zone, click Reset.

Privacy Tab

The Privacy tab is used to configure privacy settings for Internet Explorer (see Figure 18.9). These settings affect the Internet content zone.

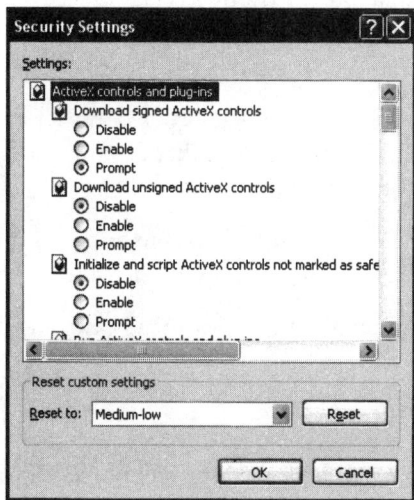

Figure 18.8   Customizing security settings.

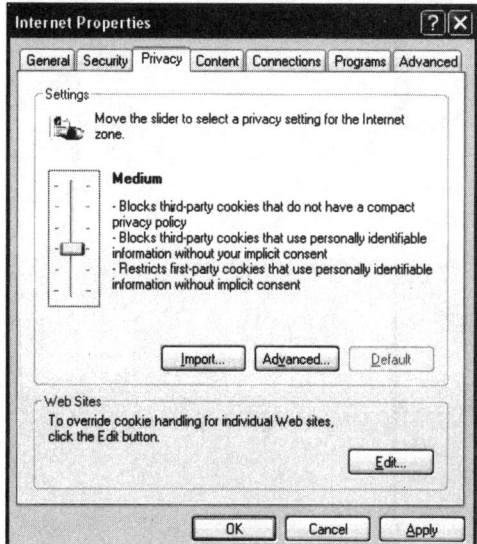

Figure 18.9   The Privacy tab.

You can choose any of the following privacy settings. To select a privacy setting, move the slider up or down until the desired privacy setting is displayed:

➤ *Accept All Cookies*—The lowest privacy setting. With this privacy setting, Web sites will be able to create and access any cookies on your computer.

➤ *Low*—Restricts third-party cookies that do not have a compact privacy policy or that use personally identifiable information without your consent.

➤ *Medium*—Blocks third-party cookies that do not have a compact privacy policy or that use personally identifiable information without your consent. It also restricts first-party cookies that use personally identifiable information without your consent.

➤ *Medium-High*—Blocks third-party cookies that do not have a compact privacy policy. It also blocks both first- and third-party cookies that use personally identifiable information without your consent.

➤ *High*—Blocks all cookies that do not have a compact privacy policy, and blocks all cookies that use personally identifiable information without your consent.

➤ *Block All Cookies*—Blocks all cookies, including cookies already existing on your computer.

Content Tab

The Content tab is used to configure what and how content will be viewed on your computer (see Figure 18.10).

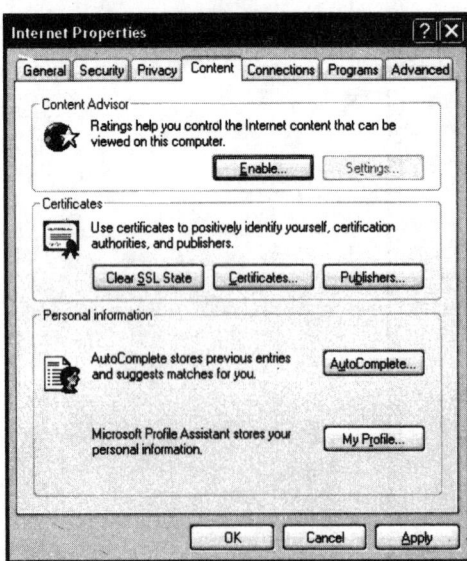

Figure 18.10 The Content tab.

The Content Advisor portion of the Content tab enables you to control how content is viewed on your computer. If any children are using your computer, you can use the Content Advisor to set rating levels for various Web sites (see Figure 18.11). These levels are maintained by the Internet Content Rating Association.

The Certificate's portion of the Content tab is used to add certificates for certificate authorities (CAs) to your computer (see Figure 18.12).

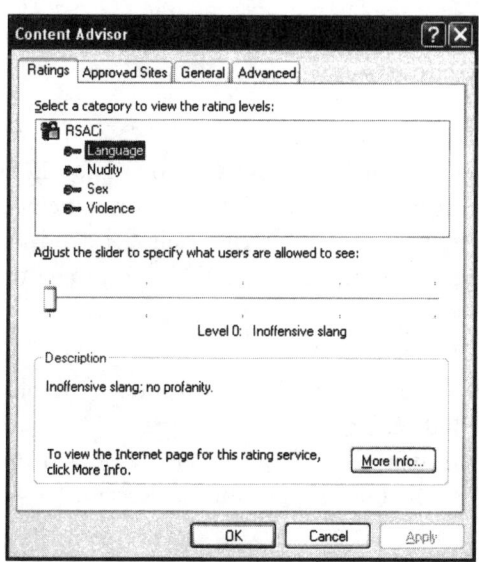

Figure 18.11   Configuring the Content Advisor.

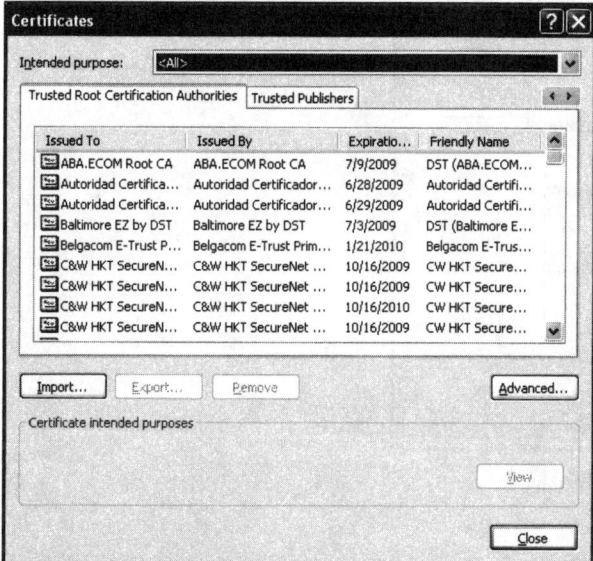

Figure 18.12   Configuring certificates.

Finally, you can also configure you personal information to be used and stored on your computer.

Connections Tab

The Connections tab can be used to specify how Internet Explorer will access the Internet (see Figure 18.13). You can specify dial-up or virtual private network (VPN) connections that will be automatically connected when Internet Explorer starts. You can also specify LAN and proxy server settings if your organization has a dedicated Internet connection.

Programs Tab

The Programs tab can be used to specify which program Windows XP will use for a particular Internet service (see Figure 18.14). Some of these settings include an HTML editor, an email client, a newsgroup reader, Internet calling, calendaring, and a contact list. You can use the default programs or specify other programs.

Advanced Tab

The Advanced tab is used to fine-tune various settings within Internet Explorer (see Figure 18.15). These settings include accessibility, browsing, HTTP, Java, multimedia, printing, searching, and security. The Advanced tab has too many settings to cover here, so only a few of the most significant are described.

Figure 18.13 The Connections tab.

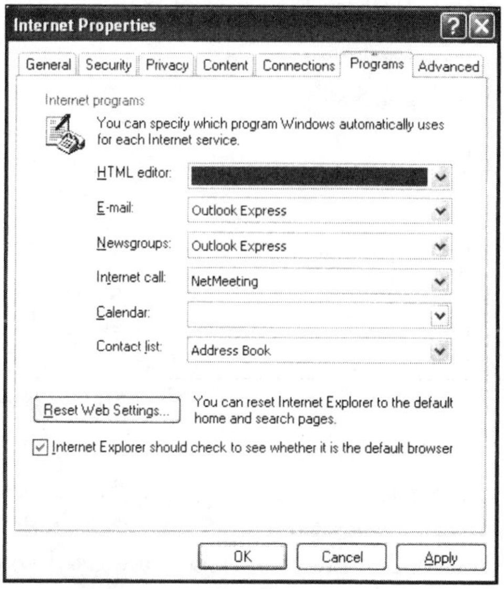

18

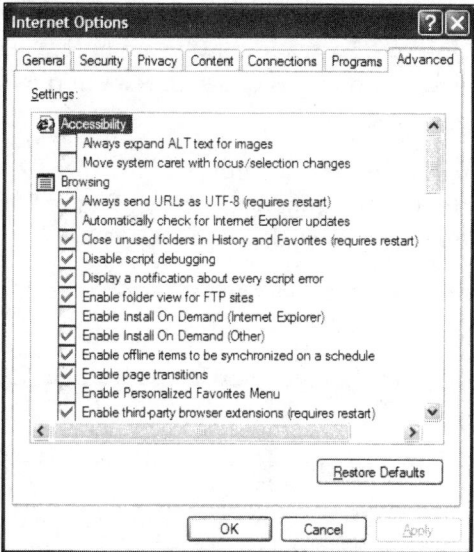

Figure 18.14   The Programs tab.

Figure 18.15   The Advanced tab.

You can configure Internet Explorer to automatically check for updates by selecting Automatically Check For Internet Explorer Updates under the Browsing section. This setting enables Internet Explorer to contact Microsoft's Windows Update Web site and determine whether an update to the Internet Explorer program is available.

Internet Explorer includes the ability to browse FTP sites. You can configure Internet Explorer to provide a folder view of FTP sites by selecting Enable Folder View For FTP Sites under the Browsing section.

Chapter Summary

Windows XP includes the latest version of Microsoft's Internet browser—Internet Explorer 6—a fully robust browser that includes numerous new features. The most obvious new feature is the look and feel of the browser. Internet Explorer 6 uses the new interface design found in Windows XP. More colorful and detailed buttons, dialog boxes, list boxes, and menus give the browser a different feel compared to previous versions of Internet Explorer.

Other new features include privacy protections and the Image toolbar. Internet Explorer 6 includes support for Platform Privacy Preferences (P3P) developed by the World Wide Web Consortium (W3C). The Image toolbar is displayed whenever your mouse is placed over an image on a Web page. It allows you to save, print, or email the image.

Out of the box, Internet Explorer meets the needs of most users and organizations. However, if a situation arises where Internet Explorer must be modified, you can configure the browser to fit your needs. To do so, customize the tabs in the Internet properties dialog box:

➤ The General tab is used to configure the general settings of Internet Explorer, such as the default Home Page, how long temporary Internet files are retained, and how items in the History folder are handled.

➤ The Security tab is used to manage content zones and security settings for Internet Explorer.

➤ The Privacy tab is used to manage and configure how cookies are handled by Internet Explorer.

➤ The Content tab is used to configure content ratings, certificates, and personal information.

➤ The Connections tab is used to specify dial-up and VPN connections, as well as LAN settings, such as proxy servers.

➤ The Programs tab is used to specify which programs Windows will use for Internet features/content.

➤ The Advanced tab is used to fine-tune many Internet Explorer settings to meet your needs.

Review Questions

18

1. Which tab is used to configure the amount of disk space used by temporary Internet files?

   a. Security

   b. General

   c. Content

   d. Advanced

2. What content zone is used for Web sites that have the potential to damage your computer?

   a. Internet

   b. Local Intranet

   c. Trusted Sites

   d. Restricted Sites

3. After reading an article in a magazine about the need to protect your privacy on the Internet, you decide that you need to block all third-party cookies while allowing access for most first-party cookies. Which privacy setting in Internet Explorer would you use to accomplish this?

   a. Accept All Cookies

   b. High

   c. Medium

   d. Block All Cookies

4. You would like to block access to certain Web sites on your computer to protect your children. Which tab is used to configure this feature?

   a. General

   b. Security

   c. Privacy

   d. Content

5. Your company has implemented a certificate authority (CA). You now need to add a certificate for the CA to Internet Explorer. Which tab is used to configure this feature?

   a. General

   b. Security

   c. Privacy

   d. Content

6. After receiving your new Windows XP Professional computer, you notice that Outlook Express is your default newsreader. You prefer to use a different newsreader from a third-party vendor. You would like to make the third-party newsreader your default newsreader. Which tab is used to configure this feature?

    a. General

    b. Programs

    c. Advanced

    d. Content

Real-World Projects

You have just been given a new Windows XP Professional-based workstation. You need to configure Internet Explorer 6 according to the current needs and requirements of your organization. First, you would like to set the Home Page for Internet Explorer to be your company's intranet Web page, **intranet.helpandlearn.com**.

Project 18.1

To set the Home Page:

1. Select Start|Control Panel|Network And Internet Connections|Internet Options to configure Internet Explorer 6.

2. On the General tab, enter the FQDN of the intranet Web page (**intranet.helpandlearn.com**). Click OK.

3. Open Internet Explorer to verify the new Home Page setting. Select Start|Internet Explorer.

Your company's intranet Web site has a Web-based timesheet application. You need to use to this application to enter the projects that you have been working on and the number of hours you have been working on each. When you open Internet Explorer, your company's intranet Web page is displayed. You select the link to the timesheet application and it does not start. After talking with the help desk, you learn that the timesheet is an unsigned ActiveX control. You need to customize your configuration to allow this application to be run.

Project 18.2

To customize security settings in content zones:

1. Select Start|Control Panel|Network And Internet Connections|Internet Options to configure Internet Explorer 6.

2. On the Security tab, select the Local Intranet content zone.

3. Click Custom Level.

4. Under ActiveX Controls And Plug-ins, and then under Download Unsigned ActiveX Controls, change the setting from Disable to Enable. Click OK.

5. Click OK to close the Internet Explorer Properties dialog box.

6. Open Internet Explorer to verify that the timesheet ActiveX control is downloaded and accessible.

After filling out and saving your Web-based timesheet, you decide to browse some Internet news sites to catch up on the latest events. When you enter the address of your favorite news Web site, an error is displayed saying that the Web page could not be found. After calling the help desk, you learn that you need to configure Internet Explorer to use a proxy server to access the Internet.

Project 18.3

To specify the proxy server:

1. Select Start|Control Panel|Network And Internet Connections|Internet Options to configure Internet Explorer 6.

2. On the Connections tab, click the LAN Settings button.

3. Place a check next to Use A Proxy Server For Your LAN. Enter the IP address and port address for the proxy server. Also, place a check next to Bypass Proxy Server For Local Addresses. Click OK.

4. Click OK to close the Internet Explorer Properties dialog box.

5. Open Internet Explorer to verify that Internet Web sites are available.

CHAPTER NINETEEN

Remote Desktop and Remote Assistance

After completing this chapter, you will be able to:

✓ Describe what Remote Desktop is and how it is used

✓ Describe the Remote Desktop Protocol

✓ Demonstrate how to configure Remote Desktop

✓ Demonstrate how to configure Remote Desktop Web Connection

✓ Describe what Remote Assistance is and how it is used

✓ Demonstrate how to send an invitation for remote assistance

Remote Desktop and Remote Assistance are two new initiatives introduced in Windows XP Professional to provide access to remote clients. These tools are based on the Windows Terminal Services technology that uses the Remote Desktop Protocol (RDP) to provide access to remote computers. Even though the technology used by both tools is basically the same, the functionality of each is different. Remote Desktop provides access to a Windows session running on a remote computer. Remote Desktop basically is the replacement for the Windows Terminal client used in previous versions of Windows. Remote Assistance enables an IT professional or helper to connect to a remote user's computer to provide assistance via chat and remote control.

Remote Desktop Overview

Remote Desktop provides users with the capability to access their company or home Windows XP Professional computer from any Windows-based client. By using Remote Desktop, users who are traveling can access their home or company computer as if they were sitting at the computer console. If a user leaves an application open on their home computer, when they connect to it via Remote Desktop, they can see and use the application just as if they were seated at the console.

When a user remotely connects to their home computer using Remote Desktop, the computer is automatically locked so that no one locally can access the files or applications. To unlock the computer, the user uses the Ctrl+Alt+Delete key combination to open a security dialog box and enter their username and password just as they would if they were at the console. If Fast Switching is enabled, multiple users can still use the computer even if someone is accessing it through Remote Desktop.

Remote Desktop requires three things:

➤ A computer that is running Windows XP Professional with a connection to a LAN or the Internet

➤ A second computer running Remote Desktop Connection

➤ User accounts and permissions for those individuals who need access to the second computer

Remote Desktop works well with both high- and low-speed network connections. The actual applications that are being accessed are hosted on the remote computer. The only data that is transmitted over the network is keyboard, mouse, and display data.

Remote Desktop is based on Windows Terminal Services and replaces the Terminal Services client in previous versions of Windows. The features provided by this service are made available through RDP.

Note: *TCP port 3389 is used by clients accessing Remote Desktop. This is the standard port for RDP and Windows Terminal Services.*

Remote Desktop Protocol

RDP 5.1 is a multichannel protocol that is an extension of the T.120 protocol family standards. RDP allows for separate virtual channels for carrying communications data with encrypted mouse and keyboard data. The version of RDP that is included with Windows XP Professional for Remote Desktop includes several features, described next.

Print Redirection

When a user logs on to a computer using Remote Desktop, any local printer on that computer is detected by Windows XP Professional. Windows XP Professional provides two types of print redirection or access to the local printer: automatic and manual.

With automatic print redirection, when a user logs on to a remote computer using Remote Desktop Connection, any local printers attached to LPT, COM, or USB ports are automatically detected. A local queue is created on the local computer for processing print jobs. When the Remote Desktop session is terminated, the printer queue on the local computer is deleted. If there were print jobs in that queue, they will be lost.

If a print driver for the printer is not found, the local queue is not created and the print drivers have to manually be installed on the local computer. Manual redirection of printers is only supported on LPT and COM ports. Printers connected to the remote computer via USB ports cannot be manually redirected in Windows XP Professional. After a printer is manually redirected for the first time on the remote computer, it will automatically redirect itself on each subsequent logon by the user. They will only have to configure it for that initial session.

Printers that have been redirected appear in the Printers and Faxes folder in the Control Panel with the following format: *Client Printer Name/ Client Computer Name/ Session Number.*

Clipboard Mapping

The Clipboard data can be shared between the Remote Desktop computer and the client computer. Data can be cut and pasted and then shared between programs running on both computers. As is normally the case on a Windows computer, information is stored in the Clipboard temporarily until something else is written to it. This information can be viewed using the Clipboard Viewer, or Clipbrd.exe. The Clipboard Viewer can also be used to cut or copy text and graphics from within the Remote Desktop Connection windows to an application on the local computer.

Audio

Any audio being played by an application on the remote computer can be outputted to speakers on the local computer.

Port Redirection

Users who are connecting to a remote computer via Remote Desktop have access to serial and parallel ports on that computer.

Configuring Remote Desktop

Before a user can connect to their home or corporate computer via Remote Desktop, it must be configured for remote access. To configure your computer for Remote Desktop access, following these steps (see Figure 19.1):

1. Open the Control Panel.

2. Double-click System.

3. Select the Remote tab.

4. Select the Allow Users To Connect Remotely To This Computer checkbox.

5. Click the Select Remote Users button to select the appropriate permissions for access, and then click OK.

6. Click the Add button.

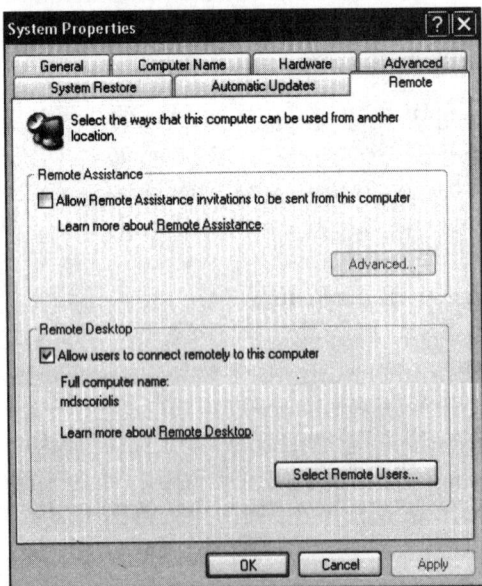

Figure 19.1 The Remote Desktop option on the System Properties dialog box.

7. Enter in the Enter The Object Names To Select box the names of the users who you want to have access, and then click OK.

8. Click OK to exit the Remote Desktop Users dialog box.

9. Click OK to exit the System Properties dialog box.

19

Connecting to a Computer

To access a remote computer using Remote Desktop, follow these steps:

1. Select Start|All Programs.

2. Select Accessories.

3. Select Communications.

4. Click Remote Desktop Connections.

5. Enter the IP address or the computer name of the computer you are trying to connect to in the Computer box.

6. Click Connect.

7. Enter the username and password in the Log On To Windows dialog box and then click OK.

Configuring Connection Settings

When setting up a Remote Desktop Connection, several connection settings can be configured and saved to enhance the remote sessions. These options are available from the Remote Desktop Connection dialog box by clicking the Options button (see Figure 19.2). When the user selects the Options button, the dialog box changes from a small window with just the Computer text box to a large window with multiple tabs. Each tab is discussed in turn in the following sections.

General

The General tab is used to enter the computer name or IP address of the remote client that the user is trying to access. In the Logon Settings section, users must enter a valid username and password for that computer. If the computer is a member of a domain, they must enter the domain name in the Domain box. The user's password can be saved for future sessions by clicking the Save My Password checkbox. In the Connection Settings section, a user can save their Remote Desktop Connection settings to a file. This file will end with an .rdp extension, which signifies that it is a Remote Desktop file. If the user has an existing connection setting file already saved, it can be opened by clicking the Open button. Users may want to have multiple Remote Desktop files for the different remote clients that they connect to.

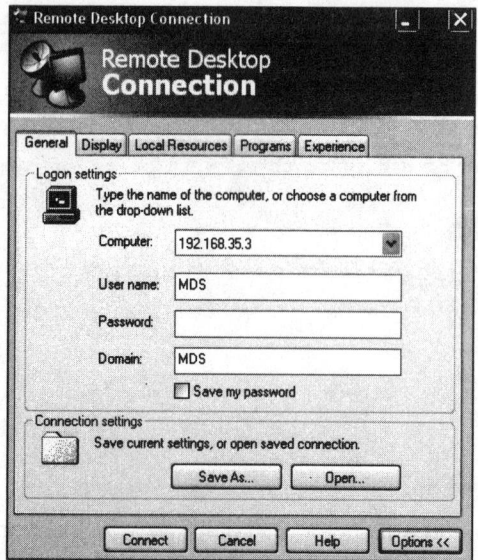

Figure 19.2 The connection settings that can be configured for Remote Desktop Connectons.

Display

The Display tab is used to control how the remote client's desktop will look when a connection is made. The first section, called Remote Desktop Size, is used to determine the overall size of the window. The second section is used to determine the color settings for the monitor. Remember that the selections that are available in this section will depend on the capabilities of the monitor. RDP 5.1 supports 15-bit, 16-bit, and 24-bit color depth when connected to a Windows XP computer. Also on the Display tab is a checkbox for displaying the Connection Bar, which can be used to minimize and maximize a full-screen Remote Desktop sessions window (see Figure 19.3).

Local Resources

The Local Resources tab is used to set audio and keyboard options. If the remote computer has sound capability, the Remote Desktop session can be configured to allow for the sound to be heard on the local computer that established the session. If the user does not want to hear audio from the remote client, they can select the Do Not Play option under Remote Computer Sound or the Leave At Remote Computer option, which will disable audio on the local computer but not on the remote client.

If the user does not want to hear audio from the remote client, they can select the Do Not Play option under Remote Computer Sound or the Leave At Remote Computer option, which will disable audio on the local computer but not on the remote client.

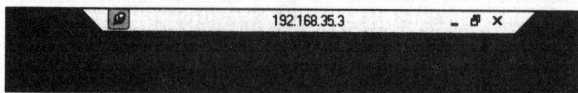

Figure 19.3 Connection Bar in a remote session.

The Keyboard section is used to configure Windows key combinations for the remote session. If On The Local Computer option is selected, all Windows key combinations will apply to the local desktop. If the On The Remote Computer option is selected, the key combinations will apply to the remote computer. If the In Full Screen Mode Only option is selected, the Windows key combinations will apply to the remote computer only when it is being viewed in Full Screen mode. If the user decides not to use the Windows key combinations during the Remote Desktop session, they can use the Terminal Server shortcut keys listed in Table 19.1.

The Local Resources tab is also used to automatically connect local devices when a connection is made to the remote computer. Local disk drivers, printers, and serial ports can all be configured to be available automatically when the Remote Desktop session is established.

Programs

The Program tab can be used to configure an application to run upon the establishment of a connection to the remote client.

Experience

The Experience tab is used to optimize the connection speed of the remote session. To improve performance, the highest possible speed should be selected for Remote Desktop Connection. The default speed for the initial connection is Modem (56 Kbps) speed. This selection should be sufficient for most network connections. The following additional characteristics can be specified if a higher-speed connection is used:

➤ Desktop background

➤ Show windows contents while dragging

➤ Menu fading and sliding

➤ Themes

➤ Bitmap caching

Table 19.1   Terminal Server shortcut keys that can be used in a Remote Desktop session.

Shortcut Key	Description
Alt+Page Up	Switches between programs from left to right
Alt+Page Down	Switches between programs from right to left
Alt+Insert	Cycles through the programs in the order they were started
Alt+Home	Displays the Start menu
Ctrl+Alt+Break	Switches the client between a window and full screen
Ctrl+Alt+End	Opens the Windows Security dialog box
Alt+Delete	Displays the Windows menu
Ctrl+Alt+- (minus symbol)	Places a snapshot of the active window, within the client, on the Terminal Server clipboard (provides the same functionality as pressing PrintScrn on a local computer)
Ctrl+Alt++ (plus symbol)	Places a snapshot of the entire client window area on the Terminal Server clipboard (provides the same functionality as pressing Alt+PrintScrn on a local computer)

When a user initially connects to a computer using the Remote Desktop Connection, all of the default settings are saved on the local computer in a file called Default.rdp.

Accessing Local Files on a Remote Session

When a user establishes a remote session, they can access local drives just as they would be able to if they were seated at the computer console. To access local drives, the Disk Drives option must be selected under Local Devices on the Local Resources tab. When this option is selected, Windows XP Professional will flash a security warning asking whether you want to connect the local drives on the remote computer. If you do not want to see this warning every time you connect, click the Don't Prompt Me Again For Connections To This Remote Computer checkbox.

Local files can be accessed through Windows Explorer within the Remote Desktop session or from a command prompt. The local drives will be displayed in Windows Explorer in the format *driver letter* on *tsclient*, wherein *tsclient* is the remote computer that is being accessed (see Figure 19.4).

Terminating a Remote Session

Users who have established a remote session can terminate the session in one of two ways. They can log off and disconnect from the remote computer or disconnect from the remote computer without logging off. If the user disconnects from the remote computer without logging off, they will automatically be reconnected to their session when they reconnect.

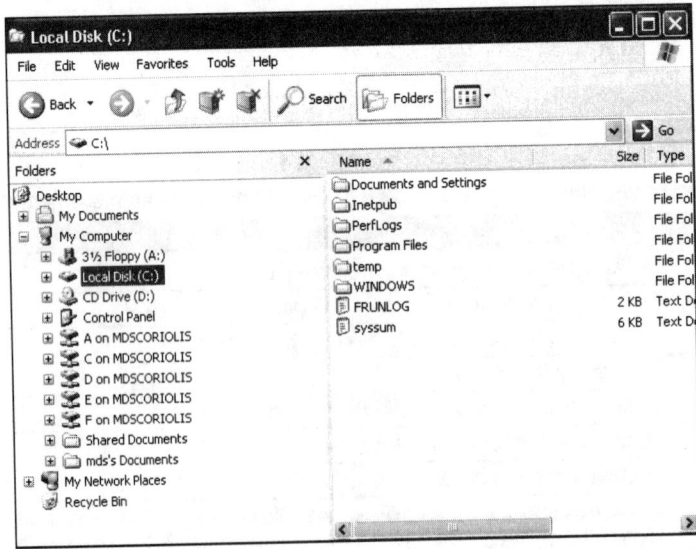

Figure 19.4 Local drives on a remote session.

To log off and disconnect from a remote session:

1. Select Start from the Remote Desktop Connection windows.

2. Select Log Off.

3. Windows XP Professional will display a dialog box asking if you are sure that you want to log off. Click the Log Off button.

To log off without disconnecting from a remote session:

1. Select Start from the Remote Desktop Connection windows.

2. Select Disconnect.

3. Windows XP Professional will display a dialog box asking if you are sure that you want to disconnect. Click the Disconnect button.

When you log back in to the remote computer, you will automatically be reconnected to your session.

You can also disconnect from the remote computer by clicking the X on the Connection Bar. Any programs that were running on the remote computer will continue to run, and you will be reconnected to your session when you log on again (see Figure 19.5).

Installing Remote Desktop Connection on a 32-bit Computer

Remote Desktop Connection replaces the Terminal Services Client that was used in previous versions of Windows. This client can be installed on Windows 95, 98, NT 4.0, and 2000 computers to allow access to a remote computer. To install the client, follow these steps:

1. Insert the Windows XP Professional CD into the 32-bit computer.

2. Select Perform Additional Tasks.

3. Select Set Up Remote Desktop Connection. The Remote Desktop Connection InstallShield Wizard will start. Click Next.

4. Select I Accept The Terms In The License Agreement and click Next.

5. Enter a username and organization.

6. Select to allow anyone who has access to use the Remote Desktop Connection or only for yourself and click Next.

7. Click Install to install the files.

8. Click Finish when the installation finishes.

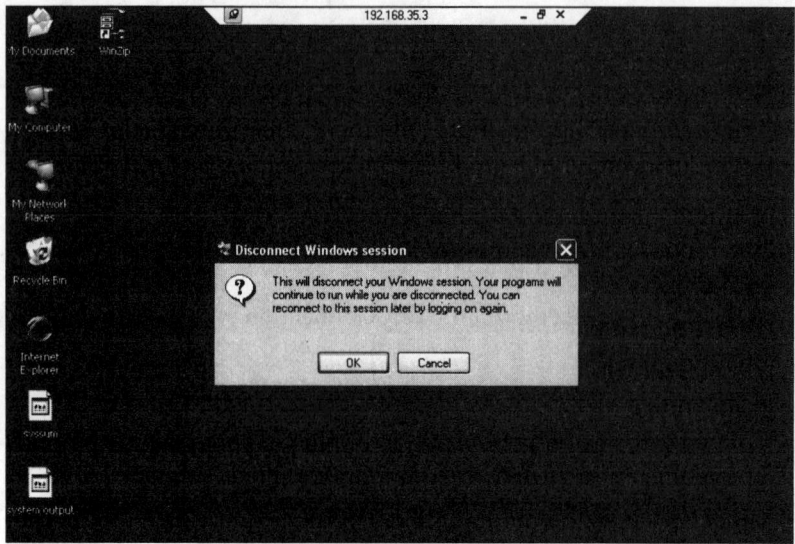

Figure 19.5 Disconnecting from a remote session using the Connection Bar.

You can now access Remote Desktop Connection by selecting Start | Programs | Accessories | Communications | Remote Desktop Connection. Enter the IP or computer name of the computer you are trying to connect to and then click Connect.

Remote Desktop Web Connection

Remote Desktop Web Connection provides the capability for users to connect to a remote computer using Internet Explorer. It consists of an Active X control and sample ASP pages. To use Remote Desktop Web Connection, IIS must be installed on the Windows XP Professional computer that is being configured for remote access.

By installing Remote Desktop Web Connection, users can access their remote computer from any Windows-based system that is running Internet Explorer. The local computer does not have to have Remote Desktop Connection installed to make a connection to the remote computer. The user can load Internet Explorer and type in the URL for the remote computer to establish a session.

To make a connection to a computer running Remote Desktop Web Connection:

1. Start Internet Explorer.

2. In the Address box, type in the URL for the remote computer and press Enter. This is typed in the format http://*remote computer name*/tsweb.

3. You will be prompted to enter the server name and to select the size of the window resolution for the connection. The default resolution is Full-screen (see Figure 19.6).

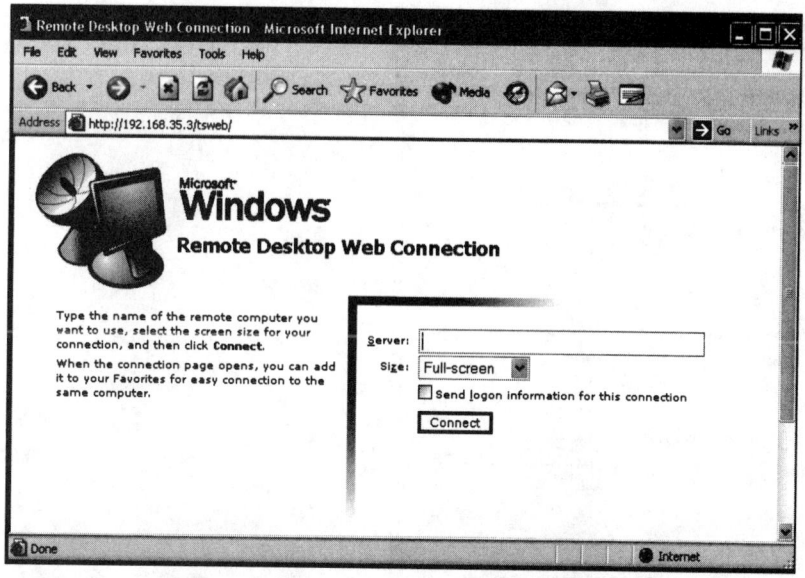

Figure 19.6 Remote Desktop Web Connection through Internet Explorer.

4. Click the Connect button to establish the remote session.

5. Enter the username and password and click OK.

Note: Some type of name resolution service, such as WINS, needs to be installed on the client computer before the user will be able to connect to the remote client. Also, Remote Desktop Web Connection requires Internet Explorer version 4.0 or higher.

Remote Assistance

Remote Assistance is a new tool introduced in Windows XP Professional that is used to assist individuals who may be having problems and need help. Remote Assistance, like Remote Desktop and Fast Switching, is based on Windows Terminal Services technology. When a user needs help, they can request assistance from a coworker or IT professional via Remote Assistance. The IT professional or helper can connect to the computer that is having problems and view the screen directly to aid in problem resolution.

Before a user can use Remote Assistance, it must be configured as follows (see Figure 19.7):

1. Open the Control Panel.

2. Double-click System.

3. Select the Remote tab.

4. Select the Allow Remote Assistance Invitations To Be Sent From This Computer checkbox.

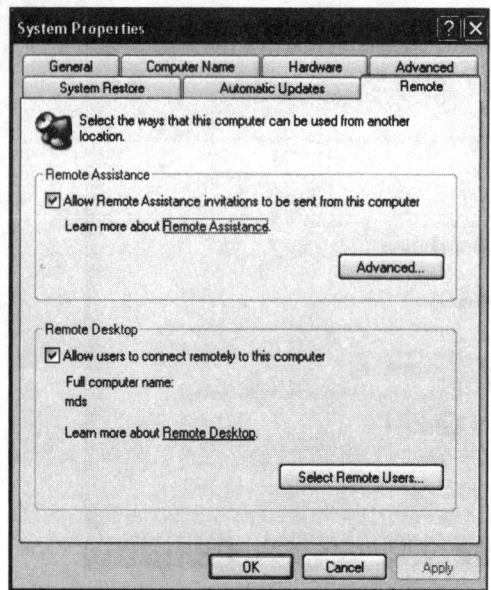

Figure 19.7   The Remote Assistance option in the System Properties dialog box.

5. Click the Advanced button to go to the Remote Assistance Settings dialog box.

6. Select the Allow This Computer To Be Controlled Remotely checkbox.

7. You can set the maximum amount of time that invitations can remain open under the Invitations section.

8. Click OK to exit the Remote Assistance Settings dialog box.

9. Click OK to exit the System Properties dialog box.

Several ways are available to request help when using Remote Assistance. An invitation for help can be sent via Windows Messenger, any MAPI-compliant email program, or a file located on a shared folder on the remote computer.

Windows Messenger

The faster way to request help is by using Windows Messenger. A user who needs help can select Tools|Ask For Remote Assistance (see Figure 19.8). They then select the email address of the Windows Messenger individual who they are requesting help from. This individual will receive an invitation as an instant message. They can accept the invitation and start the Remote Assistance session.

Email

Users needing help can send an email request via any MAPI-compliant email program, such as Outlook or Outlook express. The user enters their name in the From text box and enters a message with the problem they are having in the Message text box (see Figure 19.9). The

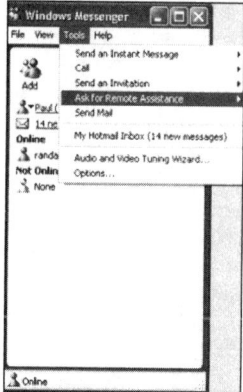

Figure 19.8   Requesting Remote Assistance in Windows Messenger.

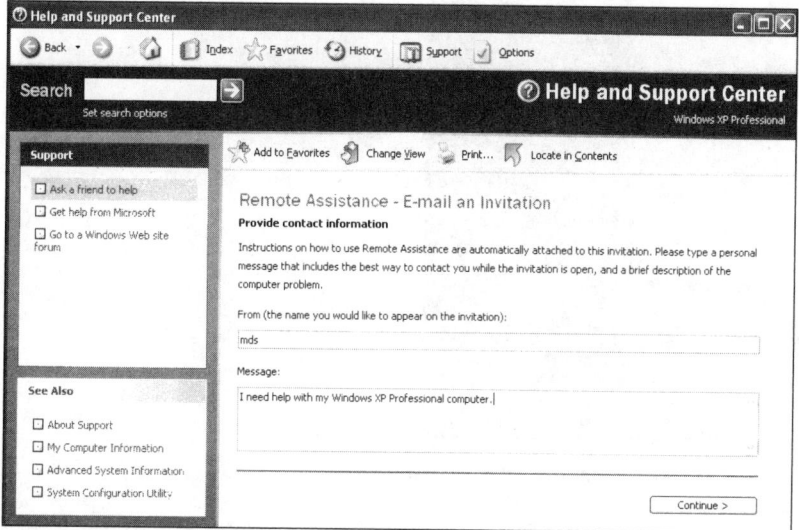

Figure 19.9   Requesting help via an email invitation in Remote Assistance.

user then clicks the Continue button and is taken to a page that is used to determine how long a recipient can accept an invitation before it expires. This page can also be used to require that the recipient enter a password before the invitation will be accepted. They then click the Send Invitation button to send the invitation to the helper.

Saved File

An invitation to request help can be saved to a file and attached to an email message. It can also be copied to a shared folder on the computer of the user who is requesting the help. The file is named RAInvitation.msrcincident. When the recipient double-clicks the file, the Remote Assistance Invitation dialog box opens. The recipient enters the password (if one is required) and clicks Yes (see Figure 19.10).

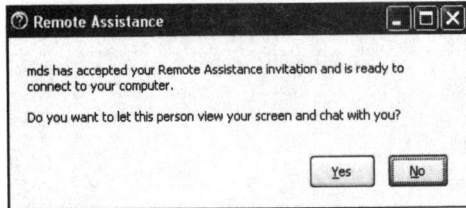

Figure 19.10   Remote Assistance Invitation file dialog box.

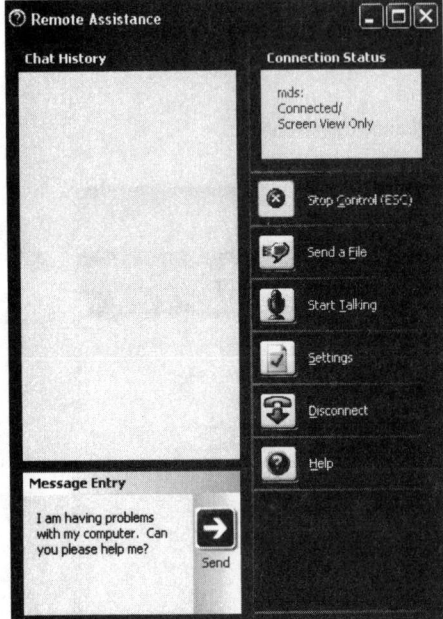

Figure 19.11   Remote Assistance Chat dialog box.

When a remote session is established, the user who requested help will see a Remote Assistance Chat dialog box (see Figure 19.11). This dialog box enables the user to communicate their problem in real time to the IT professional who is helping them.

The dialog box has three sections. The first section, Chat History, displays the chat text that has been sent between the two users. The second section, called Message Entry, is used to input text that is sent to the remote helper. The user does this by inputting the text and then clicking the Send button. The third section, on the right side of the dialog box, has several buttons. The Stop Control (ESC) button is used to terminate mouse and keyboard control of the helper. The Send A File button opens a dialog box that can be used to locate a file that can be sent to the helper. If both computers have audio capability, the Start Talking button can be used to initiate an audio session between the two computers. The Settings button is

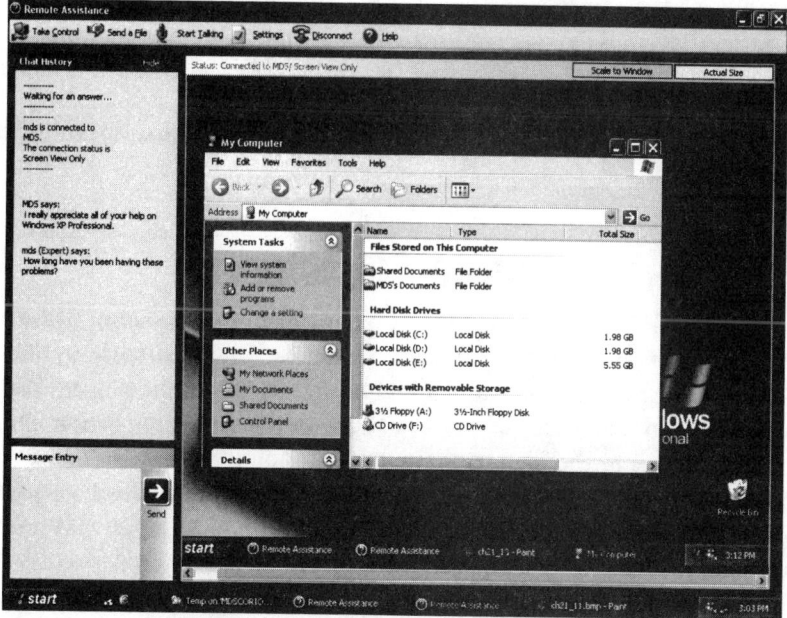

Figure 19.12 Remote Assistance windows for the helper.

used to configure the sound and video quality for the session. The Disconnect button is used to terminate the Remote Assistance session.

Figure 19.12 shows the Remote Assistance window that the helper sees when connected to a Remote Assistance Session. This window has all the sections that are included in the Remote Client Chat window plus a large window that displays the desktop of the remote client. From this window, the helper can move around the remote computer as if they were seated at the console. Instead of a Stop Control button, the helper window has a Take Control button. This button enables the helper to take control of the keyboard and mouse functions on the remote client.

After the helper is given access to the remote desktop, both users still have access to the keyboard and mouse at the same time. Only one user should try to control the computer at a time. The user requesting help can terminate the helper's control at any time by clicking the Stop Control button in their Remote Assistance window.

For added security, several key features are implemented in Remote Assistance to protect against unauthorized access:

➤ The user who is sending an invitation to request help can require that a password be provided before the helper can connect to the session. This is normally enabled by default.

➤ When an invitation is initiated from the remote client, an XML-based encrypted ticket is sent to the helper. This ticket can only be decoded and used by the target recipient.

➤ The duration of the remote session is based on a time specified by the user who is requesting help. The default period for this is one hour, but it can be as short as a minute or as long as 99 days.

➤ All authentication information for a remote session is deleted when the remote session expires.

Group Policy and Remote Assistance

If the Windows XP Professional computer is part of a domain, Group Policy can be used to enable helpers or IT professionals to offer Remote Assistance to individuals without a request from them for it (see Figure 19.13). When the helper tries to connect to the remote client, the user can allow or deny the connection. The helper cannot attach to the remote computer unannounced nor can they control the desktop without the user's permission. If the Offer Remote Assistance Group Policy is enabled, two options can be configured. The helper can be allowed to remotely control the remote computer, or they can be allowed only to view the desktop, without the ability to control the keyboard and mouse.

This policy can also be used to specify which users or groups of users can offer remote assistance

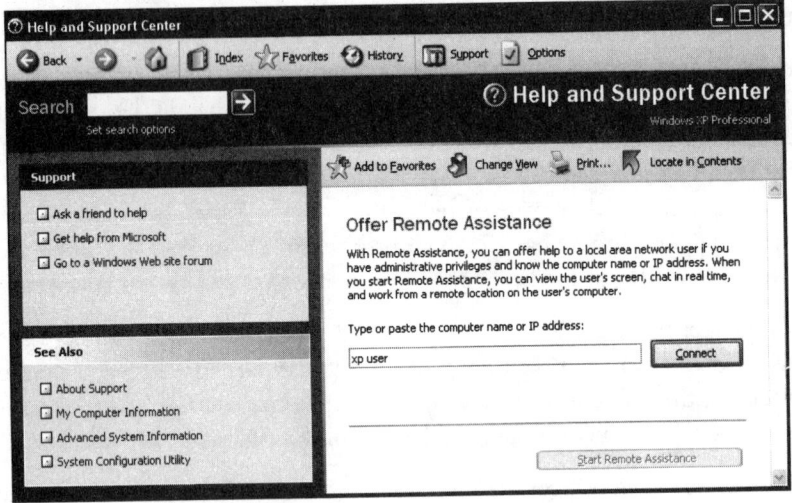

Figure 19.13 Offer Remote Assistance in the Help and Support Center.

Remote Desktop and Remote Assistance Differences

19

Even though both Remote Desktop and Remote Assistance are based on Windows Terminal Services, they do have several distinguishing features:

➤ When a user connects to a computer using Remote Desktop, they do so by establishing a new session. When a user connects to a computer using Remote Assistance, they are connecting to an existing session.

➤ When using Remote Assistance, both the helper and the individual who is requesting help must be present at their computers.

➤ When using Remote Assistance, both computers must be running Windows XP Professional.

Chapter Summary

This chapter looked at two tools introduced in Windows XP Professional, Remote Desktop and Remote Assistance. Both of these tools are based on the Windows Terminal Services technology. Remote Desktop provides users with the capability to access their home or corporate computers remotely. When a Remote Desktop Connection session is established to the remote computer, the user can use the mouse and keyboard just as if they were seated at the console.

To use Remote Desktop, three things are required: a computer running Windows XP Professional with a LAN or Internet connection, a second computer running Remote Desktop Connection, and user accounts and permissions for accessing the second, or remote, computer.

Remote Desktop uses the Remote Desktop Protocol to provide remote access services. This protocol includes features such as printer and port redirection, clipboard mapping, and audio. When a user establishes a session to a remote computer, they can access local drives and files just as they could if seated in front of the computer console.

Remote Desktop Web Connection allows a remote computer to be accessed over the Internet via Internet Explorer. The local computer that is trying to make the connection to the remote client does not have to have Remote Desktop Connection installed to establish the remote session. The user can load Internet Explorer and type in the URL for the remote computer that they need to use.

Remote Assistance is based on the same technology as Remote Desktop Connection but has a different function. Remote Assistance is used by Windows XP Professional users to request help from "helpers" or IT professionals who have been designated to provide support. These requests can be sent via Windows Messenger, an email program such as Outlook, or a file saved to a share on the remote computer. After a helper accepts the invitation to provide help, their screen shows the remote computer's desktop. If the user requesting help allows it, the helper can take control of the desktop's mouse and keyboard and use them to aid in the problem resolution.

Review Questions

1. Remote Desktop is based on what Windows technology?

   a. Active Directory

   b. EFS

   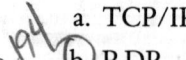 c. Terminal Services

   d. Group Policy

2. What is the protocol used for providing Remote Desktop services in Windows XP Professional?

   a. TCP/IP

   b. RDP

   c. IPX/SPX

   d. MS-CHAP

3. Rondy needs to connect to his home computer using Remote Desktop to get some information from files he was working on last night. He wants to cut and paste some information from the files to an application he has open on the local computer he is currently working on. Rondy has the capability to cut and paste information from the remote computer using Remote Desktop. True or False?

   a. True

   b. False

4. Josh has created several Remote Desktop Connection settings that he saved to his hard drive. For some reason, he cannot seem to find the location where he saved them. What file type or extension should Josh search for on his computer to locate the configuration files for the Remote Desktop Connections?

   a. .txt

   b. .exe

   c. .rdp

   d. .cmd

497

5. Sally is setting up her home computer to run Remote Desktop Connection so that she can access it from her office. She wants Microsoft Word to be started automatically every time she establishes a remote session to her home computer. Where can she configure this?

   a. On the Programs tab of the Remote Desktop Connection dialog box.

   b. On the General tab of the Remote Desktop Connection dialog box.

   c. On the Local Resources tab of the Remote Desktop Connection dialog box.

   d. On the Experience tab of the Remote Desktop Connection dialog box.

499

6. Hattie wants to be able to listen to the audio on a remote computer that she is connecting to via Remote Desktop Connection. What option should she select to enable her to hear the audio on the speakers on her local computer?

   a. She should select the Display The Connection Bar When In Full Screen Mode checkbox on the Display tab of the Remote Desktop dialog box.

   b. She should select Bring To This Computer under Remote Computer Sound on the Local Resources tab of the Remote Desktop Connection dialog box.

   c. She should select Leave At Remote Computer under Remote Computer Sound on the Local Resources tab of the Remote Desktop Connection dialog box.

   d. She cannot listen to audio from a remote computer when connected via a Remote Desktop Connection.

7. Both local hard and floppy drives can be accessed when a user is connected to a remote computer with Remote Desktop Connection. True or False?

   a. True

   b. False

8. Benson has a Windows NT 4.0 machine that he uses at work. He would like to connect to his Windows XP Professional computer at home so that he can access a project he was working on. How can he establish a remote session to his Windows XP Professional computer?

    a. Benson can load Remote Desktop Connection on his NT 4.0 workstation and use it to connect to his Windows XP Professional computer at home.

    b. Benson can use Telnet to connect to his Windows XP Professional computer.

    c. Benson can load a third-party remote connection program to make the connection.

    d. Benson can configure the Call Back feature on his Windows XP Professional and have it connect to his Windows NT 4.0 workstation at the office.

9. What tool will allow a user to connect to a Windows XP Professional computer using Internet Explorer?

    a. Remote Desktop Web Connection

    b. Telnet

    c. RRAS

    d. IntelliMirror

10. Jill needs to request help from the IT technical staff for her Windows XP Professional computer. She has Windows Messenger installed on her computer and has been told that she can request help from the IT staff from it. What option should Jill select to request help for her computer?

    a. She should select Send Mail.

    b. She should select Send An Instant Message.

    c. She should select Send An Invitation.

    d. She should select Ask For Remote Assistance from the Tools menu.

11. Which of the following Group Policy features can be enabled to allow IT professionals or "helpers" to offer help to users on their network?

    a. Allow configuration of connection sharing

    b. Offer Remote Assistance

    c. Solicited Remote Assistance

    d. Turn off Resultant Set of Policy logging

12. When a user connects to a computer that is running Remote Desktop Connection, any printers that are connected to the LPT or COM ports will be automatically detected. True or False?

495

    a. True

    b. False

13. What item is displayed on the remote computer desktop during a session that can be used to minimize and maximize the remote session windows?

    a. Control Panel

498   b. My Computer

    c. Taskbar

    d. Connection Bar

14. Sam disconnects from a remote session he has established to his Windows XP Professional home computer without logging off. When he reconnects to the computer, his session will be reestablished. True or False?

501

    a. True

    b. False

15. What is required on a Windows XP Professional computer before Remote Desktop Web Connection can be installed on it?

    a. Certificate Services

502   b. Cluster Services

    c. Internet Information Services

    d. Message Queuing Services

Real-World Projects

William is the system administrator for a company that provides insurance services to several large corporations. It has recently upgraded its network to Windows 2000 from Windows NT. It has decided to upgrade all of its company workstations from Windows 98 and NT 4.0 to Windows XP Professional.

Several of the top staff members work from both home and the office. Windows XP computers have been installed at both locations for these workers. William realizes that he has an incredible task ahead of him, because many of the users have not used Windows 2000 or Windows XP before. A lot of them have limited knowledge of Windows 98 and NT. William wants to utilize the tools provided in Windows XP to ease the transition from the older Windows workstations to this new XP operating system. He wants to give the staff members the capability to access their computers at home from their workstations at the office. He also wants to be able to remotely provide support to users when they need it.

Project 19.1

To configure Remote Desktop to automatically connect to local drives when a remote session is established:

1 Select Start|All Programs.

2. Select Remote Desktop.

3. Click the Options button.

4. Select the Local Resources tab.

5. Under Local Devices, check the Disk Drives checkbox and click Connect.

6. Click OK when the Security Warning dialog box appears.

Project 19.2

To create a Remote Connections settings file and save it to your local hard disk:

1 Select Start|All Programs.

2. Select Remote Desktop.

3. Click the Options button.

4. Select the Display tab.

5. Uncheck the Display The Connection Bar When In Full Screen Mode checkbox.

6. Select the Local Resources tab.

7. Under Keyboard, select On The Local Computer.

8. Under Local Devices, select the Disk Drives and Printers checkboxes. Select the Experience tab.

9. Select the Show Contents Of Window While Dragging checkbox.

10. Select the Themes checkbox.

11. Select the Bitmap Caching checkbox.

12. Select the General tab.

13. Click the Save As button.

14. Select the location to save the file in the Save In text box.

15. Enter a name for the file in the File Name text box and click Save.

Project 19.3

To install IIS on the client computer so that it can be accessed with Remote Desktop Web Connection:

1. Log on as Administrator or as a user with administrative privileges.

2. Open the Control Panel.

3. Double-click Add Or Remove Programs.

4. Click Add/Remove Windows Components.

5. Select Internet Information Services (IIS) and click Details.

6. Select World Wide Web Service under Subcomponents Of Internet Information Services (IIS) and click Details.

7. Under Subcomponents Of World Wide Web Service, click Remote Desktop Web Connection and click OK.

8. Click OK and then click Next. The installation of IIS is started. You may have to insert the Windows XP Professional CD to continue the installation.

9. Click the Finish button and then click Close to exit from Add or Remove Programs.

10. From within the Control Panel, double-click Administrative Tools.

11. Double-click Internet Information Services.

12. Double-click Add Or Remove Programs.

13. Click the plus sign (+) by the local computer name to expand it.

14. Click the plus sign by Web Sites to expand it.

15. Click the plus sign by Default Web Site to expand it.

16. Right-click tsweb and select Properties.

17. Select the Directory Security tab.

18. Click Edit under Anonymous Access And Authentication Control.

19. Check the Anonymous Access checkbox under Authentication Methods and click OK.

20. Click OK again to close the tsweb Properties dial box.

21. Exit from Internet Information Services.

Project 19.4

To create a Remote Assistance file and store it in a shared folder for helper access:

1. Create a shared folder on your local computer and name it "RemoteAccess".

2. Select Start | All Programs.

3. Select Remote Assistance.

4. Click Invite Someone To Help You under Remote Assistance.

5. Select Save Invitation As A File (Advanced).

6. Enter your name in the From text box.

7. Set a duration for the invitation under Set The Invitation To Expire and then click Continue.

8. Make sure that the Require The Recipient To Use A Password checkbox is checked.

9. Enter a password and click Save Invitation.

10. Select the shared folder you created in step 1 and click Save.

Project 19.5

To configure Local Group Policy to allow helpers to offer remote assistance:

1. Select Start | Run.

2. Type "gpedit.msc" in the Run dialog box and then click OK.

3. Click the plus sign (+) by Computer Configuration.

4. Click the plus sign by Administrative Templates.

5. Click the plus sign by System.

6. Select Remote Assistance.

7. Double-click Offer Remote Assistance.

8. Click Enabled under the Settings tab.

9. Select Allow Helpers To Remotely Control The Computer under Permit Remote Control of this computer.

10. Click the Show button.

11. Click the Add button.

12. Enter the name for the helpers who will be providing remote assistance and then click OK after each entry.

13. Click OK to close the Show Contents dialog box.

14 Click OK to close the Offer Remote Assistance Properties dialog box.

15. Exit from Group Policy.

19

Sample Test

Question 1

You are the network administrator for a large financial company. You need to prepare 100 Windows XP Professional computers. These computers will be distributed to the regional field offices. You have learned that there are several non-Plug and Play hardware devices in each computer. What sysprep.exe command-line option should be used to prepare the machines for disk imaging?

- O a. **Sysprep.exe -quiet**
- O b. **Sysprep.exe-forceshutdown**
- O c. **Sysprep.exe -pnp**
- O d. **Sysprep.exe -nosidgen**

Question 2

Of the following file types, which cannot be encrypted using EFS (Encrypting File System)?

- O a. Word files
- O b. Bitmaps
- O c. Compressed files
- O d. XML files

Question 3

David just purchased a new internal cable modem from his local computer store. The documentation that comes with the modem states that it is Plug and Play. Following the directions in the manual, David proceeds to physically install the modem into his Windows XP Professional computer. What else does David need to do to start using the modem?

○ a. Install the driver

○ b. Run the Plug and Play Manager

○ c. Have the computer detect the new hardware

○ d. Nothing

Question 4

Caroline needs to add another volume to her Windows XP Professional workstation. Unfortunately, Caroline's network environment requires the use of many mapped drives. Therefore, her workstation has no drive letters available. How can Caroline still add this volume to her workstation?

○ a. By adding a Volume Mount Point to her NTFS drive

○ b. By removing a mapped drive

○ c. By adding a Volume Mount Point to her FAT32 drive

○ d. By adding a Volume Mount Point to her FAT drive

Question 5

You need to manage disk storage on a group of computers located in a data center in San Diego. You are located in New York. Of the following, to which groups do you need to be a member? [Check all correct answers]

❑ a. Power Users

❑ b. Server Operators

❑ c. Computer Operators

❑ d. Administrators

Question 6

You are attempting to access resources on a TCP/IP-based network. You are not able to connect to any other computers. You are not sure if DHCP is related to the problem. To rule out DHCP, you want to obtain a new IP address from the DHCP server. What commands allow you to receive a new IP address? [Check all correct answers]

❑ a. **ipconfig /registerdns**

❑ b. **winipcfg /renew**

❑ c. **ipconfig**

❑ d. **ipconfig /renew**

20

Question 7

Colleen is the network administrator for a large corporation. Her company has recently acquired a smaller company whose network uses both Windows 2000 and Novell NetWare 4.11 servers. Although the management of the company wants employees to access the data on the NetWare servers, they do not want another network client deployed. What should Colleen do?

○ a. Install Client Services for NetWare on all computers

○ b. Install a Windows XP Professional computer with Gateway (and Client) Services for NetWare

○ c. Install a Windows 2000 Server with Gateway (and Client) Services for NetWare

○ d. Migrate all NetWare data to Windows 2000 Servers

Question 8

Convert the IP address, 192.168.12.10 to binary.

○ a. 11000000.10101000.00001100.00001010

○ b. 11000000.00010101.00110000.11101000

○ c. 10100011.10010001.10110000.10101000

○ d. 11000000.10010111.10100111.11010011

Question 9

You need to access data on a Windows 2000 Server with the IP address of 192.168.1.210. Your Windows XP Professional computer is configured with the IP address 192.168.5.64 and the subnet mask 255.255.255.0. Is the Windows 2000 Server located on your local subnet or a remote subnet?

○ a. Local

○ b. Remote

Question 10

You are the network administrator for a medium-sized company. You need to automate the installation of Windows XP Professional for approximately 500 laptops. These laptops have already been distributed to sales representatives across the United States. You need to create a customized Windows XP Professional compact disc that will be distributed to all sales representatives. What else must you distribute with each CD for the installation to be successful?

○ a. A floppy disk with the winnt.cmd file

○ b. A floppy disk with the UDF file

○ c. A floppy disk with the answer.txt file

○ d. A floppy disk with the winnt.sif file

Question 11

You have been told by a friend about a cool new feature in Windows XP called Fast User Switching. You would like to check out this feature on your office computer, but it is not available. Why?

○ a. The network administrator has disabled the feature.

○ b. Your computer is configured as a member of a workgroup.

○ c. Fast User Switching is available only in Windows XP Home Edition.

○ d. Your computer is configured as a member of a domain.

Question 12

When using the CHAP authentication protocol, when is a user's password transmitted across the network?

○ a. During the challenge

○ b. During the response

○ c. During both challenge and response

○ d. Never

20

Question 13

Your Windows XP Professional computer is configured with the IP address 210.169.8.12 and the subnet mask 255.255.248.0. On what subnet is your computer located?

○ a. 210.0.0.0

○ b. 210.169.0.0

○ c. 210.169.4.0

○ d. 210.169.8.0

Question 14

In Windows XP Professional, which protocol is used to access files on a Windows 2000 Server from across the network?

○ a. NCP

○ b. CIFS

○ c. IPX

○ d. IP

Question 15

From the following list, which authentication protocol is considered the most secure?

○ a. PAP

○ b. MS-CHAP

○ c. SPAP

○ d. MS-CHAPv2

○ e. EAP

○ f. CHAP

Question 16

You are a consultant to a company that wants to deploy Windows XP Professional on all its desktops. One project requirement is to remotely install Windows XP Professional. You decide to have desktops boot directly from the network card and perform the install from the RIS server. To use this solution, what must the network card support?

○ a. PXE

○ b. Ethernet

○ c. TCP/IP

○ d. PCI

Question 17

What is the minimum amount of RAM required to install Windows XP Professional?

○ a. 32MB

○ b. 64MB

○ c. 128MB

○ d. 256MB

Question 18

You need to connect to the NetWare 4.11 server MARKETING_DATA. This server is using NDS for user authentication. How does Client Services for NetWare need to be configured? [Check all correct answers]

❑ a. Default Tree

❑ b. Context

❑ c. Preferred Server

❑ d. NDS Name

20

Question 19

You need to perform a backup of your Windows XP Professional workstation. You also want to back up the Registry files. What do you need to do?

○ a. Boot using the installation CD-ROM and then copy the Registry files to a floppy disk.

○ b. Perform a backup using the Backup utility and select the System State.

○ c. Export the Registry files to a comma-delimited text file, and then copy the Registry files to a floppy disk.

○ d. Boot the system in Safe Mode, and then use the Backup Registry option.

Question 20

You have recently been issued a Windows XP computer. You have attended a 5-day technical class on Windows XP. In which tool do you configure and administer disk storage space in Windows XP Professional?

○ a. In the Computer Management Console, Disk Management

○ b. In the Computer Management Console, Disk Administrator

○ c. In the Control Panel, Disk Management

○ d. In the Control Panel, Disk Administrator

Question 21

From the following list, identify the network protocols supported by Windows XP. Next, place each characteristic in one of three groups with its corresponding network protocol.

   a. TCP/IP

   b. Internet

   c. NWLink

   d. Novell NetWare

   e. Small Networks

   f. Non-routable

   g. MAC Address used for host address

   h. No error correction

   i. Highly configurable

   j. DNS

   k. NetBEUI

   l. SAP

Question 22

The administrator for your network has sent you, via email, a HOSTS file and an LMHOSTS file. She wants you to use these files until she resolves some DNS and WINS issues. Where do these files need to be placed for your Windows XP Professional workstation to use them?

   ○ a. %systemroot%\system32

   ○ b. %systemroot%\system32\tcpip

   ○ c. %systemroot%\system32\drivers\etc

   ○ d. %systemroot%\

Question 23

You are responsible for desktop technical support for your company. A company executive has come to you with a major problem. His laptop won't boot up and his presentation to the CEO is located on the laptop's hard drive. His presentation is in two hours. After troubleshooting, you suspect that the boot sector on the system partition is damaged. Using the Recovery Console, what command allows you to create a new boot sector?

- ○ a. fixmbr
- ○ b. fixbootsector
- ○ c. fixboot
- ○ d. sys

20

Question 24

Sally is an administrative assistant in a large legal firm. She has several Windows 98 applications that she uses daily. Her computer has been recently upgraded to Windows XP Professional. Sally has noticed that the applications do not seem to run properly under the new operating system. How can Sally continue to use the Windows 98 applications without having to uninstall Windows XP Professional?

- ○ a. Sally could contact the maker of the application for the version that is compatible with Windows XP Professional.
- ○ b. Sally can download a patch for the application from the developer's Web site.
- ○ c. Sally can use the Windows 98 applications by using the Application Compatibility Wizard in Windows XP Professional.
- ○ d. Sally will not be able to use the applications with her Windows XP Professional computer.

Question 25

The manager of your department has assigned you the role of Deployment Engineer. You would like to install Windows XP Professional on 1,200 workstations. You would also like to automate the install on all the computers. What do you need to use to give each workstation a unique computer name? [Check all correct answers]

- ❑ a. UDF
- ❑ b. PXE
- ❑ c. UNATTEND.TXT
- ❑ d. RIS

Question 26

You have been assigned a Windows XP Professional laptop. In the office, you connect to the network that has Windows 2000 and Novell NetWare 4.11 servers. You are told that most of the data you need is located on the Windows 2000 servers. The NetWare servers are being migrated to Windows 2000. When connecting remotely, you only require access to a Windows 2000 Server running Exchange Server for email. From the following list, select the correct binding order to achieve maximum performance for your remote connection.

○ a. Local Area Connection, TCP/IP

○ b. Local Area Connection, TCP/IP, NWLink

○ c. Remote Connection, TCP/IP

○ d. Remote Connection, TCP/IP, NWLink

Question 27

Your company, a large media company, has decided to upgrade all desktop and laptop computers to Windows XP Professional. They are currently using Windows NT 4 Workstation. Instead of upgrading, they decided to purchase new computers to take advantage of some of the new multimedia features that are provided with Windows XP. What tool in Windows XP Professional can be used to easily transfer employee files and settings from the older computers to the new Windows XP workstations?

○ a. User State Migration Tool

○ b. Add/Remove Profiles

○ c. Remote Assistance

○ d. Removable Profiles

Question 28

What is the minimum amount of free disk space required to install Windows XP Professional?

○ a. 650MB

○ b. 2.2GB

○ c. 1.5GB

○ d. 128MB

Question 29

You need to manage network shares on a group of remote computers located in Seattle. Of which groups do you need to be a member? [Check all correct answers]

○ a. Power Users

○ b. Server Operators

○ c. Computer Operators

○ d. Administrators

20

Question 30

From the following list, select the steps that are used in NetBIOS name resolution. Next, arrange the steps in the order in which they occur. The computer where name resolution is occurring is configured as an h-node. Also, it is configured to use DNS and LMHOSTS for NetBIOS name resolution.

○ a. Query WINS servers

○ b. Check local HOSTS file

○ c. Query DNS servers

○ d. Check the NetBIOS name cache

○ e. Send a remote broadcast

○ f. Send a local broadcast

○ g. Clear NetBIOS name cache

○ h. Check local LMHOSTS file

Question 31

You are the head of network security for your company. You suspect that unauthorized people are attempting to hack into the network. You have requested that the network administrators enable auditing for unsuccessful logon attempts. After enabling it, where can you view the results?

○ a. Event Viewer, System Log

○ b. Event Viewer, Security Log

○ c. System Monitor, Audit Log

○ d. System Monitor, System Log

Question 32

Marshall is attempting to connect to a couple of NetWare servers on the network. One NetWare server, NWSRV1, is a NetWare 3.11 file server. The other NetWare server, NWSRV2, is a NetWare 4.11 file server. What does Marshall need to install and configure to access these file servers? [Check all correct answers]

❏ a. Client Services for NetWare

❏ b. NWLink

❏ c. Frametype 802.2

❏ d. Frametype 802.3

Question 33

You are the network administrator for your company. You are reviewing data that was created from a log file in System Monitor. You would like to export this data to another program so you can present the data to people throughout your company. What file types can be used to export this data? [Check all correct answers]

❏ a. .doc (Word)

❏ b. .html (Web page)

❏ c. .xls (Excel)

❏ d. .tsv (tab delimited)

Question 34

You need to propose a VPN solution for your company, a large agripharmaceutical company. What does the tunneling protocol L2TP rely on for data encryption?

○ a. PAP

○ b. EAP

○ c. IPSec

○ d. MS-CHAP v2

Question 35

You are the lead network administrator for a large company. You discovered in one of your reports, that another administrator was downloading non-business related images to his computer. After discussing the issue with Human Resources, you decided to fire him. Before leaving, the fired administrator changed the permissions on many sensitive documents, revoking all access to the files. He also took ownership of the files. What can you do to gain access to the files?

○ a. Take ownership and grant access

○ b. Grant access

○ c. Restore from backup

○ d. Format the volume containing the files and restore from backup

20

Question 36

Which command displays the NetBIOS name cache?

○ a. **nbtstat -r**

○ b. **nbtstat -R**

○ c. **nbtstat -c**

○ d. **nbtstat**

Question 37

The Windows XP Professional workstation you are using receives its IP configuration via a DHCP server. You are having difficulty accessing resources on the network. You suspect that your system's IP configuration is wrong. How can you view your current IP configuration?

○ a. **winipcfg /view**

○ b. **ipconfig /all**

○ c. **show ip config**

○ d. **ipconfig /view**

Question 38

Up to how many processors can be supported by Windows XP Professional?

○ a. 2

○ b. 4

○ c. 1

○ d. 8

Question 39

You are responsible for managing printing in your company. A user's Windows XP workstation has stopped printing for no apparent reason. The print jobs are just sitting in the spooler. You decide that you want to stop and start the spooler service on the computer. What snap-ins can you add to the console to accomplish this? [Check all correct answers]

❑ a. Services

❑ b. System Information

❑ c. Printers

❑ d. Computer Management

Question 40

You have several desktop computers that do not support PXE.99c. How can you deploy Windows XP Professional via RIS to these computers?

○ a. Replace the network interface cards in the computers with ones that support PXE.

○ b. Use the Remote Boot Disk Generator to create RIS boot disks for the computers that do not support PXE remote-boot ROMS.

○ c. You cannot upgrade the computers if they do not have PXE support.

○ d. Change the System BIOS on the computers to enable PXE .99c support.

Question 41

Max has recently upgraded his Windows 98 laptop to Windows XP Professional. Talking with colleagues around the water cooler one day, he hears about several capabilities that Windows XP has that Windows 98 did not. He wants to add disk quotas, file compression, and file and folder encryption. A coworker attempts to show Max how to configure encryption for a folder, but there is no option in Windows Explorer to accomplish this. How can Max gain the ability to encrypt his files and folders?

O a. Windows XP does not support encryption.

O b. Max needs to convert his Windows 98 FAT32 file system to NTFS before he can use NTFS features.

O c. Max's computer is experiencing some corruption.

O d. Max needs to make a Registry change before he can encrypt the folder.

Question 42

You are the network administrator for your company. Your boss, the CIO, has asked you to assign a software package to all workstations in the environment. Which of the following are characteristics of assigning software packages via Group Policy? [Check all correct answers]

❑ a. Assigned software appears as a shortcut on the user's menu.

❑ b. Software assigned to a user is advertised when the user logs on but not installed until she double-clicks the icon for the software package.

❑ c. Software assigned to a computer is not advertised by default.

❑ d. Published software is installed through Add/Remove Programs in Control Panel.

20

Question 43

Your company has 200 computers that it wantsto upgrade to Windows XP Professional. Your boss has assigned you the task of managing the upgrade for the company. The company has a mix of older Windows operating systems that include the following:

➤ Windows 3.1

➤ Windows 95

➤ Windows 98

➤ Windows NT 4

➤ DOS

You are concerned that you might not be able to directly upgrade some of the computers with older operating systems to Windows XP Professional. Which of the following operating systems will you not be able to directly upgrade to Windows XP Professional? [Check all correct answers]

❑ a. Windows 3.1

❑ b. Windows 95

❑ c. DOS

❑ d. Windows 98

Question 44

Mike is preparing for an unattended installation of Windows XP Professional, and he wants the installation to go as smoothly as possible with no interruption for the users. He does not want Dynamic Update to interrupt the installation and wants to disable it so that it can finish as quickly as possible. What can Mike do to prevent Dynamic Update from running during the unattended installation?

○ a. Use the **/debug** switch in Setup to disable Dynamic Update.

○ b. Use the **/dudisable** switch in Setup to disable Dynamic Update.

○ c. Use the **/nodynamicupdate** switch in Setup to disable Dynamic Update.

○ d. Use the **/nointerrupt** switch in Setup to disable Dynamic Update.

Question 45

You are the network administrator for your company. You want users to be aware if they are using applications that are trying to download and install unsigned device drivers. How should you configure each workstation on the network so that users are prompted before an application attempts to install an unsigned driver?

○ a. Configure the Driver Signing option to Ignore so that it displays a message before installing an unsigned file.

○ b. Configure the Driver Signing option to Warn so that it displays a message before installing an unsigned file.

○ c. Configure the Driver Signing option to Block so that it displays a message before installing an unsigned file.

○ d. This feature is not available in Windows XP.

20

Question 46

You have been asked by the CIO of your company to design a VPN solution using L2TP. Which of the following are characteristics of L2TP? [Check all correct answers]

❑ a. Header Compression is supported.

❑ b. Can only be used with TCP/IP-based networks.

❑ c. Uses IPSec for encryption.

❑ d. Uses built-in MPE encryption.

Question 47

Samuel has recently downloaded a new device driver for his computer from a vendor's Web site. After he installs the driver, his computer begins to malfunction. He would like to use Windows XP's driver rollback option to restore the device driver back to its original state. Where can Samuel access the ability to roll back the driver?

○ a. The Driver Rollback Wizard in Control Panel.

○ b. Windows XP does not support driver rollback.

○ c. He has to remove the device driver using the Add/Remove Hardware Wizard.

○ d. The Device Manager.

Question 48

Your company has a large installed base of Windows NT 4 Workstation computers. You need to determine if these computers are compatible with Windows XP Professional. How can you accomplish this? [Check all correct answers]

❑ a. Hardware Compatibility List

❑ b. The **/checkupgradeonly** utility on the Windows XP Professional CD

❑ c. Scandisk

❑ d. Device Manager

Question 49

You have been tasked with designing a deployment capability using RIS for your company. Which of the following services are required before Remote Installation Services can be used to install Windows XP Professional on network workstations? [Check all correct answers]

❑ a. WINS

❑ b. DHCP

❑ c. DNS

❑ d. AD

Question 50

What is the minimum processor speed requirement for computers running Windows XP Professional?

○ a. 166MHz

○ b. 233MHz

○ c. 300MHz

○ d. 1GHz

CHAPTER TWENTY-ONE

Answer Key

1. c	19. b	35. a
2. c	20. a	36. c
3. d	21. a, b, i, j	37. b
4. a	c, d, g, l	38. a
5. b, d	k, e, f, h	39. a, d
6. a, d	22. c	40. b
7. c	23. c	41. b
8. c	24. c	42. a, b, c
9. b	25. a, c	43. a, b, c
10. d	26. c	44. b
11. d	27. a	45. b
12. d	28. a	46. a, c
13. d	29. a, d	47. d
14. b	30. d, a, f, h, b, c	48. a, b
15. e	31. b	49. b, c, d
16. a	32. a, b, c, d	50. b
17. b	33. b, d	
18. a, b	34. c	

Question 1

Answer c is correct. The **–pnp** switch in the Sysprep utility allows for the detection of non-Plug and Play devices. Answer a runs Sysprep in Silent mode, without dialog boxes. Answer b forces the computer to shut down instead of power off. Answer d causes Sysprep to not regenerate the computer's SID during a reboot.

Question 2

Answer c is correct. Compressed files cannot be encrypted. To encrypt compressed files, uncompress the file and then encrypt it. The remaining answers can be compressed.

Question 3

Answer d is correct. David does not need to do anything. When the system boots up, it will detect the Plug and Play compatible device and automatically install associated device drivers. There is no such thing as the Plug and Play Administrator.

Question 4

Answer a is correct. Volume Mount Points allow you to add a volume to a system without using a separate drive letter for the new volume. The Volume Mount Point must be placed in an empty folder on the hosting system's NTFS volume.

Question 5

Answers b and d are correct. To remotely manage disk storage, you need to be a member of the Administrators or Server Operators groups. Power Users and Computer Operators can perform most, but not all, administrative duties.

Question 6

Answers a and d are correct. Two commands allow you to obtain a new IP address. **Ipconfig /renew** is the more commonly known command. **Ipconfig /registerdns** is meant to be used to register the workstation with DNS, but it will also renew the IP address with the DHCP server. Winipcfg is the Windows 9x utility used to manage the IP configuration.

Question 7

Answer c is correct. Because management did not want another network client installed, Colleen's only choice was to use the Gateway (and Client) Services for NetWare. The gateway can only be installed on a Windows 2000 Server. Windows XP Professional cannot act as a gateway to NetWare.

Question 8

Answer a is correct. The IP address 192.168.12.10 displayed in binary is 11000000.10101000.00001100.00001010.

Question 9

Answer b is correct. The first three octets are part of the Network ID. The third octet in the IP addresses of the Windows 2000 Server and your Windows XP computer have different values. Therefore, they are located on different subnets.

Question 10

Answer d is correct. To perform an unattended installation using an installation CD-ROM, you need to rename your unattended answer file to winnt.sif and save it to a floppy disk. This disk, along with the CD-ROM, must be distributed to the users. UDF files are Uniqueness Database Files and are used to supply unique information during an unattended install. Answer.txt is an unattended answer file. It is normally named unattend.txt.

Question 11

Answer d is correct. Only Windows XP computers that are configured to run in a workgroup can use Fast User Switching.

Question 12

Answer d is correct. CHAP operates by having the server send a challenge to the client computer. The client computer, using MD5, hashes both the challenge and the password and sends it to the server. The server, knowing the challenge and the user's password from its security database, creates its own hash. The server then compares the two hashes. If the hashes match, the requested access is permitted. As you can see, the password itself is never transmitted across the network.

Question 13

Answer d is correct. By examining the subnet mask, you can see that the first three octets are part of the network ID. The computer's IP address is 210.169.8.12, so its subnet must be 210.169.8.0.

Question 14

Answer b is correct. CIFS (Common Internet File System) is the protocol used to open, close, read, and write to files on Windows 2000 and Windows XP computers across the network. CIFS is also known as SMB (Server Message Block) protocol, which is found in earlier Windows operating systems. NCP (NetWare Core Protocol) is used for file and printer sharing on NetWare networks. IPX (Internet Packet Exchange) is the core network protocol for NetWare 4.x and earlier. IP is the network protocol for the Internet and is the default network protocol for Windows NT/2000/XP and NetWare 5.x.

Question 15

Answer e is correct. EAP (Extensible Authentication Protocol) is the most secure authentication protocol, because it provides a way for vendors to incorporate additional authentication methods, such as smart cards or Secure ID. PAP is the least secure authentication protocol, because it provides no encryption for data or passwords.

Question 16

Answer a is correct. PXE (Preboot eXecution Environment) is an industry standard that allows a system to boot from the network card. RIS requires a network adapter that is PXE .99c compliant. Ethernet is a network topology/technology. TCP/IP is a network protocol suite. PCI (Peripheral Component Interconnect) is a bus technology found in most computers.

Question 17

Answer b is correct. 64MB of RAM is the official minimum requirement from Microsoft, although we highly recommend that you have at least 128MB of RAM for better performance.

Question 18

Answers a and b are correct. When connecting to a NetWare server using NDS, Client Services for NetWare must be configured with the Default Tree (i.e., the name of the NDS tree) and the Context (the location in the tree where the user's account information is located). Preferred Server is used when connecting to a bindery-based NetWare server (typically NetWare 3.x or earlier).

Question 19

Answer b is correct. To back up the Registry, use the Backup utility and select the System State. The System State includes a number of items related to the system configuration, including the Registry files.

Question 20

Answer a is correct. Disk Management is the utility that allows you to configure and manage disk storage. It is found in the Computer Management Console. Windows XP also includes a command-line utility called DISKPART. Disk Administrator is the name of the same utility in Windows NT.

Question 21

The items should be placed in the following groups and orders:

a, b, i, j

c, d, g, l

k, e, f, h

From a design standpoint, it is important to know the different network protocols and their characteristics. Although the world is quickly becoming IP-only because of the Internet, you will undoubtedly come across other network protocols from time to time. Although NetBEUI is not displayed by default when adding protocols to Windows XP Professional, it can still be installed. It is found in the VALUEADD\MSFT\NET\NETBEUI folder on the Windows XP Professional CD-ROM.

Question 22

Answer c is correct. The HOSTS and LMHOSTS files need to be placed in %systemroot%\system32\drivers\etc. %systemroot% is a system variable that represents the directory Windows XP Professional was installed in (i.e., C:\WINDOWS).

Question 23

Answer c is correct. The Recovery Console command **fixboot** will create a new boot sector for the system partition. **Fixmbr** fixes the master boot record of the system partition. **Sys** is an MS-DOS command that places the MS-DOS operating system files on a drive. **Fixbootsector** does not exist.

Question 24

Answer c is correct. Windows XP's Application Compatibility Wizard will configure Windows XP to present itself to the application as an earlier operating system.

Question 25

Answers a and c are correct. You need to use a UDF (Uniqueness Database File) file and an answer file, UNATTEND.TXT. The UDF file will override the answer file (UNATTEND.TXT) with unique answers for each workstation. PXE (Preboot eXecution Environment) is an industry standard that allows a system to boot from the network card. RIS (Remote Installation Services) is a Microsoft imaging solution found in Windows 2000. It supports Windows 2000 Professional and Windows XP Professional.

Question 26

Answer c is correct. When configuring multiple connections, it is important to bind only the network protocols that are required on the connection. In the question, you need TCP/IP only to access the Exchange Server. For the local network, you need both TCP/IP and NWLink to access the Windows 2000 and Novell NetWare servers.

Question 27

Answer a is correct. The User State Migration Tool can be used to transfer the employees' files and configuration settings from the older computers to the new Windows XP Professional computers. Remote Assistance is a feature that allows a user to request assistance from another user or support personnel. Add/Remove Profiles and Removable Profiles do not exist.

Question 28

Answer a is correct. Windows XP Professional requires 1.5GB of free disk space.

Question 29

Answers a and d are correct. To remotely manage disk storage (i.e., create shares), you need to be a member of the Administrators or Power Users groups.

Question 30

The items should be placed in the following order:

d, a, f, h, b, c

There are many factors to consider when a Windows XP Professional workstation is performing NetBIOS name resolution. Items such as node type and configuration settings can greatly affect how resolution occurs. For example, in the question, if the workstation was configured to be a b-node and was not configured to query DNS, it would have sent a local broadcast and checked the LMHOSTS file. It would not query WINS or DNS.

Question 31

Answer b is correct. You need to use the Event Viewer and select the Security Log to view audited events. System Monitor is used to monitor system objects' performance.

Question 32

Answers a, b, c, and d are correct. All items need to be installed and configured. NetWare servers use NWLink (IPX/SPX) as their network protocol. Windows XP and Windows 2000 computers wanting access to the NetWare servers need to use Client Services for NetWare. By default, the frametype is set to autodetect. However, because the two NetWare servers are using two different frametypes (802.2 for NetWare 4.11 and 802.3 for NetWare 3.11), Marshall must manually configure the frametypes.

Question 33

Answers b and d are correct. System Monitor can export files as either HTML or TSV. HTML files can be viewed via a Web browser such as Internet Explorer. TSV files can be imported into Microsoft Excel. The other file types are not supported.

Question 34

Answer c is correct. L2TP (Layer 2 Tunneling Protocol) does not have any inherent way of encrypting data. To get data encryption, L2TP always relies on IPSec. PAP, EAP, and MS-CHAPv2 are authentication protocols.

Question 35

Answer a is correct. If you are the Creator/Owner of a file, you can still change permissions even if your access was revoked. By taking ownership, you become the Creator/Owner.

Question 36

Answer c is correct. **nbtstat –c** will display the NetBIOS name cache. **nbtstat –r** will list all names resolved by WINS or broadcasts. **nbtstat –R** will purge the cache and reload the remote cache name table (NetBIOS names marked #PRE in the LMHOSTS file).

Question 37

Answer b is correct. **ipconfig /all** will display all the IP configuration settings on the workstation. Winipcfg is the Windows 9x utility used to manage the IP configuration. The remaining answers are not possible.

Question 38

Answer a is correct. Windows XP Professional supports two processors. Windows XP Home Edition supports only single processor operation.

Question 39

Answers a and d are correct. The Services snap-in gives you direct access to all services. The Computer Management snap-in also contains the Services snap-in.

Question 40

Answer b is correct. The Remote Boot Disk Generator is used to create RIS boot disks for the computers that do not support PXE remote-boot ROMS. This allows the computer to receive a DHCP IP address and connect to the RIS Server.

Question 41

Answer b is correct. When Max upgraded his computer from Windows 98, he did not convert the partition to NTFS. Windows 98 uses FAT32 for its file system.

Question 42

Answers a, b, and c are correct. All are characteristics of assigning software packages.

Question 43

Answers a, b, and c are correct. You can not directly upgrade this operating systems to Windows XP. You will need to either do a interim upgrade to an OS that can be directly upgraded or perform a clean install.

Question 44

Answer b is correct. The **/dudisable** switch will disable Dynamic Update during the installation process. The other switches are not possible.

Question 45

Answer b is correct. By configuring the Driver Signing option to Warn, users will see a message displayed before installing an unsigned driver or file. This option can also be set to Ignore or Block.

Question 46

Answers a and c are correct. L2TP supports Header Compression and uses IPSec for encryption.

Question 47

Answer d is correct. The driver rollback option is found in Device Manager by selecting the device's properties.

Question 48

Answers a and b are correct. You can check the computer's hardware devices against the HCL or you can use the **/checkupgradeonly** utility. Scandisk is a Windows 9*x* utility to check hard drives. Device Manager is used to check device and driver settings.

Question 49

Answers b, c, and d are correct. RIS requires that DHCP and Active Directory be installed on the network. Active Directory also requires DNS, so DNS would also be required for RIS. WINS is not required for RIS operation.

Question 50

Answer b is correct. 233MHz is the minimum processor speed for Windows XP Professional. It is recommended that 300MHz or higher processors be used.

Appendix A
Answers to Review Questions

Chapter 1 Solutions

1. **b.** System Restore uses restore points to recover a system to its previous state after it crashes.

2. **a.** Ronald must use Windows Product Activation to register Windows XP Professional.

3. **c.** Joann can run Windows Update to ensure that she has the latest service packs installed.

4. **d.** WebDAV allows users to share and collaborate on files on the Internet.

5. **a.** NetCrawer will search a network for printers and other network devices.

6. **c.** Microsoft Passport allows a user to log on to multiple secure Web sites with an email address and password.

7. **a.** IPSec allows users to send sensitive data securely over the public Internet.

8. **b.** Offline Files and Folders will allow Marshall to work on his corporate documents when he is not connected to the company network.

9. **d.** ClearType provides clear text display on LCD screens in Windows XP Professional.

10. **a.** The Automatic Recovery Wizard will allow Jeff to back up the System State data on his network.

Chapter 2 Solutions

1. **c, d.** A VGA monitor and at least 2GB of hard disk space are some of the minimal requirements for installing Windows XP Professional.

2. **a.** Sally should check the HCL to see if her computers are on it.

3. **d.** John can run Winnt32.exe with the **/checkupgradeonly** command-line option.

4. **b.** NTFS is the best file system for Windows XP Professional.

5. **a, b, c, d.** File encryption, disk quotas, compression, and file permissions are all benefits of using the NTFS file system.

6. **a.** Because Sally is upgrading from a Windows 95 computer, she would start the installation with Winnt32.exe.

7. **b.** Marshall could connect the computers to a network share and install the Windows XP Professional operating system.

8. **d.** Sysprep uses an answer file called Sysprep.inf for installing Windows XP Professional.

9. **a, c.** The Setupcl.exe file starts the Mini-Setup Wizard and generates a new security ID when used with Sysprep.

10. **a, c, d.** DHCP, Active Directory, and DNS are all required Windows XP Server services for installing Windows XP using RIS.

11. **a, d.** CD-based and RIPrep are both images that can be used by RIS to deploy Windows XP Professional.

12. **b.** SMS uses SMS packages to distribute software to SMS clients.

13. **c.** The User State Migration Tool (USMT) can be used to transfer user settings to a new Windows XP Professional computer.

14. **a.** Scanstate.exe is used to scan user state settings on a computer being migrated to Windows XP Professional.

15. **b.** After Billy installs Windows XP Professional, he must use Windows Product Activation to register the newly installed operating system.

Chapter 3 Solutions

1. **a, b.** MMC by default launches in Author Mode. Mmc.exe is the executable, and, if you want to make absolutely sure you are in Author Mode, you must use the /a switch.

2. **a, b, c, d.** You can create all of these tasks.

3. **a.** User Mode–Full Access is the best answer because it meets the restrictions and gives the users the most functionality. However, answers b and c could be correct, but they are not the best answers.

4. **a, b.** Either of these modes will restrict the adding of new snap-ins, and allow new windows to be used.

5. **d.** Only Author Mode will allow users full access to customize the console.

6. **b.** This mode will allow users to use multiple windows but not remove these windows from the console.

7. **b, c.** Device Manager allows you to manage the hardware on your system. The Computer Management snap-in also contains the Device Manager.

8. **c.** The MMC saves its consoles with an .msc extension.

9. **a.** By selecting the option Do Not Save Changes To This Console, users will see the same console every time they start the console.

10. **c.** You can check the extensions that are loaded with a particular snap-in. Sometimes, you might be able to remove some of the functionality by unloading an extension.

11. **b, d.** When you load the snap-in Link To Web Address, you can connect through HTTP or FTP.

12. **d.** Favorites will assist you in navigating to often-used areas of your console tree.

13. **a.** Tasks will allow you to run a script file from within the MMC.

14. **c.** If the Console drop-down menu is not available, you are probably in one of the User Modes. You must open the MMC in Author Mode to make these options available.

15. **b.** False. You can use the MMC to connect to other computers and have full functionality from wherever you are located.

16. **a, b.** You would use the Event Viewer snap-in. The Computer Management snap-in also contains the Event Viewer.

17. **a, d.** You would use the Disk Management snap-in to modify your partitions. The Computer Management snap-in also contains the Disk Management snap-in.

18. **a, b.** You would use the Device Management snap-in to disable a device. The Computer Management snap-in also contains the Device Management snap-in.

19. **a, c.** You would use the Local Users And Groups snap-in. The Computer Management snap-in also contains the Local Users And Groups snap-in.

20. **a, b.** The Services snap-in will accomplish this goal. The Computer Management snap-in also contains the Services snap-in.

Chapter 4 Solutions

1. **b, c.** A disk can contain primary and extended partitions.

2. **c.** A logical drive is created through an extended partition.

3. **a, c.** RAID-5 and mirrored volumes are not supported in Windows XP Professional.

4. **c.** Basic disks support three primary partitions and one extended partition.

5. **b.** A spanned volume can utilize disk space on up to 32 drives.

6. **a.** Bob can use the DiskPart command-line tool to perform disk management.

7. **c.** A disk status of Foreign indicates that the disk came from another computer.

8. **b.** GPT disks are only supported on the 64-bit version of Windows XP Professional.

9. **b.** The master boot record contains the master boot code, the disk signature, and the partition.

10. **c.** The DiskPart tool can be used to convert a basic disk to a dynamic disk in Windows XP Professional.

11. **b.** A basic disk can have only one active partition.

12. **c.** Sheila needs a minimal of 15 percent free disk space to run Defrag.exe.

13. **a.** John can run Defrag.exe with the **/a** command-line option to get an analysis report on the drive.

14. **b, c.** FAT and FAT32 file systems do not support file permissions.

15. **a, b, c, d.** NTFS supports disk quotas, compression on files and folders, and EFS.

16. **d.** Disk quotas will allow administrators to control how much disk space users have on the volumes.

17. **a, c, d.** The Disk Cleanup utility can delete temporary Internet files, Setup log files, and Recycle Bin files.

18. **b, d.** Disk quotas can be applied to the NTFS 4.0 and 5.0 file systems.

19. **b.** The Fsulti.exe utility can be used to set disk quotas from a command line.

20. **d.** The correct syntax is **convert.exe d: /fs:ntfs**.

Chapter 5 Solutions

1. **c.** John should use the Mandatory profile.

2. **a.** Julia can add a Web site shortcut to her desktop.

3. **d.** Mary can implement FilterKeys..

4. **b, c.** The Utility Manager can provide users with access to the Magnifier and the On-Screen Keyboard.

5. **b.** William can pin the programs to his Start menu.

6. **b.** Samantha should add the Links toolbar to the taskbar.

7. **a.** He can configure the settings in the Environment Variables dialog box.

8. **a, b, c, d.** The system can write an event to the system log. It also can be configured to send the administrator an alert and to automatically reboot itself after the crash. Debugging information can be written to a memory dump file for later analysis.

9. **b, c.** Bonnie can use Dumpchk.exe and Dumpexam.exe

10. **b.** Remote Assistance will enable Alicia to remotely help those users who are having problems with their computers.

11. **a.** Sally did not save the theme with a unique name when she created it.

12. **a.** They can implement Internet Connection Sharing on the computer that has Internet access.

13. **b.** Fast Switching will allow multiple users to share the same computer.

Chapter 6 Solutions

1. **c.** Donavan should check the My Music folder. By default, all music files are stored in this folder.

2. **c.** The History folder will allow users to track Web pages they have visited.

3. **c.** If Jenny wants to view her files as images she should choose the Thumbnail option for viewing.

4. **a.** The Read permission is the most restrictive. Users who have been assigned the Read permission can only read a file and view its attributes.

5. **a, c.** Read Attributes, Write Attributes are special file and folder permissions.

6. **c.** Access control entries are entries in the ACL that determine what actions are allowed or denied by users or groups.

7. **b.** The system access control list (SACL) is used to audit object access.

8. **d.** Before files and folders can be audited, the success or failure of Audit Object Access must be enabled.

9. **b, c, d.** Full Control, Read, and Change are valid shared folder permissions.

10. **c.** The ADMIN$ share is provided by default to give administrators access to the system root folder

11. **b.** The Sessions section of Shared Folders can be used by administrators to see what users are accessing shared folders on the network.

12. **a.** The command line to allow an administrator to delete a share name OLDSHARE is **net share oldshare /delete.**

Chapter 7 Solutions

1. **d.** The print driver supplies device-specific information to the GDI. The GDI in turn uses this information to create the print job that is sent to the spooler.

2. **a.** Because print jobs are sent to any available printer that is a member of the printer pool, the printers need to be identical. If the printers differ, the print job may call for a specific printer function, such as duplexing, that is not supported by one of the printers in the printer pool. Choice b is incorrect because printers in a printing pool can use serial or parallel cables.

3. **a, d.** Windows XP supports Point and Print, which allows a user to simply select the printer, and Windows XP will automatically install the printer driver. Windows XP can install printer drivers for Windows XP, Windows 2000, Windows NT 4 and 3.51, and Windows 95/98. Additional printer drivers can be installed in two places: the Sharing tab in the printer's Properties dialog box, and the Drivers tab in the Print Server Properties dialog box.

4. **c.** Internet Printing requires the use of Internet Information Services (IIS) on the print server. IIS, through the function of Active Server Pages, supplies the Web-based interface that users can use to connect, install, and manage print jobs. Answer a is incorrect because Internet Printing is based (and relies) on the TCP/IP protocol suite. IPX is not compatible with TCP/IP. Answer b is incorrect because Internet Printing is a standard that is documented in a number of RFCs. Answer d is incorrect because Internet Printing does not require SQL Server.

5. **b.** The default spooler location for Windows XP printers is %systemroot%\
System32\spool\PRINTERS. This location can be changed if the boot
partition (where %systemroot% is located) is running out of disk space.

6. **b.** Windows XP supports the following print job formats: Enhanced Metafile
(EMF), RAW, RAW (FF Appended), RAW (FF Auto), Text, and PSCRIPT1.

7. **a.** The print spooler service controls the print router, remote print provider,
local print provider, and port monitors. By restarting the print spooler service,
all of these components will restart. They will then restart any jobs located in
the spool directory. The print spooler service can be restarted by selecting
Control Panel | Administrative Tools | Services or by entering NET STOP
SPOOLER followed by NET START SPOOLER at a command prompt.

8. **b.** Standard TCP/IP Port Monitor (SPM) is the preferred port monitor for
Windows XP. It uses the Simple Network Management Protocol (SNMP) to
configure and monitor ports. Answer a is incorrect. NetWare Link State
Protocol (NLSP) is a routing protocol used with IPX. Answer c is incorrect.
Although SPM uses SNMP to monitor the ports, Windows XP relies on SPM
to provide the functionality. Answer d is incorrect. TCP/IP is a protocol suite
that consists of many protocols.

9. **a.** The logical printer represents the software-based printing process in Windows XP. The physical printer represents the actual hardware printing device.

10. **c.** Clients using Windows 3.x or DOS can only see network printers that
conform to the 8.3 file name standard. Use 8 characters for the file name plus 3
for the extension for a total of 11 characters.

11. **d.** Using Resume from the Document menu will allow the print job to
continue printing. Answer a will start the print job from the beginning. Answers b and c are not possible.

12. **a.** True. Because Internet Printing relies on TCP/IP, TCP/IP must be installed
on the workstation.

13. **a.** The default spooler location for Windows XP printers is
%systemroot%\System32\spool\PRINTERS. This location can be changed if
the boot partition (where %systemroot% is located) is running out of disk
space. This setting can be changed from Server Properties.

14. **b.** The Pause Printing command stops the print queue from sending data to the
print device. The print device will continue to print any data that it has in
memory. Once the data in memory is printed, the print device will stop
printing.

15. **a.** To enable Windows NT 3.51 clients to use the printers, the Windows NT 3.51 print drivers need to be installed on the print servers. Once installed, the clients can use Point and Print services to install and use the printers.

16. **c.** Remember that priorities go from 99 (highest) to 1 (lowest). By configuring your supervisor's logical printer to 99 and leaving the remaining logical printers at the default setting of 1, the supervisor's print jobs will print first.

17. **c.** Forms can be added using the Forms tab in the Print Server Properties dialog box. On this page, a form can be defined by specifying the margins and paper size.

18. **a.** By default, CREATOR/OWNER is granted the Manage Documents right. With this right, users can manage their own print jobs, but not the print jobs of other users. The Print right, granted to the Everyone group by default, allows users to submit jobs, but they cannot manage the print jobs. The Manage Printers right allows the user to pause or stop the printer. This right is granted to Administrators and Power Users by default.

19. **b.** False. Windows XP supports printing in a wide variety of network environments, including TCP/IP, IPX/SPX, and NetBEUI.

20. **a.** Auditing can be accessed via the Security tab in the Printer Properties' dialog box . Click the Advanced button and then the Auditing tab to configure auditing.

21. **a.** When an individual print job is paused, the remaining print jobs in the print queue continue to print as they normally would.

22. **b.** The print spooler service can be restarted by selecting Control Panel | Administrative Tools | Services. Another way of restarting the print spooler is by entering "NET STOP SPOOLER" followed by "NET START SPOOLER" at a command prompt.

23. **c.** When FILE is selected as the print port, Windows XP prompts the user for a file name. The print job is then written to disk using the supplied file name.

24. **b, c.** The local print provider contains two subcomponents, the print processor and the separator page processor. The print router and the GDI are two separate components.

Chapter 8 Solutions

1. **c.** The maximum number of devices that can be connected to one USB port is 127.

2. **a.** WDM or Windows Driver Model is used by developers to create device drivers that are supported across multiple operating system platforms. WDM supports Plug and Play, and is used for most multimedia device types and many other newer device types such as USB and 1394 devices and.

3. **a, c.** Isochronous and asynchronous data transfer modes are supported by both USB and IEEE 1394 devices.

4. **b, c.** IEEE 1394a devices can support data transfer speeds of 100 and 400 Mbps.

5. **a.** XML or Extensible Markup Language is a system for defining, validating, and sharing document formats and is replaced HTML as the universal format for data on the Web.

6. **b.** UPnP or Universal Plug and Play which is introduced in Windows XP offers automatic peer-to-peer network detection, connectivity and configuration of PC hardware devices.

7. **d.** Ronald can connect up to 63 devices to one IEEE 1394 bus in Windows XP Professional.

8. **b.** TCP/IP is the default protocol that is used by Universal Plug and Play and is the foundation for the UPnP initiative.

9. **b.** IEEE 1394 devices cause the least amount of degradation on the system's processor because they handle and respond to device request directly. They do not use the system's central processor unit when handling device requests.

10. **a.** The first thing the device has to do is to obtain an address in order to participate on the network. Therefore Addressing is the first step that occurs when a UpnP device is connected to the network for the first time.

11. **b.** SSDP stands for Simple Service Discovery Protocol. SSDP is used by control points and UPnP devices and defines how network services can be discovered on the network.

12. **c, d.** Windows XP Professional and Windows 2000 Professional have the capability to share data using IrDA connections. Computers running Windows 98 and ME will not be able to share data with Julie's Windows XP Professional computer.

13. **b.** Windows XP Professional supports the 9-Wire service class for IrCOMM.

14. **c.** Rashed can use Scanners and Cameras tool in the Control Panel applet to control the parameters for his newly installed scanner.

15. **c.** A computer that is running the 64–bit version of Windows XP Professional can have up to 16GB of usable RAM.

16. **b.** Windows Media Player 8, which is an upgrade to Windows Media Player 7, can be used by Winston to view his DVDs in Windows XP Professional.

17. **c.** Digital Video Disc or DVD is based on the Universal Disk Format or UDF. This format is also used for CD-recordable and CDRW (CD rewritable) drives.

18. **c.** Power management in Windows XP Professional is based on the ACPI specification. ACPI ACPI is an acronym that stands for Advanced Configuration and Power Interface and is power management specification that was introduced in Windows 98.

19. **a.** Dxdiag.exe is the diagnostic tool that is used for troubleshooting DirectX problems.

20. **a.** Jim can configure driver signing on each computer. This will allow Jim block unsigned drivers from being loaded.

Chapter 9 Solutions

1. **c.** The Password Authentication Protocol (PAP) is the authentication protocol that transmits the password in an unencrypted or plaintext form.

2. **b.** A hub is a network device that provides a central point of connectivity to a physical network. Each individual computer connects to the hub via its own network cable. Network traffic that enters the hub is then replicated and sent back out every port in the hub.

3. **d.** A workgroup is a group of computer resources in name only. All members of a workgroup maintain their own user account databases. In this situation, users need a username and password for each network resource they desire access to.

4. **d.** QoS (Quality of Service) Packet Scheduler allows an administrator to control bandwidth on the network. For example, if a user needs to use a network-intensive application, such as Voice over IP (VoIP), QoS can be implemented to prioritize VoIP traffic over regular network traffic.

5. **b, c.** Windows XP ships with support for the two most popular local area networks: Client for Microsoft Networks and Client Services for NetWare.

6. **a.** Windows XP provides support for two tunneling protocols: PPTP and L2TP. L2TP relies on IPSec to provide data encryption at a machine level.

7. **c.** With the Challenge Handshake Authentication Protocol (CHAP), the password is never transmitted across the network. CHAP uses the hashing method known as Message Digest 5 (MD5). CHAP operates by having the server send a challenge to the client computer. The client computer, using MD5, hashes both the challenge and the password and sends it to the server. The server, knowing the challenge and the user's password from its security database, creates its own hash. The server then compares the two hashes. If the hashes match, the requested access is permitted. The password itself is never actually transmitted across the network.

8. **c.** The Network Driver Interface Specification (NDIS) layer provides a way for a network transport (such as TCP/IP, NWLink, or NetBEUI) to communicate with a network adapter. This layer contains the drivers that communicate directly with the network adapters.

9. **b.** The Extensible Authentication Protocol (EAP) is an extension to PPP that works with dial-in, PPTP, and L2TP clients. EAP allows additional authentication methods with PPP. These methods include smart cards, such as Secure ID, public key authentication, and certificates. EAP is generally used in VPN networks that require stronger authentication methods.

10. **a.** A bridge is a network device that connects two or more physical networks. The bridge maintains a table consisting of hardware addresses. When the bridge receives a frame from one physical segment, it checks the destination hardware address for the frame against the table. If the hardware address is located on the other side of the bridge, it allows the frame to cross. If it isn't, the frame is not permitted to cross.

11. **b.** False. When ICS is enabled on Windows XP, it configures the Windows XP computer with a static IP address of 192.168.0.1.

12. **d.** When third-party software is being used to connect to a network and you are not sure which authentication protocol it uses, the simplest authentication protocol, PAP, should be used. Most software packages support PAP. Another authentication protocol can be used on the server after figuring out what other authentication protocols are supported by the third-party software.

13. **a, b.** NetWare 5.0 is the first version of NetWare to provide support for both IPX/SPX and TCP/IP. Previous versions of NetWare supplied limited TCP/IP support.

14. **a.** The Windows XP Component Architecture is comprised of software components, such as network adapter drivers, protocols, and APIs.

15. **d.** A router is a network device that connects two or more logical networks. The router maintains a routing table that tells the router which logical networks it knows the routes to. When the router receives a packet, it analyzes the packet's logical destination address to determine where it should route the

packet. If the router is aware of a route to the destination, it forwards the packet out the port closest to the destination. If the router is not aware of a suitable route, the router discards the packet and sends a notification to the sender that the destination was not reachable.

16. **b.** False. Windows XP supports local area, remote, VPN, and direct connections.

17. **c.** Windows XP supports a number of network media, including Ethernet, Token Ring, ATM, cable modem, and DSL. X.25 is used for remote dial-up connections.

18. **c.** A switch is a network device that combines the features of bridges and hubs. Like a hub, a switch contains ports that interconnect multiple computers or physical networks. Like a bridge, the switch analyzes the destination hardware address in a frame and sends the frame out the appropriate port. Because the frame is not replicated on all ports like a hub, using a switch results in greater bandwidth for individual workstations.

19. **a.** NWLink, more commonly known as IPX/SPX, is a proprietary network protocol designed to be used by Novell NetWare networks.

20. **c.** Windows XP does not ship with support for Localtalk. Localtalk is a simple protocol used with the Apple Macintosh.

21. **a.** A domain-based network model provides a centralized user account database. Any members of the domain use the domain user account database to verify network access. A user needs only one user account to access any resources in the domain.

22. **a.** The Network Protocol layer provides services that allow data to be sent across the network. These protocols include TCP/IP, NWLink, NetBEUI, AppleTalk, IrDA, ATM, and DLC.

Chapter 10 Solutions

1. **b.** 00100101.10100010.00101111.01100000 is the proper conversion.

2. **d.** 11011010.00101111.11101100.01110110 is the proper conversion.

3. **c.** 00010010.11110111.10001000.10000000 is the proper conversion.

4. **a.** 217.253.38.238 is the proper conversion.

5. **d.** 153.252.39.110 is the proper conversion.

6. **a.** 157.204.63.222 is the proper conversion.

7. **b.** This is a remote network because the third octet is part of the network ID and it has a different value than your source IP address.

8. **a.** This is a local network because only the first two octets are part of the network ID and they have the same value.

9. **b.** This is a remote network because the third octet is part of the network ID and it has a different value than your source IP address.

10. **a.** This is a local network because only the first two octets are part of the network ID and they have the same value.

11. **a.** The WINS entry is the one used here because WINS is checked before the LMHOSTS file.

12. **b.** The HOSTS entry is the one used here because the HOSTS file is checked before the DNS entry.

13. **c. ipconfig /renew** requests a new address from the DHCP server, although **ipconfig /registerdns** refreshes the DHCP lease as well. It also registers the computer again with the DNS server.

14. **a. ipconfig /registerdns** refreshes the DHCP lease and registers the system with the DNS server.

15. **d. ipconfig /all** displays all of the settings for your TCP/IP configuration.

16. **a, b, c, e.** The client first attempts to renew the address at half the lease time; if unsuccessful, it tries at seven-eighths the time. The client will also renew the address whenever the system reboots.

17. **b.** Running **NBTSTAT –R** purges the local NetBIOS name cache and allows the new IP address to be resolved.

18. **d.** The HOSTS file is the first item checked to resolve a hostname.

19. **d.** ARP maps an IP address to a MAC address.

20. **c.** c:\windows\system32\drivers\etc is the path where these files need to be for the system to find and use them.

Chapter 11 Solutions

1. **b.** Hardware profiles can be used to create multiple hardware configurations depending on whether the user is at home or connecting to a network at the office.

2. **d.** Jeannie could purchase a docking station for her notebook computer. The docking station basically turns her notebook computer into a desktop computer.

3. **c.** A cold dock occurs when a notebook computer is inserted into a docking station when it is not turned on.

4. **c.** BAP, or Bandwidth Allocation Protocol, works with PPP Multilink to provide administrators the capability to add and delete links dynamically.

5. **a.** Ron can use the Callback feature for dial-up connections if it has been configured for his use by his network administrator. He can call the company remote access server, which will disconnect the call and then call him back on a predefined number.

6. **a, b.** IPSec uses the DES and Triple DES encryption algorithms. DES uses a 56-bit encryption key, and Triple DES uses a 168-bit encryption key.

7. **c.** Regina can use the Stored User Names and Passwords feature of Windows XP to create a unique logon name and password for each server she needs connectivity to.

8. **a.** Julie could use Direct Connections to create a connection to the computer that she is trying to transfer the files to. This connection could be via a serial, parallel, or infrared port.

9. **d.** The Wake-on-LAN feature of Windows XP will allow Betsy to install the software on the notebook computers. If they were in Standby mode, it would put them in a wake state so that Betsy could install the software. After the software installation is finished, the notebook computers would go back into Standby mode.

10. **b.** Wills can use the Synchronization Manager to configure a schedule that will synchronize the files when it detects inactivity on his computer.

11. **b.** Jill could make a VPN connection to her company network and securely transfer the files.

12. **c.** MS-CHAPv2 supports mutual, or two-way, authentication.

13. **c.** SLIP is a protocol that was originally designed for use with Unix systems and that is primarily used today with the Telnet application.

14. **b.** Jonathan can configure his computer to go into Hibernation mode when the batteries are reaching a low-power state. Any data that he was working on would be saved when the computer goes into Hibernation mode.

15. **c.** PPTP can only be used on IP-based networks.

16. **d.** The Remote Desktop feature of Windows XP will allow Morris to connect to his desktop computer at work. After he has connected to his desktop, he can use any applications on it.

17. **a.** Susan can use Dualview to connect a second monitor to her notebook computer. She can run the presentation on the second monitor and continue working on her other project using the LCD monitor on her notebook.

18. **a.** Windows XP Professional allows users to encrypt the offline files database using Encrypting File System (EFS).

19. **d.** If Ronald uses the Presentation power scheme, the notebook computer will not go into Standby mode during his presentation.

20. **c.** RDP is the protocol that is used to provide the Terminal Services features of Remote Desktop.

Chapter 12 Solutions

1. **b, c, d.** If Jerrold installs the highly secure template on his computer, he will only be able to communicate with computers that are also configured with that template. He will not be able to communicate with any computers that are running Windows 95, 98, or NT.

2. **b.** William can be made a member of the Guests group, which will give him one-time access to the network.

3. **c.** The Security Configuration and Analysis snap-in tool is used to analyze security on a computer system and apply security configurations to the system.

4. **a, b.** Interactive logon and network authentication are the two authentication methods used in Windows XP.

5. **c.** The Backup Operators group members can back up and restore all files on a network. The Administrators group members could also perform this task, but putting Joan in the Backup Operators group gives her the appropriate permissions to perform the task.

6. **c.** Kerberos v5 is the default protocol for authenticating Windows XP Professional computers to Windows 2000 domains.

7. **b.** False. Members of the Users group can only delete local groups that they create. Jill will have to delete the local groups she created. Rena will not be able to do it.

8. **d.** If Mary is made a member of the Power Users group, she will be able to create user accounts.

9. **c.** John should configure the computer to audit object access to determine who is accessing the files.

10. **a.** Any user who is accessing a computer over the network is considered a member of the Network group.

11. **a.** The Key Distribution Center (KDC) is responsible for issuing ticket-granting tickets for obtaining authentication in a domain.

12. **d.** EAP is the protocol that is used to provide authentication when using smart cards.

13. **a.** The IPSec driver compares inbound and outbound packets against a filter list.

14. **a.** True. In Windows XP, both compressed and encrypted files can be shown in an alternate color in Windows Explorer. In Windows 2000, only compressed files can be shown in an alternate color.

15. **b.** False. Encrypted files and folders cannot be compressed.

16. **a.** The certificate store is a permanent storage location for certificates, certificate revocation lists, and certificate trust lists.

17. **c.** The Security Association (SA) determines the type of encryption that is used by IPSec on a VPN connection.

18. **b.** False. Andrew must convert his file system to NTFS if he wants to encrypt files. EFS is not supported on FAT or FAT32 volumes.

19. **d.** X.509 version 3 is the standard certificate format used in Windows XP.

20. **a, d.** Public keys and private keys are the two types of encryption used in public key security.

Chapter 13 Solutions

1. **c.** The Scheduled Tasks tool can be used to run applications or programs at a predefined time.

2. **b.** Bill can go to the Network tab on Task Manager and get statistics on any network connections on his computer.

3. **b.** Devices that have to be manually installed on the computer are displayed in the Forced Hardware section of the System Information tool.

4. **b, c.** Both Available Bytes and Pages/sec are memory counters that can be used by Tom to determine if his computer is experiencing a memory problem.

5. **a.** The Security Log monitors all successful and failed logon attempts to the server.

6. **b.** An Error event is a critical event in the Event Logs and would warrant immediate attention.

7. **a.** True. Event log data can be saved for analysis in several log formats.

8. **b.** False. Any schedule that William creates using the **AT** command will be usable in Scheduled Tasks.

9. **a.** The Components section of the System Information tool provides information abut hardware devices such as disk drives, CD-ROM drives, displays, and so forth.

10. **a, c.** Tasks can be scheduled to run monthly and weekly. They can also be scheduled to run daily, at system startup, and one time only.

11. **a, b.** Greg can save the data from the event log in event log format (EVT) and text format (TXT).

12. **b.** To start Task Manager from a command line, type "taskmgr.exe".

13. **b.** The Applications section of the System Information tool is available only if a version of Office 2000 is installed on the computer. This can be any version of Office 2000, including the Small Business version.

14. **a.** True. All applications show up in Task Manager as being in either a Running or Not Responding state.

15. **b.** The User tab is available in Task Manager only if Fast Switching is enabled on the computer.

16. **b.** Virtual memory or the paging file can be configured to provide more memory than is physically available on the computer.

17. **d.** To ensure that the database is not interrupted during its processing, the processing scheduling should be set to optimized for applications. This will ensure that the application that is running in the foreground will receive the most attention from the processor.

18. **a.** Event Viewer is used to view event logs.

19. **b.** Stan can determine the amount of memory that is being used by each process by checking the Mem Usage measure under the Processor tab of Task Manager.

20. **b.** False. The Event Log is a service that is started automatically when the computer is booted.

Chapter 14 Solutions

1. **b.** False. The ASR disk is not bootable. To use the ASR disk, you must boot the system using the Windows XP Professional installation CD-ROM and begin the ASR restore process.

2. **c.** Use the Automated System Recovery (ASR) process to recover missing or corrupt boot files. To use the ASR disk, you must boot the system using the Windows XP Professional installation CD-ROM and begin the ASR restore process.

3. **d.** Perform a backup using the Backup utility, and select the System State. By selecting the System State, Backup backs up the Registry files. It also places a copy of the files in %systemroot%\repair\regback.

4. **c.** When booting in Safe Mode, only essential drivers and services are loaded. These include the mouse, keyboard, basic VGA, the Event Log, Remote Procedure Call (RPC), and the Logical Disk Manager services.

5. **b.** The Recovery Console can be started by booting the system either with the Windows XP Professional installation CD or with the Windows XP Professional Setup floppy disks. Once booted, select C to start the Recovery Console.

6. **c.** Device drivers can be disabled by using the **disable** *servicename* command found in the Recovery Console, where *servicename* is the name of the device driver or service to be disabled.

7. **d.** Backup in Windows XP Professional supports the following media types: QIC tape, DLT tape, 8mm tape, digital audio tape, floppy disks, hard disks, optical disks, CDR, and CDRW.

8. **a, b, c, d.** By default, the Recovery Console only permits access to %systemroot%, the root directory of local disks, \cmdcons and any subdirectories, and directories on floppy disks and CD-ROMs. Access can be gained to other directories by changing the local Group Policy setting named Allow Floppy Copy And Access To All Drives And Folders.

9. **a.** The log file is stored in the %systemroot% folder and is called Ntbtlog.txt.

10. **d.** The Safe Mode With Networking option loads the minimum required device drivers, including device drivers required for network connectivity.

11. **b.** Although it was found in Windows 2000 and earlier versions of Windows NT, the Emergency Repair Disk (ERD) is not supported in Windows XP Professional. To restore the Registry, you must use either the Backup utility with the System State or ASR with the System State.

12. **a.** The Safe Mode options can be accessed by pressing the F8 key when the OS selection menu is displayed.

13. **d.** The Emergency Repair Disk (ERD) Process restores the Registry files from the %systemroot%\repair directory. The Registry files stored in this directory are the Registry files created after the initial install of Windows 2000.

14. **b.** False. Individual components in the System State cannot be selected. The System State is restored as a whole because there are dependencies that occur between the different components.

15. **a.** The **enable** command can be used to set the start type for a device driver or service. The syntax of the **enable** command is as follows:

```
enable servicename start_type
```

16. **b.** Enable Boot Logging boots the system under normal conditions (all device drivers and services designated to start automatically will be loaded). It creates a log file called Ntbtlog.txt that logs the name and status of device drivers in memory. The log file is stored in the %systemroot% folder.

17. **b.** The Recovery Console command **fixboot** creates a new boot sector on the system partition.

18. **c.** The regback directory is created when the System State is backed up. The regback directory is used to store backup copies of the Registry at the time that the System State is backed up.

19. **d.** CDFS is the file system for CD-ROMs. As such, only read-only access is possible, not full access.

20. **a.** The Recovery Console can be installed as a startup option. To install, insert the Windows XP Professional installation CD into your CD-ROM drive. At the command prompt, type "D:\I386\WINNT32 /cmdcons", where D: is the drive letter of the CD-ROM drive.

Chapter 15 Solutions

1. **d.** DHCP can provide an IP address, a subnet mask, a default gateway, DNS server addresses, and WINS server addresses. MAC addresses are configured in the network adapter at the factory.

2. **a.** The User Principal Name looks exactly like an Internet email account. The UPN consists of the username followed by the @ sign followed by the user principal name suffix.

3. **b.** Kerberos v5 authentication protocol is the default authentication method. Kerberos is a standard security protocol supported by many vendors and operating systems.

4. **a.** True. A domain-based network is a logical grouping of computers that all share a common security database. This allows a user to have a single user account that can employ, when granted the proper access, any resources in the domain.

5. **a.** IPX/SPX, or NWLink, uses the 802.5 frametype when operating on a Token Ring network.

6. **d.** WINS is used to resolve NetBIOS names to IP addresses.

7. **a, b.** The key word here is nonrouted. The default gateway is the IP address of a router. When the workstation needs to send data on another subnet, it sends the data to the default gateway.

8. **a, b.** Connectivity between Windows XP Professional and NetWare requires the networking protocol NWLink, also known as IPX/SPX, and Client Services for NetWare, which provides access to NetWare file and print services.

9. **c.** The Distinguished Name uniquely identifies an object in Active Directory by including the full path to its Active Directory location. For example, the Distinguished Name of Samuel Watson, a member of the Marketing department at mycompany.com, is cn=SamuelWatson, ou=Marketing, dc=mycompany, dc=com (cn designates the common name, ou designates the organizational unit, and dc designates the domain component).

10. **b.** Because an IP address is a property of TCP/IP, selecting Obtain An IP Address Automatically from the Internet Protocol (TCP/IP) Properties dialog box will configure TCP/IP in Windows XP to use DHCP.

11. **c.** Windows XP Professional first attempts to use Kerberos. Because the Windows NT 4 domain does not contain the Kerberos Key Distribution Center on the domain controller, it then attempts to use NTLM and the SAM.

12. **c.** DNS is used to resolve hostnames to IP addresses.

13. **d.** Windows XP uses the Common Internet File Service (CIFS) protocol to access file and print resources on a Microsoft network. CIFS is identical to the Server Message Block (SMB) protocol that is used in earlier Microsoft network operating systems such as Windows NT. The other protocols listed are network protocols that facilitate communication between computers on a network.

14. **d.** Windows XP Professional stores Group Policy objects in the %systemroot%\System32\GroupPolicy directory.

15. **a.** Only a member of the Administrators group can change workgroup or domain membership.

16. **d.** Windows XP does not include a client for the AS400.

17. **d.** When accessing a network with multiple frametypes, you must specify each frametype. AutoDetect sets the frametype to the first one it detects.

18. **b.** False. A workgroup is a logical grouping of computers without a centralized security database. The purpose of a workgroup is to make it easier for users to identify network resources. To access these resources, a user needs a separate logon and password for each resource.

19. **a, d.** Windows XP supports two types of logons: SAM Account Name, which is provided for backward compatibility with Windows NT 4, and User Principal Name, found in Windows 2000 and Active Directory.

20. **b.** The common name, or cn, is the default Relative Distinguished Name.

Chapter 16 Solutions

1. **a.** To configure Gateway (and Client) Services for NetWare, you need to have a valid NetWare user account that is a member of the NTGATEWAY group on NetWare.

2. **b.** False. The Bindery is a standalone object. In other words, if you wanted to log on to two separate NetWare 3.12 servers, you would need a valid user account on each server. NDS, however, is replicated and distributed among the NetWare servers on the network.

3. **d.** The context represents the NDS location of a user's account. For example, if a user account called Lisa is located in an OU called Marketing and is also located in the Phoenix OU, Lisa's context would be MARKETING.PHOENIX.

4. **a, d.** To connect to a NetWare server, a Windows XP Professional workstation needs to have Client Services for NetWare and NWLink installed. CSNW permits the Windows XP Professional workstation to speak the same language of the NetWare servers—NCP. NWLink is the network protocol used by NetWare 3.12 servers.

5. **a.** If a NetWare 4.*x* or NetWare 5.*x* server is running with a Bindery context, you must specify the Preferred Server in Client Services for NetWare properties. A Bindery context simulates the Bindery found in NetWare 3.12.

6. **b, c.** Novell changed the default frametype following NetWare 3.11. NetWare 3.11 and earlier use Ethernet 802.3; NetWare 3.12 and later use Ethernet 802.2. Autodetect sets the frametype to the first one detected. Once set, it doesn't change "on the fly."

7. **a.** The NetWare group NTGATEWAY is given trustee assignments to NetWare resources. This allows the gateway to connect and authenticate to the NetWare resources.

8. **c.** The **net use** command can be used to map network drives and printer ports to network resources. Always remember to specify a resource's location using the UNC path: *Servername**Volumename*.

9. **b.** False. The Windows XP Professional workstations do not need NWLink unless that is their network's protocol. The only computer that needs NWLink installed is the Windows 2000 server that is running Gateway (and Client) Services for NetWare.

10. **a.** True. The internal network number is used for internal routing purposes, in other words, amongst the network-related processes within the computer. This is used only if you are running an application such as File and Print Services

for NetWare. By default, Windows XP sets the internal network number to 00000000. Normally, the internal network number does not need to be changed.

11. **c.** The **net use** command maps network drives to NetWare resources, much as it is used to map network drives to shares on a Microsoft network. The **net use** command uses UNC paths to locate the NetWare volume. UNC syntax is *Servername**Volume*.

12. **a.** The external network number is used for addressing and routing purposes. This is analogous to the network portion of an IP address.

13. **c.** When you are connecting to a NetWare 3.12 server, Client Services for NetWare needs to know which NetWare 3.12 server's Bindery contains the user account. CSNW uses the Preferred Server setting to locate the NetWare 3.12 server.

14. **b.** Novell introduced NDS with NetWare 4.*x*. NDS is a directory service that contains all network objects, such as user accounts, printers, servers, and so on.

15. **c.** The Bindery contains all user and group accounts, passwords, and trustee assignments in NetWare 3.12 and earlier.

16. **a.** Writing the context as a typefull name means that you notate each container object with its type. For example, ou= designates that the object named is an organizational unit. o= designates that this is the name of the NDS tree. cn= designates the common name of the object, although that is not used in a context. Only container objects are specified in the context.

17. **c.** Management doesn't want Client Services for NetWare installed, so you must install a Windows 2000 server running Gateway (and Client) Services for NetWare. This setup allows existing Microsoft clients to access the NetWare servers.

18. **b.** Gateway (and Client) Services for NetWare translates CIFS requests from Microsoft clients into NCP requests that NetWare servers understand.

19. **a.** When you are using Gateway (and Client) Services for NetWare, the Windows 2000 server maps network drives to the NetWare server. These mapped drives are then turned into shares on the Windows 2000 server that Microsoft clients can connect to.

20. **c.** The **net view** command by default lists resources on a Microsoft network. By adding the switch **/network:nw**, you can also view NetWare resources.

21. **c.** Novell changed the default frametype following NetWare 3.11. NetWare 3.11 and earlier use Ethernet 802.3. NetWare 3.12 and later use Ethernet 802.2.

22. **a, d.** NetWare 5.*x* relies on NDS for user authentication. The Default Tree specifies the NDS tree, whereas the context identifies the location where the user account can be found.

23. **d.** Feeling the competitive effects of the Internet, Novell redesigned NetWare 5.*x* to use TCP/IP as its core network protocol. Previous versions of NetWare relied on the network protocol IPX/SPX.

24. **a, c.** Objects in NDS can be either container objects or leaf objects. Container objects can contain other container objects and leaf objects. Leaf objects are objects such as user accounts, group accounts, servers, printers, and volumes.

25. **d.** NetWare 3.12 relies on the Bindery for storage of user and group account information.

Chapter 17 Solutions

1. **a.** Linux is a freely distributed operating system that runs on Intel-based computers.

2. **b.** Client for NFS allows Windows NT/2000/XP computers to access NFS files directly. You can browse the NFS network by double-clicking NFS Network in My Network Places.

3. **b.** False. Services for Unix is an add-on package that must be purchased separately from the operating system.

4. **d.** To install Services for Unix 2, you need 60MB of free disk space.

5. **d.** NFS is a standard client/server protocol used to access files across a Unix-based network. NFS is defined in Request for Comments (RFCs) 1094 and 1813.

6. **b.** Server for NIS integrates Active Directory and NIS by allowing an Active Directory domain controller to act as a master NIS server. This permits an Active Directory administrator to create, modify, and delete user accounts in both security domains.

7. **a.** User Name Mapping provides a way to create maps between Windows and Unix user and group accounts. For example, a Windows user account is mapped to a Unix account. When a user (running either Client for NFS, Server for NFS, or Gateway for NFS) attempts to access data on a Unix server, the client contacts a User Name Mapping server, which in turn matches the Windows account to the appropriate Unix account.

8. **c.** The Telnet Server is limited to 10 connections when installed on a Windows 2000/XP Professional or Windows NT Workstation 4 computer.

9. **d.** Server for NFS is not installed when performing a standard installation on a Windows XP Professional computer. If your computer is running Windows NT Workstation 4 or Windows 2000/XP Professional, the following components are installed during a Standard Installation: Telnet Client, Telnet Server, Unix Shell and Utilities, and Client for NFS.

10. **d.** The Telnet Client allows a user to connect to a remote computer and execute programs. The Telnet Client uses port 23 (the Telnet protocol).

11. **a.** Server for NFS allows a Windows NT server or a Windows 2000 server to act as an NFS server, exporting Windows directories as NFS file systems.

12. **c.** AT&T started the development project that eventually became Unix. Sun and HP are vendors who produce two separate variations of Unix.

13. **b.** The Telnet Client command to create a new connection to a Telnet Server is **open *hostname***, where *hostname* is the name of the Telnet Server.

14. **b.** The Telnet Client allows a user to connect via the Telnet protocol (port 23) to a remote computer over a TCP/IP-based network. It provides a command-line interface to execute applications remotely.

15. **a.** Server for PCNFS allows a user to supply his or her Unix username and password to be authenticated. Once verified, the Windows 2000 server running Server for PCNFS returns the user identifier (UID) and group identifier (GID). The user's computer then connects to the Unix server. This component is included in Services for Unix 2 to provide support for earlier Services for Unix clients.

16. **b.** False. A user accessing files on an NFS share must have a valid NIS user account.

17. **b.** If your computer is also a domain controller, Server for NFS Authentication is also installed when performing a standard install.

18. **b.** False. The Gateway for NFS component can only be installed on Windows NT Server or Windows 2000 Server computers.

19. **c.** The C programming language was adopted by the architects of Unix to enhance the operating system by introducing new capabilities, such as scripting.

20. **c.** Gateway for NFS creates connections to NFS servers and in turn hosts these connections as Windows shares. When Windows-based clients want to access NFS servers, they make a connection to the appropriate share found on the Gateway server using the native CIFS protocol.

Chapter 18 Solutions

1. **b.** The General tab is used to configure temporary Internet file settings. To configure the amount of disk space used, you must click the Settings button under the temporary Internet files section.

2. **d.** The Restricted Sites content zone should contain sites that you do not trust and that could potentially damage your computer. The security settings for this content zone disable all ActiveX controls, file downloads, and Java support.

3. **c.** The Medium-High privacy setting blocks third-party cookies that do not have a compact privacy policy. It also blocks both first- and third-party cookies that use personally identifiable information without your consent.

4. **d.** The Content tab is used to configure parental rules. You can use the Content Advisor to set rating levels for different Web sites.

5. **d.** The Content tab is used to configure certificates.

6. **b.** Internet Explorer 6 enables you to specify different Internet programs to meet your needs. The Programs tab is used to configure this capability.

Chapter 19 Solutions

1. **c.** Remote Desktop is based on the Windows Terminal Services. Fast Switching and Remote Assistance also use this technology.

2. **b.** RDP, or Remote Desktop Protocol, is the protocol used to provide remote access via Remote Desktop.

3. **a.** True. Remote Desktop supports copy, cut, and paste operations from the remote client to a local application.

4. **c.** Remote Desktop Connection settings files end in the .rdp extension.

5. **a.** Sally can configure an application such as Microsoft Word to run automatically when she connects to her remote session via the Program tab of the Remote Desktop Connection dialog box.

6. **b.** If Hattie wants to be able to listen to the audio of the remote computer she is accessing she should select Bring To This Computer under Remote Computer Sound.

7. **a.** True. When a remote session is established using Remote Desktop Connection, all of the local drives can be made accessible on the remote computer.

8. **a.** Benson could load the Remote Desktop Connection on his Windows NT 4 workstation and use that to connect to his Windows XP Professional computer at home. Remote Desktop Connection is the replacement for the Terminal Services client used in previous versions of Windows.

9. **a.** If Remote Desktop Web Connection is installed on the Windows XP Professional computer, a user can access it using Internet Explorer from any Internet connection.

10. **d.** From within Windows Messenger, Jill should select Ask For Remote Assistance from the Tools menu.

11. **b.** The Offer Remote Assistance group policy feature, if enabled, will allow helpers to offer assistance to users running Remote Assistance.

12. **a.** True. Printers that are connected to LPT or COM ports are automatically detected when a connection is established using Remote Desktop.

13. **d.** The Connection Bar can be used within a full-screen remote session to maximize and minimize the window.

14. **a.** True. If Sam did not log off before he disconnected, he will be reconnected to his old session when he reconnects his Windows XP Professional computer. Any applications that were running when he disconnected will still be running when he reconnects.

15. **c.** Internet Information Services is required on the Windows XP Professional computer before Remote Desktop Web Connection can be installed.

Appendix B
Objectives for Exam 70-270

Installing Windows XP Professional	Chapter(s)
Perform an attended installation of Windows XP Professional	2
Perform an unattended installation of Windows XP Professional	2
• Install Windows XP Professional by using Remote Installation Services (RIS)	
• Install Windows XP Professional by using the System Preparation Tool	
• Create unattended answer files by using Setup Manager to automate the installation of Windows XP Professional	
Upgrade from a previous version of Windows to Windows XP Professional	2
• Prepare a computer to meet upgrade requirements	
• Migrate existing user environments to a new installation	
Perform postinstallation updates and product activation	2
Troubleshoot failed installations	2

Implementing and Conducting Administration of Resources	
Monitor, manage, and troubleshoot access to files and folders	6
• Configure, manage, and troubleshoot file compression	
• Control access to files and folders by using permissions	
• Optimize access to files and folders	
Manage and troubleshoot access to shared folders	6
• Create and remove shared folders	
• Control access to shared folders by using permissions	
• Manage and troubleshoot Web server resources	
Connect to local and network print devices	7
• Manage printers and print jobs	
• Control access to printers by using permissions	
• Connect to an Internet printer	
• Connect to a local print device	
Configure and manage file systems	6
• Convert from one file system to another file system	
• Configure NTFS, FAT32, or FAT file systems	
Manage and troubleshoot access to and synchronization of offline files	6
Configure and troubleshoot fax support	8

Implementing, Managing, Monitoring, and Troubleshooting Hardware Devices and Drivers	Chapter(s)
Implement, manage, and troubleshoot disk devices	8
• Install, configure, and manage DVD and CD-ROM devices	
• Monitor and configure disks	
• Monitor, configure, and troubleshoot volumes	
• Monitor and configure removable media, such as tape devices	
Implement, manage, and troubleshoot display devices	8
• Configure multiple-display support	
• Install, configure, and troubleshoot a video adapter	
Configure Advanced Configuration Power Interface (ACPI)	8
Implement, manage, and troubleshoot input and output (I/O) devices	8
• Monitor, configure, and troubleshoot I/O devices, such as printers, scanners, multimedia devices, mice, keyboards, and smart card readers	
• Monitor, configure, and troubleshoot multimedia hardware, such as cameras	
• Install, configure, and manage modems	
• Install, configure, and manage Infrared Data Association (IrDA) devices	
• Install, configure, and manage wireless devices	
• Install, configure, and manage USB devices	
• Install, configure, and manage handheld devices	
Manage and troubleshoot drivers and driver signing	8
Monitor and configure multiprocessor computers	8

Monitoring and Optimizing System Performance and Reliability	
Monitor, optimize, and troubleshoot performance of the Windows XP Professional desktop	13
• Optimize and troubleshoot memory performance	
• Optimize and troubleshoot processor utilization	
• Optimize and troubleshoot disk performance	
• Optimize and troubleshoot application performance	
• Configure, manage, and troubleshoot Scheduled Tasks	
Manage, monitor, and optimize system performance for mobile users	11
Restore and back up the operating system, system state data, and user data	14
• Recover system state data and user data by using Windows Backup	
• Troubleshoot system restoration by starting in Safe Mode	
• Recover system state data and user data by using the Recovery Console	

Configuring and Troubleshooting the Desktop Environment	
Configure and manage user profiles	5
Configure support for multiple languages or multiple locations	5
• Enable multilanguage support	
• Configure multilanguage support for users	
• Configure local settings	
• Configure Windows XP Professional for multiple locations	
Manage applications by using Windows Installer packages	5
Configure and troubleshoot desktop settings	5
Configure and troubleshoot accessibility services	5

Implementing, Managing, and Troubleshooting Network Protocols and Services	Chapter(s)
Configure and troubleshoot the TCP/IP protocol	15
Connect to computers by using dial-up networking	9
• Connect to computers by using a virtual private network (VPN) connection	
• Create a dial-up connection to connect to a remote access server	
• Connect to the Internet by using dial-up networking	
• Configure and troubleshoot Internet Connection Sharing	
Connect to resources using Internet Explorer	18
Configure, manage, and troubleshoot Remote Desktop and Remote Assistance	19
Configure, manage, and troubleshoot an Internet connection firewall	9

Configuring, Managing, and Troubleshooting Security	
Configure, manage, and troubleshoot Encryption File System (EFS)	12
Configure, manage, and troubleshoot local security policy	12
Configure, manage, and troubleshoot local user and group accounts	12
• Configure, manage, and troubleshoot auditing	
• Configure, manage, and troubleshoot account settings	
• Configure, manage, and troubleshoot account policy	
• Configure and troubleshoot local users and groups	
• Configure, manage, and troubleshoot user and group rights	
• Troubleshoot cache credentials	
Configure, manage, and troubleshoot a security configuration	12
Configure, manage, and troubleshoot Internet Explorer security settings	18

Appendix B

Appendix C
Study Resources

Books

Microsoft Corporation. *Microsoft Windows XP Professional Resource Kit Documentation.* Microsoft Press, Redmond, WA, 2001. ISBN 0-7356-1485-7. Contains comprehensive technical information and insights direct from the Microsoft Windows XP product development team.

Microsoft Corporation. *Administering Microsoft Windows XP Professional Operations Guide.* Microsoft Press, Redmond, WA, 2001. A one-stop resource direct from Microsoft covers all major topics of Windows XP, including deployment, desktop management, and security.

Minasi, Mark. *Mastering Windows XP Professional.* Sybex, Inc., Alameda, CA, 2001. ISBN 0-7821-2981-1. This book is from the leading Windows authority, Mark Minasi, and includes information about installing, configuring, and administering Windows XP.

Stanek, William R. *Microsoft Windows XP Professional: Administrator's Pocket Consultant.* Microsoft Press, Redmond, WA, 2001. ISBN 0-7356-1381-8. A pocket-sized resource that provides fast answers to Microsoft Windows XP-based desktop administration. Includes quick-reference tables, lists, and step-by-step instructions.

Microsoft Windows XP Step by Step. Online Training Solutions, Inc., Redmond, WA, 2001. ISBN 0-7356-1383-4. This book provides step-by-step instructions for many features of Windows XP, including adding and removing programs, hooking up printers and other devices, and managing files and folders.

Periodicals

Certification Magazine, MediaTec Publishing, Oakland, CA. Monthly magazine slanted toward certified professionals of information technology. Its aim is to provide IT professionals and technical trainers with a comprehensive look at all platforms of IS/IT certification and training.

Microsoft Certified Professional Magazine, Microsoft Corporation, Irvine, CA. A monthly magazine for Windows NT experts that is also a good resource for Microsoft certification information.

Windows and .NET Magazine (formerly *Windows 2000 Magazine*), Duke Communications, International, Loveland, CO. Covers the technical aspects of Windows XP, Windows 2000, Windows NT, and Windows BackOffice.

Microsoft-Approved Test Providers

MeasureUp, Inc.—**www.measureup.com**

Self Test Software, Inc.—**www.selftestsoftware.com**

Online Resources

www.microsoft.com/windowsxp—Microsoft's default site for Windows XP. This site has links to how-to articles, technical information, and resources for end users to learn about Windows XP.

www.microsoft.com/hwdev/Whistler—A developer site with information about driver and hardware development for Windows XP. Includes a section on the white papers for various hardware and software components when developing for Windows XP.

www.wxperience.com—This site has current news about Windows XP and an archive of articles about Windows XP from ZDNet and CNET. In addition, downloads are available as well as access to forums for discussion of issues such as drivers and hardware and application compatibility.

www.wxperience.com/links.php—Excellent site that provides links to other Windows XP sites, hardware and software manufacturers, and game manufacturers.

support.microsoft.com—Microsoft Knowledge Base, which you can search for technical support information and self-help tools for Microsoft products. This site is great for problem solving. Users can search the Microsoft Knowledge Base with specific questions on all of Microsoft's products.

www.microsoft.com/technet—Microsoft TechNet home page. TechNet provides technical resources for Windows professionals. Technical information is provided for all of Microsoft's products.

www.windows2000experience.com—This page gives IT professionals the how-to knowledge, resources, and product information needed to evaluate and deploy Windows 2000. This site is provided by *Windows 2000 Magazine*, and it has current news on Windows 2000, reprinted articles from *Windows 2000 Magazine,* and a

Windows 2000 discussion forum for posted questions. This site is a good one-stop resource.

www.labmice.net—LabMice.net prides itself on being "the definitive online resource for IT Professionals who deploy, manage, and support Microsoft Windows 2000 products and services." The site consolidates information from other technical sites into one user-friendly resource. LabMice.net also has reviews of the must-have books for keeping current with the latest technology.

www.windows2000faq.com—A Windows 2000 Frequently Asked Questions resource from *Windows 2000 Magazine*. This site, which is updated weekly, contains a lot of useful information about all aspects of Windows 2000. Users can search the site for specific topics.

www.winsupersite.com—Site provided by *Windows 2000 Magazine* that has reviews of the latest Windows products. This site prides itself on being the one site you need to evaluate, administer, and use Microsoft's Windows operating systems.

www.win2000mag.com—Online version of *Windows 2000 Magazine*. This is a searchable site with access to back issues of *Windows 2000 Magazine*. Detailed information is accessible only to subscribers of the hard copy version of the magazine.

www.i386.com—Good resource for Windows 2000 information. This site gives brief synopses of various components of Windows 2000.

www.microsoft.com/traincert—Microsoft's training and certification page; lists requirements for all Microsoft certifications. It also provides links to training resources and the latest news on training and certification for Microsoft products.

www.windowsitlibrary.com—A free online technical reference source for Windows NT, 2000, and XP. This site lists subjects by topic and has brief online chapters on each topic. All material is original technical content or is selected content licensed from computer book publishers.

www.microsoft.com/seminar—Microsoft Seminar Online resource center. Contains online seminars and presentations, which cover IT topics, such as product features, planning, deployment, development, and strategic assessment.

www.mcpmag.com—Online version of *Window Microsoft Certified Professional Magazine*. Very thorough site, with an MCP chat area and discussion groups. Users can view current and previous issues of *MCP Magazine*. It also has salary surveys for all levels of Microsoft certification.

www.cramsession.com—Certification and training site that provides free study guides (or Cramsessions), free exam practice questions, and free information on IT topics.

Appendix C

www.examcram.com—The Coriolis Group's certification site. Here, you can access training courses and materials, read the latest industry news, get study tips, find questions and answers, find out about mentor programs, join discussion groups, take real-world exam practice questions, and more.

www.microsoft.com/traincert/mcp—Microsoft Certification Program news and certification track requirements.

www.ittutor.com—ITTutor.com offers free online training for Windows NT and 2000. Users must download the ITT2000 applications to use the free test.

www.brainbuzz.com—BrainBuzz.com labels itself the IT Vortal (a vertical portal—a comprehensive Web site that provides information, resources, and services targeted to a specific industry). BrainBuzz.com is the vertical portal for IT career enhancement.

www.mcmcse.com—The MC MCSE certification site has three areas: (1) a certification section that contains practice exams, study notes, and links; (2) a knowledge area that provides links to TechTutorials.com, which is a free Web site that provides a searchable index of over 1,000 terms; and (3) an employment section that provides career advice and resources as well as access to a database of over 220,000 tech jobs.

www.mcsetutor.com—The MCSETutor.com site provides solutions for MCSE self-study needs. It has a forum area where users can post questions about various topics relating to certification. It also has a book list of recommended books for Windows NT and 2000.

www.microsoft.com/partner—Microsoft Direct Access is designed to help consultants get the information they need to support Microsoft products. Listings are available for local Microsoft news and events. The Microsoft Direct Access training programs offer discounted technical training and free online courseware that enables individuals to study at their own pace. Evaluation tools and quarterly briefings are also available to help users stay up-to-date on the latest products.

mspress.microsoft.com—Microsoft Press is a good source for information about Microsoft products. The **mspress.microsoft.com** site is the starting point for locating Microsoft-approved books, study guides, and other resources for Microsoft's certification tests.

windows2000.about.com—This site provides book reviews, access to Windows 2000 forums, and the latest Windows 2000 news.

Appendix D
Windows XP Professional
Keyboard Shortcuts

This appendix contains 13 tables that are divided into separate areas of useful keyboard shortcuts.

Table D.1 Windows XP keyboard shortcuts.

Shortcut Key	Description
Ctrl+C	Copy
Ctrl+X	Cut
Ctrl+V	Paste
Ctrl+Z	Undo
Delete	Delete
Shift+Delete	Delete selected item permanently without placing the item in the Recycle Bin
Ctrl while dragging an item	Copy selected item
Ctrl+Shift while dragging an item	Create shortcut to selected item
F2	Rename selected item
Ctrl+Right Arrow	Move the insertion point to the beginning of the next word
Ctrl+Left Arrow	Move the insertion point to the beginning of the previous word
Ctrl+Down Arrow	Move the insertion point to the beginning of the next paragraph
Ctrl+Up Arrow	Move the insertion point to the beginning of the previous paragraph
Ctrl+Shift with any of the arrow keys	Highlight a block of text
Shift with any of the arrow keys	Select more than one item in a window or on the desktop, or select text within a document
Ctrl+A	Select all
F3	Search for a file or folder
Alt+Enter	View properties for the selected item
Alt+F4	Close the active item, or quit the active program
Alt+Enter	Display the properties of the selected object
Alt+Spacebar	Open the shortcut menu for the active window
Ctrl+F4	Close the active document in programs that allow you to have multiple documents open simultaneously
Alt+Tab	Switch between open items
Alt+Esc	Cycle through items in the order they were opened
F6	Cycle through screen elements in a window or on the desktop

(continued)

Table D.1   Windows XP keyboard shortcuts *(continued).*

Shortcut Key	Description
F4	Display the Address bar list in My Computer or Windows Explorer
Shift+F10	Display the shortcut menu for the selected item
Alt+Spacebar	Display the System menu for the active window
Ctrl+Esc	Display the Start menu
Alt+underlined letter in a menu name	Display the corresponding menu
Underlined letter in a command name on an open menu	Carry out the corresponding command
F10	Activate the menu bar in the active program
Right Arrow	Open the next menu to the right, or open a submenu
Left Arrow	Open the next menu to the left, or close a submenu
F5	Refresh the active window
Backspace	View the folder one level up in My Computer or Windows Explorer
Esc	Cancel the current task
Shift when you insert a CD into the CD-ROM drive	Prevent the CD from automatically playing

Table D.2   Dialog box keyboard shortcuts.

Shortcut Key	Description
Ctrl+Tab	Move forward through tabs
Ctrl+Shift+Tab	Move backward through tabs
Tab	Move forward through options
Shift+Tab	Move backward through options
Alt+underlined letter	Carry out the corresponding command or select the corresponding option
Enter	Carry out the command for the active option or button
Spacebar	Select or clear the checkbox if the active option is a checkbox
Arrow keys	Select a button if the active option is a group of option buttons
F1	Display Help
F4	Display the items in the active list
Backspace	Open a folder one level up if a folder is selected in the Save As or Open dialog box

Table D.3   Accessibility keyboard shortcuts.

Shortcut Key	Description
Right Shift for eight seconds	Switch FilterKeys on and off
Left Alt+Left Shift+Print Screen	Switch High Contrast on and off
Left Alt+Left Shift+Num Lock	Switch MouseKeys on and off
Shift five times	Switch StickyKeys on and off
Num Lock for five seconds	Switch ToggleKeys on and off
Windows logo key+U	Open Utility Manager

Table D.4   Microsoft Natural keyboard shortcuts.

Shortcut Key	Description
Windows logo key	Display or hide the Start menu
Windows logo key+Break	Display the System Properties dialog box
Windows logo key+D	Show the desktop
Windows logo key+M	Minimize all windows
Windows logo key+Shift+M	Restore minimized windows
Windows logo key+E	Open My Computer
Windows logo key+F	Search for a file or folder
Ctrl+ Windows logo key+F	Search for computers
Windows logo key+F1	Display Windows Help
Windows logo key+L	Lock your computer if you are connected to a network domain, or switch users if you are not connected to a network domain
Windows logo key+R	Open the Run dialog box
Windows logo key	Display the shortcut menu for the selected item
Windows logo key+U	Open Utility Manager

Table D.5   Windows Explorer keyboard shortcuts.

Shortcut Key	Description
End	Display the bottom of the active window
Home	Display the top of the active window
Num Lock+asterisk on numeric keypad (*)	Display all subfolders under the selected folder
Num Lock+plus sign on numeric keypad (+)	Display the contents of the selected folder
Num Lock+minus sign on numeric keypad (-)	Collapse the selected folder
Left Arrow	Collapse current selection if it's expanded, or select parent folder
Right Arrow	Display current selection if it's collapsed, or select first subfolder

Table D.6   Help Viewer Keyboard shortcuts.

Shortcut Key	Description
Alt+Spacebar	Display the System menu
Shift+F10	Display the Help viewer shortcut menu
Alt+Tab	Switch between the Help viewer and other open windows
Alt+O	Display the Options menu
Alt+O, and then press T	Hide or show the navigation pane
Ctrl+Tab	Switch to the next tab in the navigation pane
Ctrl+Shift+Tab	Switch to the previous tab in the navigation pane
Up Arrow	Move up one topic in the table of contents, index, or search results list
Down Arrow	Move down one topic in the table of contents, index, or search results list
Page Up	Move up one page in the table of contents, index, or search results list
Page Down	Move down one page in the table of contents, index, or search results list

(continued)

Appendix D

Table D.6   Help Viewer Keyboard shortcuts *(continued).*

Shortcut Key	Description
F6	Switch focus between the navigation pane and the topic pane
Alt+O, and then press R	Refresh the topic that appears in the topic pane
Up Arrow or Down Arrow	Scroll through a topic
Ctrl+Home	Move to the beginning of a topic
Ctrl+End	Move to the end of a topic
Ctrl+A	Highlight all text in the topic pane
Alt+O, and then press P	Print a topic
Alt+O, and then press B	Move back to the previously viewed topic
Alt+O, and then press F	Move forward to the next (previously viewed) topic
Alt+F4	Close the Help viewer

Table D.7   Search tab keyboard shortcuts.

Shortcut Key	Description
Alt+S	Display the Search tab
Alt+L	Start a search
Alt+D or Enter	Display the selected topic

Table D.8   Index tab keyboard shortcuts.

Shortcut Key	Description
Alt+N	Display the Index tab
Up Arrow or Down Arrow	Select a keyword in the list
Alt+D or Enter	Display the associated topic

Table D.9   Contents tab keyboard shortcuts.

Shortcut Key	Description
Alt+C	Display the Contents tab
Right Arrow	Open a book
Left Arrow	Close a book
Backspace	Return to the previous open book
Up Arrow or Down Arrow	Select a topic
Enter	Display the selected topic

Table D.10   MMC main window keyboard shortcuts.

Shortcut Key	Description
Ctrl+O	Open a saved console
Ctrl+N	Open a new console
Ctrl+S	Save the open console
Ctrl+M	Add or remove a console item

(continued)

Table D.10 MMC main window keyboard shortcuts _(continued)_.

Shortcut Key	Description
Ctrl+W	Open a new window
F5	Refresh the content of all console windows
Alt+Spacebar	Display the MMC window menu
Alt+F4	Close the console
Alt+A	Display the Action menu
Alt+V	Display the View menu
Alt+F	Display the File menu
Alt+O	Display the Favorites menu

Table D.11 Navigation in MMC.

Shortcut Key	Description
Tab or F6	Move forward between panes in the active console window
Shift+Tab or Shift+F6	Move backward between panes in the active console window
Ctrl+Tab or Ctrl+F6	Move forward between console windows
Ctrl+Shift+Tab or Ctrl+Shift+F6	Move backward between console windows
Plus sign (+) on the numeric keypad	Expand the selected item
Minus sign (-) on the numeric keypad	Collapse the selected item
Asterisk (*) on the numeric keypad	Expand the entire console tree below the root item in the active console window
Up Arrow	Move the selection up one item in a pane
Down Arrow	Move the selection down one item in a pane
Page Up	Move the selection to the top item visible in a pane
Page Down	Move the selection to the bottom item visible in a pane
Home	Move the selection to the first item in a pane
End	Move the selection to the last item in a pane
Right Arrow	Expand the selected item; if the selected item doesn't contain hidden items, behaves like Down Arrow
Left Arrow	Collapse the selected item; if the selected item doesn't contain exposed items, behaves like Up Arrow
Alt+Right Arrow	Move the selection to the next item; performs the same function as the Forward button on the toolbar
Alt+Left Arrow	Move the selection to the previous item; performs the same function as the Back button on the toolbar

Table D.12 MMC console window keyboard shortcuts.

Shortcut Key	Description
Ctrl+P	Print the current page or active pane
Alt+Minus sign	Display the Window menu for the active console window
Shift+F10	Display the Action shortcut menu for the selected item
F1	Open the Help topic, if any, for the selected item

(continued)

Appendix D

Table D.12   MMC console window keyboard shortcuts *(continued)*.

Shortcut Key	Description
F5	Refresh the content of all console windows
Ctrl+F10	Maximize the active console window
Ctrl+F5	Restore the active console window
Alt+Enter	Display the Properties dialog box, if any, for the selected item
F2	Rename the selected item
Ctrl+F4	Close the active console window; when a console has only one console window, this closes the console

Table D.13   Terminal Server shortcut keys.

Shortcut Key	Description
Alt+Page Up	Switch between programs from left to right
Alt+Page Down	Switch between programs from right to left
Alt+Insert	Cycle through the programs in the order they were started
Alt+Home	Display the Start menu
Ctrl+Alt+Break	Switch the client between a window and full screen
Ctrl+Alt+End	Open the Windows Security dialog box
Alt+Delete	Display the Windows menu
Ctrl+Alt+Minus sign (-) on the numeric keypad	Place a snapshot of the active window, within the client, on the Terminal Server clipboard (provides the same functionality as pressing Print Screen on a local computer)
Ctrl+Alt+Plus sign (+) on the numeric keypad	Place a snapshot of the entire client window area on the Terminal Server clipboard (provides the same functionality as pressing Alt+Print Screen on a local computer)

Appendix E
Windows XP Professional
Command-Line Utilities

Windows XP Professional includes an impressive number of commands that can be executed directly from a command prompt. These tools can be incorporated into batch files or scripts to further enhance the functionality of Windows XP. This appendix describes these commands and their usage.

arp

The **arp** command displays and modifies entries in the Address Resolution Protocol (ARP) cache, which contains one or more tables that are used to store IP addresses and their resolved Ethernet or Token Ring physical addresses.

Syntax

```
arp [-a [InetAddr] [-N IfaceAddr]] [-g [InetAddr] [-N IfaceAddr]] [-d
InetAddr [IfaceAddr]] [-s InetAddr EtherAddr [IfaceAddr]]
```

The following table describes the switches for the **arp** command.

Parameter	Description
-a [*InetAddr*] [-N *IfaceAddr*]	Displays current ARP cache tables for all interfaces
-g [*InetAddr*] [-N *IfaceAddr*]	Identical to -a
-d *InetAddr* [*IfaceAddr*]	Deletes an entry with a specific IP address, where *InetAddr* is the IP address
-s *InetAddr EtherAddr* [*IfaceAddr*]	Adds a static entry to the ARP cache that resolves the IP address *InetAddr* to the physical address *EtherAddr*
/?	Displays help at the command prompt

at

The **at** command schedules commands and programs to run on a computer at a specified time and date. You can use **at** only when the Schedule service is running. Used without parameters, **at** lists scheduled commands.

Syntax

```
at [\\ComputerName] [{[ID] [/delete]|/delete [/yes]}]
at [[\\ComputerName] hours:minutes [/interactive] [{/every:date[,...]|/
next:date[,...]}] command]
```

The following table describes the switches for the **at** command.

Parameter	Description
\\ComputerName	Specifies a remote computer. If you omit this parameter, **at** schedules the commands and programs on the local computer.
ID	Specifies the identification number assigned to a scheduled command.
/delete	Cancels a scheduled command. If you omit *ID*, all the scheduled commands on the computer are canceled.
/yes	Answers yes to all queries from the system when you delete scheduled events.
hours:minutes	Specifies the time when you want to run the command.
/interactive	Enables you to interact with the desktop of the user who is logged on at the time the command runs.
/every:	Runs on every specified day or days of the week or month (for example, every Thursday, or the third day of every month).
date	Specifies the date.
/next:	Runs on the next occurrence of the day (for example, next Thursday).
/?	Displays help at the prompt.

cacls

The **cacls** command displays or modifies access control lists (ACLs) of files.

Syntax

```
cacls filename [/t] [/e] [/c] [/g user:perm] [/r user [...]] [/p user:perm
[...]] [/d user [...]]
```

The following table describes the switches for the **calc** command.

Parameter	Description
filename	Displays ACLs of specified files.
/t	Changes ACLs of specified files in the current directory and all subdirectories.
/e	Edits an ACL instead of replacing it.
/c	Continues changing ACLs, ignoring errors.
/g user:perm	Grants specified user access rights. Possible values for *perm* are **n** (None), **r** (Read), **c** (Change or Write), and **f** (Full Control).
/r user	Revokes specified user access rights.
/p user:perm	Replaces specified user access rights. Possible values for *perm* are **n** (None), **r** (Read), **c** (Change or Write), and **f** (Full Control).
/d user	Denies the specified user access.

chkdsk

The **chkdsk** command creates and displays a status report for a disk based on the file system. **chkdsk** also lists and corrects errors on the disk. Used without parameters, **chkdsk** displays the status of the disk in the current drive.

Syntax

```
chkdsk [volume:][[Path] FileName] [/f] [/v] [/r] [/x] [/i] [/c] [/l[:size]]
```

The following table describes the switches for the **chkdsk** command.

Parameter	Description
volume:	Specifies the drive letter (followed by a colon), mount point, or volume name.
[Path] FileName	Specifies the location and name of a file or set of files that you want **chkdsk** to check for fragmentation.
/f	Fixes errors on the disk. The disk must be locked. If **chkdsk** cannot lock the drive, a message appears that asks you if you want to check the drive the next time you restart the computer.
/v	Displays the name of each file in every directory as the disk is checked.
/r	Locates bad sectors and recovers readable information. The disk must be locked.
/x	Use with NTFS only. Forces the volume to dismount first, if necessary. All open handles to the drive are invalidated. **/x** also includes the functionality of **/f**.
/i	Use with NTFS only. Performs a less vigorous check of index entries, reducing the amount of time needed to run **chkdsk**.
/c	Use with NTFS only. Skips the checking of cycles within the folder structure, reducing the amount of time needed to run **chkdsk**.
/l[:size]	Use with NTFS only. Changes the log file size to the size you type. If you omit the *size* parameter, **/l** displays the current size.
/?	Displays help at the command prompt.

cipher

The **cipher** command displays or alters the encryption of folders and files on NTFS volumes. Used without parameters, **cipher** displays the encryption state of the current folder and any files it contains.

Syntax

```
cipher [{/e|/d}] [/s:dir] [/a] [/i] [/f] [/q] [/h] [/k] [/u[/n]] [PathName
[...]] | [/r:PathNameWithoutExtension] | [/w:PathName]
```

The following table describes the switches for the **cipher** command.

Parameter	Description
/e	Encrypts the specified folders.
/d	Decrypts the specified folders.
/s: *dir*	Performs the selected operation in the specified folder and all subfolders.
/a	Performs the operation for files and directories.
/I	Continues performing the specified operation even after errors occur. By default, **cipher** stops when it encounters an error.
/f	Forces the encryption or decryption of all specified objects. By default, **cipher** skips files that have been encrypted or decrypted already.
/q	Reports only the most essential information.
/h	Displays files with hidden or system attributes. By default, these files are not encrypted or decrypted.
/k	Creates a new file encryption key for the user running **cipher**. If you use this option, **cipher** ignores all of the other options.
/u	Updates the user's file encryption key or recovery agent's key to the current ones in all of the encrypted files on local drives (that is, if the keys have been changed). This option only works with **/n**.
/n	Prevents keys from being updated. Use this option to find all the encrypted files on the local drives. This option only works with **/u**.
PathName	Specifies a pattern, file, or folder.
/r:*PathNameWithoutExtension*	Generates a new recovery agent certificate and private key, and then writes them to files with the file name specified in *PathNameWithoutExtension*. If you use this option, **cipher** ignores all the other options.
/w:*PathName*	Removes data on unused portions of a volume. *PathName* can indicate any directory on the desired volume. If you use this option, **cipher** ignores all the other options.
/?	Displays help at the command prompt.

compact

The **compact** command displays and alters the compression of files or directories on NTFS partitions. Used without parameters, **compact** displays the compression state of the current directory.

Syntax

```
compact [{/c|/u}] [/s[:dir]] [/a] [/i] [/f] [/q] [FileName[...]]
```

The following table describes the switches for the **compact** command.

Parameter	Description
/c	Compresses the specified directory or file.
/u	Uncompresses the specified directory or file.
/s:*dir*	Specifies that the requested action (compress or uncompress) be applied to all subdirectories of the specified directory, or of the current directory if none is specified.

(continued)

Parameter	Description
/a	Displays hidden or system files.
/i	Ignores errors.
/f	Forces compression or uncompression of the specified directory or file. This is used in the case of a file that was partly compressed when the operation was interrupted by a system crash.
/q	Reports only the most essential information.
FileName	Specifies the file or directory. You can use multiple file names and wildcard characters (* and ?).
/?	Displays help at the command prompt.

convert

The **convert** command converts FAT and FAT32 volumes to NTFS.

Syntax

```
convert [volume] /fs:ntfs [/v] [/cvtarea:FileName] [/nosecurity] [/x]
```

The following table describes the switches for the **convert** command.

Parameter	Description
volume	Specifies the drive letter (followed by a colon), mount point, or volume name to convert to NTFS.
/fs:ntfs	Required. Converts the volume to NTFS.
/v	Specifies verbose mode; that is, all messages are displayed during conversion.
/cvtarea:*FileName*	For advanced users only. Specifies that the Master File Table (MFT) and other NTFS metadata files are written to an existing, contiguous placeholder file.

defrag

The **defrag** command locates and consolidates fragmented boot files, data files, and folders on local volumes.

Syntax

```
defrag volume
defrag volume [/a]
defrag volume [/a] [/v]
defrag volume [/v]
defrag volume [/f]
```

The following table describes the switches for the **defrag** command.

Parameter	Description
volume	The drive letter or a mount point of the volume to be defragmented.
/a	Analyzes the volume and displays a summary of the analysis report.
/v	Displays the complete analysis and defragmentation reports. When used in combination with /a, displays only the analysis report. When used alone, displays both the analysis and defragmentation reports.
/f	Forces defragmentation of the volume regardless of whether it needs to be defragmented.
/?	Displays help at the command prompt.

DiskPart

DiskPart is a command-line tool used to manage disks, partitions and volumes.

The following table describes the switches for the DiskPart command.

Parameter	Description
active	Marks the partition as active.
add disk =n	Adds a disk.
assign [{letter=dlmount=path}]	Changes the drive letter associated with a removable device.
break disk=n	Breaks the mirrored volume with focus into two simple volumes; applies only to dynamic disks.
clean	Removes all partition or volume information.
iconvert basic	Converts an empty dynamic disk to a basic disk.
convert dynamic	Converts a basic disk to a dynamic disk.
convert gpt	Converts an empty basic disk with the MBR partition style to a basic disk with the GPT partition style; Itanium-based computers only.
convert mbr	Converts an empty basic disk with the GPT partition style to a basic disk with the MBR style; Itanium-based computers only.
create partition efi [size=n] [offset=n]	Creates an EFI system on a GPT disk; Itanium-based computers only.
create partition extended [size=n] [offset=n]	Creates an extended partition on the current drive.
create partition logical [size=n] [offset=n]	Creates a logical drive in an extended partition.
create partition msr [size=n] [offset=n]	Creates a Microsoft Reserved (MSR) partition on a GPT disk; Itanium-based computers only.
create partition primary [size=n] [offset=n]	Creates a primary partition on the current basic disk.
create volume raid [size=n] [disk=n]	Creates a RAID-5 volume on the specified dynamic disks.
create volume simple [size=n] [disk=n]	Creates a simple volume.
create volume stripe [size=n] [disk=n]	Creates a striped volume.
delete disk	Deletes a missing dynamic disk from the disk list.
delete partition	Deletes the partition with focus on a basic disk.
delete volume	Deletes the selected volume.

(continued)

Parameter	Description
detail disk	Displays the properties of the selected disk.
exit	Exits DiskPart.
extend [size=n] [disk=n]	Extends the volume with focus.
help	Displays a list of available commands.
import	Imports a foreign disk group into the local computer's disk group.
list disk	Displays a list of disks and information on the disks.
list partition	Displays the partition of the current disk.
list volume	List basic and dynamic volumes on all disks.
rem	Used to add comments to a script.
remove [{{letter=d|mount=*path*[all]}}]	Removes a drive letter from the volume with focus.
rescan	Used to locate new disks that have been added to the computer.
retain	Prepares an existing dynamic simple volume to be used as a boot or system volume.
select disk=[n]	Shifts focus to the specified disk.
select partition=[{n/d}]	Shifts focus to the specified partition.
select volume=[{n/d}]	Shifts focus to the specified volume.

expand

Appendix E

The **expand** command expands one or more compressed files. This command is used to retrieve compressed files from distribution disks.

Syntax

```
expand [-r] Source [Destination]
expand -d source.cab [-f:files]
expand source.cab -f:files Destination
```

The following table describes the switches for the **expand** command.

Parameter	Description
-r	Renames expanded files.
-d	Displays a list of files in the source location. Does not expand or extract the files.
-f:*files*	Specifies the files in a cabinet (CAB) file you want to expand. You can use wildcards (* and ?).
Source	Specifies the files to expand. *Source* can consist of a drive letter and colon, a directory name, a file name, or a combination. You can use wildcards (* and ?).
Destination	Specifies where files are to be expanded. If *Source* is multiple files and -r is not specified, *Destination* must be a directory. *Destination* can consist of a drive letter and colon, a directory name, a file name, or a combination.
/?	Displays help at the command prompt.

format

The **format** command formats the disk in the specified volume to accept Windows files.

Syntax

```
format volume [/fs:file-system] [/v:label] [/q] [/a:UnitSize] [/c] [/x]
format volume [/v:label] [/q] [/f:size]
format volume [/v:label] [/q] [/t:tracks /n:sectors]
format volume [/v:label] [/q]
format volume [/q]
```

The following table describes the switches for the **format** command.

Parameter	Description
volume	Specifies the mount point, volume name, or drive letter of the drive you want to format.
/fs:file-system	Specifies the file system to use: FAT, FAT32, or NTFS. Floppy disks can use only the FAT file system.
/v:label	Specifies the volume label. I
/a:UnitSize	Specifies the allocation unit size to use on FAT, FAT32, or NTFS volumes.
/q	Performs a quick format. Deletes the file table and the root directory of a previously formatted volume but does not perform a sector-by-sector scan for bad areas.
/f:size	Specifies the size of the floppy disk to format.
/t:tracks	Specifies the number of tracks on the disk.
/n:sectors	Specifies the number of sectors per track.
/c	NTFS only. Files created on the new volume will be compressed by default.
/x	Causes the volume to dismount, if necessary, before it is formatted. Any open handles to the volume will no longer be valid.
/?	Displays help at the command prompt.

fsutil

The **fsutil** command can be used to perform many FAT and NTFS file system–related tasks, such as managing reparse points, managing sparse files, dismounting a volume, or extending a volume.

The following table describes the switches for the **fsutil** command.

Parameter	Description
Behavior	Enables or disables the settings for generating 8.3 character-length file names..
Dirty	Queries if a volume's dirty bit is set.
File	Finds a file by its SID; sets a file's short name; queries files system statistics.

(continued)

Parameter	Description
fsinfo	Lists all drives; queries volume information; queries file system statistics.
hardlink	Creates a hard link, which is a directory entry for a file.
objected	Manages object identifiers.
quota	Manages disk quotas on NTFS volumes.
reparsepoint	Queries or deletes reparse points.
sparse	Manages sparse files.
Usn	Manages the update sequence number change journal.
volume	Manages a volume; dismounts a volume; queries a volume for available disk space.

ftp

The **ftp** command transfers files to and from a computer running a File Transfer Protocol (FTP) server service, such as Internet Information Services. The **ftp** command can be used interactively or in batch mode by processing ASCII text files.

Syntax

```
ftp [-v] [-d] [-i] [-n] [-g] [-s:FileName] [-a] [-w:WindowSize] [-A] [Host]
```

The following table describes the switches for the **ftp** command.

Appendix E

Parameter	Description
-v	Suppresses the display of FTP server responses.
-d	Enables debugging, displaying all commands passed between the FTP client and FTP server.
-i	Disables interactive prompting during multiple-file transfers.
-n	Suppresses the ability to log on automatically when the initial connection is made.
-g	Disables file name globbing. **Glob** permits the use of the asterisk (*) and question mark (?) as wildcard characters in local file and path names.
-s:FileName	Specifies a text file that contains **ftp** commands. These commands run automatically after **ftp** starts. This parameter allows no spaces. Use this parameter instead of redirection (<).
-a	Specifies that any local interface can be used when binding the FTP data connection.
-w:WindowSize	Specifies the size of the transfer buffer. The default window size is 4,096 bytes.
-A	Logs on to the FTP server as anonymous.
Host	Specifies the computer name, IP address, or IPv6 address of the FTP server to which to connect. The host name or address, if specified, must be the last parameter on the line.
/?	Displays help at the command prompt.

help

The **help** command provides online information about system commands. Used without parameters, **help** lists and briefly describes every system command.

Syntax

```
{help [command]|[command]/?}
```

The following table describes the switches for the **help** command.

Parameter	Description
command	Specifies the name of the command about which you want information.

ipconfig

The **ipconfig** command displays all current TCP/IP network configuration values and refreshes Dynamic Host Configuration Protocol (DHCP) and Domain Name System (DNS) settings.

Syntax

```
ipconfig [/all] [/renew [Adapter]] [/release [Adapter]] [/flushdns] [/
displaydns] [/registerdns] [/showclassid Adapter] [/setclassid Adapter
[ClassID]]
```

The following table describes the switches for the **ipconfig** command.

Parameter	Description
/all	Displays the full TCP/IP configuration for all adapters.
/renew [*Adapter*]	Renews DHCP configuration for all adapters (if an adapter is not specified) or for a specific adapter if the *Adapter* parameter is included.
/release [*Adapter*]	Sends a DHCPRELEASE message to the DHCP server to release the current DHCP configuration and discard the IP address configuration for either all adapters (if an adapter is not specified) or for a specific adapter if the *Adapter* parameter is included.
/flushdns	Flushes and resets the contents of the DNS client resolver cache.
/displaydns	Displays the contents of the DNS client resolver cache, which includes both entries preloaded from the local Hosts file and any recently obtained resource records for name queries resolved by the computer.
/registerdns	Initiates manual dynamic registration for the DNS names and IP addresses that are configured at a computer.
/showclassid *Adapter*	Displays the DHCP class ID for a specified adapter. To see the DHCP class ID for all adapters, use the asterisk (*) wildcard character in place of *Adapter*.
/setclassid *Adapter* [*ClassID*]	Configures the DHCP class ID for a specified adapter. To set the DHCP class ID for all adapters, use the asterisk (*) wildcard character in place of *Adapter*.
/?	Displays help at the command prompt.

mountvol

The **mountvol** command creates, deletes, or lists a volume mount point. The **mountvol** command is a way to link volumes without requiring a drive letter.

Syntax

```
mountvol [Drive:]Path VolumeName
mountvol [Drive:]Path /d
mountvol [Drive:]Path /L
mountvol Drive: /s
```

The following table describes the switches for the **mountvol** command.

Parameter	Description
[Drive:]Path	Specifies the existing NTFS directory folder where the mount point will reside.
VolumeName	Specifies the volume name that is the target of the mount point. The volume name is of the form \\?\Volume{*GUID*}\, where {*GUID*} is a globally unique identifier (GUID) (for example, \\?\Volume\{2eca078d-5cbc-43d3-aff8-7e8511f60d0e}\).
/d	Removes the volume mount point from the specified folder.
/L	Lists the mounted volume name for the specified folder.
/s	Use for Itanium-based computers only. Mounts the EFI System Partition on the specified drive.
/?	Displays help at the command prompt.

msinfo32

The **msinfo32** command displays a comprehensive view of your hardware, system components, and software environment.

Syntax

```
msinfo32 [/?] [/pch] [/nfo FileName] [/report FileName] [/computer
ComputerName] [/showcategories] [/category categoryID] [/categories
categoryID]
```

The following table describes the switches for the **msinfo32** command.

Parameter	Description
FileName	Specifies the file to be opened. This can be an NFO, XML, TXT, or CAB file.
/?	Displays help for the **msinfo32** command.
/pch	Displays the history view.
/nfo FileName	Saves the exported file as an NFO file.
/report FileName	Saves the exported file as a TXT file.

(continued)

Appendix E

Parameter	Description
/computer *ComputerName*	Starts System Information for the specified remote computer.
/showcategories	Starts System Information with all available category IDs displayed.
/category *categoryID*	Starts System Information with the specified category selected. Use **/showcategories** to display a list of available category IDs.
/categories *categoryID*	Starts System Information with only the specified category or categories displayed.
/?	Displays help at the command prompt.

nbtstat

The **nbtstat** command displays NetBIOS over TCP/IP (NetBT) protocol statistics, NetBIOS name tables for both the local computer and remote computers, and the NetBIOS name cache.

Syntax

```
nbtstat [-a RemoteName] [-A IPAddress] [-c] [-n] [-r] [-R] [-RR] [-s] [-S]
[Interval]
```

The following table describes the switches for the **nbtstat** command.

Parameter	Description
-a *RemoteName*	Displays the NetBIOS name table of a remote computer, where *RemoteName* is the NetBIOS computer name of the remote computer.
-A *IPAddress*	Displays the NetBIOS name table of a remote computer, specified by the IP address (in dotted-decimal notation) of the remote computer.
-c	Displays the contents of the NetBIOS name cache and the table of NetBIOS names and their resolved IP addresses.
-n	Displays the NetBIOS name table of the local computer.
-r	Displays NetBIOS name resolution statistics. On a Windows XP computer that is configured to use WINS, this parameter returns the number of names that have been resolved and registered using broadcast and WINS.
-R	Purges the contents of the NetBIOS name cache and then reloads the #PRE-tagged entries from the Lmhosts file.
-RR	Releases and then refreshes NetBIOS names for the local computer that is registered with WINS servers.
-s	Displays NetBIOS client and server sessions, attempting to convert the destination IP address to a name.
-S	Displays NetBIOS client and server sessions, listing the remote computers by destination IP address only.
Interval	Redisplays selected statistics, pausing the number of seconds specified in *Interval* between each display. Press Ctrl+C to stop redisplaying statistics.
/?	Displays help at the command prompt.

net config

The **net config** command displays the configurable services that are running, or displays and changes settings for a service.

Syntax

```
net config [service [options]]
```

The following table describes the switches for the **net config** command.

Parameter	Description
None	Type **net config** without parameters to display a list of configurable services.
service	Specifies a service (**server** or **workstation**) that can be configured with the **net config** command.

net print

The **net print** command displays or controls print jobs and printer queues.

Syntax

```
net print \\computername\sharename
net print [\\computername] job# [/hold | /release | /delete]
```

The following table describes the switches for the **net print** command.

Parameter	Description
computername	Specifies the name of the computer sharing the printer queue(s).
sharename	Specifies the name of the printer queue. When including the *sharename* parameter with the *computername* parameter, use a backslash (\) to separate the names.
job#	Specifies the identification number assigned to a print job in a printer queue. A computer with one or more printer queues assigns each print job a unique number.
/hold	When used with *job#*, holds a print job waiting in the printer queue. The print job stays in the printer queue, and other print jobs bypass it until it is released.
/release	Releases a print job that has been held.
/delete	Removes a print job from a printer queue.

net send

The **net send** command sends messages to other users, computers, or messaging names on the network. The messenger service must be running to receive messages.

Appendix E

Syntax

```
net send {name | * | /domain[:name] | /users} message
```

The following table describes the switches for the **net send** command.

Parameter	Description
name	Specifies the user name, computer name, or messaging name to send the message to.
/domain[:name]	Sends the message to all the names in the computer's domain. If name is specified, the message is sent to all the names in the specified domain or workgroup.
/users	Sends the message to all users connected to the server.
message	Specifies text to be sent as a message.

net session

The **net session** command lists or disconnects the sessions between a local computer and the clients connected to it.

Syntax

```
net session [\\computername] [/delete]
```

The following table describes the switches for the **net send** command.

Parameter	Description
None	Type **net session** without parameters to display information about all sessions with the local computer.
\\computername	Identifies the computer for which to list or disconnect sessions.
/delete	Ends the computer's session with computername and closes all open files on the computer for the session. If \\computername is omitted, all sessions on the local computer are canceled.

net share

The **net share** command creates, deletes, or displays shared resources.

Syntax

```
net share sharename
net share sharename=drive:path [/users:number | /unlimited] [/
remark:"text"]
net share sharename [/users:number | unlimited] [/remark:"text"]
net share {sharename | drive:path} /delete
```

The following table describes the switches for the **net share** command.

Parameter	Description
None	Type **net share** without parameters to display information about all resources being shared on the local computer.
sharename	The network name of the shared resource. Type **net share** with a share name only to display information about that share.
drive:path	Specifies the absolute path of the directory to be shared.
/users:number	Sets the maximum number of users who can simultaneously access the shared resource.
/unlimited	Specifies an unlimited number of users who can simultaneously access the shared resource.
/remark:"text"	Adds a descriptive comment about the resource. Enclose the text in quotation marks.
/delete	Stops sharing the resource.

net start

The **net start** command starts a service, or displays a list of started services. Service names of two or more words, such as Net Logon or Computer Browser, must be enclosed in quotation marks.

Syntax

```
net start [service]
```

The following table describes the switches for the **net start** command.

Parameter	Description
None	Type **net start** without parameters to display a list of running services.
service	Includes alerter, client service for netware, clipbook server, content index, computer browser, dhcp client, directory replicator, eventlog, ftp publishing service, hypermedia object manager, logical disk manager, lpdsvc, media services management, messenger, Fax Service, Microsoft install server, net logon, network dde, network dde dsdm, nt lm security support provider, ole, plug and play, remote access connection manager, remote access isnsap service, remote access server, remote procedure call (rpc) locator, remote procedure call (rpc) service, schedule, server, simple tcp/ip services, site server ldap service, smartcard resource manager, snmp, spooler, task scheduler, tcp/ip netbios helper, telephony service, tracking service, tracking (server) service, ups, Windows time service, and workstation. The following services are available only on Windows 2000 Server: file service for macintosh, gateway service for netware, microsoft dhcp service, print service for macintosh, and windows internet name service.

net statistics

The **net statistics** command displays the statistics log for the local Workstation or Server service, or the running services for which statistics are available.

Syntax

```
net statistics [workstation | server]
```

The following table describes the switches for the **net statistics** command.

Parameter	Description
None	Type **net statistics** without parameters to list the running services for which statistics are available.
workstation	Displays statistics for the local Workstation service.
server	Displays statistics for the local Server service.

net stop

The **net stop** command stops a Windows 2000 network service.

Syntax

```
net stop service
```

The **net stop** command has one switch, **service**, which includes the following services:

➤ alerter

➤ network dde dsdm

➤ simple tcp/ip services

➤ client service for netware

➤ nt lm security support provider

➤ site server LDAP service

➤ clipbook server

➤ ole

➤ snmp

➤ computer browser

➤ remote access connection manager

➤ spooler

➤ directory replicator

➤ remote access isnsap service

➤ tcp/ip netbios helper

➤ ftp publishing service

➤ remote access server

➤ **ups**

➤ **lpdsvc**

➤ **remote procedure call (rpc) locator**

➤ **workstation**

➤ **messenger**

➤ **remote procedure call (rpc) service**

➤ **net logon**

➤ **schedule**

➤ **network dde**

➤ **server**

net time

The **net time** command synchronizes the computer's clock with that of another computer or domain. Used without the **/set** option, the **net time** command displays the time for another computer or domain.

Syntax

```
net time [\\computername | /domain[:domainname] | /rtsdomain[:domainname]]
[/set]
net time [\\computername] [/querysntp] | [/setsntp[:ntp server list]]
```

The following table describes the switches for the **net time** command.

Parameter	Description
None	Displays the current date and time at the computer designated as the time server for the local computer's Windows Server domain.
computername	Specifies the name of a server you want to check or with which you want to synchronize.
/domain[:*domainname*]	Specifies the domain with which to synchronize time.
/rtsdomain[:*domainname*]	Specifies the domain of the Reliable Time Server with which to synchronize time.
/set	Synchronizes the computer's clock with the time on the specified computer or domain.
/querysntp	Displays the name of the Network Time Protocol (NTP) server currently configured for the local computer or the one specified in *computername*.
/setsntp[:*ntp server list*]	Specifies a list of NTP time servers to be used by the local computer. The list may contain IP addresses or DNS names, separated by spaces. If multiple timeservers are used, the list must be surrounded by quotes.

net use

The **net use** command connects a computer to or disconnects a computer from a shared resource, or displays information about computer connections. The command also controls persistent Internet connections.

Syntax

```
net use [devicename | *] [\\computername\sharename[\volume]] [password |
*]] [/user:[domainname\]username] [[/delete] | [/persistent:{yes | no}]]
net use devicename [/home[password | *]] [/delete:{yes | no}]
net use [/persistent:{yes | no}]
```

The following table describes the switches for the **net use** command.

Parameter	Description
None	Used without parameters, **net use** retrieves a list of network connections.
devicename	Assigns a name to connect to the resource or specifies the device to be disconnected. There are two kinds of device names: disk drives (D through Z) and printers (LPT1 through LPT3). Type an asterisk instead of a specific device name to assign the next available device name.
\\computername\sharename	Specifies the name of the server and the shared resource. If **computername** contains blank characters, enclose the entire computer name from the double backslash (\\) to the end of the computer name in quotation marks. The computer name may be from 1 to 15 characters long.
\volume	Specifies a NetWare volume on the server. You must have Client Service for NetWare (Windows 2000 Professional) or Gateway Service for NetWare (Windows 2000 Server) installed and running to connect to NetWare servers.
password	Specifies the password needed to access the shared resource.
/user	Specifies a different username with which the connection is made.
Domainname	Specifies another domain.
Username	Specifies the username with which to log on.
/delete	Cancels the specified network connection. If the user specifies the connection with an asterisk, all network connections are canceled.
/home	Connects a user to the home directory.
/persistent	Controls the use of persistent network connections. The default is the setting used last. Deviceless connections are not persistent.
Yes	Saves all connections as they are made, and restores them at the next logon.
No	Does not save the connection being made or subsequent connections. Existing connections are restored at the next logon. Use the **/delete** switch to remove persistent connections.

net user

The **net user** command adds or modifies user accounts or displays user account information.

Syntax

```
net user [username [password | *] [options]] [/domain]
net user username {password | *} /add [options] [/domain]
net user username [/delete] [/domain]
```

The following table describes the switches for the **net user** command.

Parameter	Description
None	Used without parameters, **net user** displays a list of the user accounts on the computer.
Username	Specifies the name of the user account to add, delete, modify, or view. The name of the user account can have as many as 20 characters.
Password	Assigns or changes a password for the user's account.
	This parameter applies only to Windows 2000 Professional computers that are members of a Windows 2000 Server domain. By default, Windows 2000 Server computers perform operations on the primary domain controller.
/add	Adds a user account to the user accounts database.
/delete	Removes a user account from the user accounts database.

net view

The **net view** command displays a list of domains, a list of computers, or the resources being shared by the specified computer.

Syntax

```
net view [\\computername | /domain[:domainname]]
net view /network:nw [\\computername]
```

The following table describes the switches for the **net view** command.

Parameter	Description
None	Used without parameters, **net view** displays a list of computers in your current domain.
\\computername	Specifies the computer whose shared resources you want to view.
/domain[:domainname]	Specifies the domain for which you want to view the available computers. If domainname is omitted, displays all domains in the network.
/network:nw	Displays all available servers on a NetWare network. If a computer name is specified, the resources available on that computer in the NetWare network are displayed. Other networks that are added to the system can also be specified with this switch.

netstat

The **netstat** command displays active TCP connections, ports on which the computer is listening, Ethernet statistics, the IP routing table, IPv4 statistics (for the IP, ICMP, TCP, and UDP protocols), and IPv6 statistics (for the IPv6, ICMPv6, TCP over IPv6, and UDP over IPv6 protocols). Used without parameters, **netstat** displays active TCP connections.

Syntax

```
netstat [-a] [-e] [-n] [-o] [-p Protocol] [-r] [-s] [Interval]
```

The following table describes the switches for the **netstat** command.

Parameter	Description
-a	Displays all active TCP connections and the TCP and UDP ports on which the computer is listening.
-e	Displays Ethernet statistics, such as the number of bytes and packets sent and received. This parameter can be combined with **-s**.
-n	Displays active TCP connections; however, addresses and port numbers are expressed numerically and no attempt is made to determine names.
-o	Displays active TCP connections and includes the process ID (PID) for each connection
-p *Protocol*	Shows connections for the protocol specified by *Protocol*. In this case, *Protocol* can be **tcp**, **udp**, **tcpv6**, or **udpv6**. If this parameter is used with **-s** to display statistics by protocol, *Protocol* can be **tcp**, **udp**, **icmp**, **ip**, **tcpv6**, **udpv6**, **icmpv6**, or **ipv6**.
-s	Displays statistics by protocol. By default, statistics are shown for the TCP, UDP, ICMP, and IP protocols. If the IPv6 protocol for Windows XP is installed, statistics are shown for the TCP over IPv6, UDP over IPv6, ICMPv6, and IPv6 protocols. The **-p** parameter can be used to specify a set of protocols.
-r	Displays the contents of the IP routing table. This is equivalent to the **route print** command.
Interval	Redisplays the selected information every *Interval* seconds. Press Ctrl+C to stop the redisplay. If this parameter is omitted, **netstat** prints the selected information only once.
/?	Displays help at the command prompt.

nslookup

The **nslookup** command displays information that you can use to diagnose Domain Name System (DNS) infrastructure.

Syntax

```
nslookup [-SubCommand ...] [{ComputerToFind| [-Server]}]
```

The following table describes the switches for the **nslookup** command.

Parameter	Description
-SubCommand ...	Specifies one or more **nslookup** subcommands as a command-line option.
ComputerToFind	Looks up information for *ComputerToFind* using the current default DNS name server, if no other server is specified. To look up a computer not in the current DNS domain, append a period to the name.
-Server	Specifies to use this server as the DNS name server. If you omit *-Server*, the default DNS name server is used.
{help|?}	Displays a short summary of **nslookup** subcommands.

ntbackup

The **ntbackup** command performs backup operations at a command prompt or from a batch file using the **ntbackup** command followed by various parameters.

Syntax

```
ntbackup backup [systemstate] "@bks file name" /J {"job name"} [/P {"pool
name"}] [/G {"guid name"}] [/T { "tape name"}] [/N {"media name"}] [/F
{"file name"}] [/D {"set description"}] [/DS {"server name"}] [/IS {"server
name"}] [/A] [/V:{yes|no}] [/R:{yes|no}] [/L:{f|s|n}] [/M {backup type}] [/
RS:{yes|no}] [/HC:{on|off}] [/SNAP:{on|off}]
```

The following table describes the switches for the **ntbackup** command.

Appendix E

Parameter	Description
systemstate	Specifies that you want to back up the System State data. When you select this option, the backup type will be forced to normal or copy.
@bks file name	Specifies the name of the backup selection file (BKS file) to be used for this backup operation.
/J {"job name"}	Specifies the job name to be used in the log file.
/P {"pool name"}	
/G {"guid name"}	Overwrites or appends to this tape. Do not use this switch in conjunction with **/P**.
/T {"tape name"}	Overwrites or appends to this tape. Do not use this switch in conjunction with **/P**.
/N {"media name"}	Specifies the new tape name. You must not use **/A** with this switch.
/F {"file name"}	Logical disk path and file name. You must not use the following switches with this switch: **/P**, **/G**, and **/T**.
/D {"set description"}	Specifies a label for each backup set.
/DS {"server name"}	Backs up the directory service file for the specified Microsoft Exchange Server.
/IS {"server name"}	Backs up the Information Store file for the specified Microsoft Exchange Server.
/A	Performs an append operation. Either **/G** or **/T** must be used in conjunction with this switch. Do not use this switch in conjunction with **/P**.
/V:{yes|no}	Verifies the data after the backup is complete.
/R:{yes|no}	Restricts access to this tape to the owner or members of the Administrators group.

(continued)

Parameter	Description
/L:{f|s|n}	Specifies the type of log file: **f**=full, **s**=summary, or **n**=none (no log file is created).
/M {*backup type*}	Specifies the backup type. It must be one of the following: normal, copy, differential, incremental, or daily.
/RS:{yes|no}	Backs up the migrated data files located in Remote Storage. The **/RS** command-line option is not required to back up the local Removable Storage database (that contains the Remote Storage placeholder files).
/HC:{on|off}	Uses hardware compression, if available, on the tape drive.
/SNAP:{on|off}	Specifies whether or not the backup is a volume shadow copy.
/M {*backup type*}	Specifies the backup type. It must be one of the following: normal, copy, differential, incremental, or daily.
/?	Displays help at the command prompt.

perfmon

The **perfmon** command enables you to open a Windows XP Performance console configured with settings files from the Windows NT 4.0 version of Performance Monitor.

Syntax

```
perfmon.exe [file_name] [/HTMLFILE:converted_file settings_file]
```

The following table describes the switches for the **perfmon** command.

Parameter	Description
.exe	Specifies the name of the file extension.
file_name	Specifies the name of the settings file.
/HTMLFILE:*converted_file settings_file*	Specifies the name of the converted files, and the name of the original Windows NT 4.0 settings file.

ping

The **ping** command verifies IP-level connectivity to another TCP/IP computer by sending Internet Control Message Protocol (ICMP) Echo Request messages.

Syntax

```
ping [-t] [-a] [-n Count] [-l Size] [-f] [-i TTL] [-v TOS] [-r Count] [-s
Count] [{-j HostList | -k HostList}] [-w Timeout] [TargetName]
```

The following table describes the switches for the **ping** command.

Parameter	Description
-t	Specifies that **ping** continue sending Echo Request messages to the destination until interrupted.
-a	Specifies that reverse name resolution is performed on the destination IP address. If this is successful, **ping** displays the corresponding host name.
-n *Count*	Specifies the number of Echo Request messages sent. The default is 4.
-l *Size*	Specifies the length, in bytes, of the Data field in the Echo Request messages sent. The default is 32. The maximum *size* is 65,527.
-f	Specifies that Echo Request messages are sent with the Don't Fragment flag in the IP header set to 1.
-i *TTL*	Specifies the value of the TTL field in the IP header for Echo Request messages sent. The default is the default TTL value for the host. For Windows XP hosts, this is typically 128. The maximum *TTL* is 255.
-v *TOS*	Specifies the value of the Type of Service (TOS) field in the IP header for Echo Request messages sent. The default is 0. *TOS* is specified as a decimal value from 0 to 255.
-r *Count*	Specifies that the Record Route option in the IP header is used to record the path taken by the Echo Request message and corresponding Echo Reply message. Each hop in the path uses an entry in the Record Route option. If possible, specify a *Count* that is equal to or greater than the number of hops between the source and destination. The *Count* must be a minimum of 1 and a maximum of 9.
-s *Count*	Specifies that the Internet Timestamp option in the IP header is used to record the time of arrival for the Echo Request message and corresponding Echo Reply message for each hop. *Count* must be a minimum of 1 and a maximum of 4.
-j *HostList*	Specifies that the Echo Request messages use the Loose Source Route option in the IP header with the set of intermediate destinations specified in *HostList*.
-k *HostList*	Specifies that the Echo Request messages use the Strict Source Route option in the IP header with the set of intermediate destinations specified in *HostList*.
-w *Timeout*	Specifies the amount of time, in milliseconds, to wait for the Echo Reply message that corresponds to a given Echo Request message to be received.
TargetName	Specifies the destination, which is identified either by IP address or host name.
/?	Displays help at the command prompt.

rasdial

The **rasdial** command automates the connection process for any Microsoft client. Used without options, **rasdial** displays the status of current connections.

Syntax

```
rasdial ConnectionName [UserName [{Password|*}]] [/domain:Domain] [/
phone:PhoneNumber] [/callback:CallbackNumber] [/phonebook:PhonebookPath] [/
prefixsuffix]
rasdial [ConnectionName] /disconnect
```

The following table describes the switches for the **rasdial** command.

Parameter	Description
ConnectionName	Required when connecting to a phonebook (PBK) entry. Specifies an entry in the current PBK file, located in the *systemroot*\System32\Ras folder.
UserName [{*Password**}]	Specifies a username and password with which to connect. If an asterisk is used, the user is prompted for the password, but the characters typed do not display.
/domain:*Domain*	Specifies the domain in which the user account is located. If unspecified, the last value of the **Domain** field in the **Connect To** dialog box is used.
/phone:*PhoneNumber*	Substitutes the specified phone number for the entry's phone number in Rasphone.pbk.
/callback:*CallbackNumber*	Substitutes the specified callback number for the entry's callback number in Rasphone.pbk.
/phonebook:*PhonebookPath*	Specifies the path to the phonebook file. The default is *systemroot*\System32\Ras*UserName*.pbk. You can specify a full path to the file.
/prefixsuffix	Applies the current TAPI location dialing settings to the phone number. These settings are configured in Telephony, which is located in Control Panel. This option is turned off by default.
/disconnect	Required when disconnecting. Disconnects the specified entry. You can also disconnect by typing **/d**.

route

The **route** command displays and modifies the entries in the local IP routing table. Used without parameters, **route** displays help.

Syntax

```
route [-f] [-p] [Command [Destination] [mask Netmask] [Gateway] [metric
Metric]] [if Interface]]
```

The following table describes the switches for the **route** command.

Parameter	Description
-f	Clears the routing table of all entries that are not host routes (routes with a netmask of 255.255.255.255), the loopback network route (routes with a destination of 127.0.0.0 and a netmask of 255.0.0.0), or a multicast route (routes with a destination of 224.0.0.0 and a netmask of 240.0.0.0). If this is used in conjunction with one of the commands (such as **add**, **change**, or **delete**), the table is cleared prior to running the command.
-p	When used with the **add** command, the specified route is added to the Registry and is used to initialize the IP routing table whenever the TCP/IP protocol is started. By default, added routes are not preserved when the TCP/IP protocol is started. This parameter is ignored for all other commands. Persistent routes are stored in the Registry location HKEY_LOCAL_MACHINE\SYSTEM\CurrentControlSet\Services\Tcpip\Parameters\PersistentRoutes.

(continued)

Parameter	Description
Command	Specifies the command you want to run. The following are the valid commands: • **add**—Adds a route. • **change**—Modifies an existing route. • **delete**—Deletes a route or routes. • **print**—Prints a route or routes.
Destination	Specifies the network destination of the route. The destination can be an IP network address (where the host bits of the network address are set to 0), an IP address for a host route, or 0.0.0.0 for the default route.
mask *Netmask*	Specifies the netmask (also known as a subnet mask) associated with the network destination.
Gateway	Specifies the forwarding or next hop IP address over which the set of addresses defined by the network destination and subnet mask are reachable.
metric *Metric*	Specifies an integer cost metric (ranging from 1 to 9999) for the route, which is used when choosing among multiple routes in the routing table that most closely match the destination address of a packet being forwarded. The route with the lowest metric is chosen. The metric can reflect the number of hops, the speed of the path, path reliability, path throughput, or administrative properties.
if *Interface*	Specifies the interface index for the interface over which the destination is reachable. For a list of interfaces and their corresponding interface indexes, use the display of the **route print** command.
/?	Displays help at the command prompt.

Appendix E

secedit

The **secedit** command is used to automatically create and apply templates and analyze system security.

Use **secedit** to analyze system security.

Syntax

```
secedit /analyze [/DB filename ] [/CFG filename ] [/log logpath] [/verbose]
[/quiet]
```

The following table describes the switches for the **secedit/analyze** command.

Use **secedit** to configure system security by applying a stored template.

Parameter	Description
/DB *filename*	Provides the path to a database that contains the stored configuration against which the analysis will be performed. This is a required argument. If *filename* specifies a new database, the **/CFG** *filename* argument must also be specified.
/CFG *filename*	This argument is only valid when used with the **/DB** parameter. It is the path to the security template that will be imported into the database for analysis. If this argument is not specified, the analysis is performed against any configuration already stored in the database.

(continued)

Parameter	Description
/log *logpath*	The path to the log file for the process. If this is not provided, the default file is used.
/verbose	Requests more detailed progress information during the analysis.
/quiet	Suppresses screen and log output. You will still be able to view analysis results using Security Configuration and Analysis.

Syntax

```
secedit /configure [/DB filename ] [/CFG filename ] [/overwrite][/areas
area1 area2...] [/log logpath] [/verbose] [/quiet]
```

The following table describes the switches for the **secedit/configure** command.

Parameter	Description
/DB *filename*	Provides the path to a database that contains the security template that should be applied. This is a required argument.
/CFG *filename*	This argument is only valid when used with the **/DB** parameter. It is the path to the security template that will be imported into the database and applied to the system. If this argument is not specified, the template already stored in the database will be applied.
/overwrite	This argument is only valid when the **/CFG** argument is also used. This specifies whether the security template in the **/CFG** argument should overwrite any template or composite template stored in the database instead of appending the results to the stored template. If this is not specified, the template in the **/CFG** argument will be appended to the stored template.
/areas *area1 area2...*	Specifies the security areas to be applied to the system. The default is "all areas." Each area should be separated by a space.
/log *logpath*	The path to the log file for the process. If not specified, the default is used.
/verbose	Specifies more detailed progress information.
/quiet	Suppresses screen and log output.

shutdown

The **shutdown** command enables you to shut down or restart a local or remote computer. Used without parameters, **shutdown** will log off the current user.

Syntax

```
shutdown [{-1|-s|-r|-a}] [-f] [-m [\\ComputerName]] [-t xx] [-c "message"]
[-d[u][p]:xx:yy]
```

The following table describes the switches for the **shutdown** command.

Parameter	Description
-l	Logs off the current user; this is also the default. -m *ComputerName* takes precedence.
-s	Shuts down the local computer.
-r	Reboots after shutdown.
-a	Aborts shutdown. Ignores other parameters, except -l and *ComputerName*. You can only use -a during the timeout period.
-f	Forces running applications to close.
-m [*ComputerName*]	Specifies the computer that you want to shut down.
-t *xx*	Sets the timer for system shutdown in *xx* seconds. The default is 20 seconds.
-c "*message*"	Specifies a message to be displayed in the Message area of the System Shutdown window. You can use a maximum of 127 characters. You must enclose the message in quotation marks.
-d [u][p]:*xx.yy*	Lists the reason code for the shutdown. The following are the different values: • **u**—Indicates a user code. • **p**—Indicates a planned shutdown code. • *xx*—Specifies the major reason code (0-255). • *yy*—Specifies the minor reason code (0-65536). • **/?**—Displays help at the command prompt.

sysprep

The **sysprep** command, or System Preparation tool, prepares a prepare Windows XP System Images as part of an automated deployment.

Syntax

```
sysprep {[-activated] [-audit] [-forceshutdown] [-mini] [-noreboot] [-nosidgen] [-pnp] [-quiet] [-reboot] [-reseal]
```

The following table describes the switches for the **sysprep** command.

Parameter	Description
-activated	Do not reset the grace period for Windows Product Activation
-audit	Reboots the computer without generating a new SID
-forceshutdown	Forces the computer to shut down after Sysprep.exe is complete
-mini	Configures XP to use Mini-Setup instead of the Windows Welcome
-noreboot	Modifies the Registry keys without the system rebooting
-nosidgen	Causes Sysprep.exe to run without generating a SID
-pnp	Used to install legacy and non-Plug and Play devices
-quiet	Runs Sysprep.exe without any onscreen messages
-reboot	Forces the computer to restart automatically after the image is installed
-reseal	Clears the Event Log and prepares the system for delivery to the customer

systeminfo

The **systeminfo** command displays detailed configuration information about a computer and its operating system.

Syntax

```
systeminfo[.exe] [/s Computer [/u Domain\User [/p Password]]] [/fo
{TABLE|LIST|CSV}] [/nh]
```

The following table describes the switches for the **systeminfo** command.

Parameter	Description
/s Computer	Specifies the name or IP address of a remote computer (do not use backslashes). The default is the local computer.
/u Domain\User	Runs the command with the account permissions of the user specified by **User** or **Domain\User**. The default is the permissions of the currently logged on user on the computer issuing the command.
/p Password	Specifies the password of the user account that is specified in the **/u** parameter.
/fo {TABLEILISTICSV}	Specifies the format to use for the output. Valid values are **TABLE**, **LIST**, and **CSV**. The default format for output is **LIST**.
/nh	Suppresses column headers in the output. Valid when the **/fo** parameter is set to **TABLE** or **CSV**.
/?	Displays help at the command prompt.

System File Checker (sfc)

The **sfc** command scans and verifies the versions of all protected system files after you restart your computer.

Syntax

```
sfc [/scannow] [/scanonce] [/scanboot] [/revert] [/purgecache] [/
cachesize=x]
```

The following table describes the switches for the **sfc** command.

Parameter	Description
/scannow	Scans all protected system files immediately.
/scanonce	Scans all protected system files once.
/scanboot	Scans all protected system files every time the computer is restarted.
/revert	Returns the scan to its default operation.
/purgecache	Purges the Windows File Protection file cache and scans all protected system files immediately.
/cachesize=x	Sets the size, in MB, of the Windows File Protection file cache.
/?	Displays help at the command prompt.

taskkill

The **taskkill** command ends one or more tasks or processes. Processes can be killed by process ID or image name.

Syntax

```
taskkill [/s Computer] [/u Domain\User [/p Password]]] [/fi FilterName] [/
pid ProcessID]|[/im ImageName] [/f][/t]
```

The following table describes the switches for the **taskkill** command.

Parameter	Description
/s *Computer*	Specifies the name or IP address of a remote computer (do not use backslashes). The default is the local computer.
/u *Domain\User*	Runs the command with the account permissions of the user specified by *User* or *Domain\User*. The default is the permissions of the currently logged on user on the computer issuing the command.
/p *Password*	Specifies the password of the user account that is specified in the **/u** parameter.
/fi *FilterName*	Specifies the types of process(es) to include in or exclude from termination. The following are valid filter names, operators, and values.

Name	Operators	Value
Hostname	eq, ne	Any valid string
Status	eq, ne	**RUNNING|NOT RESPONDING**
Imagename	eq, ne	Any valid string
PID	eg, ne, gt, lt, ge, le	Any valid positive integer
Session	eg, ne, gt, lt, ge, le	Any valid session number
CPUTime	eq, ne, gt, lt, ge, le	Valid time in the format *hh:mm:ss*; the *mm* and *ss* parameters should be between 0 and 59, and *hh* can be any valid unsigned numeric value
Memusage	eg, ne, gt, lt, ge, le	Any valid integer
Username	eq, ne	Any valid username ([*Domain*]*User*)
Services	eq, ne	Any valid string
Windowtitle	eq, ne	Any valid string

Parameter	Description
/pid *ProcessID*	Specifies the process ID of the process to be terminated.
/im *ImageName*	Specifies the image name of the process to be terminated. Use the wildcard (*) to specify all image names.
/f	Specifies that process(es) be forcefully terminated. This parameter is ignored for remote processes; all remote processes are forcefully terminated.
/t	Specifies to terminate all child processes along with the parent process, commonly known as a tree kill.
/?	Displays help at the command prompt.

Appendix E

tasklist

The **tasklist** command displays a list of applications and services with their process ID (PID) for all tasks running on either a local or a remote computer.

Syntax

```
tasklist[.exe] [/s computer] [/u domain\user [/p password]] [/fo
{TABLE|LIST|CSV}] [/nh] [/fi FilterName [/fi FilterName2 [ ... ]]] [/m
[ModuleName] | /svc | /v]
```

The following table describes the switches for the **tasklist** command.

Parameter	Description
/s Computer	Specifies the name or IP address of a remote computer (do not use backslashes). The default is the local computer.
/u Domain\User	Runs the command with the account permissions of the user specified by **User** or **Domain\User**. The default is the permissions of the currently logged on user on the computer issuing the command.
/p Password	Specifies the password of the user account that is specified in the **/u** parameter.
/fo {TABLE|LIST|CSV}	Specifies the format to use for the output. Valid values are **TABLE**, **LIST**, and **CSV**. The default format for output is **TABLE**.
/nh	Suppresses column headers in the output. Valid when the **/fo** parameter is set to **TABLE** or **CSV**.
/fi FilterName	Specifies the types of process(es) to include in or exclude from the query. The following table lists valid filter names, operators, and values.

Name	Operators	Value
Status	eq, ne	**RUNNING|NOT RESPONDING**
Imagename	eq, ne	Any valid string
PID	eq, ne, gt, lt, ge, le	Any valid positive integer
Session	eq, ne, gt, lt, ge, le	Any valid session number
SessionName	eq, ne	Any valid string
CPUTime	eq, ne, gt, lt, ge, le	Valid time in the format of *hh:mm:ss*. The *mm* and *ss* parameters should be between 0 and 59, and *hh* can be any valid unsigned numeric value.
Memusage	eq, ne, gt, lt, ge, le	Any valid integer
Username	eq, ne	Any valid username ([*Domain*\]*User*)
Services	eq, ne	Any valid string
Windowtitle	eq, ne	Any valid string
Modules	eq, ne	Any valid string

Parameter	Description
/m [ModuleName]	Specifies to show module information for each process. When a module is specified, all the processes using that module are shown. When a module is not specified, all the processes for all the modules are shown. Cannot be used with the **/svc** or the **/v** parameter.

(continued)

Parameter	Description
/svc	Lists all the service information for each process without truncation. Valid when the **/fo** parameter is set to **TABLE**. Cannot be used with the **/m** or the **/v** parameter.
/v	Specifies that verbose task information be displayed in the output. Cannot be used with the **/svc** or the **/m** parameter.
/?	Displays help at the command prompt.

tracert

The **tracert** command determines the path taken to a destination by sending Internet Control Message Protocol (ICMP) Echo Request messages to the destination with incrementally increasing Time to Live (TTL) field values. The path displayed is the list of near-side router interfaces of the routers in the path between a source host and a destination. The near-side interface is the interface of the router that is closest to the sending host in the path. Used without parameters, **tracert** displays help.

Syntax

```
tracert [-d] [-h MaximumHops] [-j HostList] [-w Timeout] [TargetName]
```

The following table describes the switches for the **tracert** command.

Parameter	Description
-d	Prevents **tracert** from attempting to resolve the IP addresses of intermediate routers to their names. This can speed up the display of **tracert** results.
-h *MaximumHops*	Specifies the maximum number of hops in the path to search for the target (destination). The default is 30 hops.
-j *HostList*	Specifies that Echo Request messages use the Loose Source Route option in the IP header with the set of intermediate destinations specified in *HostList*.
-w *Timeout*	Specifies the amount of time in milliseconds to wait for the ICMP Time Exceeded or Echo Reply message corresponding to a given Echo Request message to be received. If not received within the timeout, an asterisk (*) is displayed. The default timeout is 4000 (4 seconds).
TargetName	Specifies the destination, identified either by IP address or host name.
-?	Displays help at the command prompt.

winnt

The **winnt** command performs an installation of or upgrade to Windows XP. If you have hardware that is compatible with Windows XP, you can run **winnt** at a Windows 3.x or MS-DOS command prompt.

Syntax

```
winnt [/s:SourcePath] [/t:TempDrive] [/u:answer file][/udf:ID [,UDB_file]]
[/r:folder][/rx:folder][/e:command][/a]
```

The following table describes the switches for the **winnt** command.

Parameter	Description
/s:SourcePath	Specifies the source location of the Windows XP files. The location must be a full path of the form *x:\[Path]* or *\\server\share[\Path]*.
/t:TempDrive	Directs Setup to place temporary files on the specified drive and to install Windows XP on that drive. If you do not specify a location, Setup attempts to locate a drive for you.
/u:answer file	Performs an unattended Setup using an answer file. The answer file provides answers to some or all of the prompts that the end user normally responds to during Setup. If you use */u*, you must also use */s*.
/udf:ID [,UDB_file]	Indicates an identifier (*ID*) that Setup uses to specify how a Uniqueness Database (UDB) file modifies an answer file (see */u*). The UDB overrides values in the answer file, and the identifier determines which values in the UDB file are used. If no *UDB_file* is specified, Setup prompts you to insert a disk that contains the $Unique$.udb file.
/r:folder	Specifies an optional folder to be installed. The folder remains after Setup finishes.
/rx:folder	Specifies an optional folder to be copied. The folder is deleted after Setup finishes.
/e:command	Specifies a command to be carried out just before the final phase of Setup.
/a	Enables accessibility options.
/?	Displays help at the command prompt.

winnt32

The **winnt32** command performs an installation of or upgrade to Windows XP. If you have hardware that is compatible with Windows XP, you can run **winnt32** at a Windows 95, 98, ME, NT, 2000, or XP command prompt.

Syntax

```
winnt32 [/checkupgradeonly] [/cmd:command_line] [/cmdcons] [/
copydir:{i386|ia64}\FolderName] [/copysource:FolderName] [/
debug[Level]:[FileName]] [/dudisable] [/duprepare:pathname] [/
dushare:pathname] [/m:FolderName] [/makelocalsource] [/noreboot] [/
s:SourcePath] [/syspart:DriveLetter] [/tempdrive:DriveLetter] [/udf:id
[,UDB_file]] [/unattend[num]:[answer_file]]
```

The following table describes the switches for the **winnt32** command.

Parameter	Description
/checkupgradeonly	Checks your computer for upgrade compatibility with Windows XP.
/cmd:command_line	Instructs Setup to carry out a specific command before the final phase of Setup.
/cmdcons	Installs the Recovery Console as a startup option on a functioning x86-based computer.
/copydir:{i386|ia64}\FolderName	Creates an additional folder within the folder in which the Windows XP files are installed. Folder_name refers to a folder that you have created to hold modifications just for your site.
/copysource:FolderName	Creates a temporary additional folder within the folder in which the Windows XP files are installed. Folder_name refers to a folder that you have created to hold modifications just for your site.
/debug[Level]:[FileName]	Creates a debug log at the level specified; for example, /debug4:Debug.log. The default log file is C:\systemroot\Winnt32.log, and the default debug level is 2. The log levels are as follows: 0 represents severe errors, 1 represents errors, 2 represents warnings, 3 represents information, and 4 represents detailed information for debugging. Each level includes the levels below it.
/dudisable	Prevents Dynamic Update from running.
/duprepare:pathname	Carries out preparations on an installation share so that it can be used with Dynamic Update files that you downloaded from the Windows Update Web site.
/dushare:pathname	Specifies a share on which you previously downloaded Dynamic Update files (updated files for use with Setup) from the Windows Update Web site, and on which you previously ran /duprepare:pathname. When run on a client, specifies that the client installation will make use of the updated files on the share specified in pathname.
/m:FolderName	Specifies that Setup copies replacement files from an alternate location. Instructs Setup to look in the alternate location first, and if files are present, to use them instead of the files from the default location.
/makelocalsource	Instructs Setup to copy all installation source files to your local hard disk. Use /makelocalsource when installing from a CD to provide installation files when the CD is not available later in the installation.
/noreboot	Instructs Setup to not restart the computer after the file copy phase of Setup is completed, so that you can run another command.
/s:SourcePath	Specifies the source location of the Windows XP files. To simultaneously copy files from multiple servers, type the /s:SourcePath option multiple times (up to a maximum of eight). If you type the option multiple times, the first server specified must be available, or Setup will fail.
/syspart:DriveLetter	On an x86-based computer, specifies that you can copy Setup startup files to a hard disk, mark the disk as active, and then install the disk into another computer.
/tempdrive:DriveLetter	Directs Setup to place temporary files on the specified partition.
/udf:id [,UDB_file]	Indicates an identifier (id) that Setup uses to specify how a Uniqueness Database (UDB) file modifies an answer file (see the /unattend entry). The UDB overrides values in the answer file, and the identifier determines which values in the UDB file are used.

Appendix E

(continued)

Parameter	Description
/unattend	Upgrades your previous version of Windows 98, Windows ME, Windows NT 4.0, or Windows 2000 in unattended Setup mode. All user settings are taken from the previous installation, so no user intervention is required during Setup.
/unattend[*num*]:[*answer_file*]	Performs a fresh installation in unattended Setup mode. The specified ***answer_file*** provides Setup with your custom specifications. ***Num*** is the number of seconds between the time that Setup finishes copying the files and when it restarts your computer.

xcopy

The **xcopy** command copies files and directories, including subdirectories.

Syntax

```
xcopy Source [Destination] [/w] [/p] [/c] [/v] [/q] [/f] [/l] [/g] [/d[:mm-
dd-yyyy]] [/u] [/i] [/s [/e]] [/t] [/k] [/r] [/h] [{/a|/m}] [/n] [/o] [/x]
[/exclude:file1[+[file2]][+[file3]] [{/y|/-y}] [/z]
```

The following table describes the switches for the **xcopy** command.

Parameter	Description
Source	Required. Specifies the location and names of the files you want to copy. This parameter must include either a drive or a path.
Destination	Specifies the destination of the files you want to copy. This parameter can include a drive letter and colon, a directory name, a file name, or a combination of these.
/w	Displays the following message and waits for your response before starting to copy files: Press any key to begin copying file(s)
/p	Prompts you to confirm whether you want to create each destination file.
/c	Ignores errors.
/v	Verifies each file as it is written to the destination file to make sure that the destination files are identical to the source files.
/q	Suppresses the display of **xcopy** messages.
/f	Displays source and destination file names while copying.
/l	Displays a list of files that are to be copied.
/g	Creates decrypted destination files.
/d[:*mm-dd-yyyy*]	Copies source files changed on or after the specified date only. If you do not include an *mm-dd-yyyy* value, **xcopy** copies all ***Source*** files that are newer than existing ***Destination*** files. This command-line option enables you to update files that have changed.
/u	Copies files from ***Source*** that exist on ***Destination*** only.
/i	If ***Source*** is a directory or contains wildcards, and ***Destination*** does not exist, **xcopy** assumes ***Destination*** specifies a directory name and creates a new directory. Then, **xcopy** copies all specified files into the new directory. By default, **xcopy** prompts you to specify whether ***Destination*** is a file or a directory.

(continued)

Parameter	Description
/s	Copies directories and subdirectories, unless they are empty. If you omit **/s**, **xcopy** works within a single directory.
/e	Copies all subdirectories, even if they are empty. Use **/e** with the **/s** and **/t** command-line options.
/t	Copies the subdirectory structure (that is, the tree) only, not files. To copy empty directories, you must include the **/e** command-line option.
/k	Copies files and retains the read-only attribute on destination files if present on the source files. By default, **xcopy** removes the read-only attribute.
/r	Copies read-only files.
/h	Copies files with hidden and system file attributes. By default, **xcopy** does not copy hidden or system files.
/a	Copies only source files that have their archive file attributes set. **/a** does not modify the archive file attribute of the source file.
/m	Copies source files that have their archive file attributes set. Unlike **/a**, **/m** turns off archive file attributes in the files that are specified in the source.
/n	Creates copies by using the NTFS short file or directory names. **/n** is required when you copy files or directories from an NTFS volume to a FAT volume or when the FAT file system naming convention (that is, 8.3 characters) is required on the destination file system. The destination file system can be FAT or NTFS.
/o	Copies file ownership and discretionary access control list (DACL) information.
/x	Copies file audit settings and system access control list (SACL) information (implies **/o**).
/exclude:*filename1*[+[*filename2*]][+[*filename3*]]	Specifies a list of files containing strings.
/y	Suppresses prompting to confirm that you want to overwrite an existing destination file.
/-y	Prompts to confirm that you want to overwrite an existing destination file.
/z	Copies over a network in restartable mode.
/?	Displays help at the command prompt.

Appendix E

Appendix F
Troubleshooting Problems in
Windows XP Professional

This chapter is a reference for troubleshooting common problems that you may encounter when using Windows XP Professional. This information was compiled from several Microsoft resources, including the Windows XP Professional Help files and TechNet.

Troubleshooters

The Windows XP Professional troubleshooters are included to help users diagnose and solve any problems that they may be having with various hardware components on their system. Several types of troubleshooters are included that walk the users through problem analysis with a series of questions that they answer about the problem they are having. The following table lists the troubleshooters included in Windows XP Professional and describes which problems each helps to resolve.

Troubleshooter	Helps Resolve Problems Related To
System Setup	Installing and setting up Windows.
Startup/Shutdown	Starting and shutting down your computer.
Display	Video cards and video adapters, including your computer screen, outdated or incompatible video drivers, and incorrect settings for your video hardware.
Home Networking	Setup, Internet connections, and sharing files and printers.
Hardware	Disk drives (including CD-ROM and DVD drives), game controllers, input devices (such as keyboards, mice, cameras, scanners, and infrared devices), network adapter cards, USB devices, modems, and sound cards.
Multimedia and Games	Games and other multimedia programs, DirectX drivers, USB devices, digital video discs (DVDs), sound, joysticks, and related issues.
Digital Video Discs (DVDs)	DVD drives and decoders.
Input Devices	Keyboards, mouse and trackball devices, cameras, scanners, and infrared devices.
Drives and Network Adapters	Hard disks, floppy disks, CD-ROM and DVD drives, network cards, tape drives, and backup programs.
USB	USB connectors and peripherals.
Sound	Sound and sound cards.
Modem	Modem connections, setup, configuration, and detection.

(continued)

Troubleshooter	Helps Resolve Problems Related To
Internet Connection Sharing	Connecting and logging on to your Internet service provider (ISP).
Internet Explorer	Browsing the Web, downloading files, saving your favorites, using IE toolbars, and printing Web pages.
Outlook Express (Messaging)	Outlook Express and Windows Messenger Service.
File and Print Sharing	Sharing files and printers between computers, connecting to other computers in a network, installing network adapters, and logging on.
Printing	Printer installation and connection, printer drivers, print quality, printer speed, and fonts.

Defragmentation

The Disk Defragmenter tool in Windows XP rearranges files, programs, and unused space on the hard drives. The following may aid in troubleshooting disk defragmentation problems.

Problem: Computer is running slowly, or opening programs on the hard disk has become slow.

Reason: The volumes on your hard disk may have become excessively fragmented.

Resolution: Analyze and then defragment the volumes on your hard disk if necessary.

Problem: The display and defragmentation report do not agree.

Reason: The displays show less detail than the Analysis and Defragmentation reports, so if you compare the results, you might notice discrepancies.

Resolution: Use the Analysis and Defragmentation displays only for a general idea of the volume's fragmentation. Use the Analysis and Defragmentation reports for precise, numerical figures.

Problem: Unmovable files appear on volumes other than the system volumes and boot volumes.

Reason: Paging files appear as unmovable files in Disk Defragmenter. On NTFS volumes, the NTFS Change Journal also appears as an unmovable file.

Resolution: This is by design, because paging files cannot be moved and therefore cannot be defragmented.

Problem: The defragmentation report on an NTFS volume shows small files with a large number of fragments.

Reason: When a file is open for write access, XP attempts to preallocate additional space to help prevent fragmentation as the file grows. When you defragment a volume, Disk Defragmenter does not allow the extra space to be moved and consolidated while the file is open. The extra space is shown as additional fragments in the report.

Resolution: Close the file to release the additional fragments and reduce the size of the file. The Size On Disk value (right-click the file and then click Properties) reports the size that you would obtain if you were to close the file.

Disks

Windows XP Professional supports both basic and dynamic disks. The following may aid in troubleshooting disk problems.

Problem: A basic disk's status is Not Initialized.

Reason: The disk does not contain a valid signature.

Resolution: Initialize the disk.

Problem: A basic or dynamic disk's status is Unreadable.

Reason: The basic or dynamic disk is not accessible and might have experienced hardware failure, corruption, or I/O errors.

Resolution: Rescan the disks or restart the computer to see if the disk status changes.

Problem: A dynamic disk's status is Foreign.

Reason: The Foreign status occurs when you move a dynamic disk to the local computer from another computer running Windows 2000 or Windows XP Professional. A warning icon appears on disks that display the Foreign status.

Resolution: Add the disk to your computer's system configuration so that you can access data on the disk. Import the foreign disk (right-click the disk and then click Import Foreign Disks). Any existing volumes on the foreign disk become visible and accessible when you import the disk.

Problem: A dynamic disk's status is Online (Errors).

Reason: The dynamic disk has I/O errors on a region of the disk. A warning icon appears on the dynamic disk with errors.

Resolution: If the I/O errors are temporary, reactivate the disk to return it to Online status.

Problem: A dynamic disk's status is Offline or Missing.

Reason: An Offline dynamic disk might be corrupted or intermittently unavailable. An error icon appears on the offline dynamic disk. If the disk status is Offline and the disk's name changes to Missing, the disk was recently available on the system but can no longer be located or identified. The missing disk may be corrupted, powered down, or disconnected.

Resolution: Repair any disk, controller, or cable problems and make sure that the physical disk is turned on, plugged in, and attached to the computer. Next, use the Reactivate Disk command to bring the disk back online.

Problem: A basic or dynamic volume's status is Failed.

Reason: The basic or dynamic volume cannot be started automatically, the disk is damaged, or the file system is corrupt. Unless the disk or file system can be repaired, the Failed status indicates data loss.

Resolution: If the volume is a basic volume with Failed status, make sure that the underlying physical disk is turned on, plugged in, and attached to the computer. No other user action is possible for basic volumes. If the volume is a dynamic volume with Failed status, make sure the underlying disks are online.

Problem: A basic or dynamic volume's status is Unknown.

Reason: The Unknown status occurs when the boot sector for the volume is corrupted (possibly due to a virus) and you can no longer access data on the volume. The Unknown status also occurs when you install a new disk but do not follow the wizard to create a disk signature.

Resolution: Initialize the disk.

Problem: A dynamic volume's status is Data Incomplete.

Reason: You moved some but not all of the disks in a multidisk volume.

Resolution: Move all of the disks that comprise the multidisk volume to the computer and then import the disks.

Problem: A dynamic volume's status is Healthy (At Risk).

Reason: The dynamic volume is currently accessible, but I/O errors have been detected on the underlying dynamic disk.

Resolution: Return the underlying disk to the Online status. Once the disk is returned to Online status, the volume should return to the Healthy status. If the Healthy (At Risk) status persists, the disk might be failing.

Problem: A mirrored volume's status is Data Not Redundant.

Reason: One half, but not both halves, of a mirrored volume was imported.

Resolution: Move all disks that span this volume to the new computer at the same time, and then import all of the disks together.

Problem: A mirrored volume's status is Failed Redundancy.

Reason: One (or both) of the members of the mirrored volume has failed, and the volume is no longer fault tolerant.

Resolution: If the dynamic disk's status is Offline or Missing (it cannot be accessed at all), an icon (X) appears in the graphical view of the Missing or Offline disk.

Problem: A mirrored volume's status is Stale Data.

Reason: If you attempt to import disks that contain a mirrored volume, but one of the volumes on the disks contains stale mirror information, the status Stale Data appears in the Import Foreign Disks dialog box. This problem can occur when the volumes on the disks you moved had a status other than Healthy before you moved them.

Resolution: Move the disks back to the computer that they came from.

Problem: A RAID-5 volume's status is Data Not Redundant.

Reason: You moved some but not all of the disks in a RAID-5 volume. You cannot import the missing disks at a later time to restore redundancy.

Resolution: Move all disks that comprise this volume to the new computer at the same time, and then import all of the disks together.

Problem: A RAID-5 volume's status is Failed Redundancy.

Reason: One (or all) of the members of the RAID-5 volume has failed, and the volume is no longer fault tolerant.

Resolution: If the dynamic disk's status is Offline or Missing (it cannot be accessed at all), an icon (X) appears in the graphical view of the Missing or Offline disk.

Problem: A RAID-5 volume's status is Stale Data.

Reason: If you attempt to import disks that contain a RAID-5 volume, but one of the volumes on the disks contains stale parity information, the status Stale Data appears in the Import Foreign Disks dialog box. This problem can occur when the volumes on the disks you moved had a status other than Healthy before you moved them.

Resolution: Move the disks back to the computer that they came from.

Appendix F

Disk Quotas

Disk quotas can be used to control disk space usage for volumes in Windows XP Professional. The following may aid in troubleshooting disk quota problems.

Problem: The Quota tab does not appear on the Properties dialog box for a FAT-formatted volume.

Reason: Because disk quotas can be set only on volumes formatted with NTFS, the Quota tab does not appear for FAT-formatted volumes.

Resolution: Format volumes for which you want to track or limit disk space usage with NTFS.

Problem: Cannot delete a quota entry.

Reason: You cannot delete a quota entry for a user account until all files that the user owns have been removed from the volume or another user has taken ownership of the files.

Resolution: Move, delete, or take ownership of all files that the user owns on that volume.

Problem: A user gets an Insufficient Disk Space message when trying to add files to a volume.

Reason: The user has exceeded the quota limit.

Resolution: Increase the user's quota limit, move or delete files from the volume, or clear the Deny Disk Space To Users Exceeding Quota Limit option in Disk Quotas.

Encrypting File System

The Encrypting File System (EFS) enables users to encrypt the files and folders on their NTFS volumes. The following may aid in troubleshooting EFS problems.

Problem: Cannot encrypt a file.

Reason: EFS only works on files and folders on NTFS file system volumes. In addition, it cannot encrypt any file that is a compressed file, a read-only file, or a system file.

Resolution: If you have the proper permissions, make sure that the file is not compressed.

IPSec

Internet Protocol Security (IPSec) is a set of standards used to provide cryptographic security services within Windows XP and 2000. The following may aid in troubleshooting IPSec problems.

Problem: Need to verify the network connection between two computers.

Reason: Separate network problems may be causing what appears to be communication failures related to IPSec.

Resolution: The TCP/IP utility, **ping**, can be used to determine if IPSec-secured communication can take place when a predefined policy is assigned to a computer. This will allow you to separate network problems from IPSec issues.

Problem: Need to verify that the IPSec policy on a computer is active and in effect.

Reason: IPSec-secured communication may not be responding as expected.

Resolution: You can use several tools to view which IPSec policy is in effect on the computer.

Problem: Basic IPSec troubleshooting must be performed.

Reason: IPSec-secured communication is failing.

Resolution: The TCP/IP utility, **ping**, can be used to separate other network issues from IPSec-related problems. Restarting the policy agent may be necessary to force a policy update.

Problem: Want to verify successful, IPSec-secured communications and statistics.

Reason: A pattern of failures occurs when attempting IPSec-secured communications.

Resolution: Use IPSec Monitor to confirm whether your secured communications are successful.

Problem: IPSec Monitor shows no security associations established.

Reason: This may be due to soft security associations between the computers, which prevent hard (secured) security associations from being established.

Resolution: You may have to restart the IPSec Policy Agent. Confirm that you need the Allow Unsecured Communications With Non IPSec-Aware Computers Filter Action option, which causes soft security associations to show up with computers that do not respond to IPSec requests.

Appendix F

Problem: IPSec component files are missing.

Reason: The files necessary for IPSec components, such as ISAKMP/Oakley, the IPSec Policy Agent, or the IPSec driver, have been removed or deleted.

Resolution: Reinstall TCP/IP.

Local Groups

Local groups are accounts that are granted permissions and rights to a computer. The following may aid in troubleshooting local group problems.

Problem: The Runas command failed.

Reason: The Secondary Logon service is not running.

Resolution: Start the Secondary Logon service.

Problem: Cannot assign a mandatory user profile.

Reason: The preconfigured user profile is not located on the specified network and needs a different file extension.

Resolution: Copy the user profile to the specified network location and change the file extension.

Modems

A modem is a hardware device that enables data to be transmitted and received over standard telephone lines. The following may aid in troubleshooting modem problems.

Problem: The modem diagnostics indicate that an external serial modem is not receiving commands.

Reason: If the modem diagnostics indicate that the modem is not receiving commands, the modem cabling may be faulty.

Resolution: Try connecting the modem with a new cable.

Problem: The modem cable is good, but the modem still does not receive commands.

Reason: The modem is installed incorrectly.

Resolution: Check the modem's documentation to make sure that you installed it correctly.

Problem: The modem works but you still cannot make a connection.

Reason: The modem is connected incorrectly to the phone line, or there is a problem with the phone line.

Resolution: Check the connection to the phone line. If the modem is connected correctly, have a telephone professional check your phone line.

Problem: Your PCMCIA modem card was not detected automatically when you inserted it.

Reason: The card's built-in COM port is not configured.

Resolution: Use Add Hardware in Control Panel to configure the card's built-in COM port. You can then install the PCMCIA modem by using the Phone And Modem Options in Control Panel.

Problem: A connection in Network Connections reports that a port is in use or not configured for remote access.

Reason: When you started Windows, a Plug and Play modem was not connected or it was turned off, so it was not detected correctly. The port is in use by another program, such as Fax or Phone Dialer.

Resolution: If the modem was disconnected or turned off, reconnect or turn on your modem, and then either restart Windows or use Device Manager to scan for new hardware. If the communications port is already in use by another connection, hang up the connection or modify the connection to use a different port.

Network and Dial-up Connections

Network and Dial-up Connections is used in Windows XP Professional to provide connectivity to the Internet or a network. The following may aid in troubleshooting Network and Dial-up Connections problems.

Problem: Unable to connect to the Internet service provider (ISP).

Reason: The ISP's server is not running.

Resolution:

➤ Ask your ISP to verify that the remote access server is running.

➤ Verify with your ISP that your user account has been established, and that you have remote access permission.

Problem: When trying to connect, a message is received that says the ISP server is not responding.

> **Reason:** At higher bits-per-second (bps) rates, your modem is incompatible with the modem of the server. A lot of static is on the phone line, which prevents a modem from connecting at a higher bps rate.

> **Resolution:** Adjust the speed of your modem to a lower bps rate.

Problem: The modem always connects at a lower bps rate than specified.

> **Reason:** The modem and telephone line are not operating correctly. Excessive static on the telephone line causes sessions to be dropped.

> **Resolution:** You can use modem diagnostics to confirm correct modem operation.

Problem: The sessions with your ISP on the network keep getting dropped.

> **Reason:** Call waiting is disrupting your connection.

> **Resolution:** Verify that the phone has call waiting. If so, disable call waiting and try calling again.

Problem: Connections are disconnecting abnormally.

> **Reason:** Your modem is unable to negotiate correctly with the modem of the ISP server. The serial port of the computer cannot keep up with the speed you have selected.

> **Resolution:** Try to connect at a lower initial port speed.

Problem: When trying to connect, a hardware error is received.

> **Reason:** The modem is turned off.

> **Resolution:**

> ➤ Verify that the modem is turned on. If the modem is turned off, turn it on and redial.

> ➤ Enable modem logging to test the connection.

Problem: Conflicts between serial ports are causing connection problems.

> **Reason:** The serial ports are conflicting.

> **Resolution:** COM1 and COM3 share interrupt request (IRQ) 4. COM2 and COM4 share IRQ 3. As a result, for serial communications, you cannot use COM1 and COM3 simultaneously, or COM2 and COM4 simultaneously.

Problem: When trying to connect by using ISDN, a No Answer message is received.

Reason: A problem exists with the hardware.

Resolution: Verify that the ISDN adapters are installed and configured correctly.

Problem: Connections made by using X.25 fail.

Reason: The dial-up PAD is configured with the wrong X.3 parameters or serial settings.

Resolution: If the remote access server is running and you cannot connect to it directly through an X.25 smart card or an external PAD, modify the dial-up PAD X.3 parameters or serial settings. Ask your system administrator for the correct settings.

Problem: Connections through PPTP fail.

Reason: TCP/IP connectivity problems are keeping you from connecting to the PPTP server.

Resolution: You or your system administrator can use the **ipconfig** and **ping** commands to verify a connection to your server.

Problem: Connections made by using PPP or TCP/IP utilities are failing.

Reason: The server does not support LCP extensions.

Resolution: If you cannot connect to a server by using PPP, or the remote computer terminates your connection, the server may not support LCP extensions. In Network Connections, clear the Enable LCP Extensions checkbox.

Problem: A specific program experiences Internet connectivity issues, and Internet Connection Sharing (ICS), Internet Connection Firewall (ICF), or both are enabled.

Reason: ICF, ICS, or both are obstructing the program or prohibiting the program from successfully establishing full, two-way communications across the Internet.

Resolution: Obtain an Internet Connection Sharing and Firewall plug-in from the program manufacturer. Internet Connection Sharing and Firewall plug-ins are designed to fix any Internet connectivity problems that you may encounter with specific programs when either ICS or ICF is enabled.

Appendix F

Problem: Connections made by using Internet Connection Sharing are failing.

Reason: The wrong LAN network adapter is shared.

Resolution: You need to ensure that ICS is enabled on the connection that connects your home network to the Internet.

Problem: When using a laptop to connect to an ISP, some or all of the programs do not run properly.

Reason: The WinSock Proxy Client may be preventing your programs from running properly when you use the ISP connection.

Resolution: If you are a mobile user and use your laptop in your corporate environment, you may need to disable the Microsoft WinSock Proxy Client (WSP Client in Control Panel) when you use the same computer to dial in to an ISP or other network.

Problem: Incoming connection clients cannot see resources beyond the incoming connection computer.

Reason: If the addresses that are being allocated to incoming clients are not a subset of the network to which the incoming connection computer is attached, you must create a route to the incoming client computers on the intranet computers.

Resolution: Reconfigure your range of IP addresses that are being allocated to incoming clients so that it is a subset of the network to which the incoming connection's computer is attached.

Printing

Windows XP Professional supports advanced printing capabilities, including the sharing of print resources among users. The following may aid in troubleshooting printing problems.

Problem: A printer connected to a computer does not print.

Reason: A problem might exist with the physical printer, the print driver, a print server, or the application you are trying to print from.

Resolution:

➤ Verify the physical printer is in a ready state, and that the correct default printer is set. Try to print a test page.

➤ Try printing from the command line (on non-PostScript printers only).

Problem: A printer connected to the network does not print.

Reason: A problem might exist with the physical printer, the logical printer setting on the client computer, the application you are trying to print from, network protocols, or hardware.

Resolution:

➤ Verify basic network connectivity.

➤ Check user rights, protocols, share names, and so on to determine whether you can see the server.

➤ Try to copy a file to the server; if you cannot access the server, you might not be able to access the printer.

Problem: Printing from an Outlook client with multiple languages is slow.

Reason: Multiple languages are installed on the client computer, but not on the print server computer.

Resolution: If clients use additional languages on their computers, you need to add these languages to the print server.

Problem: You get an Access Denied message when trying to configure a printer from within an application.

Reason: You do not have the appropriate permission to change the printer configuration.

Resolution: You need Manage Printer permission to change the printer's setup.

Problem: The document does not print completely, or comes out garbled.

Reason: The printer's driver is either corrupted or incorrect.

Resolution: Verify or reinstall the correct printer driver on the client's computer.

Problem: Hard disk problems occur, and the document does not reach the print server.

Reason: The hard disk might not have enough space for spooling the document.

Resolution: Make sure the hard disk has enough disk space, or relocate the spool folder to another volume.

Appendix F

Problem: Documents on the print server will not print and cannot be deleted.

Reason: The print spooler might be stalled.

Resolution: On the print server, try to stop and restart the Print Spooler service.

Problem: A document sent to the printer from an MS-DOS–based program on a Windows XP or Windows NT 4 client does not print.

Reason: Some MS-DOS programs will not print until you close the program.

Resolution: Close the application you tried to print from. In addition, make sure the correct printer driver is installed on the client computer.

Problem: A driver is not listed in Windows XP.

Reason: The printer was not on the market when Windows XP was released, or a newer version of the print driver has only recently become available.

Resolution: Windows printer drivers are developed through cooperation between Microsoft and the independent hardware vendor (IHV) that manufactures the print device. Windows XP supports all print devices listed in the latest Hardware Compatibility List.

Problem: A new print driver downloaded from the Internet needs to be installed.

Reason: The print driver is not listed in the Add Printer Wizard's list of printers, but instead was downloaded from the Internet.

Resolution: Download the printer driver to an empty folder. Expand the files by typing the name of the executable followed by the **–d** switch.

Problem: With printer location tracking enabled, some printers cannot be located.

Reason: After printer location tracking is enabled, the default behavior is that the user will find only those printers whose location attribute matches the naming convention.

Resolution: You need to set the location string again for this printer.

Remote Access

Remote Access in Windows XP is part of the Routing and Remote Access Service that connects mobile users to their company networks. The following may aid in troubleshooting remote access problems.

Problem: A remote access client can't establish a connection with the remote access server.

Resolution: If using a modem, verify that the correct telephone number is being dialed. If attempting to establish a VPN connection, make sure the Internet connection is working properly by pinging the FQDN of the VPN server.

Problem: The remote access user is denied access by the remote access server.

Resolution: Verify that the user has the appropriate permissions.

Problem: Callback configured by the remote access server is not calling back.

Resolution: Make sure that the correct Always Callback To telephone is configured.

Problem: A remote access client is unable to make a VPN connection when using L2TP.

Resolution: Ensure that certificates are installed on both the remote access client and the remote access server.

Remote Desktop

Remote Desktop is a new feature of Windows XP Professional that utilizes terminal services to provide users with remote access to their corporate or home computers. The following may aid in troubleshooting Remote Desktop problems.

Problem: The following error message appears: Because of an error in data encryption, this session will end. Please try connecting to the remote computer again.

Reason: Data encryption provides security for data traveling over network connections. A data encryption error can end a session for security reasons.

Resolution: Try connecting to the remote computer again.

Problem: The following error message appears: The remote connection has timed out. Please try connecting to the remote computer again.

Reason: The terminal server disconnected your session because you did not send a response within the time limit set for responses.

Resolution: Try connecting to the terminal server again. If you again receive this error message, try to reconnect at a later time. If you continue to receive this error message, contact the server administrator.

Appendix F

Problem: The following error message appears: The remote session was disconnected because the total logon time limit was reached. This limit is set by the server administrator or by network policies.

Reason: A slow network connection, caused by excessive network traffic, has delayed your response to the terminal server.

Resolution: Try connecting to the terminal server again. If you receive this error message again, try to reconnect at a later time. If you continue to receive this error message, contact the server administrator.

Problem: The following error message appears: The specified computer name contains invalid characters. Please verify the name and try again.

Reason: The name of the remote computer is incorrect. This might be a typing error.

Resolution: Try typing the name of the remote computer again. If you receive the same message, contact the server administrator to be sure you are using the correct name for the remote computer.

Problem: The following error message appears: The specified remote computer could not be found. Verify that you have typed the correct computer name or IP address, and then try connecting again.

Reason: The name or IP address of the remote computer is incorrect. This might be a typing error.

Resolution: Try typing the name or IP address of the remote computer again. If you receive the same message, contact the server administrator to be sure you are using the correct name or IP address for the remote computer.

Problem: The following error message appears: The local computer is low on memory. Close some programs, and then connect to the remote computer again.

Reason: Not enough RAM is available on your computer. If your computer has too little RAM available, it cannot free enough processing capacity to start new functions, such as applications or connections.

Resolution: Close all unnecessary programs, and try your connection again.

Problem: The following error message appears: The connection was ended because of a network error. Please try connecting to the remote computer again.

Reason: A network error prevented your computer from communicating with the terminal server.

Resolution: Try connecting to the remote computer again. If you receive the same message, be sure that your computer is connected to the network. If you are still unable to connect to the remote computer, contact the server administrator.

Problem: The following error message appears: The client could not connect. You cannot connect to the console from a console session of the same computer.

Reason: You are logged on to a computer, and you are trying to connect to that same computer.

Resolution: If you are not on the same computer, contact the server administrator.

Problem: The following error message appears: The client could not connect to the remote computer. Remote connections might not be enabled or the computer might be too busy to accept new connections. It is also possible that network problems are preventing your connection. Please try your connection again later. If the problem continues to occur, contact your administrator.

Reason: The remote computer might not be set up to accept remote connections.

Resolution: Try connecting to the remote computer at a later time. If you receive the same message, contact the server administrator.

Problem: The following error message appears: Error: Out of memory. The remote session will be disconnected. Close some programs on the local computer, and then try connecting to the remote computer again.

Reason: Not enough RAM is available on your computer. If your computer has too little RAM available, it cannot free enough processing capacity to start new functions, such as applications or connections.

Resolution: Close all unnecessary programs, and try your connection again. Not enough disk space is available on your hard drive. If the hard drive on your computer is full, there might not be enough space available to allow the swap file to operate correctly. The swap file allows your computer to perform some RAM functions even when not enough RAM space is available.

Problem: The following error message appears: An internal state error has occurred. The remote session will be disconnected. Your local computer might be low on memory. Close some programs, and then try connecting to the remote computer again.

Reason: Not enough RAM is available on your computer. If your computer has too little RAM available, it cannot free enough processing capacity to start new functions, such as applications or connections.

Resolution: Close all unnecessary programs, and try your connection again. Not enough disk space is available on your hard drive. If the hard drive on your computer is full, there might not be enough space available to allow the swap file to operate correctly. The swap file allows your computer to perform some RAM functions even when not enough RAM space is available.

Problem: The following error message appears: Because of a protocol error, this session will be disconnected. Please try connecting to the remote computer again.

Reason: A protocol specifies the way a computer communicates with other computers. A protocol error prevents your computer from communicating with the terminal server to which you were connected.

Resolution: Try connecting to the remote computer again. If you receive the same message, contact the server administrator.

Problem: The following error message appears: Client and server versions do not match. Please upgrade your client software and then try connecting again.

Reason: Remote Desktop Connection does not function unless the version of software on your computer matches the version of software on the server.

Resolution: Contact the server administrator for assistance with upgrading the software on your computer.

Problem: You cannot copy text from an application on the terminal server to another application that is on your local computer.

Reason: It is possible that Remote Desktop Connection was not installed correctly.

Resolution: Uninstall and then reinstall Remote Desktop Connection. If you need assistance, contact the server administrator.

Problem: You minimized the Remote Desktop Connection dialog box, and then your screen went blank.

Reason: Using a password-protected screen saver can cause this problem. Your applications are still running on the remote computer, but you can no longer use them.

Resolution: Do not use a password-protected screen saver on your local computer.

Problem: The screen saver on your Remote Desktop is blank.

Reason: By default, when a screen saver is activated on Remote Desktop, it is blank. This is true regardless of whether you have previously selected a different screen saver.

Resolution: Continue to use the blank screen saver.

Problem: Remote Desktop Connection is very slow.

Reason: A low-bandwidth connection can slow Remote Desktop performance.

Resolution: On the remote computer, set the background selection to None.

Remote Installation Services

Remote Installation Services (RIS) is used to install Windows XP Professional client computers remotely. The following may aid in troubleshooting RIS problems.

Problem: I am not sure whether I have the correct PXE ROM version.

Resolution: When the Net PC or client computer containing a remote boot ROM starts, the version of the PXE ROM appears on the screen. RIS supports .99c or greater PXE ROMs, except in a few situations that require the .99L version.

Problem: I am not sure whether the client computer has received an IP address and has contacted the Remote Installation Services server.

Resolution: When the client computer boots, you will see the PXE boot ROM begin to load and initialize.

Appendix F

Security Templates

Security templates are provided in Windows XP Professional as a method for defining different levels of security on computers. The following may aid in troubleshooting security template problems.

Problem: Security policy is not propagating correctly.

> **Reason:** Any number of reasons.

> **Resolution:** A Registry value creates a log file during policy propagation, located in systemroot\Security\Logs\Winlogon.log. You can examine this log file to identify specific errors that occur during policy propagation to the computer.

Problem: The following error message appears: Event message: Event ID 1202, Event source: scecli, Warning (0x%x) occurs to apply security policies.

> **Reason:** Group Policy was not refreshed after changes were made.

> **Resolution:** Trigger another application of Group Policy settings or local policy refresh by using the Secedit command-line tool to refresh security settings.

Problem: The following error message appears: Failed to open the Group Policy Object.

> **Reason:** The most likely causes for this error are network-related.

> **Resolution:** Make sure that no stale entries are in the DNS database, and resolve local DNS servers and Internet service provider (ISP) DNS server entries.

Problem: Modified security settings are not taking effect.

> **Reason:** The Group Policy model specifies that any policies configured locally may be overridden by like policies specified in the domain. If your setting shows up in local policy but not in effective policy, it implies that a policy from the domain is overriding your setting.

> **Resolution:** Manually do a policy refresh by typing the following at the command line: **secedit /refreshpolicy MACHINE_POLICY**.

Shared Folders

Shared folders provide a way for users to share files and folders on their local computer with others on the network. The following may aid in troubleshooting shared folder problems.

Problem: Cannot access shared resources.

> **Reason:** The Internet Connection Firewall is enabled.

> **Resolution:** If the Internet Connection Firewall is enabled, you cannot view shared resources.

Problem: Cannot view shared resource information in shared folders.

> **Reason:** You are not logged on to the target computer as a member of the Administrators or Power Users group for computers that are running Windows XP Professional.

> **Resolution:** Log on to the target computer with the appropriate credentials.

Virtual Private Networks

Virtual private networks (VPNs) provide users with the ability to connect to remote access servers on a private network over the Internet. The following may aid in troubleshooting VPN problems.

Problem: Unable to establish a remote access VPN connection.

> **Reason:** The Routing and Remote Access Service is not started on the VPN server.

> **Resolution:** Verify the state of the Routing and Remote Access Service on the VPN server.

Problem: VPN clients are unable to access resources beyond the VPN server.

> **Reason:** The LAN protocols used by remote access VPN clients are not enabled to allow access to the network to which the VPN server is attached.

> **Resolution:** Configure the LAN protocols used by the remote access VPN clients to allow access to the network to which the VPN server is attached.

Appendix F

Windows Installer

Windows Installer is used in Windows XP to manage the installation and removal of applications. The following may aid in troubleshooting Windows Installer problems.

Problem: The installation package will not install correctly.

Reason: This can be caused when the installation package has become corrupted.

Resolution: Repair the installation package by using the Windows Installer repair option.

Problem: The installation process stops before completing the installation.

Reason: Windows Installer was not able to read the installation package, or conditions on your computer prevented the package from successfully installing.

Resolution: Windows Installer creates entries in the Windows XP event log.

Stop Messages

Stop messages that are generated by the operating system usually indicate some type of fatal error has occurred. The Stop messages described in this section are the most common ones that users may encounter when using Windows XP if a problem occurs that could affect the operation of the computer for one reason or another.

Stop Message 0x0000000A on an Existing Installation

Error description: IRQL_NOT_LESS_OR_EQUAL

Reason: Drivers using improper memory addresses.

Resolution:

➤ Check Event Viewer for additional information that might help determine the device or driver causing the problem.

➤ Disable any newly installed drivers and remove any newly added programs.

➤ Remove any newly installed hardware.

➤ Ensure that you have updated drivers for your hardware devices.

> ➤ Check the Microsoft HCL to verify that your hardware and its drivers are compatible with Windows XP.

> ➤ Disable memory caching in the BIOS.

Stop Message 0x0000000A on a New Installation

Error description: IRQL_NOT_LESS_OR_EQUAL

Reason: Drivers using improper memory addresses.

Resolution:

> ➤ During the installation process, at the Setup Is Inspecting Your Computer's Hardware Configuration message, press F5. Select the correct computer type when prompted.

> ➤ Disable memory caching in the BIOS.

> ➤ Remove all adapters and disconnect all hardware devices that are not absolutely required to start the computer.

> ➤ Run the system diagnostics supplied by your hardware vendor, especially the memory check.

> ➤ Check the Microsoft HCL to verify that your hardware and its drivers are compatible with Windows XP.

Stop Message 0x0000001E

Error description: KMODE_EXCEPTION_NOT_HANDLED

Resolution:

> ➤ Check that you have adequate disk space, especially for new installations.

> ➤ Disable the driver identified in the Stop message or any newly installed drivers.

> ➤ If you have a non-Microsoft-supplied video driver, try switching to the standard VGA driver or to a suitable driver supplied with Windows XP.

> ➤ Ensure that you have the latest system BIOS.

> ➤ Restart your computer. At the startup screen, press F8 for Advanced Startup options, and then select Last Known Good Configuration.

Appendix F

Stop Messages 0x00000023 and 0x00000024

Error description: FAT_FILE_SYSTEM or NTFS_FILE_SYSTEM

Reason: Heavily fragmented drive, heavy file I/O, some types of drive-mirroring software, or some types of antivirus software.

Resolution:

➤ Disable any antivirus or backup programs, and disable any defragmentation utilities.

➤ Check for hard drive corruption by running **CHKDSK /f** and then restarting the computer.

➤ At the startup screen, press F8 for Advanced Startup options, and then select Last Known Good Configuration.

Stop Message 0x0000002E

Error description: DATA_BUS_ERROR

Reason: A parity error in the system memory.

Resolution:

➤ Run system diagnostics supplied by your hardware vendor, especially a memory check.

➤ Disable memory caching in the BIOS.

➤ Try starting in Safe Mode.

➤ Ensure that you have updated drivers for your hardware devices and the latest system BIOS.

➤ Remove any newly installed hardware.

➤ Restart your computer. At the startup screen, press F8 for Advanced Startup options, and then select Last Known Good Configuration.

Stop Message 0x0000003F

Error description: NO_MORE_SYSTEM_PTES

Reason: A driver is not cleaning up properly.

Resolution: Remove any recently installed software, including backup utilities or disk-intensive applications, such as defragmenting, virus protection, and backup utilities.

Stop Message 0x0000007B

Error description: INACCESSIBLE_BOOT_DEVICE

Reason: A problem is occurring during the initialization of the I/O system (usually the startup device or the file system).

Resolution:

➤ Check for viruses on your computer. This Stop message is frequently displayed when there is a virus in the boot sector.

➤ Remove any newly added hard drives or controllers.

➤ Run CHKDSK.

➤ Restart your computer. At the startup screen, press F8 for Advanced Startup options, and then select Last Known Good Configuration.

Stop Boot Sector 0x0000007F

Error description: UNEXPECTED_KERNEL_MODE_TRAP

Reason: Hardware or software problems; most often, a hardware failure.

Resolution:

➤ Run system diagnostics supplied by your hardware vendor, especially a memory check.

➤ Disable memory caching in the BIOS.

➤ Check the Microsoft HCL to verify that the hardware and its drivers are compatible with Windows XP.

➤ Restart your computer. At the startup screen, press F8 for Advanced Startup options, and then select Last Known Good Configuration.

Stop Message 0x000000B4

Error description: VIDEO_DRIVER_INIT_FAILURE

Reason: The video driver is bad, corrupted, missing, or disabled.

Resolution:

➤ Try starting your computer in Safe Mode or enable VGA Mode.

➤ If you can start your computer in Safe Mode, uninstall the video driver by using Add/Remove Hardware.

➤ After completing the previous step, reinstall the video driver.

Appendix F

Stop Message 0x000000BE

Error description:
ATTEMPTED_WRITE_TO_READONLY_MEMORY

Reason: A driver is bad or corrupted or does not function correctly.

Resolution:

➤ Disable the driver identified in the Stop message or any newly installed drivers.

➤ Try to replace the driver, either with a good copy from your installation media or with an updated version from the manufacturer.

Stop Error 0x00000058

Error description: FTDISK_INTERNAL_ERROR

Reason: A primary drive in a fault-tolerant set has failed.

Resolution: Using the Windows XP Setup disks to start your computer, boot from the mirrored (secondary) system drive.

Stop Error 0x00000050

Error description: PAGE_FAULT_IN_NONPAGED_AREA

Reason: Memory error (data cannot be swapped out to disk using the paging file).

Resolution:

➤ Remove any newly installed hardware.

➤ Run any system diagnostics supplied by your computer manufacturer.

➤ Verify that any new hardware or software is properly installed.

➤ If the computer is formatted with NTFS, restart your computer, and then run **Chkdsk /f /r** on the system partition. If you cannot start the system due to the error, use the Command Console and run **Chkdsk /r**.

➤ Disable or uninstall any antivirus programs.

➤ Disable BIOS memory options such as caching or shadowing.

Stop Error 0x00000077

Error description: KERNEL_STACK_INPAGE_ERROR

Reason: The requested page of kernel data from the paging file could not be read into memory.

Resolution:

➤ Using a current version of your virus-protection software, check for viruses on your computer.

➤ If the computer is formatted with NTFS, restart your computer, and then run **Chkdsk /f /r** on the system partition. If you cannot start the system due to the error, use the Command Console and run **Chkdsk /r**.

➤ Run any system diagnostics supplied by your computer manufacturer.

➤ Disable BIOS memory options such as caching or shadowing.

Stop Error 0x00000079

Error description: MISMATCHED_HAL

Reason: Hardware Abstraction Layer and the kernel or the machine type do not match (usually when single-processor and multiprocessor configuration files are mixed on the same system).

Resolution: Use the Command Console to replace the incorrect system files on your computer.

Stop Error 0x0000007A

Error description: KERNEL_DATA_INPAGE_ERROR

Reason: The requested page of kernel data from the paging file could not be read into memory (usually due to a bad block in a paging file, a virus, a disk controller error, or failing RAM).

Resolution:

➤ Using a current version of your virus-protection software, check for viruses on your computer.

➤ If the computer is formatted with NTFS, restart your computer, and then run **Chkdsk /f /r** on the system partition. If you cannot start the system due to the error, use the Command Console and run **Chkdsk /r**.

➤ Run any system diagnostics supplied by your computer manufacturer.

Appendix F

Stop Error 0xC000021A

Error description: STATUS_SYSTEM_PROCESS_TERMINATED

Reason: The user mode subsystem, such as Winlogon or the Client Server Runtime Subsystem (CSRSS), is fatally compromised and security can no longer be guaranteed.

Resolution:

➤ Remove any newly installed hardware.

➤ If you are unable to log on, restart your computer. When the list of available operating systems appears, press F8. On the Windows 2000 Advanced Options Menu screen, select Last Known Good Configuration, and then press Enter.

➤ Run Recovery Console and allow the system to repair any errors that it detects.

Stop Error 0xC0000221

Error description: STATUS_IMAGE_CHECKSUM_MISMATCH

Reason: A driver or a system DLL has been corrupted.

Resolution:

➤ If the computer is formatted with NTFS, restart your computer, and then run **Chkdsk /f /r** on the system partition. If you cannot start the system due to the error, use the Command Console and run **Chkdsk /r**.

➤ Run Recovery Console and allow the system to repair any errors that it detects.

➤ If the error occurred immediately after RAM was added to the computer, the paging file might be corrupted or the new RAM might be either faulty or incompatible. Delete the Pagefile.sys and return the system to the original RAM configuration.

➤ Run any system diagnostics supplied by your computer manufacturer, especially the memory check.

Glossary

Accelerated Graphics Port (AGP)
A dedicated bus developed by Intel, AGP allows operating systems like Windows XP to have high quality video and graphics. This expansion slot can only be used for AGP video cards.

access control entry (ACE)
An entry in the access control list (ACL) for a user or group. The ACE, containing the security identifier (SID) along with an access mask, establishes which operations are allowed, denied, or audited for a particular object. See also access control list, security ID, and access mask.

access control list (ACL)
A list of ACEs that apply to a particular object and/or the object's properties. See also access control entry, security ID, and access mask.

access mask
One of two parts of the access control entry, the access mask is a 32-bit value that specifies rights that are allowed or denied for a particular object. See also access control entry, access control list, and security ID.

access token
A security object that identifies a user to the security subsystem in Windows XP. The access token contains security information such as the user's security ID (SID) and the SIDs of all groups of which the user is a member. It also contains the user's list of privileges on the local computer. See also access control entry, access control list, access mask, privileges, and security ID.

accessibility
The ability of a user interface to provide alternative methods of functionality for people with hearing, visual, and physical disabilities.

account lockout
A Windows security feature that locks a user account if a number of failed logon attempts occur within a specified amount of time, based on security policy lockout settings. Locked accounts cannot log on.

Active Directory
Directory service found in Windows XP and 2000 that stores and distributes information about network objects. Using a single logon, users can use Active Directory to access any network object, such as printers, servers, shares, and so on. See also directory service.

active partition
A partition from which an x86-based computer starts up. The active partition must be a primary partition on a basic disk. If you use Windows exclusively, the active partition can be the same as the system volume.

active volume
The volume from which the computer starts up.

ActiveX
A set of technologies that allows software components to interact with one another in a networked environment, regardless of the language in which the components were created.

address (A) resource record
A resource record used to map a DNS domain name to a host IP address on the network.

address classes
Predefined groupings of Internet addresses with each class defining networks of a certain size. The range of numbers that can be assigned for the first octet in the IP address is based on the address class. Class A networks (values 1 to 126) are the largest, with more than 16 million hosts per network. Class B networks (128 to 191) have up to 65,534 hosts per network, and Class C networks (192 to 223) can have up to 254 hosts per network.

Address Resolution Protocol (ARP)
In TCP/IP, a protocol that uses broadcast traffic on the local network to resolve a logically assigned IP address to its physical hardware or media access control layer address.

Administrator
The most powerful user object found in Windows XP. The Administrator user object can create other objects such as users, shares, printers, and so on. The Administrator can also reconfigure and install device drivers and system files.

Advanced Configuration and Power Interface (ACPI)
An industry specification used to define power management in computers. ACPI is an open standard embraced by many hardware and software vendors, including Microsoft in Windows XP.

Advanced Power Management (APM)
A proprietary interface developed by Microsoft and Intel used between hardware-based power management software (BIOS level) and an operating system.

answer file
A text file used to automate the installation of a Windows XP computer. The answer file provides user input for questions presented by the installation routine during setup. The default answer file in Windows XP is unattend.txt.

application programming interface (API)
A standard set of routines that an application or operating system uses to provide basic functionality. For example, an API may contain the routines to open and write to a file. A programmer writing an application can call the API's routines to perform that operation without the need to create a new routine.

asynchronous communication
A form of data communication where the sender must notify the receiver when the transmission of data begins and ends.

Asynchronous Transfer Mode (ATM)
A connection-oriented protocol that can be used to transport many different types of network traffic, such as video, voice, and data. It is known for its high speed.

attribute

For a file or directory, an attribute can be used to mark a file as read-only or archiveable. In Active Directory, an attribute can be used to describe the characteristics of an object. The schema defines which attributes an object can have.

audio input device

An audio input device records music and voice input into your computer. Examples of audio input devices are CD-ROM players and microphones.

auditing

Used to track the activities of users or processes. Audited events are stored in the security log.

authentication

Used to identify users and objects, whether accessing the resource locally or remotely. When a user logs on, his or her username and password are checked by the security subsystem of the workstation or domain.

automated installation

The process of using one of several methods (Remote Installation Services, Sysprep, bootable CD) to perform an unattended setup in Windows XP.

Automatic Private IP Addressing (APIPA)

Found in Windows XP, Windows 2000, and Windows 98, APIPA allows a DHCP-enabled workstation to still receive an IP address if DHCP is unavailable. The network range used for APIPA is 169.254.0.1 through 169.254.255.254, along with the subnet mask 255.255.0.0.

B-channel

A single channel of an ISDN line that is used to carry either voice or data information. ISDN Basic Rate Interface (BRI) has two B-channels.

backup

A copy of data used for disaster recovery purposes.

backup operators

One of the built-in groups in Windows XP whose members have the right to backup and restore files and folders regardless of access permissions, encryption settings, or ownership.

backup types

Used to determine how data is backed up. There are five backup types found in Windows XP: normal, copy, differential, incremental, and daily.

bandwidth

In analog communications, the difference between the highest and lowest frequencies in a given range. In digital communications, bandwidth is expressed in bits per second (bps).

Bandwidth Allocation Protocol (BAP)

A PPP control protocol that is used on a multiprocessing connection to dynamically add and remove links.

base priority

A precedence ranking that determines the order in which the threads of a process are scheduled for the processor. Use Task Manager to view and change base priorities.

basic disk

In Windows XP, a physical disk that contains primary partitions or extended partitions with logical drives. Basic disks can also contain volume sets or RAID sets.

Glossary

Basic Input Output System (BIOS)
A collection of software routines used to test and startup hardware in a computer. The BIOS is stored in read-only memory (ROM). This allows the computer to be turned off without the loss of the BIOS.

basic storage
A storage method in MS-DOS, Windows, Windows NT, Windows 2000, and Windows XP for primary partitions, extended partitions, and logical drives.

basic volume
A volume found on a basic disk in Windows XP.

batch program
An ASCII (unformatted text) file that contains one or more operating system commands. A batch program's file name has a .cmd or .bat extension. When you type the file name at the command prompt, or when the batch program is run from another program, its commands are processed sequentially. Batch programs are also called batch files.

baud rate
The speed at which a modem communicates. Baud rate refers to the number of times the condition of the line changes. This is equal to bits per second only if each signal corresponds to one bit of transmitted data.

binary
A base-2 number system in which values are expressed as combinations of two digits, 0 and 1.

boot
The process of starting or resetting a computer. When first turned on (cold boot) or reset (warm boot), the computer runs

the software that loads and starts the computer's operating system, which prepares it for use.

boot files
The system files needed to start Windows. The boot files include Ntldr and Ntdetect.com.

boot logging
A process in which a computer that is starting (booting) creates a log file that records the loading of each device and service. The log file is called Ntbtlog.txt, and it is saved in the system root directory.

boot sector
Located at sector 1 of each bootable disk, it contains the executable code to access data on the disk.

bootable CD
Automated installation method found in Windows XP that is used to run Setup from a CD-ROM.

bottleneck
A condition resulting from a poorly performing component that results in the slow performance of the entire system.

broadcast
An address that is destined for all hosts on a particular network segment.

browser
Software that interprets the markup of files in HTML, formats them into Web pages, and displays them to the end user.

buffer
A region of RAM reserved for use with data that is temporarily held while waiting to be transferred between two locations, such as between an application's data area and an input/output device.

bus

A communication line used for data transfer among the components of a computer system.

bytes

A unit of data that typically holds a single character, such as a letter, a digit, or a punctuation mark. Some single characters can take up more than one byte.

cable modem

A modem used to access broadband Internet service used on cable TV infrastructures. It operates in the range of 10Mbps to 30Mbps.

cache

A local store of recently resolved names for remote hosts used to speed IP address resolution times. Typically the cache is used for DNS and WINS.

callback number

The number that a remote access server uses to call back a user.

CD-R

Recordable compact disc. Data can be copied to the CD on more than one occasion; however, data cannot be erased from the CD.

CD-RW

Rewritable compact disc. Data can be copied to the CD on more than one occasion and can be erased.

central processing unit (CPU)

The heart and brain of a computer that is used to retrieve data from other hardware devices in the system. It can then interpret the data and execute the required instructions.

certificate

A digital document used to authenticate users and their transactions. See also Certificate Services, certificate authority.

certificate authority (CA)

An entity responsible for establishing and verifying the authenticity of certificates.

Certificate Services

A service in Windows XP that issues certificates for a certificate authority (CA). See also certificate, certificate authority.

Challenge Handshake Authentication Protocol (CHAP)

An authentication protocol for Point-to-Point Protocol (PPP) connections.

Class A IP address

A unicast IP address that ranges from 1.0.0.1 through 126.255.255.254. The first octet indicates the network, and the last three octets indicate the host on the network.

Class B IP address

A unicast IP address that ranges from 128.0.0.1 through 191.255.255.254. The first two octets indicate the network, and the last two octets indicate the host on the network.

Class C IP address

A unicast IP address that ranges from 192.0.0.1 through 223.255.255.254. The first three octets indicate the network, and the last octet indicates the host on the network.

client

A computer or program that connects to another computer or program to access resources.

Glossary

COM port

A communications or serial port used to connect peripherals such as modems, printers, and scanners.

Common Internet File System (CIFS)

A protocol used on Microsoft networks to perform file operations on a remote computer. CIFS is formerly known as Server Message Block (SMB).

Compact Disc File System (CDFS)

A file system found in Windows XP, Windows 2000, and Windows NT that provides access to data stored on CD-ROM drives.

compact disc recordable (CD-R)

A type of CD-ROM that can be written to via a CD recorder and read via a CD-ROM drive.

copy backup

A backup type that copies the selected data to backup media but does not set the archive bit on the file. By not setting the archive bit, the file is shown as not having been backed up.

CPU time

In Task Manager, the total processor time, in seconds, used by a process since it started.

CRC errors

Errors caused by the failure of a cyclic redundancy check. A CRC error indicates that one or more characters in the data packet received were found garbled on arrival.

cryptography

The processes, art, and science of keeping messages and data secure. Cryptography is used to enable and ensure confidentiality, data integrity, authentication (entity and data origin), and nonrepudiation.

daily backup

A backup type that copies data that has been created or modified the day the daily backup is performed. It does not set the archive bit on the file. By not setting the archive bit, the file is shown as not having been backed up.

Data Link Control (DLC)

A network protocol used for IBM mainframe computers and HP network printer connectivity.

data packet

A logical unit of data transmitted from one network device to another.

decryption

The process of making encrypted data readable.

default gateway

The IP address of a router located on the host's local subnet.

defragmentation

The process of rewriting parts of a file to contiguous sectors on a hard disk to increase the speed of access and retrieval.

desktop

The screen working area where icons, menus, applications, and dialog boxes are displayed.

device conflict

A conflict that occurs when the same system resources have been allocated to two or more devices. System resources include interrupt request (IRQ) lines, direct memory access (DMA) channels, input/output (I/O) ports, and memory addresses.

device driver

A software component that provides the operating system with routines to access a hardware device.

Device Manager

An administrative tool that you can use to manage the devices on your computer.

dial-up connection

The connection to your network if you are using a device that uses the telephone network. This includes modems with a standard phone line, ISDN cards with high-speed ISDN lines, or X.25 networks.

differential backup

A backup type that copies data that has been created or modified since the last normal or incremental backup. It does not set the archive bit on the file. By not setting the archive bit, the file is shown as not having been backed up.

digital audio tape (DAT)

A magnetic tape medium used to back up data as well as digital audio data.

digital linear tape (DLT)

A magnetic tape medium used to back up data. DLT is known for its high storage capacity and speed.

digital signature

A means for originators of a message, file, or other digitally encoded information to bind their identity to the information.

digital subscriber line (DSL)

A type of communication line used for high-speed data transfer over traditional copper telephone wires.

digital video disc (DVD)

A type of optical storage technology known for its high data capacity. DVDs can hold full-length movies with alternate soundtracks, scenes, and so on. It also has the capacity to contain multiple CD-ROMs.

direct cable connection

A link between the I/O ports of two computers created with a single cable rather than a modem or other interfacing devices.

direct memory access (DMA)

Used for data transfer directly between memory and the hardware device, without the intervention of the CPU.

directory

Used to hold information about computer files (a file system) or network objects (a directory service such as Active Directory).

directory service

The entity or service that is used to present directory information to other objects.

DirectX

An extension of the Microsoft Windows operating system. DirectX technology helps games and other programs use the advanced multimedia capabilities of your hardware.

discretionary access control list (DACL)

The part of an object's security descriptor that grants or denies specific users and groups permission to access the object. Only the owner of an object can change permissions granted or denied in a DACL; thus, access to the object is at the owner's discretion.

disk

A storage device that is attached to a computer.

disk quota

The amount of disk space available to a particular user.

Glossary

Distinguished Name

A method of uniquely identifying an object in a directory. This method uses the Relative Name along with the names of container objects and domains that contain the object.

Distribution Folder

A folder used to distribute the Windows XP setup files.

DNS server

A server that responds to Domain Name System (DNS) queries from DNS clients. A DNS query is a request to resolve a host name to an IP address.

DNS zone

An adjoining portion of the DNS namespace that is administered separately by a DNS server.

dock

Used to connect a laptop or notebook computer to a docking station.

docking station

A unit for housing a portable computer that contains a power connection, expansion slots, and connections to peripherals, such as a monitor, printer, full-sized keyboard, and mouse. The docking station turns the portable computer into a desktop computer.

domain

A collection of computers and resources that share a common security database.

domain controller

A Windows XP, Windows 2000, or Windows NT Server that authenticates domain logons and maintains the security database.

domain name

The name given by an administrator to a collection of networked computers that share a common directory.

Domain Name System (DNS)

A service and hierarchical naming system used for locating and resolving host names on a TCP/IP-based network.

dual boot

A computer configuration that can start two or more operating systems. A dual boot computer will display an operating system selection menu upon startup.

duplex

A system capable of transmitting information in both directions over a communications channel.

DVD decoder

A hardware or software component that allows a digital video disc (DVD) drive to display movies on your computer screen.

DVD drive

A disk storage device that uses digital video disc (DVD) technology. A DVD drive reads both CD-ROMs and DVDs; however, you must have a DVD decoder to display DVD movies on your computer screen.

dynamic disk

A physical disk that has been upgraded by Disk Management. Dynamic disks cannot contain logical drives or partitions. They can only contain dynamic volumes created by Disk Management. Dynamic disks can only be accessed by Windows XP and Windows 2000 computers.

Dynamic Host Configuration Protocol (DHCP)

A protocol used on TCP/IP-based networks to supply IP configurations dynamically to TCP/IP hosts. It is used to automate and simplify the configuration of a TCP/IP network.

dynamic link library (DLL)

A file containing a library of executable routines used by the operating system and associated applications. These routines work together to perform a specific software function.

dynamic storage
A storage method in Windows that allows disk and volume management without requiring operating system restart.

dynamic volume
A logical volume created using Disk Management and residing on a dynamic disk. Dynamic volumes can be one of the following: simple, spanned, striped, mirrored (RAID-1), and striped with parity (RAID-5).

emergency repair disk (ERD)
A floppy disk that contains files necessary in the Emergency Repair Process for Windows XP. Files from the *%systemroot%*\repair directory are copied to the ERD. The ERD is created using the Backup utility.

Encrypting File System (EFS)
Used to protect sensitive data on a Windows XP computer, EFS uses symmetric key encryption along with public key cryptography to encrypt files on an NTFS partition.

encryption
The process of disguising a message or data in such a way as to hide its substance.

environment variable
A string consisting of environment information, such as a drive, path, or file name, associated with a symbolic name that can be used by Windows.

error detection
A technique for detecting when data is lost during transmission.

Ethernet
A networking technology that uses Carrier Sense Media Access with Collision Detection (CSMA/CD) to manage network traffic. Ethernet is used in either a bus or star topology across coaxial, twisted-pair, or fiber-optic cabling.

event
Any significant occurrence in the system or an application that requires users to be notified or an entry to be added to a log.

Event Log service
A service that records events in the system, security, and application logs. The Event Log service is located in Event Viewer.

event logging
The process of recording an audit entry in the audit trail whenever certain events occur, such as services starting and stopping, or users logging on and off and accessing resources.

Event Viewer
A component you can use to view and manage event logs, gather information about hardware and software problems, and monitor security events.

Extensible Authentication Protocol (EAP)
An update to Point-to-Point Protocol (PPP), EAP allows additional authentication mechanisms to be employed during PPP connection validation, such as smart cards and secure ID.

Extensible Markup Language (XML)
A meta-markup language that provides a format for describing structured data.

extract
When you extract a file, an uncompressed copy of the file that is created in a folder you specify. The original file remains in the compressed folder.

Glossary

FAT32

An enhanced version of FAT that supports smaller cluster sizes. This results in more efficient use of disk space.

fault tolerance

The ability of computer hardware or software to ensure data integrity when hardware failures occur.

Fiber Distributed Data Interface (FDDI)

A networking technology that uses fiber-optic cabling.

file allocation table (FAT)

One of the most universal file systems, FAT employs a file allocation table to keep track of various portions of a disk.

file system

The method by which files and folders are named, organized, and stored on a disk.

File Transfer Protocol (FTP)

A protocol used to transfer files from one computer to another computer on a TCP/IP-based network.

FilterKeys

A keyboard feature that instructs your keyboard to ignore brief or repeated keystrokes.

firewall

A combination of hardware and software that provides a security system, usually to prevent unauthorized access from outside to an internal network or intranet.

folder

A container for programs and files in graphical user interfaces, symbolized on the screen by a graphical image (icon) of a file folder.

font

A graphic design applied to a collection of numbers, symbols, and characters. A font describes a certain typeface, along with other qualities such as size, spacing, and pitch.

fragmentation

The scattering of parts of the same disk file over different areas of the disk. Fragmentation occurs as files on a disk are deleted and new files are added.

gateway

A device connected to multiple physical TCP/IP networks capable of routing or delivering IP packets between them. A gateway translates between different transport protocols or data formats.

gigabyte (GB)

1,024 megabytes, though often interpreted as approximately one billion bytes.

group

A collection of users used for organizational purposes as well as to administer rights to other objects.

Group Policy

A utility that allows an administrator to define certain rights and capabilities for users and groups on a computer or domain.

Guest account

A built-in account used to log on to a computer running Windows when a user does not have an account on the computer or domain, or in any of the domains trusted by the computer's domain.

GUID partition table (GPT)

A disk-partitioning scheme that is used by the Extensible Firmware Interface (EFI) in Itanium-based computers.

half-duplex

A system capable of transmitting information in only one direction at a time over a communications channel.

handshaking

A series of signals acknowledging that communication can take place between computers or other devices.

hard disk

A device, also called a hard disk drive, that contains one or more inflexible platters coated with material in which data can be recorded magnetically with read/write heads.

hardware

The physical components of a computer system, including any peripheral equipment such as printers, modems, and mouse devices.

Hardware Abstraction Layer (HAL)

Part of the modular design of Windows XP, the HAL is composed of many software components, such as device drivers and system files. These components work together to manage and interact with the hardware components in a computer. By employing the HAL, Windows XP can easily be ported to other hardware platforms without the need to rewrite the entire operating system.

Hardware Compatibility List (HCL)

A list of hardware devices that have been certified by Microsoft to be used in Windows XP. The HCL can be found on Microsoft's Web site.

hardware profile

A profile used to load a different set of device drivers. A hardware profile is typically used when the hardware characteristics of a computer change rather frequently. For example, a laptop used with a docking station would have two hardware profiles. One would include the hardware for the docking station and the laptop, while the other would simply be the hardware configuration of the laptop.

hash

A fixed-size result that is obtained by applying a one-way mathematical function (sometimes called a hash algorithm) to an arbitrary amount of data. If there is a change in the input data, the hash changes.

hibernation

A state in which your computer shuts down after saving everything in memory on your hard disk. When you bring your computer out of hibernation, all programs and documents that were open are restored to your desktop.

high contrast

A display feature that instructs programs to change the color scheme to a high-contrast scheme and to increase legibility whenever possible.

HOSTS file

A local text file that maps host names to IP addresses. It is stored in the \%systemroot%\System32\Drivers\Etc folder.

hot docking

The process of attaching a laptop computer to a docking station while the computer is running, and automatically activating the docking station's video display and other functions.

hub

A common connection point for devices in a network.

hyperlink

Colored and underlined text or a graphic that you click to go to a file, a location in a file, an HTML page on the World Wide Web, or an HTML page on an intranet.

Hypertext Transport Protocol (HTTP)

A protocol used to transfer files and data between a Web server and a Web browser. HTTP is the protocol for the World Wide Web.

icon

A small image displayed on the screen to represent an object that can be manipulated by the user. Icons serve as visual mnemonics and allow the user to control certain computer actions without having to remember commands or type them at the keyboard.

IEEE 1394

A standard for high-speed serial devices such as digital video and digital audio editing equipment.

incremental backup

A backup type that copies the selected data that has changed since the last normal or incremental backup to backup media and sets the archive bit on the file. By setting the archive bit, the file is shown as having been backed up.

infrared (IR)

Light that is beyond red in the color spectrum. While the light is not visible to the human eye, infrared transmitters and receivers can send and receive infrared signals.

Infrared Data Association (IrDA)

The industry organization of computer, component, and telecommunications vendors who establish the standards for infrared communication between computers and peripheral devices, such as printers.

infrared device

A computer, or a computer peripheral such as a printer, that can communicate using infrared light.

infrared port

An optical port on a computer that enables communication with other computers or devices by using infrared light, without cables.

inheritance

A mechanism that allows a given access control entry (ACE) to be copied from the container where it was applied to all children of the container.

inherited permissions

Permissions on an object that are automatically inherited from its parent object. Inherited permissions cannot be modified.

Integrated Services Digital Network (ISDN)

A type of digital phone line used for the conveyance of both voice and data communications. ISDN can operate up to 128Kbps.

IntelliMirror

This feature allows a user's desktop, application, and user environments to follow them throughout the network environment.

interactive logon

The process of logging on to a Windows XP computer via that computer's keyboard.

Internet

The TCP/IP-based network whose public infrastructure is available practically worldwide.

Internet Control Message Protocol (ICMP)

A required maintenance protocol in the TCP/IP suite that reports errors and allows simple connectivity. ICMP is used by the Ping tool to perform TCP/IP troubleshooting.

Internet Group Management Protocol (IGMP)

A protocol used by IP hosts to report their multicast group memberships to any immediately neighboring multicast routers.

Internet Information Services (IIS)

Software services that support Web site creation, configuration, and management, along with other Internet functions. Internet Information Services include Network News Transfer Protocol (NNTP), File Transfer Protocol (FTP), and Simple Mail Transfer Protocol (SMTP).

Internet Printing Protocol (IPP)

A protocol used for printing documents across the Internet. IPP uses HTTP to transfer the print jobs to printers.

Internet Protocol (IP)

A protocol that is responsible for the routing of data across a TCP/IP-based network. It is also responsible for IP addressing and the segmenting and reassembly of IP packets.

Internet Protocol Security (IPSec)

A set of cryptography standards used to protect data transmitted using the TCP/IP protocol suite.

Internet service provider (ISP)

A company that provides Internet access to individual users and organizations via either a dial-up, cable modem, or DSL connection.

Internetwork Packet Exchange (IPX)

A protocol that is responsible for the routing of data across an IPX/SPX-based network. More commonly known as the native protocol for Novell NetWare networks.

interrupt

A request for attention from the processor.

Interrupt Request (IRQ)

A signal sent from a hardware device to the central processing unit (CPU) to notify the CPU that the device wishes to send or receive data. Each hardware device is assigned a unique IRQ number from 0 through 15.

intranet

A TCP/IP-based network used within an organization that employs Internet technologies such as HTTP and FTP.

IP address

A 32-bit binary address used to identify a host on a TCP/IP-based network. Each host must have a unique IP address. IP addresses are shown in dotted-decimal format; for example, 192.168.0.10.

Itanium

An Intel microprocessor that uses explicitly parallel instruction set computing and 64-bit memory addressing.

junction point

A physical location on a hard disk that points to data located at another location on your hard disk or another storage device. Junction points are created when you create a mounted drive.

Kerberos

The default authentication protocol used for the verification of users in Windows XP. Windows XP employs Kerberos v5.

kernel

The heart of the modular architecture of Windows XP, this software component comprises the core software that manages basic operating system and CPU operations.

keyboard language

The language you want to use when you type.

Glossary

Layer 2 Tunneling Protocol (L2TP)

An industry-standard Internet tunneling protocol. L2TP does not require IP connectivity between the client workstation and the server. L2TP requires only that the tunnel medium provide packet-oriented point-to-point connectivity.

Lightweight Directory Access Protocol (LDAP)

The primary access protocol for Active Directory.

Line Printer Daemon (LPD)

A service on the print server that receives documents (print jobs) from Line Printer Remote (LPR) utilities running on client systems.

liquid crystal display (LCD)

A type of display used in digital watches and many portable computers.

LMHOSTS file

A local text file that maps NetBIOS names (commonly used for computer names) to IP addresses for hosts that are not located on the local subnet. In this version of Windows, the file is stored in the *%systemroot%*\System32\Drivers\Etc folder.

local area network (LAN)

A network of computers located within a relatively small geographic area.

local computer

A computer that is accessed directly without the use of a network or a modem.

local group

A group that resides on the local computer. A local group can only be granted access to resources on the local computer where the local group resides. Local groups can contain users from the local computer, as well as users and global groups from trusted domains.

logical drive

A volume created on an extended partition of a basic disk.

logon script

A batch file that contains a set of commands typically used to configure a user's working environment. The logon script is executed whenever the user logs on.

long name

A folder name or file name longer than the 8.3 file name standard (up to eight characters followed by a period and an extension of up to three characters) of the FAT file system.

loopback address

The address of the local computer used for routing outgoing packets back to the source computer. This address is used primarily for testing.

mandatory user profile

A user profile that is not updated when the user logs off. It is downloaded to the user's desktop each time the user logs on, and is created by an administrator and assigned to one or more users to create consistent or job-specific user profiles.

master boot record (MBR)

The first sector on a hard disk used to start the process of booting the computer. The MBR contains the executable code for booting as well as the partition table for the hard disk.

Master File Table (MFT)

An NTFS system file on NTFS-formatted volumes that contains information about each file and folder on the volume. The MFT is the first file on an NTFS volume.

media

Any fixed or removable objects that store computer data.

media pool

A logical collection of removable media that have the same management policies.

memory address

A portion of computer memory that can be allocated to a device or used by a program or the operating system. Devices are usually allocated a range of memory addresses.

Microsoft Challenge Handshake Authentication Protocol (MS-CHAP)

An authentication protocol, similar to CHAP, for Point-to-Point Protocol (PPP) connections.

Microsoft Challenge Handshake Authentication Protocol version 2 (MS-CHAP v2)

An authentication protocol, similar to CHAP and MS-CHAP, for Point-to-Point Protocol (PPP) connections. MS-CHAP v2 employs stronger security mechanisms than CHAP or MS-CHAP.

Microsoft Management Console (MMC)

A software-based console used for administration. An MMC is defined by the administrative utilities, also known as snap-ins, that it contains.

Microsoft Point-to-Point Encryption (MPPE)

An 128/40-bit encryption algorithm, which uses RSA RC4 for packet security between two computers employing tunneling technologies.

mirrored volume

A volume that duplicates (or mirrors) data to two separate physical disks, resulting in fault tolerance. Also known as RAID-1.

modem (modulator/demodulator)

A device that allows computer information to be transmitted and received over a telephone line.

mount

To place a removable tape or disc into a drive.

mounted drive

A drive attached to an empty folder on an NTFS volume.

MouseKeys

A keyboard feature that enables you to use the numeric keypad to move the mouse pointer and to click, double-click, and drag.

MS-DOS (Microsoft Disk Operating System)

An operating system used on all personal computers and compatibles.

multicasting

The process of sending a message simultaneously to more than one destination on a network.

multihomed computer

A computer that has multiple network adapters or that has been configured with multiple IP addresses for a single network adapter.

multilink dialing

The combination of two or more physical communications links' bandwidth into a single logical link to increase your remote access bandwidth and throughput by using remote access multilink.

Musical Instrument Digital Interface (MIDI)

A serial interface standard that allows for the connection of music synthesizers, musical instruments, and computers.

My Documents

A folder that provides you with a convenient place to store documents, graphics, or other files you want to access quickly.

Glossary

name resolution

The process of having software translate between names that are easy for users to work with and numerical IP addresses, which are difficult for users to work with but necessary for TCP/IP communications.

NetBIOS Extended User Interface (NetBEUI)

A network protocol used on small local area networks with fewer than 200 computers. It is a nonroutable protocol.

NetWare

A network operating system produced by Novell.

network

A group of computers and other devices, such as printers and scanners, connected by a communications link, enabling all the devices to interact with each other.

network adapter

A hardware device used to connect a host to a network.

network administrator

A person responsible for planning, configuring, and managing the day-to-day operation of the network.

Network Basic Input Output System (NetBIOS)

A network application programming interface (API) that is used to request lower level network services.

Network Driver Interface Specification (NDIS)

A software component that provides a common interface between network protocols and network adapters.

Network Filing System (NFS)

A file system found in Unix that allows computers to share files across a network.

Network Information Service (NIS)

A distributed database used in Unix that contains shared configuration files, such as password and hosts files.

Network News Transfer Protocol (NNTP)

A member of the TCP/IP suite of protocols used to distribute network news messages to NNTP servers and clients (newsreaders) on the Internet.

normal backup

A backup type that copies the selected data to backup media and sets the archive bit on the file. By setting the archive bit, the file is shown as having been backed up.

Novell Directory Services (NDS)

A distributed database that contains user, group, and network object information. NDS is found in Novell NetWare 4.x and 5.x.

nslookup

A command-line tool used to diagnose Domain Name System (DNS) infrastructure.

NT File System (NTFS)

A file system used in Windows 2000 and Windows NT that uses transaction logging to ensure data integrity. NTFS also supports encryption and compression.

NTLM

An authentication protocol that uses challenge/response. It was the default authentication protocol for Windows NT 4 and earlier. Windows XP uses Kerberos as its default authentication protocol.

NWLink

Microsoft's implementation of Novell's IPX/SPX protocol suite.

Open Systems Interconnection (OSI) reference model

A networking model introduced by the International Organization for Standardization (ISO) to promote multi-vendor interoperability. OSI is a seven-layered conceptual model consisting of the Application, Presentation, Session, Transport, Network, Data Link, and Physical layers.

packet assembler/disassembler (PAD)

A device that connects a non-X.25 device, such as a modem, to an X.25 packet switching network.

packet switching

A technology for breaking data into packets and then sending the packets over a network.

page fault

A situation where data is requested but cannot be found in physical memory. As a result, the operating system must look in the paging file for the data.

paging file

A file on a hard disk that Windows 2000 uses to store data and code that can either no longer fit into physical memory or has not been used recently.

parallel port

The input/output connector for a parallel interface device.

parity

A calculated value that is used to reconstruct data after a failure.

partition

The logical division of a physical disk used to organize data. A partition can only be formatted for a single partition; thus, a single physical hard disk with multiple partitions can contain multiple file systems.

Password Authentication Protocol (PAP)

The simplest authentication protocol, PAP merely transmits the user's username and password in plaintext format.

PC card

A removable hardware device that is placed in a Personal Computer Memory Card International Association (PCMCIA) slot. They are typically found in laptops.

performance counter

A data object that is incremented according to the characteristics of the performance object it is associated with. Performance counters can be viewed in System Monitor.

performance object

A logical collection of performance counters that are associated with a hardware or software resource. Performance objects can be viewed in System Monitor.

peripheral

A device, such as a disk drive, printer, modem, or joystick, that is connected to a computer and is controlled by the computer's microprocessor.

peripheral component interconnect (PCI)

A specification introduced by Intel Corporation that defines a local bus system that allows up to 10 PCI-compliant expansion cards to be installed in the computer.

ping

A TCP/IP utility used to verify the connection between two TCP/IP hosts.

Plug and Play

A standard set of specifications that allows a computer to automatically detect new hardware devices and install the corresponding device drivers.

Point and Print

A method of installing network printers and their associated device drivers on a computer.

Point-to-Point Protocol (PPP)

A protocol used for dial-up connections.

Point-to-Point Tunneling Protocol (PPTP)

Networking technology that supports multiprotocol virtual private networks (VPNs), enabling remote users to access corporate networks securely across the Internet or other networks by dialing into an Internet service provider (ISP) or by connecting directly to the Internet.

policy

The mechanism by which desktop settings are configured automatically, as defined by the administrator.

port

A connection point on your computer where you can connect devices that pass data into and out of a computer.

Post Office Protocol 3 (POP3)

A popular protocol used for receiving e-mail messages. This protocol is often used by ISPs.

power scheme

A group of preset power-management options.

primary partition

A volume created from unallocated space on a basic disk, a primary partition is the partition used to start an operating system such as Windows XP.

print job

The source code that contains both the data to be printed and the commands for print.

print queue

A list of documents waiting to be printed on the printer.

print server

A computer that is dedicated to managing the printers on a network.

print spooler

Software that accepts a document sent to a printer and then stores it on disk or in memory until the printer is ready for it.

printer

A device that puts text or images on paper or other print media.

printer driver

A program designed to allow other programs to work with a particular printer without concerning themselves with the specifics of the printer's hardware and internal language.

printing pool

Two or more identical printers that are connected to one print server and act as a single printer.

private key

The secret half of a cryptographic key pair that is used with a public key algorithm.

protocol

A set of specifications used to allow two or more computers to communicate across a network.

public key

The nonsecret half of a cryptographic key pair that is used with a public key algorithm.

public key cryptography

One form of cryptography where two different keys are used, one public, one private.

public key encryption

A method of encryption that uses two encryption keys that are mathematically related. One key is called the private key and is kept confidential. The other is called the public key and is freely given out to all potential correspondents.

public key infrastructure (PKI)
The term generally used to describe the laws, policies, standards, and software that regulate or manipulate certificates and public and private keys.

Public Switched Telephone Network (PSTN)
Standard analog telephone lines, available worldwide.

Quality of Service (QoS)
A method of guaranteeing bandwidth to critical or time-sensitive data transmissions.

queue
A list of programs or tasks waiting for execution.

random access memory (RAM)
Memory that can be read from or written to by a computer or other devices. Information stored in RAM is lost when the computer is turned off.

read-only memory (ROM)
Information stored in memory (usually a computer chip or CD) that cannot be erased or modified.

recovery agent
A person who is issued a public key certificate for the purpose of recovering user data that is encrypted with Encrypting File System (EFS).

recovery console
A text mode interface found in Windows XP that allows an administrator to troubleshoot and recover a Windows XP computer.

redundant array of independent disks 1 (RAID-1)
Also known as mirroring, RAID-1 duplicates data to two separate physical disks to provide fault tolerance.

Redundant Array of Independent Disks 5 (RAID-5)
Also known as striping with parity, RAID-5 stripes data across three or more physical disks to provide fault tolerance. One of the stripes includes parity information, which allows the RAID set to continue to function even in the event of a drive failure.

Registry
A database that contains computer configuration and user information. The registry is found in Windows XP, Windows 2000, Windows NT, and Windows 9x.

relative ID (RID)
The part of a security ID (SID) that uniquely identifies an account or group within a domain.

remote access server
A Windows-based computer running the Routing and Remote Access service and configured to provide remote access.

Remote Authentication Dial-In User Service (RADIUS)
A security authentication protocol based on clients and servers and widely used by Internet service providers (ISPs) on remote servers in non-Windows-brand operating systems.

Remote Installation Services
Software services that allow an administrator to set up new client computers remotely, without having to visit each client. The target clients must support remote booting.

Glossary

removable storage

A service used for managing removable media (such as tapes and discs) and storage devices (libraries).

replication

The process of copying data from a data store or file system to multiple computers to synchronize the data.

Request for Comments (RFC)

An official document of the Internet Engineering Task Force (IETF) that specifies the details for protocols included in the TCP/IP family.

reservation

A specific IP address within a scope permanently reserved for leased use to a specific DHCP client.

restore point

A representation of a stored state of your computer.

right-click

To position the mouse over an object, and then press and release the secondary (right) mouse button.

roaming user profile

A server-based user profile that is downloaded to the local computer when a user logs on and that is updated both locally and on the server when the user logs off.

router

A network device that routes packets between two or more LANs. A router can interconnect LANs of differing network technology (for example, Ethernet to Token Ring).

Router Information Protocol (RIP)

A protocol used by routers to communicate and share routing tables. RIP can be found in both IP and IPX networks.

routing table

A list of routes that contains network IDs and the interfaces they can be reached from.

RS-232-C standard

An accepted industry standard for serial communication connections.

Safe Mode

A startup option found in Windows XP, Windows 2000, and Windows 9x that loads a limited set of device drivers. Safe Mode is used to troubleshoot and recover a computer.

scalability

A measure of how well a computer, service, or application can grow to meet increasing performance demands.

Secure Hash Algorithm (SHA-1)

A message digest hash algorithm that generates a 160-bit hash value.

Secure Sockets Layer (SSL)

A proposed open standard for establishing a secure communications channel to prevent the interception of critical information, such as credit card numbers.

security

On a network, protection of a computer system and its data from harm or loss, implemented especially so that only authorized users can gain access to shared files.

Security Accounts Manager (SAM)

A subsystem and database that is used to store and authenticate users in Windows NT 4, Windows 2000 Professional, and Windows XP Professional.

security descriptor

A data structure that contains security information associated with a protected object.

security group

A group that can be listed in discretionary access control lists (DACLs) used to define permissions on resources and objects.

security ID (SID)

A variable that identifies a user, group, or computer. Every SID is unique.

security log

An event log containing information on security events that are specified in the audit policy.

serial port

An interface on the computer that allows asynchronous transmission of data characters one bit at a time. Also called a communication or COM port.

server

In general, a computer that provides shared resources to network users.

Server Message Block (SMB)

A protocol used for file sharing on Microsoft networks. SMB is now known as CIFS in Windows XP.

service

A program, routine, or process that performs a specific system function to support other programs, particularly at a low (close to the hardware) level.

shared folder

A folder on another computer that has been made available for other people to use on the network.

Shiva Password Authentication Protocol (SPAP)

A proprietary authentication protocol used for dial-up connections that utilize Shiva equipment.

shortcut

A link to any item accessible on your computer or on a network, such as a program, file, folder, disk drive, Web page, printer, or another computer.

ShowSounds

A feature that instructs programs that usually convey information only by sound to also provide all information visually, such as by displaying text captions or informative icons.

Simple Mail Transfer Protocol (SMTP)

A member of the TCP/IP suite of protocols that governs the exchange of electronic mail between message transfer agents.

Simple Network Management Protocol (SNMP)

A network protocol used to manage TCP/IP networks. In Windows, the SNMP service is used to provide status information about a host on a TCP/IP network.

Simple Network Time Protocol (SNTP)

A protocol used to synchronize clocks over the Internet. SNTP enables client computers to synchronize their clocks with a time server over the Internet.

Single Sign-On (SSO)

A process that allows a user with a domain account to log on to a network once, using a password or smart card, and to gain access to any computer in the domain.

Small Computer System Interface (SCSI)

A standard high-speed parallel interface defined by the American National Standards Institute (ANSI).

smart card

A device (about the size of a credit card) that is used to authenticate a user.

smart card reader

A device that is installed in computers to enable the use of smart cards for enhanced security features.

Glossary

socket
An identifier for a particular service on a particular node on a network. The socket consists of a node address and a port number, which identifies the service.

SoundSentry
A Windows feature that produces a visual cue, such as a screen flash or a blinking title bar, whenever the computer plays a system sound.

spanned volume
A dynamic volume consisting of disk space on more than one physical disk.

speech recognition
The ability to interpret spoken words and convert them into computer-readable text.

spooling
A process on a server in which print documents are stored on a disk until a printer is ready to process them.

static routes
Routes in the routing table that are permanent.

StickyKeys
A keyboard feature that enables you to press a modifier key (Ctrl, Alt, or Shift), or the Windows logo key, and have it remain active until a non-modifier key is pressed.

subnet
A portion of a divided network.

subnet mask
A method of annotating the network ID portion of an IP address. It is represented by a 32-bit binary value, where contiguous 1's represent the network ID.

symmetric encryption
An encryption algorithm that requires the same secret key to be used for both encryption and decryption.

system access control list (SACL)
The part of an object's security descriptor that specifies which events are to be audited per user or group.

system disk
A disk that contains the MS-DOS system files necessary to start MS-DOS.

system files
The critical files that are used to run the Windows XP operating system.

system partition
The partition that contains the hardware-specific files needed to load Windows (for example, Ntldr, Osloader, Boot.ini, and Ntdetect.com).

System Policy
A Group Policy that is used to configure user and computer settings in the Registry.

system volume
The volume that contains the files needed to boot the operating system.

Task Manager
A utility that provides information about programs and processes running on the computer.

taskbar
The bar that contains the Start button and appears by default at the bottom of the desktop.

Telephony Application Programming Interface (TAPI)
An API used by communications programs to work with telephony and network services.

Telnet
A terminal-emulation protocol that is widely used on the Internet to log on to network computers.

terminate-and-stay-resident (TSR) program
A program running under MS–DOS that remains loaded in memory even when it is not running, so that it can be quickly invoked for a specific task performed while any other application is operating.

ToggleKeys
A feature that sets your keyboard to beep when one of the locking keys (Caps Lock, Num Lock, or Scroll Lock) is turned on or off.

toolbar
In a program in a graphical user interface, a row, column, or block of on-screen buttons or icons.

Transmission Control Protocol / Internet Protocol (TCP/IP)
A protocol suite used to interconnect network computers. It is the network protocol for the Internet.

Transport Layer Security (TLS)
A standard protocol that is used to provide secure Web communications on the Internet or intranets.

Trivial File Transfer Protocol (TFTP)
A protocol used to download the initial files needed to begin the installation process.

tunnel
A logical connection over which data is encapsulated.

uniform resource locator (URL)
An address that uniquely identifies a location on the Internet. A URL for a Web site is preceded with http://.

uninterruptible power supply (UPS)
A device connected between a computer and a power source to ensure that electrical flow is not interrupted.

Universal Naming Convention (UNC)
A convention for naming files and other resources beginning with two backslashes (\\), indicating that the resource exists on a network computer.

universal serial bus (USB)
An external bus that supports Plug and Play installation. Using USB, you can connect and disconnect devices without shutting down or restarting your computer.

user account
An account that contains information pertaining to a particular user, such as username, full name, password, and so on.

User Datagram Protocol (UDP)
A TCP complement that offers a connectionless datagram service that guarantees neither delivery nor correct sequencing of delivered packets.

user profile
A file that contains configuration information for a specific user.

users
A special group that contains all users who have user permissions on the server.

virtual memory
Also known as the paging file, a file on a hard disk that Windows XP uses to store data and code that can either no longer fit into physical memory or has not been used recently.

virtual private network (VPN)
A connection to a private network that utilizes a public network infrastructure such as the Internet. VPNs employ tunneling protocols such as PPTP and L2TP.

volume
A partition on a physical disk that has been formatted with a file system.

Glossary

Web Distributed Authoring and Versioning (WebDAV)
An application protocol related to HTTP 1.1 that allows clients to transparently publish and manage resources on the World Wide Web.

Web server
A computer that is maintained by a system administrator or Internet service provider (ISP) and that responds to requests from a user's browser.

wide area network (WAN)
A network that consists of diverse geographic areas interconnected with routers.

Windows File Protection (WFP)
A feature that protects system files by checking modified system files for the correct version. If it is not the correct version, the modified file is replaced.

Windows Internet Naming Service (WINS)
A service found in Windows NT, Windows 2000, and Windows XP that resolves NetBIOS names to IP addresses.

Windows Update
An online extension of Windows XP that consists of a Web site that can be used to automatically locate and download updated portions of Windows XP.

workgroup
A grouping of computers for identification and resource location purposes only.

Index